THE NEW CAMBRIDGE MODERN HISTORY

ADVISORY COMMITTEE
G. N. CLARK J. R. M. BUTLER J. P. T. BURY
THE LATE E. A. BENIANS

VOLUME V

THE ASCENDANCY OF FRANCE
1648–88

THE NEW CAMBRIDGE MODERN HISTORY

VOLUME V

THE ASCENDANCY OF FRANCE

1648–88

EDITED BY

F. L. CARSTEN

CAMBRIDGE
AT THE UNIVERSITY PRESS
1961

PUBLISHED BY
THE SYNDICS OF THE CAMBRIDGE UNIVERSITY PRESS
Bentley House, 200 Euston Road, London, N.W.1
American Branch: 32 East 57th Street, New York 22, N.Y.
West African Office: P.O. Box 33, Ibadan, Nigeria

Printed in Great Britain at the University Press, Cambridge
(*Brooke Crutchley, University Printer*)

PREFACE

The first eight chapters in this volume are devoted to the more general aspects of European history in the second half of the seventeenth century. They are followed by nine chapters on the countries of western Europe—France, the United Provinces, Britain, Spain, and Portugal—with their possessions in America and Asia and the contacts which existed between Europe and other continents. The final eight chapters describe the countries of central, south-eastern, north-eastern and eastern Europe, a world very different from that of the West where trade and enterprise were developing fast during this period. The volume covers the years from 1648 to 1688; but it has not always been possible to adhere strictly to these dates, especially where they do not mark a well-defined period. In the chapters on France and on Britain, as well as in the chapter on Europe and North America, it has been found more logical to leave the description of the disturbances of the Fronde and of the Interregnum to volume IV and to start this volume with the personal rule of Louis XIV and the restoration of Charles II. Several other chapters begin with the accession of a new ruler or end with the death of a king, thus transgressing to some extent into the period before 1648 or after 1688: thus the chapter on Scandinavia extends to the death of Charles XI of Sweden, and that on Poland to the death of King John Sobieski. The chapters on Philosophy, Political Thought, Art and Architecture, Europe and Asia, the Empire after the Thirty Years War, and the Rise of Brandenburg cover the years from 1648 to 1715, the periods of volumes V and VI, because it has been found more convenient to treat both together. Some other aspects of the period, such as music, will be discussed in volume VI.

The editor wishes to express his gratitude to those of his colleagues in the University of London who have undertaken the arduous task of translation which, in many cases, has also meant adaptation and interpretation: to Dr J. F. Bosher of King's College who has translated the chapter on French Diplomacy and Foreign Policy; to Mr A. D. Deyermond of Westfield College who has translated the chapters on Spain and on Portugal; to Dr Ragnhild Hatton of the London School of Economics and Political Science who has translated the chapter on Scandinavia; to Dr J. L. H. Keep of the School of Slavonic and East European Studies who has translated the chapters on Poland and on Russia; to Mr W. Pickles of the London School of Economics and Political Science who has translated the chapter on Political Thought; and to Mrs P. Waley of Westfield College who has translated the chapter on Italy. The editor's greatest debt of gratitude is due to his wife who has assisted him throughout in the work of editing, comparing and checking the contributions of so many historians.

WESTFIELD COLLEGE, LONDON F.L.C.
March 1960

CONTENTS

CHAPTER I

INTRODUCTION: THE AGE OF LOUIS XIV

By F. L. Carsten

Reader in Modern History, Westfield College, University of London

CHAPTER II

ECONOMIC PROBLEMS AND POLICIES

By D. C. Coleman, *Reader in Economic History at the London School of Economics*

CHAPTER III

THE SCIENTIFIC MOVEMENT

By A. R. HALL, *Professor of the History of Science, University of California*

CHAPTER IV

PHILOSOPHY

By W. VON LEYDEN, *Senior Lecturer in Philosophy in the Durham Colleges, University of Durham*

CHAPTER V

POLITICAL THOUGHT

By Stephan Skalweit, *Professor of Modern History in the University of Saarbrücken*

CHAPTER VI

CHURCH AND STATE

By Anne Whiteman, *Fellow and Tutor of Lady Margaret Hall and Lecturer in Modern History in the University of Oxford*

CHAPTER VII

ART AND ARCHITECTURE

By R. WITTKOWER, *Professor of the History of Art, Columbia University*

CHAPTER VIII

THE SOCIAL FOUNDATIONS OF STATES

By Sir George Clark, *Fellow of All Souls College, Oxford*

CHAPTER IX

FRENCH DIPLOMACY AND FOREIGN POLICY IN THEIR EUROPEAN SETTING

By G. Zeller, *Emeritus Professor of Modern History at the Sorbonne*

CHAPTER X

FRANCE UNDER LOUIS XIV

By J. LOUGH, *Professor of French in the Durham Colleges, University of Durham*

CHAPTER XI

THE ACHIEVEMENTS OF FRANCE IN ART, THOUGHT AND LITERATURE

By DAVID OGG, *Emeritus Fellow of New College, Oxford*

CHAPTER XII

THE DUTCH REPUBLIC

By E. H. KOSSMANN, *Reader in Dutch History and Institutions in the University of London*

CHAPTER XIII

BRITAIN AFTER THE RESTORATION

By David Ogg

CONTENTS

CHAPTER XIV

EUROPE AND NORTH AMERICA

By E. E. Rich, *Master of St Catharine's College and Smuts Professor of Imperial History in the University of Cambridge*

CHAPTER XV

SPAIN AND HER EMPIRE

By JUAN REGLÁ, *Professor of Modern History in the University of Valencia*

CHAPTER XVI

PORTUGAL AND HER EMPIRE

By V. M. GODINHO, *Professor of Economic and Social History at the Institute of Overseas Studies, Lisbon*

CHAPTER XVII

EUROPE AND ASIA

I. THE EUROPEAN CONNECTION WITH ASIA

By J. B. HARRISON, *Lecturer in the History of Modern India, School of Oriental and African Studies, University of London*

2. THE ENGLISH AND DUTCH EAST INDIA COMPANIES

By C. D. COWAN, *Lecturer in the History of South-East Asia, School of Oriental and African Studies, University of London*

CHAPTER XVIII

THE EMPIRE AFTER THE THIRTY YEARS WAR

By F. L. Carsten

CONTENTS

CHAPTER XIX

ITALY AFTER THE THIRTY YEARS WAR

By Giorgio Spini, *Professor of History in the University of Florence*

CHAPTER XX

THE HABSBURG LANDS

By R. R. Betts, *Masaryk Professor of Central European History in the University of London*

CHAPTER XXI

THE OTTOMAN EMPIRE UNDER MEHMED IV

By A. N. KURAT, *Professor of History in the University of Ankara*

CHAPTER XXII

SCANDINAVIA AND THE BALTIC

By JERKER ROSÉN, *Professor of History in the University of Lund*

CHAPTER XXIII

THE RISE OF BRANDENBURG

By F. L. Carsten

CHAPTER XXIV

POLAND TO THE DEATH OF JOHN SOBIESKI

By HORST JABLONOWSKI, *Professor of East European History in the University of Bonn*

CHAPTER XXV

RUSSIA: THE BEGINNING OF WESTERNISATION

By WERNER PHILIPP, *Professor of East European History in the Free University of Berlin*

CONTENTS

CHAPTER I

INTRODUCTION: THE AGE OF LOUIS XIV

THE Peace of Westphalia, concluded in the year with which this volume begins, not only brought to an end one of the most devastating wars in the history of Europe; it also terminated one of the most decisive periods of European history, that of the Reformation and Counter-Reformation. Although religious events and motives continued to be of vital importance in the history of many European countries—such as France, England and the Habsburg territories—there were no further changes in the religious frontiers: the European countries and principalities retained the religion which was established there in 1648. Only religious minorities—such as the Austrian Protestants and the French Huguenots—might be forced to leave their native countries; or they might receive official recognition—as the Non-Conformists did in England. It is true, of course, that the rule of Islam was broken in south-eastern Europe during the period covered by this and subsequent volumes, but this was a political change; it freed the Hungarians and other Balkan Christians from Turkish overlordship, but did not change the religious loyalties of the population. Even in much-divided Germany the religious frontiers remained stable after the peace of 1648. Although several German princely houses changed their faith during the subsequent decades—mainly from Lutheranism to Roman Catholicism—their subjects did not follow this example, but kept their religion. Very slowly—perhaps only through mutual exhaustion after many years of fighting—the religious conflicts began to subside and religious hatred started to recede: to be fanned into new flames by the *dragonnades* and the Revocation of the Edict of Nantes (1685). Some of the leading thinkers and writers of Europe were attempting a *rapprochement* between the different Christian faiths or dreaming of one all-embracing religion. A more rational approach to the world and its problems can be observed in many a field. The great advances in science and learning were working in the same direction. The way was beginning to be prepared for the rationalism and the enlightenment of the eighteenth century.

The Peace of Westphalia also marked the end of the dreams of reform and unification of the Empire which had been cherished by Maximilian I and Charles V, and which the Emperor Ferdinand II had once more tried to transfer into the realm of reality in the course of the Thirty Years War. Henceforth the Empire was a loose federation of many States, which indeed survived into the early nineteenth century, but even nominally ceased to be the leading Christian State. Although many further reforms were attempted after 1648, they produced little practical result. What is even more important, the great alliance which had dominated Europe for more than a century—that of the Spanish and the Austrian Habsburgs—was no longer a powerful combination. The defeat of the 'invincible' Spanish army at Rocroi (1643) by the French under Condé not only marked the decline of Habsburg power, but was a portent of things to come. The Austrian Habsburgs were much less affected than their Spanish cousins by this decline, in spite of the continuing disintegration of the Empire. Yet they were hard pressed by the Turks, who reverted to a policy of conquest under the efficient administration of the Köprülüs. It was only after the siege of Vienna of 1683 that the tide in the Balkans turned and the Habsburg armies conquered large territories in Hungary and Transylvania; yet no unified Habsburg State came into being. The Austrian Habsburgs continued to be one of the leading families of Europe—far longer indeed than any other ruling house; for their rivals in Berlin and Moscow were only beginning to lay the foundations of their future greatness during the second half of the seventeenth century. Pride of place, however, without any doubt belonged to the Bourbons: it was the ascendancy of France which was most clearly marked by the Peace of Westphalia, although Louis XIV was only ten years old when the peace was signed, and although the war between France and Spain was to continue for another eleven years.

When the young Louis XIV surveyed the European scene in 1661, at the beginning of his personal government, his secretary could write at his behest with much justification:

> *Spain* was unable to recover so quickly from her great losses: she was not only without funds, but without credit, incapable of any great effort in terms of money or man-power, occupied with the war against Portugal....Her king was old and in dubious health; he had but one son, young and rather feeble....
>
> I had nothing to fear from the *Emperor*, who was elected only because he was a member of the House of Austria and tied in a thousand ways by a capitulation with the Estates of the Empire....[1] The Electors, who above all had imposed upon him such harsh conditions and could hardly doubt his resentment, lived in continuous distrust of him; a party of the other princes of the Empire was working in my interest.
>
> *Sweden* could have true and durable relations only with me; she had just lost a great king,[2] and all she could aspire to was to maintain her conquests during the infancy of her new king. *Denmark* was weakened by the preceding war with Sweden, in which she had almost succumbed, and thought only of peace and recovery.
>
> *England* could hardly breathe after her past ills and only tried to strengthen the government under a newly re-established king who was, moreover, well-inclined towards France.

[1] See below, ch. XVIII, p. 446.

[2] See below, ch. XXII, pp. 522–3, 526, for the death of Charles X and the defeat of Denmark.

The whole policy of the Dutch and of those governing *Holland* had only two aims: to sustain trade and to abase the House of Orange; the least war would hinder them in the one as well as in the other aim, and their greatest support rested on my goodwill....[1]

If this was the state of affairs at the beginning of Louis's rule the balance of power changed even more strongly in favour of France during the following years. This was a period during which France dominated Europe more completely than it has ever been dominated by a single power since Roman days. When she repeated this feat under Napoleon I it was for a much briefer spell of time; and Napoleon's power remained severely limited to the Continent, while Louis's embraced parts of America and strongly influenced Stuart England. After the victorious conclusion of the war of 1672–8 Louis was able to write:

In the course of this war I flatter myself that I demonstrated what France, unaided, can achieve. France supplied my allies with millions and I poured out money freely; I found the means of striking terror into the hearts of my enemies, of astounding my neighbours and making my detractors despair. All my subjects supported me to the best of their ability: in the armies, by their valour, in my kingdom, by their zeal, and in foreign lands, by their industry and skill; in short, France proved the difference between herself and other nations by her achievements....[2]

The strength of France rested on the weakness of her neighbours, deeply divided among themselves, as well as on her own resources, her wealth, her population, her army and her navy. With eighteen or nineteen million inhabitants, she had more than thrice the population of Spain, Italy or England, more than eight times that of the United Provinces or Portugal, more even than Muscovite Russia. This large population and her wealth enabled France to maintain an army which in peacetime reached a strength of more than 100,000, and much higher figures in time of war. Led by great generals—Condé, Turenne, Luxembourg—it set the pace for its opponents and became a model for the armies of other European countries. It gave an example in military education and the art of siege and fortification, as well as in efficient military administration. The *intendants de l'armée*, introduced by Le Tellier, the Secretary of State for War, brought order into the chaotic system of army finances and of levying contributions in occupied countries. The French army ceased to consist of semi-independent units and was on its way to becoming a national army, although many regiments of foreign mercenaries continued to serve in it; a much larger number of French noblemen chose the career of professional officer, a factor indicating the same trend of development. The weight of France's military effort remained concentrated in Europe and on land. Yet Colbert created a navy which made France the third maritime power in the Atlantic and the first in the

[1] *Œuvres de Louis XIV* (Paris, 1806), I, 14–16 (1661).

[2] *Ibid.* III, 130–1.

Mediterranean; and the French system of conscription, the *inscription maritime*, which applied to all seamen and fishermen, gave her an advantage over her rivals at sea.

France's fertile soil was able to maintain a large and comparatively dense population, in spite of primitive methods of agriculture and the heavy burdens imposed upon the peasantry. While there was no improvement in these conditions during the later seventeenth century, French industry made great progress under the efficient direction of Colbert. Intervention, direction and support by the State were almost inevitable in a country where the members of the *bourgeoisie* invested in land, *rentes* and offices rather than in trade and industry. It was the great merit of Colbert that he provided the capital and, even more, the initiative which French industry needed, and that he supplied Louis XIV with the financial means which his ambitious foreign policy required. Colbert's example was the inspiration for many countries of Europe, especially for those where (even more than in France) State action had to be substituted for the spontaneous activities of the middle classes. In France it was not only the luxury industries which benefited from State subsidies and protection, but also the basic cloth and silk industries, the foundries and ironworks, as well as the arsenals and dockyards. The construction of the *Canal des Deux Mers* and other canals greatly improved the internal system of communications. French trade with other European countries, with Asia, and especially with the West Indies expanded greatly; but the trading companies founded by Colbert on the model of the Dutch and English companies tended to rely on the State which had created them and were hampered by government interference.

The leading role of France was not only marked in the political and military fields, but extended into those of literature, thought, art, education, manners and fashion. Much as everything French was criticised and condemned in the countries directly menaced by France, such attacks were unable to halt the victorious advance of French culture during its *grand siècle*. French increasingly became the language of polite society, of the educated, and of the upper classes in many parts of Europe. The salons of Paris, presided over by the most accomplished ladies of Europe, set a pattern soon to be imitated even in Muscovite Russia; while Versailles, its art and architecture, its operas and ballets, its ceremonial and its style, was the model which every crowned head of Europe strove to imitate to the best of his ability. French fashions became dominant in dress and hairstyles, in cooking and gardening, in furniture and interior decoration, as far as the wealthy and the upper classes were concerned. Even the dispersal of the Huguenots brought about as an entirely unpremeditated result the establishment of French luxury and other industries, the diffusion of the French language and way of life, the spread of French art and literature to their adopted countries, on the development of which the exiles exercised a most profound influence. The scions of the European princes and nobility in their turn were sent to France to admire the marvel of Versailles and to study French accomplishments and manners at the source. The first performance of the ballet *Le Triomphe de l'Amour* at Versailles in 1681 was attended by the margrave of Ansbach, the dukes of Hanover, Holstein and Württemberg, as well as other princes.

Owing to the impoverishment of Rome and the decline of the Italian city republics and the papal curia, France became the centre of the arts and, within France, Paris and Versailles their new capitals. The Court alone could mobilise the resources and the patronage required for a massive development of the arts such as had been provided by the Italian cities until the Thirty Years War. Colbert made the king the foremost patron of the arts and the Royal Academies, which were controlled by Colbert, the chief arbiters of taste. The State organised the production of art as an integral part of the system of absolutism which permeated every sphere of society, and which tried to regulate everything from above. In France the culture of the Baroque became almost a prerogative of the court, which laid down the principles guiding the arts. Like the government of the State, the arts should be uniform, exact and clear; they should be governed by binding regulations; the individual artist, like any other member of society, should not be allowed any freedom, but should serve the State and obey its rules. The duty of the arts was the glorification of Louis XIV, and the Academies were entrusted with the execution of this task. The painter Lebrun was appointed the director of the *Académie Royale de Peinture et de Sculpture* as well as of the *Académie de France* in Rome, the *premier peintre du roi*, and the manager of the Gobelin tapestry works, where he developed an enormous activity. He supervised the execution of all their plans of production and drafted many of them himself. In their workshops the decorations and statues for the royal palaces and gardens were produced. There the art of Versailles developed on the basis of Lebrun's authoritarian rules and principles. In this way the primacy of the State was clearly established, and French culture became the handmaiden of French absolutism. Innumerable large busts, statues, reliefs and paintings of the *roi soleil* emanated from the workshops or were commissioned by the State to spread the glory of the king. The dictatorship of the Royal Academies, which became the model of similar academies in many European countries, exercised an even more unfortunate influence. Lebrun was a superb craftsman, but the *style Louis XIV* was dull and monotonous. The examples of our own century show only too vividly that the arts cannot be marshalled like an army without disastrous consequences.

It was, however, in the field of literature that France above all showed her native genius during this period. No other country could boast of so many brilliant names as those of Molière and Racine, La Fontaine and

Madame de Sévigné, Pascal and Bossuet, Boileau and La Rochefoucauld, within so short a period. Many, but by no means all of them, owed their rapid success to the exercise of royal patronage. Indeed, Louis XIV exercised a much more beneficial influence on literature than on art and architecture, where his pronounced taste for the grandiose and the colossal had rather unfortunate results, precisely because it impressed his contemporaries to such an extent and set the standard for the official art of so many European countries. Yet it remains true that under his patronage and supervision the arts and literature flourished and that France became the leading country not only in the military field.

What was the king like who gave his name to his age, what were his motives, and how did he rule France? Even his critics and his enemies had to admire him. The duc de Saint-Simon, who hated Louis because of his abasement of the French nobility, wrote in his *Mémoires*:

> Louis XIV was made for a brilliant court. In the midst of other men, his figure, his courage, his grace, his beauty, his grand mien, even the tone of his voice and the majestic and natural charm of all his person, distinguished him till his death as the King Bee, and showed that, if he had only been born a simple private gentleman, he would equally have excelled in fêtes, pleasures and gallantry, and would have had the greatest success in love....[1]

Another observer, the Venetian ambassador Primi Visconti, reported somewhat later:

> The King maintains the most impenetrable secrecy about affairs of State. The ministers attend council meetings, but he confides his plans to them only when he has reflected at length upon them and has come to a definite decision. I wish you might see the King. His expression is inscrutable; his eyes like those of a fox. He never discusses State affairs except with his ministers in council. When he speaks to courtiers he refers only to their respective prerogatives and duties. Even the most frivolous of his utterances has the air of being the pronouncement of an oracle....[2]

Louis XIV had indeed drawn one lesson from the rule of the two cardinals and the experiences of his childhood: never to have a prime minister, and never to admit a high ecclesiastic or a high nobleman to his inner council. One of the first passages in the *Mémoires*, written at the beginning of his personal rule in 1661, emphasised: 'Since my childhood the very name of idle kings [*rois fainéans*] and mayors of the palace has given me pain when mentioned in my presence....'[3] From the outset Louis was determined to rule himself and to shoulder the vast burden of work which this entailed—devotion to duty was by no means a trait exclusive to certain eighteenth-century rulers. His day was regulated and filled to the minutest detail from the moment of waking to that of retiring

[1] *The Memoirs of the Duke of Saint-Simon*, translated by Bayle St John (London, 1900), II, 357.

[2] Quoted by Louis Bertrand, *Louis XIV* (New York and London, 1928), pp. 292–3.

[3] *Œuvres de Louis XIV* (Paris, 1806), I, 6.

to bed. Many hours were taken up by work and the even more tiring elaborate court ceremonial, which was introduced during his reign after the example of the Spanish court. As the king put it for the benefit of the Dauphin: 'But I would tell you quite simply that I feel for this labour, however unpleasant it may be, less repugnance than others, because I have always considered it the sweetest pleasure of the world to find satisfaction in doing one's duty. I have often wondered how it could happen that, while love of work is a quality so essential to a sovereign, it is nevertheless one of those which is found so seldom among them....'[1] Although this picture may be rather a rosy one, there can be no doubt that Louis throughout his life submitted himself to an extremely arduous routine without ever voicing a complaint, and that for more than half a century he was the real ruler of France. Unfortunately, in the eighteenth century Louis's admonitions were not heeded and the kings of France once more became *des rois fainéans*.

Louis considered it his duty to supervise all the details of government and administration, but the system of government remained unchanged. Although it was refurbished and made more efficient by Colbert and other ministers, nothing was done to reform the basic features of the *ancien régime*, which eventually were to cause its downfall. The tax-exemptions of the privileged classes, especially the nobility, remained in force, although Colbert strove to limit the number of those exempted from the *taille* and other taxes and to enforce payment by those who were not entitled to claim privilege. Louis, however, needed more and more money to carry out his ambitious foreign policy. Thus offices continued to be sold, thousands of useless offices continued to be created, and their holders could claim exemption from taxation. The bureaucracy became huge and unwieldy, a clog to economic and social development. The monopolies of the gilds were extended and new branches of industry subjected to their control, while the artisans were forced to join the gilds, again for purely fiscal reasons. If private initiative and private capital investment were lacking, this was partly due to the fact that the French State provided opportunities for investment which carried no risk with them and led to social advancement. The holders of the highest offices might finally be entitled to enter the ranks of the nobility, the leading social group, or to intermarry with it; for French society was dominated by the standards of the nobility, in spite of its decline, and not by those of the *bourgeoisie*.

Louis XIV was not a reformer, nor was he a great general. William of Orange, Charles X and Charles XI of Sweden, Frederick III of Denmark, John Sobieski of Poland, the Great Elector of Brandenburg led their armies in battle; but Louis appeared a military genius only in the eyes of his courtiers and servants. After the fall of Maastricht in July 1673 even

[1] *Ibid.* I, 105 (1661).

the great Colbert flattered the king: 'All Your Majesty's campaigns have that character of surprise and astonishment which takes hold of the spirit and leaves to it only one liberty, to admire....One must admit that such extraordinary means to acquire glory have never been thought of by any-one but Your Majesty....'[1] Ten months later, after the capture of Besançon, Colbert wrote: 'One has, Sire, to be silent, to admire, to thank God every day that we have been born in the reign of a king such as Your Majesty, who has no limits to his power but his own will....'[2] Louis intervened with the details of military administration and jurisdiction, perhaps because he was conscious of his own shortcomings as a military leader and wanted to assert his will in this sphere too; for it was during his reign that the authority of the State over the army was established. In 1674, when a sergeant of the de Dampierre regiment was commended for distinguished service in Holland, his general was informed: 'His Majesty desires that Lafleur be promoted lieutenant in the regiment de Dampierre when there is a vacancy, and that in the meantime he be given a gratuity of five hundred *livres*.'[3] When in 1683 a soldier was court-martialled and shot for organising a protest against illegal deductions from the men's pay, Louvois was instructed to write: 'His Majesty regards what has been done to the soldier as murder....There was nothing that justified such an example being made of him....I am sending orders to M. de La Chétardie to suspend the officers who sat on the court-martial and to imprison the commanding officer who permitted the retention of the men's pay....'[4] It is a king somewhat different from the clichés of the textbooks who emerges from such actions. Even if they were undertaken as a means of asserting his control, they show a personal interest in the men who were gaining glory for him.

The acquisition of glory was indeed Louis's primary motive in the conduct of his foreign policy. As the royal *Mémoires* put it for the benefit of the Dauphin: 'You will always observe in me the same constancy in work, the same firmness in my decisions, the same love for my people, the same passion for the greatness of the State, and the same ardour for the true glory....'[5] To these considerations even the royal love affairs had to be sacrificed, for Louis held that 'the time which we give to our love must never be taken to the prejudice of our affairs, because our primary objective must always be the conservation of our glory and our authority, neither of which can be maintained absolutely without assiduous labour...'.[6]

The pursuit of glory was not only undertaken through war and conquest, but also applied in the diplomatic sphere. At the very beginning of

[1] *Œuvres de Louis XIV*, III, 412–13. [2] *Ibid.* p. 503.
[3] Quoted by W. H. Lewis, *The Splendid Century* (London, 1953), p. 149.
[4] Quoted by W. H. Lewis, *Louis XIV, An Informal Portrait* (London, 1959), p. 129.
[5] *Œuvres de Louis XIV*, II, 4 (1666). [6] *Ibid.* p. 292 (1667).

Louis's personal government the issue of precedence between the Spanish and the French ambassadors to the Court of St James's led to an affray in the streets of London during which the French, in spite of the help of some officers and soldiers especially sent over, were badly beaten. Philip IV of Spain was forced to apologise for this insult and had to concede precedence at all courts to the French diplomatic representatives. Louis's comment after this 'victory' was: 'and I do not know whether since the beginning of the monarchy anything more glorious has ever occurred,... this has been for me a long and enduring subject of joy...'. The following admonition to the Dauphin was added: 'if there is a question, as on the occasion which I have just mentioned to you, of the rank you hold in the world, of the rights of your Crown, of the king thus and not of the private individual, make bold use of the loftiness of which your heart and spirit are capable; never betray the glory of your ancestors nor the interest of your successors, of which you are but the depository....'[1]

Again and again Louis's *Mémoires* emphasise the enormous importance attached to the splendour and might of kingship, the elevation of the king above all others, the 'pre-eminence which constitutes the principal beauty of the place which we are holding'. This is the picture of the king seen through Louis's eyes:

> All the eyes are fixed on him alone; it is to him that all the wishes are addressed; he alone receives all the respects; he alone is the object of all hopes....Everyone regards his good graces as the only source of all benefits; no one can raise himself but by gradually coming closer to the royal person or estimation; all the rest is mean, all the rest is powerless, all the rest is sterile, and one can even say that the splendour emanating from him in his own territories spreads as by communication into the foreign provinces. The brilliant image of the greatness to which he has risen is carried everywhere on the wings of his reputation. As he is the admiration of his own subjects, so he soon arouses the amazement of the neighbouring nations, and if he makes any use of this advantage, there will be nothing, either inside or outside his empire, which he cannot obtain in course of time....[2]

Kings are not only absolute rulers, but 'have naturally the full and free disposition of all the goods owned by the clerical as well as the secular Estates'.[3] Any revolt against a prince, however bad he might be, Louis held to be infinitely criminal, for 'He who has given kings to men has desired that they be respected as His lieutenants, reserving to Himself alone the right to examine their conduct. His will it is that, whoever is born a subject, must obey without any discrimination; and this law, so clear and so universal, has not been made only in favour of the princes, but it is salutary even for the peoples on whom it is imposed; they can never violate it without exposing themselves to far greater evils than those which they pretend to guard against....'[4] God alone is the judge of

[1] *Ibid.* I, 132, 139 (1661).
[2] *Ibid.* II, 66–9 (1666).
[3] *Ibid.* p. 121 (1666).
[4] *Ibid.* p. 336 (1667).

princes; for them alone it is to deliberate and to resolve; the other members of society have but one function: to execute the orders given to them by the head.[1] The Divine Right of kings could not be formulated more trenchantly, more forcefully, than it was done by its most powerful protagonist.

Convinced of his divine appointment and task, Louis XIV would brook no criticism or opposition, be that from his servants or his allies. They simply received instructions which they had to obey. In 1684 Duke Victor Amadeus of Savoy was curtly informed that the king counted on the speedy extermination of the heretics in the Waldensian valleys of Piedmont, and that he would lend him French troops and a general for this purpose. Catinat then invaded the valleys and treated the Waldensians in such a manner that even the French ambassador in Turin protested; but the royal reply was: 'It is fortunate for the Duke of Savoy that illness is saving him a great deal of trouble with the rebels of the valleys, and I have no doubt that he will easily console himself for the loss of subjects who can be replaced by others far more dependable.'[2] Louis was to experience to his own cost that—although France lost only a small percentage of her population through the emigration of the Huguenots—it was far from easy to replace their skills, or to compensate for the loss of the Protestant sailors who had served in the French fleet. Catholic Frenchmen could not fill the gap created through the Revocation of the Edict of Nantes. The horror which the king's policy aroused in Europe was the cement that bound together the coalitions formed against him, and many distinguished Huguenot soldiers, such as Marshal Schomberg, served in the allied forces against France. If Louis sincerely believed that he was executing God's will, it was not France but her enemies who reaped the benefit from it. It is true that none of the European States of the time granted political rights and citizenship regardless of creed. The Popish Plot showed to what lengths victimisation of Catholics could go even in England, but by comparison with the *dragonnades* its terror rather paled. Since the Thirty Years War Europe had not seen religious persecution applied on such a scale and accompanied by such horrors, and it was to be the last of its kind until the persecution of the Jews two hundred and fifty years later. If much of the outcry against Louis was partisan and biased, it was also true that he was personally responsible for this policy, and at least in the Protestant countries diversity of belief was becoming more accepted. Some small principalities, such as Transylvania, were outstanding in the religious tolerance which they granted; and the very fact that in a number of countries the religion of the ruler differed from that of the majority of his subjects made for a more tolerant attitude on the side of the authorities. The writings of Pierre Bayle, Locke and

[1] *Œuvres de Louis XIV*, II, 26 (1666).

[2] Quoted by W. H. Lewis, *The Splendid Century*, p. 46.

Leibniz had a similar effect. In spite of the policy of Louis XIV, a more tolerant spirit began to spread and the storms of religious passion abated.

In a different sphere, however, the rulers of Europe not only admired the system of Louis XIV, but eagerly sought to follow his example in their own countries: in the field of government and administration. France possessed the most highly developed bureaucracy in Europe, a factor essential for the strengthening of princely power. Charles II in 1660 returned from his 'travels' deeply impressed by the French precepts of government which he tried—without much success—to introduce in England. Everywhere outside France the machine of the State was still rudimentary, and what machinery there was was often controlled by great noble families and more feudal than royal in character. By her example France showed how the power of *les grands* could be curtailed, how the king could make himself independent of Estates and great families alike, how he could become absolute, basing his power on a bureaucracy and a standing army. In Bavaria, where Maximilian I had made himself absolute in the course of the Thirty Years War, his successor, Ferdinand Maria (1651–79), summoned the diet for the last time in 1669 and henceforth ruled without the Estates, in spite of their willingness to grant him large sums of money. In Brandenburg, the Great Elector, Frederick William (1640–88), broke the power of the Estates and created a powerful military bureaucracy, the prototype of which was furnished by the French *intendants de l'armée*. It was the exhaustion and economic decline of his territories after the Thirty Years War that enabled him to impose his will upon the country. In the devastated Palatinate and the equally devastated margraviate of Baden-Durlach, the prince for similar reasons could make himself absolute. The diet of the margraviate met for the last time in 1668, that of the duchy of Holstein in 1675. Everywhere in the Empire princely officials began to supplant the machinery provided by the Estates, and the State assumed an importance which it had not possessed before the Thirty Years War. Even where the Estates did not disappear as an institution, their powers declined. In the Habsburg territories the same process was inaugurated through the victories of Ferdinand II and the Counter-Reformation over the local, largely Protestant, Estates in the course of the Thirty Years War and continued through the conquest of Hungary from the Turks, although there the Estates retained some influence.

In Denmark too, it was after a war, during which the country had been conquered and defeated, that absolutism was introduced; for the ruling class, the nobility, refused to participate in the taxation required to reduce the enormous debts resulting from the war. After the nobility's resistance to any constitutional change had been weakened, power was transferred to King Frederick III (1648–70) by a treaty concluded with the three Estates, and in 1665 the new constitution was completed and promulgated as the 'King's Law'. In Sweden also, an unsuccessful war and the large debts caused by it brought about the adoption of absolute government, a quarter of a century later than in Denmark. His financial plight forced Charles XI (1660–97) to compel the nobility to return the alienated Crown lands, a policy which was supported by the other Estates, so that in both Scandinavian countries absolutism grew on the basis of an alliance of the monarchy with the unprivileged classes. In Brandenburg, on the other hand, and to a certain extent also in Bavaria, absolute government was established on the foundation of a working alliance between the prince and the nobility: its privileges, especially exemption from taxation, were confirmed, and it became a service nobility which filled the higher posts in State and army; while in France Louis XIV excluded the nobility from the government, in which he employed members of the *bourgeoisie*. In Sweden, as in Bavaria and Brandenburg, the transition to absolute government took many years, during which the diets gradually lost their importance and met for shorter and shorter sessions. The introduction of absolutism often seems to have been due less to a premeditated policy on the side of the prince than to the force of circumstances, especially to the great impoverishment of the Crown after a devastating or unsuccessful war; of equal importance was the ruler's desire to possess a standing army so as to strengthen his position at home and abroad. Thus absolutism was often established step by step, almost imperceptibly, and without any declaration to that effect.

In many countries the Estates continued to meet, but they were only a shadow of the past—such as the Cortes of Spain and Portugal, or the diets of the Habsburg territories in central Europe. Even in England Charles II, at the end of his reign, succeeded in making himself independent of parliament and in remodelling the borough charters, a step designed to guarantee him willing parliaments in the future; the opposition party, the Whigs, overreached themselves, were defeated by the king's astute tactics and crushed by persecution. It was only James's stubbornness which ruined his brother's achievements. Until the revolution of 1688 England's constitutional development was not so divergent from that of the Continent, but showed similar traits. The establishment of a standing army strengthened the hands of Charles II, as it did those of Charles XI of Sweden and of the Great Elector. Absolute government seemed to triumph all over Europe, and the doctrine of the Divine Right of kings reached its apex. French and other political writers as well as the teachings of the established churches provided the ideological basis on which the new type of monarchy could be erected. It was the Glorious Revolution and the writings of John Locke that marked the end of the dominance of the accepted doctrine.

There were some European States—such as Switzerland, Venice and Poland—where there was no trend towards greater centralisation or greater monarchical power; but these were declining and comparatively small countries, without much influence outside their own frontiers. There was only one power which provided an exception from the general trend: the United Provinces, an aristocratic republic with a federal constitution. Indeed, its constitution was so federal that it was only the predominance of the province of Holland which gave some coherence and purpose to the whole structure, and the fact that in time of war—after the revolution of 1672—the House of Orange strongly reasserted its influence and furnished the leadership which the provinces needed. Throughout the seventeenth century the Dutch predominated in the Baltic trade, which provided the fleets of Europe with timber and naval stores, and in the trade with the East, which they conquered from the Portuguese and from which they attempted to exclude the other nations. If the French model was followed in other fields, in commerce and shipbuilding the Dutch example was paramount. Their great trading companies, especially the Dutch East India Company, found imitators from France to Brandenburg, from Sweden to Portugal.

The strength of the United Provinces rested on their sound finances; at a time when the revenues of all other European countries were weak and unstable the Dutch were the great lenders and the payers of subsidies to many countries. The Republic was always solvent; the companies were always able to mobilise new financial resources; shares and stocks were bought and sold as in no other European country. The Bank of Amsterdam was the financial hub of Europe (and not only of Europe) and was unrivalled by any similar institution in England or France. England might try to exclude the Dutch from trade between her and the colonies, but with little effect. As the governing class, the Regents, was closely connected with the merchants and the money-lenders, the policy of the Republic could be shaped in accordance with their interests. Success in trade and enterprise led to an astonishing prosperity, still visible in the patrician houses and along the *grachten* of Amsterdam, Delft, Dordrecht, Haarlem, Leiden and other towns. It also led to a great flowering of the arts, partly caused by the demand of the wealthy Dutch burghers for portrait groups and interior decorations and their investment in paintings. The portraits, the landscapes and seascapes, the pictures of inns and burgher houses, of ships and urban life, immortalise the golden age of the Dutch Republic. If French culture was severely aristocratic and if it influenced above all the upper classes of Europe, Dutch culture was largely middle-class; but the Dutch influence in Europe was confined to the sphere of trade and finance.

Even Dutch prosperity, however, was unable to stand the strain of almost continuous warfare; for the second half of the seventeenth century, like the first, was an extremely belligerent period. In western Europe the great struggle between France and Spain continued until 1659, and was renewed in 1667 when Louis XIV invaded the Spanish Netherlands after the death of Philip IV. An enfeebled Spain also had to wage war against the Portuguese who were fighting to gain their liberty: Portugal's independence was recognised only after twenty-eight years of war, in 1668, never to be questioned again. The Portuguese in their turn were engaged in long-drawn-out conflicts with the Dutch, during which they lost most of their eastern empire, but succeeded in retaking Brazil. Only a few years after the end of these wars in western Europe, Louis XIV once more started a general conflagration by his invasion of the Dutch Republic in 1672, a war which lasted until 1678. The Republic was also engaged in three naval wars with England. It was only during the last decade of the period 1648–88 that peace returned to western Europe. It was soon to be broken again by yet another attack of Louis XIV, which was foreshadowed during the interval of peace by the *Réunions*, the seizure of Strassburg, and the claims which he put forward to the Palatinate. Warfare was not only almost continuous, but often extremely ruthless. The behaviour in particular of the French soldiery in the Netherlands and the Palatinate caused a European outcry. That there was an outcry does perhaps indicate that such military methods were no longer considered normal. Yet the worst excesses of the time occured just after the end of this period, during the early months of 1689, in the course of the second devastation of the Palatinate.

Warfare was equally common in northern and eastern Europe; but—apart from the issue of Baltic supremacy which concerned all the Western powers—these wars were on the whole waged quite separately from those in the West. The War of the North from 1655 to 1660 was not only a war of Sweden against Poland and Denmark for supremacy in the North, but gradually Russia, Brandenburg, the Habsburgs, and even Transylvania were drawn into it; and a Dutch fleet intervened to help the Danes against Holland's rival in the Baltic, Sweden. The end of the war saw Sweden at the height of her power and in the possession of the southern parts of the Scandinavian peninsula; while Brandenburg had gained the sovereignty over the duchy of Prussia—an acquisition of great importance for the future, preparing the way for the foundation of the kingdom of Prussia at the beginning of the eighteenth century. Another war between Denmark and Sweden was unable to break the Swedish power in the Baltic which remained dominated by the Swedish navy. Sweden's extensive and scattered empire around its coasts remained firmly under her control until the end of the century and provided her with considerable revenues and a flourishing trade. Although westernisation began in Russia under the tsars of the House of Romanov in the second half of the seventeenth century, there was as yet no sign of the destruction of the Swedish Empire, soon to be accomplished by the most famous tsar of the Romanov family. Only in the struggle between Poland, the Ottoman Empire and Russia for the control of the Ukraine did Russia make substantial progress, to reach the Dnieper, to gain Kiev on its western bank, and to establish her control over the Cossacks to the south. While Russia was not yet a great power, her future greatness was beginning to reveal itself, unnoticed by the West. The West was vitally interested in the Baltic trade, and Sweden, through her trade and her acquisition of territory in Germany at the Peace of Westphalia, had become closely linked to the West; but the struggle for the Ukraine and the approaches to the Black Sea was entirely outside the purview of the Western powers.

There was, however, another great conflict in eastern Europe which did find an echo in the West: the struggle against the Ottoman Turks, who at this time experienced a remarkable revival under the able Grand Viziers of the Köprülü family. In the long-drawn-out war between the Republic of Venice and the Turks over the possession of the island of Crete the Venetians did not receive any effective help. The fortress of Candia was finally surrendered in 1669, after great naval victories by the Turks which transformed the eastern Mediterranean into a Turkish lake. Their advance up the valley of the Danube, however, evoked some response when it began to threaten Vienna. A French and numerous German contingents participated in the battle of St Gotthard on the Raab (1664), where General Montecuccoli inflicted an important defeat on the Turks; this was followed by a peace lasting almost twenty years. The next great advance of the Turks, in 1683, led them to Vienna itself, a feat which they had not accomplished since the days of Suleiman the Magnificent. The news of the siege of Vienna caused dismay in western Christendom. The Committee of the Württemberg Estates interrupted its proceedings on account of the 'sad tidings that the Imperial residence Vienna was truly besieged by 200,000 Turks and Tatars and the great consternation which this caused'.[1] Yet little military help was sent from the West, Louis XIV had no intention of extricating the Habsburgs from their difficulties, and it was King John Sobieski of Poland who came to their rescue. This was the last time that the Turks posed any threat to Europe: the period of the decline of the Ottoman Empire had begun.

Unable to adapt themselves to the changing military tactics of the West and to absorb the advances in science and technology made there, the Turks were speedily driven from Hungary. The army which fought them was not only Austrian or Habsburg in its composition, but contained contingents of many German States and was led by Duke Charles of Lorraine, the Elector Max Emanuel of Bavaria, Margrave Louis of Baden, and Prince Eugene of Savoy. The States of the Empire recovered some of their lost unity in the struggle against the Infidel; perhaps it was the last time that the crusading spirit manifested itself in Europe. Only the Most Christian King chose to attack the Empire from the west so as to relieve

[1] State Archives Stuttgart, *Tomus Actorum*, vol. XCI, fo. 7 (12 July 1683).

the Turks from Habsburg pressure, and thus revived the old alliance between Francis I and Suleiman the Magnificent. Nor can it truthfully be said that the Christians welcomed their liberators with open arms. The Protestants and Dissenters of Hungary and Transylvania feared that the Habsburgs would introduce the Counter-Reformation, and the Magyar nobility, which had been engaged in continuous intrigues and revolts against the Habsburgs, suspected that these would suppress the political liberties of Hungary. One of those who fought in the battle of St Gotthard complained bitterly, 'because the population is anyhow desperate and rather wishes for the arrival of the Turks than ours; they are banding together everywhere, slaying and killing those who fall into their hands, and thus they are doing almost more damage to us than the arch-enemy himself...and it is impossible to describe in words the unreliability of the treacherous Hungarians and Croats...'.[1] The Christian armies were indeed superior to those of the Muslims; but the Balkans continued to present problems to the victors which they were unable to solve, and which could not be solved by military means.

Europe was still very largely self-centred, and the European countries traded principally among themselves. Yet this was the age of the great overseas companies, and colonial conflicts began to play an increasingly important part in the struggle between the great powers. In the East, the Dutch East India Company had ousted the Portuguese from the Indonesian archipelago and established a monopoly of the valuable spice trade and of the trade with Japan; just after the middle of the seventeenth century it occupied the Cape of Good Hope and the island of Ceylon, thus securing the route to the Indies. In the trade with the East the English East India Company occupied but the second place; in 1682 it was expelled from Bantam in Java by the Dutch and thus lost its principal foothold in Indonesia. The French and Portuguese were even weaker in Asia, although in their missionary work there the Catholic countries were far ahead of the Protestants. In America the picture was very different. There the Portuguese were successful in recapturing Brazil from the Dutch West India Company, which surrendered its last possessions to them in 1654. Although the Dutch as well as the English and the French succeeded in establishing themselves in the West Indies, the Spanish colonial empire in America remained virtually intact. The decline of Spain in Europe had no direct political repercussions in America, but much of its trade passed into the hands of the interlopers.

In North America the Dutch were even more unsuccessful. New Amsterdam and its outposts, founded at the beginning of the century, did not develop into large Dutch settlements; before the outbreak of the second Anglo-Dutch War (1665–7) they were occupied without much resistance by the English, whose American colonies were much larger and

[1] State Archives Stuttgart, *Tomus Actorum*, vol. LXIV, fos. 573–4 (letter of 8/18 August 1664).

more populous, and thus the gap between the English possessions along the coast was closed. Although the Dutch succeeded in retaking New Amsterdam, the Treaty of Breda (1667) confirmed it in English hands, and as New York it became one of the most important towns of the English American empire. For it was an empire which English statesmen were building in America, and an imperial policy was slowly being evolved, in spite of the centrifugal tendencies among the colonies and their proprietors. The main threat to the English colonies did not come from the Dutch, but from France. Even at a time when England and France were close allies in Europe, the French threatened to bar English progress across the Alleghenies and into the hinterland of their colonies. The French position in Canada, however, was much weaker than that of the English colonies, its population much smaller, much more dependent on immigration and support from France (which were but meagre), and continuously hindered by interference from there. In North America it was proved beyond doubt that State action and State intervention were not a substitute for the spontaneous efforts of the English colonists and the financial support which they received from the middle classes at home. The Huguenots, who might have provided this spontaneous support for the French colonies, were not permitted to emigrate to America. Even French military support for Canada remained woefully inadequate, for Louis's preoccupation with Europe did not permit such a dispersal, so that at the end of the period the colony was contracting, not expanding. France remained above all a European power, and her influence, in the main, confined to Europe.

It was only in the two maritime countries, where commerce and industry were able to develop more freely, that we can truly speak of a 'rise of the middle classes' during this period. Only in these two among the major European States did the nobility and its standards not dominate the life of society, did the State not interfere with the details of economic life, was there sufficient 'social mobility' up and down the scale of society to permit a spontaneous growth, did individual entrepreneurs engage in new ventures at home and overseas on their own initiative, and did the trading companies flourish without strong State support and protection. Even the Whig aristocrats and Tory squires of Restoration England were closely linked to the urban middle classes and their economic activities. In other European countries, such as Spain, or Italy, or the Empire after the Thirty Years War, the middle classes were declining; in eastern Europe they had not yet come into being. In France, their ambitions were too much confined to the buying of offices and titles and to becoming State officials; there was too little private investment and private capital accumulation; what surplus there might have been available was absorbed by the large army and the heavy burdens imposed by almost continuous warfare. Hence France, although much more advanced than the countries of central or eastern Europe, fell behind in the competition with the maritime countries. In another vital field, that of science and technology and its application to industry, Holland and England were also leading; and that again seems to be connected with the more spontaneous economic climate which existed in these two countries, and with the social progress which was being made there. For England, indeed, with Isaac Newton, Robert Boyle, William Harvey, Richard Lower, Christopher Wren, and the Royal Society (founded in 1660) this was a great age, hardly matched by any other. France had her Descartes and Pascal, but both belong to an earlier generation: that of Louis XIV did not produce any great French scientists.

The period from 1648 to 1688 was the period of the greatness of France, not only in the political and military sphere, but also in culture, literature and art. Yet there were other fields which, from a more general point of view, mattered most for the future—finance and economics, the social structure, the development of the middle classes and of industry, overseas trade and colonies, more diversity and tolerance in religion. In these, it was not France who was leading Europe, but the two maritime powers, Holland and England. That Holland would soon yield second place to England was indicated, during this period, by the loss of her colonies in America; but it was due, above all, to her more limited resources and her smaller population, and also to the long-drawn-out wars in which the United Provinces were involved because of the attacks of Louis XIV. It was one of the ironies of history that they did not benefit France, but Holland's greatest commercial rival, another Protestant power which Louis in vain hoped to lead back into the Catholic fold. In England the result of this policy was not a strengthening of Catholicism, but a Protestant revolution which led her firmly into the ranks of Louis's enemies and thus materially contributed to the failure of his ambitious plans. Thus Louis XIV overreached himself, and upon the ascendancy of France there followed the period of her decline. England and Holland, joined together under the House of Orange, succeeded in defeating the greatest military power of Europe. The year with which this volume closes was the year of the Glorious Revolution: the writing was already on the wall.

CHAPTER II

ECONOMIC PROBLEMS AND POLICIES

It is sometimes said that the landmarks of political history, such as those which serve to delimit the period to which this volume is devoted, have little or no relevance to economic history. This is a half-truth. And it is especially mischievous if it leads to the supposition that the economic history of nations can somehow be written without reference to the actions of governments, as though economic life existed in a vacuum, emptied of political contamination. It remains true that in certain aspects of economic life political events and personalities made no real mark. In the day-to-day or year-to-year life of English husbandman or Spanish peasant it mattered little then that Charles of England should lose his head or Charles of Spain his empire. In the forty years between the Peace of Westphalia and the English Revolution, no innovation significantly altered costs, output, or methods of production in any of the main economic activities of Europe. It was not always for want of effort: what science does today, the State tried vainly to stimulate then. This is not to say that economic life remained wholly static; it is simply to stress both that continuity and change have to be carefully balanced, and that if at certain levels a slow evolution paid little heed to the explosions of political history, at others those explosions were real enough. And for all the inventions of ingenious men, there is no set of historical laws to guide us.

The first section of this chapter consists of a broad survey of the main trends in population, agriculture, industry, trade, and finance. Here the impact of State policy is virtually ignored. The second section examines the nature of certain economic and social problems as they presented themselves to the governments of the time, and the efforts made to solve those problems. Finally, there is a brief discussion of the idea of 'mercantilism' and its relationship to economic policy and economic thought.

From the sparse and heterogeneous population statistics which have survived for the seventeenth century, it is possible to get a rough impression of the general demographic trends.

The sixteenth-century upsurge of population seems to have spent itself by the 1630's, in some areas still earlier, and there followed, in the middle and later decades of the seventeenth century, a period of decline, stagnation, or at best only slow growth over most of Europe. From the 1630's to the 1690's, plague, war, famine, and other agents of death struck periodically, and with more than usual harshness, at the peoples of Europe, though their incidence varied markedly from area to area.

After the severe attacks of plague in the 1630's, many parts of Europe were again visited in the following three decades. London, Chester and other English towns suffered further attack in 1646–8; parts of Spain in 1648–50, Munich in 1649–50, Copenhagen in 1654, Amsterdam and Leiden in 1655. Far more killing was the epidemic which broke upon many regions of Italy in 1656–7. Liguria and the kingdom of Naples were the worst hit: the town of Naples itself may have lost some 50 per cent of its population. When the plague made its last spectacular appearance in England in 1665–6, it is thought to have resulted in the deaths of perhaps 100,000 persons in Greater London. Elsewhere the attack was less severe, though some other towns in the south-east suffered heavily. The Great Plague in England marked the last of the big outbreaks in our period though it certainly did not disappear from the European scene. Danzig, for instance, which had suffered heavily in 1653 and 1657, was again attacked in 1660, Amsterdam and Frankfurt in 1664 and 1666, southern Spain in 1679–80, and Magdeburg and Leipzig, urban casualties of the Thirty Years War, in 1680–1.

Recurrent and especially bloody warfare is one of the major themes of seventeenth-century history. Yet as a direct killer war was of slight importance; as an indirect agent of death some wars were very important. The predominantly naval Anglo-Dutch Wars had almost certainly no effect whatever on the demographic development of England and Holland; but the Thirty Years War or the various wars which, during the next three decades, swept across Poland and Prussia had significant demographic and economic consequences for some areas of some of the countries involved. Almost certainly far fewer people fell to the soldiery than to the conditions which the soldiery helped to create. Warfare conducted in the manner of the Thirty Years War had three main sorts of impact on population. First, it stimulated emigration from the war zones to more happily placed towns. Second, by placing a heavy burden on food supplies and at the same time disrupting agriculture, it could readily turn a harvest failure into a local famine. And third, by thus increasing population movement and helping to lower already low standards of nutrition, it provided ready channels for the growth and spread of infectious diseases.[1]

The losses incurred during and after the Thirty Years War were thus extremely complex in their nature and causation. In magnitude they varied sharply from area to area. North-western Germany, north of a line from Luxemburg to Lübeck, as well as the alpine areas of Switzerland and Austria were hardly affected at all. Bohemia, Saxony, Silesia and Moravia sustained only very moderate losses, though some towns, such as Freiberg, lost heavily. The worst-affected regions lay along a line running across Germany south-west to north-east, roughly from Strassburg to Stralsund. Average losses of about 50 per cent have been estimated for

[1] For further details, see below, ch. XVIII, pp. 434–5.

Brandenburg, Magdeburg, Thuringia, Bavaria and Franconia; and of 60–70 per cent for Mecklenburg, Pomerania, Coburg, Hesse, Württemberg and the Palatinate. But these figures do not command general agreement amongst historians and may well be too high. Nor are such losses necessarily to be ascribed wholly to the war, its attendant circumstances or aftermath. The population of Augsburg, for example, averaged some 45,000 during the first three decades of the century and only about 22,000 between 1630 and 1680, but it was already falling before the war. Wide-ranging warfare did not end with the Peace of Westphalia, nor were its effects confined to Germany. Parts of eastern France suffered from the Thirty Years War; from Poland during the long years of fighting after 1648 comes the same dreary tale of devastated villages, deserted holdings, migration and economic decline; and so, too, from Prussia after the Swedish-Polish war of 1655–60. Farther west, the long-suffering Spanish Netherlands suffered again in 1667. And with the wars which Louis XIV let loose in 1672 the theme is taken up yet again: whereas peasants had migrated to Holland from Saxony and Westphalia during the Thirty Years War, now they fled thence to escape the advancing French; the Palatinate, recovering only slowly from earlier devastations, was ravaged once more in 1674 and yet again, and even more savagely, in 1688–9.

The harm wrought by warfare on population and economic life in seventeenth-century Europe has been exaggerated, and this is especially true of Germany and the Thirty Years War. War has been blamed for much that was too readily assumed to mean death and was probably migration; losses in one area have not been balanced against gains in another; the extent of subsequent recovery has often been minimised; and much has been ascribed to war that was mainly due to other causes.

Between the later sixteenth and early eighteenth centuries lie some of the worst crop failures in European history. Caused in part by worsening climatic conditions, especially violent rainstorms alternating with severe drought, they had important demographic consequences. The most far-reaching and destructive of the famines—such as those in the 1590's and 1690's—occurred outside the years from 1648 to 1688; these years include, nevertheless, three periods of harvest failures, some of which were severe and widespread. Between 1648 and 1652 the crops failed in one country after another. In Amsterdam and Paris, in Leipzig and Danzig grain prices soared to famine levels. In England they reached their highest point of the century in 1649; in Spain and Sweden alike the harvests were disastrous. A decade of good harvests and falling prices was ended by further crop failures in many parts of Europe, mainly between 1660 and 1663. The varying severity of this crisis reached a high point of seriousness in France where there were local famines. A doctor from Blois wrote in March 1662: 'I have never seen anything that approaches the desolation now existing at Blois, where there are 4000 [poor] who have flowed in from neighbouring parishes. In the country the dearth is greater. The peasantry have no bread. They pick up all kinds of meat scraps, and the moment that a horse dies, they fall upon it and eat it.'[1] Such descriptions are not unique to France nor to 1662. After a longer period of better harvests, the third wave of failures appeared around 1675–9. They were less widespread and less acute: although, for example, food prices rose sharply in Florence, Spain and parts of Germany and Sweden, England and France were scarcely affected. Towards the end of the period there were sporadic crop failures at various times, 1683–5 being poor years in some countries, but there was little severe or pervasive shortage.

The significance of plague, war and famine is not to be measured simply in population loss. The shifting and stirring of the population helped alike to exacerbate the pressing problems of vagabondage, poverty, and poor relief and to change the patterns of economic prosperity or decay. The continuance of these patterns was in turn related to growth in numbers after the killing waves had passed. Some areas, of course, did not recover from their losses, but others experienced surges of population growth as the birth-rate rose rapidly. And this could bring further burdens as the proportion of children, already high, rose still higher, and the need for food and work gained a fresh edge. Here, then, was the European population of the time—numbering somewhere about 100 million in the continent as a whole—unstable, violently fluctuating, with a high proportion of young people, and the low expectation of life (about 30 to 32 years, at birth) resulting from high mortality rates.

The areas of loss and gain can be indicated only very generally. Spain, Italy, the Spanish Netherlands, parts of Germany and the Habsburg Empire, Poland and Hungary seem to have been areas both of net population loss and of economic decline. But within these countries all was not loss. Though Spain's population is estimated to have fallen from about 8 million to about 6 million in the course of the century, most of this fall occurring before the 1660's, and although many of the towns of Castile shared in this, Cadiz and Madrid both grew notably. Though Naples is thought to have decayed from nearly 300,000 when the plague struck in 1656 to 186,000 in 1688, Venice, despite the plague of 1630, recovered, and its population of about 130,000 in the 1690's was not much less than before 1630. As Milan decayed, so did Turin and Leghorn rise rapidly. In Germany, whilst Augsburg, Erfurt and Nuremberg sank, Berlin, in spite of earlier losses, grew rapidly to some 20,000 people in 1688; though Danzig and Lübeck declined, Hamburg, Bremen and Vienna grew; though many districts of Westphalia were hard hit, the town of Essen expanded.

France, England and Holland present broadly the opposite picture. These were the rising countries, economically and politically, and their

[1] Quoted by A. P. Usher, *The History of the Grain Trade in France, 1400–1710* (Harvard, 1913), p. 210.

populations, whatever precisely may have happened to them, probably grew slowly or at worst only stagnated. They were spared the fiercest excesses of war; France suffered no epidemics comparable to those which ravaged Italy; in England harvest failures, after 1649, were relatively mild in their impact; Dutch towns continued to grow and there was probably a net immigration into the country, especially after the Revocation of the Edict of Nantes, which helped to maintain the population. London certainly grew, probably doubling its population between the 1630's and 1690's to reach about half a million—a much more rapid growth than in England as a whole—and thus making it and Paris the only European cities of over 400,000 persons. The slightly upward movement in these countries seems to have been shared, in the century as a whole, by Sweden, Norway and Switzerland.

Throughout Europe agriculture continued to be the main economic activity for most people; and its methods remained in 1688 very much what they had been in 1648. Indeed, the period is too short to be able to pin-point meaningful changes in an age of very gradual technical evolution. In some regions new crops or new techniques, often introduced in the course of the sixteenth century, spread further afield, more land was brought under cultivation, specialisation made some progress, and farming was a profitable business. Dutch advances in the practice of land drainage and reclamation, for example, already demonstrated successfully in earlier decades, continued to be copied in England and France. In other regions nature reasserted itself, the weeds came back and the ploughman was gone; or, if he stayed, his methods remained crude and inefficient, and his lot poverty-stricken and wretched even by the low standards of the time. In Spain, for instance, the area under tillage fell and wool-growing was not improved by the continued decay of the already crumbling organisation of the Mesta; in Germany and Poland some of the ravaged districts did not easily recover their agrarian potentialities in this period.

Over great areas of Europe the ancient arrangement of strips, open fields and two- or three-yearly fallowing still prevailed, in one form or another; it was interspersed, as in parts of northern France and western Britain, with field systems derived from the Celtic in-field and out-field cultivation, or with great areas of marsh, woodland, waste and rough grazing, barely within any recognisable system of cultivation. Variations abounded: differences by region and by nation, in farming methods and in tenurial relationships. The Netherlands, and especially Flanders, appeared to contemporaries as models of small-scale, intensive cultivation of such specialised crops as vegetables, hops and fruit. The use of clover and other 'artificial grasses' to improve the quality of pasture spread from the Low Countries to England at about this time. Another important agrarian advance, often ascribed to the eighteenth century but which in fact made its appearance in eastern England during this period, was the growing of such fodder crops as turnips within a field rotation. These practices were as yet very far from common, though they were being increasingly advocated by agricultural writers. The latter were a sign of the times almost peculiar to England: Sir Richard Weston, John Worledge, William Blith, Samuel Hartlib were some of a number of English authors active in the mid-seventeenth century and with few counterparts elsewhere in Europe. They drew heavily on the practices prevailing in parts of Flanders and Holland, yet these countries themselves do not seem to have produced a comparable literature of agrarian improvement.

The pattern of European specialisation and trade in foodstuffs was modified during these years in a manner which matched the changing fortunes of the different areas. Although eastern Europe remained the major grain-growing region, grain exports from the Baltic ports declined. Shipments from Danzig, chiefly of rye, reached their peak in 1618; after severe fluctuations during the Thirty Years War and a very high figure in 1649, they fell off sharply in the 1650's, and despite some recovery did not again reach the levels of the earlier years of the century. Nevertheless, these cereals remained vitally important to the European economy. The trade in grain continued to be dominated by the Dutch, who carried it home to help feed their own dense population, or re-exported it, especially to the Mediterranean countries. France and England were normally self-sufficient in cereals. Though still drawing on eastern European grain in bad years, they produced during this period a growing surplus for export. French grain periodically found its way to Holland, Spain or Portugal; and in the 1670's and 80's, a consistent, though small, surplus was shipped from London, mainly to Holland and the American colonies. Animal products or special crops continued to enter into foreign trade in amounts which, although normally small, sometimes constituted important proportions of the trade of the exporting country: butter and cheese from Holland, hops from Flanders, cattle and beef from Ireland and, on a larger scale, wines from France.

As would be expected from the nature of the demographic trends sketched above, this period saw a temporary reversal of the steep and century-long rise in food prices. After reaching their then highest points in most countries of Europe between 1620 and 1650, grain prices for the next forty years showed a stationary, or gently falling trend, despite some very sharp year-to-year fluctuations. These conditions had varying impacts upon different classes in the communities. The small peasant producer, with inadequate reserves and selling on a generally depressed market, was adversely affected; the wage-earning labourer may have enjoyed some slight increase in real wages, provided that there was work for him, and in the disturbed economic condition of the time there often was not; for the landed proprietor there is little indication that the change in the course of prices was in itself sufficiently marked to present any serious problem or challenge. And, in the main, the relations between landlord and tenant continued to evolve along the lines which had been hammered out during the fifteenth and sixteenth centuries.

In Germany east of the Elbe, in Poland, and elsewhere in eastern Europe the grip of the landowning nobility on a peasantry already reduced to serfdom was not relaxed. In spite of some temporary reverses, the Junkers of Brandenburg and Prussia were able to consolidate their power, political and economic, and further to tighten their hold over their labour force. Farther west, the French peasantry, though mainly untrammelled by serfdom, was increasingly saddled with feudal burdens as landlords continued to reconstitute their demesnes and, by a variety of practices, secure a bigger share in the profits of the soil. The *noblesse de robe* and the *bourgeoisie* increased their holdings of landed property. In the fertile grain and vineyard areas around Dijon, for instance, the *bourgeoisie* by investing in land contrived to improve both their social position and their profits, as well as to help revive a region hit by the wars. For an important section of the Swedish peasantry the threat of serfdom was dispersed as a result of the reacquisition by the Crown of lands formerly alienated to the nobility. Started in 1654 and continued more vigorously after 1680, this policy of 'reduction' (from the Swedish *reduktion*) was largely financial in intent; although certainly not ruining the nobility, it had the effect of markedly reducing their share of the land.[1] Everywhere there was variety: alongside the large estate with a crop-sharing system—*métayage* in France, *latifundia* in Spain or Italy—were prosperous, landowning peasantry, themselves employing wage labour and hovering on the verge of a higher social class; alongside the free peasantry of the province of Holland were those in Overyssel and Guelderland whose freedom was curtailed by sundry feudal burdens. In England, the manor and its feudal structure more and more lost their significance, alike in estate management and in tenurial relationships, as the landed estate and the leasehold farm continued their gradual but triumphant progress. Many open fields still remained, but enclosure, becoming notably more respectable in this period, was increasingly for arable rather than for pasturage; it was much advocated by the agricultural writers as a means to improved husbandry which, in practice, it sometimes was. The modest yeoman and small husbandman were hard pressed by falling prices and the inadequacy of smallholdings, though their lot probably remained better than that of many of their continental European counterparts. In the landed gentry, reinforced regularly by prospering *bourgeoisie*, by lawyers and merchants, living on and interested in the farming of their estates, England possessed a unique rural class, the growing importance of which, as a whole, was little disturbed in this period, despite the Civil War and its aftermath.

The distribution of change in industry and trade followed a geographical

[1] See below, ch. XXII, pp. 521, 533–4.

pattern similar to that in population and agriculture. The decaying industries of Italy and Spain were already well set on the downward path; they were not rescued during this period. Venetian cloth output, for instance, already falling sharply in the 1620's, had sunk by the 1680's to little more than a tenth of its level a century or so earlier. Even in the markets of the Levant it was being ousted by English, Dutch and, increasingly, French cloth. Nor was the situation any better in Florence or Milan; though some of the older centres kept their importance as producers of luxury wares, and although some rural industry developed in the north of Italy, there was not enough to counterbalance the general decay. The brightest spot on the Italian scene was Leghorn. But it owed much of its prosperity to a liberal policy which encouraged foreign merchants, and to the business which they, especially the English, brought to the port as it became the main distributing centre for English trade in the Mediterranean. Linked to the fate of Italian industry was the continued decay of the Spanish market, as the decadence of Spain—political, military, and economic—became even more evident under Philip IV and Charles II.[1] The textile and metal industries languished; the wool export trade suffered from the falling Italian demand and, though continuing to supply the northern industries, it was increasingly controlled by foreign merchants. The colonial trade became more and more a bone to be quarrelled over by any mercantile dogs other than Spanish—mainly Dutch, English and French. The Spanish Netherlands, too, slipped still further from their ancient glory. Ravaged by repeated wars, menaced by France, superseded by Holland, their trade and industry declined. Hondschoote, for example, with its famous textile industry already in decay, was finally despoiled by the French in 1657; and Antwerp's decline was further sealed by the continued closing of the Scheldt, insisted on by the Dutch in 1648.

To the east the decline in the economic fortunes of the miscellaneous jurisdictions which made up the Empire also continued. The business life of the great south German cities was waning before the fury of war attacked them; and if Nuremberg and Augsburg recovered little of their former wealth during these years, it was in part due to the general shift of trade from the Mediterranean to the Atlantic. The Hanseatics had lost the battle before war and the Swedes came to make matters worse. But foreign powers and foreign merchants—Dutch, English, Swedish and Danish—further tightened their hold on the great northern outlets of German trade, from the Rhine to the Oder. The barriers to economic advance were formidable: isolation from the new and expanding areas of trade; inability to participate in the scramble for colonies; an economic and political fragmentation which riddled the great riverine trade routes with a multiplicity of toll stations, and saddled the lands of the Empire with a confusing diversity of weights and measures and coinages; and an

[1] See below, ch. xv, pp. 369–77.

impoverished and servile peasantry. The sensational nastiness of the Thirty Years War must not be allowed to obscure the reality of these barriers. Nor must the extent of absolute decline be exaggerated. The Silesian linen industry became one of the leading textile manufactures of Europe; Leipzig regained much of its prosperity, and Hamburg rose to major commercial and financial importance; and the growing demand for timber from the mercantile nations of western Europe played an increasingly important role in sustaining the economy of the Baltic hinterland.

Sweden's spectacular foray into European power politics continued to find most of its economic strength in copper and iron. Copper output reached a peak in 1650 and, though falling slightly thereafter, remained at a high level until 1687. After the technical innovations of the later sixteenth century, the iron industry advanced rapidly and Swedish exports dominated European supply in this period. The remaining, though less important, staples of Swedish trade were tar and timber. Much of the tar came from the forests of Swedish Finland; and in this commodity, so vital for shipbuilding, Sweden enjoyed a near-monopoly, as in copper and iron. In timber, Norwegian production continued to overshadow that of Sweden.

Woollens and worsteds still dominated English industry and trade. Their lead shortened, however, especially towards the end of the period, as metal wares, coal and grain took a larger, though still small, share in exports; and, above all, as the re-export trade advanced rapidly. Imports of tobacco and sugar from America and of calicoes and silks from India rose strikingly, and London became the centre of a growing trade in the re-export of these wares to Europe, as well as of the shipment of European wares to the colonies.

These changes in the pattern of English trade were not peculiar to England; similar developments were occurring in France. They were part of the first real challenge to Dutch commercial supremacy, a supremacy which reached its zenith in the years around 1649 and which survived, though not unscathed, the years here considered. Dutch ships and merchants still dominated the grain and timber trades of the Baltic, the spice trade from the East, the slave trade to the West Indies, and—that 'chiefest trade and principal Gold Mine of the United Provinces'—the herring fishery of the North Sea. But, if much of French commerce was in Dutch hands in the 1640's and 1650's, far more of it was in French hands in the 1670's and 1680's; merchants from Bordeaux and Nantes, as well as from London and Bristol, began to play a growing role in the complex trade with the Caribbean and West Africa; and international rivalry in Asia was stiffened by the continued advance of the English East India Company and the launching in 1664 of the French East India Company.[1]

[1] See below, ch. XVII, pp. 418–21, 427–9.

Traffic within the European seas still accounted for easily the largest share of Europe's trade. But the new spurt in English and French commercial expansion brought a small but growing demand from the planters and settlers in America or the factories in India and Africa which helped to stimulate the various home industries supplying the ordinary wants of life: cloth or pots and pans, nails or paper. The growing entrepôt trade also encouraged processing industries to rival those in Holland, sugar refining, for example, developing in France and England during these years; and, though the greatest impact of imported Indian textiles was not felt until later, their inflow was sufficiently large in England in the 1680's to provoke complaints and further efforts to diversify the domestic products. At the same time as the output, and import into Europe, of these Indian and American wares was rising their prices were falling. The price of Virginian tobacco in London fell drastically between the early years of the century and the 1680's; sugar and calico were the subject of similar trends. These downward movements reinforced the fall in agricultural prices and the mainly static, or only very slightly falling, level of most industrial prices. Meanwhile some industries thrived behind protective barriers. In France the dreary aftermath of the Fronde was succeeded by a new vigour in industrial and commercial life, with renewed and more assertive State support. Many of Colbert's new industrial foundations—tapestries, lace, mirrors, luxury fabrics—were often artificial and uneconomic; but the linen, silk, woollen, paper and metal industries were feeding a widening export trade; and, though they and other branches of economic life were hit by the folly and tragedy of the Revocation of the Edict of Nantes in 1685,[1] by that time France was probably the greatest industrial producer in Europe.

The organisation of industry and trade underwent little basic change during this period. In spite of certain large enterprises the unit of activity remained generally small, appropriate to the technical and financial circumstances of the time.

The existence of a number of large, State-chartered, monopolistic trading-companies must not blind one to the steady advance of individual merchants or partnerships, sometimes encroaching, 'interloping', on the preserves of a company, sometimes operating outside its ambit. Within European waters the giant organisation, joint-stock or 'regulated' in form, lost power or failed to justify hopes. The English Merchant Adventurers—who transferred their mart to Dordrecht in 1655—were already retreating in face of both the advancing interlopers and the general opposition to privileged trade, when their monopoly was ended in 1689; the Levant, Eastland and Russia Companies were also on the wane, the Baltic trade, for instance, being in effect freed from the Eastland Company's grip in 1673. The high hopes placed by Colbert on the various trading-

[1] See below, ch. VII, p. 141.

companies which he founded were least fulfilled by those concerned with European trade. In the struggle for colonial trade, on the other hand, the big companies still dominated; and new ones appeared, notably in France, to join the Dutch and English giants.[1] Even here, however, though State-sponsored concerns, such as the English Royal African Company, made headway in establishing trade, none achieved the wealth and prestige still attaching to the great Dutch East India Company, and none was untroubled by merchants working illegally outside their control who gradually secured more and more business.

In industry, whenever techniques allowed, some type of domestic or putting-out arrangement was increasingly to be found. The great majority of textiles, in Flanders or Languedoc, in Devonshire or Silesia, were made by the wage-labour of spinning and weaving peasants working in their homes, and finished by skilled, urban artisans. Throughout Europe thousands of tiny mills testified to the growing possibilities of harnessing wind or water (mainly the latter) to industrial processes: corn-grinding, fulling or paper-making, slitting iron or crushing ore. And the occasional larger unit, as in iron- or glass-making, reflected the technical need for concentration. There were, of course, a few giant enterprises. Some were State-supported, such as the great arsenals and dockyards made necessary by the growing navies of the age; others owed their scale to the character of some outstanding entrepreneur. One of the most striking was that built up in Sweden by the Dutch merchant, financier, industrialist and arms magnate, Louis de Geer. The greatest ironmaster in Sweden, shipper, shipbuilder and manufacturer of various wares, he supplied arms from his Amsterdam warehouses to contestants in the Thirty Years War, to Portuguese revolutionaries and to English royalists. And, though he founded a famous Swedish noble house, it was in his native Amsterdam that he died in 1652.

At one end of the scale of finance were still the countless petty dealings of ordinary men: peasants, labourers, weavers, usually in debt to local tradesmen or farmers or merchant putters-out of yarn; and as industry grew or the peasant was burdened with dues and taxes, so, whether in Wiltshire or in the Beauvaisis, the credit network grew. At the other end of the scale, just as de Geer made a fortune from the military needs of ceaselessly belligerent States, so did great financiers, such as Barthélemy Hervart, banker to Mazarin, prosper on their financial needs. The emergence of the London bankers, some from the ranks of the goldsmiths, is perhaps the main theme in English financial history during this period; private bankers handling public debts rose to importance after the Restoration. Yet, in spite of projects, neither in England nor in France were there established at this time public banks such as the famous Bank of Amsterdam, the ancient foundations at Genoa and Venice, the pros-

[1] See below, pp. 36–7.

pering Bank of Hamburg, or the bank which, founded in Sweden in 1656, was to produce, five years later, the first short-lived issue of paper money in Europe, and in 1668 to become the Bank of Sweden. In 1683 the Bank of Amsterdam started making advances against bullion deposits for which were issued receipts that then came to circulate widely in the merchant community. The outbreak of war in 1672, meanwhile, had brought something of a financial crisis: the Hamburg bank had temporarily to suspend payments; the Stop of the Exchequer brought losses to some of the London goldsmiths, though it certainly did not ruin them. No State could afford to offend too many financiers too often.

The problems of public finance presented themselves urgently and repeatedly to all governments: how to raise money for mounting national or dynastic ambitions, for courtly extravagances, above all for war. Attempts to economise were sporadic and feeble; expenditure normally rose and income had to match it. And the bigger revenues had to be raised rapidly in societies with national incomes which grew only very slowly; and moreover in which wealth was mainly held by small groups or classes with claims to privilege and power which rulers none too secure could not lightly ignore. The diverse solutions found to these problems often had important consequences for the social and economic development of countries, and fiscal needs left their mark on many wider aspects of policy.

To increase direct taxes on land and property was a familiar gambit, but one with limited possibilities. For where, as in France or Spain, the nobility and clergy were exempt from much taxation, to try to tax them thus was either dangerous or unthinkable, and it was not always easy to squeeze more from the poorer classes; whilst in England the power of a parliament dominated by landowning payers of property taxes was a real brake on both royal and Cromwellian ambitions.

As the largest single source of French revenues, the *taille* was of obvious interest to Colbert's reforming zeal. Levied variously and riddled with anomalies and exemptions, it was in effect paid by the mass of the ordinary country people, above those at the very bottom, of whom it was pointless to demand revenue. The nobility and clergy were exempt, and it was evaded by a great number of the rich, the powerful and the somehow privileged. Colbert managed to reduce the rates and improve the collection of the *taille*. But war demands pushed it up again, slightly in 1667–8, more in 1674–8; nevertheless it remained at the end of his administration about 20 per cent lower than the high level it had reached under Fouquet. Yet, even when reduced, Colbert's more rigorous enforcement and collection had the effect of making its weight more onerous to a class bearing a growing burden of other dues and taxes. So when wartime increases came, protest grew, tension was screwed up, and unpaid arrears mounted. In contrast to the *taille*, the English direct taxes did not exempt the rich at the expense of the poor, and their yield was thus potentially the more elastic. None of these early taxes tapped efficiently the incomes of merchants, financiers or lawyers—people in whose hands the accumulation of wealth was probably at its most rapid. But the monthly assessment, introduced in 1644, continuing as the main tax of the Protectorate and sometimes used under Charles II and William III, may well have been better than most. The heavy demands of Cromwell's wars kept it at a high level; not until the last years of the Interregnum, however, did its collection fall seriously in arrears, and it was not the subject of major complaints. The same cannot be said of the hearth-tax, introduced in 1662 to supplement the evidently inadequate revenue granted to Charles II at the Restoration. Penetrating farther down the social scale than did either the assessment or the ancient subsidy, it rapidly caused trouble, proved difficult to collect, and was further disliked as an innovation from the Continent.

Still more fruitful of public outcry and discontent were some of the indirect taxes and varied fiscal expedients to which the rulers of the day had frequent resort. Some form of excise or sales tax increasingly commended itself to governments during this period. There were various reasons for this. The limited possibilities of direct property taxes left customs or excise duties with an especial value as sources of tax revenue. But to push up the yield of the customs demanded a vigorously growing overseas trade or great scope for increases in rates above their current level, or both. Few countries were in such a position, though England was probably nearest to it. Tariff manipulation was also, precisely at this time, becoming increasingly important as a weapon in international economic rivalry, sometimes to the detriment of its importance in domestic finance. Moreover, antiquated methods of customs administration sometimes effectively barred any attempt to raise revenues appreciably, without thoroughgoing reform. So the tax on internal production or sales of goods in everyday consumption, tapping a wider range of wealth than land or property taxes, and leaving room for reduction in export duties, or other manœuvres in the customs field, was introduced or its use extended.

A most formidable array of excise duties, levied upon a great range of ordinary wares, formed a vital part of the Dutch taxation system. Fiscal measures which would have burdened overseas trade were normally eschewed in favour of those which passed the burden on to the cost of living of the ordinary man. The generally low level of customs duties—essential to the country's mercantile economy—had, however, to be increased on the outbreak of war in 1651. But Dutch trade was no longer expanding rapidly, and the customs revenue tended to decline. This was, therefore, an unpromising source of State finance, even had manipulation of it for fiscal purposes been politically or economically expedient. Consequently, excise duties were raised and extended during this period; they were increasingly resented, and they made the United Provinces in the age of their greatness one of the most heavily taxed nations of Europe.

A similar story of rising indirect taxation can be heard from other countries. Spanish courtly extravagance as well as persistent and unsuccessful warfare conducted within a declining economy and a decaying empire meant taxation on a scale which could not fail to make matters worse. Both the *millones* and the *alcabala* were raised during this period; the latter reached 14 per cent by 1664, and as a sales tax payable on all transactions represented a stifling burden on economic life. In France, whilst Colbert was reducing the *taille*, he was raising the much-hated *gabelle* and the *aides*, quadrupling the yield of the latter between 1661 and 1683.[1] With little foreign trade, and much of that stagnant, and a nobility largely exempt from taxation, the lands of the Great Elector could hardly yield him much money from customs or direct taxes. So taxation in general and the excise in particular—the latter accounted for over 60 per cent of all the taxes of the duchy of Prussia in the 1670's—loomed large in his struggle with the Estates. The price of his victory and his wars was a heavy burden of taxation most of which was borne by the towns and the peasantry. Although in England the yield of the customs was made to rise, both Cromwellian and Stuart revenues would have been woefully inadequate without the excise. Introduced in 1643 to finance the Civil War, it rapidly became a prop for the finance of other wars, as well as the object of riots. At the Restoration only the excise on beer and certain other beverages was retained as an internal indirect tax, but its yield rose substantially so that by the 1670's it accounted for about one-third of total revenue.

That well-tried method of raising urgent revenue, the sale of offices, continued to be most extensively exploited in France. Many carried exemption from the *taille*; many were created and sold in an effort to tide over the virtual State bankruptcy at the time of the first Fronde; and Colbert, despite the reforms which he introduced before the war against Holland made a swift increase of revenue urgent, found himself ultimately unable to dispense with a device which, by aiding a revenue-hungry State, created a place-hunting *bourgeoisie*. Elsewhere this practice, though far from unknown, did not usually provide a significant share of State income, although the fiscal woes of the Spanish government brought its office-selling activity to a maximum during this period. Akin to the sale of offices was the farming-out of the right to collect taxes. It remained a standard technique of achieving two ends: screwing-up the yield of taxes, and anticipating the revenue by borrowing from the tax-farmers—who were naturally, therefore, amongst the most-hated men of the time. In Holland the excise had long been farmed out and continued to be. In England the customs-farmers, removed during the Interregnum, returned in 1662, though departing for ever in 1671; but for much of the period the excise

[1] For the French taxes, see below, ch. x, pp. 230–1, 242.

was farmed and so was, intermittently, the hearth-tax. The collection of the French indirect taxes remained in the hands of tax-farmers; and in spite of his zeal in clearing up Fouquet's mess, Colbert was soon adding to their numbers. In 1674, for example, a State monopoly of the sale of tobacco was created and farmed to a syndicate of financiers: it brought riots and it brought a growing revenue. And his important edict of 1673 requiring that all trades should be organised into gilds to which statutes would be granted in return for a fee—the collection of which he duly farmed out—was a fiscal device wholly akin to the numerous grants for industrial regulation or gild monopolies made in England under Elizabeth I and the early Stuarts.

Fiscal measures could be enumerated at length: in England the sale by the Long Parliament of Crown, episcopal and delinquents' lands; in Sweden the re-acquisition of Crown lands; Colbert's reorganisation of the royal demesne, with a resulting massive increase in its income; Oropesa's attempts in the 1680's to bring order to Spanish finances, efforts ending inevitably in unpopularity, dismissal and the obstinate refusal of Spanish revenues to rise. But there remains to be considered the important question of State borrowing.

The Dutch were far ahead of the rest of Europe in the efficiency of their system of public borrowing: without it they would not have survived. Despite the burden of taxation and great size of the national debt, not only did people continue to invest in public loans at low rates of interest, but it proved possible to lower the rates still further. Following the example of the province of Holland, the States General lowered their rate in 1649 to 5 per cent; after the increase of debt arising from the first Anglo-Dutch War, de Witt managed, not without opposition, to lower it to 4 per cent in 1655; and another conversion operation reduced it to 3¾ per cent in 1672. Meanwhile, some city loans were subscribed to at still lower rates, such as that of Amsterdam floated at 3 per cent in 1664. By contrast, their English rivals, with no effective system of public funded debt, muddled along as before. During the Protectorate sundry merchants advanced money against the security of specific taxes; and Charles II borrowed from goldsmiths' banks or East India Company magnates. The 'public faith bills' of the Interregnum were a dreary failure at 8 per cent; and an over-issue of Exchequer orders culminated in the 'Stop' of 1672. This failure to organise effective public borrowing was an important element in weakening English power, and thereby fostered the ignominious scrambles of royal diplomacy by which after 1675 Charles II became a pensioner of Louis XIV. In their own arrangements for public borrowings the French made no notable advance during this period. Failure to pay interest due on the *rentes* helped to precipitate the Fronde of 1648–9; corruption, venality and disorder marked French finances under Mazarin and Fouquet. Colbert attacked *rentes* and *rentiers*, and substantially reduced the interest burden of the State. But the negligible response to a public loan offered at 5½ per cent in 1672 and to an issue of *rentes* at 6¼ per cent in 1674 may serve to illustrate the weak credit of *le roi soleil* at a time when he was attacking the nation with the best credit in Europe.

Closely allied to the problem of State finance was that of money: how to maintain or preferably increase the amount of specie within the country. Shortage of money could hinder the payment of taxes or lead to deflation and depression in economic life. The influx of gold and silver from America had dribbled down into insignificance. Taken in conjunction with the probably increasing volume of economic activity in Europe as a whole, the certainly growing need for precious metals as trade with the East, the Levant, and the Baltic expanded, and the marked rise in government tax collection and expenditure, this meant an increasing demand for, and a decreasing supply of, precious metal for circulating media. There was, therefore, in the course of the century, a notable growth in the use both of credit transactions and of non-precious coinage metals, especially copper.

In Spain Philip IV inflated still further the already large quantities of *vellón*. This copper coinage seems to have accounted for over 90 per cent of the money used there throughout the period; precious metals virtually disappeared from circulation; the premium on silver in terms of *vellón* multiplied fivefold between 1650 and 1680; and a vacillating policy of alternating inflations and deflations added extreme monetary instability to economic decadence.[1] In France Colbert was troubled by a shortage of money in the economy, despite a great increase in coinage between 1640 and 1680 and some inflow of bullion from Spain. Much of the circulating media, especially in the 1660's and 1670's, comprised debased silver and copper coins (there was a large coinage of copper between 1655 and 1658), and there were many complaints of good gold and silver leaving the country. The best Dutch coins were in demand everywhere and were exported to be used in commercial transactions in Scotland or India, in Russia or the Mediterranean. By a reform of 1659 the Flemish rixdollar and ducatoon, which had been finding their way in increasing numbers into Dutch circulation, were formally included in the monetary system of the Republic; and the long prevailing difference between the 'bank money' and 'current money' was legalised. In England the guinea made its début—a product of the gold of the newly formed African Company; coins with milled edges—already used in France—were introduced in 1663; mint charges were abolished; and in 1672 and 1684 halfpennies and farthings of copper and tin were added to the coinage. The most bizarre development took place in Sweden. Here the introduction in 1625 of what was virtually a copper standard—intended both to raise the foreign

[1] See below, ch. xv, pp. 370–2.

price of copper and maintain the level of production—rapidly led to a copper coinage, largely displacing silver, and with coins of fantastic size and weight: the 10-*daler* piece weighed about 43 lb. and the standard, rectangular 2-*daler* coin in 1649 measured about 9½ inches across.

Reactions to the problem of controlling the flow of precious metals over national frontiers varied from country to country. Although the Dutch made occasional gestures of control, in practice they continued to allow almost full freedom for such movements: gold and silver from Europe and the New World flowed into Holland and much of it flowed out again to finance the trade or supply the mints of the Western world. In England the old prohibition of the export of bullion was at last abandoned in 1663, partly under the pressure of the East India Company, and partly as a belated recognition in law of what had long happened in fact.

The continuing Spanish prohibition on export remained an example of legislative futility in the face of an outflow evident to all Europe. In France, too, 'bullionist' views still prevailed in government circles; as much alarm was generated by the outflow of treasure in the Levant trade, as was approval by its inflow through the trade with Cadiz.[1] Though allowing certain exceptions, Colbert continued the policy of banning the export of coin and bullion, and strove, usually vainly, to ensure that French commerce should everywhere be carried on through the export of French wares rather than of French money.

These efforts formed an integral part not simply of monetary, but also of commercial policy. To the governments of the day two interrelated tasks presented themselves for solution: how to acquire the largest national share of what was commonly seen as a more or less fixed amount of international trade; and how so to control the national share that it resulted in a favourable balance of trade and a net import of precious metals. A further complication for those engaged in a wider struggle was the need to extend the control to colonial trade. None of these problems was new to this period, nor were the answers without historical precedent. But it was at this time that some of the first and biggest blows were struck in the battle for economic supremacy in Europe.

The English Navigation Act of 1651 required that all imports should come directly from their country of production or normal first shipment; that all products of Asia, Africa and America were to be imported only in ships owned and manned by Englishmen or men of the colonies; and it had various provisions designed to keep the fishing and coastal trades in English hands. It drew upon national aspirations—readily identifiable with public interest—as well as upon the claims of trading groups, such as the Levant and Eastland Companies, who were eager for a diminution of competing foreign imports. Its timing, and that of the war which followed, owed something to current business depression. The Act struck at the

[1] Cp. below, ch. xv, p. 376; ch. xvii, p. 402.

Dutch; and in the war which it helped to precipitate Dutch trade and shipping suffered more than English. But in the long run, by proving unworkable, it paved the way for the modified and more enforceable Navigation Act of 1660 which, with the related Acts of 1662, 1663, 1664 and 1673, formed the core of what was later rationalised as the 'Navigation Laws' or the 'Old Colonial System'.

By these laws trade with the colonies was to be limited to English or colonial ships with predominantly English crews; and it was required that certain enumerated goods—sugar, tobacco, cotton, ginger, indigo and other dye-woods—be exported from the colonies only to England or another English colony. The Staple Act of 1663 applied the old formula of the staple town to colonial trade in the interests of English businessmen: European wares were not to be shipped directly to the colonies, but taken first to the mother country, and then shipped thence in English-built ships. Certain specified European goods were to be brought to England only in English ships or ships of the country of origin; the import of certain goods from Hamburg and Amsterdam was prohibited completely. The Act of 1673, imposing duties on enumerated goods when shipped from one colony to another, was mainly concerned with setting up a staff to enforce the restrictions on colonial trade.

In this body of legislation there was scarcely a new idea. Spain had long sought to keep foreigners out of her colonial trade; and plenty of precedents can be found, in England, France and elsewhere, for efforts to encourage native shipping. The English legislation, however, earned a greater and more enduring importance: because English industry, trade and shipping were growing rapidly it was becoming possible for England to supply her colonies with more and more of their needs, and thus in turn possible to secure some enforcement of the laws, such as was quite impossible for Spain. Although the English Navigation Laws were often broken and had often to be amended, and although they probably made little difference to English commerce in Africa, Asia or the Levant, there can be little doubt that by effectively linking colonial trade to the mother country they did benefit English trade in America, that they warded off competition in Europe, and helped to build up London's entrepôt trade.

French policy was equally active in this international economic struggle. The well-tried technique of creating chartered companies with monopolistic powers and the promise or reality of State support in pushing national trade against foreign rivals was exploited by various countries, and not least by Colbert. Liquidating the remnants of earlier companies, and with an envious eye on the Dutch East India Company, he set up both East and West India Companies in 1664, a company for trading in North Africa in 1665, the Company of the North in 1669, and Levant and Senegal Companies in 1670 and 1673 respectively. Of the first two, launched on a lavish scale, with vast powers and royal subscriptions, the

Compagnie des Indes Orientales was a financial failure in this period, though it provided the basis for later French achievements in India; the *Compagnie des Indes Occidentales* was dissolved in 1674 and the French plantations became royal colonies.[1] Nevertheless, French Caribbean trade and sugar production grew rapidly (though much of it was outside the company) and the Dutch grip was weakened. As in the Spanish and English colonies, an exclusive system was adopted: all foreign ships were to be excluded from the French Antilles, a policy vigorously pursued by Colbert with naval support. Again, as in English but not Spanish commerce, because French trade and shipping were growing and increasingly able to play many of the parts assigned to them, some fair degree of success in enforcement was achieved, though not without periodic strife. Of the remaining companies, the *Compagnie du Nord* was the most important. Its creation was part of Colbert's massive efforts to build up the navy; its main intended role was to dislodge the Dutch hold upon the trade in Baltic timber and naval stores, a task in which it did not really succeed. By the later 1670's the company was virtually defunct though its privileges were not finally revoked until 1689.

Sweden, Denmark and Brandenburg all apparently possessed companies for trade in Africa, India or the West Indies, sporadically active in this period; but in fact they were largely enterprises by Dutch merchants seeking to operate outside the ambits of the Dutch East and West India Companies. In England, the growing dislike of monopolistic organisation prevented much recourse to the creation of new companies. The only major creations—apart from the inevitable and unsuccessful fishing companies designed to capture the fishing business from the Dutch—were the Hudson's Bay Company, chartered in 1670, and the Royal African Company, launched in 1672. The former spent much of its early life fighting for existence with French settlers in Canada;[2] and the African Company until about 1689 enjoyed a success which, economically, was probably more apparent than real, though, in terms of the international trade struggle, it certainly helped to increase English participation in the slave trade.

In the intervals between wars, commercial treaties tried by negotiation to secure ends unachieved by more drastic means. Between 1654 and 1656 Cromwell signed treaties with Portugal, Denmark, Sweden, Holland and France, of which the most important was probably that with Portugal, negotiated from a position of strength in 1654.[3] It forced the Portuguese to grant substantial freedom of trade to English merchants in Portugal and in Portuguese colonies; and it marked the start of English dominance in Portuguese commerce, a dominance unimpaired by the treaty between Holland and Portugal in 1661 by which the Dutch were also admitted to

[1] See below, ch. XIV, pp. 357, 361.
[2] See below, ch. XIV, pp. 359–66.
[3] See below, ch. XVI, p. 394.

Portuguese trade. The Franco-Dutch and Anglo-Dutch treaties of 1662 did little to stem the tide of growing commercial enmity; and that which ended the second Anglo-Dutch War in 1667 was partly a tribute to mutual financial exhaustion in warfare. In a sense it marked the end of an era in Anglo-Dutch economic conflict, not because wars or treaties had solved the problems, but because they were to fall into the background in the face of the looming ambitions of Louis XIV and Colbert. The treaties which the latter negotiated with Denmark and Sweden in 1663 formed a minor part of his efforts to push French trade in the Baltic. Growing economic tension between France and England was reflected in the futile negotiations for a commercial treaty which went on intermittently between 1663 and 1674. And after the Franco-Dutch conflict, such political gains as Louis XIV secured at Nymegen in 1678 must be set off against that important blow to Colbert's economic ambitions: the abandonment of the tariff of 1667.[1]

Tariffs, tariff wars, and trade embargoes are multi-purpose economic weapons. During this period they were used in the interest of revenue, the balance of trade, and shipping, or in order to encourage and protect industry.

Colbert was a major exponent of their use. He sought, first, to bring order to the muddled accretion of tariffs and dues, internal and external, which hampered French economic life; and, second, to deploy tariffs as defensive weapons around French industry and as offensive weapons against Dutch and English trade. The main instrument for his first task was the tariff of 1664; for his second, that of 1667. Neither of these tariffs was primarily concerned with raising revenue. Although the 1664 reform applied only to the area of the *cinq grosses fermes* it went a long way towards consolidating the many and various duties of that area into a single, simplified tariff. Its general tendency was slightly protective, rather more than slightly for textiles. The 1667 tariff was protective to the point of aggression. It applied to fewer goods, but rates of duty were often doubled and it was particularly directed against imported textiles. Although leaving undisturbed the confusion of duties outside the *cinq grosses fermes*, it covered the whole of France. And it led to a heightening of international economic tension, a tension further aggravated in 1670–1 by Colbert's strengthening of the preferential sugar duties established in 1665, thus encouraging French refineries and plantation trade and hitting at the important Dutch sugar interests. Retaliatory measures against French wines and brandies followed in 1671–2. Just as this intensifying economic rivalry was a most important element in precipitating the ensuing war, so was the abandonment of the 1667 tariff a severe blow to Colbert who, in the first flush of war enthusiasm, had regaled his master with a detailed dream of what French might would do with Dutch commerce.

[1] See below, ch. IX, p. 219; ch. XII, p. 296.

In Anglo-French rivalry, too, the 1667 tariff was a landmark. A short volley of trade embargoes in 1648–9 was followed by a temporary truce in commercial hostilities. But increases in French duties on English cloth in 1654, 1664 and, especially, 1667 fanned the flames of an anti-French agitation amongst influential mercantile interests in London. Anglo-French trade was represented, with more heat than accuracy, as having an unfavourable balance for England and as causing thereby a drain of precious metals to France. In 1678 the main French imports into England were prohibited on the grounds that they 'exhausted the treasure of the realm'. Although repeal came in 1685, this was only a brief pause in a worsening situation. From 1689 onwards embargoes or prohibitive duties were piled upon Anglo-French trade. And it was not until then that English tariffs, as a whole, showed any markedly protectionist character.

Tariffs not only invite retaliation but, as a device for industrial protection, they suggest the pre-existence of industries worth protecting. Perhaps only France could hope to use them successfully at this time, for it came nearest to the contemporary ideal of a country blessed with all its needs, as well as possessing a great industrial potential. In Holland protective industrial tariffs were incompatible with other demands of this entrepôt empire; the English could not afford to invite more retaliation against a commerce already provided with the armament of the Navigation Laws. But if few governments could hope successfully to foster industry by these methods this did not stop them trying. Yet even France found itself unable to dispense with Dutch-supplied wares; and the government of Brandenburg was forced drastically to modify the many prohibitions on imported manufactures which, imposed in the first flush of the Great Elector's success, failed to nourish the desired growth of native industries. In many countries, unable or unwilling to adopt measures of Colbertian rigour, the same general tendency was apparent: duties on the export of manufactured wares and the import of necessary raw materials were lowered; and those on the import of manufactured goods and the export of necessary raw materials raised. Such a trend was apparent in Sweden, especially from the 1650's and 1660's onwards: exports of copper and brass wares, for example, were taxed less than exports of unworked metal; even in Spain where, under Philip IV, customs policy had come in effect to favour imports by foreign merchants, efforts were made in the 1680's to protect native silk and woollen industries. The English prohibition on the export of wool, fuller's earth and other raw materials was continued by Cromwell and embodied in an Act of Parliament after the Restoration, although efforts to prevent the export of unwrought leather were abandoned in 1668.

Methods more direct than commercial policy were currently in vogue for the encouragement, protection or regulation of economic activity, and Louis XIV's France provides the most striking example of their use. In

Colbert's vast vision of an ordered and majestic economy industry loomed large. In pursuit of his vision, gilds were supported, monopolies created, privileges granted, subsidies paid out, and industrial life bombarded with an unrelenting barrage of highly detailed regulations. Most spectacular were the workshops set up for the making of luxury wares: tapestries, elaborate furniture, rugs, pottery, Venetian glass and mirrors. To this end, new life was put into the Gobelins and the Savonnerie which flowered into *manufactures royales*; similar enterprises were set up or supported at Beauvais and Aubusson; Venetian workers were lured to France (despite the efforts of the Venetian republic to ensure that they stayed in Venice) and a privileged mirror-making company started: by 1680 Colbert was boasting that this particular *manufacture royale* was depriving Venice of one million *livres* per year. In fact, however, these luxury manufactures had more splendour than economic importance to France as a whole; their economic value is not to be confused with their great aesthetic and cultural influence in Europe.

To Colbert's way of thinking it also seemed important that his countrymen should not have to buy foreign cloth. So Van Robais was lured from the Netherlands and the large, highly privileged and soon famous establishment developed at Abbeville to make types of cloth then produced in England and Holland; a company was set up and subsidised to make serges in Burgundy; and the Languedoc industry was given bounties to stimulate its exports to the Levant. The Lyons silk industry prospered on vast royal orders arranged by Colbert himself; the iron industry was given some protection (Swedish iron could not be dispensed with); State foundries were created for cannon manufacture; and at Rochefort, Toulon and Brest were set up the immense arsenals and dockyards which were amongst the biggest industrial establishments of the age. In striving for the regulation of industry as a part of its promotion, Colbert exhibited his usual economic conservatism. He took the existing creaky machinery and fashioned from it a vast apparatus, centrally controlled and operating through the *intendants*, the newly created inspectors of manufactures, and the gilds. No industry attracted more of his regulative zeal than woollen textiles. In the 1660's detailed rules in the medieval manner were sent out to numerous towns; they were followed by corresponding national regulations, stressing the maintenance of uniform standards and the need for gild organisations. Although the edict of 1673[1] was primarily fiscal in intent, it was wholly in the logic of Colbert's industrial views. The number of gilds increased during his era and continued to do so afterwards. At the same time they were tending to become exclusive organisations of gild masters, used by the central government to discipline the workers. This was in turn paralleled by the growth of journeymen's organisations. Some of these, especially in such skilled crafts as papermaking, began to

[1] See above, p. 33.

conduct strikes; and the heightening of industrial tension came to be answered by further *règlements*.

Varied examples of similar but lesser attempts to promote industry and trade may be culled from all over Europe. Economic authorities were set up: the Council of Trade in England in 1650, the *Kommerskollegium* in Sweden in 1651, the *Kommerzkolleg* in Vienna in 1665. There were efforts to sustain or create economic activity with State support in Saxony, the Palatinate, and Brandenburg; foundations of privileged companies included that for silk manufacture set up in Munich in 1665; the immigration of skilled artisans was encouraged with particular vigour in England, Holland and Brandenburg, to attract Protestant refugees, both before and after the Revocation of the Edict of Nantes; the nobility was permitted or encouraged to participate in trade or industry, as in France and Spain; canals were built, none such vast undertakings as the *Canal des Deux Mers* constructed between 1666 and 1681, but including that which the Great Elector had built to join the Spree and the Oder—and thus link Berlin and Breslau. Almost everywhere regulation was seen as the inseparable brother of industrial encouragement. The Dutch, for example, minutely regulated their fishing industry so as to maintain the quality, reputation, and price of products known and sold throughout Europe. Their textile industry, in Leiden and Amsterdam, remained subject to gild control, with its halls where cloth was inspected and sealed to check its conformity to carefully regulated specifications. Similar control exercised in Venice and other urban centres of textile manufacture in Italy, though continued with the intention of benefiting the industry by maintaining quality, in practice hampered it from adaptation to new demands by insisting on the continued manufacture of old and expensive types of cloth no longer in demand. Although in many areas rural textile manufacture was slipping away from gild control, and although newer industries such as sugar-refining or gunpowder-making were often free of it, it was only in England that there was a continuing and nation-wide move away from State or municipal regulations. The gilds continued to decline and the English government, though no less anxious than others to promote national economic power, tended more and more to do this by commercial policy rather than direct industrial subventions or similar devices. Characteristically, its biggest direct interest in industrial activity was represented by the naval dockyards at Chatham, Woolwich and Deptford, which were greatly expanded during this period.

To divorce economic from social history is neither fruitful nor sensible. As governments grappled with economic problems, so were they involved with social questions. In practice they were affected in three main ways at this time: poor relief, the maintenance of employment, and the provision of food in time of emergency. Their efforts must be seen against a background of chronic under-employment and widespread poverty; of societies in which much labour was casual, and mobs and riots an endemic threat to a public order often precariously maintained by authoritarian régimes. To keep people from 'stealing and starving', as a contemporary put it, was a policy which commended itself for more reasons than those of morality. And the confusion and instability of these decades brought, in many parts of Europe, a notable activity in social policy.

Particularly evident in this war-torn era was a new vigour imparted to old policies aimed at repressing beggars, vagrants, idlers—the able-bodied unemployed. It could be seen in England after the Civil War and the murky years of 1648–9, and it was embodied in the Settlement Act of 1662; in France Colbert pursued the idle with edicts depressingly familiar in content; alike in the Bohemia of the Emperor and the Sweden of the Vasas there were complaints about beggars and policies for their suppression. Corporal punishment and/or expulsion from town or parish remained the standard recipe, and increasing ferocity was no prerogative of countries embracing the severer sorts of Protestantism. The period saw a striking increase in the erection of various types of workhouses and the more or less compulsory incarceration therein of poor people. The famous Hôpital of Paris was set up in 1656; in 1673 it contained over 6400 inmates, as well as others in various annexed foundations, and catered for a range of persons stretching from prostitutes to foundling children, from the old and infirm to the able-bodied poor who worked at various trades. Many other workhouses, similar in type but smaller in size, were founded, particularly from the 1650's onwards, not only in other French towns but in towns all over Europe: in Holland and Switzerland, in Prussia and Austria. In England the establishment of Houses of Correction had made little progress by the Restoration; thereafter, criticism of the growing burden of the poor-rate for out-relief led to the setting up of public workhouses, similar to the London Bridewell. The motives for starting all these institutions were mixed: religious charity; the desire to sweep the streets clear of a growing flock of potentially dangerous vagrants; the hope that the practice of a trade by the inmates would contribute to the country's industry, usually textiles. In practice they did little to relieve poverty by the provision of work, and still less to augment wealth by the encouragement of industry.

Attempts to control the trade in foodstuffs mainly followed traditional lines. There was much regulation of internal trade, though practices varied greatly; but the familiar alternation of permitted exports during periods of good harvests, and forbidden exports during periods of bad, remained the customary technique. That these decades saw a more than usual freedom of export was due primarily to the falling grain prices and the comparatively long series of good harvests between the failures, rather than to any general access of 'free trade' ideas. The crisis years around

1647–50, when the links between dear food and rioting were demonstrated in many parts of Europe, were followed by the widespread removal of export prohibitions during the good harvests of the 1650's. The bad failure of 1661–3 brought renewed controls, but then came long periods of freedom: in the lands of the Great Elector there were no prohibitions on grain exports from 1663 to 1673, few from 1677 to 1683, and none from 1685 to 1688; in France export was free from 1669 to 1674, alternated with prohibitions from 1675 to 1683, and was free again from 1686 to 1689. Socially motivated though this policy was, other influences bore upon it: Spain's dire need of grain forced her to encourage imports; Holland's interest in the international grain trade kept her trade in it substantially free; the exporting interest of the Junkers told against ready export prohibitions in the ports of northern Germany.

Few nations could or did attempt any consistent policy of agricultural protection: Holland did protect its dairying with a stiff tariff on imports; Denmark's efforts at agrarian protection alternated with export prohibitions; Sweden's protective attempts in 1672 were short-lived; aside from his efforts to stimulate grain exports by allowing them to be mainly duty-free, Colbert's agrarian interests lay less with foodstuffs than with timber, as manifested by the celebrated and comprehensive ordinance of 1669 (*Ordonnance des Eaux et Forêts*). The general tendency in most countries was towards the sporadic use of controls in the immediate interest of consumers rather than of producers or merchants. Only one country showed a noteworthy move in a different direction. From 1654 to 1670 English grain exports were allowed when prices were not above certain specified levels; in 1670 export was permitted whatever the price; and in 1673 there was introduced the system of granting bounties on export which, although it lapsed in 1681, was revived in 1689. Meanwhile, high duties were imposed on grain imports when prices were low, and low duties when prices were high. Thus was laid down the Corn Law policy which was to last for so long and give protection to English farmers. At the same time various restrictions on corn-dealing were also lifted. Although controls were later temporarily imposed during emergencies, the new policy survived and marked a clear step away from the older method of trying to ensure distributive justice by controls to a new one of protected expansion for the producer and reliance upon increased production to meet the needs of the consumer.

The economic policies of this era, as indeed of the three centuries from about 1500 to about 1800, are often assessed in terms of 'mercantilism' or 'the mercantile system'. In first developing the notion of the mercantile system, Adam Smith in 1776 systematised certain aspects of the commercial policies of the seventeenth and early eighteenth centuries and presented them as an absurdity in terms of economic efficiency; rather over a century later Schmoller and Cunningham gave mercantilism a lease of intellectual life by presenting it as an ideal in terms of State-building. Thereafter, the idea of mercantilism grew into a nebulous and all-embracing entity, explaining little and concealing much. What does it mean?

Behind the acts of policy considered here there certainly lay a mass of attitudes and beliefs, common to many countries, about social and economic matters. These notions, expressed in sundry books, pamphlets, letters or edicts have been labelled in the history of economic thought, as 'mercantilism', just as have the policies themselves. But this miscellaneous assortment of ideas, assumptions and prejudices was quite different from the systematic analysis which is today called economics. It was different in content, in its nature, its practitioners, and its relationship to policy. It drew heavily upon two interrelated sources: empirical observations by statesmen or merchants concerned with particular problems or engaged in special pleading; and long-held and little-questioned assumptions about economic life. The former included, for example, such practical matters as the export of bullion and the shortage of coin, problems besetting businessmen and finance ministers alike. There seems little need to distinguish them as peculiarly mercantilist. They have acquired this label largely because the answers then found to those problems were judged by later generations, anachronistically, in terms of classical liberal economics. The first source drew, sometimes unconsciously, upon the second, the underlying assumptions. Amongst the most important of these were: that there was a more or less fixed volume of commerce, money, and economic activity generally; that the circumstances of both supply and demand were normally fairly inelastic; and that governments should govern in economic matters as in political.

Such notions were not peculiar to this period or even to the sixteenth and seventeenth centuries. Some were assumptions far from unreasonable in the general circumstances of economic life outside modern industrialism; some were even then becoming out of touch with reality. All were given particular historical significance by their continuing influence on the minds of those who were busy guiding the emergent States and growing international rivalries of contemporary Europe. They cannot be used alone to explain policy; they did not determine it. Economic policy in practice was (and often still is) an indeterminate product of economic assumptions and immediate problems, shaped by the personalities of outstanding men and timed, in part, by the transient prosperity or depression of economic life. To attach so simple a label as 'mercantilism' is to conceal the variety of forces which bore upon its formulation. But an historical label once attached is difficult to detach; and this particular label may serve some classificatory purpose if tied on simply to those attitudes, assumptions, and unsystematic notions which informed contemporary actions. For they were certainly drawn upon, and their rigidity, their essentially static and conservative nature helped to worsen the tensions and conflicts of the time.

The period was fruitful in writings on economic matters, and many of them showed an increasing interest in proposals for surveying and exploiting national resources. With such many-sided authors as Johann Joachim Becher, scientist and economist, active in the Vienna *Kommerz-kolleg*, or Sir William Petty, doctor, inventor, economist, and much else besides, we seem to be on the borderland between the new world of scientific discovery and the old one of traditional assumptions. Petty, along with John Graunt, pioneered in the 1660's the field of social statistics known at the time as 'political arithmetic'; he was active in the newly founded Royal Society which itself was only one of a number of academies—the *Académie des Sciences*, the Florentine *Accademia del Cimento*—which helped to bring a new stimulus to interest in economic as well as scientific matters.

But in fact the influence on economic policy of this dawning scientific world was negligible in this period. Nor were its basic economic ideas much different then from the conventional assumptions embodied in most contemporary writings. Such a work as *Het Interest van Holland* (published in 1662, largely written by Pieter de la Court, but usually ascribed to John de Witt under whose name it later appeared in French and English translations) seems to breathe an air of economic liberalism. But it was largely a patriotic tract in terms of the economic interests of a merchant republic. There were exceptional writings, such as those of Roger Coke. More typical was the sentiment expressed in the title of von Hornigk's *Österreich über Alles wann es nur will* (1684), or the revealing sub-title of Andrew Yarranton's *England's Improvement by Sea and Land; or How to beat the Dutch without fighting* (1677). And the vigorous activity of such a man as Sir George Downing, pursuing his anti-Dutch policy and shaping the Navigation Laws, typified the reality of mercantilism in practice.

Towering over all else as the embodiment of mercantilist policy was Colbert. An administrator of genius, his perception of economic life nevertheless differed from the ordinary in no way save in its comprehensiveness. His views show all the rigidities of conventional mercantilist writings; and some were decreasingly relevant to the slowly changing world in which he wielded such power. Whilst the rapid opening-up of new branches of trade in America and the East was palpably beginning to make the ancient picture of fixity untrue, and while he himself was busy founding companies to pursue those trades, he could still cling to the idea of a fixed volume of commerce and regard the discovery of some new trade as virtually impossible. And so logically, as he informed his master in 1669: 'le commerce cause un combat perpétuel en paix et en guerre entre les nations de l'Europe, à qui en emportera la meilleure partie. Les Hollandois, Anglois et François sont les acteurs de ce combat.'[1] In his internal policy as well as his external, in his attitude to trade, industry and poverty, all the generalised characteristics of mercantilism appear. And his memory and influence perpetuated them. Just as Louis XIV's France provided political and cultural models for aspiring princelings, so was Colbert's economic *étatisme* a model for their orthodox economic conservatism. Colbert was perhaps the only true 'mercantilist' who ever lived.

[1] *Lettres, Instructions et Mémoires de Colbert*, ed. P. Clément (Paris, 1861 ff.), VI, 266.

CHAPTER III

THE SCIENTIFIC MOVEMENT

To the year 1648 belongs one of the dramatic experiments of the scientific revolution. F. Perier, brother-in-law of Blaise Pascal by whom the experiment had been proposed to him, climbed the Puy-de-Dôme in Auvergne bearing some glass tubes and a quantity of mercury. He found as he ascended the mountain that at each successive station the height of the mercury in his barometer was less, until at the summit it stood at only 23 inches. This was ocular testimony to the truth of the view that the column of mercury within the barometric tube was supported by the pressure of the atmosphere outside the tube: the column fell as it was carried higher in the ocean of air, so reducing that pressure. The phenomenon itself had been discovered in Italy; there was nothing very original in Pascal's prediction that the height of the mercury would decrease above sea-level; the experiment to test it was simple in the extreme. Yet it had not been made before, it was made in France, and it was widely publicised. It was characteristic of the time that it should be so, for this was the peak of one of the great creative periods in French science. The transformation of science had been first undertaken in Italy and in Germany; religious fanaticism had stultified the promising renaissance of the sciences in the Paris of the mid-sixteenth century and postponed to the reign of Louis XIII the development of anti-Aristotelian philosophy, the pursuit of the great Copernican debate, and the introduction of experimental inquiry. From this time, however, as in politics, manners and the arts of civilisation Paris became the arbiter of Europe, so in science France rose to a commanding position, to retire in turn before the challenge of English empiricism.

In thinking of French science in the seventeenth century it is inevitably and correctly the name of Descartes that comes first to mind.[1] His works and their influence have been discussed in the preceding volume, yet the period from 1648 to 1688 may fittingly be called the age of Cartesianism. Descartes died in 1650, six years after the publication of his *Principia Philosophiae*, the bible of his followers; it was in the next generation that the forms of scientific explanation he had offered were assimilated and questioned. They were accepted and taught most eagerly by his native countrymen (with whom his relations had been kept close, during his residence abroad, by the indefatigable Père Marin Mersenne (1588–1648)) and by his adopted countrymen, the Dutch. That, so far as science is concerned, the Netherlands were a province of France paradoxically

[1] For Descartes, see below, ch. IV, pp. 74–7; ch, XI, pp. 251–2.

rendered justice to the influence which the Dordrecht schoolmaster, Isaac Beeckman (1588–1637), had exercised over the intellect of the youthful Descartes. Yet if his was the predominant new influence in France, it was not the only one. Mersenne and others had equally drawn the attention of French scientists to the discoveries of Galileo; Bacon and Harvey had been read by them; the new school of chemical philosophers was active. Gassendi's revival of Lucretian atomism was almost contemporaneous with Descartes's assertion of mechanistic principles, and he had able mathematical rivals in Roberval, Desargues and Fermat. By mid-century the French achievement in science was solid, and Mersenne's provincial correspondents testify to its strength beyond its centre in the capital.

By comparison the England of the boyhood of Newton, Boyle, Wren, Ray and Hooke, riven by religious and political controversy, could boast of little intellectual distinction. Bacon's grand design remained unimplemented. The aged Harvey had abandoned science for the service of his king, though in *De Generatione Animalium* (1651) the fruit of earlier years of study was preserved. In London Gresham College was almost moribund, while the ancient universities had been distracted by civil war and religious purges. Only an audacious spirit could have foretold, from the meetings of a philosophical club in London that began about 1645, and from Cromwell's later patronage of such men as John Wilkins and John Wallis, the scientific eminence of the future Royal Society. Into England also the influence of Descartes penetrated strongly, providing almost as much evidence as there is of a stirring scientific outlook at this time. The philosopher Thomas Hobbes and the diplomat Sir William Boswell were among his correspondents; Henry More of Cambridge challenged him on important points. A few years later Cambridge students were to complain of the neglect of modern thinking there, because Descartes was not read as he was at Oxford. Nevertheless, at either university the younger Fellows of the early Royal Society like Newton and Hooke were brought up on Descartes, to become uncompromising mechanical philosophers.

Few of Galileo's friends and pupils in Italy outlived him; his death in 1642 (the year of Newton's birth) marked the end of the epoch in which Italy made her greatest contribution to the growth of modern science. Elsewhere in Europe no serious scientist or philosopher any longer submitted inevitably to the force of Aristotelian arguments, or doubted the greater plausibility of the Copernican hypothesis. In Italy the deadening effect of clerical attitudes, foreseen by Galileo himself, became apparent. Though there were gifted Italian scientists in the second half of the seventeenth century, their work was confined to non-controversial matters. An Italian astronomer, Giovanbattista Riccioli, produced the last great defence of the old world-view (*Almagestum Novum*, 1651)—a massive and by no means foolish book—but no astronomer in Italy contributed notably to the advancing flood of contrary observations and theory. As might be expected, the most active scientific centre was Florence. There Vicenzo Viviani (1621–1703), one of Galileo's last pupils, was energetic in perpetuating his master's fame. He was a major figure in the *Accademia del Cimento*, a scientific society which under the patronage of the Medici and with their financial support flourished in Florence from 1657 to 1667. It was a small and select society, and able to acquire some excellent apparatus; but when ducal interest flagged it collapsed. As its name suggests, the business of the society was to try experiments, mostly in relation to physics, which it did in rather a planless fashion. Many of the experiments on the motions of bodies suggested but not actually performed by Galileo were tried—not always with success; the Torricellian vacuum provided promising topics, and a number of experiments described by Boyle in 1660 were repeated. Beautiful thermometers were made for the academicians' experiments on heat and cold; thermal expansion, the incompressibility of water, the force of gunpowder, and capillary attraction were examined. The *Saggi di Naturali Esperienze* (1667), in which the proceedings of the academy were described, give an interesting picture of the routine type of scientific experimenting of the time. It yielded much new information—not least on the difficulty of making and interpreting experiments; it confirmed much that was already believed; but it settled no important questions, except perhaps the question of whether or not 'nature abhors a vacuum'. Much of the experimentation at the Royal Society's meetings in its early years was of the same kind: the results were curious rather than conclusive.

The *Saggi* are striking examples of pure experimental reporting; in its object it is a book quite unlike anything published in the first phase of the scientific revolution, just as the *Accademia del Cimento* is the first example of a society existing simply to make co-operative experiments. The best-known of older scientific societies, the *Accademia dei Lincei* of which Galileo had been proud to be a member, had been more of a fraternity: it never met in session, and its members never undertook a common enterprise. The much larger scientific societies of the second half of the century were, in varying degrees, all more 'Verulamian' in design. In Germany scientific interest was virtually limited, till the end of the century, to the activity of such clubs in various cities; there were also mathematicians and philosophers working at the universities, but none was a major figure until Leibniz (1646–1716) emerged, a few years before the end of this period.[1] Some of the German societies were devoted solely to medicine; others were preoccupied (in a manner already rather old-fashioned) with exploring the 'secrets' of nature by experiment, studying physical phenomena that were still regarded as mysterious or paradoxical. One or two of the books to which they gave rise, like Caspar Schott's *Magia universalis naturae et artis* (1657–9), had a fairly general currency.

[1] For Leibniz, see below, ch. IV, pp. 82–5, ch. V, pp. 114–17, and ch. VI, pp. 145–6.

In France, also, local scientific clubs existed beside the *Académie Royale des Sciences*, whereas England was wholly dominated by the Royal Society. The founders of the latter were deliberately mindful of Bacon's programme, though they were never to enjoy the financial endowment that it required. The Royal Society undertook the compilation of the accounts of craft-methods he had advocated; sent to the provinces and abroad papers of *Quaeries* to be answered; drew up notes of advice to travellers; and made lists of experiments that ought to be performed. Their procedure demanded that an original experiment be performed at each weekly meeting, and no conjecture or theory was to be advanced for discussion unless suitable experiments were offered to substantiate it. Experiments, anatomical dissections or natural curiosities reported by the Fellows were ordered to be shown at Gresham College before the eyes of all. Like the *Saggi*, the minutes of the Society's meetings fill the reader with bewilderment: it is clear that the Fellows wished to make and understand experiments, but there is no continuity, no sense of scheme or purpose, no connection between one topic of discussion, or one meeting, and the next. There are obvious signs that experiment for its own sake could obstruct organised, coherent, scientific investigation. In the end the Fellows ceased trying to do any important work in common, in order to pursue their own researches on which they still reported from time to time.

In fact, the Royal Society never had formulated a detailed programme, nor committed itself to a tight organisation. Having its origins in an informal club of astronomers, physicians and mathematicians meeting in or near Gresham College somewhat before 1648, some of whose members moved in Cromwell's time to Oxford where they encouraged scientific pursuits in a number of brilliant young men, becoming first a formal and then a chartered society (in 1660 and 1662), it yet never lost its easy, general character. By no means all of the Fellows who assiduously participated in the meetings were erudite in science, or professionally concerned with scientific affairs. It is misleading to emphasise the amateurishness and credulity of this body—though it revealed both qualities on occasion—for generally discussion was sensible and well informed; yet it was a society willing to devote itself to any topic that seized its fancy of the moment, one in which any serious speaker might utter his mind, and one largely independent of outside influences. In its independent and liberal character the Royal Society was very different from the French academy. This was of slightly later formation, though again there is a long prehistory of regular scientific meetings in Paris. The men who met from about 1648 under the presidency of the atomist philosopher Gassendi (1592–1655) and the patronage of Habert de Montmor adopted a constitution for their academy in 1657, and from about that time were in touch with the founders of the Royal Society in England. The accession to personal power of Louis XIV, occurring at a time when dissension within the academy was strong, provided an opportunity for reorganisation under the most exalted patronage. An appeal was made to Colbert, and the *Académie Royale des Sciences* took shape in 1665–6. No earlier constitution than that of 1699 is extant, but it seems that the number of academicians was limited; they were appointed by the Crown, received pensions, and were expected to be constant in their attendance at meetings, which were not normally open to visitors. There was no room for virtuosi like Evelyn and Pepys. The *Académie* was an institution of the State in a sense which the Royal Society was not, and though its members were for the most part free to deliberate as they chose, they were on occasion subject to official demands. The most distinguished of them, the Dutch physicist Christiaan Huygens (1629–95), ultimately resigned and left Paris because of Louis XIV's militarist policies. In compensation, the *Académie* enjoyed some facilities that the Royal Society lacked. The State financed an excellent astronomical observatory for its use, where physical experiments were also made. Costly enterprises, like the measurement of the length of meridian degrees in France and the astronomical expedition to Cayenne, could be embarked upon with State aid.[1]

Scientific societies, especially the national societies of England and France, did not merely confer a local distinction upon scientific talent, nor an opportunity for discussion and joint experiment; they had an international importance too. The *Académie* numbered besides Huygens two foreign astronomers, the Italian Cassini and the Dane Roemer; the Royal Society elected foreign Fellows and maintained an extensive correspondence with Europe and New England. What was accomplished in Paris was regularly discussed in London, and vice versa. Latin, as well as French, was still an effective international language among the learned; the works of Robert Boyle, for instance, published in English, were reprinted in Latin at Amsterdam, as were the *Philosophical Transactions of the Royal Society*. (The *Académie* issued no official memoirs until after 1699.) Scientists had long been linked by a close network of private correspondence, and the device of making important results or arguments known in this way was older than Galileo. Journals like the *Journal des Savants*, the *Philosophical Transactions* (both begun in 1665) and the German *Acta Eruditorum* (1684) gave the systematic letter, in the form of a scientific article, a wider currency. Some of the most important work of the second half of the seventeenth century was first described in the *Philosophical Transactions*, which was adopted as a vehicle for publication by Malpighi in Italy and Leeuwenhoek in Holland. This development in communication was the most important that had occurred since the

[1] Crown support for the Royal Observatory at Greenwich (1675) was by contrast always meagre; on the other hand, naval resources were given to Edmond Halley to enable him to plot the position of stars in the southern sky.

invention of printing, and one peculiarly adapted to scientific needs. News, journals, and even books travelled much more rapidly than formerly, when, for instance, reports of Galileo's work were long in arriving in France and northern Europe. The number of those who could potentially take part in the scientific movement was enlarged accordingly, the new journals being above all responsible for broadening its base.

This rapid expansion of scientific activity and publicity, marked by royal visits to the academies, participation in them of the nobility, controversies over the merits of old and new ways and opinions, propaganda to farmers, manufacturers and navigators, and vehement international rivalry among the leading scientists themselves, occurred mainly in the sixth and seventh decades of the century. This was the great time of hope, to be in turn followed by a slackening of vigour and enthusiasm. It was in part one aspect of the recovery of Europe, in part an expression of the national confidence otherwise well marked in France and England; more particularly, it was the product of a feeling of triumphant emergence. The men of Galileo's time were still struggling against the oppression of the past, and harassed by conservative criticism. They had had to aspire to achievement; their successors were buoyed up by the consciousness of what had been achieved. They had but to go on, and did not doubt their ability to progress in ways already proved successful. This did not mean, however, that at mid-century solider proofs of the 'new philosophy' were not still required. A demonstration of the motion of the earth was still desired; the telescope's revelation of the heavens was still imperfect; the speculations of chemical philosophers and physicians were still in hot debate; the circulation of the blood had still to be vindicated and interpreted; the fundamental theory of dynamics was still in urgent need of exact statement. Above all, new ideas on the secret springs of nature embraced in the mechanical philosophy were conflicting and insecure. Cartesianism had still to be explored and tested. The mechanical philosophy was the heart of the new scientific outlook. Much else, of outstanding importance in contributing to a new picture of the natural world, was limited to the range of observational description, pure mathematical theory, or empirical experiment. Discoveries of this kind, however important, could not by themselves offer the more profound explanations of natural phenomena, such as Descartes had sought; they could not elucidate the unchanging attributes of matter, nor the forces by which nature invariably operates. To this extent, therefore, the deeper tenets of the old philosophy like the schoolmen's distinctions of form and substance would be left inviolate unless they were challenged by a theoretical structure of equal universality. Here was the real problem of ideas, in the completion of the replacement of the old conception of the natural order by a new one: a task that could necessarily be vindicated only by its dramatic success.

The success was to be won in Newton's *Philosophiae Naturalis Principia Mathematica* of 1687; won, in fact, in opposition to Cartesianism though not to the scientific attitude that Descartes had inculcated. And this success of the scientific revolution summarised many of its most recent developments, though it was not immediately dependent on all of them. Some of these, therefore, must be described first.

Galileo's advocacy of Copernican astronomy had been brilliantly effective; it had nullified all physical objections to the motion of the earth and had brought forward fresh observational evidence against Ptolemy's heliostatic system, but it left a geometrical chaos. His celestial physics was far too simple to be true. Descartes's cosmology explained the nature of stars, sun, planets, and earth; it stated the cause of gravity, explained why the planets revolved, and how their orbits preserved their stability; but Descartes was no more concerned for the exactitude of astronomical geometry than was Galileo. Neither physical theory could satisfy a mathematical astronomer. While the key to the problem lay unperceived in Kepler's laws, planetary theory (the chief preoccupation of astronomers for over 1500 years) was neglected; the telescope commanded all attention. For many years it remained a small, crude instrument, with which others often failed to see what Galileo had observed through his favourite *occhiale*. Improvements were effected by using a magnifying convex eye-lens in place of the concave lens of the Galilean telescope, and through refinement of glass-working techniques. By about 1680 telescopes 40 or 50 feet long were not uncommon, and monsters of 100 or 200 feet had been attempted. Magnification increased to the point where the strange mystery of Saturn's variable appearance could be resolved,[1] and even the division of its ring observed. Five satellites of this planet were discovered, to add to the four famous 'Medicean stars' circling Jupiter. Their orbits and periodic times could be measured accurately with the aid of micrometers placed in the telescope's field of vision; from such observations on the satellites of Jupiter, Roemer deduced in 1676 that light took about 20 minutes to traverse the earth's orbit. Hevelius at Danzig studied comets and selenography; Flamsteed at Greenwich re-mapped the fixed stars and observed the motion of the moon. Nearly another century was to elapse before the exploring telescope could reach beyond the limits of the solar system, but already enough, and accurate, information had been collected by 1687 to enable the theory of universal gravitation to be verified from the behaviour of planets, comets and the moon. Indeed, astronomy permitted wider speculation: might not these other new worlds it disclosed be inhabited too, as Fontenelle suggested in 1686? The most powerful telescopes, leading the eye into the Milky Way and the farthest depths of space could detect no propinquity in the stars, nor suggest any

[1] It was caused by the varying inclination of the ring, which had caused Saturn sometimes to appear as though accompanied by two adjacent stars.

limit to their remoteness: might not the universe be infinite? Thus the imaginings of Giordano Bruno became in a century transposed into sober scientific conjecture.

Observational astronomy could falsify or support an explanation of its complex, yet clearly patterned, phenomena; much else was required to devise an explanation: not least was a suitable mathematical analysis. Kepler at the beginning of the century had strained the resources of conventional geometry in his struggle to determine the true shape of a planetary orbit, yet the problems involved in setting out a physical theory of planetary motions in mathematical form were far more severe. Descartes had not attempted it; he had asserted that the planets were borne around the sun in an ethereal vortex, without examining mathematically the conditions of such motion. (Newton undertook this, and proved that a vortex could not impart to the planets their observed velocities.) The marriage of algebra and geometry effected by Descartes, however, furnished the basis for mathematical procedures by which his own physics could be disproved. The essence of the matter is that the problem of handling mathematically the motions of bodies in curves was advanced far towards solution.[1] The Greek geometers had solved this problem for circular motion, the simplest case of all; the later seventeenth-century mathematicians were able to deal with more complex curves—the parabola, ellipse and hyperbola (also well understood in antiquity), the cycloid, the catenary and many more—and their methods were convenient and general. As it happened, the main features of the developments in pure mathematics that interested most mathematicians—developments leading to the differential and integral calculus—were brought sharply into focus by solving mechanical problems: the properties of the curve traced by a point on a wheel rolling along a plane, or of the curve assumed by a perfect chain, suspended by its ends. Though the solution of such problems as these was mathematically difficult at the time when they were proposed, the results were trivial for physics; whereas the analogous problems arising when the action of forces on bodies was studied were very important in physics.

Advanced mathematics was essential for the development of dynamical theory, and in turn dynamical theory was essential to celestial mechanics. In the earlier part of this period Huygens's work in dynamics excelled; though he did not display the highest genius for invention in pure mathematics, Huygens's accomplishments, like those of Newton, would clearly have been impossible for anyone lacking great mathematical ability. These accomplishments, not fully published until 1673 (*Horologium*

[1] As the *Principia* shows, this does not mean that *every* mathematical problem encountered in physics could be solved. Important areas of pure mathematical thought relevant to contemporary physics were still almost unexplored at the end of the century. But in the work of Huygens, Newton, Leibniz and their successors the major immediate obstacles were overcome.

Oscillatorium), were the result of researches begun early, about 1657. Huygens made a full study of the dynamics of oscillating bodies (from which incidentally he obtained a very accurate value for the acceleration due to gravity) and went on to discover how to calculate the centripetal acceleration of a body revolving in a circle. He also investigated the impact of elastic and inelastic bodies, correcting the faulty principles enunciated by Descartes. Huygens did not endeavour, however, to apply his dynamical reasoning to the motions of celestial bodies; strangely enough the problems they presented do not seem to have interested him, although he was a keen observer and devoted much labour to the construction of his own telescopes. Well aware as he was of the many errors in Descartes's *Principia Philosophiae* and of the *a priori* character of Descartes's theorisation, he nevertheless remained essentially a Cartesian, above all in cosmology. Thus he stood firm in the conviction that terrestrial gravity and the planetary revolutions were caused by an ethereal vortex, and consequently the line of thought that Newton followed was closed to him.

Possibly Huygens, like most scientists, was still insensitive to the crucial significance of Kepler's laws. About 1645 some astronomers recognised that Kepler had solved the age-old problem of the true paths followed by the planets, though in general the controversial issue was seen in terms of the opposition of Copernicus and Galileo to Ptolemy and Tycho Brahe; this polemical issue tended to obscure the merit of Kepler's intricate mathematical labours. The ellipticity of the orbits was commonly accepted only from about 1660, as for example by the Italian Cartesian, Alphonso Borelli, in 1666. More important, Kepler's third law was familiar to Newton at about the same moment. Like Huygens, Newton calculated (in either 1665 or 1666) the centripetal acceleration (*conatus a centro*) of a body revolving in a circle; combining this information with Kepler's third law of planetary motion,[1] he recognised that the centripetal acceleration of each planet is proportional to the inverse square of its mean distance from the sun.

Once this was understood, it was possible to introduce a great and transforming conception. Descartes had been very well aware that, unless they were impelled towards the sun by some force, the planets would move in straight lines out into space—in fact it was Descartes who had first correctly stated the law of inertia, of which this is a consequence. He had accordingly explained how (as he thought) the ethereal vortex about the sun would press the planet inwards, so that it could not escape but must for ever revolve in an orbit. Newton had now satisfied himself that this force towards the sun must always be inversely as the square of the distance from the sun: he adventured into a totally new realm of ideas in

[1] This states that among the planets there is a constant ratio between the cubes of their mean distances from the sun, and their periods of revolution.

proposing to identify it with that other force known as gravity on the earth's surface. If the earth had this gravitating power, why should it not also belong to the vastly more massive sun, and to the other planets as well? And why should not this power extend far from the immediate vicinity of the body, indeed indefinitely into space? By a simple calculation, Newton again satisfied himself that if the earth exerted a gravitational pull upon the moon, like that which it exerted upon heavy objects near its surface, but reduced in the squared ratio of the moon's distance, this pull would be 'pretty nearly' of the magnitude necessary to prevent the moon escaping from the earth altogether by its own motion. (If Newton had known the size of the earth more correctly in 1666, the agreement would have been almost complete.) If all these suppositions were correct, there would be no function for the Cartesian ether to fulfil in accounting for the planetary motions.

In 1666 Newton was by no means confident that they were correct; for his trial on the lunar motion seemed to indicate a discrepancy. Other means of checking them were not readily available at this point. He lacked information on the detailed astronomical facts; more serious still, his initial crude investigation was founded on the rough assumption of circular motions, whereas he knew from Kepler that the planetary paths are elliptical, and from the English astronomer Horrox that the moon's orbit is elliptical also. To analyse these actual motions dynamically raised formidable mathematical difficulties. And there was a further serious problem, which again relates Newton's work to that of his predecessor, Descartes. For it is certain that Newton was a mechanical philosopher: that he believed all matter to be composed of particles, and every property or attribute of matter to be explicable in terms of its component particles. Gravity could be no exception; if aggregates of innumerable particles possess a gravitating power, it must belong to each component particle. Again, it would be far from easy to show how the gravitating properties of large bodies arise from the gravitational power of the particles.

For such reasons Newton kept his ideas on celestial mechanics to himself for twenty years. He spoke to no one of a hypothesis that he knew he could not prove; he seems even to have undervalued its importance. There were really two tasks before him: one was to explore dynamics more thoroughly, especially the dynamics of bodies moving under the action of central forces (this he was to do in Book I of the *Principia*), and further to show that these dynamical principles apply to the celestial motions (this he did in Book III); the second task was to place the gravitational force in its proper context as one of the fundamental natural forces, associated with the ultimate particulate structure of bodies and hence with their aggregate masses. This would have provided, to put it crudely, the explanation of gravity. If he had done this, Newton's work would have been completely parallel to that of Descartes, though mathematically and dynamically far superior; but he was never able to accomplish the second task to his satisfaction, and so was compelled to refer to the universal gravitating power of bodies (whose laws of operation he defined) as something that *de facto* exists, though it cannot be accounted for. Following this policy, when he published the *Principia* Newton struck out a *Conclusion* he had drafted in which gravitation was boldly handled as a mechanical principle.[1] Newton's status as a mechanical philosopher is still clear in the *Principia*, but it was not to be exhibited in the form of conjectures about the cause of gravitation. It is hard not to believe that it was a policy that Newton adopted with reluctance, that he would not have preferred to be as complete as Descartes in explaining gravitation mechanically, and it seems very likely that he did over these twenty years search for such an explanation.

Newton's thoughts on the mechanical cause of gravitation illustrate the complexity of his reaction to Cartesian principles—a complexity evident in the theorisation of other English scientists at this time. They accepted and found useful the basic Cartesian premises: that matter is particulate; that all the phenomena of nature arise from the interacting motions of the particles; that these motions are in accord with dynamical laws. They even believed in an ether, a medium whose particles were immensely more minute and more widely separated than those composing ordinary matter, and might have other properties differentiating them from material particles. (Newton himself postulated such an ether in his more speculative pronouncements.) They were as convinced of the mechanism of the universe as was Descartes himself: effect followed from cause in an unbroken chain till the first causes were found in the structure and properties of matter and ether. God was the First Cause, and His creation of the universe not mechanical, but as the physiologist Nehemiah Grew wrote (using a simile repeated over and over):

> [We need not think] that there is any Contradiction, when *Philosophy* teaches that to be done by *Nature*; which *Religion*, and the Sacred *Scriptures*, teach us to be done by *God*; no more, than to say, That the Ballance of a *Watch* is moved by the next *Wheel*, is to deny that *Wheel*, and the rest, to be moved by the *Spring*; and that both the *Spring*, and all the other *Parts*, are caused to move together by the *Maker* of them. So *God* may be truly the *Cause* of *This Effect*, although a Thousand other *Causes* should be supposed to intervene: For all Nature is as one Great *Engine*, made by, and held in His Hand.[2]

These were broad ideas that all scientists of the later seventeenth century held in common. Within their loose framework it was possible to move more or less far away from the explanations of particular phenomena devised by Descartes himself; to reject the Cartesian ether, the vortices,

[1] Some of the content of the rejected *Conclusion* is reflected in the *Quaeries* added to Newton's *Opticks* about twenty years later.

[2] *The Anatomy of Plants* (London, 1682), p. 80.

the Cartesian conception of light, and so forth, while remaining a mechanical philosopher and faithful to the basic tenets of Cartesian science—perhaps more faithful than Descartes and some of his followers. Thus to favour mechanical explanations did not necessarily mean that one was content (as Gassendi was) with Greek atomism, or the closely woven Cartesian system.

One of the first to make this abundantly clear was Robert Boyle (1627–91). His adhesion to the mechanical philosophy was never in doubt: he proclaimed it constantly, regarded the mechanical explanation of phenomena as the core of the scientific revolution, and strove constantly to illustrate its validity by experiment. Yet Boyle claimed to have refrained from reading both Descartes and Gassendi in his early days as a scientist in order to deliver his mind from the tyranny of systems. (One might perhaps wonder how, then, he learnt to be a mechanical philosopher.) In his first important scientific work (*New Experiments Physico-Mechanical touching the Spring of the Air and its Effects*, 1660) Boyle displayed the ingenuity in the design, execution and interpretation of experiments, whether in physics or chemistry, that was to illuminate science in the next thirty years; he showed also scepticism concerning the hypothetical or dogmatic conceptions of Descartes. He doubted the Cartesian definition of matter by extension; he doubted the Cartesian denial of the vacuum. His experiments did not permit him to deny the Cartesian hypotheses outright; but he demanded that experiment be brought forward to prove them. He himself, however, could not see how the elasticity of air could be accounted for save by a mechanical hypothesis based on its particulate composition.

The titles of Boyle's later works themselves indicate the bent of his theory: *The Origin of Forms and Qualities* (1666), *The Excellency and Grounds of the Mechanical Philosophy* (1674), *The Mechanical Origin of Volatility* (1675), *The Mechanical Production of Electricity* (1675), *The Mechanical Origin of Heat and Cold* (1675), and numerous others illustrate for various aspects of science the merits of mechanical explanations. It was chemistry that especially attracted Boyle's interest. Van Helmont in the preceding generation had tried to frame a chemical philosophy; but Boyle was the first to borrow the ideas of *his* natural philosophy—the mechanical or corpuscular philosophy—and use them to explain chemical phenomena. His object, he declared, was to try 'whether I could, by the help of the corpuscular philosophy...associated with chymical experiments, explicate some particular subjects more intelligibly, than they are wont to be accounted for, either by the schools or the chymists'.[1] Boyle's theory of chemistry was essentially a physical one: it would explain a chemical reaction by considering the physical structure of the reagents

[1] *Some Specimens of an Attempt to make Chymical Experiments useful to illustrate the Notions of the Corpuscular Philosophy: Works* (1772), I, 356.

and the motions of their particles. He neither employed nor invented specifically chemical concepts—he rejected the notion of chemical elements for example—except as these were necessary to describe the materials he used and the experiments he made.

In this endeavour Boyle differed doubly from the chemists of his own and earlier generations. In the first place chemical phenomena were mainly of interest to him as evidence for a new philosophy of nature—though he became indeed enormously interested in them for their own sake; neither, however, did he regard chemistry as being primarily an art or technique. Those chemical writers of the recent past who had ventured upon elaborations of theory, such as Paracelsus and the less extravagant van Helmont, had developed mysterious and esoteric explanations that owed something to alchemy but little to rational philosophy. Reciprocally, the philosophers had paid little attention to them. Other chemists, writing as plain men undeceived by theoretical fancies, looked upon their science as merely a complex of techniques—solution, distillation, precipitation, sublimation, crystallisation and so on—applied to specific materials in order to obtain specific products. To most of these, chemistry was the art of preparing effective medicaments, a function which they treated in a wholly empirical fashion. Chemistry appeared in a similar light to those who were interested in the scientific aspects of metallurgy, dyeing, glass-making and other industries, in which notable empirical advances were occurring at this time. Yet again, natural philosophers like Descartes had paid little attention to the techniques of chemistry until their significance was emphasised by Boyle. Working just at the moment when existing explanations of chemical changes—such as combustion—whether Aristotelian or Paracelsan, were beginning to seem rather feeble, and when at least the manipulative part of chemistry was being described in a full and rational manner, Boyle was able to demonstrate that this neglected form of experiment could yield valuable information about the nature of matter, and that an adequate theory of matter might account for all the facts known to chemists. No other chemist had seen as deeply as this. Boyle was indeed attempting to extend to the chemical range of experience the ambition already dominant in physics: the explanation of everything in terms of corpuscular structure and properties. This would have made chemistry strictly parallel to, or even dependent upon, physics; and the influence of Boyle's mechanical philosophy applied to chemistry explains why Newton in turn devoted so much attention to chemical experiments and their explanation in terms of corpuscular structure and forces.

It is easy to judge that this attempt to account for chemical facts in terms of physical theory was premature. Though it was possible to account for many single experiments—such as those on the solution of metals in acids with the formation of salts—within the corpuscular hypothesis, and such explanations afforded useful insights into the general nature of chemical reaction, neither Boyle nor Newton succeeded in framing a complete theory solidly based on experimental facts. Their loose texture of hypotheses never consolidated into a theory in a way comparable with the theories of physical science. But this first attempt to render chemistry a rational, mechanical science should not be regarded as wholly futile. It was henceforward considered a proper branch of natural philosophy, one that rapidly ceased to be marked by the singularities of its early development. Moreover, the philosophical chemists like Boyle proved themselves not less able than their empiricist colleagues in the operations of the science, and so did much to remove from chemical experimentation the atmosphere of workshop and kitchen.

A special problem, attracting much attention then as later, was that of combustion. This could be described as a special kind of fermentation, which like other examples of fermentation (and putrefaction) produced heat by bringing about a violent agitation of the particles. This could again be compared with the heat evolved in some chemical reactions as a result of a similar agitation. Combustion, however, has a peculiar association with a luminous glow or flame, and unlike other heat-producing processes it can normally take place only in the presence of air. The fact that some apparently cold substances—phosphorescent ones—are also luminous was an additional complication. The English mechanical philosophers (Hooke, Mayow, Boyle, and Newton) all had their say on this subject, which was neither to be solved by their corpuscular hypothesis nor in the seventeenth century. Nevertheless, their theories were consonant with a purely kinetic idea of heat (whereas the eighteenth-century chemists had to describe heat as an impalpable fluid). They ascribed combustion to the presence of a particular type of 'sulphureous' particle in all combustible matter, and they further recognized that the agitation of heat resulted from the violent interaction of this type with a second, 'nitrous' type found in air and other substances, especially nitre. Thus combustion and flame-producing were explained by appeal to the same sort of mechanism that was supposed to operate in other chemical reactions; and to some extent the appearance of light itself was accounted for mechanically.

Light and its laws, its transmission and the formation of colours had always offered a challenge to science, one that the Middle Ages had faced more successfully than antiquity. Geometrical optics—the tracing of a ray of light as represented by a straight line through reflections and refractions—had reached a fair degree of precision while ideas about the origin and nature of light were still crude. For geometrical optics does not explain what light is, or how it is capable of giving rise to the sensation of colour, or why it is reflected and refracted by liquid and solid bodies. Physical theories accounting for such properties of light virtually begin in the second half of the seventeenth century, upon a basis of Cartesian speculation. Descartes had done notable work in geometrical optics; in his theory of light he explained it as a pressure in the material ether emanating from the luminous source; physiologically the sensation of light was caused by the action of this pressure on the optic nerve. His successors were divided in opinion between two theories, each owing something to his. In the emission theory light was regarded as a stream of particles, issuing from the source in all directions. In the pulse theory (where the analogy was with the transmission of sound) the source was regarded as creating a pulsatory or vibratory motion in the ether, travelling outwards from its centre. Both conceptions were, like that of Descartes, mechanical; both involved particulate motions, and there was not to be for a long time any possibility of experimental discrimination between them.

Newton was the most powerful and fertile supporter of the emission theory, though he recognised at length that no simple analogy between a light-ray and a stream of particles could be made to work. He held that a pulsatory theory could not account for the rectilinear propagation of light. The reception of his optical discoveries, described in the *Philosophical Transactions* in 1672, was hampered by his supposed attachment to the emission theory. Against his critics Newton argued that his discoveries were experimental facts or necessary inferences from these facts standing entirely independent of hypotheses. From neat and conclusive experiments he reasoned that white light was not simple and homogeneous, as had always been supposed, but was a mixture of coloured constituents; these, when properly distinguished from each other—as by passing a white beam through a glass prism—proved to be truly simple and homogeneous: therefore, colour was not caused by a modification of white light, as had been believed in the past. To each coloured constituent, moreover, belonged an unvarying potentiality for refraction; however large or small the angle of refraction, the blue rays were always bent more than the red. The separate constituents could be recombined to give white light identical with the first, but no ordinary white light could be formed without all of them.

Like Hooke and Grimaldi—respectively the first to describe interference (as we now call it) and diffraction bands, both in 1665 when Newton was making his own early optical experiments—Newton discovered that colours could be obtained from white light by other means than refraction. His studies of all these phenomena were profound; but his mechanical hypotheses to account for the separation of the coloured constituents were less successful, and unverifiable. His best effort was in suggesting that when white light falls on an object, one or more of the coloured constituents of the light may be more strongly reflected than the rest, because of the corpuscular nature of the object's surface. If for instance green is reflected strongly and the rest weakly the object will appear green, and similarly with transmission through transparent materials.[1] In the *Principia* Newton showed how a stream of particles falling on a surface could be so bent round as to re-emerge, that is, be reflected, the angles obeying the correct optical law. He always supposed that refraction, interference and diffraction were caused by a force in or near bodies acting upon the beam of light and bending it;[2] colours appeared because the force acted more strongly on some constituents of the beam than on others, and so caused them to diverge.

Newton was always—or very nearly always—careful to distinguish in print between direct inference from experiment and explanatory hypotheses of light which had not been demonstrated. The lasting scientific merit of his work lies in the former, though his hypotheses had a century-long influence, and in them his constant recourse to concepts of corpuscular structure, and of attraction between the particles of bodies and those of light, is perfectly clear. Once again physics was reduced, in principle, to corpuscular dynamics, as in the theory of gravitation. Since the exponents of the alternative pulse-theory shared similar notions of structure (though they did not admit Newton's intracorpuscular forces of attraction and repulsion) they were at a disadvantage: it was less easy to connect a vibratory motion in the ether with the corpuscular structure of reflecting and refracting bodies. Hooke's ingenious hypothesis in the *Micrographia* (1665), explaining how colours were produced by disturbance of the pulses constituting white light, was invalidated by Newton's paper of 1672. Huygens worked out correctly the geometry of reflection and refraction for the pulse-theory (*Traité de la Lumière*, 1690) but did not attempt to explain the formation of colours. Though later theorists were to build upon Huygens's analysis, from the point of view of contemporary mechanical philosophers Newton's hypotheses were more readily acceptable, and explained far more. They seemed successful because they satisfied current expectations of what a theory or hypothesis in physics should do; expectations both too narrow in their range and too ambitious in their pretensions that set the bounds of the scientific thought of the age.

Discussion of fundamental theories and hypotheses was the subject of only a small fraction of the scientific writing of the second half of the seventeenth century. For the most part the physical sciences were treated either mathematically or experimentally; Boyle was exceptional in his explicit and detailed defence of the mechanical philosophy, and yet the great bulk of even his work was devoted to the consideration of his experiments. The publications of other physicists like Huygens, Newton, Mariotte were also chiefly concerned with the reporting of experiments or

[1] Newton showed that, when illuminated by a monochromatic light, objects (variously coloured in white light) appear of the same colour, more or less brightly.

[2] *Opticks*, Quaery 5, etc.

the development of propositions in mathematical form. On the other hand, the expositors of Cartesian natural philosophy (as distinct from mathematicians and experimenters who adopted Cartesian ideas where they seemed useful) made scarcely any use of mathematical demonstration, and employed experiments only to illustrate their doctrines. After initial resistance, attributable to partiality towards Aristotle combined with a dislike of mechanism, the scientific principles of Descartes had become fashionable. They were taught by the Jesuits, one of whom, Jacques Rohault, wrote the outstanding textbook of Cartesian science, which was popular until well into the next century (*Traité de Physique*, 1671). Adding little theoretically but something experimentally to Descartes's *Principia Philosophiae* (1644), Rohault expounded Cartesian physics and cosmology plausibly, and with a greater air of certainty than its originator. Cartesian physics was a system, whose metaphysical postulates had been deliberately defined: hence in teaching it as a system there was necessarily a considerable emphasis on its manner of explaining phenomena universally by corpuscular mechanism. And as a system its purpose was to explain the universe as a whole, not to describe or analyse in detail particular phenomena (as Descartes himself had done in other works). Even with this class of writing set aside, however, together with the writings of those who clearly subscribed to Cartesian mechanism though they cannot be numbered among its expositors, the mechanical philosophy was undoubtedly dominant among physical scientists; as Hooke wrote of his colleagues in the Royal Society, 'they found some reason to suspect that those effects of Bodies which have been commonly attributed to [scholastic] *Qualities*, and those confessed to be *occult*, are perform'd by the small machines of Nature'. The 'small machines', the wheels within wheels of material bodies, were corpuscular mechanisms. With common agreement on the basic idea and its application, and much common language, analogy, and elementary illustration of the truth of the mechanical philosophy, each scientist (again excepting the professed Cartesians) produced his own variants in dealing with particular phenomena—optics, chemical reaction, pneumatics, combustion, magnetism. Mechanical explanations were not fixed or determined.

The great originality of Newton was to lie in the suggestion that various forces of attraction and repulsion—he did not define their nature or number—operate between the component particles of bodies. 'Have not the small Particles of Bodies certain Powers, Virtues, or Forces by which they act at a distance, not only upon the Rays of Light...but also upon one another for producing a great Part of the Phenomena of Nature?' he was to ask years later. This broad hypothesis was by no means conspicuous when the *Principia* was published in 1687; on the other hand, the notion of gravitational 'attraction' was itself enough to disturb the strict mechanists, especially the Cartesians. That corpuscles and masses of matter should attract each other, and not be impelled together by the pressure of a material ether, seemed to many a revival of discredited occult forces. (Newton was careful later to insist that in referring to 'attractive' and 'repulsive' forces he did not mean to deny that these forces might be produced by mechanical impulses still unknown.) Newton's version of corpuscular mechanism, which had taken definite shape at the time when the *Principia* was written though his ideas were known to few, was more subtle and powerful than any that preceded it; but the primitive billiard-ball simplicity of the earlier forms of mechanical philosophy was sacrificed. However, the dispute between Cartesians and Newtonians must be left for the present.

What should be said here is that the *Principia*, a book in which the mechanical philosophy and the corpuscular structure of matter are treated as common assumptions requiring no argument, provided the best exemplification of mechanism. The universe of Newton is neither more nor less mechanistic than that of Descartes. But Descartes had composed 'un beau roman de physique' (as Huygens said): its machinery was imaginary. The universe of the *Principia* is mathematically and observationally impeccable;[1] for the hypothetical machine-world of Descartes Newton had substituted a testable and verified theory. The satellites of Jupiter and Saturn, the revolutions of the planets, the motions of the moon and of the tides, the oscillations of the pendulum, the descent of heavy bodies, the flow of liquids, and the echo itself testify to its truth. And as Newton reminded his readers more than once, what is true of the whole is true of the parts: we can only deduce mathematically the laws governing observable phenomena from our certainty that the invisible world of microscopic particles is mechanistic, just as we confirm our certainty by the experiments on macroscopic bodies which alone are feasible. In his concept of *force*, as governing the motions of particles, Newton went far beyond Descartes, preparing the way for the nineteenth- and twentieth-century concept of *field*. He believed in the existence of many different forces operative at the microscopic and the observable levels alike: three (gravity, magnetism, and electricity) were directly demonstrable; others, like the force by which bodies act on light, and that involved in chemical reaction, could be inferred from experiments; others again, like the force of cohesion rendering bodies hard, seemed necessary but even less susceptible to experiment. These forces would explain both why a world made up of infinitesimal particles immensely thinly scattered in space was nevertheless stable and solid, and why such a world was capable of revealing motion, change, growth, and decay. Of all the forces only one, gravity, was mastered by Newton; only gravity was comprehended within a mathematical system, with its laws and their operation securely proved

[1] At least in principle! The *Principia* was not without error, as Newton's critics pointed out.

from observation and experiment. Newton's universe of particles and forces was a mechanistic one, and he revealed the mechanism of gravitation. This was the triumph of the mechanical philosophy; yet in comparison with Newton's ambitions it was, perhaps, 'the shadow of a noble experiment'. As he wrote in the preface to the *Principia*:

I wish we could derive the rest of the phenomena of Nature by the same kind of reasoning from mechanical principles [as he had derived the phenomena of gravitation] for I am induced by many reasons to suspect that they may all depend upon certain forces by which the particles of bodies, by some causes hitherto unknown, are either mutually impelled towards one another, and cohere in regular figures, or are repelled and recede from one another.

Many passages in Newton's writings make it plain that, like other followers of the mechanical philosophy and of Descartes, he saw the intricacy of particulate structure as applicable, in increasing complexity of explanation, to the understanding not merely of physics and chemistry but of biological processes too. The quotation from Nehemiah Grew[1] shows that a naturalist need find nothing abhorrent in the physicist's picture of the universe. Perception and muscular control; nutrition and growth; respiration and the motion of the heart; these and other characteristic attributes of living beings were also regarded as explicable on mechanical principles—though philosophers did so at the cost of maintaining the Cartesian dichotomy between mind and matter.[2] The analogy between physiological processes in the living being and chemical processes *in vitro* had been emphasised earlier, by Paracelsus and van Helmont, for example; if now chemistry was to be given a mechanistic theory, it was natural that it should be extended to physiology. The progress of experiment offered a very natural opportunity for this. Boyle's experiments with the air-pump, and other related ones, suggested a close similarity between respiration and combustion in keeping with a much older simile between life and flame. Animals and flame both needed air—or as it was later proved, some constituent of the air; neither could survive in an atmosphere vitiated by the other. Further, an animal rendered incapable of normal breathing could be kept alive by filling its lungs with fresh air from a bellows. It was consistent with anatomical knowledge to suppose that it was the function of the lungs gradually to expose the whole blood in the body to fresh air; and the clinching argument was supplied by Lower's demonstration that the change in appearance between venous blood (entering the lungs) and arterial blood (leaving the lungs) was effected by exposure of the former to air, and could be reproduced *in vitro*. Hence, it was argued, something present in the air—some particles, of course, usually qualified as nitrous—entered the blood and were necessary

[1] See above, p. 57.

[2] Newton (for example) did not applaud the manner in which this distinction was upheld by Descartes, but he did not challenge its basic necessity.

to life, as they were to fire. These particles were purely hypothetical entities, and no plausible role could be assigned to them in altering the appearance of the blood or in physiology generally; but within the terms of the mechanical philosophy the new theory gave a fresh significance to Harvey's discovery of the circulation, just as Malpighi's actual observation of the passage of the blood through capillary vessels from the artery to the vein completed its anatomical confirmation. The blood was not only seen to move: its movement through the lungs and then about the body had been given a purpose.

The study of respiration affords an example, somewhat rare in the seventeenth century, of the fruitful transplantation of the ideas of physical science into a biological environment. This transplantation is the core of the work of the English physician John Mayow, published in 1668 and 1674, who elaborated on the groundwork of Boyle, Hooke and Lower. Mayow attempted a complete exploration of the physiological functioning of the 'nitro-aerial' particles, which he regarded as also instrumental to various phenomena in physics and chemistry; and in this the danger of such transplantation becomes apparent, for it had the effect of slurring over the distinction between a relatively simple effect in physics and a far more complex one in biology. It was a long-standing weakness of chemical theory and practice that chemists tended to regard an involved organic operation—say the distillation of vegetable matter or of blood—as though it were exactly like a simple inorganic process; it was even worse to suppose that a plant 'grew' like a crystal, or that an animal could be represented by a marionette of wheels and wires. The *principle* was sound, but in reading Lower's words (1669): 'If you ask me for the paths in the lungs, through which the nitrous spirit of the air reaches the blood, and colours it more deeply, do you in turn show me the little pores by which that other nitrous spirit, which exists in snow, passes into the drinks of gourmets and cools their summer drinks...', one becomes aware of the frailness of the shoot that was to be transplanted, and of the dimness of the philosophers' realisation of the change of environment involved. Intellectually, the situation is not unlike that which existed in actual fact when some experimenters (including Lower) attempted to transplant an animal's blood into man: if the experiments had worked better their results would have been more often fatal.

Studies of other biological questions—of the ingestion and digestion of food in men and animals, of the growth of plants from soil and water, or forms of perception, especially vision, of the development of the mammalian foetus and so forth—either attempted the use for different purposes of the new techniques of physical science, or sought to make better sense of what was known in the light of physical ideas. None was very successful, though one might note the future promise of such endeavours as Nehemiah Grew's to determine the composition of vegetable materials by chemical analysis. An enormously greater activity in biology, falling into three wide categories, was directed less to the understanding of function and growth than to enumeration and description.

There was first the continuing interest of medical men (for the most part) in the structure of man and other species. Broadly speaking, the general topographic anatomy of the human body had been fairly well established by the mid-seventeenth century, and, apart from microscopic investigation to be mentioned later, the emphasis was now on comparative anatomy, or on more specialised and detailed examination of particular organs or structures such as had been begun long before by Fabricius and Casserio. A very large body of zoological knowledge was built up by Claude Perrault (1613–88) and other members of the French academy, who dissected mainly mammals and birds; by Gerard Blasius (*c.* 1625–92), who described in three books over a hundred species, and others associated with him in Amsterdam; by the members of the *Academia Naturae Curiosorum*, especially Johannes von Muralt of Zürich (1645–1733); and in England by John Willis (1621–75; oyster, lobster, earthworm) and Edward Tyson (1651–1708), the first English zoological anatomist of real importance, who (besides others) dissected three American species: the rattlesnake, peccary and opossum. His work on the 'pygmy' (chimpanzee) showed that, if less than a man, it was not a monkey. Technique advanced rapidly. Effective methods for injecting specimens with wax and mercury were introduced by Jan Swammerdam; anatomical museums came into existence, and of course illustration was freely used. Some of the zoologists, like Swammerdam (and Hooke, Lower and Wren in England) were led from dissection to experiment; thus the contraction of the muscle of a frog on applying a mechanical stimulus to the nerve provoked a good deal of curiosity. Descartes, who had considerable experience as an anatomist, had attempted to account for the transmission of a sensation from the external sense-organs to the brain and of the 'message' from the brain to the muscles by the motions of a subtle fluid; and Alphonso Borelli in *De motu animalium* (1680–1) attempted to develop a purely mechanistic approach even further. Yet Swammerdam had already demonstrated that the volume of a muscle does not increase on contraction; rather, he thought, it diminished.

All this work on zoology did much to correct old errors and clear up old problems, even though zoologists could still, despite the anatomical evidence before their eyes, refuse to classify the porpoise and other cetacea with the animals rather than the fishes. The swim-bladders of fish were well understood, for instance, as was the insect eye; it was possible to understand and compare the circulatory and reproductive mechanisms in the different classes of mammals, amphibia, reptiles and fishes, though many gaps were left and many mistakes made. Some simple generalisations could be drawn, like that associating the type of stomach and the length of intestine with the food normal to the creature. A very striking confutation of traditional zoological fallacy was provided by Francesco Redi (a member of the *Accademia del Cimento*) in 1668. It had long been believed, even the great Harvey having contradicted himself on this point, that numerous creatures—frogs, bees, 'barnacle geese', insects, and above all insect parasites—were spontaneously generated from dirt and rottenness. Like summer flies, they appeared and disappeared without trace. By simple observations and experiments (like allowing meat to putrefy under muslin, so that flies were denied access to it) as well as dissection, Redi proved that the supposedly spontaneously generated creatures were reproduced by normal means. Putrescent matter generated maggots only after flies had settled on it; the maggots in turn became pupae from which hatched flies of the same kind. He asserted roundly (and was joined in this by most naturalists of the later seventeenth century, though the controversy was revived later in a new form) that all kinds of plants and animals arise only from seeds or eggs produced by parents of the same kind. Since it followed that the continuity of species is preserved not by chance but by transmission, Redi effectively removed the last obstacle to the acceptance of the concept of immutable specific descent, like descending from like without significant variation.

From quite a different quarter came other support for the same concept. The second category of biological description, that dependent on the microscope, gave rise to ideas that seemed to establish the immutability of species as almost a logical inevitability. After the early observations of Stelluti (1618) the microscope resumed its role as the biologist's indispensable tool about 1660, in the hands (nearly at the same time) of Marcello Malpighi, Robert Hooke, Jan Swammerdam, and Henry Power. The first two used the compound microscope, optically and mechanically more elaborate, but cumbersome, unstable and limited to a workable magnification of about 60 or 80 times. The technical problems in making a really efficient, high-power microscope were not solved before about 1830. Swammerdam, like Leeuwenhoek later, used simple biconvex lenses, easy to manipulate and capable of yielding an equal enlargement. Leeuwenhoek, an artist in making very small lenses and adapting them to his purposes—he made over 400 microscopes for his own use, since he adapted each one to a particular purpose—achieved magnifications of the order of 300 by which he was able to see some bacteria. Even the less powerful devices of Malpighi (1628–94) and Swammerdam (1637–80) were enough virtually to bring new branches of biology into existence. The former has the stronger claim to be considered the founder of animal and plant histology; together they created insect morphology in their studies of the silkworm (Malpighi) and the may-fly (Swammerdam) through their respective life-cycles. Malpighi's description of the developing heart of the chick has been described as 'perhaps the most remarkable observational achievement of any biologist in the seventeenth century',[1] while Swammerdam was undoubtedly its greatest entomologist. Both were brought to the same ideas on generation: Malpighi by tracing back the structure of the chick, Swammerdam by his discovery that at a certain stage in the development of an insect the larval, pupal, and imaginal forms may co-exist one within the other; they concluded that the embryo is preformed in the egg. Its structure did not take shape, and change, as a consequence of fertilisation and during growth; it merely swelled and became visible. On this theory specific variation was impossible, because the female parent had preformed its progeny independently of the male and of any other circumstance; indeed, in the later variation of preformation (*emboîtement*) all eggs were held to have been created from the beginning of the world, encapsulated one within the other until each successive adult became mature.

Antoni van Leeuwenhoek (1632–1723), the third of the great trio of microscopists, was no less a preformationist. He claimed to have seen the perfect form of a sheep in an embryo an eighth of the size of a pea; but the discovery of spermatozoa (1677) convinced him that the male was the true source of the preformed foetus: as he wrote to Grew, 'If your Harvey and our De Graaf[2] had seen the hundredth part they would have stated, as I did, that it is exclusively the male semen that forms the foetus, and that all the woman may contribute only serves to receive the semen and feed it'.[3] No one ever saw a 'homunculus' in the head of a sperm, though pictures of it were published; yet Ovists and Animaculists debated for over a century.

Leeuwenhoek is more justly remarkable in other respects. Untrained in science and writing only in Dutch, he sent to the Royal Society and his friends during a period of fifty years, beginning in 1672, about 300 letters, many very extensive and mostly on his microscopic observations. In microscopic anatomy he worked on mite, flea, lobster, louse, gnat and aphis, though never demonstrating the mastery of Swammerdam. He made elaborate comparative studies of spermatozoa. He discovered parthenogenesis (in aphids). He examined the 'globules' of milk and blood and the regular structure of plant matter—appearances which gave ocular credibility to the corpuscular theory. Like other early microscopists, he turned his gaze to almost anything that seemed a promising subject, so that his letters seem to leap from one observation to the next without order or coherence, though Leeuwenhoek was clearly capable of more continuous and purposive observation than appears on the surface. Thus, one day, applying his instrument to a drop of rainwater, he was

[1] F. J. Cole, *A History of Comparative Anatomy* (London, 1949), p. 180.

[2] Discoverer of the uterine follicle, then misinterpreted as the mammalian egg (first seen by von Baer in 1827).

[3] 18 March 1678: *Collected Letters* (Amsterdam, 1941), II, 335.

astonished to find it full of *animalcula* (protozoa), of which he described numerous recognisable species; on another occasion, examining scrapings from his teeth, he observed objects that were clearly bacteria, and of these also he depicted several identifiable species obtained from various sources. Impelled by a rich sense of curiosity, which he possessed the technique to gratify, and a painstaking and percipient observer besides, Leeuwenhoek is the founder of protozoology. His microscopes opened up a new world of minute living things whose existence imagination had never suspected, more strange than animals in the moon; so strange indeed that many of his reports met with incredulity at first, for only a few of his observations (like those of 'vinegar-eels'—nematode worms) were easily repeatable with other instruments, if at all.

As yet this new subcreation imposed no problems of taxonomy, though it is possible to see occurring at once those problems arising from the lack of a suitable descriptive terminology and a means of identification which had long been familiar in the older natural history. This constitutes the third category of biological description. By the middle of the seventeenth century the problems of taxonomy created enormous difficulties here, for knowledge was inadequate to devise a 'natural' classification (using many specific characters), and no workable 'artificial' system (one based on a few selected characters) had been devised. In the last of the traditional herbals (an English example is Parkinson's *Theatrum Botanicum*, 1640) thousands of types of plants and their varieties were described; the language of technical description was inadequate for its purpose, and though the herbal might be conveniently enough arranged for pharmaceutical use, it was a poor botanical compendium, concealing the natural affinities of species and the 'plan' of creation. The problem of classification was especially acute in botany, but the case of mammals, reptiles, fish, birds, and so forth was hardly better. Hence, in spite of all that had been done by naturalists since the Renaissance, a great task of orderly enumeration and description awaited their seventeenth-century successors, freshly conditioned by the awakened interest of botanists in plants for their own sake, and not as sources of drugs, and of zoologists in animals as such, and not as imperfect models of the human frame. It was possible for this task to be reduced to the narrower one of collecting and cataloguing, as though these were the only functions of the naturalist; but this happened less in the seventeenth century than in the eighteenth.

In particular, the outstanding naturalist of its latter half, John Ray (1627–1705), is notable for the breadth of his discussions of taxonomical principles, for his attention to ecology, and for his interest in comparative anatomy and physiology. His scope was almost universal: besides his vast work on plants and his incomplete entomology, he wrote (with Francis Willughby) on birds and fishes as well. He was thus the last of the great natural encyclopaedists, for he was neither a taxonomic specialist (like Linnaeus later, whose work tended to overshadow Ray's), nor a monographic writer like the contemporary zoologists. Although not primarily a student of function, Ray sensibly adopted the discoveries of others. Like Redi, he realised the absurdity of the common notion of spontaneous generation; like Grew, he believed in the sexuality of plants, a question more fully cleared up by Camerarius (1694); and he was absorbed into the controversy over the nature and purpose of the flow of sap. Nor was he committed to any highly dogmatic view of the immutability of specific forms; on the contrary, like Hooke and, most impressively, the Dane Niels Stensen (or Steno, 1638–86), he believed that fossils were authentic organic remains. The argument for this latter view inevitably rested upon the virtual indistinguishability of some of the fossils—like Steno's sharks' teeth—from similar structures in extant species, and so tended to diminish the problem of accounting for those that were obviously dissimilar from extant species. But it was already well known that the latter did occur and must represent creatures that had lived only in the past, perhaps in some earlier creation.

Undoubtedly the quantity and quality of descriptive work in biology will stand comparison with, if it does not in intrinsic complexity surpass, anything that was done in the same period of a like kind in the physical sciences. In biology, too, experiment was almost as necessary as observation, and in some respects the relationship between theory and facts, though not mathematical, was hardly less intricate than in physics. But if one might judge that physical science, in the universality of Newton's *Principia* and the mechanical philosophy, was tending to become a huge, geometrised superstructure erected on a relatively slender basis of precise ascertained fact, conversely biology tended to pile up its factual foundations without creating a theoretical superstructure. Seventeenth-century biologists were far less engaged in thinking than were physicists or (less markedly) chemists; far more devoted to doing—collecting, dissecting, drawing and making notes. And the texture of biological thinking, despite the new strands woven into it, contained a multiplicity of threads that were traditional, indefinite or derivative. Its concepts lacked the definition and authority that those of the physical sciences were fast acquiring. To say this is to indicate the difference between the two broad aspects of science, and the different features of their historical evolution, not to regard one as more progressive than the other. Seventeenth-century biologists did effect a revolution in science; but it was not of the same kind as the revolution effected by the experimenters, mechanical philosophers, astronomers and mathematicians. It did not bring about a vast and all-pervasive revolution in thought; it did not alter the dimensions and quality of the stage on which the players strut.

Hence, although a contemporary historian of seventeenth-century science, such as William Wotton (*Reflections on Ancient and Modern*

Learning, 1694), might more often refer to its biological than to its physical aspects, and though he might be more impressed by the discoveries of Harvey and the accomplishments of Ray than those of Galileo and Newton, it was the novelties of physical and mathematical science that seized the attention of philosophers (as is still largely the case today). It was the majesty of Newton's achievement in setting out the fundamental mechanical laws of the universe that commanded the admiration of Locke and Bentley, as it later provoked the criticisms of Leibniz and Berkeley, and later still inspired Voltaire and the French *philosophes*. For Locke, Newton devised a simpler proof than that published in the *Principia* that dynamical reasoning entailed the elliptic orbit; for Bentley he provided a detailed explanation of his idea of gravitation. Apart from the more technical questions of philosophy raised by the *Principia* (such as the problem of induction, expressly discussed by Newton in more than one passage, and that of the relation between mathematical reasoning and physical reality), it impelled the reader to inquire into the role of God in the mechanistic universe that Newton had depicted: a question that Descartes had similarly aroused in the minds of his readers. The devoutly religious Newton was far from believing that God had abandoned His creation when it was complete; rather he opened himself to the criticism of Leibniz that, for Newton, God was an imperfect workman who had constantly to tinker with His machine in order to keep it running. So, it seemed, either God's intervention in the creation is needless, or else He has made it less perfect than He might. This was an irresolvable antithesis that philosophers might debate as long as they chose, but for physics the practical answer was that God had been driven from the universe with the planetary intelligences. However impious Laplace's legendary quip might sound, it no more than stated an accepted position. In biology it was otherwise as yet: no one could divorce the concepts of life and intelligence from that of divinity. There, this more complicated and emotional debate was postponed to a still remote future.

CHAPTER IV

PHILOSOPHY

In the history of philosophy the seventeenth century is associated with the names of Descartes, Hobbes, Spinoza, Leibniz and Locke. The doctrines of these philosophers mark a momentous turning-point in European thought: they were developed in close interrelation with the contemporary 'scientific revolution';[1] they introduced new basic concepts and methods of knowledge; they also had a profound effect upon the course of modern philosophy as a whole.

The process which led to the Cartesian interpretation of the world had two main aspects. In the first place, the conception of nature as an organism, characteristic of the early phase of Renaissance thought, gave way to the view that all phenomena are to be conceived on the analogy of the movements of a machine. Accordingly, on this view, causes were antecedent motions and, as such, efficient causes: all physical change was explained as the effect of the motions and impacts of matter in space and time. In proportion as the mechanistic view prevailed, the appeal of the traditional doctrine of final causes, namely the doctrine that processes in nature are directed by a tendency to attain a specific end, diminished. The new method of explanation was also attractive because it seemed particularly successful. It enabled a scientist not only to interpret but, in Francis Bacon's phrase,[2] to dominate nature. The underlying assumption was that, if it is known how phenomena are generated, it is possible to predict them on any particular occasion and in this sense to gain power over nature.

Secondly, with motion accepted as the principle of all natural processes, it became clear, particularly to Kepler (1571–1630) and Galileo (1564–1642), that the structure of reality was fundamentally quantitative and not, as for Aristotle, reducible to qualitative distinctions; that therefore the appropriate method of scientific explanation was to formulate the laws of motion with the help of mathematics. Much that is characteristic of mathematics naturally enhanced its prestige in the past: its terms are easily intelligible and its definitions precise; its propositions are interconnected and its proofs conclusive. On no other basis did it seem possible to render the formulation of truths both necessary and universal. For this reason, and because of its success in the solution of scientific problems during the seventeenth century, the mathematical method was applied to other fields of study such as ethics, political theory, jurispru-

[1] For this, see ch. III, above.

[2] *Novum Organum* (1620), Bk. I, Aph. III.

dence, and theology. It was regarded as above all the model for philosophical reasoning. The rationalist philosophy of the day, at any rate, consisted in an eagerness for clear intellectual intuitions and tight deductive systems. What was furthermore expected of philosophers was that they should settle conclusively, that is, by *a priori* argument, particular matters of fact as well as questions concerning the ultimate nature of reality as a whole. The differences in kind between a philosophical and a scientific problem had thus not yet become apparent. Often also, as is shown by the wide range and variety of their correspondence, philosophers were either polymaths like Leibniz, or at least conversant with many branches of knowledge, like Hobbes. The general tendency, however, was to accumulate knowledge not for its own sake as in the Renaissance, when wisdom had often been identified with learning, but in order to unify it and to arrive at a judgement that recommended itself to reason and the methods of geometrical demonstration.

Philosophy then was universal in yet another sense. It permeated the whole of society, including the *salons* of educated women. Its chief tool was alleged to be good sense,[1] or the 'natural light' of reason, and this could be presumed to exist in every ordinary person alike. The truths of philosophy should therefore be generally intelligible and acceptable everywhere without question. Moreover, as the greatest philosopher of the time, the Frenchman René Descartes (1596–1650), had shown in the *Discours de la Méthode* (1637), it was possible for a philosophical book to be written in the vernacular and to be lucid as well as forceful. His own philosophy reigned supreme, not only in France and in Holland, where he had lived for many years and had written all his important works, but also, after his death at the court of Queen Christina of Sweden, in other countries. None the less, the authority of Cartesianism was by no means unlimited: it was at all times and everywhere faced with powerful criticism and opposition. This was the 'century of genius',[2] glorying in a great number of eminent thinkers. Even such a close friend and admirer of Descartes as Princess Elizabeth of the Palatinate (1618–80),[3] to whom he dedicated his *Principles of Philosophy* (1644), admitted that she found several of his doctrines both strange and difficult. Besides, the Cartesian philosophy had itself been instrumental in undermining respect for orthodoxy and fostering the spirit of critical discussion, and it is significant from this point of view that the first edition of Descartes's *Meditations* (1641) included six sets of *Objections* written in criticism of this work, together with his *Replies*. Among those who contributed to the *Objections* were Thomas Hobbes and Pierre Gassendi. Indeed, those most critical of

[1] Descartes, *Discourse on Method*, Pt. I, *ab init.*; Hobbes, *Leviathan*, ch. 13, *ab init.*

[2] For the phrase see A. N. Whitehead, *Science and the Modern World* (Cambridge, 1926), ch. III.

[3] A daughter of Frederick V, Elector Palatine, and a granddaughter of King James I.

Descartes were the founders of modern empiricism. They too were inspired by the new developments in science. But they believed that all knowledge was based ultimately not on *a priori* and deductive arguments, but on sensory evidence and generalisations from experience. The empiricist approach, accordingly, though by no means anti-mathematical, proved hostile to the metaphysical and speculative ambitions characteristic of Cartesianism.

There was more than one reason for the central position of the Cartesian philosophy in the seventeenth century. In the first place, unlike the old-style philosophy of the Renaissance, it was systematic and technically adequate. Descartes was himself a mathematician of genius; and by his invention of analytical or co-ordinate geometry he promoted the mechanistic description of nature in terms of extension, figure and motion. Secondly, he thought that knowledge of the external world depends not so much on what is known as on self-knowledge and the capacity to know. Two assumptions led him to this belief: first, that he could deduce his own existence solely from the fact that he was thinking; secondly, that what he immediately experienced was necessarily mental so that it was impossible to experience physical objects independently of ideas. His teaching that knowledge of the real is relative to the mind gave rise, on the one hand, to idealism and phenomenalism—the tendency to merge the objects of knowledge with ideas—and, on the other, to psychologism in philosophy—the claim to solve the problem of knowledge by means of introspecting mental states and operations. By initiating a preference for the 'how' over the 'what' of knowledge, for epistemology over ontology, Descartes was responsible for the modern 'bifurcation' of knowledge.

His starting-point was an attitude of scepticism which, however, he used as a weapon with which to fight the sceptics on their own ground. Even the most general doubt, he argued, implies thinking and this in turn the existence of whoever thinks: *cogito ergo sum*. The great merit of his methodological doubt was that it acted as a filter: it separated what one has a right to believe from what prejudice or authority make one believe. And indeed to say 'I am thinking' as also to say 'I exist' is to say what is in some sense indubitable: to doubt or to deny either precisely proves it to be true. Modern existentialists, on the other hand, have paid tribute to Descartes because he began from an existential premise, a factual truth.[1] If his starting-point was a fact, however, it was not logically necessary, and if it was a truth of reason it was not sufficiently informative. Descartes's predicament was that his system lacked the foundation which he thought he had provided.

In order to give his system the necessary additional support Descartes set himself to prove the existence of an omnipotent and veracious God. He employed three arguments, of which one was the so-called ontological

[1] K. Jaspers, *Descartes und die Philosophie* (Berlin, 1937), pp. 15, 30.

proof made famous by Anselm of Canterbury in the eleventh century. The argument from design, also called the physico-theological argument, found no favour with Descartes: it involves the concept of final causes, which he excluded from his mechanistic explanation of nature. All traditional arguments have been declared invalid, especially the ontological one, which rests on the assumption (refuted by Hume and Kant) that existence is a predicate. Nevertheless it would be difficult to point to any seventeenth-century philosopher in whose system God was not a necessary postulate. A mechanic was required for Newton's physics, and even such a materialist as Hobbes accepted, though reticently, the idea of God as a first cause and a supreme legislator.

The advantage of allying theology to philosophy was that problems arising in either field could be solved more easily. But there were also a number of specific reasons why the concept of God, even if it retained little of its traditional meaning, remained of fundamental importance in seventeenth-century, and particularly in Descartes's, philosophy. One was the general interest in substance. Descartes defined substance as that which, like God, can exist of itself, or which needs only the concurrence of God in order to exist. Then there were the epistemological difficulties created by the two-substance doctrine of mind and matter, which, according to Descartes's disciple John Clauberg (1622–65), justified an appeal to divine intervention. If, as for Descartes, the world of mind and that of matter are fundamentally distinct substances, knowledge cannot be the effect of contact or interaction between the two: it must be the result of an innate disposition on the part of the human mind, founded ultimately upon the arbitrary, inscrutable will of God.

By arguing from the necessity that every event has a cause Descartes believed he could show that material things exist independently of our minds, that they are atomic in structure, and that their essential properties are extension and its modes, namely shape, size, position, and motion. In common with Galileo and indeed with most contemporary thinkers, empiricists as well as rationalists, he held that these so-called primary qualities, being quantitative characteristics, are susceptible of mathematical treatment and therefore the only proper objects of scientific understanding. On the other hand, neither he nor the other thinkers believed that such sensible qualities as colour, sound, or taste could represent the real character of material things, since in their view this consists of nothing but atoms in motion. Descartes's approach was particularly radical in that for him all sense perception, including that of the primary qualities, if taken as an indication of what things are in themselves, is at least partially illusory and of only biological use. Though he occasionally stressed the value and necessity of experience in physics, his tendency was to maintain that we know the true nature of the real by *a priori* intuition and deductive inference alone.

The main feature of Descartes's physics, his equation of matter with extension, was particularly important. In the first place, this doctrine proclaimed, as against Aristotle, that there is one uniform substance spreading everywhere and common to every material thing, celestial as well as terrestrial. Secondly, it implied that since the world is homogeneous and infinite it can have no centre or fixed points. Descartes's achievement was to provide this view with a consistent scientific formulation, as is best shown by his theory of motion. Since in an infinite, homogeneous space no place has an absolute meaning, he thought that movement could not be conceived as locomotion in the strict sense, that is as the activity of a body wandering from one place to another, but only as transference of a body from one vicinity to another. By making motion consist in a geometrical change Descartes proved it to be relative: he could show that there is as much motion in bodies leaving their surroundings as in the surroundings themselves. With this idea of the reciprocity of motion Descartes formulated a principle which Newton recognised only in a limited sense, restricting it as he did to unaccelerated motion, and which it was left for Einstein to demonstrate.

There was, in the seventeenth century generally, a growing interest in problems of relativity, arising partly as a result of the implications of travellers' tales, partly in connection with the spread of sceptical ideas. Hobbes expressed it in his remark that a constant impression is the same as no impression; Leibniz in his belief that the universe is a system of perspectives; Pascal and Malebranche in speculations centred on the notion that 'nothing is in itself either great or small'. The idea had appealed to Shakespeare, who found that time 'travels in divers paces with divers persons',[1] and it was to be furnished with a general illustration in Dean Swift's 'elementary treatise on relativity',[2] *Gulliver's Travels* (1726).

Many parts of Descartes's physical theory, particularly those described by his first biographer, the abbé Baillet, as his 'romance of nature', soon became obsolete. One of these was his theory of vortices, an explanation of the origin and constitution of the universe in accordance with mechanistic principles. Another was his cumbersome explanation of the interaction between soul and body and of their union in the pineal gland, and his assertion that animals are mere automata. A further stumbling-block was his equation of matter with extension, which gave rise to difficulties concerning the doctrine of the Eucharist and that of Creation.

As a result, charges of atheism were brought against Descartes, and in 1663 his works were placed on the Roman Index of forbidden books, where they have remained ever since. Hence also Blaise Pascal (1623–62),

[1] *As You Like It*, III, ii, 326.

[2] For the phrase see A. S. Eddington, *Space, Time and Gravitation* (Cambridge, 1920), p. 32.

in his *Pensées* (1670), complained: 'I cannot forgive Descartes: he would have liked, throughout the whole of his philosophy, to be able to do without God.'[1] To Descartes's mechanistic view and his axiom of the supremacy of reason Pascal, in an almost modern 'existentialist' fashion, opposed the 'reasons of the heart' and the 'truths of fact'. Though brought up a Cartesian and an eminent mathematician himself, he firmly believed that the scientific approach could never yield certainty in its own right. He was particularly haunted by the two 'abysses' of the infinitely small and the infinitely great, and since the ambitions of the intellect proved to him self-defeating he became sceptical and derisive of philosophy and, instead, a staunch believer in the revealed mysteries of faith.

It fell to Descartes's chief disciple, Nicolas Malebranche (1638–1715), to make Cartesianism appear more palatable to the ecclesiastical authorities. He achieved this by combining the teaching of Descartes with doctrines of St Augustine and the Neo-Platonists. Following Louis de la Forge and Géraud de Cordemoy, two older disciples of Descartes, he stressed the importance of the Cartesian theory that everything requires divine support in order to continue in existence; and hence he inferred that God is the sole real cause and force in the world. From this he was able to derive two further doctrines. The first, the theory of occasionalism, explained the apparent interaction of mind and body as the result of divine intervention: God moves my body each time I decide to move it, and similarly He produces an experience in my mind on the occasion of a change in my body. The theory became common property among Cartesians, though it was Arnold Geulincx (1625–69) of Antwerp who, in his *Ethics* (1665), first elaborated it into a system. There were two versions of occasionalism. The argument was either that God interfered directly on each particular occasion, or that His intervention happened indirectly and once for all at the moment of creation. Malebranche eventually adopted the second version, which came very near Leibniz's theory of pre-established harmony.

In close dependence on occasionalism Malebranche developed his second principal doctrine, that of seeing all things in God. This was based on three assumptions: (1) that all we know is ideas; (2) that those of sense are false; (3) that since there cannot be in each mind an infinite number of innate ideas, knowledge must consist in a divine illumination of the intellect. The Platonic and idealist epistemology of Malebranche's main work, the *Recherche de la Vérité* (1674–5), and the acute criticism of it in Antoine Arnauld's (1612–94) *Traité des Vraies et des Fausses Idées* (1683) gave rise to a bitter controversy, one of the most famous of the time. Not long afterwards a similar polemic developed in England between John Locke, a critic of the *Recherche*, and John Norris (1667–1711), a prominent disciple of Malebranche.

[1] *Pensées*, fr. 77 (ed. Brunschvicg).

The influence of Malebranche was indeed considerable. He supplied the premises of Pierre Bayle's (1647–1706) scepticism as well as for Bishop Berkeley's conclusion that things are ultimately ideas in the mind of God. He also provided a stimulus for David Hume's (1711–76) phenomenalism and his denial of necessary connections in experience. But though Malebranche was himself a student, nay the founder, of empirical psychology, being like Francis Bacon particularly interested in the causes of human error, he was ultimately a metaphysician, without the common-sense approach and the analytical methods characteristic of British empiricists. Undoubtedly he was the most original, and certainly the acknowledged leader, of Descartes's followers, most of whom were regarded by Leibniz as mere commentators.[1] Yet none of the varieties of Cartesianism was capable of holding its own against the rival systems of Spinoza, Leibniz, Newton and Locke. Particularly inauspicious was the tendency, apparent in Geulincx's *Metaphysics* (1691) and the *Essay upon Reason* (1694) of his disciple Richard Burthogge, to undermine Descartes's basic realism by unfolding the idealistic implications in his thought. The only really persistent influence of the Cartesian system lay in its method, which was everywhere adopted by educated men in Western Europe. The main principles of this method found their way into the most influential textbook of Cartesianism, the Port-Royal *Logic* or *L'art de penser* (1662), edited by the Jansenists Antoine Arnauld and Pierre Nicole (1625–95).[2]

Some, but not all, of the difficulties inherent in the Cartesian philosophy were overcome by Baruch, or Benedict, de Spinoza (1632–77), a Jew whose family, originally from Portugal, had settled in Holland. He owed his main inspiration to Descartes, but he was also indebted to Neo-Platonism, Renaissance philosophers like Giordano Bruno, and of course Hebrew traditions. His main work, the *Ethics* (1677), published after his premature death at the age of forty-four, presents difficulties to the uninitiated and is indeed in several respects like a sacred text. But there are many who have found relish in its breadth of vision, the substance of its thought, and the power and subtlety of its moral teaching. A particular characteristic of the work is its geometrical presentation in terms of definitions, axioms, proofs, and corollaries. Spinoza's aim to secure scientific objectivity was furthered also by 'regarding human actions and emotions just as if he were dealing with lines, planes, or bodies'.[3]

His first step was to show that there can be only one substance, God, and that this is necessarily infinite, for if there were two they would limit one another and neither could then claim to be, like a true substance,

[1] Letter to Malebranche, 22 June 1679, in *Sämtliche Schriften und Briefe*, ed. Preussische Akademie der Wissenschaften (Darmstadt, 1926), series II, I, 473.

[2] For Port-Royal and Jansenism, see below, ch. VI, pp. 132–6.

[3] *Ethics*, Pt. III, Preface; *Tractatus Politicus*, ch. I, para. 4.

self-explanatory. A most unorthodox doctrine followed from this, namely that there could be no creation on the part of God since such an act would involve the distinction between God and nature, that is, two substances. This application of logic to theology, as also Spinoza's critical exegesis of the Bible in his *Tractatus theologico-politicus* (1670), which revealed Christianity as a historical phenomenon, struck at the roots of traditional dogma. As he explained nature mechanistically and rejected all anthropomorphic views of God and freedom of will in man, he came to be decried as an atheist, even by a Cartesian such as Malebranche and a sceptic such as Bayle. No doubt he was often insufficiently understood, and Novalis's appraisal of him as the 'God-intoxicated man',[1] though itself not wholly unbiased, was probably more correct. Spinoza himself regarded his heterodoxy as an expression of intellectual independence, which he prized so much that in 1673 he declined the offer of a chair of philosophy at Heidelberg, which he feared would impose on his teaching the necessity of becoming officially respectable. Though an outcast from both the Christian and Jewish communities he was a happy and tolerant man. He earned his livelihood as a lens-grinder, true to his maxim that a free man who lives among ignorant people should try to do without their charity.

All the remaining features of Spinoza's philosophy can be deduced from his notion of substance. Obsessed as he was with the idea that substance must be absolutely infinite, he argued that it is not infinite in one respect only, for example, in space, but must have an infinite number of attributes. In his view, only two of these are known to the human intellect: extension and thought. That is to say, whatever is spiritual in the universe is at the same time part of extension and, conversely, whatever occurs as a physical event also occurs as a mental event. The problem of how soul and body can be said to interact causally thus did not arise for Spinoza. For him mind and matter were inseparably correlated aspects of one and the same state of affairs in the one substance. A strange implication of this view was that in Spinoza's opinion we perceive a physical object only in so far as our body is affected by it so that the perception is really of a change in our body. A further implication was that the order of extended things or of material changes is the same as the order in which ideas follow one another in God's mind or in the minds of men. This led Spinoza to hold that all connections in the world can be discovered by *a priori* reasoning alone, without the least help from observation. He thereby obliterated the distinction between the factual relation of cause and effect and the logical relation of ground and consequence. It was the price—a costly one, as Hume and Kant would have thought—he paid for his solution of the problem of the relation between mind and matter.

Spinoza's ethics is deducible directly from his metaphysical principles.

[1] *Fragmente*, ed. Kamnitzer (Dresden, 1929), fr. 1730.

Like the ancient Stoics, whose doctrines had been revived by Michel de Montaigne (1533–92), Justus Lipsius (1547–1606), and William Du Vair (1556–1621), he would hold that in order to know the nature and goal of man it was indispensable to know his place in the universe. He believed that to the extent that finite beings are acted upon by their environment they experience emotions which upset their internal balance. The problem, as he envisaged it, was how to evade this 'human bondage'. He solved it through his theory of *conatus*. Like Hobbes and Leibniz he thought that it is of the essence of every individual thing to *endeavour* to preserve its own being. In the case of men and their comparatively developed thinking power, this tendency is expressed by a desire to counteract their dependence on external causes, which makes them slaves of passion, by behaviour which is active and which springs from their own nature. This is the case whenever we think logically or, in Spinoza's terms, form 'adequate' ideas of ourselves, our environment, and our relation to God. Man's freedom and happiness therefore, Spinoza argued, increase with the number of adequate ideas in his mind.

Two important qualifications have to be borne in mind. First, a man is free, on Spinoza's view, not in the sense that his behaviour is undetermined, but in the sense that it is unconstrained, that is, undetermined by external factors. Secondly, though he believed that a man is free only if his behaviour is dictated by his reason, he was too much a man of the Renaissance[1] not to appreciate the delightful and useful emotions. Moreover, he challenged the intellectualist thesis of the Stoics that it is within the power of reason to expel an emotion. His psychological insight made him realise that a passion can be checked or replaced only by another and stronger passion. This doctrine carried a message of great educational importance: vice is to be avoided not by fighting against it, but by arousing the active emotions of love and pleasure. Similarly, knowledge, Spinoza thought, must appear as intellectual love, *amor intellectualis Dei*.

One of the most convincing of his recommendations for moral progress and individual happiness was that we can make an obsessive passive emotion harmless by forming a clear and distinct idea of it. The most important part of his ethical theory, however, was that everything must be viewed in the light of its necessary relation to the whole order of nature, that is 'under a certain form of eternity'.[2] Morality, he considered, was concerned with the truth of scientific laws, undistorted by praise and blame or the myopia inherent in subjective points of view. By eliminating from the moral sphere all authority, dogma, reward and punishment he made ethics in this sense autonomous. On the other hand, there was no room in his thought for the concept of duty; besides, his monistic conception of substance blurred the ordinary distinctions

[1] *Ethics*, Pt. IV, prop. 45, note ii.

[2] *Sub quadam aeternitatis specie: Ethics*, Pt. II, prop. 44, coroll. ii.

between ethics, physics and logic. It was chiefly this unitary and all-comprehensive character of his system which earned him the label of a pantheist. It also caused his fame among the English romantics and the German idealists at the end of the eighteenth century.

Spinoza had much in common with the German philosopher Gottfried Wilhelm Leibniz (1646–1716), but there was also a marked contrast between the two philosophers, noticeable in the manner of their lives. While Spinoza was a solitary and almost saintly man, intent on one single purpose, Leibniz was a courtier and a diplomat, whose energies were dispersed in worldly plans and official commitments as well as in an extraordinary variety of intellectual pursuits. Similarly, as philosophers, they differed in their dominating vision. Unlike Spinoza, Leibniz did not start with one all-inclusive category, the divine substance, but with many individual substances, which he called monads and which explain the title of one of his chief works, the *Monadology* (1720). All substances, he believed, are spiritual and what seems to be matter, motion, and extension is really mind. Though in his early years he considered himself a follower of Gassendi and Hobbes, he abandoned their mechanistic systems during his sojourn in Paris (1672–6), which was one of the most stimulating events in his life. He found the notion of atoms on which these systems were based particularly unsatisfactory. A true substance, he argued, must be a unitary thing and therefore unextended, indivisible, and organic; it must be an immaterial centre of energy, immune from external influences.

Leibniz arrived at his conception of a multitude of individual substances chiefly as a result of two mistaken assumptions. The first was that all statements can be properly expressed in the subject–predicate form. The second was that the predicate of any true affirmative statement is included in the concept of the subject, so that all true statements become analytic. The two beliefs in conjunction explain Leibniz's conviction that the concept of an individual substance virtually contains, once for all, everything that can ever happen to it. He broached the question for the first time in his *Discourse on Metaphysics* (1685–6), but this important work was not published until 1846. However, a summary was sent to Arnauld, who in the famous correspondence that ensued (1686–90) objected to its main doctrines because he thought they entailed the denial of all liberty to man and to God.

But Leibniz's metaphysics was not exclusively built upon his logic.[1] Monadism was attractive in that it represented an open and dynamic system instead of the closed and static one of Spinoza. God's omnipotence, Leibniz came to think, was most conspicuously revealed in a world of the widest variety and composed of the maximum number of

[1] Though this is the principal thesis of the pioneer works by B. Russell, *A Critical Exposition of the Philosophy of Leibniz* (London, 1900), and L. Couturat, *La Logique de Leibniz d'après documents inédits* (Paris, 1901).

substances. He and many of his contemporaries were obsessed by the notion of the infinite. In mathematics this led him, independently of Newton, to the discovery of the infinitesimal calculus (1676). In metaphysics it made him postulate, within each monad, myriads of mental states, conscious and subconscious, representing a miniature universe which only an infinitely prolonged analysis could fully reveal. No wonder he was excited over the new microscopical discoveries of cells and spermatozoa, for he was himself trying to explain what it must be like inside an indivisible organism. The characteristics of substances, according to him, were perceptions following one another continuously by the action of some internal principle which he called 'appetition'.

Leibniz made much of the law of continuity according to which there are no leaps in nature, and this was to play an important part in modern science. However, on his view it applied to developments within monads only, not to anything external to them. A monad, he in fact asserted, can neither act nor be acted on by anything outside itself. Each is 'windowless', that is, living in complete isolation from any other. He was convinced that this self-sufficiency of substances was a guarantee of the soul's liberty as well as of its immortality, and that this gave his philosophy a great advantage over its mechanistic rivals. Such an advantage, however, was accompanied by a great disadvantage. The rigid Cartesian dichotomy between thought and extension reappeared in the gulf between any two monads.

The difficulty for Leibniz was to explain how on his premises a tree, for instance, which is an island colony of monads, can be perceived by a mind, which is another such island colony, and similarly how a man can move his arm or kick a ball. The solution of the problem—the great philosophical problem of the age—was provided by his famous doctrine of pre-established harmony. His view was that for every one of the infinitely many perceptions or internal states arising spontaneously within a monad at any given time there invariably happens to be a corresponding perception or state in every other monad; what appears as interaction between mind and matter and between soul and body is in reality the result of a gigantic miracle of adaptation or synchronisation between developments of mutually independent souls. Hence Leibniz came to speak of monads as 'mirroring' the universe each from its own point of view.

The reason why, for Leibniz, perspectives must differ from one another was his 'principle of sufficient reason', from which he deduced most of his physics and natural theology. The principle stipulated that there is always a sufficient reason why a thing should be as it is, the course of its development being completely determined by a rule arising from God's choice of what is best. As Leibniz wished his fatalism to leave room for free will, he argued that sufficient reasons 'incline without necessitating'.

Few, it seems, were convinced by this argument, and Voltaire spoke derisively of Leibniz's *raison insuffisante*.[1] Another famous principle advanced by Leibniz was that of the identity of indiscernibles (or of the dissimilarity of the diverse). This had occupied his mind ever since his doctor's dissertation of 1663, the *De principio individui*. In a philosophy like his it must indeed be a necessary truth that if things are *two* they are discernible, while if they are *indiscernible* they are not really two but one. For the only way in which it is possible, on his premises, to refer to a substance uniquely is in terms of attributes which it does not have in common with other substances. Among attributes Leibniz included circumstances of time and place. He regarded these as a kind of order among phenomena and as purely perceptual. As a result of this view he became involved, at the end of his life, in the celebrated and, on his part, brilliant correspondence with Samuel Clarke (1675–1729), who defended Newton's theory that space and time are real entities, that is, existing in their own right and not ideally in thinking substances. This theory, in the eyes of Leibniz, was pure fiction, and though plausible to the ordinary man, science has in fact discredited it.

Leibniz took a decisive step forward in the ideal of science as a unified encyclopaedia, beyond the artificial symbolisms of Raymond Lully (1235–1315) and his own contemporaries Athanasius Kircher, George Dalgarno and John Wilkins. His aim was to construct not so much a universal language as a system of rules by means of which the connections between the several parts of knowledge become self-explanatory and all reasoning is reduced to calculation. In his youthful thesis *De arte combinatoria* (1666) and subsequent papers he elaborated a logical calculus, a 'universal characteristic', which included shrewd methods of estimating probabilities. His symbolic logic became the forerunner of modern logistic, though its fruits were either forgotten or remained unpublished until almost two hundred years after his death, by which time they had been worked out independently by subsequent logicians. The major defect of Leibniz's logic was his failure to take into account the independent nature of relations, which he believed were reducible to predicates. This is the more astonishing as his analysis of mathematical reasoning should have made him aware of the mistake. Besides, he knew and admired the *Logica Hamburgensis* (1638) of Joachim Jung, the first to inquire into the logic of relations and non-syllogistic forms of inference, which was perfected two hundred years later by Boole, Frege, Peirce and Russell. Another difficulty was Leibniz's claim that his calculus could be usefully applied to domains other than mathematics and, indeed, to all branches of knowledge. The claim is unjustifiable, since abstract calculi operate only within deductive systems, that is, those starting from a few

[1] *Correspondance*, letter to Mairan of 5 May 1741, ed. Besterman (Geneva, 1955), XI, 108.

precisely definable concepts. They can never exhibit the full range and flexibility of meaning characteristic of general empirical discourse, nor the different kinds of implication that form part of it.

The reason for Leibniz's claim was his belief in a harmonious and inherently rational universe. On his view, therefore, the boundaries between different spheres of thought should not only be passed over but effaced. In his *Systema Theologicum* (1686), accordingly, he worked out a universal rational theology on which to base the reunion of the Christian Churches, for the conflict between them had certainly not been resolved by the Peace of Westphalia. With his many-mansioned mind he was doubtless the last truly universal man and hence also the first to see future scientific advance as the work not of individual geniuses but of co-operative enterprise. And just as his vast correspondence animated the whole contemporary republic of letters in Europe, irrespective of wars and religious differences, so was he the moving spirit behind schemes for the foundation of academies in Germany, Austria and Russia. Furthermore, throughout his life he encouraged Jesuit missionaries in China to work for a cultural union between Europe and the East. But though his own system was extraordinarily comprehensive, it was too much of an attempt to reconcile opposites—such as mechanism and purposive explanation, or contingency and necessity—to be convincing. There was no less of the miraculous in his world than in that of the Cartesians, even though the miracles filling his universe were, on his interpretation, miracles of reason.

His most emphatic conclusion was that God had created the best, at least the most perfectible, of all possible worlds. He expressed this optimism in his *Essais de Théodicée* (1710), a critique of Pierre Bayle the sceptic. Four years after the Lisbon earthquake Voltaire, in his *Candide* (1759), ridiculed it in the person of Doctor Pangloss, though in his *Siècle de Louis XIV* (1751) he fully recognised Leibniz's outstanding significance. On account of its popular exposition the *Théodicée*, together with Bayle's *Dictionary*, became one of the most influential books of the eighteenth century. In this way it contributed to the decline of the hegemony of Cartesianism in European intellectual life. At the same time its monadism provided a metaphysical prop for the Protestant dogma of direct communication between God and each individual believer.[1]

Under the influence of Christian Wolff (1679–1754), professor of mathematics at Halle, Leibniz's doctrine was narrowed into a school philosophy on which Immanuel Kant (1724–1804) was brought up. The latter took over from Leibniz the criticism of Locke's empiricism and the doctrine of the *a priori* character of the notions of the intellect. Leibniz likewise stimulated the romantic reaction by his views of individuality and development; however, these have ceased to satisfy because of their connection with the traditional belief in substance and the subject–predicate

[1] *Monadology*, paras. 83 ff.

logic. The use he made of the notion of perspectives, on the other hand, has had a striking effect on modern theories, especially those of Whitehead and Russell.

One of Leibniz's major works, the *Nouveaux Essais sur l'entendement humain* (written in 1703 and published posthumously in 1765), was an answer to John Locke's *Essay concerning Human Understanding* (1690). It expresses, more conspicuously than any other, the issues involved in the controversy between the metaphysical rationalists of the time and the contemporary school of empiricism. During the seventeenth century the latter had established itself as a leading tradition and had even begun to challenge the supremacy of Cartesianism. The principal reason for rivalry between the two schools was that each favoured and, in its own way, owed much to the contemporary scientific movement. An additional reason was that they formed different geographical associations: rationalism with the Continent and empiricism with England. The new scientific outlook obtained a particularly prominent expression in the London Royal Society (founded in 1660), which took its stand squarely on the philosophy of Francis Bacon. The achievements of British empirical science, especially those of Isaac Newton, were sufficiently impressive for Voltaire to suggest that the century might be called the 'Age of the English' as well as that of Louis XIV.[1] The remark illustrates the significance of the contemporary English contribution to the course of European thought; previously this had been moulded chiefly by the Latin tradition in Italy, Spain and France.

None the less, an important forerunner of the British empiricists was Pierre Gassendi (1592–1655), a Frenchman like his contemporary Descartes. He was not himself a very important scientist, having no training in mathematics, nor any discoveries to his credit except for the first clear formulation of the law of inertia. Yet he was a scrupulous observer, particularly in the field of astronomy, and an admirer of Copernicus and Galileo. His reputation was based on his restoration and defence of the doctrines of the ancient Greek atomists, Democritus and Epicurus. He published this combination of scientific and historical inquiry in separate works between 1647 and 1649; it appeared as *Syntagma Philosophicum* in the posthumous edition of his collected works (1658). Originally the atomistic hypothesis had derived most of its plausibility from the *a priori* argument that the only substances in the world are an infinite number of imperceptible, simple, and incorruptible particles of matter, since their motions and interrelations would be sufficient to account for all processes of generation and destruction in nature. In Gassendi's time experimental evidence recommended the theory to

[1] *Siècle de Louis XIV*, ch. 31: *Œuvres Complètes* (Paris, 1878), XIV, 535. For the Royal Society and Newton, see above, ch. III, pp. 50–1, 55–7, 61–5.

physicists and chemists, and his own particular achievement was to have adapted ancient atomism, of which there had been earlier expositions, to the findings of the new science. All the same he superimposed on the mechanistic philosophy a Christian theology and a belief in final causes and the spirituality of the soul, thus making it far from homogeneous and systematic.

One of his leading doctrines was that the source of our knowledge lies in sense perception. Since he also taught that the qualities of bodies that strike our senses give rise only to appearances, he was led to the conclusion that matter, though independently real, is ultimately unknown. He derived support for this teaching, which reappeared in Locke and subsequent developments of English thought, from the ancient sceptic Sextus Empiricus and Pierre Charron (1541–1603). As a consequence he adopted a pragmatic outlook, founded on probabilities, and opposed this, in the important fifth set of *Objections* to the *Meditations* (1641), to Descartes's initial systematic doubt as well as to his final notion of the demonstrability of science. An implication of his sceptical attitude was that the alleged knowledge of atoms and the void, that is, the very foundation of his philosophy, could not itself be empirical but must be derived from a postulate of reason. The intellect, he in fact came to argue, must transcend and correct experience. On the other hand, he refused to accept theories which were not in the last resort confirmed by observation. His failure was to show exactly how reason and sense perception are related to one another.

Gassendi's influence was enhanced by his conceptions of space and time which he thought are absolute entities though without being either substance or attribute. On the one hand, this view made a breach in the time-honoured Aristotelian system of categories; on the other, it constituted, together with similar theories of Henry More and Isaac Barrow, the metaphysical framework of Newtonian science. Another scientist who profited from his doctrines was Robert Boyle (1626–91), though his corpuscular philosophy differed from Gassendi's in that he denied that motion was an intrinsic property of matter. It was precisely this dynamic aspect of Gassendi's philosophy that attracted the young Leibniz. Although Locke rarely acknowledged his debts to previous thinkers, it is obvious, if only from the testimony of Leibniz,[1] that he owed to Gassendi the idea of the mind as *tabula rasa* and the suggestion that matter might be able to think—two notions which struck at the foundation of Cartesian orthodoxy. While, apart from a few medical men like Samuel Sorbière, Gassendi had no real disciples, many read him with approval in the abridged and more intelligible representation of his system by François Bernier, which appeared in 1675. One of the reasons why he has been rarely discussed as one of the pioneers of empiricism is the elusive

[1] *Nouveaux Essais*, Bk. I, ch. I, *ab init.*

character of his thought;[1] another is that much of his system soon appeared obsolete in comparison with the more up-to-date pronouncements of British empiricists.

The first to draw up and advertise persuasively a map of knowledge and scientific method along the lines of the new experimental philosophy, but entirely separate from religious truth, was Francis Bacon (1561–1626). He assumed that the ultimate elements of things and also the sum total of phenomena were finite in number. Nature should therefore be capable of being exhaustively known with the help of an adequate theory of induction. In his *Novum Organum* (1620) he formulated a method for the discovery of causal laws, the so-called method of elimination, which he claimed was far more satisfactory than the traditional argument by simple enumeration. The basis of inductive proof, he considered, was the observation and collection of empirical facts. However, he recognised that there must also be *deliberate* experiments, a careful sifting of instances, and an unhampered application of the new method. In his opinion, the union of the experimental and rational faculty served the ultimate end of knowledge, that is, the practical one of increasing the dominion of man over nature. In his celebrated doctrine of the 'idols', moreover, he outlined the causes of error and prejudice which he thought lay in the way of truth and progress. Although Bacon's general conception of the 'advancement of learning' was of considerable importance, his notions of the functions of theory and scientific reasoning were limited. Hobbes, Spinoza and Leibniz found little in his system that interested them philosophically; his influence was felt particularly among the early members of the Royal Society and the French Encyclopaedists of the eighteenth century.

Thomas Hobbes (1588–1679) was a more subtle and forceful thinker than Bacon, though during and after his lifetime he was repudiated as a radical and an atheist on account of his materialism, his egoistic theory of human nature, and the man-made political order which he envisaged in his *Leviathan* (1651).[2] He spent part of the Civil War in Paris, where on a previous visit (1634–7) he had been introduced to Father Mersenne (1588–1648), the centre of a wide and varied intellectual circle. Mersenne himself was an eclectic and the author of several second-rate books on natural philosophy. He endeavoured to propagate together reason, experience, and faith, being as little satisfied with Bacon's one-sided empiricism as with Descartes's high-flown metaphysical ambitions. On his initiative Gassendi and Hobbes each submitted his own criticism of Descartes's *Meditations*. These two in fact were drawn towards one another not so much by their common empiricism as by their being adversaries of Descartes—and harshly treated ones at that. But Hobbes

[1] For controversial points in connection with his theory see the addresses in *Pierre Gassendi*, Centre International de Synthèse (Paris, 1955).

[2] For Hobbes and the *Leviathan*, see below, ch. v, pp. 103–5.

was a better trained mathematician than Gassendi and taught a materialism as consistent in principle as the great eighteenth-century systems of Holbach and La Mettrie. He not only rejected Descartes's dualism but also preferred to conceive of matter in terms of motion rather than extension. His mechanistic philosophy had none the less much in common with Descartes's—so much indeed that their correspondence in 1641 was marred by mutual charges of plagiarism.

Hobbes was particularly stimulated by the problem of sense perception which, he believed, is motion in external bodies as well as in the organs of our body. And while pleasure was for him 'motion about the heart' and thinking 'motion within the head', he defined a good object as what arouses motion towards itself, and endeavour as an incipient movement. This emphasis on motion was of great significance. In the first place, it excluded from his conception of science the immobile, immaterial objects of religious faith. Secondly, it suggested the idea of a purely geometrical view of nature.

In fact, Hobbes wrote his *Short Tract on First Principles* (*c.* 1630), the forerunner of one of his major works, the *De Corpore* (1655), a year after he had become interested in Euclid's *Elements.* His claim was that scientific or philosophical knowledge is exclusively a deductive inquiry into the efficient causes of motion, as though the relation of cause and effect were identical with that between the premises and the conclusion of an argument. This rationalism on his part differed widely from the new experimental philosophy ushered in by Bacon and practised by the Royal Society, which in his view in fact was 'natural history', not 'natural philosophy'. He was doubtless influenced in this connection by Galileo's and Harvey's resolutive–compositive method which formed part of the Averroistic tradition of the School of Padua. This suggested to him the idea of causal or genetic definitions according to which phenomena, including such things as the nature of men or that of civil society, could be reconstructed rationally from first principles like a geometrical figure. Hobbes's problem, of course, was to explain which of several alternative definitions or causal explanations of a phenomenon was to be accepted as the right one. For he realised that an hypothesis concerning the causes underlying an effect is the result of conjecture and may indeed be false, though the demonstration on which it is based is valid. But while throwing into relief the empirical basis of knowledge Hobbes, it appears, was not really interested in experimental verification or factual truth; at any rate, he failed to show how these are related to the *a priori* deductions of science.

Hobbes's super-nominalism, as Leibniz[1] called it, and his conventionist theory of truth point in the same direction. In his opinion rational knowledge is concerned with universals and hence must begin and end with the

[1] Preface to an edition of Nizolius, in *Philosophical Papers and Letters*, ed. Loemker (Chicago, 1956), I, 199.

use of words; for there is, he thought, 'nothing in the world universal but names'.[1] Furthermore, he regarded the imposition of names upon objects as arbitrary and, accordingly, all definitions as stipulative. In the absence of real meanings of words, truth in his view must lie in the logical connection between words in sentences, to be grasped by a process of formal 'reckoning': unlike the Cartesian intuition by clear and distinct ideas, it tells us nothing about the real nature of things.

Hobbes's analysis of language, none the less, promoted the cause of empiricism. It helped to rid philosophy and science of the belief in universal essences. In this, as well as in his view that no deductive reasoning is itself descriptive of reality, Hobbes was a precursor of Hume and modern positivism. But in addition to being a staunch empiricist and materialist he was unquestionably also one of the most thoroughgoing rationalists of the seventeenth century.

Most other British rationalists of the time adopted a spiritualist metaphysics and a belief in certain 'anticipations of the soul', that is, basic concepts supposed to be independent of experience. Their target in fact was Hobbes. Not surprisingly, Descartes's influence in England had spread ever since his correspondence with Henry More and the publication of Sir Kenelm Digby's treatise on the soul's immortality (1644). Another trend of thought which accounted for the rising tide of idealism and the intellectualist outlook was more particularly ethical and religious in character. It began with Lord Herbert of Cherbury (1583–1648) and flourished in the remarkable school of Cambridge Platonists, whose founder was Benjamin Whichcote (1610–83) and whose main representatives were Henry More (1614–87) and Ralph Cudworth (1617–88). A common characteristic of the Platonists was that, unlike Bacon, Hobbes, Pascal and Bayle, who all advocated a sharp separation of theology from philosophy, they sought to form a synthesis between them. After all, this was an age which, though still dominated by religion, had succeeded in explaining much that had hitherto appeared mysterious. The general appeal was to reason or, in Whichcote's favourite phrase, 'the candle of the Lord'.

Thus Lord Herbert, in his *De Veritate* (1624), argued for a religious truth underlying the many particular forms of faith which the mind cannot help but assent to because it is inborn in man. Acceptance of a natural rather than a revealed religion was characteristic of deism and also of the latitudinarian divines of the Church of England. What proved particularly attractive to the pioneers of eighteenth-century enlightenment was the contention that moral judgements and all eternal truths are valid in their own right and not, as Calvin and Descartes had taught, because they are the expression of a divine decree. This Platonic approach to ethics was the most important contribution to moral philosophy in the seventeenth century. Leibniz had a share in it, and also Cudworth with his two books,

[1] *Leviathan* (London, 1651), p. 13.

The True Intellectual System of the Universe (1678) and *A Treatise concerning Eternal and Immutable Morality*, posthumously published in 1731. His inquiry into the logical issues involved in moral theory set the stage for the subsequent development of ethical rationalism in England. It was poles apart from the moral psychology in which the contemporary French maxim-writers La Rochefoucauld and La Bruyère delighted. The metaphysical writings of the Cambridge Platonists, on the other hand, were not always free from strange and obscure doctrines such as Cudworth's theory of 'plastic natures' or More's notion of the spiritual nature of space. Their work also suffered from a diffuseness of thought and a mass of antiquated erudition. It might never have become the intellectual force that it did in the following century had it not been given a more polished and informal expression in the *Characteristics* (1711) of the third Earl of Shaftesbury (1671–1713) ,who particularly relished the Platonic doctrines of love and beauty.

John Locke (1632–1704), at one time Shaftesbury's tutor, was brought to philosophy by questions very similar to those discussed by the Cambridge Platonists; as shown by his *Reasonableness of Christianity* (1695), he remained under the influence of the Latitudinarians until the closing years of his life. At the same time the empiricism of Gassendi had made an early impression on him, even before his visit to France (1675–9) where, among scientists and scholars of every kind, he met the populariser of Gassendi, François Bernier. Personal as well as professional ties also connected him with Robert Boyle and the group of experimental scientists responsible for the establishment of the Royal Society; besides he was a friend and disciple of Thomas Sydenham, the distinguished physician. Locke was a doctor of medicine himself, preserving throughout his life an equal interest in the body and in the mind. He wrote with authority on such different subjects as philosophy, religion, politics, economics, education, and medicine. He was drawn into public life by Anthony Ashley Cooper, first Earl of Shaftesbury, after whose downfall he fled to Holland (1683), whence he returned early in 1689 in the retinue of William of Orange.[1]

In one of his first writings, the Latin *Essays on the Law of Nature* (composed in 1664), he chose for discussion a topic which was to form the basis of his influential political teaching in the *Treatise of Civil Government* (1690).[2] Two questions were of particular interest to him: the epistemological question of how natural law is known, and the moral question of the extent to which this law is binding. His answer to the first question was an empiricist theory of knowledge, which he developed at length in his *Essay concerning Human Understanding* (1690). This work has been his chief title to fame, not least on account of his method of investigation, which proved as important as the issue between empiricism

[1] For the first Earl of Shaftesbury, see below, ch. XIII, pp. 306, 314–19; ch. XIV, pp. 332–4, 344–5.

[2] For Locke and the *Two Treatises of Government*, see below, ch. V, pp. 119–21.

and rationalism that it was designed to settle. He was the first to regard philosophy not as a super-science, essentially similar to the other special sciences, but as a purely critical inquiry with problems of its own. His object was to study the nature, origin and extent of knowledge. In adopting this 'historical, plain method' and the position of an 'under-labourer' he proved himself courageous as well as unpretentious, for many of his over-rational contemporaries thought that to be without large-scale metaphysical aspirations was a declaration of philosophical bankruptcy. Another important though little appreciated contribution to philosophy was his study of the nature of words and definition in Book III of the *Essay*; he expected this to lead to a new 'sort of logic and critic'.

However, Locke created confusion at the very outset of his inquiry. Influenced as he was in several important ways by Descartes, he as well as Berkeley and Hume after him were convinced that not only when a man thinks, but also when he perceives an object he is confronted not with real things immediately but only with his own mental processes or ideas. In Locke's use this key-term 'idea' remained dangerously vague, denoting such a variety of things as objects of perception, images, acts of mind, and concepts. A further difficulty arose in connection with his well-known doctrine, attacked by both Leibniz and Kant, that all our knowledge is *derived* from experience, either sensory or introspective. He weakened his case by offering a psychological account of the origin of ideas, instead of arguing that in order to be meaningful concepts must be testable, at least indirectly, by sensory observation.

Irrespective of how it was formulated, Locke's denial of innate ideas in Book I of the *Essay* was nevertheless significant. It led to the rejection of the *a priori* premises from which Descartes and many theologians of the time had claimed to be able to argue about the universe by the deductive method alone. Admittedly, like Descartes and Leibniz, he assumed that the basic constituents of knowledge are simple elements. His achievement was to be the first to practise with any seriousness a technique of analysis in conjunction with a thoroughgoing empiricism. Nevertheless he laid himself open to the charge that the simplicity of the simple ideas of sense at which he arrived was a mere assumption and not, as he himself thought, the result of philosophical analysis.

Another consideration underlying Locke's 'new way of ideas' had equally puzzling consequences. He argued that, if the distinction between illusory and veridical perceptions was to be preserved, some ideas at least must be presumed to refer to things really existing outside of us on which they causally depend and which they also resemble. It was natural for him to single out as real the so-called primary qualities of bodies such as extension, figure, and motion: they could be regarded as both the necessary and sufficient conditions of sensory perception. On the other hand, the Cartesian doctrine that a mind cannot directly know material objects but only its own ideas was too deep-seated to be relinquished. Hence there arose a crucial difficulty, noticed already by John Sergeant in his *Solid Philosophy Asserted* (1697): how we are to believe in material entities, know their qualities, and speak of ideas as resemblances of these, if the entities and qualities in question are not and never could be, even in principle, directly experienced. The theory was not merely an unplausible hypothesis: it was a philosophical myth. Bishop Berkeley (1685–1753), a more consistent empiricist than Locke, evaded the difficulty by an outright rejection of dualism: in his most important book, the *Principles of Human Knowledge* (1710), he denied that there was anything but 'spirits' and their ideas. Locke, however, though a phenomenalistic analysis of reality was never far from his mind, felt unable to abandon the traditional belief in physical qualities and, hence, in material substance. None the less he looked upon this belief as a mere hypothesis of reason, unjustifiable on strictly empiricist premises. He admitted that, though the concept of material substance pointed to some real existence, it was imperfect and obscure, standing for 'something, he knew not what'.[1] His startling suggestion, hotly disputed by Edward Stillingfleet, bishop of Worcester (1635–99), that God might have endowed matter with the power of thinking arose, as was rightly seen by Voltaire,[2] not from a desire to deny the immateriality of the soul, but precisely out of his recognition that, *pace* Descartes, the nature of material substances remained outside the reach of knowledge.

Accordingly, Locke made much of the distinction between real and nominal essences. His contention was that, whereas we are ignorant of the real essence of, for example, gold, we know its nominal essence, that is, the ideas of those of its properties that are found regularly conjoined with one another. However, he noted that no appeal to experience, which provides us with ideas of particulars but never with any concepts or general ideas, could explain what qualities are consistently found together in our concept of a thing. The task, he recognised, could be achieved only by relying again upon reason. The position he took up in the traditional dispute concerning the nature of universals was that of conceptualism—a theory opposed alike to Platonic realism, the Aristotelian doctrine of substantial forms and Hobbes's nominalism. On his view, the meaning of a general name such as 'gold' is an abstract general idea in the mind, derived in the last analysis from the similarities between objects in nature. His mistake was to assume that for an idea to be general it must display characteristics that are themselves general. It was Berkeley's achievement, so highly praised by Hume, to discover that the generality of an idea lies entirely in its use and the relation it has to other ideas. Locke regarded abstract ideas as extremely important, for knowledge, according to him,

[1] *Essay*, Bk. II, ch. XXIII, sect. 2.

[2] *Lettres philosophiques* (1734), letter xiii, ed. Lanson (Paris, 1909), I, 170.

consisted in the perception of the agreement or disagreement of such ideas. Apart from our own existence and the existence of 'a God', of both of which he claimed to be certain, he accorded certainty of knowledge to those sciences only which do not refer to real existences. Pure mathematics is of this kind and, in his opinion, moral philosophy too; whence arose his favourite, though curious view, held also by Hobbes, Hugo Grotius, and Spinoza, that ethics is a demonstrable science.

Locke was generally an empiricist, at least in the sense that he rejected the Cartesian assumption that *a priori* deductions are descriptive of the world. Instead he maintained, rightly no doubt, that knowledge of matters of fact rests on the evidence of particular observations. He never went so far, however, as to hold that all reasoning is inductive or that we can ever attain certainty in the natural sciences, for he was by no means a strict empiricist. The mingling of reason and experience in his theory no doubt widened its scope, but it also had certain demerits. He failed to explain satisfactorily the role of each of these two elements in his system and, although he must have been aware of the tension between them, already so noticeable in the doctrines of Gassendi and Hobbes, he did not attempt to eliminate it. His dislike of extremes prevented him from becoming a consistent idealist or phenomenalist. On the other hand, he was in some measure a sceptic and thus need not have been unduly disturbed by the neglect of system in his thought. But while he was not a dogmatist and the least metaphysically inclined of the seventeenth-century philosophers, he resolutely adhered to certain assumptions. One of these was his common-sense approach to philosophical problems. This was attractive in its apparent simplicity, though it lacked the technical ingenuity necessary for the treatment of some at least of the complicated questions with which he dealt.

None the less, Locke was a pioneer in a variety of ways. His epistemology profoundly stimulated the young Berkeley and came to be exploited for innovations in religion by Anglicans no less than deists. Voltaire, Condillac, and afterwards the so-called Ideologues regarded him as of all philosophers the wisest: he had not, like his rationalist predecessors, written a 'romance of the soul' but modestly offered the 'history' of it. Hence on the Continent his method no less than his teaching were either faithfully propagated or transformed into the principles of the new sensationalism and associationist psychology.

Very broadly, then, the great rationalist systems of metaphysics, on the one hand, and the rise of empiricism, on the other, were the chief characteristics of philosophy in the period from Descartes to Locke. The central issue throughout was that of the relationship between immaterial minds and physical bodies and of the validity of knowing by way of ideas. The rationalist philosophers, eager for abstract speculation, started from two far-reaching presuppositions. One was that philosophical questions, like those in mathematics, can be settled by arguments which are not only plausible but logically compelling. The other was that philosophical reasoning, though regarded as *a priori* and deductive, is nevertheless descriptive of reality. The tendency of the empiricists was to assume that all the material of knowledge, that is, the meaning of our concepts as well as the truth of our beliefs, is ultimately derived from observation and that no conclusions about the world are demonstrable. An undoubted achievement of empiricism was its elimination of the more abstruse kind of traditional metaphysics and the substitution of questions which could be approached on the basis of psychological data, inductive generalisation, or an analysis of language. The rationalist metaphysicians, on the other hand, were in their own way equally progressive. Though still dominated by religious concepts, they were no longer in a strict sense theologians. In fact their critical and scientific study of man, nature and truth exercised a considerable leavening influence on traditional theology. The close alliance, nay fusion, of philosophical thought with the newly developed root concepts of science—a general feature of the seventeenth century and unique to Europe—was particularly prominent in Descartes, Hobbes and Leibniz. These thinkers boldly anticipated subsequent developments in scientific theory by their mathematical conceptions of space and motion and their emphasis on the importance of an adequate logic and methodology. One defect of the metaphysical systems was that their comprehensive grandeur no less than their aim to render reality completely intelligible were achieved largely at the cost of artificiality. Difficulties also arose on account of the still prevalent metaphysical notion of substance and the common failure to distinguish the idea of causal connection from that of logical implication. And while, in the field of moral theory, some rationalist philosophers, such as Spinoza, excelled in new insights, others, such as Descartes, contributed surprisingly little. On the other hand, the widespread contention that moral judgements are valid because of their inherent equity and rationality still had an appeal for the Age of Enlightenment. Seventeenth-century philosophy, generally, both in its rationalist and empiricist forms, prepared the way for the ideals of the eighteenth century—Reason and Humanity. Not that the French Encyclopaedists, such as Diderot and d'Alembert, or any of the other so-called *philosophes* were primarily philosophers. In point of fact they were, even in scientific inquiry, more historically minded than any of the seventeenth-century philosophers. All the same, the latter had raised, and passed on, important new questions: they had made a start which, even if it was not always the right one, remained fruitful. For, though many of the doctrines of Descartes and Leibniz, Hobbes and Locke have become obsolete, their impact, particularly on the theory of knowledge, is still felt three centuries later.

CHAPTER V

POLITICAL THOUGHT

THE seventeenth century has been called the heroic age of rationalism in Western Europe, and the term does indeed accurately express the three essential features of the thought of the period. These were, first, the alliance between the traditions of Galileo and of Descartes—between the new mathematico-mechanical science and the idea of natural law—second, the divorce of political thought from theology, and finally, the capacity of its great minds for creative thought. For there are few centuries so rich in creative philosophic ability, or in which political theory so boldly aspires to the utmost heights of intellectual speculation. But the spell cast by the great philosophers of the period presents a danger to the historian of its thought. He tends much too easily to confuse their originality with their influence, their future importance with their authority among their contemporaries. Many of their most important ideas are far ahead of their time—ideas which could not be fully developed in the intellectual climate of the age and did not leave their full mark on the history of thought until much later. The importance of Spinoza was first fully revealed by Goethe, that of Leibniz by the German idealists. That is why, more than in any other period since then, the history of ideas cannot be considered *in vacuo*, but must be related to the changing conditions of an age in which the basic problems of political life constantly take on new forms.

This is particularly true of the period covered by this volume. In the events with which it deals, the contrast between the two basic political attitudes around which the conflicts of the seventeenth century took place is strikingly expressed—the conflict between the glorification of the idea of Divine Right, which was incarnated in the monarchy of Louis XIV, and the theory of a social contract based on reason, to which the Glorious Revolution gave a new and much wider historical significance. These same events also bring out clearly the shifts in the claim to leadership among nations in the field of political theory. It is not by accident that there is no Frenchman among the leading political thinkers of the period. The ascendancy of France, which in other ways leaves its mark on the whole period and extends to the most varied fields of artistic and intellectual life, does not apply in the rarefied atmosphere of political thought. Bodin's great discovery, the concept of State sovereignty as a unified and indivisible power, independent of any other, represents the sole original contribution of France for a whole century to the doctrines of the age. It was sufficiently clear and embracing to provide a justification for the claim of absolute monarchy to internal and external domination. From then onwards, absolutist political theory did no more than develop and clarify it.

It has often been emphasised that the moment chosen by Louis XIV for his decision in favour of personal rule was quite unusually favourable, both inside and outside France, to the strengthening of royal authority, since the decision was made at a time of international *détente*, following upon two major peace treaties, when religious conflicts were becoming less insistent; while the institution of monarchy was becoming more and more firmly established, as 'the King in Council' freed himself from the tutelage of all-powerful prime ministers and himself became the visible focus of all governmental activity. Throughout Europe the revolutionary upheavals and other signs of crisis of the mid-century left behind them an overwhelming desire for peace, which was reflected in the world of ideas and only served to emphasise in men's minds the advantages of undisputed monarchical authority.

All this must be borne in mind if we are to understand the powerful attraction exerted by the monarchy of Louis XIV in its own time—an attraction based in part on his successes in the field of power politics, but corresponding also, to some extent at least, to a common and unifying concept of the ideal ruler, which set its stamp on every European monarchy. The student of the history of political ideas must therefore take into account Louis's own conception of himself and of the profession of monarchy. The active statesman—especially if he is successful—will only rarely feel the need to theorise about the purpose and the juridical basis of his position. His conception of the limits, the duties and the ethics of his calling arises normally from his practical experiences; it is put into writing only in the documents associated with that activity, which are destined for day-to-day practice. So it was with Louis XIV, whose political ideas and concepts can be deduced, if at all, only from a source of this kind—from the *Instructions pour le Dauphin*, which date from 1666 and 1667. These are generally referred to under the misleading title of 'Memoirs of Louis XIV', though they belong rather to the category of 'political testaments'; for their most important content is a portrait of the model king, such as France needed, the quintessence of principle and experience, which the king wished the heir to the throne to take to heart. It is true that this work was not the product of the king's own hand; it was worked up by secretaries from notes and general indications, but it can fairly be considered, in spite of much ornamentation and literary embellishment in its drafting, as the mirror of his ideas and of his concept of monarchy.

In its concept of absolute power, the work follows traditional lines: the king is the viceregent of God upon earth; his guiding star is the *salus publica*; his rule of conduct is dictated by his own conscience, for which he is answerable to no mortal being. In this document, however, the divine mission has become little more than a conventional formula. The ways in which he fulfils the function of a ruler and the scope of its possibilities are explained, not by attributing them to the inspiration of a divine and mystic grace, but by means of an eminently rational psychology. The position of the monarch, superior to all mortals, is seen as the source of special qualities, which the ruler possesses irrespective of any ability and experience he may have. He acquires his profound political insight and capacity for decision as a result of the unparalleled range of vision which he alone possesses—because he is born to rule and called to the office by birth and by right of inheritance. This enables the monarch to get extraordinary results from the intelligence and common sense which he shares with other mortals. Indeed, this elevated viewpoint puts him in a position to do even more: to observe with a certain detachment the conflict between reason and passion within himself, and to take the right side at the right moment. It is, however, only the concurrent effect of his own zealous labours, of *l'action* and of *le grand travail*, which gives meaning to *la place élevée* of the ruler and justifies it before God and man. Thus, the *Instructions pour le Dauphin* becomes simply an admonition to unceasing activity in the practice of the *métier du Roi*, an attempt to inspire loathing of mere regal dignity, divorced from the active functions of monarchy.

It has often been pointed out that the whole work proclaims only the glory of Louis XIV himself. His effort to be seen everywhere as the sole source of decision goes so far that not one of those ancestors who prepared the way for absolute monarchy in France is mentioned by name. Yet it would be an error to see in this work only an inflated picture of Louis's search for power and glory. Its real emphasis is on the total identification of State and ruler. Even the apocryphal 'l'État, c'est moi' loses the frivolous undertone often attributed to it if one sees the phrase in the fuller form which Louis XIV himself gave to it in the *Mémoires*: 'Quand on a l'État en vue, on travaille pour soi. Le bien de l'un fait la gloire de l'autre.' The *moi* of the ruler expresses itself in action, in hard work, and so becomes the essence, the mainspring of the State; and in the same way, the State is bound up with the king's person; his *gloire* increases its power and prestige, and nothing gives him such a sense of fulfilment as tireless labour in the service of the State. There is no conceptual separation between the personal sphere and that of the State, between the desire for glory—the ruler's *passion dominante*—and the interest of the State.

In this respect, the *Mémoires* may be seen as typical evidence of a certain 'modernisation' of the doctrine of absolutism. Beneath the surface, even of Louis's ideas, a certain traditional notion of religious duty is still clearly discernible; but this is emptied of its true content by a new and purely psychological interpretation of the natural self of the ruler and its development—an interpretation which, even at this stage, appears to require scarcely any support from theological and ethical arguments. The old theory of the monarchy *jure divino* is, as it were, supported and corroborated by arguments much closer to those of seventeenth-century rationalism, in a way which links the *Mémoires* with one of the great literary traditions that reached their peak in the France of Louis XIV, the 'moralising' observation of human nature in its psychological relationship to its social environment. In any case, the problem of the juridical, ethical and religious limits which this 'highest self' of the ruler might, at a pinch, be compelled to recognise is not seriously raised. The reduction of all political rights and all political wisdom to his 'natural self' foreshadows the exaggeration and degeneration of the later years of Louis's reign. In the rosy dawn of the *grand règne*, in the intoxication of his first impetuous successes, the young ruler could not yet understand the basic moral problem of absolute monarchy, the inevitable discrepancy between the limited abilities of a mortal monarch and the theoretically unlimited power which he wielded. Nor could the rational psychology of the *Mémoires* solve this problem either; at best, it could conceal it. The search for a theoretical solution could not begin until the problem itself had become clearly visible, and that was not possible until the French supporters of absolutism had looked back and thought hard about the divine mission of monarchy. This precisely was the method chosen by the most brilliant and eloquent interpreter of the monarchy of Louis XIV, by Bossuet.

It is characteristic of the range of Bossuet's mind that his activities covered the most varied fields and were expressed in the most varied literary forms. A thorough appreciation of his political thought would have to cover all of them—the theologian and historian of the *Discours sur l'histoire universelle* as well as the polemical theologian of the *Histoire des Variations*, the specialist in ecclesiastical policy of *De l'Église Gallicane*, the eloquent preacher of the *Oraisons funèbres* and the interlocutor of Leibniz in the great interconfessional argument of the century. Here, however, we must limit ourselves to the only one of his works which was political in the narrower sense, the *Politique tirée des propres paroles de l'Écriture sainte*, which was begun in the prime of his life—in 1677—and occupied him until his death.

Bossuet's *Politique* is not a work of pure theory. On the contrary, it served an eminently practical purpose, the education of the Dauphin, a matter which, in an absolute monarchy, was a matter of public interest. The unusual title is both misleading and rooted in the conditions of the time. It gives the impression that Bossuet wished to deny to politics, and therefore also to the State, the right to exist independently of theology. It seems to put the authority of the Bible in the place of rational and systematic examination of the nature of the State, and indeed the title has often been so understood; or rather misunderstood, for, in fact, the biblical foundation of Bossuet's argument, if not precisely superficial, is certainly not a basic one. One might say that the biblical basis serves less to support his own arguments than to refute those of his opponents, and especially the Protestant theories of the right of resistance, which claimed biblical justification and so had to be refuted from the Bible.

Yet Bossuet's frequent use of biblical quotations cannot conceal the fact that the view of history and politics developed in the *Politique* is certainly not inspired by Holy Writ. The Bible is used only to emphasise what Bossuet in any case believes to be true. Basically, reason suffices, in his view, both to reveal the *principes primitifs qui ont fondé les empires* and to answer the great question of the century, the problem of the origin and nature of State and society. Bossuet is thus able to allow the secular world, within certain limits, to determine its own laws and to explain history and politics from knowledge of itself and of human nature—for the theologian in him knows these things to be subject to a divine plan of salvation, beyond human understanding. In Bossuet's view, the power of the State has its origin not only in divine ordinance, but also in natural necessity. It is only nature's inevitable subjection of everyone to the sovereign that makes the anarchic *multitudo* into a State. This view is strikingly reminiscent of Hobbes; so much so, indeed, that a direct influence of Hobbes on Bossuet has been suggested. The existence of such an influence can be neither proved nor disproved. Bossuet certainly knew Hobbes, whose works were known in the France of Louis XIV in several translations. It is therefore quite possible that the most revolutionary thinker of the century supplied the conservative Bossuet with arguments which the latter adapted to his own needs and reconciled with the dogma of original sin—a strange intellectual cross-current which, however, looks less strange if it is seen against the background of its own time. For what most impressed the continental readers of Hobbes and what they most easily understood was not the hidden revolutionary content of his teachings, the rational derivation of absolute power from the contract of submission, but the way in which it could be used to disprove the subversive theories of the right of resistance and so to support the authority of the legitimate ruler.

Bossuet, of course, knows that there have been many forms of State and government since classical times, and he is careful not to present monarchy as the only form of legitimate authority. Basically, in his view, any form of authority is beyond criticism once it has become hallowed by tradition and has achieved a certain degree of stability. But monarchy comes nearest to divine intention, because it is farthest removed from anarchy and offers the best guarantees of peace and order. In the *Politique*, Bossuet sees in monarchy four essential characteristics: it is sacred, paternal, absolute, and in harmony with reason. The first of these characteristics describes its origin, the third its range, while the second and fourth, which are references to the duties of the ruler, can be no more than moral qualities; they have no *vis coactiva*, only a *vis directiva*, for the conduct of the monarch, but they are of quite special importance in Bossuet's political thought, since they form the basis of the vital distinction which he makes between *gouvernement absolu* and *gouvernement arbitraire*. For *gouvernement arbitraire*, in Bossuet's view, is the exact contrary of any ordered régime, and therefore the contrary also of *gouvernement absolu*, properly understood. All that the two have in common is that, in both, the supreme power is subject to no human control. But in the one, the subjects are slaves, sacrificed to a lawless arbitrariness which makes it *barbare et odieux*; while in the other, they enjoy the effective protection of an authority bound by the specific traditions and commands of reason, a rule which accepts the limitations set by God for all mortals. And Bossuet described these limits with all the vigour of his rhetoric, when he said to the kings, 'Vous êtes les enfants du Très Haut; c'est lui qui a établi votre puissance pour le bien du genre humain. Mais, ô dieux de chair et de sang, ô dieux de boue et de poussière, vous mourrez comme des hommes'.

This distinction between *gouvernement arbitraire* and *gouvernement absolu* contains an implicit tribute to the particular *Etat monarchique* in which Bossuet lived and for which he wrote. For there, in its oldest and most venerable form—in the French hereditary monarchy—the links between *gouvernement absolu* and a traditional juridical order must have seemed to him to be revealed in exemplary fashion. Bossuet also knew and used the concept, which in France in particular had so many different meanings, of *lois fondamentales*, but he extended its meaning beyond those usual in his age, by including in it not only personal freedom, but also the inviolability of private property. In this, Bossuet set himself apart from the most extreme exponents of absolutism, who insisted that the absolute power of the monarch extended to the life and property of his subjects. La Bruyère described this idea, in a well-known passage of his *Caractères* as 'le langage de la flatterie'; but he knew perfectly well that it was used not only by flatterers, but also by serious writers, to whom it appeared to be derived with a certain logic from the notion of *pouvoir absolu*. And Louis XIV, in his *Mémoires*, himself accepted the notion in principle.

Bossuet's *Politique* cannot be classed among the greatest and most profound political writings of the century. It is too eclectic in its mixture of theology and *raisonnement*, too full of special pleading, to be included among the writings of the great thinkers of the period. In particular, it is not a work of philosophy, but belongs rather, like its author and the State which it served, to the old world in which politics and theology were one, and which the new age was leaving behind. Yet it is precisely its intellectual contradictions which make it the faithful expression of a form of authority which found its *raison d'être* and its legal justification in its own existence, in the imposing weight of power which it embodied, in its own achievements, in the capacity for survival which it promised, and in the radiance of religious inspiration which surrounded it. All this was brought together and developed in Bossuet's *Politique* and supported by two arguments which, together, must have seemed illuminating and compelling to his contemporaries: he justified the institution of monarchy by appealing both to the will of God and to earthly utility. On the one hand, he pointed to the incomparable stability which made absolute monarchy superior to all other forms of government. On the other, by making tradition the most effective basis of all legality, he was also able to show how its beneficent influence in the day-to-day working of government made the unlimited power of the monarch bearable—how it allowed the humblest of the king's subjects to feel himself part of an ordered society, based on law and sanctified by tradition, and so binding also on the absolute ruler, for whom the care and protection of his subjects was the highest duty. Bossuet's *Lieutenant de Dieu* is no Leviathan, whose power extends in terrifying uniformity over a mass of isolated individuals; his authority extends over the State and a complex hierarchy of subjects, to whom he is bound by a common respect for ancient customs and well-tried institutions.

Bossuet's weakness, which he shares with all the great traditionalists of political thought, is that, in his eyes, law and habit become confused, so that the survival of a régime is the decisive criterion of its legitimacy. It is significant that the focal point of his political theory is the idea of 'prescription', which a hundred years later was to become the key word of Burke's conservative view of politics. When Bossuet wrote, absolutism in France had reached a peak which could not be surpassed, either in reality or in theory. Bossuet stands at the end of a long process of historical maturation, and the theories which he had formulated supplied, right up to the end, the theoretical justification of the régime which he exalted. But the principle of the sovereignty of the people, the force which ultimately defeated the monarchic régime of which Bossuet painted so radiant a picture, was clearly and menacingly visible in the background. Bossuet lived to see the challenge of this force in the polemical works of Jurieu and Levassor. When the *Politique* was written, however, at the peak of the *grand règne*, the dangerously explosive power of the newer theory appeared to have been held in check, as it had never been before, by the conquering and driving force of the monarchic idea. This was the greatest hour of that absolutist doctrine which, indeed, was to reach the peak of its appeal in the very country in which it had been most seriously challenged —in England.

To the historian, and in the light of later developments, the English Restoration looks like a short-lived constitutional compromise; but to contemporary observers it was very much more. Its easy and bloodless victory looked like the passing of a divine judgement against anarchy and rebellion—a judgement in favour of hereditary monarchy, which had found its anointed martyr in the person of Charles I. It is perhaps surprising that the theory of the Divine Right of kings was most pungently formulated, not in the France of Louis XIV, but in the England of Charles II—a fact which can be understood only if one looks back to the great constitutional conflict which shook England in the first half of the century. Part of the essence of this conflict was that it was bound to illustrate more clearly than in any other country the two great conflicting political principles of the age. Nobody ever proclaimed the absolutist theory of government in more striking or more challenging fashion than the extraordinary royal savant who ruled when the argument began, and nowhere else was the contrary notion of the right of resistance stated with such emphasis. In the Great Rebellion this theory carried all before it and conquered the State itself, until it created its own negation in the Cromwellian dictatorship. The right of resistance, however, would never have been able to develop its overwhelming force had it not been intimately linked with the impulses of a religious mass movement: the Stuart monarchy was foredoomed to defeat in the struggle with parliament because it had identified itself with the hated episcopacy and so challenged the religious beliefs of the mass of the population. The acute mind of Thomas Hobbes was quick to grasp the connection between the two, and if, as is possible, it was this perception that first gave a revolutionary turn to his thought, then we may say that this too was a product of the conditions of the time.

Although Hobbes's greatest political work, the *Leviathan*, was not published until 1651, it is a part of a comprehensive philosophical system, of which the essential features had been formulated at an earlier date. It grew out of Hobbes's conviction that the relationships between human activities can be stated as accurately as geometry states the relationships between the sizes of given figures. In this work the mathematical thought of the period, of which Hobbes was one of the pioneers, is applied with the greatest boldness and the most rigorous logic to the phenomena of social and political life. In Hobbes's view, only pure reason and the mathematical method derived from it can validly be applied to the observation of public life; all previous philosophising about the State, law and society appears to him to be determined by passion and dogmatic prejudice. Starting from this conviction, the powerful mind of Thomas Hobbes develops a pessimistic anthropology, which was not uninfluenced by the depressing experience of the English Civil War. The natural impetus of fear, the power of which Hobbes had himself experienced, becomes the fundamental principle of a system of political thought in which all human activities, including political behaviour, are seen as deriving from the need for security and self-preservation. This is a fundamental rejection of the classic Aristotelian theory of natural law. What has led man to create the State is not his social nature, but the demands of reason, which teach him to avoid violent death as the worst evil. Like every other permanent human relationship, the State arises, not from benevolence, but from mutual fear. In order to avoid the state of nature, the *bellum omnium contra omnes*, the individual accepts unconditional subjection to the will of one singular individual, who thus becomes the 'great Leviathan', invested with supreme power. In these circumstances, the precise form of government represented by Leviathan is comparatively unimportant, but Hobbes makes it clear that he regards monarchy as being in practice the best, because it is in monarchy that the merging of State and sovereignty is most clearly embodied.

It was Hobbes who gave the widest interpretation to this concept of sovereignty, so popular among his contemporaries, and who attributed to the sovereign the most complete right of domination ever conceded by one man to another; his power, in Hobbes's view, is quite literally unlimited. Sovereignty is the fountain of justice, the creator of law, and its powers extend to the most intimate spheres of private life. For Hobbes's Leviathan knows no freedom of property, of thought, or of religion. The State is the sole interpreter of all laws, spiritual and profane. God's commandments are transmitted through the mouth of the civil power. The Church and its services have no genuine religious mission; their function is solely to provide the all-powerful State with the appearance of religious authority. In the last analysis, the State itself is deified, for its authority destroys any personal responsibility, even in religious matters. This merciless 'mortal God' owes its *raison d'être* to the services it performs and to the need for security felt by the individuals subject to its power without any rights. That is the strange paradox to which Hobbes's political philosophy can ultimately be reduced. Its beginning and end are the self-interest of the isolated individual, who by cold calculation entrusts himself to the protection of an all-powerful State. This utilitarian motive in Hobbes's thinking sharply distinguishes his doctrine from all the modern forms of totalitarianism, with which it is often wrongly compared.

The teaching of Hobbes thus defends the most extreme form of absolutist thinking and at the same time deprives it of its spell-binding power. In his materialist and hedonistic philosophy, the State loses the last shred of that divine consecration with which the imagination of even the boldest thinkers had found it necessary to surround the God-given authority and its anointed instrument. This, more than anything else, reveals the unbridgeable gulf between Hobbes and his national environment, that of Restoration England, under which his long life, spanning three generations, came to its end. While in continental Europe he was long considered one of the greatest thinkers—so much so that others totally hostile to him nevertheless borrowed ideas from him—the English persisted in seeing in him 'the father of unbelief' and in his notorious myth of Leviathan the Medusa's head of despotism and arbitrary government. Did not Leviathan find its only empirical realisation in the dictatorship of Cromwell, to which Hobbes half rallied, thus betraying the royal cause? Thus, in English eyes, there was attached to the already doubtful reputation of Hobbes the memory of the great break with tradition from which his own theory of the State had in fact arisen. It was the healing of this breach with tradition that gave meaning and purpose to the restored monarchy. The only theory on which the Restoration could and must be based was the buried tradition of the English monarchy—a tradition authoritarian, but not tyrannical, appealing both to sentiment and to political reason, and based on natural succession instead of on some artificially created sovereignty. Such a system could afford less than any other to renounce divine institution as the source of its legitimacy. All these advantages were united in the old theory of the Divine Right of kings, now revived in a form more appropriate to its time. The royalist slogans of the civil war—non-resistance, indefeasible hereditary rights, passive obedience—became significantly fashionable slogans expressing loyalty to the restored monarchy.

It is typical both of the popularity of the theory of Divine Right and of its limited potentialities that in Restoration England it had innumerable devotees, but no new theoretician of the first rank. In Sir Robert Filmer's *Patriarcha*, dating from the Civil War, the doctrine found its manifesto. Published posthumously as late as 1680, this work ran rapidly through several editions and became widely known. It is noteworthy neither for profundity of thought nor for any literary quality. Presumably, it would long ago have been forgotten if Locke's famous refutation of it in his *First Treatise of Civil Government* had not ensured it a place in the history of political thought. The fact, however, that Locke thought it worth the effort of refutation shows the importance of the place it occupied in the political literature of its time.

Not the least of the reasons for the success of the *Patriarcha* was its especially skilful linking of the two major arguments for the supremacy of monarchy: its divine origin and its justification in nature and reason. Filmer unequivocally laid his main emphasis on the second of these arguments, for he probably vaguely felt that it carried greater conviction than the arbitrary mixture of biblical quotations on which his proof of the divine origin or monarchy inevitably rested. While the majority of the defenders of the theory of divine right based their proof of the legitimacy of hereditary monarchy and of its divine sanction on the existence of kingship in biblical history, Filmer chose the opposite route. Since (he says) monarchy is in harmony with nature, it must be inspired and created by God. His whole argument rests on the equation of monarchy and family, of royal and paternal authority. In this thesis, the ancient metaphor which made of the king the father of his people is used to provide reasoned proof of the absolutist doctrine, so that Filmer became in fact the founder of a patriarchal theory of State and society. This theory provided the defenders of monarchy with a new argument, which called in the aid of natural law, without casting doubt on the divinity of monarchy. For Filmer, too, the Bible remained the ultimate source of all political wisdom, but he saw it, not as a mere arsenal of quotable texts, but as an authentic account of the origin and character of early society and its monarcho-patriarchal form of government. He felt what had not occurred to Hobbes and Locke and all the supporters of the contract theory—that society is the natural and necessary condition of the existence of individual human beings, and not the artificial creation of an individual or group decision. This belief took him back to something very like the great Aristotelian theory of the origin of the State. But, by claiming that the patriarchal society described in the Old Testament was in fact the only natural model for all times, he put himself into a dangerously exposed position, in which his theory was destined sooner or later to fall victim to the remorseless logic of the modern theory of natural law. The critical eye of Locke was quick to see that the weak spot in his theory was the unbridgeable gulf between modern society and the primitive form of the patriarchal State, and he had no difficulty in proving that the beginnings of political society, as shown in the Bible, are anything but natural. The force of Filmer's argument was inevitably weakened by his attempt to make patriarchal authority the source of all political rights and to trace the modern State—which to Filmer meant hereditary monarchy—back to Adam. The fact that this was indeed the rational culmination of the theory of Divine Right helped to create a reaction against it, and so led to a movement which ultimately replaced Divine Right by new and more logical conceptions of the origin of State and society.

There is a certain historical significance in the fact that, while Bossuet was writing his *Politique* in France and the theory of the Divine Right of kings was attaining the status of an official doctrine in England, in Holland died a lonely thinker who also found himself justifying absolute power, though he started from quite different premises and reached his conclusions in spite of himself. Baruch Spinoza has often been closely likened to Hobbes—even by his contemporaries, who misunderstood him, and saw him, above all, as a great atheist; and indeed, the similarities between Spinoza and Hobbes were by no means superficial. They had in common an urge to find a rational explanation of the universe, belief in a method of thought based on the *more geometrico*, the great importance they attached to power and the will to power, and a basically pessimistic view of human nature, which they both saw as governed by passion and desire. But this community of views had as its background two totally different conceptions of the universe. While in the Hobbesian system all relationships are interpreted in materialist and mechanistic terms, in Spinoza's they are rooted in a transcendental universal system, in which God and nature are fused into a single whole and all the dissonances of the world of nature are linked *sub specie aeterni* in a heavenly harmony. Even the 'war of all against all' in the state of nature, which the mechanistic thinking of Hobbes saw simply and brutally as a fact, is illuminated in Spinoza's theory by a philosophy, monistic and pantheistic at the same time, which raises the power of natural things to an instrument of the eternal power of God. It is this notion, leading, as it does, to Hegel, which gives to Spinoza's thought its historical significance and assigns to him a special place among the thinkers of his time. And yet this stern, cool mind, apparently so independent of environmental influences, clashed with the political reality of the times of which, as a thinker, he was far ahead. His basic political ideas were the product of the tension between his ethical ideal and the real world as he saw it: indeed, there is much to suggest that his ideas changed along with reality.

Spinoza discussed political problems in detail in two works: the *Tractatus theologico-politicus*, which he wrote before 1665, and the *Tractatus politicus*, which was still unfinished when he died in 1677. Between these two dates, experience added to his understanding of politics, and the result was a certain number of characteristic modifications in his later work. Spinoza acquired his experience in a country which, in its time, was regarded as the bastion of political liberty and the pioneer of religious toleration. It was in the Netherlands, and perhaps only in the Netherlands, that those who had been expelled on religious grounds from their own countries could live unmolested. Even there, however, they lived totally withdrawn from the world, under the jealous eye of an orthodox clergy, their contacts limited to a few patrons and friends. Spinoza's *Tractatus theologico-politicus* was judged in the most severe terms by both the spiritual and secular authorities of the Republic, and this fact soon brought him to a certain community of fate with followers of sects like the Mennonites, who enjoyed a limited and perpetually threatened toleration and were in close contact with the Independents and Congregationalists, who represented English Puritanism. It seems certain that he became familiar with them and came to know something of their ideal of a democratically governed Church: how far this in turn affected his basic political beliefs is a much-discussed question. One cannot help noting that, in the *Tractatus theologico-politicus*, direct democracy—majority rule at meetings of equal citizens—is presented as the 'most natural' form of government, and is used by Spinoza to explain the origin of the State and the nature of sovereignty. It must be admitted that the State which originates in this way has all the essential characteristics of that of Hobbes; but its basic political democracy remains an ideal, even though in practice it leads to the same type of omnipotent State as in Hobbes. In a celebrated phrase of the *Tractatus theologico-politicus*, 'the true purpose of the State is liberty', the same notion emerges as the ultimate purpose of all forms of political organisation.

Spinoza's final answer to the question, 'What is the best kind of State?' will never be known, since the surviving fragment of the *Tractatus politicus* breaks off at the decisive point, when Spinoza comes to the problem of democracy. But his original attitude must by then have become somewhat less dogmatic, as is shown by the fact that, at this point, he brings into the argument the other two classical types of régime, monarchy and aristocracy, and uses them as pegs on which to hang a discussion of the nature and functions of the best possible régime. There is, indeed, much to suggest that this modification was prompted by his experience of the particular régime under which he was living. As in all the 'republics' of the time, both the political structure and the social basis had a markedly aristocratic stamp; this became even more marked in Spinoza's day, as the popular and dynastic counterweight to aristocracy—the institution of the Stadholderate under the Princes of Orange—yielded much of its power and influence to the patrician merchant class, whose spokesman, the Grand Pensionary John de Witt, was the leading figure in the States General.[1] This widely cultured and philosophically minded statesman had contacts with Spinoza which have often been overestimated. It is nevertheless certain that Spinoza was one of de Witt's admirers and became familiar with the politics of his elective homeland after he had settled in The Hague in 1669. He was living at the political centre of a prosperous State which encouraged a flourishing culture. It may well be that the evidence of his own eyes suggested to him that the intellectual freedom to which he attached so much importance was better protected under such a régime than in a democracy, with the unpredictable emotional mass movements which in his century were nearly always closely linked with religious passions.

Spinoza must himself have witnessed the collapse of this régime, to which he was so favourably disposed, amid the frightening violence of a fanatical mob. He appears actually to have been an eye-witness of the assassination of John de Witt and his brother after the French invasion of the Netherlands in 1672.[2] This event was the starting-point of a long war, in which for the time being Louis XIV was victorious. And this victory was the victory also of absolute monarchy over an aristocratic republic, of a continental great power over a nation of merchants and sailors, of an offensive over a defensive policy, of material strength over moral principles. The whole affair revealed that not even the freest constitution can guarantee internal and external security. Even an intellectual recluse like Spinoza could not escape this conclusion, and it was certainly his own

[1] See below, ch. XII, pp. 279–91. [2] See below, ch. XII, pp. 293–4.

distressing experience which led to the striking modification of his political thought in his last work: 'the function of the State is purely and simply to guarantee peace and security; it follows that the best State is that in which men live their lives in concord and in which their rights are inviolate'.

Thus, Spinoza too ends his great monologue on the place of reason in the State with the resigned allocation of the intellectual to the private sphere of freedom of thought. This was, in essence, a deliberate compromise which the rational free-thinker of the age concluded with the all-powerful State of the century. Power belongs to the State and—since might and right are synonymous—the State also has the right to do whatever contributes to its own survival. Precisely for that reason, however—in the interests of *raison d'état*—it will concede the right of freedom of thought to the individual who unreservedly recognises its authority. At bottom, what leads Spinoza to justify the all-powerful State is the same individualistic motive as that of Hobbes, the idea of the State as guarantor of one's own security and of freedom of thought, though in Spinoza's case the notion was more deeply felt and perhaps more fully thought out. In spite of the idealistic impulse that lay behind his philosophy, Spinoza could not free his mind from the utilitarian tangle to which the limitations of seventeenth-century thought condemned him. These limitations are, first, the habit, induced by the acceptance of natural-law theories, of looking at the State in the light of the common needs of individuals, and second, the political and constitutional circumstances of the time, which made even the most original and independently minded thinker permanently conscious of the threat to his right to think and, indeed, to his very existence. No political thinker could escape the problem of security which dominated the whole epoch and constituted an important, though often hidden and unadmitted, basis of their confrontation with political reality. Spinoza encountered political reality in one of the principal storm-centres of a period of great decisions. A contemporary, a man of exactly the same age, Samuel von Pufendorf, met it in the relative calm of the German and Scandinavian principalities. This fact alone throws a significant light on the special features which historical and national factors gave to the natural-law theories of the seventeenth century in Germany.

In Germany, as elsewhere, the middle of the century constitutes a great historical turning-point: indeed, it was in Germany that the change was, perhaps, most marked and most visible. The Peace of Westphalia confirmed the long and difficult rise of the German principalities to the rank of independent States. It was on the ruins left by war that the victorious power of the absolute princely State was built, and it was in these small German States, rather than in the great monarchies, that the individual felt most keenly the pressure of absolutism. Yet the narrowness of political life in these States was not wholly constricting; in some ways, German political thought gained by it. German political thinkers accepted as gladly as those elsewhere the combination of the new mathematical science and natural law; but the special conditions in which they worked in Germany led them to add a new current, of some importance in the history of political ideas, to the great philosophic stream of West European thought. Within the easily surveyed area of the small German State, political thinkers were inevitably in close contact with facts. Precisely because the State intervened in every aspect of life, and because this made any secure intellectual life or scientific activity possible only in the form of service to the princes—as university teacher, legal adviser or diplomat—political theory was almost always concerned with day-to-day political experience, and so tended more easily than elsewhere to absorb the results of empirical studies, like history and finance, which provided it with assured fields of knowledge and brought it down nearer to earth.

The consequences of the Thirty Years War helped to cement this alliance between political theory and day-to-day political experience; for the war and its results both presented the German principalities with a whole series of practical problems as well as problems of constitution and public law, which had first of all to be considered and resolved on the theoretical plane. In their attempts to meet both types of problem, the governments of the principalities found an ideal ally in the greatest intellectual force of the century, the concept of secularised natural law. This offered the strongest possible support to a claim to sovereignty which could not appeal, as the older monarchies had done, to the doctrine of Divine Right. Its undenominational character also gave it a special value at a time when the religious energies of the country in which the Reformation was born had been exhausted. And in principalities which were too small and too poor to leave much scope for the growth of power politics, the material and moral welfare of their subjects was considered the highest and indeed the true purpose of the State. As early as the seventeenth century, the influence of the theory of natural law was thus responsible for bringing about in Germany—and in Germany only—an alliance between absolutism and the enlightenment. It was no accident that, when Spinoza was being slandered by ecclesiastical circles throughout Europe, he was offered a university chair by a German Elector, Charles Louis of the Palatinate, son of the 'Winter King', who tried to compensate for the misery caused by his father, not only by repairing the material damage of war, but also by a far-seeing policy of toleration.

Such was the political and intellectual background of the work of the most constructive German political thinker of the time, Samuel von Pufendorf, who was born in the middle of the war, in 1632. His family circumstances were modest; his father was a Protestant clergyman in

Saxony, who wanted his son to become a theologian; but Pufendorf turned to the study of law, philosophy and the natural sciences. At Jena, he came under the influence of the mathematician and philosopher Weigel, who later also taught Leibniz. It was he who introduced Pufendorf to Descartes's *Discours de la Méthode* and perhaps also to Galileo's picture of the physical world. Thus Pufendorf came into contact with the new and dominant intellectual current of his age, and at the same time, in the works of Hugo Grotius and Thomas Hobbes, he encountered the new world of natural law. As tutor in the family of the Swedish Ambassador at Copenhagen, he came into involuntary contact with world affairs, for on the outbreak of the Danish–Swedish war in 1659 he was arrested and spent eight months in captivity. He used his enforced leisure to write his first book, the *Elementa Jurisprudentiae Universalis*. To Pufendorf, as to the other great legal mind of the age, Grotius, imprisonment without cause and for purely political reasons provided an experience which formed the background to reflections on the principles of natural law. On his release, he went to Holland where his political and historical horizon was much widened. But it was not by accident that he found his professional fulfilment in the service of a German prince, as holder of the chair of Politics and Natural Law in the University of Heidelberg. In this post, however, Pufendorf was not so much an academic lawyer as a philosopher and political writer. It was not until he went to Lund, whither he was called by the king of Sweden, that he became Professor of Natural and International Law. It was in Sweden in 1672 that he published his chief work, under the title of *De jure naturae et gentium*, and established his European reputation. During the later years of his life his transformation into a historian was accomplished: while in the service of the king of Sweden he wrote a history of the Swedish Empire, and he died as court historiographer of the Elector of Brandenburg.

These facts indicate the circumstances, in some respects typical of the age, within which a German scholar and publicist could move in the seventeenth century. They also reveal the special place to which Pufendorf is entitled in the development of the theory of natural law. His aim was to develop it into a system by bringing together various disciplines and their methods. He combined the studies of philosophy, history and the mathematical sciences and sought to fuse into a single new union the different approaches of these disciplines. This combination of mathematical proof and empirical investigation is his most original contribution to knowledge, but it also imposed limitations on his field of vision; for it is part of the nature of these completely contrary methods that no attempt to combine them and to apply the result to the field of natural law could be wholly successful. The effect was to bring the rationalist and the empiricist within him into conflict, though he was himself unaware of it. The rationalist believed in his own capacity to find a way, by the light of reason, to those natural and basic principles of law to which man is subject in moral, legal and political matters. But the empiricist found himself faced at the outset with a problem—that of the origin of natural law—which, though recognisable by reason, could not be solved by reason alone. Precisely because it seemed to him to be in contradiction with the experience of history, he rejected both the theory of Grotius, according to which law arises from the social instinct, and the contrary theory of Hobbes, which derived all human society from the instinct of self-preservation. He therefore refused to assume any contract of society, because this assumption is incapable of historical proof, but postulated instead a natural state of helplessness, or 'imbecillitas', which exists at all times and in all places and forces individuals into society. In this secularised form the Lutheran doctrine of the origin of the State as a divinely instituted expedient clearly found an echo in the mind of Pufendorf. For him, too, law is basically a product of necessity, the expression, not of anything divine, but of something specifically human. This raised the problem which preoccupied Pufendorf throughout his life, of the connection between natural law and the real State as it existed in history. It is true that he did not, like Hobbes, reach a position in which he saw the power of the State and the commands of nature as synonyms; but he nevertheless went near enough to this view—again in contrast with Grotius—to see natural law, realised in the State, as the sole source of positive law.

His system is a synthesis of earlier views, for Pufendorf too, as a political thinker, was a disciple of Bodin and still more of Hobbes. He too conceived of the State after the fashion of his century, as the repository of unlimited sovereignty, free from any ecclesiastical or political authority and equal in rights with all other States. This is shown most clearly in his well-known attitude to the special constitutional problem of Germany, the relationship between the Empire and the principalities.

Deeply rooted in German history there lay an inevitable conflict between the Germans' sense of being one people and the new conception of the State, which they encountered in the political reality of the century. In France, the absolute authority of the king, with its religious basis, had long been fused with the nation's need for unity; even in England, the interest of the nation and the prerogative of the ruler were never in fundamental conflict with each other, despite the bitterness with which the extent and limits of the royal power were contested. In Germany, on the other hand, the new conception of sovereignty benefited only the principalities and inevitably tended, as it took deeper hold, to empty the concept of the Empire of all content. The growing contrast between the *raison d'état* of the autonomous princely States and the venerable edifice of the Empire which embraced them all, between a princely and an Imperio-monarchic interpretation of the traditional constitution of the Empire, increased the need, in theory and in practice, for a new and clearly formulated definition of the relationship between the Empire and its loose components. Pufendorf was among those who tackled this topical problem. Preceding his comprehensive system of natural law, he published an analysis and critique of the Imperial constitution which became his most popular work and still ranks among the classic works of German political literature.

There were, of course, earlier important and widely read treatises on the idea and constitution of the Empire, and of these Pufendorf made extensive use; but they were products of the political struggle and thus, in the widest sense, partisan. Pufendorf, on the other hand, claimed to have produced something much more modern and, indeed, revolutionary: he aimed at a scientific approach, involving, therefore, a reasoned critique of the existing State. He may have realised the danger of such an enterprise, for he gave his work the colourless title of *De Statu Imperii Germanici* and published it under the pseudonym of an Italian traveller, Severinus de Monzambano. The originality of this brief work lay, not in the much-quoted description of the Empire as a constitutional 'monster', but rather in its new and striking independence of all the political authorities of the time. He defended neither the special interests of the princes and Estates nor those of the Habsburg Emperors. His *ratio status* was exclusively that of the Empire, but of an Empire which—because of its lack of any single sovereignty—in Pufendorf's opinion was an international federation rather than a single State. However much the politician in him may have regretted it, the historian could not fail to see how historical development had led the Empire permanently away from the single-State structure, and that something durable could develop only within the framework of the new territorial principalities. For that reason, he saw the Empire as a federation of States, and this view for long exercised a decisive influence upon German constitutional thought.

This sober assessment of the irrevocable facts of historical reality was connected with a further characteristic of Pufendorf's political thought: his *bourgeois* attitude to the problems of the political world. He was already thinking as a matter of course in terms of the modern antithesis between 'ruler' and 'subject'. His detailed proposals for reform breathe the same *bourgeois* spirit. Many of his demands—a common currency, abolition of customs and trade barriers—particularly affected the German burghers, their legal status and economic interests. In this respect, Pufendorf may be classed among the forerunners of the urban civilisation of the eighteenth century, which in Germany developed under the protection of, and to some extent in alliance with, enlightened despotism. His name is therefore indissolubly linked with this typically German version of absolutism, for which, it has been said, his theory was 'made to measure'. The extent to which he accepted the absolute princely State should, however, not be overestimated. In Pufendorf's view, the prince is less important than the State and is required to put its interests before his own. He also clung to the idea of the transcendental character of Christianity, though he rejected the narrowing influence of dogma. The State certainly does not exist for the sake of the Church, but neither has it any right of compulsion in matters of faith. Pufendorf saw the Church as a part of that more comprehensive body, the State; but he also conceived of every organised political community as Christian—and by Christian he meant Protestant. A purely philosophic *religio naturalis* did not provide an adequate ethical basis for the State as he conceived it. This, in particular, distinguished him both from the French enlightenment and from the dogmatic rationalism and hostility to revealed religion of Thomasius, who none the less remains, among all later German political thinkers, his nearest and closest disciple.

Pufendorf embodies in striking fashion the trends of political thought which are characteristic of the century in which he lived and of his German environment. He was significant and original enough to express all these tendencies; but he was not a creative genius. This, indeed, explains the extraordinary range of his influence and his reputation which, in Germany, remained undimmed until the appearance of Christian Thomasius and Christian Wolff. He followed the fashion of system-building which dominated the age, but showed the practical sense and down-to-earthness which the century demanded of its political writers. He shared to the full its optimistic belief in the power of reason and yet remained rooted in his Protestant traditions. The philosophic insight of the great thinker was denied to his sober, unspeculative, sometimes rather dry and pedantic mind, and these intellectual limitations were recognised by no less a person than Leibniz, who said of him: 'vir parum jurisconsultus, sed minime philosophus'.

These limitations are shown most clearly by a comparison with the much more eminent author of this criticism. There can be no doubt that Leibniz also represented his century, and in a much more important sense than Pufendorf. But it is part of the tragedy of every genius that he can never live in complete agreement with his time; he looks far beyond it, and often enough is broken by it. The first of these characteristics applies in a quite special degree to Leibniz; the second only in so far that, although destined to great happiness, he died in solitude and disappointment. The greater part of his work was left half finished. It was not granted to him to set down all the results of his life's work and present them as a single whole, so that his political thought is interwoven into the general content of his basic philosophic, scientific and religio-ethical ideas. It never took the form of a precise and independent theory, capable of giving him a well-defined place in the history of political ideas. His thought was also in part determined and directed by the often passionate desires of a man who was involved in the processes of political decision, even if only on the fringe. This too distinguishes Leibniz from the other great thinkers of his time; for him the data of politics and government constitute not only an immense field of observation, but he feels compelled, within the limited possibilities available to him, actively to intervene. Although never a statesman in the professional sense of the term, he did not hesitate to use political weapons in the service of his great plans, so that his life appears to be bound up with the political and diplomatic issues of his time. He used up some of the best of his powers in varied missions and in the drafting of memoranda for princely employers. Indeed, nothing illustrates more clearly the narrowness and poverty of conditions in Germany than the fact that the owner of the richest and freest mind of the age was dependent on service to a prince and ended his days in almost humiliating dependence, as historiographer to the House of Guelph. Many of his political writings were therefore written merely in order to further dynastic interests, or referred to purely topical matters.

This is true even of the best-known of his political works, the *Consilium Aegyptiacum* and the *Mars Christianissimus*. Therefore, these two works are best seen as source-books of contemporary history rather than vehicles of Leibniz's deepest convictions. These are concerned with fields of thought far removed from those of mere day-to-day politics, which, indeed, they touch on only superficially—with Leibniz's conception of a European culture, with his plans for a comprehensive organisation of science and with his Christian sensibilities. These lead him to three great problems: the first is the relationship of Germany, that is, the Empire, to the other nations and States; the second is that of the surmounting of religious divisions; and the third, the growing conflict between Christian belief and the teachings of mechanistic science. It is when one measures the attitude of Leibniz to these problems against the customary categories of thought of his time that one becomes most acutely conscious of the intellectual paradox which he embodied. On the one hand, he appears almost as the prophet of coming centuries, as the far-seeing guide to developing intellectual and political forces whose future significance was hidden from his contemporaries, and on the other hand, his thought continues to lean on traditional concepts which his age as a whole had left behind.

This is particularly evident in his attitude to his own political environment in Germany. For him the medieval concept of the Emperor has still some meaning; the Empire is something infinitely greater than a mere confederation of States; it is a monarchic body of a Christian character. Though he undoubtedly wished it to be primarily German, he saw it also as a symbol of the West as a whole and of that intellectual unity of Europe in which he so profoundly believed. For him, the 'idea' of the Empire, as he wished to see it understood, signified in the political field the same thing as the central idea of 'harmony' in his philosophy—a higher unity, within which every part retains its own special characteristics. For this reason, and especially on account of the many types of State power which it included, he wished to see the historic constitution of the Empire preserved. For this reason, too, he sees in the Empire an essential element of the European community of States, of the *balance de l'Europe*. Both the Empire and Europe, in his view, would be most seriously threatened if the whole Continent came to be ruled by the French monarchy, and the changes in the power relationships of his day seemed to him to bring this within the range of possibility.

Here we find the roots of his 'Imperial patriotism', which of necessity was directed against France and her expansionist foreign policy; but to him Europe, and beyond Europe the unity of the whole world, were more important than the Empire. From the time of his meeting with Peter the Great, Russia seemed to him to offer a new and promising field for the European spirit. At the same time he looked towards distant China as a possible participant in a world-wide civilisation based on European and Christian concepts. The national and the universal trends of his thought—German patriotic feeling, together with a consciousness of Europe as a whole—are constantly merging. Just as his plans for an Academy embraced both the old Empire and the whole of the civilised world, so his patriotic aims culminated in the search for an essentially universal civilisation, so that even at the end of a life full of disappointments he was still able to write: 'I consider Heaven my mother country, and all right-thinking men my fellow-citizens.' But this cultural citizenship of the world, with its philosophic guiding-star of universal harmony, was not limited to the sphere of mind. Despite its unmistakably rationalist colouring, it has a Christian background, against which it must be seen.

Outwardly, Leibniz always remained a Lutheran Protestant, but his Christianity had a universal content, capable of bursting the bonds of any dogma; and no country was so well suited as Germany, with its sharp religious divisions, to bring home to him the tragic significance of the division of Christendom. He saw this division both as a national misfortune for Germany and beyond that as an obstacle to religious and political peace in Europe. He devoted years of his life to active collaboration in the 'irenic' attempts at the reunion of Christendom, as a step on the road to his own supreme goal, a Christian community of all peoples, ruled by reason. It was in the course of this effort that he crossed swords with Bossuet in a remarkable correspondence—he, the greatest representative of the 'new science' and of Protestant Germany, pitting himself against the greatest intellectual exponent of the Catholic monarchy of Louis XIV. The 'irenic' campaign failed, as it was bound to fail, in its clash with the facts of a political reality in which State and Church were still interlinked and with the immovable dogmatic basis of post-Tridentine Catholicism.[1]

While Leibniz was striving vainly to heal the old breach between the rival religions, he saw a new and dangerously wide breach opening at the feet of both religious communities—the breach between Christianity and modern science. His recognition of this fact and his assessment of its future significance prove his great percipience. Leibniz accepted in full the rationalist optimism of his time, and his belief in the intellectual and moral power of scientific knowledge never left him, nor did his conviction that he could make the human race happier and better by his combined philosophic and scientific endeavours. In this sense, Leibniz always belonged to the 'enlightenment'; but at the same time he foresaw the distant consequences of a trend of which he knew himself to be one of the agents, and which owed to him something of its driving force. He recognised the dangers that lay hidden in the intellectual presumption of rationalism, and he tried to warn its adepts that they 'were preparing everything for the general revolution with which Europe is threatened'. These astonishing words were written at the turn of the century, in a polemic against John Locke. It was not chance that led him to produce this work in the second half of his life, for it embraced that significant transition period which we have come to call, after the title of a famous book, *La crise de la conscience Européenne*. It included the last two decades of the old century and the first of the new and was a period of preparation for sudden change in every field of intellectual life, a period in which the current of political ideas was noticeably quickened.

The political views discussed in this chapter differ from each other in important respects, and they emerged from widely differing philosophic, personal and national circumstances. And yet they possess one striking, though perhaps superficial, common characteristic: they all help to justify the existence of a powerful State. Even those authors who avoided all historical and theological argument and relied only upon natural law saw in natural law the rational justification of a strong monarchy, in which, for the seventeeth-century mind, both the legality and the utility of absolute power were most impressively demonstrated. Such is the nature of the dialectic of natural law, however, that it inevitably contained from its very beginnings all that was required to justify a diametrically opposite political concept, provided only that the 'natural' rights of the individual were set above the association into which he was merged and that one moved forward to the claim that the State rests on and is sustained, not by the sovereignty of the princes, but by that of the people. This doctrine had lain for long in the intellectual arsenal of mankind. It was conceived in the Middle Ages, but became a political weapon only during the religious wars of the sixteenth century. It was not the percep-

[1] Cp. below, ch. VI, pp. 145–6.

tive mind of the philosophers, but the ethical and religious demands of the Calvinists that turned it against a hostile State and filled it with the passion of religious certainty. It was developed into a comprehensive doctrine of State and society by a German Calvinist, Johannes Althusius, at the beginning of the century.

Even this doctrine, however, could not dispense with the most important methodological principle of the thought of the age, the contract theory; this theory ensures to the individual a number of rights, above all religious rights, felt by every individual to be his own inborn possession, which can be neither lost nor surrendered. A whole series of concrete and pregnant political demands found a characteristic justification in this theory—demands which, as in the England of the Great Rebellion, almost led to a destruction of the State itself. And, indeed, the bogy of anarchy, which seemed to raise its head along with the principle of the sovereignty of the people, became one of the most powerful arguments of the defenders of monarchical absolutism, which reached its peak, in theory and practice, between 1660 and 1685. Sovereignty of the people remained, none the less, the most powerful and dominant political concept of the time. It was not defeated, but only held in check by conditions unfavourable to its development, and a change in these conditions was enough to revive it.

This change was introduced by two events which happened in the same year, though there was no causal connection between them. All they had in common was the fact that, in different ways, they threatened the right of large sections of the people to worship in their own way. One was the Revocation of the Edict of Nantes by Louis XIV, the other the accession of James II in England. The persecution of the Huguenots, the final and belated action of the Counter-Reformation, awakened the intellectual resistance of world-Protestantism to the French monarchy, and the French Calvinists took the ideological offensive against absolutism from their new base in Holland. In England, the policy of James II had the effect on a Protestant nation of a call to battle and brought the doctrine of the Divine Right of kings face to face with a challenge which it was not equipped to meet. In both cases, there arose demands for political and for religious freedom which combined to give revolutionary power to the principle of the sovereignty of the people. While, however, in France the consequences of the persecution of the Huguenots were not seen until much later and therefore did not visibly weaken French absolutism, the consequences of the change of ruler in England were immediate and revolutionary; for in the Glorious Revolution a monarchy was born which no longer rested on divine ordination and the right of succession, but owed the throne to the call of parliament, despite all the efforts made to hide this fact. This was not the least of the causes of the widespread influence in Europe of the revolution settlement. It was not only the final and successful solution of an almost secular constitutional struggle, not only the starting-point of a general shift in the balance of power; it was also a milestone in the history of political ideas, and would have been even if it had not found in John Locke an influential interpreter, who presented it to all Europe as a model of the rational organisation of the State.

There have been few occasions in history on which a major political event and its interpretation by a contemporary thinker have so happily coincided with and complemented each other as did the Glorious Revolution and Locke's *Treatises of Civil Government*. Yet the student would be wise to beware of seeing in Locke's essay a mere *pièce d'occasion*, written with the conscious intention of justifying for party purposes the revolution of 1688. It was not merely under the influence of the revolution that Locke's basic political ideas were formed. They had been ripening in his mind before he wrote the *Treatises*. Moreover, the English Whig politicians had not been dependent on his arguments, for the intellectual weapon which they needed and used had long been available in the extensive polemical literature which was born of the English constitutional conflict. It is also too often forgotten that Locke's theory is by no means in complete conformity with the traditional Whig standpoint. One of the best-known arguments of the 'Revolution-Whigs' was 'the original contract between king and people', which—in their view—James II had broken. In Locke's theory, on the other hand, there is no 'contract of government' between king and people, but only a 'social contract' between individuals who have joined together to form 'civil society'. Locke's contract is thus pre-political; the power of the State arises, not from a contract, but from a revocable 'fiduciary power' which the people entrusts to the rulers.

Locke remains nevertheless in a deeper sense what he was to his contemporaries and to posterity, the philosophical apologist of the constitutional principles of the Whigs. For the justification which he offered for these principles was not only their suitability to the material and political needs of the time, but also their conformity with the eternally valid commands of pure reason. In so doing, he gave to the revolution settlement, in his own clear, readable and unassuming prose, an interpretation admirably adapted to the temper of the times. His astounding influence, first upon his contemporaries and then upon the whole eighteenth century, rests on the combination of these two qualities. For his political philosophy was certainly not wholly new, but rather the fruit of prolonged and wide reading. The raw materials from which he constructed his system are to be found in the writings of numerous forerunners and contemporaries. Indeed, many of his basic views had been more carefully considered or more brilliantly presented by others. But, by reformulating them with greater clarity and moderation and linking them with an attractive picture of man in the state of nature, he fashioned a theory which incorporated the whole spirit of the changing order of things in political life. Locke's theory, indeed, mirrored to perfection the character of an age in which the passion of the constitutional conflict had given way to the sober desire for a settlement, an age whose temperate piety found the religious passion of Milton as uncongenial as the so-called 'atheism' of Hobbes, and which saw in 'government by consent' the best guarantee of the secure and peaceful enjoyment of private property.

The teachings of Locke, and in particular his contradictions, become self-explanatory, or at least lose some of their contradictions, if they are measured against the political reality of which Locke never lost sight when he was writing his *Treatises*. It is true that he clothed his political theories in general philosophic concepts, but these cannot hide the historic features of the English constitution of the seventeenth century. Behind the fiction of a mass of exactly similar individuals equipped with natural rights there lies the hidden reality of Locke's compatriots in England, and what he describes, in the language of the political philosophy of his time, is the machinery and the working of the English constitution, as he knew it from his own observation and as it was then understood. Even his much-discussed theory of the separation of powers conveys in fact an accurate general picture of the actual distribution of authority in England between the highest organs of the State. Where the picture appears to be wrong, it has merely been overtaken by later constitutional developments; in its own time it was very close to reality. The fact that the theory laid its emphasis on the separation of powers and overlooked the possible links between the powers is due to the conditions of a period in which the ever-wakeful mistrust of the Crown seemed to point to the need for the greatest possible degree of separation between legislative and executive. And if, in his mind, the judicial and administrative powers merge into one—the executive—when set against the legislature, that fact too merely reflects the greater strength of the legislature, as embodied in parliament.

It may at first sight seem confusing that Locke should first have made parliament the 'supreme power' and then limited its authority by the creation of another 'supreme power', the people; but this is in fact no more than the typical contemporary presentation of the distinction between 'legal' and 'political' sovereignty. Locke avoided the word 'sovereignty' with something akin to fear, because it seemed to him to have been discredited by Hobbes, but he knew what it meant and could be made to mean. The 'supreme power' of the legislature is simply the 'legal sovereignty' of parliament, in the form into which it had developed in the seventeenth century and in which it had been confirmed by the Glorious Revolution. In the same way, the 'supreme power' of the people is simply the 'political sovereignty', to which, in the last resort, the legislature is answerable. But the power of the people does not manifest itself in normal circumstances; it affirms its existence by the act of creating the

State and does not act again, except when there is no legitimate political authority. In the intervening periods it remains passive, and the legislature is the 'supreme power'. The only right which Locke accords to the people as a political society is a qualified right of revolt, when the formerly legitimate authority has broken its trust; for he was by no means a democrat. Like the Whigs whose views he shared, he accepted in its entirety the traditional constitution, which—in their unshakeable view—had simply been restored by the Glorious Revolution.

What the eighteenth century saw in the works of Locke was, then, the English constitution, an essentially complete and therefore inviolable structure: this is the reason for the almost canonical status which later generations accorded to him. It is equally the source of the profound misunderstandings to which his ideas gave cause. They were still seen as the last word in political wisdom when the circumstances from which they had arisen had long since changed. The myth of the English constitution, which he so effectively helped to create, trailed like a cloud of glory behind him and made him the spiritual father of the West European enlightenment and of its far-reaching ideological and political consequences. In England itself, on the other hand, he was seen as the eloquent defender of stability and of tradition—which explains why clearly discernible threads of influence run from him to Rousseau as well as to Burke.

CHAPTER VI

CHURCH AND STATE

For both Catholics and Protestants, the Peace of Westphalia was a bitter disappointment. Recourse to the sword, instead of bringing final victory as the extremists of each confession had hoped, had merely ensured the perpetuation of religious division; and now Catholics, Lutherans and Calvinists had to accept co-existence in a Europe where ideas, and the institutions embodying those ideas, were markedly changing. But the forty years after the peace were not characterised only by interdenominational hatred and attempts to end it; they were also years of tension between Church and State in several countries of western and southern Europe. In some the conflict was a simple one between the secular authority and one officially recognised Church; in others the situation was complicated by the existence of religious minorities, either Catholic, or Protestant, or both.

At first sight there might appear to be little reason in this period for an intensification of, or even a notable alteration in, this endemic problem of the relationship of Church and State. The mid-seventeenth century was not shaken by an acute and general crisis, such as the Reformation. Yet important if not spectacular changes were taking place. One of the most significant was the tendency in several countries, Protestant as well as Catholic, for government to become more absolute and thus less inclined to tolerate rival or extraneous authorities, of which the churches, with their claim to men's deepest loyalties, were the most important. Louis XIV put the case for the State thus: 'Kings are absolute *seigneurs*, and from their nature have full and free disposal of all property both secular and ecclesiastical, to use it as wise dispensers, that is to say, in accordance with the requirements of their State'; and again, 'those mysterious names, the Franchises and Liberties of the Church...have equal reference to all the faithful whether they be laymen or tonsured, who are all equally sons of this common Mother; but...they exempt neither the one nor the other from subjection to Sovereigns, to whom the Gospel itself precisely enjoins that they should submit themselves'.[1] The slow growth of a clearer idea of sovereignty as an attribute of the State, however it was expressed, left little room for the conception of the Church as an equal partner, and none at all for a theocracy. For the most part the forms which the inevitable conflicts took were the traditional ones. Opposition to clerical immunities and ecclesiastical jurisdiction was not new, but the State was now better

[1] *A King's Lessons in Statecraft: Louis XIV: Letters to his Heirs*, ed. J. Longnon, transl. Herbert Wilson (London, 1924), p. 149.

able and more inclined to make it effective. Taxes paid by the clergy were already an important part of the revenue of most countries, yet the churches' untapped wealth was a standing temptation to governments finding it hard to meet the cost of their expensive wars. Kings and their more influential subjects had long tried to accumulate ecclesiastical patronage and use it for their own ends, and such exploitation was ruthlessly extended. While *raison d'état* dominated more openly the policies of European rulers, both in foreign and domestic affairs, theories of Divine Right, somewhat paradoxically, emphasised the unchallengeable source of royal authority and gave the State its own independent religious sanction. The Church thus increasingly appeared as a useful but, in the last resort, scarcely essential prop of secular government, although its influence was nowhere underestimated: all rulers were aware, for example, that tuning the pulpit was one of the basic arts of politics. An inclination to treat the Church as a department of State was not new, but its realisation was becoming more feasible.

In some ways, however, the most important change was that in intellectual climate. The tendency towards secularisation and rationalism in thought and outlook, which certainly began in the first half of the century, was quickened, and with it came a new scepticism, healthy in some ways, but inevitably destructive of much in the old order. Cartesianism opened up paths which Descartes himself never thought to tread. The empirical approach fostered by experimental science slowly led to the questioning of written authority, and the treatment of history became more critical. The full results of these new methods of thinking were apparent rather after, than before, 1688, although they were already bearing fruit. Of more immediate importance in this period was the fact that arguments of social convenience and material prosperity were winning a new respectability and influence where the middle classes, with their direct interest in trade, got more political power, as in the United Provinces and, to a lesser degree, in England. Even in theological circles the idea that it might be more profitable to emphasise what men could agree upon than to argue about their differences was gaining ground, whether this took the form of Syncretism in Germany or Latitudinarianism in England. Catholics and Protestants alike were aware of the scandal presented by a deeply divided Church and sought to promote plans for reunion; Protestants in particular began to take seriously arguments for toleration, although this was regarded as a second best to the elimination of all religious differences.

However, neither the new claims of the State nor the growing liberalism in thought as yet betokened any widespread falling-off in the intensity of religious life, which under such forms as Jansenism, Quietism, Pietism and Puritanism in all its varieties showed the vigour of Christianity in finding new forms of expression. Indeed, it has plausibly been argued that the full force of the Counter-Reformation was only at this time attained in certain countries, notably France and Austria. It was, in fact, precisely the ambitions of the secular rulers coupled with this intensity of religious conviction that gave much of its distinctive character to this period in the relationship of Church and State, sandwiched as it was between the violence of the religious wars and the exhausted somnolence of the eighteenth century. Of course the conflict was not felt everywhere with the same force, and in some countries constant friction was its manifestation rather than formulated antagonism.

The religious forces ranged against the secular powers varied in strength. Lutheranism, lacking an international organisation, had always leant heavily on secular support, but was by no means always subservient. Since the break-up of its unity in the early seventeenth century, Calvinism had begun to lose something of its drive, and by 1648 no longer exacted a super-national loyalty, although it remained extremely powerful within narrower limits. Rome still maintained widespread influence and commanded a large and faithful following trained to respect her authority. Ultramontanism was steadily upheld by the international agencies of the Jesuits and the Mendicant Orders and by the papal nuncios. In stimulating the offensive against the Turks, the papacy remained a force of some importance, but in other ways its political power was on the wane: the total disregard of the pope in all the main peace treaties from Westphalia onwards demonstrates both its lost prestige and the growing secularisation of European life. Every papal election and every nomination of new cardinals underlined the vulnerability of the Curia to pressure from the great powers of France, Spain and Austria. Yet under an able or vigorous pope Rome was still very much a force to be reckoned with, for Protestant as well as Catholic powers. For different reasons neither Innocent X (1644–55) nor Alexander VII (1655–67) was impressive, but Clement IX (1667–9) and Clement X (1670–6) won more general respect through their attempt to uphold moderation and justice. Innocent XI (1676–89), however, was a pope in the great tradition in spite of certain weaknesses, and his quiet obstinacy was fully a match for all Louis XIV's diplomacy and violence, while his character excited general admiration throughout Europe.

In Germany the history of Church and State in this period is in many ways a commentary on the Treaty of Osnabrück, concluded on 24 October 1648 between the Emperor Ferdinand III and the Swedes and their respective allies, and essentially, in its main religious provisions, an amplification rather than a revision of the Peace of Augsburg (1555). Under its terms, Calvinists were at last, after years of controversy, given the same privileges as adherents of the Augsburg Confession, and Calvinist territorial lords held to enjoy the same right as Catholics and Lutherans to decide the religion of their lands (the *jus reformandi*). Special plans were made to ensure the continuation of an established religion when a ruler changed his faith, as had happened, for example, when in 1613 John Sigismund of Brandenburg abandoned Lutheranism for Calvinism. Although the terms of the treaty were ambiguous, there were also provisions to permit some practical toleration for those living under a ruler of different faith, but except for certain specified areas these did not apply to any Habsburg dominions. Whatever freedom of worship, public or private, had existed in 1624 was (except in the diocese of Hildesheim) to be perpetuated, until reunion could be achieved. Those who in 1624 had not been allowed any free exercise of religion, unless it were the same as the ruler's, were now granted the right of private worship and of educating their children in their own faith; nor were such persons to be subject to any civil disability nor denied Christian burial. Another clause, however, seemed to permit the forced emigration of religious dissentients. How far these provisions were really effective in practice it is hard to say, but in theory a fairly liberal settlement had been achieved, which compared favourably with the situation in many other parts of Europe.

Particularly important was the ruling on ecclesiastical territories and reservations, so hotly disputed during the Thirty Years War. In the lengthy negotiations on this point the main difficulty had been to fix the year which should be decisive in settling the possession of the various lands. 1 January 1624 was at last chosen (although it did not apply to the Emperor's hereditary lands), a date favouring the Protestants since it ignored the results of the Edict of Restitution of 1629[1] and some notable military acquisitions of the Catholics, but left in Catholic hands many churches coveted by their rivals. Accordingly, whichever confession had held a bishopric, religious foundation or ecclesiastical estate on this date was to keep it, unless it was specifically disposed of in the treaty, until reunion should take place. Permanency was sought for this ruling by the decision that if the occupant of an ecclesiastical office changed his religion, his tenure would end at once; moreover, if a cathedral chapter were divided in religion, the same proportion of Catholics and Protestants was henceforth to be kept. Thus further secularisations were prevented, and the main material inducement to conversion to Protestantism was taken away. As a result, Protestantism remained strong in the north; but in the south Catholicism was dominant, the duchy of Württemberg and the Palatinate constituting the only large Protestant areas there.

That Innocent X condemned the settlement in his brief *Zelo Domus Dei* of November 1648 was in practice meaningless, since German Catholics had no alternative but to accept the peace. Neither side, of course, was wholly satisfied, and in some areas the treaty provisions proved difficult to implement: in Württemberg, for example, where after 1634 the monasteries had been restored, the Catholics gave up their newly acquired possessions with slow reluctance. That the Protestant position and the peace in general

[1] For this, see vol. IV, ch. XI.

was in danger was a recurrent fear excited both by the vigour of Catholic missionary activity and the political power of the Habsburgs, and often fanned by France's readiness to intervene in German affairs as the 'Protector' of the 'German Liberties'. The ineffectual *corpus evangelicorum* set up by Protestant members of the Diet in 1653 and the League of the Rhine of 1658, with Catholic and Protestant adherents, both sought, among other and more specifically political aims, to uphold the religious provisions of the Osnabrück treaty. But in spite of mutual distrust, the letter of the peace was not substantially violated, however often its spirit was ignored.

Within the German States the current problems of Church and State differed widely. A strong belief that religious uniformity was a prerequisite of civil unity continued to dominate the Catholic rulers, although the provisions of the 1648 treaty and, especially within the Habsburg dominions, the exigencies of politics combined to prevent complete re-Catholicisation. In areas where the war had caused most disturbance, a thorough ecclesiastical reorganisation was sometimes necessary, such as that of the Calvinist or Reformed Church in the Rhine Palatinate on the return of the Elector Charles Louis in 1649. The consistory was reinstated the same year, but some ambiguity in the peace terms led to a constant dispute as to whether Calvinism was to be regarded as the official religion or not, while the Elector's tolerant outlook and interest in reunion deprived the Reformed Church of whole-hearted princely support. In Hesse-Cassel, serious difficulties arose between the Calvinist Landgrave William VI and the commission set up to decide on church order, and the plan finally made law in 1657 was carried in spite of strong opposition from the Reformed pastors. The Great Elector of Brandenburg, himself a Calvinist, found it hard to keep the peace between the Lutherans (the overwhelming majority of his subjects) and his co-religionists in Brandenburg and Prussia. His own indifference to theological disputes was not shared by the Lutheran ministers, and serious trouble flared up in 1662, when a conference of Lutheran and Calvinist representatives, summoned to Berlin to discuss reunion, failed to reach agreement. The practice of abusing opponents from the pulpit by name grew so scandalous that an edict of 1664 forbade such personal attacks, prohibited public criticism of other confessions, and required ministers to submit to its terms in writing or suffer ejection. Resistance came from a vigorous minority of Lutherans which included Paul Gerhardt, a notable preacher and hymn-writer; Frederick William did his best to get him reinstated, but he resigned again in 1666 and went to Saxony, where his avowal, 'I cannot regard the Calvinists as Christians', was more in line with official policy. Support for the recalcitrants came from the Brandenburg diet and the town of Berlin. In the duchy of Prussia, where Lutheran orthodoxy was particularly strong, Calvinism was only slowly tolerated at all and Calvinists were excluded from most important offices. In Cleves, on the other hand, the Great Elector was forced to protect Lutherans from the Calvinist majority. Although opposed to Catholicism, Frederick William was generally tolerant of the Catholic minorities in his lands, as he was also of Socinians and Mennonites. A desire to increase the population and prosperity of his dominions was probably as potent a cause of his toleration edicts of 1662 and 1664 as religious and intellectual conviction, but he was genuinely interested in reunion and tried, though unsuccessfully, to promote it in his own territories. His approach to ecclesiastical problems was predominantly authoritarian and secular, and he considered himself, within his realms, the supreme bishop.

If the political leadership of Protestant Germany had to some degree now passed to Brandenburg, Saxony (whose Elector had protested vigorously against the admission of Calvinists to equality in the Empire in 1648) stood for Lutheran orthodoxy, and the Saxon University of Wittenberg as the fount of uncorrupted Lutheran truth. 'If things are to go on according to the intentions of Electoral Saxony...we shall have a new papacy and a new religion', was the comment in 1650 of the mild theologian George Calixtus of the liberal Brunswick University of Helmstedt, where Syncretist ideas were strong. Very different was the climate of opinion in Hanover, whose ruler, Duke John Frederick, had been converted to Catholicism in 1651. He was not able to give his co-religionists much relief, but he drew round himself excellent men of all confessions, including the great Leibniz. The wife of his successor Ernest Augustus, Sophia, the daughter of the unfortunate Elector Frederick V of the Palatinate, continued to encourage projects for reunion, and her influence helped to make Hanover the home of calm and reasonable discussion.

Throughout this period great families continued to monopolise both Catholic and Protestant bishoprics and ecclesiastical properties. Thus the Bavarian Wittelsbachs dominated a group of North German bishoprics, members of the Habsburg family often occupied another group of sees, and Protestant dynasties had an even firmer hold in the secularised bishoprics, mostly in North Germany. The requirement of a certain social rank, even if not always noble blood, for the holding of many prebends in German cathedrals and collegiate churches also strengthened the control of the aristocracy over both the Catholic and the Protestant churches. But high birth and political entanglement did not necessarily make for inefficiency: two of the most notable administrators of this period were Christopher Bernard von Galen, bishop of Münster, and Ferdinand von Fürstenberg, bishop of Paderborn.

The histories of Spain and her European possessions, of Portugal (who gained her independence in 1640), and of Venice illustrate well the various difficulties concerning the relations of Church and State which might arise even when both rulers and people were firmly Catholic, the problem of religious minorities absent, and new ideas made comparatively little impact. In Spain, Church and State were so closely connected that the Spanish Church is sometimes described as a State-Church, and the Spanish State as a Church-State; that the Inquisition was under royal and not papal control typifies this relationship. But the coincidence of interests may easily be exaggerated. It was agreed by all discerning critics that in Spain there were too many priests and monks, the Church owned too much property (perhaps about a fifth of all the land), and the amount it paid in taxation was disproportionate to its wealth, although it contributed much to the government and the Crown was generally in debt to the funds of the Inquisition. Nor was the state of the Church satisfactory. Most of the country priests were poor and many of them very ignorant, since the post-Tridentine movement for the foundation of seminaries had made little advance in Spain. The episcopate mainly consisted of hard-working and serious-minded men, without that aristocratic predominance so marked in contemporary France and Germany; but there was an unhealthy contrast between rich sees, such as Seville and Valencia, and poorer ones like Lugo and Oviedo. It is noteworthy that, unlike the kings of France, Spanish kings had comparatively little patronage outside the Indies, and some even of what they exercised came to them only by papal grant. As in other countries, ecclesiastical administration in all its forms provided profitable openings for the nobility and *hidalgos*, and abuses were probably as much enjoyed as they were condemned.

It is therefore not surprising that, in spite of the fervour of Spanish Catholicism, Philip IV sought in some ways to limit the wealth and powers of the Church. He inaugurated, partly with papal support, a movement for the reform of the clergy and the religious orders, forbade any further increase of property in mortmain, and extended certain taxes to the clergy. But the forces against any fundamental reform were too powerful for much success to be achieved, and Philip himself (who came under the strong influence of Sor María de Ágreda in 1643) did not pursue it wholeheartedly. During the minority of Charles II and later under his pathetic personal rule little further was done, and indeed the rise to political power of the Queen's confessor, the Austrian Jesuit, Father Nithard, from 1665 to 1669, marked the resurgence of clerical domination in the highest counsels of the land. But in 1677 reform of the religious orders was again debated, and the founding of new religious houses made more difficult. The powers of the Inquisition were also slightly curtailed, in spite of an *auto de fe* in 1680 to celebrate the marriage of Charles II with Marie Louise of France, when a hundred and eighteen persons were sentenced and some later burnt; in 1677 Charles declared excommunication illegal in matters concerning laymen or temporal possessions only, and so sought to curb the Inquisition's excessive jurisdictional powers. But such measures did not portend any real diminution of Catholic zeal in Spain. On the contrary the missionary work that was such an important consequence of the Counter-Reformation went steadily forward, and Jesuit activities were particularly successful.

In the Spanish Netherlands Jansenist doctrines (of which more will be said later) spread widely, especially under the influence of Louvain University, and gave rise to peculiar difficulties between Church and State, especially over what authority should promulgate papal orders, whether a Bull had any validity unless endorsed by a royal *placet*, and the extent of Rome's jurisdiction in the country. The Spanish authorities clashed with the papacy also in Naples and Milan, primarily over jurisdiction, rights of asylum, and the disposal of lands of suppressed religious houses, the last a matter of contention as well between Rome and the republics of Venice and Genoa. But for all the talk of interdict and other ecclesiastical penalties, the proximity of Spanish territory to the Papal States was a powerful deterrent to decisive action, and friction rather than open conflict characterised everywhere the relations of Spanish-controlled governments with the papacy.

The Portuguese Church in the earlier part of this period was in a peculiar sense the victim of politics. King John of Braganza, who was leading Portugal's struggle for independence from Spain, had in 1645 sent the Prior of Sodofeita to Rome to promote his claim to nominate bishops, both for reasons of prestige and to consolidate his hold on the country. For the pope to have agreed to this demand, thus acknowledging John's legitimacy as a ruler, would have been perilous in view of Spain's still formidable strength, and Innocent X decided instead to provide bishops to the vacant sees of Guarda, Miranda and Viseu, *motu proprio*. With the support of France, John (who had threatened to call a national council) then appointed bishops to three other sees without papal confirmation and so shut the door on compromise. While a bitter struggle between the Spanish and French factions took place at Rome over his recognition, the state of the Portuguese Church grew steadily worse. By 1649 there was only one bishop of undoubted validity in the country. The deadlock persisted until, in 1668, peace with Spain made it possible for the vacant sees to be canonically filled, the king's right of nomination for the future settled, some order re-established in the Church, and the threat of schism ended. Another crisis arose when the incompetent Afonso VI was deposed in 1667 and succeeded by his brother Pedro II.[1] Afonso's wife, Marie Françoise of Savoy, who was under French influence, applied, not to Rome, but to Lisbon, for an annulment so that she could marry Pedro; moreover, the dispensation for her to marry her former husband's brother was obtained, with very doubtful legality, from her uncle the

[1] See below, ch. XVI, p. 396.

Cardinal Vendôme while he was in France, and not from the pope. Louis XIV, who relied on her to maintain French interests in Portugal, did all in his power to prevent Rome's intervention; but as a result of the queen's scruples Clement IX finally submitted the question to a Congregation which confirmed the new marriage. Not until this matter had been settled could Portugal and Rome resume full diplomatic relations. In the latter part of the century there was comparatively little friction.

Difficulties between Venice and the papacy were endemic throughout the period. Papal support for the Venetians in their fight against the Turks led to generous grants from ecclesiastical property and clerical taxes for the expenses of war, for example in 1653, 1657, 1660 and 1667; but constant trouble occurred over jurisdiction, nomination to bishoprics, the curbing of the Inquisition, and (till 1657 when they were readmitted) the banishment of the Jesuits. Venice's adherence to the Holy League in 1684[1] was to some extent a triumph for Innocent XI's crusading policy against the Turks, but in ecclesiastical matters the Venetians were determined to maintain their own traditions of independence and tension continued.

France was the scene of varied and bitter conflicts between Church and State. This is scarcely surprising. In the first place, Louis XIV was by far the most ambitious ruler of his time, and his assumption of an overriding authority, based on Divine Right, historical tradition and *raison d'état* came into conflict at many points with the papacy; it was a conflict, moreover, with elements in it of an ecclesiastical civil war, since the king could depend on Gallican sections in the French Church to support his cause against Rome. Secondly, Louis's respect for orthodoxy and preference for uniformity accorded ill both with the well-established toleration of his Protestant, and the Jansenism of some of his Catholic, subjects. Thirdly, the remarkable vigour and variety of religious life in France at this period, and the no less remarkable devotion which so many Frenchmen of all classes and creeds felt towards their king, caused many to face a clash of loyalties in the most acute form. Neither papal nor royal policy was consistent. Rome's attitude to Jansenism, for example, differed considerably under Innocent X and Innocent XI; the king's desire for uniformity forced him into both inviting and repelling papal interference in the religious affairs of France.

The Gallican tradition of the French Church conditioned to a greater or lesser degree all the ecclesiastical controversies of the reign. But the Gallican standpoint cannot easily be summarised. Neither the word 'Gallicanism' nor any precisely defined theory to deserve that name existed in 1648, nor, in spite of the Four Articles of 1682, even by 1688. Contemporaries, however, spoke of the 'Gallican Church' and its 'Liberties' and saw these as contrasted with papal pretensions and ultramontane claims, both suspect to Frenchmen who feared the hand of

[1] See below, ch. XIX, p. 471; ch. XX, p. 498.

Spain behind them. Yet for the king of France, the Faculty of Theology at Paris, the *Parlements* and the French bishops, the import of these phrases was not the same. Royal Gallicanism was concerned with the maintenance of the Concordat of Bologna of 1516 and other agreements, and, as circumstances demanded, with further claims to control the French Church based on the proud boast that the kings of France held their authority direct from God without any intermediaries and had at their disposal all property both secular and ecclesiastical. The Faculty of Theology at Paris sought to uphold various maxims, including the defence of the authority of councils against papal superiority, and of the divine institution of bishops against the claim that the pope was *episcopus universalis*, and the Church an absolute monarchy under him, from whom all other authority was merely delegated. Far less forceful was the Gallicanism of the bishops who, relying on the king for support against either papal or secular encroachment, were frequently sacrificed to the dictates of political exigency. The *Parlements* in their turn were anxious to secure the king's independence in temporal matters and to rebut any suggestion that the Gallican liberties were founded on any privilege, revocable by the pope, or on any dispensation or mere custom. Relying on the evidence of early ecclesiastical history, they used their learning to challenge later papal claims and made much of the project that the king should exercise over the Church the same powers that Constantine and particularly Charlemagne had once enjoyed. The five-yearly meetings of the General Assembly of the Clergy, at which the valuable *dons gratuits* were voted to the Crown, provided regular and widely publicised occasions for the propagation of these points of view.

Not all Frenchmen, however, were Gallican in their sympathies. Indeed some groups, such as the Jesuits and the Mendicant Orders, held strongly ultramontane opinions, upholding the pope as the source of all authority in the Church, belittling the importance of bishops and councils, and stressing papal infallibility in controversies of the faith. But while the Friars were of little significance in educated circles, the Jesuits, though widely distrusted for their moral theology, enjoyed a considerable reputation, directing through the confessional the spiritual life of many Frenchmen including the king, and in their schools training boys from the leading French families. Ultramontane ideas were only slightly less strong in the various centres for spiritual reform where the *dévots* exerted their powerful influence. Fervently religious, scrupulously correct in their Catholicism, obedient to the dictates of their spiritual directors and deeply imbued with a sense of their personal responsibility for advancing the Kingdom of God on earth, the men and women to whom this term was applied were in no sense a homogeneous body. They owed their inspiration to such notable individualists as Pierre de Bérulle (1575–1629), the founder of the Oratory in France, St Vincent de Paul (*c.* 1580–1660), the tireless reformer with his emphasis on charity, Jean-Jacques Olier (1608–57) who set up the seminary of Saint-Sulpice, and St Jean Eudes (1601–80), the devout missionary whose name is remembered for his work in promoting the better training of priests and in fostering devotion to the cult of the Sacred Heart of Jesus. At once practical in their attack on human problems and mystical in their approach to God, inspired by the ideal of self-abnegation and yet aware that a religious life spent in good works was highly fashionable, the *dévots* worked through various societies, the most famous of which, founded in 1627, was the *Compagnie du Saint-Sacrement*, suppressed in 1666 by a government suspicious of its secret ways and unknown powers. Through its influential membership, which included many laymen of high social standing, the *Compagnie* intervened in all departments of life, seeking to reform morals, promote missions, exercise charity and counter actual heresy in the guise of Protestantism or the potential dangers of Jansenism. With such emphasis on good works and direct action, most *dévots* were mistrustful of learning and of the historical and legal arguments behind so much Gallican theory. Politically as well as socially they were a powerful body, supported by the queens Anne of Austria and Marie Therèse and many others at Court. Their influence, coupled with Mazarin's subtle diplomacy, probably goes far to explain France's comparatively peaceful relations with the papacy until Louis XIV, in reaction against his mother, changed in 1661 the tone of French policy.

Jansenism was the occasion of the first crisis in this period in the relations of Church and State. The movement took its name from Cornelius Jansen who had died, as bishop of Ypres, in 1638. In Louvain in 1640, and in Paris in 1641, was published his *Augustinus*. Although its influence was considerable in the Spanish Netherlands, its effect was most marked in France where Jansen's lifelong friend, Jean du Vergier de Hauranne, Abbot of Saint-Cyran, had for the last twenty years been building up a party to promote the work of the Counter-Reformation on foundations of disciplinary and ascetic ideas, which owed much to Bérulle and the Oratory and, theologically, to the teaching of St Augustine. By 1640 the most important elements in it included the Cistercian convent of Port-Royal, dominated by the *parlementaire* family of Arnauld, and a group of friends and admirers of Saint-Cyran who approved of his attacks on the Jesuits and their laxist theology. Jansenism was no more than Gallicanism a coherent or unified movement. But its sympathisers shared certain convictions, notably a belief in conversion, which could only be effected by the descent of grace, and in predestination, which condemned to perdition those upon whom grace did not fall. This apparently harsh teaching was given the force of a moral and spiritual revolution by the publication, in 1643, of Antoine Arnauld's widely influential *De la Fréquente Communion*, criticising laxist and Jesuit ideas and advocating abstention from communion until the penitent's contrition had been proved. In spite of the condemnation of the *Augustinus* by the Bull *In eminenti*, published in 1643, the party continued in the next few years to gain in strength; it could normally expect support from the *Parlement* of Paris and a section in the Faculty, but the opposing forces were strong. Not only were the Jesuits implacable and powerful foes, but the government's latent mistrust was to ripen into open hostility when highly placed Jansenists and their sympathisers, including Cardinal de Retz, the coadjutor of the Archbishop of Paris, were suspected of complicity in the Fronde.[1] The movement's threat to uniformity in the Church and unity in the State could scarcely be ignored; but one of the results of governmental interference was the strengthening of those elements in Gallicanism that were least easily controlled by the Crown, and most likely to give rise to new friction.

A new phase began in 1649 when Nicolas Cornet, syndic of the Faculty, put forward for censure by his colleagues certain propositions, five of them allegedly drawn from the *Augustinus*; despite appeals for intervention by the *Parlement* all were condemned. Further opposition from Gallican forces arose when the pope was asked to confirm this sentence. Innocent X appointed a commission whose long labours were summed up in the Bull *Cum occasione* of May 1653, in which the five propositions were censured. The Jansenists retorted that although the Church, infallible in matters of faith, had legitimately condemned them, the propositions were not in fact to be found in the *Augustinus* and in such a matter of fact the Church did not enjoy infallibility; this distinction between law (*droit*) and fact (*fait*) was henceforth to be of prime importance in the controversy. Mazarin, fearful of Rome's anger at the imprisonment of de Retz, agreed to the publication of the Bull, although it was bound to excite Gallican criticism. Only after considerable difficulties was a Particular Assembly of the French clergy induced, in March 1654, to declare that the Five Propositions had been censured 'in their proper sense, which was the sense of Jansenius', and this decision was sanctioned by Innocent's brief of September. These rulings struck at the root of the Jansenist distinction between law and fact, and the chances of any compromise were further weakened by a plan of Mazarin and Pierre de Marca, archbishop of Toulouse, that a formulary against Jansenist tenets should be signed by all ecclesiastical persons, a measure ratified in September 1656 by a General Assembly of the Clergy, which also confirmed the acts of the Particular Assembly of 1654. Meanwhile the Jansenist party was subject to conflicting fortunes. In January 1656 Antoine Arnauld was expelled from the Faculty, but the *Lettres Provinciales* of Blaise Pascal (one of the 'messieurs' living in close contact with Port-Royal), written to defend him and the cause, were to be the stimulus of further endeavour.

[1] For this, see vol. IV, ch. XVI.

But although the formulary was not yet generally enforced and the Jansenists enjoyed much Gallican support, government hostility to the party was intensified even before the death of Mazarin in 1661.

Louis XIV's accession to personal power began a period of severe persecution. Measures were taken against Port-Royal, where resistance to the subscription of the formulary was widespread, even while the distinction between law and fact was still condoned; after this concession had been overruled, the nuns refused to sign again, 'purely and simply', and were joined in their recalcitrance by four bishops (of Angers, Beauvais, Alet and Pamiers). To put an end to the ridiculous position in which a handful of women and a few bishops and theologians withstood the dictates of pope, king and assembled national clergy, Louis in February 1665 asked Alexander VII to provide a constitution with a formulary and to command, *ex cathedra*, that all ecclesiastics and nuns should sign it. The king's appeal was curiously out of character with his recent humiliating policy towards Rome. After a clash in 1662 between the pope's Corsican Guard and the French ambassador's suite at the Palazzo Farnese (then the French embassy in Rome) Louis had refused all attempts at apology or settlement, invaded Avignon, and threatened the Papal States; finally, Alexander had been forced to agree in 1664 to the shameful Treaty of Pisa, according to which a pyramid was to be erected in Rome to mark papal acceptance of the French demand that Corsicans must never again be employed by the Holy See.

Nevertheless the pope, consistently hostile to Jansenism, could hardly refuse Louis's request, though the wording of the Bull *Regiminis apostolici*, of 15 February, subtly emphasised the impotence of the French king and bishops to deal with the controversy, which was represented solely as a matter of submission to Rome. A *lit de justice* was needed to induce the *Parlement* of Paris to register the edict based on the Bull, with the addition forbidding the employment of any 'distinction, interpretation, or restriction' in the signing of the formulary, which was to be done within three months. The four bishops refused to accept this royal qualification, and in asking their subordinate clergy to sign, left it open to them to make the distinction between law and fact. The election of Cardinal Rospigliosi as Clement IX, largely as the result of French diplomacy, facilitated the temporary settlement of a controversy by now confused and partly meaningless. Through the able and at times unscrupulous negotiations of de Lionne, the four bishops were persuaded in 1668 to make their apology to the pope and to give a 'sincere' signature to the formulary. At the beginning of 1669 a medal was struck to celebrate this 'Peace of the Church', Arnauld was received by the king and the nuncio, and the nuns of Port-Royal were readmitted to communion. For the next ten years the Jansenist problem was quiescent; but other controversies involving Church and State played their part in the later history of the movement.

The conflict over the *régale* involved questions of a different kind. The French Crown had long received the so-called *régale temporelle*, that is, the revenues of certain sees during vacancy, but four ecclesiastical provinces claimed exemption and the extent of the right was hotly debated. By an edict of 1673, reinforced in 1675, Louis extended this demand to the whole kingdom. He also put forward a new claim to the *régale spirituelle*, that is, the right to nominate, while a see was vacant, to certain convents and to benefices without cure of souls. The reason was not financial; indeed, the revenues so received were almost always kept for the use of the next bishop and, from 1641, the custom was to allow two-thirds to revert to the see and a third to go towards the conversion of the Protestants. More likely Louis was convinced that the *régale temporelle* was an inalienable natural prerogative of the Crown and wanted, in addition, administrative uniformity in his dominions; it was also clearly advantageous to extend his patronage. His wish to apply the terms of the Concordat fully had already been shown in its extension in 1668 to the bishoprics of Metz, Toul and Verdun, and the question also arose in newly acquired Artois and Roussillon.

The decrees of 1673 and 1675 were issued without the concurrence of, but equally without any immediate protest from, Rome. Effective opposition came from two bishops, Nicolas Pavillon of Alet and François de Caulet of Pamiers, both associated with Jansenism and both remarkable as energetic reformers; in their remote Pyrenean sees both stood aloof from the fashionable world of Versailles which exerted such a hold on their richer episcopal brethren. The government joined issue by making new nominations to all benefices which had fallen vacant in both dioceses since the two bishops had occupied their sees, on the grounds that since neither had taken the oath of allegiance now demanded from all prelates in the areas into which the *régale temporelle* had been extended, their temporalities had never been restored. Pavillon and later Caulet excommunicated all who accepted these new appointments from the king. Both men appealed to their respective metropolitans and also to the pope, but in 1677 Pavillon died. Louis then made a move calculated to prolong the conflict indefinitely. He ordered the confiscation of Caulet's temporalities, and Innocent XI intervened directly by sending a series of critical briefs to the king and setting up a special congregation to consider the *régale* as a whole.

Suspicions as well as incidents widened the breach. The new pope's high regard for Antoine Arnauld and approval of the strict moral content in Jansenist teaching and certain indiscretions of the Jansenists in France resuscitated Louis's fears of the movement, which in 1679 lost influential supporters by the deaths of Madame de Longueville and de Retz and the disgrace of the king's minister Pomponne, a member of the Arnauld family. But the balance of forces was now altered, since the king could expect little help from the papacy; one of the most remarkable results of Louis's policy over the *régale* was the association of Jansenism with ultramontane rather than Gallican forces. The revival of royal hostility to Jansenism was manifested in a series of petty persecutions: expulsions from Port-Royal, the prohibition against receiving new novices and the exile of Antoine Arnauld. Louis's enmity was also directed against the pope himself who was as firmly convinced of the danger of secular encroachment as was Louis of papal interference. The Most Christian King, whose policy after 1679 was dominated by the violent Colbert faction in place of the more moderate Le Telliers, was to find Innocent a dangerous and determined opponent.

By 1681 affairs appeared to have reached a deadlock, a situation less serious for the pope than for Louis, who wanted a number of concessions from Rome and was, moreover, genuinely afraid that he might be excommunicated. But negotiation was difficult since diplomatic relations had almost ceased, and Louis's special envoy to Rome, Cardinal d'Estrées, was a man more likely to exacerbate than to compose a quarrel. There remained one possibility: to create a crisis in which the pope would be compelled to ask the king for help in quelling Gallican criticism, by encouraging the French clergy to show their resentment at the recent condemnation by Rome of a book by Jean Gerbais, written at the request of the Assembly of 1665 and praised by that of 1670. But to think that such a situation, once manufactured, could be controlled at will was to prove a costly delusion, and time was to show that Innocent XI, far from seeking Louis's help in restoring order among the clergy, was perfectly prepared to let the French Church fall into chaos rather than abandon his principles.

In the spring of 1681 an informal assembly of bishops considered Gerbais's book and Innocent's recent briefs and advised the calling either of a National Council or a General Assembly of the Clergy; the second alternative was preferred, since the first might well lead to a totally unwanted schism. As these threats left Rome unmoved, Louis was driven on 16 June to summon a General Assembly for October; ten days later the king learnt that Innocent had instructed Cardinal Cibo to begin talks with d'Estrées. Preparations for the General Assembly were entrusted to the ambitious Archbishop Harlay, a skilful manager, while behind him was Colbert, the implacable enemy of Rome. The Chancellor Le Tellier and his son the Archbishop of Rheims, sincerely anxious for a settlement, hoped that this might be achieved by the arbitration of the French clergy between the pope and the king; possibly Bossuet's famous sermon at the opening of the Assembly, with its emphasis on the unity of the Church and praise of both Gallican liberties and the authority of the Roman see, was composed with this plan in mind. Two presidents were chosen, the Archbishops Harlay and Le Tellier, mutually suspicious and jealous.

Over the *régale* the Le Tellier party won a signal victory in persuading Louis to agree to modify his claims to the *régale spirituelle*, while the clergy accepted the extension of the *régale temporelle*. Archbishop Le Tellier wrote a letter to the pope which, it was hoped, would end the conflict, but Innocent merely sent it on to the Congregation for the *régale*.

The Assembly then turned to the second part of their business, the approval of the famous Four Articles. Political and clerical opinion was divided on the expediency of making such a declaration; but Colbert finally persuaded the king that, while Rome and Paris were on bad terms, it would be valuable to redefine French doctrine as to the extent of papal power. Yet if the immediate re-establishment of peace was really wanted, the declaration was a strange miscalculation. The Four Articles (finally drafted by Bossuet) asserted, first, that kings and secular princes were not subject to any ecclesiastical power in temporal affairs; secondly, that the decrees of the Council of Constance (concerning the superiority of a council over the pope) were and are still valid; thirdly, that the pope must exercise his authority in conformity with the canons and respect the customs of the Gallican Church; and lastly, that although the pope had the preponderant part in questions of faith and his decrees were binding on the Church, his judgement was not unalterable (*irreformabile*) if it did not meet with the assent of the Church. They had much in common with the Six Propositions put forward by the Faculty in 1663, though the wording of similar phrases was often subtly changed; but the real innovation was that such 'maxims' were published for the first time by the bishops in the name of the French Church. The king made them an integral part of the theological teaching of the country by an order of March 1682.

The Assembly's anger against the pope increased after receiving Innocent's brief *Paternae charitati* on the *régale*. In scathing words he denounced the agreement with the king and castigated the French bishops for their cowardice in surrendering the rights of the Church; in full session the affronted prelates unleashed their wrath against Rome. Lest worse befall, Louis decided to end the Assembly. He, at any rate, wanted peace with the pope, just as Innocent, obsessed with the Turkish menace, wanted peace with Louis. But the Four Articles were a serious impediment. Throughout France they excited widespread opposition; even worse, the Faculty of Theology at Paris proved so troublesome that Louis's boast that all the French clergy were behind him was ignominiously and publicly disproved. At Rome, divisions among the cardinals and Innocent's fear of provoking a schism delayed a formal condemnation, but the practical consequences of Rome's displeasure were bad enough: Innocent refused Bulls of institution to bishoprics to all those who had taken part in the Assembly, and since Louis would not recognise any difference between participants and others, no sees could canonically be filled, with the result that by 1688 thirty-five were vacant.

Deadlock had again been reached. Innocent remained adamant and unimpressed even by Louis's suppression of heresy in 1685. A new phase opened with the Affair of the Franchises on the death of the French ambassador in Rome, the duc d'Estrées, in 1687. Three years earlier Innocent had announced that he would receive no new ambassador until France agreed to renounce the extensive diplomatic immunities which made the maintenance of law and order in Rome impossible. Disregarding this request, Louis dispatched the brutal Marquis de Lavardin, who ignored a sentence of excommunication passed on him and denied that he could even fall under it when executing his master's orders. Accordingly, at the beginning of 1688 the Most Christian King was secretly told that he had incurred the long-dreaded sentence of excommunication.[1] In France there was much talk of ignoring the Concordat altogether and of assembling a National, or appealing to a General Council; the advocate-general, Talon, in the *Parlement* of Paris attacked the pope for threatening to use a spiritual weapon in a temporal quarrel. But again Louis had strong political reasons for attempting a settlement. He wanted the pope's support for his candidate, William von Fürstenberg, in the forthcoming election at Cologne, and hoped to surrender the right of diplomatic quarter in exchange for this and the confirmation of the bishops. Negotiations again broke down. The king then decided on violent measures, including the capture of Avignon and the invasion of the Papal States; he launched a vast press campaign to undermine the pope's authority and reputation in Europe. Innocent was accused of favouring heretics, including Jansenists and Quietists, and, in the temporal sphere, of trying to deflect the Emperor's arms from the Turks to turn them against France. The French clergy were virtually cut off from all communication with Rome, and everywhere there was talk of schism; it was said that Harlay, still influential in the royal counsels and having lost all chance of a cardinal's hat, was not averse to assuming the office of Patriarch of the Gauls, an ambition Richelieu had also entertained. But although Avignon was invaded in October 1688, Louis's commitments to a European war and the death of Innocent in August 1689 prevented any extreme measures. Under Alexander VIII conciliatory moves were made by both sides, but the brief *Inter multiplices*, condemning the competence of the Assembly of the Clergy to make such a declaration as that of 1682, showed how far the quarrel was from settlement. Under Innocent XII, however, a compromise was reached. In 1692 he confirmed in their sees the French bishops who had not taken part in the 1682 Assembly, and the participants a year later, after every member had sent him a letter of apology. The king withdrew the order that the Four Articles should generally be taught, although they were not specific-

[1] L. von Pastor, *The History of the Popes* (transl. E. Graf, London, 1940), XXXII, 363–4; J. Orcibal, *Louis XIV contre Innocent XI* (Paris, 1949), pp. 11–13.

ally forbidden. The conflict over the *régale* lapsed rather than found a solution; but in this Louis enjoyed a practical victory, since except at Cambrai and Lyon he kept the *régale temporelle*, while the *régale spirituelle* was still in dispute.

Although official policy towards the Huguenots was closely connected with other political and ecclesiastical questions, the history of French Protestantism must be separately considered, since it involves a different problem, that of the relations of the State with a religious minority. In the middle of the seventeenth century the prospects for Huguenotism did not appear unpromising, since the main provisions of the Edict of Nantes had survived fifty years of stress and strain. But in fact the omens were not good. The edict had been accepted by both Catholics and Protestants not because they believed in toleration, or that a country should have two religions, but because at that time neither had an alternative. Since 1598, however, much had changed. The government had grown more authoritarian, the Counter-Reformation had burst tardily but forcefully into French Catholicism, and Huguenotism had lost something of its original impulse, as it changed from a fighting community led by nobles into a party dominated by law-abiding officials and men of the middle class. Among the more liberal Catholics and many of the Protestants there was a nostalgia for unity. Admirable as such irenic sentiments were, however, they blunted the sword of the Huguenots in the strife to come, as did their growing Erastianism and the almost idolatrous praise and flattery which many of them lavished on the king. Nevertheless, well into the personal reign of Louis XIV the Huguenot party retained considerable social and political significance. Turenne did not become a Catholic until 1668, Ruvigny and Schomberg never recanted, and up to the Revocation the Protestants included men of wealth and standing, influential in the law and other professions and powerful as bankers; in the south they owned much of the land.

During Mazarin's ascendancy official policy changed little, in spite of pressure for the reduction of Huguenot privileges from the Assemblies of the Clergy and the *Compagnie du Saint-Sacrement*. But Louis, if as yet only conventionally religious, was firmly convinced that more than one confession in the State destroyed national unity and compromised authority, while the churchmen appealed to him 'to walk in the steps of the great Constantine' and repress heresy. The king's first intention was to maintain the terms of the Edict of Nantes, but to interpret them strictly through special commissioners, and in addition, to refrain from showing any favour or giving any promotion to Protestants. Louis was also well aware that a healthy and respected Catholic Church would itself encourage conversions; in fact the polemical skill of men like the Jansenists Arnauld and Nicole and especially Bossuet, in his *Exposition de la foi catholique* (1671), was of great importance. Precision was given to this policy of enforcement by a declaration of February 1669, which among other orders restricted Protestant worship to places already annexed to the Crown in 1598 and decreed the destruction of churches built since that date, which led, for example, to the demolition of eight in Dauphiné, sixty-four out of seventy-four in Poitou, and thirteen in La Rochelle.

The severity with which these orders were enforced fluctuated according to the exigencies of the king's policy; but the government still hoped that persuasion rather than violence would be effective. Turenne had plans to win over the more accommodating Huguenot ministers at a synod, while discussions between Bossuet and the Huguenot Ferry took place in 1666, and between Bossuet and Claude in 1678. Financial as well as theological considerations were also thought to hinder conversions; abjuration meant an inevitable loss of livelihood for pastors and might also do so for laymen. The sums already set aside from government funds and voluntary subscriptions were quite insufficient to relieve such cases. Accordingly the *Caisse des Conversions*, with funds drawn from vacant abbeys and benefices and a share of the revenues of sees in *régale*, was established in 1676, under the control of Paul Pellisson, himself a convert; Étienne Le Camus had already proved the value of adequate resources by his many conversions in his diocese of Grenoble. Pellisson's methods were much criticised; it was difficult to distinguish sincere from opportunist conversions and to avoid the imputation of simony; the cynicism of many of the converts could not be disguised.

A combination of circumstances finally led Louis XIV to a policy of violent persecution which was not even to end at the Revocation of the Edict of Nantes. A desire to eradicate heresy once and for all certainly lay behind it. But even more urgent was his need to embarrass Innocent XI; the greater his endeavours for Catholicism, the more must the pope either express his gratitude or appear to all Christians as the favourer of heretics. To be more Catholic than the pope suited also his anti-Habsburg policy; if Leopold I toyed with papally-supported schemes of reunion, Louis would impress the German Catholic princes with his fervent care for the maintenance of orthodoxy. To see himself as the reincarnation of Constantine and Charlemagne was also in harmony with his passion for glory. But that his personal conversion, not really influential till 1686, was the major—or indeed even a minor—factor in this policy is not supported by the evidence; moreover his confessor, Father La Chaise, who is sometimes accredited with devising it, had probably very limited political importance. Nor does the persecution owe its origin or continuation to the persuasions of Madame de Maintenon who in her authentic correspondence expressed disapproval of the violent methods advocated by her enemy Louvois; the letters so often quoted to prove her complicity have been shown to be an eighteenth-century forgery.[1]

[1] For a review of the evidence, see J. Orcibal, *Louis XIV et les Protestants* (Paris, 1951), pp. 91–4.

The quickening tempo of action against the Huguenots is illustrated by the fact that between 1661 and 1679 about twelve Acts were passed against them, compared with no less than eighty-five between 1679 and 1685. Many of these concerned petty but cumulatively intolerable restrictions on religious and personal liberty and affected children as well as adults. In 1681 Marillac, the *intendant* of Poitou, systematised the notorious plan by which dragoons were forcibly quartered on Huguenot households, and although there was criticism of the violence used, it was in 1685 extended to other areas; as a result large parts of the south of France and other districts were nominally returned to Catholicism, including the generalities of Toulouse, Bordeaux, La Rochelle, Poitiers and Montpellier as well as the towns of Marseilles, Aubusson, Loudun and Rouen. Many Huguenots emigrated, thereby causing alarm in the *Conseil d'en haut* at the loss to commerce and industry. Simultaneously continued confused attempts at reunion or comprehension, partly sincere and partly mere political manœuvres; there was some faith, some hope and even a little charity behind the treatment of the Huguenots, as well as the degrading use of force. And even force could be justified by the high authority of St Augustine who had taught that, although coercion cannot make a conversion, it may prepare a man to receive it. So argued Bossuet in his sermon *Compelle intrare* (1685).

The Edict of Fontainebleau, registered in *Parlement* in October 1685, killed the Reformed Church in France on the grounds that it was no longer necessary since the majority of Frenchmen were now Catholics. By its terms, which did not apply to Alsace, all Protestant churches were destroyed, public and private worship proscribed, and all ministers ordered to leave the country within fifteen days, although adult laymen were forbidden to emigrate. Recent concessions, such as tax-exemption for the newly converted, came to an end. Liberty of conscience was allowed, but this meant nothing. Foremost among the opponents of the treatment of the Huguenots was Le Camus of Grenoble who attacked the idea of forced communions and the continuing use of the *dragonnades*. The future was to show that Protestantism had been cowed rather than killed. And as soon as the first spontaneous pleasure at the Revocation had passed, king, clergy and laymen could see that new problems had taken the place of the old.

One of the most important consequences was the revulsion that affected many parts of Europe where Louis was in fact most anxious to bear a good reputation, such as England and certain States in Germany. But the daily arrival of Huguenot refugees was more persuasive than Louis's propaganda. It is impossible to establish with certainty the total number of emigrants, but it may have reached two hundred thousand or more. The United Provinces, England, Brandenburg, Switzerland, North America and South Africa received many and, through them, the means of building up their prosperity at the expense of France. Irreparable harm was done to French religious life. Violence, forced and sacrilegious communions and bribery brought Catholicism into disrepute, and libertine ideas, comparatively unimportant since the first half of the century, gained strength. Equally serious in another sphere was Innocent's refusal to be suitably impressed with Louis's extinction of heresy. His brief was cool and offered no concessions over the *régale*, and the solemn *Te Deum* and formal celebrations at Rome were offset by the elevation to the purple of Le Camus, the opponent of Louis's methods of violence. The king's policy towards Protestantism did not, in the main, bear the fruits expected of it, any more than had his treatment of the Jansenists or his plans for the *régale*. The elements of contradiction in all of them were too strong, and in every case the capacity of the ecclesiastical forces for resistance had been seriously underestimated by the secular arm.

In the officially Protestant countries of Western Europe—the United Provinces, England and Scotland—the relationship of Church and State was affected by different factors. In the first place, the established or officially approved Churches in these countries were free from the supervision, as well as the support, of an international organisation such as the papacy, but it would be misleading to think of them as consequently under complete State control; the theocratic tradition of Calvinism, for example, was but one of the bulwarks against secular domination. Secondly, the fissiparous character of Protestantism, with its emphasis on the individual's responsibility for his own salvation and lack of respect for authority, led to the growth of sects outside the approved Church, whose existence in an age when ideas of uniformity were still strong could not be ignored by the rulers of either Church or State. Lastly, the Catholic minorities in these countries often excited a fear disproportionate to their size, though not always to their social standing: this was natural in the light of current suspicions of Roman Catholics as agents of foreign powers out to destroy both Protestant and national liberties.

After the bitter ecclesiastical quarrels of the first few decades of the century, the United Provinces acquired the well-deserved reputation of being the most tolerant country in Europe. This was achieved more by failing to put the law into execution than by altering it, a policy followed both during the stadholderless régime (1650–72) and under William III. Thus the Arminians, proscribed and exiled by the Synod of Dort, but strongly supported by the Regent class, were in practice widely tolerated, and in Amsterdam and perhaps elsewhere enjoyed complete liberty of worship; their connections with the Cambridge Platonists and John Locke are proof of their high intellectual standing. Sir William Temple, in his *Observations upon the United Provinces* (published in 1673), described them as 'rather the distinction of a Party in the State, than a Sect in the

Church', but this is hardly borne out by the dispute over the doctrine of grace and forgiveness which broke out about 1660 between the latitudinarian Coccejus of Leiden and the strict Calvinist Voetius, although both Regents and Orangists took sides, as they did in the controversy over public prayers for the Prince of Orange. Protestant sects flourished and Jewish synagogues existed in Amsterdam and Rotterdam. The position of the Catholics, who were numerous in the eastern provinces, in the Generality Lands and in Amsterdam, was more complicated. Although they had no legal protection for worshipping publicly, in practice they enjoyed considerable freedom to do so on payment of fines; equally in practice, though not in theory, they were normally allowed civic rights. Temple was not the only observer to be struck by the prevailing lack of coercion and general air of tolerance shown by a government interested primarily in keeping order and fostering prosperity; that the Dutch were prosperous partly because they were tolerant was a lesson often noted but as yet seldom followed by the rest of Europe. But the publicity given to this experiment in secularisation, helped greatly by the lack of press censorship which was another characteristic of the United Provinces, was in the long run to have the most important consequences. The Dutch presses became the presses of liberal Europe, while Dutch cities gave shelter to intellectual refugees of all creeds and nationalities.

In England the revolutionary period without an established Church came to an end at the Restoration in 1660, when Anglicanism was surprisingly quickly re-established. As a result of the consummate skill of Clarendon and Gilbert Sheldon (from 1663 Archbishop of Canterbury) the Presbyterians, who for their services in bringing about the king's return reasonably expected some concessions, were thoroughly outmanœuvred. With the least possible delay diocesan and parochial administration was resumed on the old lines, and Church lands, sold during the Interregnum, were restored. In April 1661 Charles II was crowned with Anglican rites; in May the newly elected Cavalier Parliament received communion according to the Prayer Book. The Savoy Conference between Anglicans and Presbyterians, which began in the former month, and the new Parliament were left little to do but accept the *fait accompli*; except for the High Commission, the Church was re-established as in 1640. One important change, the taxation of the clergy through parliament instead of through Convocation, resulted not from the Interregnum, but from a private agreement in 1664 between Clarendon and Sheldon. Henceforth Convocation, the power of the purse lost, was easily set aside, and for long periods the Church had no official mouthpiece.

By the Act of Uniformity of May 1662 Puritans were excluded from the Church, and the names Dissenter and Nonconformist explain their new status outside the establishment. Less affront was done to the sects, whose belief in a select brotherhood of the converted did not require political domination for its realisation, than to the Presbyterians with their theory of a comprehensive State-Church. Exclusion was also to mean persecution, intermittent but sometimes violent, as central politics and the resentment of local officials and their varying efficiency dictated. Henceforth to be a Nonconformist entailed loss of certain civil rights, as well as the prohibition of public worship: the Corporation Act (1661) kept Dissenters out of the government of the towns where their main strength lay, as it did the Catholics whose worship was also proscribed. Within the first twelve years of Charles's reign, and again in the period of reaction after the Popish Plot and the Rye House conspiracy,[1] the Nonconformists suffered severely in many places as a result of the Conventicle Acts of 1664 and 1670, the Five Mile Act of 1665, and older laws still on the Statute Book, as well as in the ecclesiastical courts. How far the government's policy was justified remains debatable. Although many Nonconformists were politically harmless, the old association of Republicanism and Dissent died hard, and the belief that discontented elements might use conventicles as a cover for seditious activities was natural.

The exact date at which Charles II was converted to Rome is less important than the fact that whenever politically possible he tried to achieve some relief for the Catholics, and was willing to include Nonconformists in his schemes as well. But Sheldon's opposition led to the stillbirth of a plan for concessions in 1662, and parliamentary criticism of the royal claim to suspend statute law, even in ecclesiastical matters, resulted in the withdrawal, a year after its issue, of the Declaration of Indulgence of 1672. A combination of factors made the next ten years particularly painful for the Catholics: news of the Duke of York's conversion, obvious to all by 1673, suspicions that the Treaty of Dover had secret clauses dangerous to English liberties and Protestantism, and fear of Louis XIV's aggression, all contributed to the anti-Catholic policy expressed in the Test Acts of 1673 and 1678 and culminated in the Popish Plot and the Exclusion Crisis of 1678–81.[2] Yet the king's masterly inactivity defeated the Whigs who tried to prevent James's succession to the throne; the Tories built up their theories of passive obedience to the monarch and the defence of the Church of England to counter the Whig programme of toleration for all Protestants, the total exclusion of Catholics from all places of responsibility, and a limited monarchy.

Restored Stuart rule did more violence to the Scottish Church. The execution of Argyle and Johnston of Warriston indicated that the Covenanters were not to be forgiven, while the Act Rescissory passed by the subservient Parliament of 1661 swept away all legislation since 1633, thus opening the way for the Privy Council to restore the hated system of episcopacy. Two other measures were to ensure twenty-eight years of

[1] For these events, see below, ch. XIII, pp. 313–14, 317.

[2] See below, ch. XIII, pp. 310–14, 316–17.

strife: the Act known as the 'Bishops' Drag-Net' imposed heavy fines on absentees from church and led to field conventicles, illegal and often violently broken up; the restoration of private patronage made it necessary for all who had received their charge direct from their congregation to seek presentation and episcopal collation. The government was surprised by the non-compliance of between two and three hundred ministers who were to form the largely irreconcilable core of opposition, both clerical and lay, which defied the settlement despite the most repressive measures, mingled with periods of conciliation. The crisis came in 1679, with the murder of the detested Archbishop Sharp and Monmouth's defeat of the deeply divided rebels at Bothwell Brig. The last-ditch defiance of the Cameronians who repudiated Charles as king was crushed by military force. The final outcome of these troubles was, at the Revolution, the formal re-establishment of non-episcopal Presbyterianism, but not the triumph of a theocracy.

While such conflicts continued to rage within many European countries, some of the best minds of the age were concerning themselves increasingly with the problems of reunion and toleration. Everyone, ecclesiastical and lay, paid lip-service to the ideal of reunion among churches, whatever suspicions might be aroused by attempts to make it a reality. On toleration there was less general agreement, for it entailed the sacrifice of the time-honoured principles of unity and uniformity, both in Church and State. Yet it was a more practicable objective. Reunion could be achieved only by widespread voluntary or forced conversion, or by the compromise of the independence of the various Churches. Toleration, on the other hand, required from the ecclesiastical point of view an acquiescence in the errors of others, and on the State's side a conviction that the abandonment of uniformity was safe and expedient. For its advance this period, with its growing secularisation and intellectual experiment, was well suited, although the progress was but slow and uneven.

The movement for reunion was not new in the second half of the seventeenth century; the cosmopolitan Scot, John Durie, had put his schemes to Gustavus Adolphus and Oxenstierna and later tried to interest Cromwell in them; in Grotius and Comenius the movement had already had two outstanding intellects behind it. In the irenic efforts of the later period three names are predominant: Leibniz, Bossuet and Cristobal de Rojas y Spinola. Leibniz, brought up a Lutheran, was apparently first attracted to the project by Johann Christian von Boineburg, a convert to Catholicism, and influential at the court of the liberal-minded Elector of Mainz, John Philip von Schönborn. In 1676 Leibniz accepted an invitation to go as librarian to the court of Duke John Frederick of Hanover, the Catholic ruler of a Lutheran State, and from then on till his death in 1716 his restless intellect was at work on finding some method of bringing the Churches together, and his restless pen in writing to the Landgrave of Hesse-Rheinfels, Pellisson, Bossuet or anyone else who might be sympathetic. He believed that by honest discussion all confessions could find agreement on the fundamental rules of faith, if they submitted themselves to the Holy Spirit as the internal, and the Word of God as the external, guide; he also placed much emphasis on the concept of an inner communion, to which men might belong without being members of the outer communion. He seemed prepared to go so far to meet the Catholic position that some wrongly believed him to be a secret convert. But his correspondence with Bossuet broke down on the question of the authority of the Council of Trent. Meanwhile Bishop Spinola was trying by personal persuasion and political manœuvre to bring about the same end. In 1673 he went round the Empire on behalf of the Emperor Leopold I to get help for the Turkish war and on his return reported to Rome on his efforts for reunion. Leopold's preoccupation with both his eastern and western frontiers and Innocent XI's interest in the Turkish question led them to favour any expedient that might further their ends, and Spinola's somewhat naïve confidence that the Protestants he met in Dresden, Berlin, Hanover and Heidelberg were enthusiastic for reunion was treated with some seriousness; but the pope's commission to examine the prospects came to a less optimistic conclusion. In 1678 and 1682 Spinola set out again, but his hopes were greater than his achievements. His main objective was to pave the way for a new General Council and, in order to get free discussion, he was anxious that the precedents of the Council of Trent and its decisions should be suspended and the Protestants should not be regarded as schismatics. But the forces against the movement were strong, and in fact the deaths of Innocent in 1689 and of Spinola in 1695 brought a serious check to its development.

More progress was made towards toleration, especially in some of the German States and in the United Provinces. Theoretically the case in its favour had often been stated. In England during the Interregnum, for example, it had been argued that the magistrate had no concern with religious matters, and that a State might safely shelter more than one Church; that there was a Christian case for the suppression of heresy was denied, and it was confidently maintained that a man should be allowed to worship how he liked provided that he kept the peace. But more was needed than such theories to persuade rulers and their subjects generally that toleration was safe and expedient. Only as materialistic considerations became increasingly important was it really believed that a man's religious convictions might be irrelevant to his loyalty and usefulness as a citizen, and that a country, to become rich and prosperous, ought to ignore religious barriers. The union of both the theoretical and practical arguments is well illustrated in the association of John Locke, whose theory of toleration was drafted by 1667, and the Earl of Shaftesbury, the dynamic politician with his belief that England could rival the Dutch as a commercial power if only she would follow the example of the tolerant United Provinces.[1] Few were prepared to allow that religious liberty ought to be universal: both Locke and Shaftesbury would have refused it to Catholics. But practice was often, as has been seen, more liberal than the law, and the foundations were at least laid for a further extension of the principle. Yet progress was far from universal: if the English Parliament passed a Toleration Act in 1689, France, four years earlier, had returned to the ideal of uniformity with the Edict of Fontainebleau.

Plans for reunion and toleration were, however, only two ways in which the distinctive temper of the times was manifested. Another development to some extent transcending national and sectarian boundaries was the fairly widespread increase in a more personal and less institutional (and, at the same time, a less intellectual) approach to religion, which to some degree coincided with the waning attraction of Calvinism in its strictest form which is a characteristic of the second half of the seventeenth century. In England, for example, the Quakers carried the Puritan conviction of the progressive revelation of the Holy Spirit to a point where they abandoned the sacraments of the Church, as well as the distinction between priesthood and laity. In Lutheran Germany the Pietist movement, led by Philipp Jakob Spener and August Hermann Francke, laid particular stress on the priesthood of all believers and thus the part to be played by the laity in the Church, and also upon religious experience in the place of doctrine and theological learning; Spener's meetings to study the Bible (the *collegia pietatis*) were only one way by which his teaching was spread. Quietism, in whose evolution the Spanish mystic Miguel de Molinos was probably most influential, rejected the validity and usefulness of all exterior activities and substituted for them an attitude of total passivity, advocating a condition of 'annihilation' in which God might work to bring the soul into a state of pure love. In spite of genuine spirituality, Molinos's teaching was condemned in 1687, while the writings of another Quietist, Madame de Guyon, were the subject of prolonged controversy in France. All such movements tended to make superfluous the traditional means by which the individual might achieve grace through an established Church. Religious developments of quite another kind were manifested in the latitudinarianism which distinguished the Arminians in the Netherlands as well as the Cambridge Platonists and liberal Anglicans in England, who sought to bring a reasonable and balanced outlook to theological and ecclesiastical problems and tried to emphasise the common grounds of agreement, rather than the differences between Christians. Their high intellectual standing and association with the most vigorous philosophical and scientific thought of the

[1] Cp. below, ch. XIV, pp. 332–3, 338–9.

day gave them a special importance at a time when these new ideas were permeating the most active minds in Europe.

All these tendencies were in some sense a reaction of exhaustion and disgust against the formalism and exclusiveness of the established Churches, both Catholic and Protestant, and contemporary critics were right in thinking that they had very real dangers: deism and atheism were to find outspoken advocates by the end of the century. But conservative forces were still very strong. The widespread hatred of the Jesuits with their allegedly easy morality, as shown in their casuistry and particularly in probabilism, was in itself a tribute to their influence. Popular superstition and piety still attracted the mass of the people more than any new ideas, and the miracles claimed at Port-Royal had a remarkable effect on men and women of a usually critical cast of mind. But everywhere the tendency towards secularisation was growing. Religion was slowly becoming more the concern of the individual and less the responsibility of the State, and the State's own *raison d'être* was in its turn changing: fewer men saw it as founded to ensure God's purpose through a divinely appointed ruler, and more believed its aim to be human security and prosperity. Against such a background it was inevitable that the relationship of Church and State should become less and less one of partners in a divinely appointed task, and increasingly a marriage of convenience in which expediency and individual advantage were the guiding aims.

CHAPTER VII

ART AND ARCHITECTURE

ROME was the centre where Baroque art originated and from where it spread. The great non-Italian artists of the first half of the seventeenth century, Rubens and Rembrandt, Velasquez and Poussin, could not have developed as they did without direct or indirect contact with the artistic events in Rome. Even though conditions radically changed after 1650, Rome must be given a large share in any consideration of European art during the second half of the century.

All the great artists of the first generation of the Baroque—Annibale Carracci (1560–1609), Caravaggio (1573–1610), Guido Reni (1575–1642), and the architect Carlo Maderno (1556–1629)—died long before 1650. The Fleming Rubens (b. 1577) died in Antwerp in 1640. Most of the great masters of the next generation, those mainly born in the last decade of the sixteenth century, were still alive, among them Alessandro Algardi (1595–1654), Andrea Sacchi (1599–1661), Francesco Borromini (1599–1667), Pietro da Cortona (1596–1669), the Neapolitan sculptor and architect Cosimo Fanzago (1591–1678), the Venetian architect Baldassare Longhena (1598–1682), and the greatest of all, Gianlorenzo Bernini (1598–1680). Of the non-Italians of this almost unbelievably strong generation Velasquez (b. 1599) died in 1660, Poussin (b. 1593) in 1665, Frans Hals (b. 1580), the oldest of this group, in 1666, Rembrandt (b. 1606) in 1669, and Claude Lorrain (b. 1600) in 1682. All these artists reached their full maturity in the fourth and fifth decades and only few lived through the third and into the fourth quarter of the century.

The masters of the third generation, born between about 1610 and 1630, are the primary concern of this chapter. They created their early works around 1650 and matured in the sixth and seventh decades. It is remarkable that there is hardly a single artist among them who can vie with the great ones of the older generation. Painters such as the Neapolitans Mattia Preti (1613–99), Salvator Rosa (1615–73), Bernardo Cavallino (1616–56), and Luca Giordano (1632–1705), the Roman Carlo Maratti (1625–1713), and the Genoese Giovan Battista Gaulli (1639–1709) were the heirs to Caravaggio and Annibale Carracci, Sacchi and Cortona. For several decades the architect Carlo Fontana (1634–1714) was the arbiter of taste in Rome. Nor did any of the sculptors of this generation approach the calibre of Bernini and Algardi. The artists of the third generation were respectable, versatile, and talented, but lacked the universality and fullness of vision of their elders.

The position was not much different outside Italy. In France the legitimate successor to Poussin was Charles Lebrun (1619–90); in Spain Velasquez was followed by Murillo (1617–82), Valdés Leal (1630–91) and Claudio Coello (1642–93). After Van Dyck's death (1599–1641), Sir Peter Lely (1618–80) became the foremost portrait painter in England. In Holland the specialists took over from Rembrandt and, by comparison, even the greatest of them, Vermeer van Delft (1632–75), shrinks in stature.

Although Bernini was alive till 1680 and enjoyed international fame to the very end, the importance of Rome as the artistic metropolis of Europe steadily declined. One can never fully account for such changes, but some factors are clearly discernible. Since the Peace of Westphalia the authority of the Holy See waned, and after the death of Alexander VII (1667) papal patronage fell off considerably. During the last decades of the seventeenth century artists in Rome were often starved of commissions, while other Italian States witnessed a considerable increase of artistic activity. In Venice the first half of the century was comparatively barren, but with the Genoese Giambattista Langetti (1625–76), the German Johann Karl Loth (1632–98), the Florentine Sebastiano Mazzoni (*c.* 1615–85), and others working there after 1650, a process of recuperation began which led to the magnificent flowering of the Venetian school in the early years of the eighteenth century. The wealthy republic of Genoa spent vast sums of money on the arts. Despite the disastrous plague of 1657 Genoa saw the rise of a vigorous school of painting and sculpture and, although some of her most gifted artists such as Giovanni Benedetto Castiglione (1610?–65) and Giovan Battista Gaulli sought their fortunes elsewhere, Genoese palaces and churches were opulently decorated at this time. But the most remarkable development took place in Piedmont and Naples. Turin entered a great phase of enlargement and embellishment under the energetic Charles Emanuel II (1638–75), whose architects Amedeo di Castellamonte, Francesco Lanfranchi, and, above all, Guarino Guarini transformed the Piedmontese capital into a splendid Baroque city. Naples had attracted outstanding Roman painters before the middle of the century: Domenichino and Lanfranco spent years of their lives there. The plague of 1656 pruned native talent very considerably; nevertheless the ascendancy of the Neapolitan school of painting was such that for two generations it had no rival in Italy.

Concurrently with this shift of gravity from Rome to the north and south of Italy, there arose the challenge of Paris as a great artistic centre. When, in 1661, the young Louis XIV decided to rule himself, Paris began to dictate the taste of Europe. In retrospect Bernini's abortive state visit to the French capital appears like a public acknowledgment of Rome's lowered prestige in artistic matters. The royal invitation was extended to the great Italian master because he alone appeared to be able to give the Louvre, the old residence of the French kings, a form worthy of the greatest monarch on earth. But already at the time of Bernini's departure from Paris in the autumn of 1665, a change of spirit had come about. In 1667 Louis decided to abandon Bernini's plans. A stately French design, the result of collaboration between Claude Perrault (1613–88), Louis Le Vau and Lebrun, was chosen for the east front of the Louvre, and the difference between its cool formality and the impetuous grandeur of Bernini's project indicates the general direction of taste in the new age.

For an understanding of the international position in the arts after 1650 it is helpful to take stock of the various styles or trends which existed side by side from the early seventeenth century onwards. There was the Baroque trend in the narrower sense of the word, a boisterous style of great vitality, the ancestry of which leads back to the 'impressionist', 'painterly' technique of the great Venetians of the sixteenth century, of Titian and Veronese, and to Correggio's bold illusionism in his dome decorations at Parma. Early in the seventeenth century Rubens had created an important aspect of this style by wedding Venetian colourism and Flemish realism. Giovanni Lanfranco and Pietro da Cortona had introduced other nuances: the former in his ceiling frescoes in Rome and Naples with their breath-taking Correggiesque wizardry, the latter in his passionate decorative manner which fused the experience of Veronese, Correggio, Raphael, and the antique into compositions of extraordinary density.

The second, more classical, trend took its cue from Annibale Carracci's grand manner which culminated in his frescoes of the Farnese Gallery; this dramatic but somewhat cool manner was buttressed by a close study of nature, antiquity, Raphael and Michelangelo, and of Venetian colourism. None of the 'Baroque' artists could overlook the potentialities of this style: it influenced Rubens as much as Pietro da Cortona and was greatly admired by Bernini; but it also opened the way to Poussin's classicism. The third important trend may generically be called 'realistic'. Realism is a term of convenience which defies precise definition. It was and is incorrectly applied to Caravaggio and, with more justice, to the northern rendering of meticulous detail. It is used to denote the choice of popular types as well as the portrayal of 'low' subjects, such as tavern scenes; the direct working from the model as well as the unembellished representation of religious imagery.

These three trends competed for recognition and primacy throughout the seventeenth century, and there is hardly a time when they cannot be found side by side. By and large, however, the Baroque current was pre-eminent during the 1620's and 1630's, while a reorientation in the direction of 'Baroque classicism' took place from the 1640's onwards. Caravaggism and realism influenced both currents to a varying degree at different times in different countries, without ever being accepted as the official style of the papacy, the courts, and the aristocracy.

A few French examples may help to throw light on some of the intricacies of the stylistic position during the critical decade. Simon Vouet (1590–1649), who for many years had travelled and worked in Italy, painted, long after his return to Paris, a *Presentation in the Temple* (1641; Louvre) in the Italian Baroque manner—a composition with sweeping diagonals, a scenographic perspective, and clusters of monumental figures emotionally charged. During the same period Poussin, living in Rome, produced such carefully arranged relief-like pictures as the *Rebecca and Eleazar* (1648; Louvre) with its evident references to Raphael and ancient models; this is a severe, classical work wholly different from Vouet's. Louis Le Nain's painting *Peasants at Supper* (*c.* 1645; Louvre) conducts the beholder into a homely scene faithfully rendered; none of the paraphernalia of 'low life'—the peasants' clothing, the torn trousers, the utensils of the kitchen, cat and dog—are left unrecorded. But compared with a Lanfranco or a Cortona, Vouet has moved away from Baroque towards classical standards; compared with a late Le Sueur (1616–55), Poussin's work still has the rich and warm palette of Baroque painting; and compared with Dutch genre painting, the monumental scale of figures and the austerity of the frontal composition show Le Nain's realism subservient to classicism. Thus a classical quality is common to the three pictures, and terminological barriers should not prevent us from noticing it.

A different line of argument may lead to associating each of the three main currents with specific national tempers and idiosyncrasies. The Italian, Bernini, may be regarded as the peerless representative of the Baroque current, the Frenchman, Poussin, as the champion of classicism, and the Dutchman, Rembrandt, as the unrivalled protagonist of northern realism. Even if this be admitted, the early careers of these great masters reveal their beliefs in similar values. The early Rembrandt's dramatic use of light, derived from Caravaggio, his composing with prominent triangles and diagonals, his interest in the great gesture and the monumental Italian form—all this has parallels in the young Bernini's interpretation of sculpture and in Poussin's painterly works of the same period. From such Baroque beginnings each master developed towards an entirely personal style. But again their late manners have something important in common: all three found a simple structure of horizontals and verticals more suited to express strong emotions than the rich Baroque compositions of their early period.

The late Poussin, obsessed by his moral and rational approach to art, clothed his convictions in puritanically severe forms and almost offensively hard colours. The London *Annunciation* of 1657 and the even later Leningrad *Rest on the Flight into Egypt* are typical examples. Bernini's late works reflect a mystic trend in Catholic seventeenth-century devotion by showing increasingly violent movement within a framework of emphatically angular forms, as evidenced in the *Blessed Lodovica Albertoni* (1674; S. Francesco a Ripa, Rome) and the bust of Gabriele Fonseca (1668–75; S. Lorenzo in Lucina, Rome). Rembrandt went the opposite way. The deeper the feeling, the more silent become his figures. He needed neither Bernini's extrovert violence nor Poussin's statuesque figures and classical compositions to express an ecstatic state of mind. In his late pictures there is complete silence; the extremely simple figures melt into space and the whole space seems to vibrate with emotion.

These three great artists echoed as well as shaped the longings of their age. They reacted as immensely perceptive sounding-boards to the society in which they lived. For over fifty years Bernini held the place of the official artist of the papacy, serving five popes in succession. His southern rhetoric and passion, his ability to conquer the minds of the public by dazzling their eyes, his mastery in rendering the physical condition of ecstasies and raptures, and his capacity of bringing home to the faithful an intense experience of the supernatural—all this predestined him to the unique part which he played as the artist of Catholic orthodoxy.

Poussin spent forty years in Rome, but most of his clientele lived in Paris. As he advanced in age his circle of patrons and friends consisted mainly of merchants and bankers, civil servants and lawyers, who embraced Descartes's rationalism as much as philosophical scepticism and stoicism. This public hailed Poussin's moral subjects and judicious classicism as a pictorial manifestation of their most cherished ideals.

Rembrandt's art had its roots in the burgher culture of Calvinist Holland. His pantheism ennobled all creation from the meanest cripple to a storm breaking in the sky. The revolution he wrought is best judged in his religious work. He was the first artist to repeal fully and irreparably the time-honoured iconography of the Catholic Church. Southern artists had always expressed Christ's divine nature by physical perfection. At the beginning of his career Rembrandt interpreted Him in these familiar terms. But gradually he conceived of Christ as ugly and humble and, at the end, his anti-heroic and personal interpretation of the biblical stories was at the farthest remove from the official art of Catholicism.

Bernini's historical mission lay mainly in the Catholic south where his influence persisted to the end of the eighteenth century. French and, indeed, European classical art of the later seventeenth and even of the eighteenth century drew its strength from Poussin's work and ideas. The further development of intimate realistic painting in northern Europe cannot be dissociated from Rembrandt's perennial achievement.

The intensity of the late styles of the great masters, however, was not fully understood by the younger generation of artists. Soon after 1650 an equalising tendency made itself felt throughout Europe, a reduction of the capacity for individual expression, and a slackening of tension, and despite the persistence of the different artistic currents an international style emerged under French hegemony. This uniform style was essentially classical, but may be more correctly termed 'Baroque classicism'. Bernini's, Poussin's, and Rembrandt's careers make it evident that the struggle for its ascendancy took on different forms in the three artistically most significant countries: Italy, France and Holland.

Since the Middle Ages Italians regarded the monumental fresco as the primary task of painters. It is in this field that late seventeenth-century painters gave of their best. With few memorable exceptions the most sumptuous Baroque decorations in Roman churches and palaces were created after 1650, often for much older buildings. The most ambitious works of this kind are Gaulli's frescoes executed between 1672 and 1683 in the late sixteenth-century Gesù, the mother church of the Jesuit Order, and Andrea Pozzo's immense ceiling (1691–4) in S. Ignazio. The dramatic effect of Gaulli's frescoes derives from the Berninesque juxtaposition of large dark and bright areas of paint and from the guidance given to the eye in penetrating step by step to the unfathomable depth of the sky, the lightest area, where the name of Christ appears amid shining rays. Another device, also owed to Bernini, requires comment: Gaulli blended fresco and painted stucco and let parts of the painted ceiling spill over on to the architecture of the vault—a contrivance meant to engage the beholder as forcefully as possible. In contrast to Gaulli, Pozzo placed a host of figures representing the apotheosis of St Ignatius into an illusionist architectural framework which expanded immensely the actual by a feigned structure. This method called *quadratura* looked back to a learned Renaissance tradition, but had never been employed on such a scale. Both types of Baroque ceiling painting—that with figures breaking through the retaining frame so that they seem to close in on the beholder, and that with the perspective widening of pictorial space so that the painted action appears to be at a great distance—found enthusiastic following, mainly in the Austrian and German Baroque of the eighteenth century.

These as well as other exuberant Baroque fresco cycles seem to belie the notion that Italian painting was developing in the direction of an international classicism. But while Gaulli was engaged on his Gesù frescoes Carlo Maratti painted a large ceiling with the *Triumph of Clemency* (after 1673) in the family palace of the Altieri Pope Clement IX. He relinquished all forms of Baroque illusionism; once again the fresco is clearly and simply framed and an attempt is made to reinstate the importance of the plastically conceived individual figure. In the struggle for primacy between Gaulli and Maratti, Gaulli's mystical Late Baroque had no chance whatever against Maratti's rationalist classicism. As early as the 1670's Maratti's success was assured. Soon even Gaulli's style began to lose its intensity; in spite of Pozzo's work in S. Ignazio, before the end of the century Rome had surrendered to Maratti's manner.

Maratti's classicism had little in common with the heroic 'Early Baroque classicism' of Annibale Carracci. To be sure, it had close points of contact with the sublime and painterly 'High Baroque classicism' which Maratti's teacher Andrea Sacchi practised in the 1640's and 1650's. But Maratti, the master of the third generation, went further towards a reconciliation of the two opposing trends, the Baroque and the classical. He steered an agreeable middle course: his paintings contain few riddles, little to puzzle the beholder or to rouse deep emotions. The admixture of just the right dose of festive splendour is characteristic of his 'Late Baroque classicism'. It was this style, to which without doubt Paris contributed, that had an all-Italian following for at least a generation.

Italians, however, never entirely submitted to a pattern. There never was a central organisation with power to dictate in matters of taste. A spirit of conformity has always been suspect in Italy. The Neapolitan Salvator Rosa, who died in Rome in 1673 after a stay there of almost a generation, is a case in point. A man of extraordinary talent, but a rebel in perpetuity, he gave his best in battlepieces, landscapes, and marine paintings: wild scenes with a romantic flavour, painted with a tempestuous brush. A number of individualists outside Rome also reacted vigorously against the rising tide of High and Late Baroque classicism. Mazzoni and Langetti, who worked in Venice, have been mentioned. Similarly, Valerio Castello (1624–59) and his Genoese successors loved violent contrasts and fiery hues. The Neapolitans Mattia Preti and Luca Giordano, both working up and down the peninsula, displayed in their paintings a dynamic power without parallel in Italy or elsewhere in the last decades of the century. All these artists as well as scores unnamed preferred work with the loaded brush and sketchy juxtapositions of small areas of colour to the smooth handling of paint, used unexpected colour contrasts rather than a harmonious scale of tones, and opposed violent movement, drama, and even a new mysticism to the facile rhetoric of the classicists.

Only up to a point is the history of Italian Baroque painting paralleled by the history of sculpture and architecture. The position of sculptors was prejudiced by the overpowering genius of Bernini. Nobody could ignore him; you had to be with him or against him, but even his opponents lived under his shadow. Before 1650, during Algardi's and Duquesnoy's lifetime, there had been much greater variety. Soon after that date the conservative Ercole Ferrata (1610–86) led the right wing and the progressive Antonio Raggi (1624–86) the left wing of the Bernini school. Their work can best be studied in the monumental marble reliefs of S. Agnese in Piazza Navona (1660). In his vast cycle of stuccoes in the clerestory of the nave and transept of the Gesù (1669–83), Raggi, the most gifted sculptor of his generation, yielded wholly to Bernini's late mystical style. But it was Ferrata who headed a large school to which sculptors from all

Italy flocked. When Ferrata and Raggi died in 1686, the only famous sculptor of their generation still alive was Domenico Guidi (1625–1701). In spite of his mediocrity he was hailed the first sculptor in Rome. It is characteristic that he maintained close contacts with the French and even obtained, in 1677, a commission for a marble group at Versailles; but since he was still steeped in Bernini's grand manner, his group gave little satisfaction at the French court.

It was at this time, after the foundation of the French Academy in Rome (1666), that French sculptors went to the Eternal City in great numbers. Some of them stayed many years and obtained important commissions, among them P. S. Monnot (1657–1733), G. B. Théodon (1646–1713), and P. Legros (1656–1719). Thus towards the end of the century the French exercised a stronger influence on Roman sculpture than on Roman painting. Camillo Rusconi (1658–1728) rehabilitated to a certain extent the autonomy of the Roman school. But his Late Baroque classicism—a forceful, belated parallel to Maratti's style in painting—did not come into its own until the early years of the next century.

Owing to Bernini's authority Rome remained the international centre for sculpture much longer than for painting. All through the seventeenth and far into the eighteenth century Roman sculptors also worked for other Italian cities and even found patrons, eager to be served by them, in Germany, Poland, Portugal, England, and elsewhere. Nevertheless, in the last decades of the century flourishing local schools sprang up in Naples, Florence, Bologna, Genoa, and Venice. The Florentine Ferdinando Tacca (1619–86) still maintained a good deal of native Tuscan reserve. With Ferrata's pupil, Giovanni Battista Foggini (1652–1737), the high-water mark of Berninesque sculpture was reached in Florence. In Filippo Parodi (1630–1702) Genoa had her first and greatest native Baroque sculptor, and the later development of the Genoese school was dependent on his distinguished achievement. Venice attracted sculptors from northern countries. The most vigorous of them was Josse de Corte (1627–79), who was born at Ypres and, after studying in Rome, settled in Venice in 1657. He introduced Baroque sculpture into Venice, and his collaborators and pupils continued his picturesque manner far into the eighteenth century.

Some of the finest buildings of the Roman Baroque fall into the period under review. Bernini's architectural commissions lay mainly between about 1650 and 1670. Of his three church buildings, the palm must go to S. Andrea al Quirinale (1658–70), a small structure over an oval ground-plan. Here one can best study Bernini's dramatic use of colour and light, and his sophisticated blending of architecture and sculpture. All the significant lines of the building converge upon the figure of St Andrew who appears soaring upward through the gilded dome. His apotheosis dominates the entire space and on entering the church the beholder immediately partakes in this 'mystery in action'. Modern critics sometimes maintain that there is a contradiction between the classicality of Bernini's architecture and the Baroque spirit of his sculpture; they evidently fail to understand that, by giving his churches an entirely non-classical meaning, Bernini endowed classical forms with a new content.

If executed, the Louvre would have been by far the most important of Bernini's secular buildings and its influence on European architecture might have been startling. Even so, the engravings after his project had an impact that was felt from Prague to Stockholm and Madrid. With the palace he built in Rome for Cardinal Flavio Chigi (1664 ff.; now Palazzo Chigi-Odescalchi), Bernini introduced a revolutionary type of palace design. The articulation by a closely set colossal order, the juxtaposition of the highly organised central block with the rusticated lower wings, the fine balance between masses (interfered with when the façade was lengthened in the eighteenth century), the subtle gradation of motifs from storey to storey—all this combined in a design of authentic nobility and grandeur. Bernini had found the formula for the aristocratic Baroque palace; it was followed and imitated in most European countries.

Between 1656 and 1667 Bernini carried out his greatest architectural work, the piazza of St Peter's. He was faced by a staggering tangle of topographical, structural, symbolic, liturgical and aesthetic problems, but he rose to the occasion and produced one of the great masterpieces of all time that has always been admired without reservation. Two wide arms of open colonnades standing four columns deep embrace a large oval piazza which forms a festive and serene forecourt to the basilica. Never before had self-contained, free-standing colonnades been used for a similar purpose. The visual impression is one of irresistible power and grandeur. No other structure of the post-Renaissance period shows an equally deep affinity to Greek architecture. Nor was it possible to handle the traditional grammar of architectural forms with such self-assurance before the seventeenth century. The Hellenic quality of the piazza could only be produced by the greatest Baroque artist, who was a sculptor at heart. For almost two hundred years Bernini's piazza remained an inspiration to urban designers.

Francesco Borromini and Pietro da Cortona created some of their finest architectural work in the first half of the seventeenth century. Although they stand for very different facets of the High Baroque, their late styles reveal a distinct simplification and broadening of architectural forms and motifs; it may therefore be claimed that they too conformed to the general trend towards classicism. This tendency was, however, not yet noticeable in S. Agnese in Piazza Navona, which Girolamo and Carlo Rainaldi began in 1652 and which a year later Borromini continued with considerable alterations. In 1657 Carlo Rainaldi in turn replaced Borromini and immediately adjusted the latter's design where still possible.

Although the completion of the church took many years and the interior decoration was not finished until the end of the century, the church must be regarded as essentially Borromini's work. It represents an important landmark in the history of architecture, for it is no less than the High Baroque revision of Bramante's centralised plan for St Peter's of which little was executed. Never before had such a rich and varied group of façade, towers, and dome been created with similarly intense spatial suggestions. The further genesis of centralised planning and of the two-tower façade in Italy and the rest of Europe is unthinkable without this key structure.

By contrast, Borromini's most important late work, the church and façade of the Collegio di Propaganda Fide (1662), was too personal a creation to exercise a significant influence. In the interior of the church he broke with the Renaissance principle, to which most Baroque architecture conformed, of giving prominence to the walls and using the orders for the rhythmic articulation. Here the orders form a coherent structural 'skeleton' reminiscent of Gothic building methods. A comparison of Borromini's façade of the Oratory of St Philip Neri (1637 ff.) with that of the Collegio di Propaganda Fide illustrates his change of style over twenty-five years. Gone is a great mass of detail, gone are the many gradations of wall surface and the almost joyful display of a great variety of motifs. All particulars are reduced to a minimum of austere forms resulting in an oppressive, well-nigh nightmarish effect. The church and façade of the Propaganda Fide with their compelling simplicity and unorthodox logic fittingly conclude Borromini's career as an architect.

Next to Bernini, Colbert had invited Pietro da Cortona to submit plans for the Louvre. They do not survive, but his design for a Chigi palace planned for the Piazza Colonna by Alexander VII may supply a clue to the character of the lost Louvre project. The design for the Chigi pope, now in the Vatican Library, shows for the first time in Baroque architecture a powerful giant order of columns screening a concave wall above a rusticated ground floor. Among Cortona's late architectural work two remarkable church façades have pride of place. The façade of Sta Maria della Pace (1656–7) presents a fascinating interplay of convex and concave forms. But perhaps even more important is the systematisation of the small piazza which is derived from the theatre: the church appears like the stage, the piazza like the auditorium, and the flanking houses like the boxes. In the façade of Sta Maria in Via Lata (1658–62) Cortona carried simplification a decisive step further. The classicising tendencies already apparent in the sober Doric of Sta Maria della Pace are strengthened; in contrast to the complexity of Cortona's early SS. Martina e Luca one finds here the crystalline clarity of a few great motifs.

Each of the three great masters, Bernini, Borromini and Cortona, had an incalculable influence on the further course of the history of architecture. In Rome Carlo Fontana (1634–1714) transformed Bernini's full-blooded style into an academic manner characteristic of the *fin du siècle*. Fontana started his career as an architectural draughtsman and clerk of works to Cortona, Rainaldi and Bernini. His own works date from the time after 1665 and his Late Baroque classicism, a precise architectural parallel to Maratti's manner, was fully formed in the façade of S. Marcello al Corso (1682). Indefatigably industrious, erudite and bookish, he produced an endless number of designs for chapels, tombs, altars, fountains, festival decorations, and even for statuary. The glamour attached to his name as the legatee of the great masters made his studio an international centre of aspiring architects. The Sicilian Filippo Juvarra (1678–1736), the Austrian Fischer von Erlach (1656–1723), the German M. Daniel Pöppelmann (1662–1736), the English James Gibbs (1682–1754)—all learned their lesson from him. Through him many Berninesque motifs became widely accepted in the early eighteenth century.

No less important was the current stemming from Borromini. He was mainly followed by non-conformist architects who were fascinated by dynamic spatial and articulating conceptions which defied traditional usage. Borromini found successors in the north and south of Italy and in Austria and southern Germany rather than in Rome. But Borrominesque mouldings, window- and door-surrounds, corner solutions, and other details soon formed part of the international language of architecture. Cortona was probably most effective through his imaginative decorative style, which culminates in the ceilings of the grand ducal apartment in the Palazzo Pitti at Florence (1640–7). It is the union of dignity and stateliness, of the festive, the swagger, and the grand, that predestined his decorative manner to be internationally followed in aristocratic and princely dwellings. The *style Louis XIV* owes more to the decorations of the Palazzo Pitti than to any other single source.

Two other architects active in the second half of the seventeenth century require special attention. Though less distinguished than the three great masters, the Roman Carlo Rainaldi (1611–91) is connected with some of the outstanding architectural tasks of his time. During the 1660's and 1670's he executed Sta Maria in Campitelli, the façade of S. Andrea della Valle, and the churches in the Piazza del Popolo. Sta Maria in Campitelli (1663–7) is one of the most interesting Baroque churches in Rome. The interior as well as the façade show a unique synthesis of North Italian scenic features with a typical Roman gravity. Never before had the North Italian 'aedicula façade' (where two canopies seem to be set one into the other) been blended with the specifically Roman increase in the volume of the orders from pilasters to half-columns and free-standing columns. This new type of Baroque façade had an immense success: it was constantly repeated and readapted to particular conditions. The churches in the Piazza del Popolo (1662–79) have a complicated building history and at some stage Bernini and Carlo Fontana had a hand in their construction. They presented a difficult town-planning problem, for they create not only a monumental front on the piazza, but also crown the wedge-shaped sites, unifying and emphasising the ends of long street-fronts. The weaving into one of street and square was a new urban device which had a future in France rather than in Italy.

The second name is that of Guarino Guarini (1624–83), whose settling in Turin in 1666 opens the era of the extraordinary flowering of Piedmontese architecture. Guarini, a Theatine priest, started his career as a theologian, philosopher, and mathematician. He began practising architecture in Messina (1660) and executed works (no longer existing) in Paris and Lisbon before accepting the call of Charles Emanuel II of Savoy. His principal works in Turin—the Cappella della SS. Sindone adjoining the Cathedral (1667–90), the church of S. Lorenzo (1668–87), and the Palazzo Carignano (1679 ff.)—are among the most remarkable creations of European architecture. He is often, incorrectly, regarded as a follower of Borromini. To be sure, both architects were non-conformists, but otherwise they had little in common. Borromini strove after the creation of homogeneous structures, while Guarini displayed deliberate contradictions, surprising dissonances, seeming inconsistencies, and complex wall boundaries. His telescoping of drum and dome into unheard of, hybrid formations, his diaphanous domes which had no tradition in western Europe, the almost unbelievable boldness of some of his creations: all show that Guarini wanted to give artistic expression to a distinct philosophical concept. It is perhaps not too bold to assume that he, the devoted student of Descartes's and Desargues's new mathematics, intended to suggest infinity by architectural devices. His longitudinal churches, of which none survive, were designed with undulating walls, an intricate system of vaulting, and baffling combinations of spatial shapes. On these designs depended to a considerable extent the development of the German and Austrian Baroque architecture.

To turn from Guarini's architecture to the artistic position in France is nothing short of an anticlimax. Guarini himself started the Theatine church of Ste Anne-la-Royale in Paris in 1662 (destroyed), precisely at the moment when a distinctly national style began to develop and Italian non-conformism and exuberance were viewed with suspicion and even disgust. The rise of French classicism between 1630 and 1660 went hand in hand with the consolidation of France as a great power. All the artists who matured during that period accomplished the transition to various facets of a classicist manner. Apart from the two greatest architects, François Mansart (1598–1666) and Louis Le Vau (1612–70), the names of the most important painters may be recalled: in the 1640's Philippe de Champaigne (1602–74) began to change his early Baroque manner, derived from Rubens, and progressively embraced an extremely austere style; George de La Tour's (1593–1652) early Caravaggesque phase was followed by a frozen and completely detached idiom; after romantic beginnings the landscapist Gaspar Dughet (1615–75) submitted to the influence of his brother-in-law, Poussin; Eustache Le Sueur (1616–55) first followed Vouet's Baroque manner and ended his career with cool and precise Raphaelesque paintings; Sebastian Bourdon (1616–71) in his early period painted in a variety of manners, but had a strictly Poussinesque late period.

These artists essentially belong to the pre-Louis XIV era. They were individualists who obeyed the call of conscience without submitting to a dictatorship of taste. Those who lived far into the third quarter of the seventeenth century (Claude died as late as 1682) were then the outmoded old guard, remnants of an age that came to an end when, after 1661, Colbert assumed control of the arts in France.

Colbert was immediately resolved to centralise all artistic activity under one head. His choice fell on the versatile Charles Lebrun (1619–90) whose easy decorative talent and first-rate organising ability stamped him as the man of the new era. In 1663 he was appointed director of the Gobelins factory the scope of which was much wider than its name reveals. He exercised full authority over an army of painters, sculptors, engravers, weavers, cabinet-makers and others. To their combined effort the world owes that rich, pretentious, pompous, and at the same time pedantic decorative style which rightly bears the name of the king whose aggrandisement it mainly served.

For the theoretical control of art production Colbert turned his attention to the academies. The Royal Academy of Painting and Sculpture, though founded in 1648, received its final constitution not until 1663. The first real academies of art with an elaborate educational programme saw the light of day in Italy at the end of the sixteenth century. Colbert built on this foundation and his Paris Academy, fenced in by a social hierarchy, a theoretical and practical syllabus, all the frills of academic training, and formal lectures in which the rules of correct art were discussed, became the model of art academies all over Europe—a development which took more than a hundred years to be completed. Colbert demanded absolute authority for the Academy. Its members were granted monopolistic privileges, and a successful career as an artist was only possible as an academician. All other intellectual activities were equally centrally controlled through newly founded academies: that of Dance in 1661, of *Inscriptions et Belles Lettres* (concerned with matters of erudition) in 1663, of Science in 1666, of Music in 1669, and of Architecture in 1671. The year 1666 also saw the establishment of the *Académie de France* in Rome for the specific purpose of giving artists a classical training at the fountain head.

When Italian Renaissance artists began to aspire to a high social standing, they opened up a gulf between the crafts and the 'fine arts'. Yet the schism between the artist as a creator in solitude and the rest of society was resolved in Louis's France. Not unlike medieval artisans, French artists again became integrated into a system of society, but not without sacrificing their hard-won freedom. No greater contrast can be imagined than that between them and Bernini at the time of his Paris visit. Italy never knew the spiritual climate of a centralised autocracy and bureaucracy. Bernini said what he thought; and his French colleagues trembled when he opened his mouth. He despised their lack of imagination and originality, their narrow dogmatism and, above all, the slavishness of their lives. 'Submission', he said, 'is necessary only in matters of faith; otherwise man has complete freedom in all spheres of life.'[1]

Nevertheless the teaching of the French Academy was deeply rooted in Italian art theory. The classical theory, derived from Aristotle and, in the Renaissance, first formulated by Leon Battista Alberti, held as its central doctrine that the synthesis accomplished in a work of art must result from a rational and selective process. Giovanni Bellori (1615–96), a learned antiquarian, librarian of Queen Christina of Sweden, a friend and councillor of the classical circle of artists in Rome, intimate of Poussin and Duquesnoy, made the supreme statement of this theory in a lecture, entitled *L'idea del pittore, dello scultore e dello architetto*, read to the Academy of St Luke in Rome in 1664. Bellori's theory was practised by Poussin. His procedure as a painter was rational; carefully calculating, he endeavoured to give his works the objective quality of ancient art, for according to the current ideology the artists of antiquity had consummated a perfect selection from nature and thus created works of ideal beauty. Poussin's method was taught and followed in the French Academy. The painter Sebastian Bourdon discussed it in a lecture to his fellow academicians. 'When a painter has made a drawing from the living model,' he said, 'he should make another study of the same figure on a separate sheet and should try to give it the character of an ancient statue.'[2] And in one of his lectures Lebrun traced the ancient models for each figure in Poussin's *Gathering of Manna* (Louvre). In the hands of such men art almost became a logical discipline. Poussin's work and Bellori's *Idea* were the two main pillars on which the edifice of the French art of the later seventeenth century rested.

The requirements of the new *bourgeoisie*, however, to which most of Poussin's friends and patrons belonged, and of the court differed. To be sure, classicism—a rational style that can easily be taught and learned, a

[1] M. de Chantelou, *Journal du voyage du Cav. Bernin en France*, ed. L. Lalanne (Paris, 1885).

[2] A. de Montaiglon, *Procès-verbaux de l'Académie royale de peinture et de sculpture* (Paris, 1875).

style that permits no vagaries and imposes conformity—may be the most adequate artistic expression for a rigorously centralised absolutism. On the other hand, grandeur, ceremonial solemnity, sublimity, and exaltation had a special place in the lives of the monarch and the court and as an artistic vehicle for such needs the Baroque style was ready at hand. Thus official art in the age of Louis XIV does not fully accord with current theory. The *style Louis XIV* can perhaps best be defined as an Italianate Baroque tamed by classicist principles. As we saw, Pietro da Cortona signally contributed to the formation of this French Late Baroque, which soon had international currency.

Louis's Versailles is the supreme achievement of this style, the hall-mark of the epoch, and the symbol of the glory of France at a heroic moment of her history. The new Versailles began to take shape between 1668 and 1671 when Le Vau incorporated an older palace into a considerably larger design. The present enormous garden front with its unrelieved horizontal of over 550 yards resulted from the alterations and extensions executed by Jules Hardouin-Mansart (1646–1708) between 1679 and 1689. To this period also belongs the celebrated Galerie des Glaces for the decoration of which Lebrun, leader of an army of artists, was responsible. Hypertrophic scale, glittering materials, the stateliness and pomposity of the interior—all this was genuinely expressive of the most ceremonial court in Europe and of a court society keyed up to extravagantly splendid and elaborate pageantries.

The French garden- and town-planning schemes of the period represent another facet of the love for the colossal, but the colossal bridled by reason and rule. André Le Nôtre (1613–1700), surveyor general of the royal works (1657), was the man of vision and genius who created the French formal garden of the Baroque. His greatest triumph was the gardens of Versailles where vast spaces are made subservient to symmetry and geometry. Straight avenues and trimmed boskets, staircase and cascade, large ponds and fountains, vases and statues are blended into a magnificent composition. It has been well said that the garden *à la française* is 'a lesson in order. At the time of Louis XIV it was also a lesson in grandeur.'[1] Le Nôtre also designed the plan of the town of Versailles. On the square in front of the château long avenues converge which find their counterpart in the garden. Thus town and park form a supreme unit with the château as focusing-point from either side.

The straight road, the vista of prodigious length with the monumental *point de vue* at its end, converging avenues, the *rond-point* with radiating streets, monuments as terminal perspectives centred on regular squares, street fronts conforming to a coherent design, the uniform planning of whole areas—though many of these elements of French town-planning had older, partly Italian pedigrees—they were never deliberately and

[1] P. Lavedan, *French Architecture* (Penguin Books, 1956).

consistently combined in designs of such magnificent scale before the age of Louis XIV. Paris was given its urban physiognomy in those years. The Champs-Élysées and the Place de l'Étoile, the Place des Victoires and the Place Vendôme, and the splendid layout of the Hôtel des Invalides, with the streets converging on the Place Vauban, set the example for no less ambitious schemes of the eighteenth and nineteenth centuries.

Next to these achievements in urban planning only a few individual buildings can be given a passing mention: the Collège des Quatre-Nations (1661–2), still close to the Roman Baroque, erected by Le Vau, the architect of the Château of Vaux-le-Vicomte; the vast Hôtel des Invalides, with its severe arcaded courts designed by Libéral Bruant (1670–6) and its high domed church over a centralised plan constructed later by Hardouin-Mansart (1679–1708); finally the austerely classical Porte Saint-Denis (1672) by Nicolas-François Blondel (1618–86), whose *Cours d'architecture enseigné à l'Académie royale* (1675–83) summarises the doctrinaire teaching at the Academy.

During the first half of the seventeenth century French sculpture was at a low ebb. Jacques Sarrazin (1588–1660) created the typically French brand of Baroque classicism with his tomb of Henri de Bourbon, Prince de Condé, at Chantilly (1648–63). The brothers François and Michel Anguier (1604–69, 1613–86) represent similar tendencies, as the latter's classicised Cortonesque decorations of the rooms of the Queen Mother in the Louvre (1655–8) as well as his famous *Nativity* (St Roch, 1665) attest. But it was three younger artists, François Girardon (1628–1715), Antoine Coysevox (1640–1720), and Pierre Puget (1620–94), who led French sculpture to new heights. Girardon in particular was a man to Lebrun's taste. He therefore played a leading part in the decoration of Versailles. His masterpiece is the many-figured group of *Apollo tended by the Nymphs* for a grotto in the park (1666) in which he skilfully blended the experience of Hellenistic sculpture with that of the late Poussin. Characteristically, the younger Coysevox found his way back to a freer, more Baroque conception of sculpture. This is less obvious in his many outdoor statues and fountains at Versailles (1679–87) than in the interior decoration, above all in the Galerie des Glaces and the Salon de la Guerre where he created his most Baroque work, the large oval with the stucco relief of the victorious Louis XIV on horseback. In some of his portrait busts Coysevox achieved a degree of freedom of expression and penetration that presaged the dawn of a new age. But the only really non-conformist artist of this period was Puget; his extreme form of individualism made it impossible for him to get commissions at court during Colbert's lifetime. Trained in Italy under Pietro da Cortona, he worked for six years in Genoa (1661–7) and spent the rest of his life at Toulon and Marseilles. His most famous works, the *Milo of Crotona* (Louvre, 1671–83) and the relief of *Alexander and Diogenes* (Louvre, 1671–93) reveal the tempestuous disposition of this great artist who owed no less to Michelangelo than to the Roman Baroque masters.

The Catholic Spanish Netherlands were closely tied to the artistic ideology of the south. Rubens and Van Dyck completely dominated the first half of the seventeenth century and their influence did not abate for several generations. Their immediate successors, painters such as Abraham van Diepenbeeck (1596–1675), Theodor van Thulden (1606–76) and Erasmus Quellin (1607–78), were entirely obscured by the greater stars. The only exception is the Antwerp master Jakob Jordaens (1593–1678) who excelled in giving full-blooded portrayals of Flemish life; but in the last phase of his career his powers declined.

Many of the Flemish painters began with an Italianising, often Caravaggiesque manner, only to embrace at the end the classicising French idiom. Bertholet Flémalle (1614–75) is a case in point. His pupil Gérard Lairesse (1640–1711), the author of a famous work on the principles of design, was entirely swayed by the French Academy. Even a genre painter like David Teniers the Younger (1610–90), who had an enormous practice at Antwerp and Brussels, did not escape the equalising tendencies of his age. Lairesse settled in Amsterdam where he enjoyed an excessive reputation. It is remarkable that at the end of the century his shallow allegories and mythologies with their courtly French imprint evoked such enthusiasm in puritanical Holland; for the course of Dutch painting had gone in a different direction.

In contrast to the Catholic south, Protestant Holland had almost no place for official painting. Freed from the patronage and tutelage of the Church of Rome as well as from the shackles imposed by sovereigns and courts, Dutch artists refuted the grand manner together with the restrictions of the traditional iconography and extended their quest far beyond the limits dictated by the southern art theory. The whole range of the visible world had become their haunt. Thus seventeenth-century Holland witnessed an unparalleled blossoming of intimate religious imagery, of the still-life, landscape and seascape; of the conversation piece and all types of genre painting; of portraiture of individual burghers and of burgher corporations. Many of the Dutch artists worked for the art market rather than for patrons. As a result the art dealer and the sales room, not totally unknown before, assumed key positions in regulating supply and demand. In this respect as in many others the Dutch constellation foreshadows that of the nineteenth and twentieth centuries. Moreover, the average Dutchman regarded pictures as an investment 'so that it is an ordinary thing to find a common farmer lay out two or three thousand pounds in this commodity' (Evelyn). Indeed, Dutch paintings were soon collected in every European country.

All the different branches of painting practised in Holland had long pedigrees; but now they developed into highly specialised fields. Jan van Goyen (1596–1656), Aelbert Cuyp (1620–91), Karel Dujardin (1622–78), Jacob van Ruisdael (1628/9–82), Adriaen van de Velde (1636–72), and Meindert Hobbema (1638–1709) painted only landscapes; Pieter Claesz (1597/8–1661), Willem Heda (1594–1680), Jan de Heem (1606–83/4), Abraham van Beyeren (1620/1–*c.* 1675) and Willem Kalf (1622–93) mainly still-lifes; the two Willem van de Velde (father and son), Jan van de Cappelle (1624–79), and Ludolf Backhuyzen (1630–1708) only marine paintings; Jan van der Heyden (1637–1712) and Gerrit Berckheyde (1638–98) only townscapes; Pieter Saenredam (1597–1665) and Emanuel de Witte (1617–92) only interiors of churches.

Specialisation was even carried a step further. Not a few painters concentrated on specialities within their chosen field. Aert van der Neer (1603–77) is the painter of moonshine and winter landscapes; Philips Wouwermans (1619–68) of landscapes with horses, and Paulus Potter (1625–54) of landscapes with cattle; Philips Koninck (1619–88) paints panoramic views, and Allaert van Everdingen (1621–75) rocky scenery with waterfalls; Jan Weenix (1640–1719) is the master of the hunting still-life, while Melchior d'Hondecoeter (1636–95) renders poultry.

Various forms of the *bourgeois* and upper-class genre and conversation piece were the preserve of a large group of artists, among them Pieter Codde (1599/1600–78), Anthonie Palamedesz (*c.* 1601–73), Gerard Dou (1613–75), Gerard Terborch (1617–81), Samuel van Hoogstraten (1627–78), Gabriel Metsu (1629–67), Pieter de Hooch (1629–*c.* 1677), Jan Vermeer van Delft (1632–75), and Pieter Janssens (*c.* 1640–*c.* 1700). The lower genre had high-class practitioners in Jan Steen (1626–79), Adriaen van Ostade (1610–85), and his pupils Cornelis Bega (1620–64) and Cornelis Dusart (1660–1704).

The result of these endless pursuits seemed a hitherto unknown revelation of microcosmic life in all its facets. Those working within the classical tenets thoroughly disapproved. Lairesse censured: 'We often hear with wonder that painters persuade one another that...it is enough to follow nature....[These painters] imitate life just as they see it, without any difference....[Whereas a painter should paint nature] not as it ordinarily appears, but as it ought to be in its greatest perfection.'[1] But in fact far from adhering to nature 'as they see it', these Dutch painters were tied to tradition in a thousand different ways. It should never be forgotten that vision is a compound of ideas, concepts, and traditions deposited in our minds and that pure vision and pure portrayals of vision must be regarded as a popular legend. It clearly follows that the Dutch painters too were fenced in by limitations which are briefly and efficiently described as 'style'.

[1] *Het Groot Schilderboek* (Amsterdam, 1707). The above digest from the English edition, *The Art of Painting* (London, 1778), p. 100.

Pieter de Hooch's career may be considered as an example for many. His early, Baroque phase characterised by strong chiaroscuro is connected with the circle of Frans Hals, with Palamedesz and Codde. Under the influence of Rembrandt's pupil Carel Fabritius (1622–54) and of Vermeer his pictures during his 'classical' phase, the decade 1655–65, have a warm and luminous quality. At this time he produced the masterly interiors with domestic scenes for which he is famed. All these works are as firmly and as solidly constructed as any Renaissance picture. A checkerboard floor parallel to the picture plane defines the space, and the composition in depth, the vista through doorways and yards is also arranged in parallel layers. Each figure of the seemingly incidental groups is firmly anchored in the picture by significant spatial co-ordinates. But now a number of pictorial devices are used to produce the impression of life 'as it ordinarily appears'. The artist always chooses a close viewpoint (for which there was a long tradition in Dutch painting), so that the picture is not relegated to an ideal sphere but draws the beholder forcefully into it. Other contrivances such as the off-centre vanishing point and the placing of the incident in one corner of the room add to the impression of casual life. Later in the 1660's and in the 1670's there follows an 'academic' phase under French influence: the compositions harden, the handling becomes facile, the tonality cool, fashionable groups and elegant anecdotes replace the domestic scenes. This development echoes three social phases: the heroic age following the wars of liberation, the comparatively peaceful phase of the thriving Dutch *bourgeoisie*, and the aristocratisation of society under the shadow of Louis XIV's supremacy.

Certain aspects of de Hooch's development may safely be generalised. Thus between the 1640's and 1660's emphasis is laid on middle-class homeliness. From then on preference is given to the rendering of polite society that follows the dictate of etiquette. Terborch, Metsu and Hoogstraten illustrate this current. Frans van Mieris (1635–81) and Godfried Schalcken (1643–1706) amplify the cool, hard, and precious character of the works of their teacher, Gerard Dou. Caspar Netscher (1639–84), Terborch's pupil, specialised in painting idealised persons clad in costly materials. Bega's pictures show that even the popular genre lost its rough conviviality.

Such observations can easily be supplemented by others. At the beginning of his career, Cuyp shows the warm palette of Rembrandt's middle period. Later his palette cools and the structure of his landscapes becomes increasingly classical. Hobbema's work appears thin and disjointed compared with the density and cohesion of Ruisdael's landscapes. Even Rembrandt's pupils perform the stylistic gyration. Nicolaes Maes (1632–93) is perhaps the most conspicuous case. A close follower of the master in the 1650's, he changed completely in the 1660's to painting portraits of high society in noble attitudes and with a palette of light broken tones. Finally, it must be said that even the great Vermeer did not work outside the pale. His early pictures reveal connections with the Italian Baroque (for example, *Christ in the House of Mary and Martha*, 1654/5; Edinburgh). Between the later 1650's and the mid-1660's, when he is most his own, his compositions are of an infinite simplicity and the velvety luminosity of his palette is insuperable. But already the *Love Letter* of about 1666 (Amsterdam) shows a peculiar disruption of the pictorial space and a frigid polish. The intensity of his vision slackened in accord with the temper of the time.

Compared with the magnificent flowering of painting, the sister arts in both parts of the Netherlands were less important; but while the south witnessed a rich development of Baroque architecture and sculpture, the north had little demand for sculptural decorations in churches and public buildings and, moreover, soon turned against the boisterous style in architecture closely associated with the Catholic Restoration. Even before the middle of the century Jacob van Campen (1595–1657) and Pieter Post (1608–69) revolutionised Dutch architecture by introducing an austere, puritanical classicism, the greatest monument of which was van Campen's Town Hall in Amsterdam (1648–55). The third great architect of the period, Philips Vingboons (1608–75), tended towards a more elegant French interpretation of the style.

The imposing southern churches of that time belong to another world. They strike the beholder as being closely tied to the Roman Baroque; but they also contain French features, and their rich, heavy-handed decoration has roots in the native tradition. Willem Hessius's (1601–90) Jesuit church, St Michel at Louvain (1650–71), Luc Fayd'herbe's (1617–97) churches, of which the unconventional Notre-Dame d'Hanswyck at Mechlin may be singled out, and the façade of the Béguinage church in Brussels (1657–76) by an unknown architect, are splendid examples of the style. The row of narrow, high houses with their profusion of miscellaneous decoration on the marvellous Grand' Place in Brussels (1696–9) reveals how completely domestic architecture preserved its local flavour.

Sculptural activity in the south was to a considerable extent in the hands of a few productive families among whom the Duquesnoy, Quellin and Verbruggen are the most important. Less influenced by French sculpture than one would expect, they blended in various ways Bernini's Italian Baroque with Rubens's Flemish realism. None came closer to translating Rubens into the plastic medium than Luc Fayd'herbe who educated a large school. The extremely productive Jean Delcour (1627–1707), by contrast, adhered to the style of the Bernini succession. The dearth of sculptors in Holland resulted in Artus Quellin the Elder (1609–68) being commissioned with the extensive decoration of the Amsterdam Town Hall, the largest task of this kind in Holland. Among his assistants was the Dutchman Rombout Verhulst (1624–96) who, together with

Willem de Keyser, was responsible for the overloaded, unaccentuated tomb of Admiral Tromp (Oude Kerk, Delft; 1655–8), the prototype of many Dutch tombs of the second half of the century. Verhulst was the most influential Baroque sculptor in Holland, but his style and that of his successors must be regarded as a dispassionate branch of the more vital Belgian school.

The position of the arts in England was very different from that prevailing in the Low Countries and France. The Restoration produced neither a splendid court patronage and an authoritative court style after the French model, nor a broad *bourgeois* public with artistic interests as in Holland. Patronage of the arts was taken in hand by the nobility and gentry, whose taste was far from sophisticated. The Civil War and Commonwealth were in fact derogatory to a continuation of the refined artistic interests which had centred in the court of Charles I. Twenty-five years after the Restoration, William Aglionby, the author of a book on painting, assessed the repercussions of the broken thread in these words: 'Our Nobility and Gentry, except some few, who have eminently showed their Kindness for this noble Art, they are generally speaking no Judges, and therefore can be no Promoters of an Art that lies all in nice Observations', and lamented 'that of all the Civilized Nations in Europe we are the only that want Curiosity for Artists'.[1]

In spite of such unfavourable prospects, there was one architect of far more than insular importance, Sir Christopher Wren (1632–1723). He had begun as a scientist. As early as 1657 he had been appointed Professor of Astronomy at Gresham College, London, and in 1661 Savilian Professor of Astronomy at Oxford. He was one of the founder members of the Royal Society[2] and never lost interest in scientific affairs. At the age of thirty he made his first somewhat amateurish architectural designs. His great opportunity came after the Fire of London (1666) when wide scope was offered to his inexhaustible creative energy. In 1669 he was appointed Surveyor-General, and the rebuilding of the destroyed churches and of St Paul's as well as the maintenance and construction of royal residences and public buildings fell to him. Between 1670 and the 1690's he partially or wholly rebuilt no less than fifty-five London churches of which thirty-four survived up to the Blitz of 1940. Many of these churches are bold essays in centralised planning (St Stephen Walbrook, 1672–87; St Swithin, 1677–85; St Mary Abchurch, 1681–6) and, although his repertory of forms is conventional, the structural principles are often new and have hardly their equal on the Continent.

Wren's greatest achievement and one of the finest post-Renaissance buildings in Europe is St Paul's Cathedral (1675–1710), crowned by a masterful dome which still dominates the silhouette of the city. The

[1] *Painting Illustrated in Three Dialogues* (London, 1685). [2] See above, ch. III, pp. 50–1.

building of the cathedral taxed Wren's ingenuity for several decades and hundreds of drawings bear witness to the many revisions which the plan as well as every detail underwent in the course of time. Thus the slow growth of the design reveals an empirical approach to architecture which reflects the spirit of the Royal Society. The same empirical, rational and anti-authoritarian spirit informed what may be called Wren's arbitrary use of the current architectural vocabulary. He incorporated in his design motifs from Serlio and Inigo Jones, Palladio and Bernini, Bramante and Michelangelo, Pietro da Cortona and Borromini, Hardouin-Mansart and many others; but the result is a homogeneous work, the cool reserve of which exactly parallels the Late Baroque classicism in vogue on the Continent.

Compared with St Paul's and the city churches most of the other Wren buildings shrink in significance. Winchester Palace erected for Charles II (1683–85) no longer exists; the magnificent plans for Whitehall Palace, made after the fire of 1698, remained on paper; Hampton Court Palace (begun 1689), an adaptation and enlargement of Cardinal Wolsey's house to serve as residence for William and Mary, is Wren's least successful creation. But the grand design for Greenwich Hospital vies with his ecclesiastical work. Queen Mary sponsored the erection of a hospital for seamen as a counterpart to the Royal Hospital for soldiers at Chelsea which Wren had built between 1682 and 1691. The palace which John Webb, Inigo Jones's pupil, had constructed for Charles II (1663–9) on the bank of the Thames was to form part of the design. Wren devised a noble layout with two successive narrowing piazzas axially orientated towards Inigo Jones's Queen's House which concludes the vista. This stately design, one of the most ambitious in seventeenth-century England, began to take shape in 1694. Its pretentious size owes not a little to Versailles, while the two long colonnades and the two high domed structures facing each other take up and transmute problems first considered in the piazzas of St Peter's and del Popolo in Rome.

Wren's work entirely dominates this period. Next to him Sir Roger Pratt (1620–85), a gentleman architect, may be mentioned, for he created the prototype of the Restoration country house at Coleshill, Berkshire (1649–62; destroyed 1952), a massive and imposing structure, less classical and more insular than Inigo Jones's buildings during the Caroline era. Hugh May (1622–84), an intimate of Pepys and Evelyn, orientated himself towards Dutch classicism. Eltham Lodge, Kent (1663–4), his finest work, might almost have been erected in Holland. The younger William Talman (1650–1719) is noteworthy for the monumental south front at Chatsworth, the palatial house of the Duke of Devonshire in Derbyshire, to which he contributed in various ways between 1687 and 1696. Talman's later work was overshadowed by the great architects Nicholas Hawksmoor (1661–1736) and John Vanbrugh (1664–1726), whose association began at Castle Howard, Yorkshire, just before the turn of the century.

It was they who for the next two decades replaced Wren's unemotional manner by an unorthodox, massive, and emotionally stirring style with conspicuous Baroque idiosyncrasies.

No British sculptor of the period can lay claim to great distinction. John Bushnell (*c.* 1630–1701), who studied in France and Rome and worked for years in Venice, practised an insipid form of Italian Late Baroque in England. Caius Gabriel Cibber (1630–1700) left a rare example of elaborate Baroque allegory in the grand manner in his relief at the base of the Monument, London (1674). Late in his life he gave proof of considerable accomplishment at both Hampton Court and St Paul's. Edward Pierce (*c.* 1630–95) has to his credit a few busts of exceptional quality, the finest of which, that of Wren (1673; Ashmolean Museum, Oxford) shows an intimacy and directness of approach reminiscent of Coysevox. Grinling Gibbons (1648–1721), finally, excelled as a woodcarver of great technical skill. The realism of his 'inhabited' garlands and hangings shows him strongly influenced by Low Country sculpture.

In contrast to the continental position in both Catholic and Protestant countries, English painting was essentially focused on portraiture. Such mediocre practitioners as Robert Walker (*c.* 1605–*c.* 1685) and Isaac Fuller (*c.* 1605–72) kept the Van Dyck tradition alive after the master's death in 1641. But already during the Commonwealth Peter Lely from Soest in Westphalia (1618–80) emerged as the foremost painter in England. His stature in the reigns of Charles II and James II can only be compared with Van Dyck's in the reign of Charles I; but his fashionable portraits, ably painted in the international facile and affected style, entirely lack Van Dyck's warmth, genius and depth of characterisation. Lely mapped out the path of English portraiture for a long time to come. Sir Godfrey Kneller (1646/9–1723) from Lübeck, who had studied in Amsterdam under Rembrandt's pupil Ferdinand Bol, settled in England in 1674 and became the heir to the Lely empire. A painter of considerable talent, he degraded his profession by innumerable glib portraits which he turned out from his 'streamlined' studio.

Most other branches of painting were also practised by foreigners who made England their home for longer or shorter periods. The allegorical fresco in the grand manner was championed by the Italian Antonio Verrio (*c.* 1639–1707) from the mid-1670's onwards and by the Frenchman Louis Laguerre (1663–1721), Lebrun's pupil, who appeared in England in 1683/4. Marine painting was introduced by the Dutchman Willem van de Velde (1611–93) and his son, Willem the Younger (1633–1707). The topographical landscape had able representatives in the Bohemian Wenceslas Hollar (1607–77), the Dutchman Leonard Knyff (1650–1721), and the Fleming Jan Siberechts (1627–*c.* 1698). It was not till the second quarter of the eighteenth century that a native British school of painting of extraordinary vitality arose.

The devastations of the Thirty Years War led to a rupture of artistic activity in Germany, and the process of recuperation was very slow. Since the autonomous development of the arts had for so long been strangled, Germans became dependent on foreign artists and foreign training. The Catholic south tended towards Italy, and the Protestant north towards Holland. Thus the mediocre Joachim Sandrart (1606–88) from Frankfurt, well known through his contemporary history of artists, the *Teutsche Academie* (Nuremberg, 1675), and the more interesting Heinrich Schönfeld (1609–75), who was mainly active in Augsburg, spent years of their lives in Italy; on the other hand, Jürgen Ovens from Slesvig (1623–79) and Michael Leopold Willmann from Königsberg (1630–1706) received their training in Holland and in their work sentimentalised Van Dyck and Rembrandt. Such rather philistine painters hardly foreshadowed the wonderful flowering of the Baroque fresco in Germany and Austria after 1700: the measure of independence, creative richness, imaginative freedom and visionary depth achieved by painters like Johann Michael Rottmayr (1654–1730), Cosmas Damian Asam (1686–1739) and scores of others.

Italian sculptors, stucco workers, and architects, not always of the first rank, had a considerable share in the German and Austrian production of the later seventeenth century; but from about 1660 native sculptors appear in fair numbers working in an Italianate Late Baroque or, on occasions, carrying on an indigenous tradition stemming from the late Gothic. Balthasar Permoser (1651–1732), outstanding among them, had a typical curriculum. Before becoming court sculptor in Dresden (1689), he spent many years in Italy and his work is permeated with recollections of Bernini, Puget, and the Venetian Baroque. Unexpectedly, Germany had in Andreas Schlüter (1664–1714) a Late Baroque sculptor of truly international format, and it is even stranger that he was a North German. In 1694 he was appointed court sculptor in Berlin. His masterpiece, the equestrian statue of the Great Elector (1692–1703), holds its own next to the great equestrian statues of all time. Stylistically it is orientated towards Italian Late Baroque movement rather than towards French classicism. Like German painting, German sculpture had a golden age in the new century. This is true mainly of Bavaria and the districts along the Danube. Sculptors now replaced Permoser's and Schlüter's international Baroque by an ecstatic, graceful, and sometimes even effeminate style of a distinctly native character.

Palace and church architecture, too, was at first almost entirely in the hands of Italians. St Cajetan, the Theatine church in Munich, the most imposing post-war structure, was begun by Agostino Barelli in 1663 after the model of S. Andrea della Valle in Rome and continued by Enrico Zuccalli after 1675. And when the Germans came into their own with Johann Dientzenhofer's cathedral at Fulda (1704–12), they first adhered to the Italian tradition. Barelli also began the palace at Nymphenburg near Munich (1663), and Lorenzo Bedogni and Girolamo Sartorio the palace at Herrenhausen near Hanover (1665), while Zuccalli designed the palace at Schleissheim near Munich (1701). Vienna lived under the shadow of the Infidel until the siege of 1683.[1] It was only after that date that a magnificent era of reconstruction began. This task was mainly in the hands of two men of genius, Fischer von Erlach (1656–1723) and Johann Lukas von Hildebrandt (1668–1745); innumerable gifted architects brought about the most brilliant architectural revival Germany and Austria had known since the Middle Ages.

While England, Germany and Austria developed into flourishing art centres at the beginning of the eighteenth century, the Low Countries and Spain saw no such renaissance. In neither case can the decline be dissociated from political and economic calamities. After the great first half of the seventeenth century the degeneration of painting in Spain was rapid and irrevocable. To be sure, throughout the second half painters of considerable talent were still at work. The reign of the last Habsburg king, Charles II (1665–1700), marks the culmination of national decay. His court painter, Don Juan Carreño de Miranda (1614–85), was but a feeble counterfeit of Philip IV's court painter Velasquez. With Claudio Coello (1642–93), Carreño's successor, the Madrid School came to an end.

The course of events in other Spanish art centres was not much different. In Valencia painting died with Ribalta's pupil, Jeronimo Jacinto Espinosa (1600–80). Granada had her last practitioners of considerable stature in the talented Alonso Cano (1601–67), painter, sculptor and architect, in Pedro de Moya (1610–66), and Juan de Sevilla (1643–95). Next to Zurbaran's pupil, Antonio del Castillo y Saavedra (1616–68), no name need be mentioned in Cordoba. Seville had a flourishing school during the seventeenth century headed by Bartolomé Esteban Murillo (1618–82). While some minor pupils carried Murillo's manner over into the eighteenth century, the death of the temperamental Juan de Valdés Leal (1622–91), a slipshod craftsman but a highly gifted colourist, brought to an end the great tradition of the Seville School.

All these painters turned Velasquez's and Zurbaran's sturdy and statuesque realism into a refined, sophisticated and, on occasion, agitated and confused manner, and replaced the compelling directness of the older masters by a virtuosity which often strikes the beholder as melodramatic, slick and insincere. Murillo, the greatest of this group, famed for his many pictures of the Immaculate Conception, developed, according to Spanish terminology, from a cool to a warm, and finally to a vaporous style; these terms indicate the course which his art took between the 1640's and his death in 1682. The muffled colours and forms and the sentimentality of his late style are characteristic of Spanish painting in the

[1] See below, ch. XXI, pp. 515–17.

last decades of the century. By and large, the general trend of the development in Spain parallels that in the rest of Europe.

Just as the most effusive decorations in Italy belong to the Late Baroque, just as France has nothing to offer that compares in splendour with the Galerie des Glaces, so Spain, during the last years of the old dynasty, began to turn to a boisterous and passionate decorative style of unexpected originality. In contrast to Spanish painting, the Spanish architecture of the seventeenth century was rather barren. Few buildings compare in grandeur and eccentricity with Cano's façade of Granada cathedral (1664). For centuries the Spanish Church had focused special attention on the high altar and the retable or altar screen, and it is here that the Spanish Late Baroque excelled. Richly ornate designs appear soon after 1650; from then all the three arts combine in producing fascinating Baroque works. Bernardo Simón de Pineda's high altar of the Caridad, Seville (1670–3), José Benito Churriguera's (1665–1725) retables in such churches as Segovia cathedral (1686–90) and San Esteban at Salamanca (1693–6) are polychrome structures of huge dimensions, vigorously organised by corkscrew columns spun over with decoration and peopled with lively statuary. The vast majority of the architectural and decorative work of these innovators, among whom besides the Churriguera family artists such as Leonardo de Figueroa (*c.* 1650–1730), Pedro de Ribera (*c.* 1683–1742), Narciso Tomé (d. 1742), and, above all, Francisco Hurtado (1669–1725) must be counted, belong to the first decades of the eighteenth century. The most fascinating monument of this style is the exuberantly decorated Sacristy of the Cartuja of Granada (1713–47) which has inconclusively been attributed to Hurtado.

Sculptors of this period gave their best in ecstatic polychrome figures of saints in which Spanish mysticism and naturalism are wedded. Pedro de Mena's (1628–88) St Francis in Toledo cathedral (1663) is the principal example. It is a characteristic sign of the time that in the work of his successor, José de Mora (1642–1724), the rendering of rapture appears more rhetorical and precious (St Bruno, Granada).

Towards the end of the seventeenth century the international classicism to a large extent imposed by the French Academy lost its attraction. A new spirit, anti-dogmatic, vigorous and enthusiastic, and at the same time distinctly national, becomes discernible in many places: witness the sudden marvellous ascendancy of Venetian painting, the rich and elegant Baroque decorations in Genoa, the rise of a luxuriant architecture in Sicily, the unexpected bloom of a typically German and Austrian Baroque, the turn to a virile and dramatic Baroque architecture in England, the exuberance of the decorative style in Spain, and, above all, the Baroque freedom aspired to by the generation of Coysevox, Permoser and Schlüter. All these roughly contemporary events have a distinct physiognomy of their own, formed by national and local idiosyncrasies, and seem therefore unconnected. None the less, fertile ideas always had an irresistible capacity of transmission. The new approach started, it may be claimed, in the stronghold of academic indoctrination, in Paris herself; that it had intra-European reverberations cannot therefore be doubted.

The first move lay with Roger de Piles, a Paris art theoretician (1635–1709), who in 1673 published his *Dialogue sur le coloris* which had the effect of a bombshell, for he maintained that Poussin, the idol of the Academy, was a failure as a colourist. He exalted Rubens, the master of the great Baroque sweep and the colourist *par excellence*, at the expense of Poussin. A heated controversy ensued between the supporters of Poussin and of Rubens, the 'Poussinists' and the 'Rubenists' as they were called. Worse was to come. In his *Conversations sur la couleur* of 1677 de Piles turned against the authority of classical antiquity itself. He maintained that the close adherence to ancient models had ruined Poussin. Before the end of the century the controversy had been decided in de Piles's favour. His friend, the painter Charles de La Fosse (1636–1716), a determined 'Rubenist', was elected Director of the Academy. So the artists themselves discredited the classical dogma and the way was open for the free development of French painting in the early eighteenth century.

Roger de Piles was capable of verbalising the problems that beset young artists of his day; he thus helped to prepare a conscious resurgence of a Baroque wave after the generation's fervent belief in the eternal values of the classical ideology. His sally against the infallibility of the Academy has another important aspect: de Piles opened the flood-gates of lay criticism. The position in Paris was unparalleled, for the French capital was not only the seat of the most powerful centralised government, but saw also the growth of a well educated and well informed middle class with a passionate interest in matters of art. This sensitive public began to enjoy discussion and controversy, and it had its own ideas about the purpose of art. An anti-rationalist tendency made its entry, for, in contrast to the principles of the Academy, the public demanded that art should please rather than instruct and should appeal to the emotions rather than to the reasoning faculties. Like the classical theory, this new position too had been prepared in Italy. It was the painter Pietro da Cortona and the Jesuit Ottonelli who, in their *Treatise on Painting* (1652), strongly advocated for the first time the hedonistic principle of delight as the purpose of painting. The inevitable sequel happened in Paris: in his *Réflexions critiques sur la poésie et la peinture* (1719) the Abbé du Bos enthroned the educated public, the art enthusiasts, as supreme judges in matters of art. Thus the late seventeenth century saw conditions arise in the relation of artists and public which had a momentous influence on the arts of the eighteenth century and, in a broader perspective, even on those of modern times.

CHAPTER VIII

THE SOCIAL FOUNDATIONS OF STATES

THE last fifty years of the seventeenth century were so eventful and saw such alterations in the outward appearance of western and central European life that prima facie this may be regarded as a significant period in the development of social classes and in the related development of institutions. This presumption may be tested by tracing some of the major changes and their connections, and it will be convenient to begin with the most obvious, the changes in the social aspects of war. It has been written, and it may be accepted as established, that from somewhere about 1560 to somewhere about 1660 Europe underwent a 'military revolution'.[1] Armament, tactics and strategy had changed. They now required new kinds of discipline, a new organisation of fleets and standing armies, new and more intensive applications of technical and general knowledge. The financial and administrative machinery of supply, the systems of political control and the social composition of the armed forces were all remodelled.

The effects of the military revolution were shown by a salient fact of social history: armies and fleets were much larger than before. Leaving out of account the armies of the Turks, we may say that the largest force ever previously united under a single command had been the 175,000 men under the orders of Gustavus Adolphus in 1632, but this was a momentary combination which was not maintained, whereas, in his navy and his army, Louis XIV kept more than double that number in service for years together. There were some countries, such as Spain, which were unable to enrol as many men as they had done before; but there were new military powers, such as Brandenburg-Prussia, which had 2000 men after it made peace in 1640 and 30,000 when it was at peace in 1688. For some of the powers naval armaments were not a standing necessity like land-armaments; but the fleets of Europe also increased. The general total of men under arms was much greater, and the increase was permanent. There have been further increases, but there has never been a general decline. Although the population of Europe was growing, and the countries where it diminished were exceptional, these armies and fleets were not only larger but they absorbed a larger proportion of the populations from which they were drawn.

These facts have been cited in support of the theory that war is primarily a means by which society is relieved from the excessive pressure of rising

[1] By Professor Michael Roberts in his inaugural lecture *The Military Revolution* (*s.a.*, published at Belfast in 1956).

population. Sociologists who accept this view have described war as deferred infanticide and have tried to prove by statistics that in certain periods the numbers of deaths resulting from war vary inversely with the rates of infant mortality. They hold that an excessively growing population builds up an explosive structure. As applied to this period the theory begins with the probably correct diagnosis that the total European population was increasing and pressing on the means of subsistence. In France, for instance, it is believed to have risen steadily from about 1600. There was some emigration, including that of the Huguenots, but from 1666 onwards Colbert legislated for the encouragement of early marriages and large families. In 1678–88 France was more populous than ever before. The slaughter and famines of 1688–1714 brought a reduction of perhaps more than 5 per cent, and no comparable explosive instability recurred until the late eighteenth century.

In the present state of knowledge regarding demographic facts it must be objected that little of this interpretation is capable of proof. For France and also for the other countries, the primary data on which contemporaries and nineteenth-century demographers relied—parish registers, taxation returns and the like—were defective, and even now critical study in this field has barely begun.[1] There is no reason to suppose that the measures of Colbert had any effect worth mentioning. Even if they had, their effect on the total population of the country, irrespective of occupations and age-groups, would not necessarily throw light on the causation of wars. Recruiting did not simply mean the withdrawal of a proportion of all French men of military age for the armed forces. It was in the main restricted to the less skilled and less firmly settled men; it was still almost entirely voluntary, except for the 'recruiting-sergeant' Hunger; and it was international. The French army included Englishmen, Scotsmen, Irishmen, Germans, Spaniards and Swiss. The armies opposed to it were equally composite. If all the facts come to be investigated it may prove that France alone had an explosive demographic situation. Such a conclusion might well have a bearing on the differences of opinion as to the relative aggressiveness of the Powers; but at present it cannot be justified. For Europe in general it has not been shown that the growth of armies absorbed the available supplies of men, nor that the pressure of numbers drove men to the colours. There is much evidence to indicate that governments were hard put to it to enrol their reluctant subjects; and there is also much to indicate that they reached the limits of their capacity to provide arms, munitions, ships, equipment, transport, rations and pay.

Demographic information can do little by itself to explain either the

[1] See P. Goubert ('Les registres paroissiaux' in *Annales*, vol. IX (1954)) who considers that information from this source only becomes good about 1730. Little is known about changes in the expectation of life, and consequently in the proportion of men of military age to total population, in any country in the seventeenth century.

causation of wars or the size of armies in this period; nor is it to be expected that it will do more than help to block out some of the conditions under which multiple social forces operated. The explosive structure which precedes the detonation of a war is a structure of the whole society, just as war is an activity of many elements in society. The military revolution was a complex of changes each of which had its part in a reciprocal interaction of causes and consequences extending throughout the life of society. Unless and until some new analysis resolves it into simpler components we may specify this revolution as one of the factors of change. Among the others the easiest to recognise are the economic factors. This period fell within the age during which capitalism was spreading through Europe. Different systems of law in relation to the family, status and heredity, along with different constitutional systems, crossed and complicated the working of economic factors, but in itself the system of private property was a perpetual source of change, if only because, when men are free to do what they like with their own, some of them will make money and some will lose it. As we have seen, broadly speaking, Europe was growing more populous. Again speaking broadly, it was growing richer. At any rate in most countries the higher strata of society collectively disposed of greater wealth and the States commanded greater resources for the purposes of war. About the fortunes of the peasants, labourers and artisans it is harder to generalise because, even apart from the disturbances of war, there were wide divergences between different localities. Interpenetrating with these economic factors were others of which one in particular was characteristic of the period. This was the movement of thought which is commonly referred to as the scientific movement.[1]

Among the social effects of the scientific movement the easiest to trace are those which it produced through improvements in technology, that is in industry, transport, agriculture and warfare. It also had direct effects in government and social organisation. These are often difficult to trace because the results of applying scientific habits of mind in such matters are much the same as those of applying common sense. The scientific movement itself was not by any means confined to natural science, and within natural science the distinction, real or unreal, between 'pure' and 'applied' had scarcely crystallised from undifferentiated 'natural knowledge'.[2] In the widest sense the movement was a tidal wave of efficient thinking, and its results resembled those of the efficiency of men of action. The determination to govern well existed quite independently of astronomy, which served to improve navigation, or metallurgy or chemistry, which were of some use in industry, though not yet in agriculture. In comparison with

[1] See ch. III, above.

[2] It was explicitly with reference to mathematics that Dr Johnson wrote in *The Rambler*, no. 14 (1750), p. 5, about 'the difference between pure science, which has to do only with ideas, and the application of its laws to the use of life'. Chambers's *Cyclopaedia* (London, 1728), I, ii, distinguishes 'Natural and Scientifical' from 'Artificial and Technical' knowledge.

this practical determination the attempts to formulate scientific principles of human nature and society had negligible, or at least scarcely traceable, results; but they did make a contribution, and there is one sphere where these results can be seen clearly. This is the sphere of mathematics, then the most precise and the most progressive of all studies. In mathematics the distinction between 'pure' and 'mixed' was already familiar,[1] and it now came to be understood that mixed mathematics included social as well as technological applications.

The simplest example of a suggestion for improving administration by directly applying mathematical knowledge is that of John de Witt's proposed reform of life-annuities. For centuries public authorities in the Netherlands had raised loans in return for which they made annual payments for the lifetime of the lenders: the town of Tournay is known to have done so in 1229. Since they did not know how long any of the lenders would live, they could not foresee how much would have to be paid out by way of annuities in any future year. The whole proceeding was speculative. By the middle of the seventeenth century, when their great wars began, the Estates of Holland were beginning to apply rational financial technique to their borrowing, and in 1655 they converted some of their loans to take advantage of a lower rate of interest. They had, however, no figures on which to base a bargain of this kind with their life-annuitants. About that time mathematicians discovered from the new study of the laws of probability how to calculate the chances of death and survival. In 1669 this idea was discussed in private letters between the great Christiaan Huygens and his brother. Whether it came round to John de Witt from either of them is not known; he may have hit upon it independently; at any rate in 1671 in a memorandum which became justly famous he laid it before his masters, the Estates of Holland. This reached the conclusion that with the rate of interest at 4 per cent a life-annuity at sixteen years' purchase was an advantageous investment. It is not to be supposed that the members of the Estates could follow the calculation. Their pensionary took the precaution of annexing to it a supporting declaration by Johannes Hudde, a mathematician who was a member of the Amsterdam municipal council and later became burgomaster there. From that beginning actuarial science grew rapidly and spread widely in public finance and private insurance business.[2]

There was indeed still no true statistical basis for de Witt's figures for the expectation of life. The first tolerably good life-table was calculated from the data of mortality in Breslau by Edmond Halley in 1693. Nor did the new principle carry all before it. In the same year, 1693, the

[1] See, for instance, J. Wilkins, *Mathematicall Magick* (London, 1648), Dedication and pp. 95–7.

[2] The memorandum was published in Amsterdam. There is a French translation by P. J. L. de Chateleux, with commentary, *Le rapport de Johan de Witt sur le calcul des rentes viagères* (The Hague, 1937).

English government, needing money badly for purposes of war, sold life-annuities of 14 per cent, and two years later it invited annuitants to convert their annuities into an 'estate' for 96 years at the low rate of 4½ years purchase. In neither case did it make any distinction for age. In Holland as late as 1810 the municipality of The Hague sold life-annuities at a rate which did not vary with the ages of the persons during whose survival they were payable. When Halley calculated his life-table, however, educated opinion had accepted the idea that mathematics as applied to government could form a regular department of knowledge. In the 1650's Sir William Petty was employed in constructing maps and tables for the allocation of land in Ireland. From this work on the ground he moved to wider reasonings, and he invented phrases which claimed that these were at least analogous to scientific thinking. In 1672 he wrote of 'political survey' and (having at one time taught human anatomy in Oxford) in 1691 he published his *Political Anatomy of Ireland.* A third phrase, which he used in the title of a book published in 1683, 'political arithmetic', passed into general currency. English governments did what they could to use statistics. The two spheres in which they hoped for valuable results were vital statistics and trade statistics, the two spheres in which governments can most easily collect large bodies of numerical facts. In vital statistics they made little or no progress, and none could well be made until the institution of a periodic national census, which came much later. In commercial statistics they did better. In 1696, at a time of war and financial crisis, they inaugurated the first statistical office successfully conducted by any western European State, that of the inspector-general of imports and exports. Commercial figures prepared in this office were used in parliamentary discussions and in negotiations with foreign powers; but the officials who handled them knew that they were defective and, throughout most of the eighteenth century, political arithmetic remained more an aspiration and a programme than an effective element in the practice of States.

The comprehensive and systematic collection of facts, the method of survey, was not a private invention of Sir William Petty but a favourite method of social inquiry at that time. One of its instruments was the questionnaire. In England the Royal Society drew up a list of headings under which travellers abroad should collect scientific information. Some of its early members reported as others had done before them on the resources of countries overseas, combining scientific with economic observations. In France science was harnessed more closely to government than in England. The *Académie des Sciences* was an essential organ of the official work of Colbert; and it devoted much attention to technology. Although it did not intrude on State concerns, there is an affinity between some of its work and some of the new methods of administration. Colbert's method of government was to submit the results of inquiry to the adjudication of common sense. He had 'un désir insatiable d'apprendre'.[1] In 1663 officials were instructed to begin a thorough inquest into the condition of the country. They were to collect all the available maps and, if necessary, have them corrected, to report on finance, economic resources and activities, taxation and everything—military, ecclesiastical and miscellaneous—that could possibly concern the government. In subsequent years Colbert and his subordinates used and improved statistics, cartography and books of reference. The *Bibliothèque Royale* was one of his creations, and he paid attention to the classification of archives. Like the English scientists he insisted on the use of a clear prose style.

The policy which was based on Colbert's inquiries was settled and put into operation by efficient machinery. A small number of ministers in close touch with the sovereign gave orders to a well-chosen body of local administrators. The *intendants* were intelligent and energetic; they had the full strength of the State behind them. France moved in the direction that Colbert desired, and, no doubt, if it had remained at peace it would have moved in the same direction to greater prosperity. But, like political arithmetic in England, Colbertism remained an unfulfilled programme, and there were other reasons for this besides the wars. The survey of 1663, which was meant to be the work of a few months, was never completed. In 1697 the duc de Beauvillier submitted an almost identical questionnaire to the *intendants*, who were to draw up memoranda on their *généralités* for the instruction of the king's grandson, the duc de Bourgogne. This was in the second period of Louis's reign, the period of unsuccessful wars, and Beauvillier belonged to a group of eminent men who were critical of the government. The greatest of them was Vauban, marshal of France, who had made his name as a military engineer, and advanced like Petty from actual survey and map-making to ideas about taxation and government. But the position of Colbert and those who thought with him a generation earlier was not fundamentally different. He was a powerful minister but he too was a reformer; he represented a spirit which was incompatible with that of many established institutions. The rational administration of the new ministerial departments was imposed upon a social and political organism which not only survived but continued to grow and to create fresh embodiments of its own principles.

There is indeed an obvious contradiction between the king's functions of government and his position as the symbolic head of the nation and its traditions. Historians no longer believe that Louis said 'L'état c'est moi'; but that was the position ascribed to him both by his extreme admirers and by his extreme opponents. Bossuet wrote: 'tout l'État est en lui',[2] and

[1] When the Abbé de Choisy wrote of this and his 'application infinie' that they 'lui tenaient lieu de science', he meant knowledge generally, not scientific knowledge: *Mémoires* (Utrecht, 1727), I, 115.

[2] *Politique tirée des propres paroles de l'Écriture Sainte* (Paris, 1709), Bk. V, art. iv, prop. I.

the most famous of Huguenot political pamphlets concurred: 'Le Roi a pris la place de l'État'.[1] The official theory of absolutism did not indeed exaggerate the part played by the king in the daily work of government, and it was written on his behalf that: 'La fonction des rois consiste principalement à laisser agir le bon sens, qui agit toujours naturellement sans peine';[2] but something like deception was practised to make it appear that everything turned on his will and his application to affairs. The four secretaries of the king's cabinet had important functions. The most influential of them *avait la plume*: he was authorised to counterfeit the king's signature, and he did it so well that no one could tell whether he or his master had written. The king devoted some of his time to empty routine, as when he checked the three financial registers in council once a month. The *contrôleur général* read the figures aloud, and after each entry the king enunciated the syllable 'bon'. There were other rulers in Europe who were more industrious and more truly men of business than Louis, and his attention to duty, although it was genuine, made less impression in France and outside it than his conspicuous expenditure.

In the *Mémoires* which were put together in his name there are some famous reflections on display as a method of winning popularity for a monarch. People judge what they do not see by what they see. Expenditure which may appear extravagant makes a very advantageous impression on the populace of magnificence, power, wealth and greatness. There is nothing about architecture in this passage, but for another the king himself jotted down a note: 'Grands bâtiments, leur magnificence.'[3] His great building works at Versailles began in 1668. The court was fully and finally installed there by 1682, after which the king seldom visited his capital fifteen miles away. From 1693 to 1700 and from 1706 until he died, he never once made the journey. The officials and courtiers who surrounded him amounted to a settlement of about 10,000 people. In the disastrous years of his last two wars the expenditure was perforce reduced, but the government of France was carried on in this extraordinary location and this extraordinary environment until the outbreak of revolution in 1789.

The official theory represented the ostentation of the French monarchy as an expression of wealth and power, and maintained that it rendered personal government more acceptable; but this justification did not convince every observer. Bernard Mandeville, born in Holland and settled in England, argued that the luxury of courts was not merely politic but was promoted and enjoyed as an end in itself. 'Where there is a real Power', he wrote, 'it is ridiculous to think that any Temperance or Austerity of

[1] *Les soupirs de la France esclave* (?Amsterdam, 1689), p. 23, formerly attributed to Pierre Jurieu, but probably mainly by Michel Levasson. No doubt the sense of the word 'état' is not exactly the same in these two passages, nor again in Louis's words on his death-bed: 'Je m'en vais, mais l'État demeurera après moi': *Œuvres* (Paris, 1806), II, 491.

[2] *Ibid.* I, 21.

[3] *Ibid.* I, 193, 225.

Life should ever render the person in whom that Power is lodg'd contemptible in his Office, from an Emperor to the Beadle of a Parish.'[1] He mentioned the contrast between the greatness of the Dutch republic and the personal simplicity of John de Witt, and this contrast had a literary history which began in de Witt's own lifetime.[2] The vast apparatus of the French monarchy was an outcome of peculiarly French conditions, and it was a sign of weakness as well as of strength.

Louis shone at Versailles at the head of the French nobility. In the civil wars of the middle of the century the hereditary nobility, feudal in origin, had been quelled. It no longer gathered in national constitutional assemblies, and in those provinces where the Estates still met to assent to taxes, the *intendants* no longer had to assert the royal power but merely went through the moves of a game of management. At court, as indeed throughout the whole nation, there prevailed a universal desire for titles, offices and marks of distinction, and this enabled the king, by an elaborately systematised etiquette, to take advantage equally of the ambitions of the prosperous and the necessities of the impoverished. In the army, commands and opportunities for promotion went largely by social rank; but the ministers Le Tellier and Louvois established the authority of the State over the army, and here the king gained another great and growing field of patronage. The nobility was not an absolutely closed caste. The highest ranks could be conferred, and there were ways of evading the genealogical restrictions which nominally closed some of the avenues to newcomers. Even if they did not rise in rank themselves, men who had become rich in other walks of life could marry their daughters to their superiors and so ennoble their descendants. On the other hand, nobility remained in essence a status of privilege. Many noblemen exercised seigniorial jurisdiction. The central government achieved nothing of importance in restraining this, and there were instances, at least in comparatively inaccessible places, where it was grossly abused. Landowners, both great and poor, encroached on common rights, and royal edicts, issued from 1667 onwards, failed to check them. Above all the nobility were exempt from taxation. In the later stages of the reign Vauban and other critics of the government saw this privilege as the main obstacle to reform of the revenue. The government itself so far recognised this as to institute in the *capitation* of 1695 the first universal tax; but this innovation of principle was on too small a scale to mitigate the evil.

The *noblesse d'épée* was thus in itself an obstacle to central control. It was also the nucleus of a growing complex of obstacles. In the first place the Church was connected with the nobility in a variety of ways. It also

[1] *The Fable of the Bees*, ed. F. B. Kaye (Oxford, 1924), II, 164–6. It appears, though there is some room for doubt, that the whole of this passage was written as early as 1714.

[2] Mandeville refers to Sir William Temple, in whose *Observations on the United Provinces* (London, 1673), it occurs on p. 113; but Temple had read the travels of Cosimo de' Medici, who also has it: ed. G. J. Hoogewerff (Utrecht, 1919), p. 247, written in 1669.

was a field of royal patronage. Ecclesiastics were employed in great affairs, especially in diplomacy. Shortly before the end of his life Louis deprived the duc de Nevers of his right to choose the bishops of the small see of Clamecy, and so completed his control of the French sees. Not all of the sees were rich, but with these and seven hundred abbeys, the king disposed of most of the major ecclesiastical offices. He used this power to gratify and control noble families and he paid little attention to the lower clergy, who, stage for stage, belonged to the less privileged or the unprivileged classes. The Church, however, was less dependent than the nobility. Every fifth year it held its general assembly to vote its own *don gratuit*, and it also made other grants and loans, which had to be negotiated for. The Gallican Church, if a faithful, was still in theory an independent ally, and it enjoyed its own privileges and exemptions. It did not provide a counterpoise to the nobility. The persecution of the Huguenots at once restricted and hardened the ecclesiastical element in social organisation.

The next group which maintained its own interests was the *noblesse de robe*. Like the feudal nobility the members of the higher courts of justice had failed to make good some of their pretensions in the civil wars, and throughout Louis's reign they were treated with disfavour: their seats were in Paris and some of the provincial capitals; Versailles was not for them. In fact, however, they and the whole legal population were still indispensable. There was no hard and fast line between the legal career and the official career. All those who held substantial positions in either belonged in a general way to the same social grouping, and there was coming and going between the two wings. The *intendants* were chosen from the corps of *maîtres des requêtes*, whose functions were partly judicial and whose number was fixed in 1689 at eighty-eight. Judicial appointments were filled by higher officers appointed by the Crown; but two things preserved both the lawyers and the officials from becoming mere functionaries. First, they also had their privileges. In the higher ranks, from which the small body of ministers almost all originated, these were the full privileges of titular nobility; but at the level of the *bourgeois* placeman there were many offices whose holders were exempt from taxation. Their number constantly grew, for they were all involved in the system of the sale of offices. This system was not confined to France. In itself it was not unreasonable: when an incoming office-holder makes a payment to his outgoing predecessor he provides something towards that predecessor's livelihood in retirement and he gives a guarantee that he will pay some attention to his new duties. But such a system may obviously generate inefficiency, extortion and corruption. Although they were aware of this and frequently tried to act on their knowledge, the government of Louis XIV could not afford financially to break away from the inherited system. The State itself sold offices, sometimes hereditary offices, and took its share when offices changed hands. Thus security of tenure, necessary to keep up the market-rates of these transactions, was coupled with the multiplication of official or nominally official posts. Those who bought or inherited them were naturally not all fit to hold them. The system was extended in the time of Colbert to many functions connected with commerce and industry, and in later years to some connected with naval administration. A decree of 1681 granted tax-exemption to a large number of office-holders. In the eighteenth century it was reckoned that there were 4000 *offices* which conferred nobility, and, for the earlier part of Louis's reign, the whole number of *offices* is estimated at 40,000 to 50,000.

During the reign of Louis XIV the expansion of government activities, especially in war and warlike preparations, created new employment at every level from that of the ruling few to the manual workers, and as the numbers of men employed increased, their tasks inevitably became more specialised. The new prosperity of industry and commerce, even if it was artificially forced at the expense of activities outside its range, had similar effects. This implies a growth of organising, clerical and trading work, of the *bourgeois* element, and in the culture of the period the rise of the *bourgeois* spirit was plainly visible. The system of privilege and of status conferred from above, however, in combination with other tendencies, cloaked and distorted the social development of the *bourgeoisie*. Municipal institutions, which showed some signs of revival after the civil wars, were weakened in the interests of royal authority. In economic affairs the great towns, with partial exceptions, as in the 'republic' of Marseilles, lost such autonomy as they had. Constitutionally their autonomy was that of narrow and selfish oligarchies, incapable of resisting the *intendants* when they intervened on behalf of the unenfranchised. In 1692 the mayors became *officiers*, and so were brought into the hierarchy of mutually jealous dependants, each with his own vested interest. In this world, as at Versailles, there was no rallying-point for ambition except the royal favour, and the rising *bourgeois* like the courtier aimed at privilege and marks of distinction. Not only lawyers but physicians and bankers secured exemption from seigniorial *corvées* for themselves, but only for themselves. The accountant's profession was emerging; but when we hear of independent accountants who work not for employers but for clients, it is in the character of *jurés teneurs de livres*, officials. It does not appear that the professional men advanced towards coherent organisations for maintaining a balance between their skill, their social services and their rewards, by controlling the relations between practitioners and clients. It was much the same with business men. Chambers of commerce and other assemblies under official auspices formed part of the machinery set up by Colbert; but the merchants, instead of trying to reform the old municipal life or build on these new foundations, returned perpetually to schemes for soliciting ennoblement, or something like it, for themselves.

Thus what might have been a rising middle class was divided and subdivided by its relation to privilege and centralised government.

The notion of society as divided into upper, middle and lower strata is indeed of little use as applied to France at that time. There was a division between privileged and unprivileged. Above it there were gradations of wealth and estimation, but the many partitions prevented the formation of classes united by similarity of functions and ways of life and conscious of common interests. Below the line there were great differences of material welfare from the upper peasants and artisans to the poorest labourers. Within the great area of France there was as much variety in agrarian and even in industrial relations as there was in soil and surface and natural resources. The worst experiences of the poorest were terrible, and not only in years of famine such as 1662, 1693 and 1709. In some places and in some years there were alarming outbreaks of rioting and even rebellion. These bulk larger in the works of modern historians than they did in contemporary writings, partly because there was no reporting of the executions and the movements of troops except in secret official correspondence. They were, however, all regional; there was never a movement of discontent through the whole nation. In 1662–3 there was trouble in the Bourbonnais, in 1664–6 in Gascony and Béarn, in 1670 in the Vivarais, in 1675 in Brittany, and so on. The repression never overtaxed the resources of the authorities; nor did they ever make concessions to discontent which implied anything but local and limited conciliation. Government was stronger than it had been in the middle of the century, and only stray phrases can be cited to show that it was beginning to consider itself responsible for the welfare of the population as a whole.

Effective central control of a State implies the absence of intermediate powers between the centre and the individual citizen. The State of Louis XIV made little progress in establishing direct contact with the citizen except in his capacity as tax-payer. When compulsory military service was introduced on a small scale with the *milice* of 1688, the selection of men was left to each parish. No civil authority kept a register of the people. The registration of baptisms, marriages and burials was done by the clergy. An edict of 1667 provided, among other things, that a copy of the register should be sent to the *greffe* or record-office of the *bailliage*, but even if they had always been well posted, which they were not, these registers would have been useless for any civil purpose. In the newly annexed territories of Flanders and Alsace, as in Brittany and the Pyrenees, the government did not seriously press the use of French at the expense of the other languages that were spoken; but this arose less from any liberal policy than from the absence of any need for the government to communicate directly with the common man. In exceptional cases there might be direct dealings, for instance in the *inscription maritime*. All seafaring men were enrolled for purposes of naval recruitment; but this was possible only because it affected a limited body of men, concentrated in the seaports and easy to identify.

Although the range and depth of its action were limited in all these ways, the monarchy of Louis XIV impressed all Europe, and in one respect or another it was taken as a model in many lands. Its armies were imitated even after the tide of victory had turned. Its architecture, its gardens, its court etiquette set the fashion. Some of its administrative successes were equally easy to follow. Perhaps the improved street-lighting of London, The Hague, Amsterdam, Hamburg and Berlin in 1670–90 was hastened by the example of La Reynie, *lieutenant général de police* from 1667, who provided Paris with 6500 reflecting candle-lanterns. In larger matters, however, the possibility of French influence depended on the prevailing social conditions. In the Spanish Netherlands, a small country, in many ways resembling the adjoining regions of France, it was possible for such a minister as Bergeyck to acclimatise the ideas and methods of Colbert. In England there had been a movement for administrative efficiency in the time of Strafford, and another had begun when the parliamentarians organised their effort in the Civil War. The exiles who returned from France at the Restoration brought no lessons with them in this field, but France was near at hand, and in the following years the abler among the supporters of prerogative power learnt from the French experience. In 1682–8 Sunderland and Godolphin stood not for native Toryism but for a continental, that is a French, ideal. Their policy was rejected for many political and constitutional reasons, but its failure was also due to social obstacles remarkably unlike those which prescribed the limits to centralised authority in France. Decisive and lasting reforms were carried out during the French war of William III, but they owed little or nothing to French inspiration.

Alexis de Tocqueville showed in a brilliant excursus that the French administrative centralisation of the *ancien régime* could best be judged in Canada. Here many of the visible and invisible obstacles to its free development did not exist. There was scarcely any nobility; the Church was not dominant; the judiciary had no roots in ancient institutions and usages; the tradition of feudalism was lost or obscured. Therefore there were no municipal or provincial institutions at all; administrative interference was ubiquitous and all initiative came from France. But in the adjoining English colonies, where there was the same freedom from European social ties, he saw exactly the opposite: vigorous local and provincial government, individualism, and no central administration worth the name.[1] The explanation of the contrast lay in the difference between the two mother countries.

The three kingdoms ruled by the English kings were constitutionally

[1] *L'ancien régime et la révolution française* (Paris, 1856), pp. 385–7.

separate. Throughout the whole period of Louis XIV it seemed possible that they might once more be divided by civil war. They actually did undergo a revolution, and for three years Ireland was a theatre of war. Even when there were no political disturbances, law and order were not much better maintained in Scotland or even in England than they were in France. French observers were taken by surprise when, in spite of all this, the three kingdoms were able to maintain great fleets and considerable armies without exhausting their finances or splitting their precarious cohesion. That they were able to do so does indeed illustrate the fact that the demands of war, even after the military revolution, did not penetrate very deeply into the structure of society. Recruiting did not interfere with the manning of industry, and even the compulsory recruiting of the navy, though it annoyed the merchant marine, does not seem to have left it short of necessary men. The supplying of the forces did not create serious shortages for the civilian consumer. The losses and inconveniences of war did not aggravate the existing discontents to the point of danger. So much might have been said of any belligerent country which was not invaded by an enemy; but there were conditions in England which made it exceptionally applicable there. England had reached a point at which economic improvement and reorganisation, so far from being set back by the wars, actually took advantage of them. Again it was true of all Europe that the demands of the State still weighed lightly on society; but in England the social structure was such that they pressed less heavily than in France.

The two great problems of relations with Scotland and relations with Ireland remained unsolved, but in the course of the period each of them was so changed that, on the basis of innumerable links of influence and interest, they became problems of management rather than of sovereignty: Ireland was reconquered, and Scotland finally came into a constitutional union (1707). They were both comparatively simple countries and changed comparatively little in social organisation. In England in some important respects there was less need than in France for any centralising reform. There were no internal economic barriers. Except for some insignificant anomalies the law was uniform and the administration of justice was under a single control. There was nothing to hinder a radical reform of finance; and, in spite of some quaint medieval survivals, this was in fact accomplished. Outside the spheres of war, justice and taxation, however, there was no corps of officials and the State had few men in its employ. It had no closer contact with the individuals who composed the mass of the population than in France. It did not interfere with the Celtic languages. During the interlude of Puritan rule before 1660, perhaps mainly for religious reasons, the registration of births, marriages and burials by justices of the peace had been substituted for the old ecclesiastical registration of baptisms, marriages and burials. The old system came back with the Restoration, but in 1695–6 the procedure of registration was somewhat improved and from that time all births were to be notified to the incumbent of the parish. Still no copies of the registers went to any civil and few to any diocesan authority. There was no approach to an *état civil*, and even attempts to imitate the French *inscription maritime* were unsuccessful. The government, lacking any officials to carry it out, could make little or no use (outside the sphere of commercial statistics) of the technique of survey. When, on one occasion, the Board of Trade wished to know how much money was levied in poor-rates throughout the kingdom, the only means of collecting this information was by very defective returns from the parish clergy.

In this instance the desire for knowledge and for a vigorous policy founded on it was frustrated partly because there were no organs through which it could act, and partly by the inertia of a conservative society. There were other instances in which this inertia showed itself capable of withstanding determined efforts of the royal authority. Two kings, Charles II and James II, used processes of law to attack the politically troublesome liberties of the boroughs. The ultimate result was the opposite of what happened in France, and the survival of the English municipal oligarchies illustrates some of the main peculiarities of the English society. The boroughs were saved by the revolution and the revolution was made, or at least led, by the nobility.

Like those of France the noblemen of England had lost something of their standing in the civil wars. The majority of them had been royalists and they had profited from the Restoration, but they were no longer feudal chieftains. In 1629 a Dutch spectator of the Garter procession at Whitehall, when each knight led his train of gentlemen, was reminded of the Polish nobility at their diet which he had seen two years before.[1] The English magnates no longer made this impression. The court was modest in its display. Rank brought privileges with it, but never either jurisdiction or exemption from taxes. The holders of hereditary titles were few in number; the younger sons of peers had distinguishing names, but nothing of the sort lasted into the third generation except for the senior line. The immediate family connections of the peerage thus ramified widely into a governing class which was even more accessible to newcomers than the French nobility and not formally separated from the upper regions of commercial and industrial wealth. There was a landed aristocracy, but it was allied on the one hand with the lesser landowners and on the other with influential men in business and the professions. It was powerful, but it exercised its power through public institutions and as the leading element of the governing class. Its members had a first claim on some of the highest offices and an advantage in competing for any of

[1] A. Boot, 'Journaal' in *Bijdragen en mededeelingen van het Hist. Genootschap*, LVII (Utrecht, 1936), 84.

them; this competition was systematised by the formation of groups and parties; but open, if unreported, discussion in constitutional assemblies assured a general control by the governing class over the appointment and conduct of ministers. There were hereditary offices of great dignity, but they no longer carried power with them, and in minor offices heredity was unimportant. Both in the army and in the State, offices were bought and sold; but this system was restricted as the finances of the State improved; in the army it was brought under a degree of supervision and it never gave the civilian placeman anything like a freehold. The resistance to centralising and innovating tendencies thus had a different basis from that in France. It was the collective conservatism of the complex social class which controlled the two houses of parliament. Through them this class dealt by legislation, often on local and particular matters, with the *agenda* which in France fell to the share of the *intendants* and their subordinates.

The position of the Church was weaker than in France. The Crown indeed chose the twenty-six bishops and exercised some minor patronage; the bishops, as members of the House of Lords, were an essential element in the conduct of business, and the clergy, who unlike the French clergy could marry, were becoming more closely associated both in the higher and lower ranks with the governing class. But the habit of appointing churchmen to high secular offices died out. In fact, and from 1689 in law, the established Church did not include the whole nation. It also surrendered its right to vote its own taxes, and after that it made no serious use of its assemblies even for purely ecclesiastical purposes. Its corporate feeling was undermined by dissensions, and its influence was exerted rather in the parishes than on the national stage.

Local government in the towns was left to its own devices sufficiently to afford room on the one hand for public-spirited initiative and on the other for disgraceful corruption. It was at its best in some of the larger towns where substantial men took part in it. The elective officers who administered the poor-law could do much, within the limits of prevailing ideas, to mitigate the hardships of poverty. National legislation failed to rationalise the system. A reformed poor-law might have been less indulgent to human weaknesses, and, in spite of many abuses, the existing law did mean that the local authorities acknowledged a responsibility at least to the 'deserving' poor.

Outside the towns the poor-law officers, like the constables and other parish officers, were subordinate in various ways to the justices of the peace. These were appointed by the Crown and primarily in order to administer justice in small matters over their humble neighbours; collectively, assembled in quarter-sessions, they not only supervised the police and administration of the parishes, but also acted as administrative authorities. In theory the county, like the parish, was 'a unit of obligation': its people owed duties to the Crown and its officers saw to their discharge. In practice it was an autonomous administrative area, and many counties were so extensive that they were rather regions than local divisions. The justices of the peace at this time were for the most part landed gentry; the magnates did not act directly in these affairs in their own localities. They left this routine work to lesser men over whom, of course, they had influence if they chose to exert it. The counties were thus governed by amateurs, who have been described, perhaps with too much disparagement, as 'an extra-legal oligarchy'. The Crown communicated with them through the circuit judges and occasionally through a secretary of state. They had personal connections with members of parliament, as well as votes in their election, so that parliamentary local legislation took account of at least some local interests and opinions. No one appears to have lamented the absence of a professional administrative hierarchy.

The demand for professional and business work, and the consequent specialisation of functions, came about in England as in France, but with different results. It made no noticeable difference to the organisation of the bar and the bench, which had their own traditions and strongly rooted corporations. In the other branch of the legal profession there were some changes. They had never had any corporate organisation: the attorneys were subdivided and more clearly separated from the solicitors, whose status was lower than theirs. Both branches of the medical profession rose in prestige: there were great improvements in the treatment of disease, and the rewards of successful practice became greater. No new professional bodies were created, but of those which existed none failed to manifest some degree of activity. Veterinary science was beginning to be studied in France, but apparently not in England. Architects were more clearly distinguished from builders, but they formed no association. There were accountants, most of them teachers as well as practitioners of accountancy. Curiously enough their profession seems to have been more fully developed in Scotland than in England.

There was nowhere any attempt to shelter the rising professions under the aegis of government. If anything they moved away from government rather than towards it. They also became more distinct from other elements of society in another way. Their work had attractions of its own, and in it advantages of education and upbringing could contribute to advancement. Their more successful members came into contact with the great and prosperous. Thus it came to be thought that certain professions were more suitable for gentlemen than trade or industry. The younger sons of landowners were now much less commonly apprenticed in London or the provincial towns. In the reign of Charles II the appropriate authorities declared that it was compatible with armorial bearings to engage in wholesale commerce, and there were magnates in business to whom all doors were open; but the Church, the bar and the army, to be followed in no long time by medicine, established a place in the public esteem which made them into strong buttresses of the social order. Of these three, the army was virtually a new career, and the habit of taking commissions in it gradually brought about a considerable change in the horizons of the landed gentry. England approximated more closely than France to the condition of a country with a developed middle class, but perhaps it would be more accurate to say that in England the middle classes, though attached by many affinities to the governing class, and nowhere rigidly separated from it, had some weight of their own.

Whatever its merit and shortcomings may have been there was nothing in the distinctively British social order which could tempt foreigners to imitation. The same is true of the social structure, and of the constitutional and administrative, as distinguished from the economic, arrangements of the other liberal State of the West, the United Provinces of the Netherlands. Here indeed, after the revolutionary period of the war of independence, there had been a successful and even a conscious effort to equal the accepted European standards of good government. By the middle of the century the federal constitution was mature and firmly established. It was destined, in spite of a succession of alarming crises, to last through the seventeenth and eighteenth centuries; but foreign observers did not expect this and pardonably failed to understand that it had a firm basis well-fitted to endure. There was unrestrained variety between the constitutions of the seven sovereign provinces, and parts of the territory of the republic were even external to these provinces. William III, sovereign in his own principality of Orange, was a high officer of the generality, and also of five of the seven provinces, with different rights and functions in each of his numerous capacities, always jealously watched when he tried to enlarge them. In each province there were special local compromises to effect a balance between town and country, between noble and other landowners, between elective and hereditary authorities, between governing assemblies and executive officers, between public authority and private influence. In the dominant province, Holland, the larger towns, and especially the great city of Amsterdam, could generally prevail over opposition; but this was not the case in any of the other provinces, and a general will of the whole republic could only be arrived at by an indescribably complicated process of management and negotiation. The union as a whole had no bureaucracy, and except for finance it had practically no civil administration. The army, consisting largely of foreign mercenaries, was federal and the naval command was unified under the admiral-general; but the dockyards, the supplies and the manning of the fleet were under five separate colleges in three of the maritime provinces.

In spite of all this, the republic exerted greater power in proportion to its population than either Great Britain or France, and in some departments of domestic government, such as prison-administration and poor-relief, it was widely admired. This paradox is not to be explained merely by the great wealth and the unique business experience of the maritime provinces. The Dutch also had special aptitudes for public life. Their governing class was anomalous and ill-defined, but it was well stocked with men fit for responsible offices, and it habitually gave them neither too little scope nor too much. It was more predominantly civilian than those of France or England. It had a professional wing in the legally educated pensionaries and 'griffiers' of the towns, the provinces and the States General.[1] It included some country landowners and many members of the urban patriciates. These were not active merchants as their grandfathers had been, but they were men of property and, along with every other kind of wealth, they owned real estate in town and country. They were well educated and well informed, and they kept a monopoly of many offices by a system of co-optation as exclusive as heredity was in other countries. Otherwise they were not socially isolated from the more prosperous among the *bourgeoisie* of merchants and professional men. The ecclesiastics belonged to this *bourgeoisie*. There was an established Church, but it had no national, only a provincial, organisation, and there was a large tolerated minority outside it. In its presbyterian organisation there were no prelates, nor were ecclesiastics employed in offices of State.

When institutions work satisfactorily in spite of being on paper apparently unworkable, the explanation is not likely to lie only on the side of those who exercise power and influence. There will probably be some relevant social and legal freedom, and some positive qualities of mind and character widely diffused through the general population. Partly because the absence of central organs made it practically impossible to impose uniformity, but also because they were valued for their own sakes, freedom of thought and of expression met with less interference among the Dutch than in any other part of Europe. So far as it is possible to make a comparison in a field where general impressions cannot be closely tested, the Dutch were a well-educated nation. Literacy seems to have been at a relatively high level, and knowledge of many kinds seems to have been widely spread. A considerable number of people of all kinds, in the country as well as in the towns, seem to have profited from a long-standing education in affairs. There were common enterprises which in their nature could only be handled by pooling the local knowledge and the good sense of all concerned, that is by allowing free discussion to run across some of the barriers of wealth and influence. The best example is

[1] The word *pensionaris* means 'stipendiary', a paid official; the office of *raad pensionaris* held by John de Witt under the Estates of Holland meant 'stipendiary councillor'. The English translations 'council pensionary' and 'grand pensionary' miss the meaning altogether. *Griffier*, the office held by the principal servant of the States General, like the French *greffier* means nearly the same as 'secretary'.

that of the authorities for diking and draining, where engineering requirements, financial considerations and conflicting local interests all had to be reconciled by authorities, partly elective, on whose decisions the livelihood and even the lives of the population depended. In experience like this innumerable little social cells, each looking after its own immediate affairs, engendered a public spirit and this burgher-organism provided a firmer base for the superstructure of the State than the societies where the ruling classes showed greater distinction and ideas took a wider range of flight.[1]

For the time being, then, the two liberal States, unlike France, were not imitated abroad. Even the influence of France and the other tendencies towards uniformity of manners and practices, though they went deeper than the surface, did little to promote any new European unity. Not only did the wars exacerbate international differences. In each of the three countries that we have examined they led the State to strengthen its own organs and to make increased demands on its subjects. As it did so under the stress of emergencies, it had to conform to its inherited social traditions, and so, although in many ways the whole Continent responded uniformly to the military revolution, the outcome confirmed each country in its idiosyncrasies and deepened the clefts between them. It contributed to the deepening of another and geographically larger social division, that between the eastern and western regions which were separated, roughly speaking, by the line of the Elbe and then by the border of Germany down to the Alps. Primarily this was a division between contrasting types of agrarian relations, but these necessarily involved corresponding contrasts in other economic and social matters. In the west the tillers of the soil were relatively free; in the east they were less free and their subjection was becoming more severe and more systematic.

In France, although royal intervention in favour of the peasants was ineffective, and although some large proprietors were consolidating and increasing their possessions, most of the peasants were personally free in the eyes of the law. The same was true of Sweden and western Germany, and also of the British Isles, where there were many large properties and landless labourers. In Spain, where such relations were even more widespread, except in Catalonia there was little active unrest among the peasantry. In Italy feudal jurisdictions and other survivals were mitigated by free economic relations between landlords and tenants. In Portugal in 1702 serfdom was abolished on the royal domains. In the east an opposite tendency prevailed and especially in the great plains where the

[1] This sentence is paraphrased from S. J. Fockema Andreae in the co-operative *Algemene Geschiedenis der Nederlanden* (Utrecht, 1953), VI, 62. This admirable chapter seems to give the first explicit account of the underlying social realities of Dutch republican institutions.

production of corn for export by sea was carried on for profit by comparatively large estates. Even in Denmark, as in eastern Germany, and southwards to Bohemia and Switzerland, the landowners depressed their tenants, not by a serfdom which bound them to the soil, but by oppressive jurisdiction and services. In the more northerly parts there was no combined resistance. In Denmark the small freeholders had disappeared long before. In 1660, when King Frederick III made the royal power absolute,[1] no attention was paid to the grievances expressed by the peasantry; an edict of emancipation for Sealand and Laaland issued by Frederick IV in 1702 was a dead letter, and during the eighteenth century the condition of the peasants continued to deteriorate. Farther south, however, there were disturbances. In Switzerland, where the masters of the peasantry were the rising town patriciates, there had been a decisive conflict in 1646–53, and there was no further disorder; something was done to alleviate discontent by concessions. In Bohemia, after a succession of local outbreaks, a serious peasant rising broke out in 1680. The Emperor put down the insurrection by force, but he also granted the Pardubitz Pragmatic or *Robotpatent*, which was intended to restrain the oppressions of the great landowners. Not, however, until a generation later did imperial edicts bring any substantial reform. In Hungary the national rebellions of 1677–1710 deflected a social movement against the landowners from its course.

Germany, half in the one region and half in the other, had already its own well-established administrative experience, and modern centralised government was first practised by some of the German States. In the sixteenth century, as *Landesherrschaft* developed into *Landeshoheit*, officials of a new type took charge of finance, justice and military administration. Austria, Bavaria, Saxony and Brandenburg made use of them and adopted the system of a single general council with subordinate, specialised commissions. The officials were for the most part educated in the legal faculties of the universities. It was not until the eighteenth century that the German universities fully recognised aspects of social study which were not related to law, and so came to train their students for official life in what came to be called *Kameralwissenschaft*; but the ground was already being prepared for that development. The scope of legal education was interpreted widely. In 1694 the University of Halle was founded, and in 1687 Thomasius lectured in German at Leipzig. The best political and economic thought in Germany emanated from the legally trained officials. Some of them broke away from the irresponsible, if stimulating, projector-mentality of which Johann Joachim Becher (1635–82) was the most prominent exponent, and wrote as practical administrators planning improvements and especially increases of revenue. They were not scientists, but they were at home with maps, with the method of survey, and with simple calculations. Since the German States

[1] See below, ch. XXII, p. 524.

were comparatively small, officials passed from one to another in the course of their careers, carrying the lessons of their experience with them, and several of the writers avowedly offered their advice to German States in general, aiming at an improvement in the standards of government throughout the Empire. A good example is Veit Ludwig von Seckendorff (1626–92), whose works were well known outside Germany. He was in the electoral service of Brandenburg, but his books were published outside the Elector's dominions and were meant for general use.

When the rulers of Brandenburg established their own system of personal and centralised government they had thus serviceable instruments ready to hand, and the military revolution favoured the attempt, as it did also in other German States. In Austria, Bavaria, Württemberg, and probably in other States, the military career began to attract members of the noble families. Brandenburg's most dangerous neighbour was Sweden, a poor country (like Brandenburg itself and Prussia) which had developed military strength by ruthlessly exploiting its resources of men and money. The Swedish example counted for something, and even in the eighteenth century it was on the Swedish pattern that conscription, based on adequate registers, was introduced in the kingdom of Prussia. The Great Elector, Frederick William (1640 to 1688) was not completely identified in origin and interests with any one part of his complex of territories. In Brandenburg itself he was the Calvinist ruler of a Lutheran population. With Prussia his connection was purely dynastic. The prosperous western bishoprics and duchies which he acquired at the Peace of Westphalia differed in social structure and economic interests from his inherited States. But the wide dispersal of these units, and the absence of defensible natural frontiers, made a strong army and tight organisation necessary. In the army the French example was paramount; French architecture and manners left their traces; but the system as a whole was fundamentally unlike that of France, and was imposed with such correct estimation of social forces that, after initial conflicts which were neither very severe nor long protracted, it remained unchallenged until the French revolutionary wars. From the army reorganisation spread to finance: the central war-fund was established in 1674. The *Intendantur der Armee*, which owed little beyond its name to the French, became the nucleus of a new central government for all the dominions: the ministries of war, finance and the interior, in fact the whole organism of State control, branched out from this stem. In the western provinces such as Cleves and Mark social relationships resembled those in the neighbouring Dutch and German territories: in a comparatively wealthy economy, with a comparatively dense population, the interests of town and country were no longer opposed to one another, and the nobility had lost much of its dominance over a free peasantry. Here, therefore, although the local institutions were weakened and although by 1672 the Elector had them at his mercy, he did not suppress them. At the price of considerable concessions in taxation, he allowed the Estates to survive. In his eastern dominions, however, where the nobility formed the strongest element, he cleared the way for the new system of finance by depriving the provincial Estates of their control. He was able to make these drastic changes because he established a two-sided alliance with the nobles. The towns were too weak to form a counterpoise to the nobility, and so he restricted their rights. He granted privileges to the nobles, including seigniorial rights and exemption from taxes. But there was never any danger that the nobility as a body would obstruct absolutism as it did in France; for the other side of the Elector's alliance with them was that he drew them into the well-rewarded but exacting service of the State. The families of the greater landowners began to provide officers for the army and officials for the bureaucracy. 'The leading positions in the Commissariats were held almost exclusively by noblemen. Of 34 *Kriegsräte* and *Geheime Kriegsräte* appointed by Frederick William, 29 were noblemen, most of them native Junkers.'[1] This powerful working nobility was not more unlike the French nobility than the monarchy it served was unlike the French monarchy. The Electors had a court and palaces, in which the influence of France could be seen; the successor of Frederick William ascended to kingly rank; but the absolute rulers of Brandenburg–Prussia were working monarchs.

From what has been said about France, Great Britain, the United Provinces and Brandenburg–Prussia some general conclusions may be drawn which seem to hold good when the neighbouring countries are also taken into account. The social structure of Europe was changing under the pressure of several major forces, none of which either originated or acted independently of the others. Knowledge, both scientific and useful, had grown; the States had strengthened their control over their subjects; they used the power so acquired in wars against one another; the resources of wealth and manpower on which they could draw had increased. For all these reasons and many others social divisions followed new lines of differentiation, especially in making room for larger and more diversified middle classes. But in each community these tendencies encountered special conditions which clothed them in unique local wrappings: in France privilege and status; in Great Britain the inertia of a governing class; in the Netherlands the paucity of central organs; in Brandenburg–Prussia the lack of a common groundwork below the centralising monarchy. These contrasts, and also the contrast between the east and the west, so far from being smoothed away, became more abrupt. While a new, cosmopolitan culture was beginning to polish manners and the arts and literature to an even surface, at the economic and social level, and in the organisation of wealth and force, differences grew greater rather than less.

[1] F. L. Carsten, *The Origins of Prussia* (Oxford, 1954), p. 264.

CHAPTER IX

FRENCH DIPLOMACY AND FOREIGN POLICY IN THEIR EUROPEAN SETTING

THE age of Louis XIV was not a time of great novelty in international relations and international law. It cannot be compared, from this point of view, with the Renaissance. Permanent embassies, for example, were first established during the sixteenth century, and it was then that the idea of an equilibrium in certain parts of Europe—later called the 'balance of power'—originated in Italy, and more particularly in Venice. For a long time sovereigns had been content to exchange ambassadors only on important occasions when, for instance, they wished to conclude a series of negotiations or to sign a treaty, the sovereign reserving to himself the right to ratify or to repudiate the decisions taken. But gradually, as ambassadors increased in number, it became common practice to send them for unlimited periods to permanent posts in the most important foreign capitals. On the death or the resignation of one of these ambassadors a successor would be immediately appointed, and in this way diplomacy became a career in which the greatest nobles sought to distinguish themselves. As ambassadors were usually loaded with honours there was no lack of candidates. The principal capitals were naturally the most sought after. Such posts called for no exceptional ability, but rather for listening, usually in silence, and only from time to time for speaking up, with a word of truth or falsehood as might be dictated by the circumstances. Yet many ambassadors became useful observers, and their despatches to their governments constitute for the historian of today one of the most important sources for the history of international relations.

It was the Italians, especially the Venetians, who from the end of the fifteenth century began to appoint permanent ambassadors. A little later the papacy followed their example: the list of its ambassadors—they were sent only to Catholic countries and were called by the Latin name of 'nuncio'—does not appear to be continuous until the second half of the sixteenth century. The last to conform to the common practice were the tsars of Russia, beginning with Peter the Great at the end of the seventeenth century.

Louis XIV kept permanent ambassadors in the capitals of all the great European States, except in Russia. In the less important States, such as the German and Italian principalities, he placed agents of subordinate rank, mere 'residents'. Wherever he judged an ambassador to be unnecessary he appointed a resident minister with more limited privileges under the title of 'Envoy Extraordinary'; this was the case in Vienna because he would not concede the right of precedence which the Austrians accorded to the Spanish ambassador. In Switzerland, a French ambassador resided permanently at Soleure; in the course of the reign he was to be seconded by a 'resident' at Geneva and another in the Grisons. The title of 'plenipotentiary' had no very precise meaning, but usually designated anyone who was charged with an important temporary mission, such as the signing of a treaty.

These various representatives of the king were for the most part chosen from the upper stratum of the *noblesse d'épée*. Not that the peers of the realm were necessarily more competent than others, but the king believed them to be capable of making a greater impression abroad; and besides, in the event of their official salaries and allowances being too small to sustain an appropriate standard of living, the noblemen, usually endowed with substantial personal fortunes, were able to draw on their own funds. Few members of the clergy were appointed, although their education equipped them with a good knowledge of Latin, the most useful international language. At the beginning of the reign, there were among the diplomats only a few members of the *noblesse de robe*, but their numbers grew as the years passed until they began to represent the king even in the more important capitals. Relations with the papacy presented special problems. In the first instance, the post in Rome was little sought after by prospective ambassadors because life in the pontifical capital was so expensive that they could easily ruin themselves; furthermore, because Paris and Rome distrusted each other, the king insisted on choosing the papal representative, the nuncio, from a list of several candidates, a formality which was imposed on no other sovereign but the head of the Church. As high officials, fulfilling mainly a representative function, ambassadors rarely took part in the life of the country in which they lived, although in Paris some of them frequented the salons either to converse or, more often, to play cards.

Louis XIV was particularly jealous of his powers as the director of foreign policy and kept his diplomatic officials in strict subordination. Even the minister who assisted him in this field, the Secretary of State for Foreign Affairs, was hardly more than an executive officer. He himself prepared, and sometimes even worded, all diplomatic correspondence; but as time passed and his difficulties increased he was to allow his collaborator greater liberty. Money played an essential part in diplomacy, especially in the diplomacy of Louis XIV. At the beginning of his reign the king spent freely in order to win friends and allies abroad. Charles II and James II were notoriously dependent on him for subsidies, and many members of parliament, as well as Dutch and English ministers, were not above bribery. 'France', a well-known Dutchman wrote in 1671, 'gives everywhere and everywhere buys what she cannot conquer.' If they were effective in Holland and England, gifts of French gold accomplished marvels in Germany, the country where consciences were most easily bought. The Great Elector of Brandenburg, one of the most needy of German princes, could never refuse anything asked of him providing it was paid for, but he and many other princes did not feel bound for long by obligations arising out of the subsidies which they received. 'It cannot be doubted', wrote an experienced ambassador on his return from a mission, 'that nearly all our success in the negotiations in Switzerland we owe to our money.' Bankers thus found themselves indispensable diplomatic auxiliaries. Yet this lasted only for a short period: after 1700 military expenditure absorbed all the available resources, and 'the shower of gold ceased'.

The idea of an international balance was first spoken of in sixteenth-century Italy, cut up into many principalities and thus a cause of dispute among the great powers. Then, during the first half of the seventeenth century, it was invoked in certain quarters to protect the German principalities threatened by French policy. In the sixteenth century international law was still in its infancy. During the seventeenth it began to inspire studies of a basic nature, but its principles were still far from constituting a proper code. It was scarcely more than a number of customs recognised and observed by all European or 'civilised' nations. If these customs were not observed, sanctions were possible, but it would be difficult to say exactly where they had ever been applied. In the sphere of international legal theory, the most outstanding early works were those of Grotius (Hugo de Groot, 1583–1630), a jurist from Delft. He acquired a great reputation, but in his own lifetime did not enjoy all the esteem he deserved.

During the reign of Louis XIV there was scarcely any progress beyond the state of affairs that had been reached before Grotius. The Congress of Münster and the treaties of Westphalia which sprang from it, although they did not mark any notable advance, were incomparably more important than any earlier ones. 'They gave', said Ernest Nys, the noted historian of international law, 'a formal consecration to the international society which was slowly being established on European soil.' Yet after 1648, as before, the notion of a balance remained in the hands of the publicists. Before it was used to define the general relations between States it was applied in a great variety of ways: people spoke of the balance of trade and navigation, or the balance of religion; and every kind of hegemony in whatever sphere it might show itself was thus condemned. Later in the century statesmen outside France used the idea of a balance to muster arguments against the policy of Louis XIV, which was visibly tending towards mastery of the Continent. With the accumulation of errors and setbacks towards the end of Louis's reign, many French people in their turn began to use similar arguments, and this maxim was to dominate the eighteenth century.

It is hardly possible to speak of international law in this period. The term 'international practices' seems more appropriate, for there existed as yet no body of law with any authority over the forms of international life. These practices were by no means very ancient and one would search in vain for them in the Middle Ages. International law was a creation of modern times, and one which evolved very slowly. Formerly, in seeking to envisage the future, it had been usual to consider the fate of Christendom as a whole. Now there was a growing tendency to think in terms of a more limited unit, of Europe, or rather of what began to be termed *le corps européen*. The hesitant beginnings of international law during this period must therefore cause no surprise. The usages of war were naturally those which first attracted the attention of the theorists; Grotius became famous by his *De Jure Belli ac Pacis*, in which war figured more largely than peace.

The most interesting aspects, for us as well as for the people of the time, were provided by naval warfare and practices. The chief maritime powers, the United Provinces, England and France, were the most vitally concerned, but others, such as Venice and Portugal, were equally interested in the solution of the problems that arose. In the struggle against the ever-present evil of piracy, regulations had been drawn up during the Middle Ages. A collection of precepts drawn from common law, the *coûtumes d'Oléron*, was made as early as the twelfth century, probably in the French islands near the coast of Poitou. Grotius, for his part, wrote his *Mare Liberum* against the Portuguese pretensions to the exclusive dominion over the Indian Ocean; and this was the origin of a bitter controversy with Portugal. Elsewhere, Venetian pretensions to the sovereignty of the Adriatic, manifested since the sixteenth century, aroused many protests and gave rise to a kind of international polemic. It was only later, in the course of the eighteenth century, that the notion of the freedom of the seas was to be generally accepted. Nys suggests that these pretensions can be explained 'by the necessities of defence and of watching the coasts, by motives arising from fiscal measures, or by the material needs of the populations'. From 1664 Louis XIV turned his attention to the Barbary pirates inflicting continuous losses on the commerce of Marseilles. He dispatched a squadron to bombard Djidjelli in Algeria and in the ensuing years made attacks on Algiers, which eventually signed a treaty in 1666, one of those ill-respected conventions which depend upon a constant readiness to use force. Tunis soon followed the example of Algiers, without showing any greater constancy in keeping its engagements.

Throughout this period the question of the naval salute preoccupied the maritime powers, especially France, Holland and England. It was customary for two ships of different nationalities to salute when they met at sea, and this could be done by firing a salvo or by dipping the colours. Such acts of courtesy caused no difficulty before the seventeenth century, that is, before the accession of James I of England who proved more sensitive in this matter than Elizabeth I. A serious incident that took place in 1603 between France and England was settled through diplomatic channels. The problem, however, became more difficult in the age of Louis XIV, the great king showing himself especially haughty whenever his own and his country's prestige was at stake. An incident early in the reign prompted Colbert, the Secretary of State for the Navy, to observe that the king was 'extremely jealous about salutes and points of honour'. His subordinates, whether admirals or mere naval commanders, were compelled to insist that every mariner pay all due respect to the French colours. Before the personal rule of Louis XIV this question had mainly divided the English and the Dutch. The Treaty of Westminster of 1654 solemnly recognised for the first time the right of salute, naturally in favour of the victorious English. And these arrangements, ambiguous though they were, were confirmed in 1667, at the conclusion of the second Anglo-Dutch War, by the Treaty of Breda. The quarrel with France was prolonged for several decades. Richelieu had failed in 1635 to secure an agreement based on an exact reciprocity of rights; it was therefore necessary to begin afresh. In the early years of Louis's rule, a diplomat was disowned because he drew up an agreement giving precedence to the English in the North Sea and to the French in the Atlantic. Negotiations were begun once again; but, pride being equally strong on both sides, it was impossible to reach an agreement. As a result the French and English avoided meeting at sea even when they were allies.

Things were no better in relations with Spain. In 1679 and 1680 the French admirals received formal orders to pursue Spanish galleys and to challenge them if they did not salute first. In 1685 Tourville and Château-Renault met a Spanish fleet near Alicante and demanded that its commander should salute the French colours. On his refusal they attacked, although France was at peace with Spain, and only retired, after killing many Spaniards, when the admiral submitted. Such incidents were frequent, all the more so because a royal order of 1671 forbade all Spanish men-of-war to salute first. The dispute with the Dutch continued even after peace had been restored between the two nations at Nymegen (1678). In 1687 Tourville, on encountering the Dutch vice-admiral, descended on him and forced him to salute. The following year a Dutch fleet and that of Tourville engaged in a veritable battle off the Spanish coast over the same issue, causing numerous casualties on both sides.

Colbert adopted the same arrogant point of view as his sovereign; he wrote in 1677: 'France claims that all other nations must bow to her at sea as at the court of Kings.' The same year a collection of 'Edicts, Declarations and Regulations concerning naval affairs' was published which began with a completely intransigent regulation on the question of the salute. Then, the following year, a stern lesson was inflicted on the Genoese who were in constant rivalry on the seas with Marseilles and refused to recognise the French pretensions. A French squadron sent to demand the first salute having met with a refusal, it launched a bombardment of more than a thousand cannon-balls. Six years later, in 1684, a great naval expedition fired a still more terrible cannonade which forced the doge himself to visit Versailles to tender his apologies.

Towards the Turks, whom it was intended to treat as friends, greater moderation was shown from the first. The ambassador who set sail for Constantinople in 1668 was instructed to have his squadron show no visible mark of nationality, in order to avoid difficulties over the salute in case of encountering any vessels of the sultan. The treatment of the Barbary States was different, although they officially recognised the suzerainty of Constantinople: an article of the treaty concluded with Algiers in 1681 stipulated that, whenever a vessel of the emperor of France (a title which the king liked to adopt in these countries) should drop anchor before Algiers, it should be saluted with more guns than a ship from any other country. After the Treaty of Ryswick (1697) the naval protocol tended to become more flexible. It was understood by then that nothing should be demanded of English vessels nor those of any kingdom: in the preceding year the ambassador in London had had to deal with the last Anglo-French incident. Henceforth the policy of intimidation was to be directed only against ships flying republican colours.

The notion of coastal or 'adjacent' waters provoked serious controversies in early maritime law. Coastal waters were conceived of in contrast to the 'high seas' or 'open sea'; but where did the coastal waters end, and how were their limits to be established? In order to define their extent there was much talk in the seventeenth century of the range of cannon-fire, and this definition was finally adopted, though not until the following century. In the meantime, the 'high seas' being thought of as the 'free seas', and the two expressions being often used interchangeably, there was a common tendency to oppose the monopolies which certain countries tried to establish over adjacent seas. The English jurisconsult and publicist John Selden published his *Mare Clausum* in opposition to Grotius's *Mare Liberum*; and Louis XIV felt obliged to define in his great naval ordinance of 1681 what was to be understood by *mer littorale*. 'All that will be counted coastal waters', it declared, 'which the sea covers and leaves bare during the new and full moons and up to where the great tides reach on the beaches.' However, as tides hardly existed in the Mediterranean, the question could not be resolved in this way and, for 'the great tides', the words 'the greatest waves of winter' were substituted.

A number of other international problems which arose in wartime were gradually coming to be resolved by common practices. Whether fighting took place on land or at sea, there were usually prisoners to be exchanged. This was done by exchanging numbers of equal ranks or one officer for several soldiers. If by chance one side could not redeem all its own prisoners held by the other side, those not claimed could be sent to the galleys like criminals in common law. Among the customs of war on land must be mentioned the right of all belligerents to force the population in a theatre of war to pay contributions in money or in kind. An excellent example of an important 'treaty of contribution' (*traité de contributions*) occurred during the Franco-Dutch War when French and Spanish commissioners, the latter representing the Netherlands, discussed the subject at length, during the years preceding the peace of Nymegen, at the little Flemish town of Deynze on the Lys. Finally, another strange custom, called the *droit de cloches*, was the right of the commander of a fleet to carry off the bells of a conquered town. Like most others, this right was flexible and open to interpretation. In 1711, when Duguay-Trouin took Rio de Janeiro he claimed this right and then declared that he would be content if the city paid him a ransom for the bells.

Of the many international institutions which arose out of maritime practices one of the most important was the consulate. It appears to have originated in a collection of maritime customs, the 'Consulate of the Sea', believed to have been written in the thirteenth century at Barcelona, which rendered the same services in the Mediterranean that the *coûtumes d'Oléron* performed on the ocean. But the origin of the institution remains rather obscure. Originally qualified representatives of the foreign merchants who frequented a certain port, consuls were to be found as early as the fourteenth and fifteenth centuries in all the great ports of Italy, later in Spain, and also in France at Perpignan, Aigues-Mortes, Montpellier and, in the sixteenth century, at Marseilles and Lyon, the thriving new centres of international trade. At first they were called 'sea consuls', then 'merchant consuls', and finally, when the consuls of France, for example, were to be distinguished from those of other countries, they became known as 'French consuls'. In the Italian ports French consuls appeared later than in the Ottoman Empire. They seem to have been royal officers from the beginning, receiving, like all office-holders, 'letters of provision' signed by the king: they were instructed to discharge their duties themselves and not to delegate them except by royal authorisation. But under Louis XIV, the posts having become venal, a General Farm of consulates appeared in 1683. Yet the Crown maintained the right to choose the occupants of certain posts, such as the one at Alexandria, later transferred to Cairo. Many obstacles had to be removed before consuls could be exchanged. The resistance of the admiralty of Guyenne to the appointment of foreign consuls at Bordeaux, on the grounds that they were an encroachment on some of its privileges, was not overcome until after the peace of 1659. Similar problems held up the exchange of consuls with the United Provinces until 1662, and with Portugal until the French prevailed in the treaty of 1667. In general, the installation of royal consuls in a certain country indicated a substantial progress of French commercial interests.

It is therefore not surprising, in view of the preponderance of French trade in the Levant, that from the beginning of the seventeenth century there were four French consulates in the Échelles: at Alexandria, Smyrna, Port Said, and Aleppo. Their rights and jurisdictions were set forth in special clauses in every agreement or 'capitulation' made with the Porte. They were instructed by the great naval ordinance of 1681—most important for our knowledge of the consular service—to exercise their powers of protection and jurisdiction in the interests not only of the subjects of Louis XIV, but of all Christians resident in the Ottoman Empire.

The institution of neutrality deserves special mention because it has since altered considerably. The word and the institution were already known in the sixteenth century. Exactly the same in the period of Louis XIV as it had been a hundred years earlier, neutrality was very different from what it became in later times. No principality had as yet been granted a permanent status of neutrality such as, for example, the Swiss Confederation has enjoyed since 1815. A country with reason to fear for its safety might receive letters of neutrality from belligerent powers, or perhaps from neighbours who foresaw war. Historians have sometimes confused 'letters of neutrality' with 'letters of safety'. The one may have been an offshoot of the other; the question has not been sufficiently studied to permit of a more definite affirmation than that in practice a guarantee of 'safety' was very similar to a guarantee of 'neutrality'. In any event, 'letters of safety', belonging to an earlier period, were not to be found in the time of Louis XIV.

The characteristic feature of early neutrality was that, although any State which undertook to take no part in hostilities might expect to be protected from the evils attendant on war, it customarily allowed belligerent powers to cross its territory on condition that they respected its integrity, its independence, and the goods of its subjects. In short, neutrality was governed mainly by the right of *transitus innoxius* (harmless passage). This right was based on usage and not on international law, as shown by the attitude of the jurists; Grotius, for instance, admitted *transitus innoxius* but stipulated a variety of guarantees to protect the inhabitants of the territories concerned, such as that troops should pass in small contingents and that indemnities should be paid, if necessary in advance, in compensation for inevitable damage. During the Thirty Years War the Free City of Strassburg obtained recognition of its neutrality by both French and German belligerents; but both used its bridge over the Rhine until 1681 when the French occupied the city. The most significant example in the reign of Louis XIV was the crossing of parts of the Spanish Netherlands by the French army in 1672, on the eve of the invasion of Holland.[1] Having no common frontier with the United Provinces, France could make contact with the enemy on land only by crossing territory

[1] See below, p. 215.

belonging to Spain. French troops, massed on the northern frontier around Charleroi, ventured over the border, apparently without meeting the least opposition, and in several stages reached the bishopric of Liège whose ruler was bound to the king by a treaty. There remained only military problems, for beyond Liège lay Dutch soil.

Latin continued to be the principal language of diplomacy, but in this sphere, as in others, its days were numbered. Already there were exceptions to the rule that all international conventions be drawn up in Latin. Such exceptions were to multiply in the time of Louis XIV and eventually to become the rule. It has been stated, incorrectly, that Latin had already been abandoned by the time of the conference of Nymegen in 1678–9. Foreign courts were setting the example—in 1663 the Elector of Brandenburg had a treaty drawn up in French as well as in Latin. Latin, however, was used in the treaty between the French and Imperial governments at Nymegen; only the simultaneous Franco-Spanish treaty was drawn up in French and in Spanish. It was not until the negotiations at Utrecht in 1714, right at the end of Louis's reign, that the Imperial diplomats employed the French language in the agreements which they concluded with France. Thereafter, French replaced Latin as the language of diplomacy.

Much has been written on the foreign policy of France during the reign of Louis XIV. In contrast with the preceding period, that of Louis XIII, there is no lack of documents, for at this time they began to be regularly preserved, being abundant especially for the Ministry of Foreign Affairs and the Ministry of War. Yet until recently they have not been systematically explored and historical writing has been based on little more than preconceived ideas. Thus it was asked whether the various enterprises of Louis XIV, like those of Richelieu, had been governed by one central idea. An historian of the mid-nineteenth century, Mignet, claimed that the whole foreign policy of the great king had as its pivot the Spanish Succession, while in fact this question dominated only the later part of the reign. This, the most outstanding attempt at systematisation, owed its short-lived success only to the talent of its author; it could not be taken seriously today.

Less notable historians, mere publicists for the most part, have claimed that Louis XIV had the ambition to complete 'French unity' by adding to the kingdom all territories of French language and civilisation that were still separated from it. It would be difficult to support such allegations by reference either to documents or to events. The men of the *ancien régime* had no notion of what we call 'French unity'; in the annexation of a new province they saw only an accretion of power for the kingdom and for the king. Neither did Louis XIV and contemporary statesmen subscribe to the celebrated programme of establishing the 'natural' frontiers of France. The idea of the Rhine frontier, like that of French unity, did not influence policy. Richelieu left a formula which helps to explain the whole, or almost the whole, policy which he directed for more than twenty years: 'to stop the course of Spanish progress'; but we look in vain for a neat formula of this kind which might be applied to the reign of Louis XIV.

It is clear, however, that the principal motive which inspired Louis XIV during the whole of his reign was the search for 'glory'. He said so on more than one occasion; and this idea emerges also from some confidential pages on foreign policy—albeit from the early years of the reign, especially 1661 and 1666—which, though written by one of his secretaries, he carefully revised and corrected in certain places. Unfortunately, he did not heed the wise advice which a man of the preceding generation, Montchrétien, gave the sovereign of the time, Louis XIII, in a work rather strangely entitled, *A Treatise of Political Economy*: 'You have, Sire, two great roads open to the acquisition of glory: one leads you directly against the Turks and infidels,...and the other is wide open to the people whom it will please you to send to the New World, where you may plant and propagate new Frances.' The quest for glory, then, took the place of a programme for Louis XIV. He measured all the opportunities which offered themselves during more than forty years in terms of their possible yield of glory. A contemporary of his youth, the Cardinal de Retz, wrote in his *Mémoires*: 'That which makes men truly great and raises them above the rest of the world, is the love of *la belle gloire*....' Yet glory was to be won only by victories, and therefore by war. War was to be the main business of his reign, all the more, as he once remarked, because all his nobility, who had no other occupation, urged him to war in which they saw opportunities to distinguish themselves and to gain benefits. He felt no scruple about declaring war, whenever a favourable opportunity occurred, and he threw himself into it with a sort of joy. On his death-bed, thus rather belatedly, he blamed himself for having 'loved glory too much'.

The France of his time was, according to the number of its inhabitants, the greatest of the European powers. The king did not know this; he could only surmise it, there being as yet no statistics of population. Historians have since calculated that there were eighteen or nineteen millions in France, as compared with perhaps five and a half or six millions in England and as many in Spain, the other two great powers of the age. If the first war, that of devolution, was directed against Spain, the following war saw France fighting Holland, a tiny country whose fault in Louis's eyes was that it had dared to oppose France in the Spanish Netherlands and by its signature of the Triple Alliance. He claimed, nevertheless, to wage only 'just' wars; and he termed 'just' those which did not contravene elementary principles of public morality, such as the maintenance of a solemn undertaking. It is only fair to state that he made ceaseless efforts to keep his engagements, though with debatable success. The great historian Ernest Lavisse could write that 'he broke nearly every promise which he ever made'. This is too sweeping an accusation, for in reality Louis XIV displayed a constant desire to keep his word, and he spoke with sincere disapproval of statesmen who did not consider themselves bound by their promises. What label would fit his extremely belligerent policy which cost France so much blood? Lavisse baptised it a 'policy of magnificence', but it may more simply be called a policy of prestige. France being the preponderant power in Europe, and the king being conscious of his position as the first sovereign, it was essential that all nations should bow to French superiority. If not, they must be forced to do so.

One result of the king's obsession with magnificence was that for his diplomatic service he often chose men not for their proven ability, but for their high rank which might uphold their position among foreign nations. The French diplomats serving in Poland at the time of John Sobieski, for example, showed a complete lack of intelligence; they understood nothing of the motives which inspired the king of Poland, and confused Louis XIV concerning the real intentions of that prince. Although Louis XIV, as we have seen, made considerable use of bribery, he appears, on the other hand, to have somewhat neglected that other means of gaining influence abroad—propaganda. Richelieu had employed teams of writers paid to explain and, if necessary, to defend his policy towards other countries. Louis XIV did not show the same interest and, although pamphleteers were never more numerous than during his reign, they served above all his enemies. The Dutch presses in particular flooded Europe with libels directed against French policy. The writers employed by the Crown were in most cases of little account, at least during the earlier and the successful part of the reign. Towards the end, when disappointments and reverses multiplied and the financial resources were exhausted, the role of money diminished, and that of propaganda by the printed word grew steadily in importance.

The personal responsibility of the king came into play only from 1661 onwards, for hitherto, during his minority, Cardinal Mazarin had continued to govern. It was Mazarin, therefore, who was chiefly responsible for the Peace of the Pyrenees (1659) which ended the long years of war against Spain. Shortly before that memorable peace Mazarin concluded a military alliance with England, according to which Dunkirk was to be handed over to England after its conquest from Spain. Thus the English co-operated in the siege of Dunkirk and occupied it in 1658. Shortly afterwards, however, the monarchy was restored in England: Louis took advantage of the financial needs of Charles II and recovered Dunkirk in return for a large indemnity. Bargaining over the price continued for more than a year, but finally the sum of 4,000,000 *livres* was agreed on, payable within three years; but only 3,500,000 (about £290,000) were actually paid, and then the young king made a solemn entry into Dunkirk.

In the same year the affairs of Lorraine furnished Louis XIV with the occasion for a great diplomatic success. The duchies of Lorraine and Bar bordered on the kingdom in two places, their western frontiers touching the three bishoprics of Metz, Toul and Verdun (annexed in 1552), and their eastern frontier meeting Alsace, most of which had become French in 1648. The French had occupied the duchies as a security measure during the Thirty Years War; but by the Treaty of the Pyrenees they restored them, retaining only the right of passage in certain circumstances. In 1661 Mazarin obtained explicit assurances that, in return for the complete restitution of Bar, the strategic roads across the duchies would become the exclusive property of the king. Duke Charles IV who ruled the principalities refused to ratify these arrangements and continued to lead in Paris the life of pleasure for which he had developed a taste during the last part of the Thirty Years War. Also in Paris, his nephew and heir apparent Prince Charles (the future Charles V) was preoccupied with the problem of the independence of the duchies. These circumstances suggested to Louis XIV the idea of a new convention with Charles IV, which was to be called the Treaty of Montmartre (1662) because it was signed in the abbey of that name, then in the hands of Mademoiselle de Guise, the last of her illustrious family. On this occasion the place became a veritable market. In return for a large indemnity Duke Charles IV consented to assign his States to the king, so that on his death they would be permanently incorporated with the French Crown. All the members of the House of Lorraine, including the Guise branch of the family, were raised to the rank of 'princes of the blood' of France.

The pride of the young king when he signed this treaty was not shared by his entourage and there was much disapproval; the deep respect for the title of 'prince of the blood', which conferred certain claims to the French throne, suffered a serious blow. At the same time that Prince Charles of Lorraine saw himself disinherited, the princes of the blood, then the highest magistrates of the kingdom and the members of the royal council, protested vigorously against what they regarded as the debasement of their rank. Louis was disappointed, but had the treaty registered by the *Parlement* of Paris, which brought it immediately into force. Furthermore, he made immediate arrangements for French officials to administer the ducal finances. The sovereign court at Nancy, however, intimidated Charles IV by declaring the treaty null and void, and in 1663 he ordered his officials to recognise the future Charles V, declaring himself released from all his engagements by virtue of a supplementary clause that the king had added to the treaty to appease the *Parlement*. Louis XIV endeavoured for some time to induce him to keep his undertakings and in 1663 seized the small town of Marsal, but that was all: the treaty was considered obsolete well before the death of Charles IV of Lorraine in 1675.

The annexations of Dunkirk and of Lorraine were not the only events which marked the policy of the new king in his relations with foreign powers. There was also the humiliation inflicted upon the Spanish government and the papal curia because the king interpreted certain incidents, arising from matters of protocol in London and Rome, as attacks on the prestige of France and her king. In Rome an obelisk was built to perpetuate the memory of the incident and of the reparations made. To so proud a man as Louis XIV, the forcing of these two powers to their knees was an auspicious beginning. Henceforth he believed that he was able to do anything he pleased.

The first war of the reign opened in 1667. This was the so-called War of Devolution, fought against Spain, the traditional enemy and the last adversary against which France had pitted herself from 1635 to 1659. The word 'devolution' must be explained: the right of devolution, which existed in various principalities of the Spanish Netherlands, including Brabant, the most important of all, meant that in the event of a second marriage the inheritance devolved upon the children of the first bed, their father remaining until his death no more than the usufructuary. The French claimed that this right should be applicable on the death of Philip IV—who was only to be considered as a usufructuary in the Netherlands—and that his principal heir, his daughter Maria Theresa, the wife of Louis XIV, should take possession of the Netherlands when her father died. It is true that she had renounced in the Treaty of the Pyrenees (1659) all her claims to the Spanish inheritance, but this renunciation had been made dependent on the payment of a dowry within eighteen months—and this was never paid.

The great question of the Spanish Succession had not yet arisen, but it could be seen just over the horizon, and it never ceased to preoccupy the French throughout the reign. From the first years onwards there was speculation whether the Spanish throne would become vacant. What excitement echoed around the world when in October 1661 the young son of Philip IV passed away after a brief children's disease and left only two sisters! But the birth of another child was expected. It was the future Charles II, who was to drag out an ailing and degenerate existence for forty years, postponing the opening of the succession question for that period. Had the child been not a prince but a princess, the history of Spain, and perhaps of all Europe, would have been very different. In view of the circumstances, Louis XIV hoped to have the Act by which Maria Theresa had renounced her patrimony annulled immediately after the death of Philip IV (September 1665), but long negotiations were necessary to bring this about. An understanding had to be reached with the United Provinces which had their own views about the Spanish Netherlands. This was soon done, for the Dutch had been friends of France ever since she had assisted them in their war of independence, and they agreed shortly before the death of the Spanish king that in this event Maria Theresa should take possession of the Spanish Netherlands.

No one was able to foresee an impending reversal of Dutch policy. In spite of an agreement in principle, the Dutch did not relish a French occupation of a part of the Netherlands. Willy nilly, Louis XIV, informed of the situation through diplomatic channels, accepted a compromise: the Dutch were to leave him the southern part of the country, including the towns of Cambrai, St Omer, Furnes and Nieuport; in return they were to obtain the entire coast up to Ostend. The negotiations lasted for a year, while Philip IV was slowly dying and the Dutch hesitated to recognise the pretended right of Devolution. After the death of the king of Spain a decision had to be reached. The situation was embarrassing, since England had just become involved in a war with Holland, and the Dutch were demanding the support of Louis XIV according to the terms of the defensive alliance of 1662. Louis, however, quibbled and invented various pretexts for avoiding his obligations. At first he gave proof of his goodwill by sending some troops to co-operate with the Dutch, who were engaged in a war against the Bishop of Münster, and by promising naval assistance against the English; but then he ordered all French warships to avoid any conflict with English forces. Thus passed the greater part of the year 1666.

At the same time, diplomatic preparations were being made for the expected war against Spain. England had to be treated tactfully, for it was said in certain quarters that she was ready to support the Spaniards. In fact, the colonial ambitions of the two powers involved them in constant conflict, and Charles II of England, after years of war with Spain, gave his support more or less discreetly to the Portuguese. Louis XIV realised that a Portuguese alliance could easily be concluded if he would only pay the price, and in April 1667 the Franco-Portuguese treaty was signed which guaranteed to the French a profitable diversion of Spanish attention for the time when hostilities would start in the Low Countries. The Spaniards do not seem to have perceived the danger which threatened them until too late, because of a certain lethargy which reigned in official circles in Madrid. All was not yet ready, for the Empire had yet to be neutralised. The Emperor Leopold I was the brother-in-law of both the king of France and the king of Spain, but it was feared in France that the old solidarity of the two branches of the House of Habsburg would once more come into play. To win the neutrality of the Emperor, Louis XIV looked for support in the Empire from those princes who were the clients of France, especially those whose territories were near the Netherlands: the Electors of Mainz and Cologne, the Duke of Jülich and Berg, the Bishop of Münster, etc. Thanks to French gold, the diplomatic efforts were successful and everything was ready by the spring of 1667, at the time when the Anglo-Dutch War was coming to an end thanks to Swedish mediation. Louis XIV avoided a declaration of war, sending to Madrid merely a treatise of justification, *Traité des droits de la reine Marie-Thérèse sur divers États de la monarchie espagnole*, in which he developed on behalf of his wife the thesis based on the law of Devolution. Then, a few weeks later, he issued a call to arms. Turenne was appointed commander-in-chief, but the king informed his entourage that he intended to accompany Turenne in order to inform himself.

With approximately fifty thousand men, Turenne marched north, in the general direction of Brussels. The Spanish general, with no more than about twenty thousand men, was obliged to sacrifice the most exposed fortifications, blowing them up, so that the French entered the country almost without firing a shot. Only a few places put up a semblance of defence. The only organised resistance was at Lille where the fighting lasted for a fortnight. After this, from the beginning of September, the army prepared its winter quarters, while it became less and less likely that the Emperor, hampered by the agreements of Louis XIV with the Rhenish Electors, would intervene. Altogether, the year 1667 was a successful one, and it was not until the following year that the difficulties began.

The Dutch, in fact, did not play the part allocated to them in the invasion of the Netherlands. An English diplomat wrote: 'The Dutch felt that once Flanders was in the power of Louis XIV their country would be nothing but a maritime province of France.' The Grand Pensionary of Holland, John de Witt, sought to mediate, requesting to know on what conditions Louis would agree to make peace. Repulsed once, he made a second attempt, this time intimating the threat of an intervention in favour of the Spaniards. Louis XIV then showed himself more conciliatory and specified that in any peace negotiations he would insist on having, besides Cambrai and a small part of Flanders, Franche Comté and Luxemburg. Soon after this first exchange of views, Louis in his turn made some proposals, the most essential of which became known as 'the alternative': either the Spaniards would cede what he had demanded from them in the preceding year and in addition would agree to make peace with Portugal, or else France would keep all the territories conquered since (mainly Lille, Tournai, Courtrai) as well as the places claimed previously, with the exception of Luxemburg. These new proposals were received very coldly by de Witt.

The reason was that he felt that England, his recent adversary, now that she had made peace with Holland by the Treaty of Breda, was ready to reverse her policy for fear of the growing power of France. If matters had been decided solely by the needy Charles II, French gold would doubtless have triumphed over English apprehensions; but parliament had to be reckoned with, and parliament, very disturbed by the French conquests—

Louvain was soon to be threatened—decided that some means must be found to stop them. The result of this parliamentary stand and Sir William Temple's diplomacy was a new Anglo-Dutch treaty, signed at The Hague on 23 January 1668, according to which the two powers were to mediate between the belligerents. To give themselves time to bring about a result, the two mediators demanded without success that hostilities should be suspended until the month of May. Shortly afterwards, they were joined by Sweden, and thus came into being the Triple Alliance of The Hague. The king of France saw three Protestant powers turning against him, powers with which he had maintained friendly relations and even alliances for many years. It was a colossal setback.

The war ended in a singular fashion, with Louis XIV trying to settle in advance with the aid of his allies the difficult question of the Netherlands. He carefully worked out a project of which he naturally would have the main benefit, and, in order not to commit himself openly, the Emperor was informed of it by Louis's intermediary, the Elector of Cologne. At first the Emperor, not wishing to irritate his Spanish friends and allies, prevaricated, but thanks to mutual concessions an agreement in principle was reached in January 1668. Hostilities did not, however, end there. In the dead of winter Louis XIV sent an army to invade Franche Comté; in less than a week Besançon surrendered to Condé and Dôle capitulated a fortnight later. Thereupon the English and the Dutch demanded an immediate cease-fire, which had to be granted without delay, especially as the two mediators had just joined forces by a permanent treaty. The terms of the peace settlement, embodied in the Treaty of Aix-la-Chapelle (2 May 1668), permitted France to keep all that was essential, her conquests in the Netherlands, and obliged her to restore only Franche Comté. In his fury at seeing the little Dutch nation take the side of his Spanish enemies, Louis swore that he would one day teach them a lesson. This was the object of the war which was to break out in 1672 and hold the attention of Europe for six years. During the years before its outbreak the king endeavoured to isolate the Dutch diplomatically, while continuing to wage against them the economic war which had been going on since the beginning of his rule.

Dutch vessels were the most numerous not only in the North Sea and the Baltic, but also in the Indian Ocean. In the Mediterranean the Dutch colours had in part supplanted the French, and there was hardly a French port where Dutch merchants were not both numerous and respected; but the result also was a smouldering hostility towards that nation. Fouquet had been induced in 1659 to take a defensive step which had caused a great stir: the establishment of a duty of 50 *sous* per ton on all foreign ships entering or leaving French ports. Colbert committed himself to the same policy. He estimated that the Dutch possessed fifteen or sixteen thousand ships, whereas there were only three or four thousand in English, and five or six thousand in French service, and he soon denounced the evils of Dutch competition. 'As we have crushed Spain on land, so we must crush Holland at sea. The Dutch have no right to usurp all commerce,...knowing very well that so long as they are the masters of trade, their naval forces will continue to grow and to render them so powerful that they will be able to assume the role of arbiters of peace and war in Europe and to set limits to the king's plans....'

The commercial war against the Dutch was thus a permanent feature of French policy from the beginning of Louis's rule. Twice, in 1664 and 1667, the customs tariffs were altered to their detriment. Refined sugar from Holland, which dominated the French market, was nearly excluded altogether. The maritime trading companies, however, formed at Colbert's instigation, languished, and everything therefore depended upon the outcome of the tariff war that broke out. In reply to the customs tariff of 1667, after the Peace of Aix-la-Chapelle the Dutch were continually raising their tariffs, for instance in 1670 and 1671. Another element in the conflict was the feeling of aversion that the Dutch nation inspired in Louis XIV. They had committed the crime of constituting themselves a republic, an unpardonable wrong in the eyes of this absolute monarch, so proud of his prerogatives. The French monarchy, which we term 'absolutist', appeared to him to be a model. He had passed his youth in the midst of the troubles of the Fronde and this exercised a profound influence on his views. After the restoration of the English monarchy Louis disliked the parliamentary régime and was shocked by the violence of the parliamentary opposition; the Dutch, who had long enjoyed a republican régime, suffered the same criticism. 'These bodies formed of so many heads', wrote a secretary charged with the preparation of his *Mémoires*, 'have no heart that could be warmed by the fire of beautiful passions....'

Nor did an aristocratic republic like Venice find greater favour in the eyes of Louis XIV who more than once showed his bad feelings towards her, especially because she felt attracted to the House of Habsburg rather than to the Bourbons. In 1680 a Venetian ambassador in Paris summed up the king admirably in a suggestive phrase: 'This prince is evidently working towards universal monarchy and is not far from achieving it....' In 1678 the town of Ragusa (Dubrovnik), a semi-independent republic closely watched by Venice and by the Ottoman Porte to which it paid tribute, attempted a *rapprochement* with France. Although its representative, a senator, was a friend of Pope Innocent XI and on friendly terms with Bossuet, this did not save him from being expelled from Paris shortly after his arrival and forced to leave French territory. Ragusa succeeded in escaping the Ottoman revenge thanks only to Austrian intervention.

There were, as has been shown, many causes of Franco-Dutch antagonism. In 1672, on the eve of the rupture, the Dutch, exasperated by the new tariffs, decided on a total prohibition of French imports for a whole year. This brought on the conflict. What was to be the attitude of the other powers towards the belligerents? During the War of Devolution, as we have seen, the struggle between France and Spain was interrupted on the one hand by England, and on the other by Sweden, the third member of the Triple Alliance of The Hague, while the Emperor Leopold I had been courted simultaneously by the Dutch and by the French. At the end of 1667, he had concluded with Louis XIV a treaty of neutrality on condition that the forthcoming war would not take place on German territory. In 1672, at the beginning of the Dutch War, he remained neutral; while the Great Elector of Brandenburg promised to assist his Dutch co-religionists and the Archbishop and Elector of Cologne sided with France. Having at first granted her the benefits of neutrality, he later concluded a treaty of alliance which authorised Louis to use the bishopric of Liège, of which he was the prince-bishop, as a base of operations. He even placed an army of about eighteen thousand at the disposal of Louis, who promised to maintain them. Shortly afterwards, one of his neighbours, the Bishop of Münster, undertook to join his troops to those of Cologne. The French took advantage of these agreements in order to prepare their attack at close quarters. Louvois, in particular, distinguished himself on this occasion. A Secretary of State since 1662 and jointly with his father, Le Tellier, responsible for military affairs, he was also, since the death of de Lionne (September 1671), acting as the Secretary of State for Foreign Affairs while waiting for the return of the newly appointed minister, the Marquis de Pomponne, from a mission to Sweden. Louvois arranged for the storage of victuals and munitions on the territory of Cologne; ironically enough, some of these had been purchased in Holland. By the end of 1671 everything was ready so that hostilities could begin in the spring of 1672.

The French passed unmolested through the Spanish Netherlands[1] to reach Liège and from there to invade the United Provinces, their right flank protected and if necessary assisted by the troops of the Elector of Cologne. It was only farther to the south that precautions had to be taken. On the left bank of the Rhine France possessed as yet only territories in Alsace, acquired in 1648, and connected with Champagne through strategic roads which were permanently under the control of Louis XIV.[2] These roads ran through the duchies of Lorraine and Bar, practically independent, owing to the fact that Duke Charles V had refused to ratify the treaty of 1662. Therefore Louis XIV in 1670 had taken care to establish military garrisons in the duchies. Nancy was to shelter French troops for the duration of the Dutch War and the Lorraine territories had to pay the heavy contributions demanded by the French government.

[1] See above, p. 205. [2] See above, p. 209.

In the course of the Middle Ages a tradition of friendship had grown up between France and her eastern neighbours which was based, according to diplomats and statesmen, on an ancient blood relationship of the Franks and the Germans. When the kings of France came into conflict with the Habsburgs, they appeared in the eyes of the German princes as the defenders of their traditional liberties threatened by Imperial ambitions; but this stage was passed by the time of the Dutch War of 1672–8. German opinion was surprised at the concessions made to France by the Treaty of Münster, and henceforth began to be opposed to all French expansion, even when it did not threaten German territory. The growth of this hostile opinion was observed in 1673 after Louis XIV had been making progress on both banks of the Rhine.

An important figure in the affairs of the Empire was John Philip von Schönborn, the Archbishop and Elector of Mainz, who combined the functions of president of the Electoral college and Imperial chancellor. Possessed of a passionate concern for the public welfare, he devoted himself energetically to the cause of peace. He very early declared himself against the influence of Spain, preponderant at the Court of Vienna, and urged that the alliance between the two branches of the Habsburgs be terminated. In 1658 he succeeded in having an 'Electoral capitulation' adopted before the election of the Emperor Leopold which forbade the new Emperor to assist Spain either in Italy or in the Low Countries.[1] Then the archbishop concluded a defensive alliance with his neighbours, which soon assumed the character of an anti-Imperial pact, the League of the Rhine, to which the young king of France adhered.[2] Many Germans, however, accused the League of playing into Louis's hands by preventing the Empire from sending help to the Netherlands during the War of Devolution; and these suspicions once aroused became stronger through several incidents. Was not a small French detachment seen crossing Germany in 1664 to subdue the town of Erfurt in Thuringia, a distant dependency of the Elector of Mainz? In 1667 a bigger affair set off a long quarrel between the nations: a lawyer of the *Parlement* of Paris published a pamphlet entitled *Des justes prétentions du Roy sur l'Empire*, in which German opinion perceived a whole programme. Such was the agitation that the king had to send the author to meditate for several weeks in the Bastille. Hostilities with the Empire appeared more and more likely, as Louis XIV and the Elector of Mainz both realised. The latter proposed to the Imperial Diet that an army of the Empire should be created, capable of defending it instead of the Habsburg forces, but the particularism and egotism of the princes defeated the proposal, while the French army pursued the conquest of the Netherlands. The idea was taken up again in 1670 when Louis XIV threw himself on the duchies of Lorraine. At the beginning of the Dutch War, the Elector of Mainz proposed a formal

[1] Cp. below, ch. XVIII, pp. 431, 446. [2] See below, ch. XVIII, p. 431.

alliance of all the princes in the vicinity of the Rhine; once again he encountered the inertia of his compatriots and he died discouraged shortly after the outbreak of hostilities. Moreover, in 1670 Bavaria entered into an alliance with France, the Elector promising his vote to the king in the case of an Imperial election. There seemed to be cause for hope in this quarter. Germany was farther than ever from achieving unity.

While military operations were in progress the Dutch on several occasions sent proposals for a settlement to Louis XIV. One of his ministers wrote to the ambassador at The Hague: 'It is well that they should continue to commit errors, for His Majesty will thereby be all the more justified in the eyes of the world if occasion arises to let them feel his heavy hand.' After 1672, however, Louis refused to let himself be drawn into negotiations, irrespective of whether the offers came from the States General or from the chief magistrate of the republic: at first the Grand Pensionary, John de Witt, then the representative of the House of Nassau, the young William of Orange.

Holland found itself beleaguered almost from the first.[1] In agreement with their French allies, the English attacked by sea, for by the Treaty of Dover (June 1670) Charles II had become Louis's pensioner and ally. The eastern frontier was imperilled by the Archbishop and Elector of Cologne and his ally, the Bishop of Münster. Two rivers, the Yssel and the Waal, served in turn as lines of defence. Then the cutting of certain dykes flooded the territory beyond, just as Louis XIV was arriving in person to watch the army commanded by Condé making a spectacular crossing of an arm of the Rhine. It was not long before the Dutch, besieged right in the heart of their country, sent ambassadors to France to offer the cession of certain towns as a preliminary to peace negotiations. Louis XIV objected that the places offered would be difficult to hold and this caused the failure of the negotiations. 'Posterity, at its pleasure,' he wrote later, 'will cast this refusal upon my ambition and my desire to avenge the insults that I have suffered from the Dutch....I shall not attempt to justify myself. Ambition and glory [*i.e.* the desire for glory] are always pardonable in a prince, and especially in a young prince so well treated by fortune as I was....' The first phase of the war, in which Louis had met with scarcely anything but success, had come to an end. The little town of Bois-le-Duc, although it looked as if it would have to suffer the same fate as the other captured places, could not be taken or even approached.

All Europe was beginning to be concerned about the fate which threatened Holland. The Emperor, in spite of his promises of neutrality, finally ceded to the entreaties of the Elector of Brandenburg and made a military pact with him (June 1672); their contingents advanced towards the Rhine into the rear of the troops of the Elector of Cologne and the

[1] For details of the campaign of 1672, see below, ch. XII, pp. 292–5.

Bishop of Münster. Turenne turned eastwards in an effort to meet them and to cut their communications with their bases; at the same time the Prince of Orange, advancing far beyond Maastricht, laid siege to the town of Charleroi which, however, he had soon to abandon on the approach of French reinforcements. In the course of the following winter, a short period of cold resulted in a forward movement of the French armies on the frozen polders, but a sudden thaw in January 1673 forced them to retreat. From that time the military situation of the Dutch tended to improve. As a result of their persistent diplomatic activities, Sweden intervened to offer her mediation and induced England and France to agree to the holding of a peace conference at Cologne. But before the discussions had begun they were broken off by Louis because he considered the Dutch proposals insufficient. It is significant, however, that just then the French had at last taken Maastricht in a spectacular operation which the king attended in person together with Vauban.

During the summer of 1673, Spain in her turn officially entered the war in her Netherlands, thus isolating the French army. Shortly afterwards, William of Orange broke through the curtain of troops which opposed him, rejoined the Imperial forces on the Rhine and took possession of Bonn, the capital of the Elector of Cologne. Louis XIV then had to decide on a partial evacuation of Holland. At the beginning of 1674 the French situation continued to deteriorate in both the diplomatic and the military spheres; furthermore, England consented to make peace with the United Provinces.[1] Most of the German States began to respond to the Emperor's entreaties and to support him against Louis XIV, and even the Elector of Brandenburg rejoined the coalition. France, forced to fight on nearly all her frontiers, was threatened by greatly superior forces. Before the end of 1674 most of the conquered places were dismantled and abandoned, the war being waged mainly against the Habsburgs. To fight against the Spanish hegemony was a tradition to which it was easy to return; but in addition the occupation of Alsace had to be completed and the remaining conquests in the Netherlands had to be defended. It was, indeed, a great battle that was waged at Seneffe, near Charleroi (August 1674), where the royal armies faced the Imperial, Brandenburg and Spanish armies; it was a defensive, yet undoubtedly successful battle, for the Prince of Orange returned to his Dutch bases. Although there were scarcely any French troops left on Dutch territory after the campaign of 1674, Maastricht remained in French hands, an advanced but isolated position.

These indecisive operations in the Netherlands continued for three years. The city of Amsterdam, protected by the inundations, was only threatened from afar. Yet the disorder in Holland was such that very soon new peace proposals were made; and once again they were disdainfully rejected. Gradually, however, the Dutch regained the initiative and in

[1] See below, ch. XII, p. 295.

1676 William of Orange attempted to retake Maastricht. This attempt failed and was followed a year later by another defeat in open country near Cassel. Meanwhile it was at last decided to hold a peace conference at Nymegen; the entire year 1676 was taken up with questions of form, etiquette and protocol. The first to negotiate were the States General who received merely moral support from England, which Charles II was unable to refuse to give in spite of all the seduction of French gold. In addition, William of Orange had just won the hand of the king's niece, Princess Mary, and this led to an Anglo-Dutch defensive treaty of friendship in March 1678. In view of this new stroke of fate Louis XIV decided that peace must be made without further delay. He let it be known in public that he would demand from the Dutch only a new commercial treaty and no territorial concessions. Accordingly, the Treaty of Nymegen (10 August 1678) restored Maastricht to the United Provinces with the reservation that the Catholic faith must be preserved there. The treaty with Spain, concluded the following month, provided for the restitution of certain places on the northern frontier acquired in 1668, others being substituted for them (Aire, Maubeuge, Ypres, etc.), which facilitated the defence of the territory. In addition, Franche Comté was confirmed as a French province. The economic difficulties which had brought on the war were settled entirely to the advantage of the Dutch, and the French customs tariffs of 1664 and 1667 were suspended. Colbert was unable to get over this setback; soon afterwards, in 1683, he died. The Empire was not a party to the treaty and did not accept the peace until six months later when, still at Nymegen, it ceded to France the town of Freiburg on the right bank of the Rhine.

After Nymegen there was a considerable interval of peace in western Europe during which Louis XIV tried to intimidate his adversaries without drawing his sword. This was the era of the *Réunions* (1680–3), the name given to annexations carried out in peacetime by decisions of the 'Chambers of Reunion', which were set up at Breisach (for Alsace), Besançon (for Franche Comté) and Metz (for Lorraine and Bar). The government ratified the *arrêts* (judgements) passed by these Chambers which were instructed to confirm the king's alleged rights in the territories close to the frontiers. The most considerable annexations were the work of the Chamber formed by the *Parlement* of Metz and instructed daily by Louvois, who was perhaps the inventor of the system itself. The territories seized as a result of the *arrêts* of this Chamber came under the jurisdiction of the *Parlement* of Metz and were attached to the three bishoprics of Metz, Toul and Verdun or to the duchies of Lorraine and Bar, at least until 1697 when most of the arbitrary annexations were annulled as a result of the Treaty of Ryswick. Among those which escaped this revision was the place on the Saar which was later fortified by Vauban and known as Sarrelouis. The most distant territory affected was below Trier in a bend of the Moselle where the fortress of Mont-Royal was built; it was restored with its surrounding territory in 1698.

In August 1680 French sovereignty was proclaimed over the whole of Alsace, with the exceptions of Strassburg and Mühlhausen. Strassburg was annexed to the kingdom in September 1681; it was still a Free Imperial City, whereas most of Alsace, of which we have come to consider it the capital, had already been annexed to the kingdom by the treaties of Westphalia. A carefully prepared plan led to the entry of French troops without a single shot being fired. The Imperial Diet, assembled at that moment at Frankfurt, attacked France with angry words and even the threat of another war; but it dispersed before these threats had given rise to any action likely to interrupt the progress of the *Réunions*.

The destiny of the France of Louis XIV was to be decided in the crucial region between the Rhine and the Scheldt. Pursuing the policy of the *Réunions* the king turned upon the Spanish territories which were affected by the *arrêts* of the Chamber of Metz. In 1684 he sent the Maréchal de Créqui to besiege Luxemburg, which the government of Madrid refused to abandon to France with the territory of the duchy of the same name. Because the city refused to surrender it was blockaded. But the siege was interrupted by an unforeseen event: it was learned that the Turks had laid siege to Vienna (July 1683).[1] Louis felt unable to remain entirely deaf to the appeals for assistance which the Emperor addressed to all Christian rulers; he also felt embarrassed because of the good relations which France had so long maintained with the Turks to the great profit of the French trade with the Levant. He decided not to intervene, resigning himself to being severely blamed abroad. When the danger threatening Vienna disappeared, thanks to the sudden intervention of King John Sobieski and the Polish army, Louis XIV rallied to the Dutch proposal of a general truce between the Powers which was being studied by the Imperial Diet assembled at Ratisbon. On account of new French successes in the Netherlands, the conquest of Luxemburg and the occupation of Trier, agreement was reached. On 15 August 1684 the truce of Ratisbon was concluded for twenty years, and France was left in possession of her conquests, including the *Réunions*.

In the following year, however, the Revocation of the Edict of Nantes (October 1685) revived dying religious passions both at home and abroad. The Protestant powers allied against Louis XIV, while Germany was, as usual, divided. The Emperor did not commit himself at first; but finally, embittered by Louis's continual interventions in German affairs, relating in particular to the Palatinate, which the king threatened to seize on behalf of his sister-in-law, *la Palatine*, he joined the league which became known as the League of Augsburg. At its inception in September 1681 the league had included only some Protestant powers: Sweden and the United

[1] See below, ch. XXI, pp. 515–16.

Provinces. Louis XIV secured the neutrality of the Elector of Brandenburg by granting him a new subsidy treaty; but Spain joined the league in 1682. The truce of Ratisbon was scarcely more than an affirmation of principle—almost an act of goodwill—for long before it expired the War of the League of Augsburg (1688–97) had come and gone. In the autumn of 1688 Louis invaded the Palatinate. After this sudden attack the Emperor decided to break with France and war broke out. England did not join the allies until after the Revolution of 1688, which broke out because James II, a Roman Catholic, alienated a large body of opinion that was attached to the Anglican faith. Because Louis XIV had chosen to invade the Palatinate, and not the United Provinces, William of Orange was able to leave for England with a fleet and an army. Under her new sovereigns, William III and Mary, England lost no time in joining the League of Augsburg.

The new chapter in the history of France which began at this time has been entitled by one author 'the Decline of French Power (1685–97)', but this is a gross exaggeration. No doubt the most brilliant years of the reign were gone. The Revocation of the Edict of Nantes permanently alienated the Protestant countries, among them two of Louis's allies, Brandenburg and Sweden.[1] To this notorious blunder he added what some historians have called 'bravado', but which was in reality little more than empty swaggering: he refused to follow the other sovereigns in renouncing the right of asylum which the ambassadors of the great powers exercised in Rome. Then, the pope having excommunicated the French ambassador, Louis ordered the occupation of Avignon, the ancient possession of the Holy See, and even threatened to send an army into Italy. In spite of his advancing years—he had now reached his fifties—Louis XIV more than ever believed any daring stroke to be possible; at the summit of his career, he felt that nothing could be refused to him. His *gloire* still shone in all its brilliance. A commemorative statue in his honour had just been erected in Paris (March 1686) in the square which was henceforth to be called the *Place des Victoires*. Having been supremely successful, both in war and by 'legal' methods of annexation, Louis did not realise that he had aroused forces which France alone was unable to withstand. In 1688 Louis stood at the summit of his power. The second part of his reign was to bring about its decline; his relentless pursuit of prestige and glory had succeeded in uniting most of Europe against France.

[1] For the relations between France and Brandenburg after the Peace of Nymegen, see below, ch. XXIII, p. 554; for those between France and Sweden, see below, ch. XXII, pp. 540–1.

CHAPTER X

FRANCE UNDER LOUIS XIV

With the death of Cardinal Mazarin in March 1661 began the personal rule of the young Louis XIV. During the eighteen years which had passed since, as a boy of five, he had succeeded to the throne, effective power had been in the hands of the cardinal, first during the regency of Anne of Austria, and then for ten more years after the king had attained his legal majority in 1651. The opening years of Mazarin's rule, down to the collapse of the Fronde in 1653, had been a period of disorder, culminating in civil war.[1] Not only had Mazarin been twice compelled to leave the country, but the absolute form of government established by Louis XIII and Richelieu had been gravely threatened; there had been barricades in Paris, and with the hostility to absolutism of the great nobles and the *Parlements*, the fate which had befallen the Stuart monarch on this side of the Channel seemed for a time to hang over his young French nephew.

Yet, thanks in part to the guile of Mazarin, the French monarchy emerged from the Fronde stronger than ever before; five years of civil war had brought nothing but devastation to considerable areas of France, and the great mass of the population longed only for peace. The opponents of Mazarin were too disunited to continue the struggle; within eight years of the collapse of the Fronde France entered upon the most absolute reign in her history. In foreign affairs Mazarin had brought to an end the war with the Emperor, begun by Richelieu, by the signing of the Peace of Westphalia in 1648; two years before his death he had concluded with Spain the Treaty of the Pyrenees which not only put an end to a quarter of a century of war between the two countries, but marked the end of Spanish hegemony in Europe and of the threat of encirclement to France through the alliance of the Spanish and the Austrian Habsburgs. Since his return to France in 1653 the cardinal had been all-powerful and, laden with treasure, had led a princely existence, surrounded by all the attributes of power and wealth.

The young king of twenty-two was determined that Mazarin should not have a successor as prime minister; he at once made it clear that he intended to govern as well as to reign, and that his ministers would take their orders direct from him. It is true that at first he retained as his advisers three men whom he had inherited from Mazarin: Lionne, an experienced diplomat, Le Tellier, Secretary of State for War, and Fouquet, the *surintendant des finances*. Fouquet, a man of boundless

[1] For the events of the Fronde, see vol. IV, ch. XVI.

ambition, had acquired under Mazarin great wealth of which his magnificent château at Vaux-le-Vicomte was the symbol: not only the interested adulation of men of letters, but above all his connections in the world of the aristocracy and of the tax-farmers, who had waxed fat on the complicated expedients by which he had administered the finances of the country, made of him a formidable figure. Yet before the year 1661 was out, he had been arrested, his post abolished, and his place in the ministry taken by his enemy, Colbert, another of the cardinal's creatures. This merchant's son from Rheims was to remain in charge of the financial and economic policy of the government from the fall of Fouquet until his death in 1683, even though it was not until 1665 that he was appointed to the newly created post of *contrôleur général.*

The period between Louis's assumption of the reins of power in 1661 and the outbreak of the Nine Years War in 1688 marks the ascendancy of France in Europe as well as the high point of absolute monarchy. Yet historians have recently established that these decades of military glory, of worship of the Sun-King, of imperishable masterpieces in literature and in the other arts were far from being a period of economic prosperity. For all the progress achieved in these years in the fields of commerce and industry, the whole life of the country continued to be dominated by agriculture. At a stage in history when the standard of living both of the masses directly engaged in the cultivation of the land and of the upper classes, whose main source of income lay in the countryside, depended on the prosperity of agriculture, the period of low prices for agricultural products which set in around 1660 and lasted, except in periods of scarcity, into the eighteenth century, exercised a crippling effect not only on agriculture itself, but on the whole economic life of France.

An English traveller like the philosopher Locke, who lived in various parts of France between 1675 and 1679, saw therefore not only the splendours of Versailles, complete with Louis XIV and his haughty mistress, Madame de Montespan, and the bonfires which celebrated the triumphs of French arms; he also lived in a country in the throes of an agricultural depression. 'The rents of lands in France', Locke noted in his journal (1 May 1676),[1] have 'fallen above half in these few years by reason of the poverty of the people and want of money.' This fall in the prices of agricultural products, in an economy in which the accident of a bad harvest could still mean not just hunger, but actual starvation for large numbers of people in the regions affected, was by no means uniform. The personal government of Louis XIV opened with a period of scarcity, comparable, in the regions affected, with the severe crises of the latter part of the reign, those of 1693–4 and 1709. In Paris the price of wheat, which had fallen steadily since the end of the Fronde, rose to over 33 *livres* a *setier* in 1661 and to nearly 39 in 1662; since these are average monthly

[1] *Travels in France*, ed. J. Lough (Cambridge, 1953).

prices, in both these years in the months of greatest shortage prices must have risen even higher than this, before they came tumbling down to a monthly average of just under 10 *livres* in 1673 and just over 8 in 1688. At Angers on the Loire the pattern of wheat prices was similar; after rising to 47 *sous* a bushel in 1661 and 38 in 1662, they oscillated between about 28 and 14 *sous* during the rest of our period. In the south-eastern province of Dauphiné, in towns like Grenoble and Romans, the movement of prices was somewhat different; in Grenoble the price of wheat was as high in 1679 and 1680 as in 1662, while in nearby Romans 1679 was also a year of high prices. At any given moment, in regions of France separated less by great distances than by a primitive and expensive transport system, prices for the different grains could vary enormously. While plenty and low prices reigned in one district, scarcity and rocketing prices could bring hardship, disease and death to the masses of a neighbouring region.

Yet the general trend in agricultural prices throughout these three decades was downwards. It is not easy to assess all the effects which this had on the French economy, even in the sphere of agriculture. No doubt the considerable part of the population which suffered severely when bread prices were high secured some relief when they fell to a lower level; but this was perhaps cancelled out by the loss of earning power brought about by the general slackening of economic activity. If the burden of feudal dues and tithes, coming on top of taxation, lay heavily on the peasantry, the incomes which the nobility and clergy drew from the land also fell and reduced their demand for goods and services. The letters of Madame de Sévigné and her cousin, Bussy-Rabutin, contain numerous allusions to the difficulties which they experienced in the 1670's and 1680's in selling the produce of their estates and extracting feudal dues and rents from the peasants. It is against this background of low prices and economic difficulties that we must consider the reign of Louis XIV. Worse was to follow in the last twenty-five years of his rule, especially in the catastrophic famine years 1693–4 and 1709; but we must bear in mind that the whole period from 1660 to 1715, and even beyond, suffered from low agricultural prices—with all that this meant in an economy still dominated by the land—interspersed with bad harvests, rocketing prices, and misery, even at times starvation, for the masses.

In examining the society in which Louis and his ministers carried on the work of government, we must not be taken in by juridical labels. Theoretically that society was made up of three orders—the clergy, the nobility and the Third Estate. In practice, though over against the masses of the Third Estate (or *roturiers*) there stood the two privileged orders of the clergy and nobility, the clergy, like the rest of society, was divided into an aristocratic minority with what was already a near-monopoly of all the best posts in the Church, and the great body of its members, drawn from the ranks of the middle classes and the peasantry. The essential division was between nobleman and *roturier*. Yet this is not the whole truth: if, as the Revolution drew nearer, it was to become increasingly difficult for the wealthy *bourgeois* to climb up into the aristocracy, in the reign of Louis XIV there were still several ladders up which rich members of the middle classes might raise themselves and their families into the nobility. The latter was far from being a closed caste, and the gulf between nobleman and *roturier* was far from being impassable, as is illustrated by the rise of the families of such ministers of Louis XIV as Colbert and Louvois; the same process, on a less striking scale, was going on throughout the period.

The clergy, nominally the first order in the State, mirrored the society of the day with its extremes of wealth and poverty. Some of the parish priests, especially in the larger towns, were fairly prosperous, but the great majority received only a miserable stipend and were often little different in outlook from the peasants in whose midst they lived. Since the best posts in the Church were used by the king to reward service to the Crown they were mostly in the hands of the younger sons of great noblemen or of the king's ministers. Many of the archbishops and bishops were first and foremost great noblemen who spent as much of the year as they could, not in their dioceses, but in their Paris mansions and the antechambers of Versailles, enjoying the social life of the capital and keeping themselves in the king's eye, on the watch for preferment or fresh favours for themselves and for other members of their families. A bishopric might be combined with a clerical post at court and with two or three abbeys, carrying with them fat incomes. For other younger sons and the daughters of the nobility all sorts of lesser posts in the Church were available; for them too a vocation, while desirable, was far from essential. The worldly lives of the court *abbés*, drawing often large incomes from the posts which they held *in commendam*, are frequently censured in the comedy and satire of the period.

Ranging as it did from the princes of the blood down to the *parvenus*, who had newly acquired noble rank by purchasing *lettres de noblesse* or an estate which carried a title with it, the nobility was an extremely mixed class. The descendants of the old feudal families, the members of the so-called *noblesse d'épée*, might continue to occupy high posts in the army and to decorate the court, though, if they were to keep up the luxurious standard of living appropriate to their class, even they were now largely dependent on the king's bounty in the form of pensions, gifts and lucrative sinecures. The less fortunate members of the old nobility often languished in the provinces in their tumble-down châteaux, too poor to purchase a commission in the army for their sons or to provide dowries for their daughters, let alone appear at court. There was thus an enormous gulf between the different members of the old *noblesse d'épée*—between the dashing courtier, dancing attendance on the king at the Louvre or Versailles, on the watch to snatch any vacant post or pension for himself and his children, and the provincial *hobereau*, often of equally or even more ancient lineage, whose fortunes had so far decayed that, but for his pride in rank, he was indistinguishable from the peasants among whom he lived.

Moreover a newer brand of nobles—the *noblesse de robe*—had grown up in the last century or so, through the purchase of all manner of official posts in the royal councils and in the high law courts such as the *Parlements*. These descendants of wealthy *bourgeois* now claimed equality with the most illustrious old noble families; in addition to having a large amount of capital invested in their posts—now hereditary like the nobility which they conferred—these men were generally wealthy landowners. Around Paris and such great provincial centres as Dijon or Bordeaux the high civil servants and judges had built up for themselves large estates. In addition to the feudal dues which they collected like any other nobleman, they drew substantial rents from the land which they had gradually acquired to round off their holdings. Keen businessmen, they saw to it that, by fair means or foul, they obtained the maximum return from the capital which they had put into the land.

The selling of official posts had opened up an enormous field of investment for the more prosperous members of the middle classes. Many of these offices offered only a small income and modest social prestige, but there were a thousand or two which enabled their possessors or their descendants to enjoy the social prestige and the associated privileges of noble rank. There were posts of masters of requests and councillors of state from which the *intendants* and secretaries of state were recruited, just as there were innumerable posts in the *Parlements* and other sovereign courts. If the nobility of the holders of such offices was relatively recent, their social position was strengthened not only by the possession of landed property, but also by intermarriage with the older noble families. The substantial dowries which they could provide for their daughters and the influence which they enjoyed in Paris or in the provinces were attractions to the parents of prospective husbands among the old nobility. A merchant's son like Colbert could become the father-in-law of three dukes, while the judges of the Paris and provincial *Parlements* were frequently connected by marriage with the court nobility. The Marquise de Sévigné, for instance, came from an old feudal family, but her grandmother on her father's side belonged to the *noblesse de robe*, while on her mother's side her grandfather was a wealthy tax-farmer.

The mingling of blue blood and wealth in the society of the age is seen also in the relations between the nobility and the world of the *financiers*—men who, whether as treasury officials or tax-farmers, grew rich on the financial needs of the Crown. The collection of both direct and indirect taxes, the raising of loans, and all manner of financial expedients such as the sale of offices and titles provided a variety of avenues to fortune and noble rank for men of often modest birth, but equipped with the necessary skill and lack of scruple. Despite their wealth and their newly acquired titles these sons of *bourgeois* or peasants (quite a number of the leading *financiers* of the period are alleged to have begun their careers as lackeys) were on paper separated by a mighty gulf from the court nobility. In practice, the handsome dowries, with a high proportion of ready cash to meet pressing debts, proved an irresistible attraction for the parents of eligible young noblemen. The duc de Saint-Simon, the author of the most famous memoirs of the reign, was compelled, despite his fanatical attachment to his rank, to confess that his duchess was the granddaughter of a wealthy tax-farmer; her father had swallowed his aristocratic pride and married the daughter of this wealthy *bourgeois* so as to be able to carry on his career in the army and to buy an estate to which he could attach his newly acquired title of duke. Again, in the letters of Madame de Sévigné we can follow the story of how, in order to restore the family fortunes, her daughter and son-in-law, the comte de Grignan, were compelled to marry their son to the daughter of a wealthy tax-farmer; no doubt this was a terrible blow to the pride of the Grignans, but they had to face the fact that, given their tremendous debts, only a marriage with a wealthy *bourgeois* family could save them from financial disaster.

These tax-farmers were not a popular section of the community; they were hated by the taxpayers who were the victims of their exactions, and despised as *bourgeois* upstarts by the aristocracy. Yet the monarchy could not survive without their assistance in raising money, and the riches which they frequently amassed put them in the very wealthiest section of the community and allowed them and their children to climb into the aristocracy by the purchase of titles and by intermarriage. By this period in French history the nobility had thus become a very mixed body in which the descendants of the old feudal families were a decided minority and had indeed often been saved from ruin by intermarriage with the daughters of new men; while the majority of its members had been recruited in the last century or so from the middle classes, thanks to the system of official posts which conferred hereditary nobility, and of *lettres de noblesse* which provided a title in return for the hard cash acquired in trade or more frequently in the handling of government finances.

The ambition of a well-to-do *bourgeois* still remained to rise out of his own despised class into the nobility. The road to great wealth lay as yet not in trade and industry, but rather in the royal finances, while much of the capital acquired in trade and industry was drained off into the purchase of *rentes*, of official posts, of land and titles. The prosperous *bourgeois* was only too anxious to leave behind such a despised calling as that of merchant, and instead of applying his capital in new fields of enterprise, he would sink it in such unproductive investments because they contributed to the social advancement of himself and his children. Many writers of the time, comparing conditions in France with those in Holland and England where the successful merchant was driven on by ambition to launch out into ever greater enterprises in the pursuit of wealth, pointed to the disadvantages from which French trade and industry suffered through the contempt in which the merchant held his profession; his one thought was to rise out of it.

Trade and industry continued to be organised largely on the basis of the gild system, with a master working in his shop with the aid of journeymen and apprentices. The regulations of the gilds laid down the number of apprentices whom a master might employ, the age of their admission and the length of their apprenticeship, the type of masterpiece which each candidate for admission to the gild had to execute, and the methods to be employed in the manufacture of the products of the particular trade. The main aim of the gild was to establish a monopoly by eliminating all competition, whether from its members or outsiders. In most large towns the different trades were organised in gilds, though, despite the efforts made by Colbert in these years to increase their numbers, since they were a very profitable source of revenue, they were by no means universal. Yet in the towns even the so-called free trades were in fact under the supervision of the municipal authority, and the difference between a trade organised in a gild and one which was not was probably not very great.

The technique of most trades had scarcely changed since the Middle Ages, so that the greater part of the industry of the country continued to be conducted on a small scale. In most cases the master would occupy only a small number of rooms which served both as dwelling-place and business-premises; there he worked with a handful of journeymen and apprentices. All shades of wealth were to be found in the gilds, ranging from the well-to-do cloth merchant or goldsmith down to such poorer artisans as shoemakers and cobblers, who often had a hard struggle to make ends meet as their numbers were very high in relation to the population of the towns.

In two respects the gild system was showing signs of disintegration. At the bottom end it was becoming more and more difficult for the ordinary journeyman to attain the rank of master, a privilege which tended more and more to be monopolised by the sons and sons-in-law of masters who were favoured in all manner of ways. The result was the formation in the towns of the nucleus of an industrial proletariat, still, of course, relatively insignificant in numbers. Although the journeymen had their associations (*compagnonnages*), which were the forerunners of modern trade unions, and although the age of Louis XIV had its strikes and even revolts, these were rare and sporadic, and were always easily and ferociously suppressed.

At the other end of the scale we see emerging in this period big merchants who stood outside, and above, the gilds. Trade, especially overseas trade, made some progress despite the obstacles presented by the slowness and high cost of transport and the dues which goods in transit inside the country had to pay, both in the form of tolls on roads, bridges and rivers and in that of customs duties which were levied by the tax-farmers on all goods passing from one province or group of provinces to another. Colbert, as we shall see, was to strive his hardest to stimulate both trade and industry in accordance with the principles of mercantilism.

The total population of the towns, even when we have reckoned in not only the middle classes and the artisans, but the masses of servants of both sexes in an age when domestic labour was cheap, and the still numerous class of people who were engaged in agriculture in the vicinity of the towns, was still small in comparison with the millions of people who lived scattered over the countryside or in villages and hamlets. The lot of the peasants in our period is not easy to describe briefly, at least if one is anxious to avoid the extremes of rosy optimism or black pessimism in presenting the very complex facts. Then as now it made a great difference in what part of France one was attempting to wrest a living from the land—whether it was in the rich corn-producing regions of the north or the mountainous or semi-mountainous regions of the centre and south. Again, it depended on the type of agriculture practised; while it was true that the fear of famine caused cereals to be cultivated in every region, however unfavourable for the purpose, and while the vine continued to be cultivated in districts altogether unsuited to it from which it has now vanished, already the beginnings of specialisation were visible; the vine was cultivated more intensively in certain favoured districts and there winegrowers put most, if not all, of their money on one crop. The lot of the winegrower could be very different, in any given season, from that of other peasants whose main interest was in cereals or dairy produce.

From district to district as inside each community the amount of land owned by peasants varied tremendously. A considerable proportion of the land was in the hands of the two privileged orders, the clergy and the nobility, and, especially in the neighbourhood of the towns, of the middle classes. The clergy's holdings varied sharply, from almost nothing to a really substantial proportion of the land though, on an average, not nearly as high a proportion as was once believed. The members of the nobility, both ancient and more recent, continued to hold a considerable share of the land, generally greater in the west than in the east, and a fair proportion was in the hands of the *bourgeois* of the towns, who were often on their way up into the ranks of the nobility. A significant area of land was, however, the property of the peasants, subject, of course, to the feudal dues exacted by the lord of the manor, lay or ecclesiastical; yet even where the peasants' share rose as high as 50 per cent, which was exceptional, their large numbers meant that the average holding was small.

A few prosperous peasants might in a given village own a high proportion of the land which was not in clerical, noble or *bourgeois* hands, but the remaining peasants would be left with only a small plot or nothing at all.

There were similar differences in the amount of land rented by the peasants. Most of the land in the hands of the privileged orders and the middle classes was let out to tenants. Some of these were well-to-do peasants with possibly a fair amount of land in their own possession, and generally with enough capital to make a good living and to enable them to pay a money-rent. But far commoner, especially in the centre and south, were the 'share-croppers' (*métayers*)—peasants who owned little or no land, and lacked the means either to pay a money-rent or to furnish the seed, implements and stock necessary for the proper cultivation of the land. These the landlord was compelled to provide; in return he received a share of the crops, generally one-half. There was an enormous gap between the poverty-stricken *métayer* and the prosperous peasant land-owner or tenant-farmer. Lower still in the scale—and a large group in some regions—were the landless or nearly landless labourers, who picked up a living as best they could by working for the better-off peasants. 'Talking in this country with a poor peasant's wife', Locke wrote in his journal (15 September 1678) after a visit to Graves, the famous wine-country near Bordeaux, 'she told us she had three children; that her husband got usually 7 sous *per diem*, finding himself, which was to maintain their family, five in number. She indeed got 3 or 3½ sous *per diem* when she could get work, which was but seldom. Other times she span hemp, which was for their clothes and yielded no money. Out of this 7 sous *per diem* they five were to be maintained, and house-rent paid and their *taille*, and Sundays and holy days provided for.'[1] It was peasants of this class who, along with their wives and children, provided a reserve of labour for the domestic industry carried on, especially in the north, under the control of the merchants of the nearby towns.

Despite all the differences between rich and poor, all peasants had in common that they owed feudal dues and services to a lord. If some dues had become much less onerous in the course of the centuries as the value of money had declined, those which were paid in kind in proportion to the peasant's crops still remained a heavy burden. Moreover, they gave rise to all manner of vexations, as did the lord's monopoly of milling and especially of hunting; the peasant's crops suffered severely at times. Moreover, feudal dues—paid in kind and in money—were not the peasant's only outgoings. There was the tithe, often collected not by his *curé*, but by the agents of a chapter or religious house. Besides, the main burden of taxation continued to be borne by the peasants. The *taille*, the principal direct tax, was essentially a tax on *roturiers* and among these the peasantry bore the heaviest burden, as the inhabitants of the towns fre-

[1] At that time a *sou* was worth a little less than an English penny.

quently secured partial or even complete exemption. There were great inequalities in the incidence of this tax between the different provinces and the different districts inside each province, and inside each village community these inequalities were repeated. Big landowners, for instance, would use their influence to secure a reduction in the amount of tax levied on their tenants—not from humanitarian motives, but so that they could charge a higher rent. 'This is that which so grinds the peasant in France', wrote Locke (26 May 1677), 'the collectors make their rates usually with great inequality.' Indirect taxes also fell heavily on the peasants. Though it varied enormously in its weight from province to province, the salt-tax (*gabelle*) could be as heavy a burden as the *taille*. Other taxes, such as customs duties and especially excise, were both vexatious and a hindrance to the sale of agricultural produce, particularly wine. When wine prices were low, as they seem frequently to have been in our period, excise duties could both reduce sales and take away most of the profit on what the peasant could manage to sell.

In assessing the ability of the peasant in the reign of Louis XIV to bear the burden of taxation imposed upon him, we must remember that the taxes which he paid, along with feudal dues and tithe, had to come out of the produce of a still primitive agriculture. The land was left fallow at least one year in three and, especially in the south, even one year in two. When a crop was obtained, the yield was appallingly low, absorbing as seed a quite disproportionate share of the previous harvest. Vast numbers of peasants did not produce for the market, but confined themselves to subsistence agriculture. Even in a year of good crops many of them did not own or rent sufficient land to keep themselves and their families in bread, the staple food of the masses both in town and country; like the landless labourers, they had to spend part of their time working for their more prosperous neighbours in order to make a living. In years of bad harvests, such as occurred over a considerable area of France at the very beginning of the personal rule of Louis XIV, prices rose to great heights even in those regions where there was not an absolute shortage, with the inevitable heavy mortality from starvation and disease. These high prices the poorer peasant had to endeavour to meet at the very time when, owing to the poor harvest, his own crops were more than usually inadequate and when, precisely because of the bad harvest, there was less work to be had in the country. The more prosperous landowner or tenant-farmer was better off up to a point—provided his own crops had not been ruined and he had at least some sort of a surplus to sell at the higher prices; but the grain needs of his family and other dependants, plus the large amount which had to be set aside for seed and the amount carted off by the agents of the lord and the clergy in the form of feudal dues and tithes, would make serious inroads into his crop, unless he was exceptionally lucky. The poorer peasants may have profited to some extent from the downward trend in agricultural prices; the grain they had to buy in to feed themselves and their families could be obtained at lower prices. On the other hand, the agricultural depression of these decades reduced the amount of work available to the poorer type of peasants, who were not necessarily entirely landless but simply dependent on a certain amount of wages to make both ends meet. On the other hand, the better-off peasants no doubt saw their prosperity diminished by the low prices which they obtained from their produce; taxes, feudal dues and tithes bore more hardly on them as prices fell, while those who rented land often found that their rents, fixed in an earlier period of higher prices, now became a heavy burden.

It would be wrong to imagine that there were not fairly prosperous peasants on the land in the reign of Louis XIV; but they were a minority. Those with a fair holding of land or able to rent a sizeable amount (they might combine this with the collection of the rents and feudal dues of a nobleman or those of an abbey, along with its tithes) formed a rural *bourgeoisie*, far above the mass of middling and poorer peasants. It was, however, the latter who predominated, and in certain regions landless labourers already formed a considerable army. The great mass of peasants lived fairly close to subsistence level, and, given the primitive agriculture of the day, went in danger not merely of hardship, but of actual starvation, if the failure of the grain crops proved really serious. A sign of the times was the continuance of peasants' revolts at the very height of the reign of Louis XIV. Sporadic and mercilessly suppressed, they still bear eloquent testimony to the latent discontent which reigned on the land.

There was, of course, nothing new in these riots and armed revolts of the lower orders of town and country; they had been numerous earlier in the century when the power of Richelieu was at its height. Yet it is significant that the Sun-King in all his glory should have encountered resistance to his ruthless taxation policy from beginning to end of his personal government. Sometimes these risings had the tacit support of the upper classes of the region, sometimes they were partly directed against the feudal exactions of the local nobility; but, however varied their origins, they show how unbearable many of the inhabitants of the France of Louis XIV found their lot. Even if we leave aside relatively minor disturbances, suppressed by hanging and the galleys, there remains a series of regional revolts which called for the use of a considerable amount of armed force before they could be suppressed. In 1662 the introduction of new taxes in the Boulogne region led to an armed revolt; in one pitched battle nearly 600 rebels were killed, wounded or taken prisoner, and some 3000 persons were arrested. Several were executed and 400 sent to the galleys. Two years later, at the other end of the country, in the Pyrenees, there broke out a revolt against the introduction of the salt-tax which lasted several years; it was led by a nobleman who was finally pardoned and given the rank of colonel in the French army. More serious was the revolt which occurred in another region of the south of France, the Vivarais, in 1670. Led by an ex-officer, the rebels, who had been incensed by the system of indirect taxation, were finally smashed by a large deployment of military force; a hundred or so were executed and several hundred sent to the galleys. The new taxes made necessary to finance the war with the United Provinces led to two particularly serious revolts in 1675—in Bordeaux and Brittany. In Bordeaux the lower orders, supported by the peasants of the neighbourhood, compelled the governor and *Parlement* to suspend the collection of taxes; as soon as the campaigning season was over, the king sent a large number of troops to take up their winter quarters in the province—a terrible punishment for the inhabitants, who were now reduced to obedience, their leaders having been hanged by the dozen. More serious still was the series of risings in Brittany, where the peasants revolted against both the exactions of the tax-collectors and their exploitation by the nobility. The repression which followed the arrival of troops was brutal; innumerable executions took place, and the soldiers robbed, tortured and killed as they made their way through the province.

Such, then, was the France over which Louis XIV began to rule in 1661 and in which in the next three decades he was to bring absolutism to its greatest height in her history. In considering the way in which he and his ministers governed France in these years we have to remember that the young king of 1661, ambitious, but raw and still unsure of himself, was a very different person from the man who, matured by events and feeding on success and adulation, led France into the Nine Years War in 1688. He was not an exceptionally gifted man; yet he brought to his *métier de roi* the qualities of industry and self-control, a rough sense of justice, a knowledge of men and an ability—shown from the beginning in the comedy he played before the arrest of Fouquet—to hide his true feelings. Physically he was endowed with a tough constitution, which stood up to all manner of excess and to the medicine of his age, and with a handsome presence which made him every inch a king; for all his politeness of manner courtiers and soldiers would tremble when called upon to converse with him. Until the death of his queen in 1683 and his secret marriage with Madame de Maintenon he flaunted before his court a succession of mistresses. When he passed through Paris in 1678 on his way to the siege of Ghent, Locke wrote in his journal (7 February): 'He was in the Queen's coach with 8 horses. In the coach with the Queen Madame de Montespan.' These mistresses were allowed to play no part in affairs, but some of their children he recognised and used to augment his meagre legitimate family.

From the first the young king was determined to be master in his own kingdom. He was king by the grace of God and responsible to God alone.

However bad a ruler might be, any revolt on the part of his subjects appeared to him an unspeakable crime. This was a far cry from the subversive theories and the rebellious conduct of princes of the blood, great nobles, the *Parlements* and common people in the civil wars of the Fronde in which Louis had spent the impressionable years between ten and fifteen. Now that Mazarin had disappeared from the scene, he meant to see to it that he was not to re-enact the role which his father had played while Richelieu had been in power. What is more, he broke with the ancient traditions of the French monarchy: there was no room in his councils for any member of the royal family, not even for the Queen Mother, Anne of Austria, who during his minority had at least nominally governed France. Louis's younger brother, Monsieur, was all his life excluded from any position of authority and was compelled to fritter away his days at court. Louis also excluded from his councils the princes of the blood, at whose head was Condé, one of the greatest generals of the age; all prelates, for he did not want to see a repetition of the rule of the two cardinals, Richelieu and Mazarin; and all great noblemen, even the great soldier Turenne, except in times of war.

'Règne de vile bourgeoisie' is how the duc de Saint-Simon sums up in his *Mémoires* the system of government under Louis XIV. The ministers whom he appointed were men of relatively humble origin, who owed their position entirely to his favour and could therefore be relied upon to show unquestioning loyalty. Under the new régime a considerable amount of government business continued to be transacted in a series of councils; but effective power was in the hands of the *contrôleur général* and the secretaries of state who worked under the direct oversight of the king. Among these officials a privileged few—a variable number, three in 1661 and occasionally rather more later in the reign—were summoned to the highest royal council, the *Conseil d'en haut*, in which the king discussed with them problems of foreign affairs and the general lines of internal policy.

The outstanding ministers of this part of the reign were Le Tellier, Secretary of State for War and then Chancellor, a post which he held until his death in 1685; his son, Louvois, who succeeded him as Secretary for War and dominated the government until he died six years later; and Jean-Baptiste Colbert who gradually came to hold the posts of *contrôleur général*, Secretary of State for the Navy and *surintendant des bâtiments* down to his death in 1683. These were all new men—Le Tellier belonging to the *noblesse de robe* and slowly making his way upwards through the various royal councils, and Colbert a mere merchant's son. The great nobles had now lost every shred of power (during the whole reign only two of their number were raised to the rank of ministers of state and even then they played a negligible part in affairs); it was with the help of members of the despised middle class that the new king ruled. These ministers were dependent on the king both for their position and for the continuation of his favours to them and their families. Their services were rewarded by their master with all sorts of honours and privileges. They were allowed to grow extremely rich in his service; their sons were permitted to succeed them or were provided with lucrative posts in the Church, while their daughters married great noblemen on whom lavish money gifts were showered; they and their sons were allowed to cover up their middle-class origins by the purchase of estates and titles. Richly as he rewarded them for their services, Louis was none the less determined to limit their power; none of them was to be allowed to attain to the influence and power which would make of him a second Richelieu or Mazarin. This end, so he imagined, was secured by taking none of them entirely into his confidence and by encouraging a keen spirit of rivalry between his ministers and also between the different families of ministers, the Le Telliers and Colberts. Every day he worked solidly for several hours with his ministers, either separately or in council; but all decisions were to be taken by him alone.

That at least was the theory underlying his government. The practice was no doubt rather different. In the panegyrics of the time and in the writings of some modern historians Louis appears as a demigod, settling all the affairs, internal and external, of the largest nation in seventeenth-century Europe with appropriate omniscience and wisdom, and dictating the answers to every problem to his humble ministers and secretaries of state. Despite his pride in carrying the whole government on his shoulders, his decisions must often have been inspired by his counsellors who, being better informed on points of detail, could present matters in the light which led to the result they desired. All along the king could be left with the impression that the decision was his, while his ministers in fact very frequently had their own way.

In order that the decisions of the king and his counsellors at the centre might be carried out all over the country, an administrative machine was necessary. The highly personal form of government set up by Louis led paradoxically, but inevitably, to the gradual establishment of a centralised bureaucratic machine. The decisions of the central government were carried out in the provinces (*généralités*) by the *intendants* who, like the ministers and secretaries of state, were men of middle-class origins and, since they were subject to recall at any moment, could be depended upon to fulfil loyally their role as agents of the royal authority. The *intendants* had already played a certain part in the government of France under Richelieu and especially Mazarin; but it was with Louis XIV and Colbert that the central government systematically established its authority in all the different provinces by employing these agents on a permanent footing. It was only gradually that this institution developed, that the *intendants* were assigned specific functions, and were given a definite district to administer until such time as they were recalled or sent elsewhere. It was not indeed until 1689 that the province of Brittany acquired an *intendant*.

The functions of these officials—the ancestors of the modern *préfets*—are summed up in their full title of *intendants de justice, de police et de finances*. The *intendant* had to watch over the administration of justice in his province so as to prevent abuses; he had the right to preside over any court within his province, and in certain circumstances he could try cases himself. A most important part of his functions was the maintenance of law and order; he had to keep a watchful eye on the influential people—the nobles, clergy and officials—who might abuse their influence to resist the royal power. He was also responsible for the repression of all riots and subversive activities. Aided by a number of part-time and unofficial assistants (*subdélégués*) whom he appointed on his own responsibility, he gradually took over a great many of the functions of the officials who were concerned with the assessment and collection of the *taille*; he came in time to direct the assessment of the different parishes in his province, to verify the lists of collectors, and to assess people who had used their influence to secure unauthorised exemptions from the tax or too light assessments for themselves or their tenants. Finally, the *intendants* intervened more and more in local government as the monarchy took advantage of the state of indebtedness of the towns and villages to assume control over their administration.

The new form of strongly centralised monarchy which grew up in the 1660's and 1670's was superimposed upon the existing social structure and political institutions; it did not destroy them. Though shorn of much of their power, those institutions which had in the past imposed some check on the power of the Crown still lingered on. The Estates General were, of course, never summoned; but they were simply forgotten, not abolished. The *Parlements* which, during Louis's minority, had attempted to take upon themselves the role of representatives of the nation in resistance to absolutism, were no longer allowed to play any part in affairs of State. Yet, though Louis did his best to humiliate them and render them powerless, he did not formally deprive them of their right to make remonstrances when royal edicts were submitted to them for registration; what he did was to strip this right of any real significance. In a series of edicts culminating in a royal declaration of 1673 he insisted that the *Parlements* should register immediately all edicts without any modification or restriction, as soon as they were presented to them, and only afterwards present their remonstrances, if they had any to make. It was not until the regency of Louis's nephew, Philippe d'Orléans, that the *Parlements* were to regain their political powers, a weapon of which they were to make more and more devastating use as the Revolution approached. In contrast to the prominent part which they had played in the Fronde, they were kept in subjection throughout the entire personal rule of Louis XIV.

Up to this time the provinces had enjoyed varying degrees of autonomy which might prove an obstacle to the advance of the authority of the Crown. Their governors had been allowed to build up a dangerous degree of prestige and influence which, as the recent example of the Fronde had once again shown, could be turned against the royal authority. To prevent this happening again, Louis no longer appointed governors for life, but only for three years at a time, a period which could be renewed if the holder behaved satisfactorily. Since the renewal of their appointments was made conditional on exemplary behaviour, the governors were unlikely to attempt to stir up trouble in their provinces, as they had done under Richelieu and Mazarin. Indeed, to make doubly sure, it was Louis's practice to keep the governors of provinces most of the time under his eye at court, while many of their functions were taken over by the *intendants*. Yet once again Louis did not abolish the old institution to make way for the new; he merely rendered the functions of governor harmless to his authority by reducing the post to a lucrative and therefore much sought after honour with which to decorate princes of the blood and great noblemen.

The towns still continued to enjoy varying powers of self-government, although they had long lost most of the freedom which they had once possessed. With the development of the power of the *intendants* the interference of the central government in local affairs grew. Here again certain of the forms of self-government were permitted to survive, but most of the substance had gone. In the end even the formal election of mayors ceased in many cities, as they now became permanent officials who acquired their posts by purchase.

The power of the *intendants* was less extensive in those provinces (*pays d'états*) which had retained their Estates or provincial assemblies, to which the nobility, clergy and Third Estate sent deputies. The most important of the *pays d'états* were Brittany and Languedoc. Their privileges were greatly envied by the inhabitants of those provinces—the great majority—which lacked Estates, because in general the amount of taxes which they were called upon to pay was less in proportion to their population. Yet it is doubtful whether in practice conditions were noticeably better there than elsewhere in the country. The *pays d'états* were never a model of democratic government, because affairs were largely in the hands of a wealthy oligarchy, drawn mainly from the ranks of the two privileged orders; and the taxes were levied with inequalities as great as elsewhere. These provinces did, however, possess the privilege of levying taxes themselves, and paying their share of taxation to the central government in the form of a *don gratuit*, the amount of which was fixed by negotiation with the king's agents.

Such remnants of provincial autonomy were hardly likely to appeal to Louis XIV. Yet once again he did not abolish the institution outright;

what he did was to deprive the provincial Estates of any real power. The deputies were bullied or bribed into submission. Moreover, Louis abandoned the old system of allowing them to present the grievances of the province before they proceeded to vote the *don gratuit*. More important, he gave up the custom of asking for more than he expected to receive and then haggling through his agents with the deputies as to the final amount to be paid over. Now the king demanded a definite sum which the deputies had to vote immediately; and from this time onwards the amount constantly rose, without anyone daring to make the slightest protest. Locke, who was in Montpellier during two sessions of the Estates of Languedoc, wrote of them (8 February 1676): 'They...have all the solemnity and outward appearance of a Parliament. The king proposes and they debate and resolve about it. Here is all the difference, that they never do, and some say dare not, refuse whatever the king demands.' That such submission on the part of the Estates was something new is well brought out in another entry (7 March 1677): 'One of the States told me that he was at an assembly twenty years ago when, the king asking 7 or 800,000 *livres tournois*, they thought it too much and gave nothing at all, but that they dare not do so now.' Things had changed since the end of the Fronde when this clash had occurred; now, with an absolute monarch at the height of his power, there was nothing for it but prompt compliance with his ever-growing demands.

Thus in the 1660's and 1670's all those institutions which might curb in some degree the power of the Crown—the *Parlements*, the governors of provinces, the provincial Estates and town councils—were gradually stripped of any effective power. The government was supreme both in the centre and in the provinces. No one class, no combination of classes could impose any effective check on the government machine. The mass of the common people—the peasants, the artisans, all those below the level of the well-to-do middle class—simply did not count in the eyes of their rulers or of the upper classes. In practice, if not in theory, the Third Estate was limited to the wealthier sections of the middle classes, the *rentiers*, the *officiers* (holders of official posts in national and local government, in the collection of direct taxes and the administration of justice), the bankers, tax-farmers and merchants. It is true that some of the most important *officiers*, the judges of the *Parlements*, had no cause to love Louis, since he had deprived them of all say in affairs of State, but with a strong king there was nothing for it but obedience. The king carried his dislike of them so far as to try to reduce the value of their posts and to make it more difficult for their sons to succeed them by insisting that no one who had a father, brother or brother-in-law in a *Parlement* could be admitted to that court; though such edicts remained a dead letter, the judges were compelled to register them. It is likewise true that the less-important *officiers*, those concerned with the collection of taxes and the administration of justice in the lower courts, were deprived of much of their power by the growing importance of the *intendants*; but their discontent was too insignificant to matter. In general, the middle classes were the firmest supporters of absolute monarchy in this period. They remembered the age-long alliance between the middle classes and the Crown which had finally broken the power of the feudal nobility. Their bitter experience of the futility of the Fronde had increased their loyalty to a powerful monarchy which alone could give them security and stability. Far from harbouring the subversive thoughts of their descendants who, a century later, were to claim a degree of political power commensurate with their importance in the economic life of the country, they considered absolutism a fair price to pay for stable government and accepted the existing social hierarchy as something divinely ordained; the one thought of an ambitious *bourgeois* was to make enough money to enable himself and his children to rise into the ranks of the aristocracy.

Of the two privileged orders the clergy alone possessed some remnants of independence. Every five years its elected representatives met together in the *Assemblée du Clergé*. It paid no direct taxes, but made instead a voluntary contribution, a *don gratuit*, the amount of which was fixed by negotiations between the king and the assembly. Yet such independence as the clergy possessed was severely limited. Ever since the Concordat of 1516 had conferred upon the Crown the right of appointing to all ecclesiastical posts of any importance, nobody who wished to make a career in the Church could afford to incur the displeasure of a strong king. The result was that, far from offering opposition to Louis's policies, the higher clergy were only too ready to play the role of courtiers.

As for the *noblesse d'épée*, their dependence on the favours of the king finally completed the transformation of the aristocracy from the turbulent, semi-feudal lords of the first half of the seventeenth century into docile courtiers. The princes of the blood and great noblemen had had their last fling in the Fronde; they no longer possessed the bands of noble retainers and the small armies which, earlier in the century, had allowed them to make war on the monarchy. Under Louis XIV they ceased to be in a position to blackmail the king by threatening to leave the court and to set up the standard of revolt in the provinces under their control. If a nobleman left the court of Louis XIV it was because the king had exiled him to his estates—a dreaded punishment which meant both the end of all favours and a life of utter boredom.

As a matter of deliberate policy Louis made his court—in a way which it never had been before and was never to be again in French history—the centre of the social life of the aristocracy, at first in the Louvre and in the other royal palaces in the Paris region and then, from 1682 onwards, at Versailles which he had transformed from his father's modest hunting-lodge into a vast palace, the residence of a monarch who was absolute at home and, after his recent victories, supreme in Europe. Versailles was the abode of the Sun-King with his proud motto *Nec pluribus impar*; the very doors bore in gold the emblem of his greatness. The palace was designed to appear to his subjects a temple dedicated to the worship of a demigod. The daily life of Louis, and therefore of the royal family and the courtiers, was regulated by the strictest etiquette, in contrast to the free and easy atmosphere of the courts of his father and grandfather. The greatest attention was deliberately paid to the regulation of the most minute details of ceremonial; everything here was of importance in Louis's eyes because it contributed to one great end, the exaltation of the king above the rest of mankind.

To keep the nobles out of mischief he insisted that they come to court. And the nobles came, not only because the life at court suited their taste for luxury and entertainment, but because it was the only way of obtaining the favours which the king had at his disposal. Unless they showed themselves at court, they had no chance of obtaining anything. 'I don't know him', the king would answer when anyone suggested the name of an absent nobleman for any favour. Crippled by debts, often reduced to augmenting their income by gambling and all manner of corrupt practices, the nobles would spend their days at court on the lookout for some post or pension which would bring them financial relief. To show their assiduity, they would try to keep themselves in the king's eye every time he appeared in public—at his *lever* and *coucher*, or when he was on the way to or from his council meetings or the chapel.

The proudest honour which a great nobleman could now receive was to possess one of the high posts in the king's household, or in those of the queen and other members of the royal family; all of these gave rise to endless intrigues whenever they fell vacant or were created as the need arose. Besides giving such posts as a reward for assiduity and obedience, the king would also confer pensions on favoured courtiers, or give them lucrative sinecures, provide dowries for their daughters, rich bishoprics or other high posts in the Church for younger sons, or even pay their debts.

The result was that the nobles were now entirely disciplined. Whatever they may have thought in private about the abject state of dependence on the king to which they were reduced, in public they outdid one another in flattery in order to curry favour with the king, piling up fresh debts in order to provide themselves and their wives with expensive costumes for the magnificent fêtes given at court, living a life of hypocrisy and intrigue beneath a veneer of refinement and politeness, for ever on the watch to snap up any of the favours which might be going. Louis had thus succeeded in reducing to utter impotence the descendants of the great noblemen who had once been the most dangerous enemies of the Crown.

For the greater part of this period of the reign the finances and the economic life of France were under the direction of Colbert. He never had things all his own way as minister. Quite apart from the difficulty of winning the king's approval for his policies, he was faced with the rivalry and often open hostility of his colleagues. This was especially the case in the last years of his life when he found himself supplanted in the king's favour by Louvois. Moreover, the practical results which he was able to achieve were limited both by the wars on which the king embarked and by the unfavourable climate of these decades of low agricultural prices and economic difficulties.

There was nothing new in the economic theories of 'mercantilism' which underlay Colbert's whole policy.[1] He aimed at creating a prosperous country in which the wealth and well-being of the people would assure the greatness of the king. This aim, he held on orthodox mercantilist lines, could be achieved, above all, by increasing to the utmost the country's stock of gold and silver. He was particularly impressed by the commercial power of the United Provinces, a tiny country compared with France, which none the less enjoyed great prosperity, thanks to its large merchant navy. Colbert aimed at wresting this commercial supremacy from the Dutch by building a large merchant fleet, by setting up new industries in France and excluding as far as possible imports from foreign countries, while at the same time selling abroad and transporting on French ships the largest possible quantity of exports.

Colbert was fully conscious of the disabilities from which France suffered in the sphere of trade and industry: the bad communications, the the internal customs-barriers, the diversity of laws and weights and measures, the lack of enterprise in the trading classes, their addiction to the purchase of official posts and to the non-productive use of their capital and, above all, the crushing burden of taxation. What he could achieve in the way of reforms and economic progress was limited by the obstacles inherent in the society of his day. As *contrôleur général* he directed all his efforts towards restoring the financial situation. The legacy which he inherited from Mazarin and Fouquet was a deplorable one: in 1661 the revenues for the following year and even part of those for 1663 had been used up in advance. Out of the 83 million *livres* paid by the taxpayer, only 31 millions found their way to the Treasury; the difference went for the most part into the pockets of the tax-collectors and tax-farmers. In order to restore the situation Colbert made the *financiers* disgorge part of their profits and also redeemed a large proportion of the *rentes*, a step which, however unpopular, was highly advantageous to the Treasury. By 1667 the gross national revenues had been raised to over 95 millions and the net revenues to 63: that is to say, in six years Colbert had succeeded in doubling the effective part of the king's income.

This result was achieved by a variety of reforms. He tried to bring some order into the Treasury accounts, and he increased enormously the

[1] For a fuller discussion, see above, ch. II, pp. 43–6.

income from the Crown lands, particularly from the forests. He had ambitious plans for a reform of the abuses in the assessment and collection of the *taille*; he dreamed, for instance, of extending to the whole country the form (a land-tax) in which it was levied in a limited number of provinces and of carrying out a survey of the whole country so as to be able to assess the value of the land on a fair basis. In practice he was compelled to confine himself to reforms of detail. He did his utmost to ferret out those who had usurped noble rank and thus exemption from the *taille* and to make them pay their share; he instructed the *intendants* to see that the rich did not abuse their local influence to push the main burden of this tax on to the shoulders of the less wealthy, and that the nobles did not have the *taille* of their peasants reduced so as to be able to extract a higher rent from them. These efforts met with only partial success, since such abuses were so deeply rooted in the society of the time, in which, as Locke said of the nobles (*Journal*, 29 September 1676), 'as well as they can, the burden is shifted off on to the peasants, out of whose labour they wring as much as they can, and rot lights on the land.' Colbert would have liked to do something to mitigate the harsh methods by which the *taille* was collected, but here again his efforts bore no fruit. It is true that he reduced the amount of the *taille*, but this brought little real advantage to the peasantry, who had to bear the main burden, as indirect taxes were increased to an even greater extent.

In short, Colbert's plans for financial reforms came to little; the abuses were too firmly rooted in the existing social system, and the wars which arose out of Louis's expansionist ambitions (and out of his own economic policy) called for heavier and heavier taxation. As soon as the wars of the reign began in 1667, money had to be raised by all manner of expedients, and taxation, both direct and indirect, soon reached a ruinous level which in turn hampered his plans for increasing the economic prosperity of the country. Despite all Colbert's expedients the net revenue for 1680 came to only 61 million *livres* against an expenditure of 96 millions, which meant a deficit of 35 millions, even leaving out of account arrears of over 12 millions from earlier years. His repeated appeals to Louis to reduce his expenditure met with no response.

In the economic sphere Colbert sought an expansion of industry to make France, as far as possible, self-sufficient. If old-established French industries were to be further developed and new ones introduced, he saw that it was necessary to have industrial undertakings possessing more capital and greater productive power than the industries organised in gilds. He set up or reorganised a number of *manufactures royales*, such as the Gobelin tapestry works in Paris, which were owned by the State; but more important were the private undertakings, bearing the same name, which he brought into being by offering the entrepreneurs such aids as subsidies, interest-free loans and a monopoly of a particular product in a given region and for a given period. Some of these new industries were concentrated in factories; more commonly they depended partly or wholly on domestic industry, employing the labour available in the towns and among the peasants of the surrounding countryside to produce such things as silk, cloth and linen, both for the home market and for export. Colbert strove by every means in his power to increase the range and output of French industry, from textiles to mining and metallurgy, not forgetting the production of weapons and ships for the army and navy. He introduced from abroad new machines and industrial processes as well as skilled workers. At Carcassonne, for instance, Locke noticed the successful use of skilled labour, imported from Holland, to build up the local cloth industry: 'They have got into this way of making fine cloth by means of 80 Hollanders which, about 5 or 6 years since, Mr Colbert got hither. They are all now gone but about 12, but have left their art behind them' (6 March 1677). He even reduced the large number of Church festivals which interfered very considerably with production. In order to improve the quality of French manufactured goods he laid down minute regulations covering such matters as the preparation of raw materials and methods of manufacture, and set up a body of inspectors to see that they were observed. 'The industry and commerce of a great country', Adam Smith wrote scornfully a century later, 'he endeavoured to regulate upon the same model as the departments of a public office.'[1]

In order to protect these new industries against foreign competition, Colbert placed fresh tariffs on imported goods. His first set of tariffs in 1664 was relatively moderate, but three years later he doubled them in order to ruin the Dutch, the great commercial rivals of France. They at once retaliated by placing heavy duties on French goods; and this economic war finally led to armed conflict between the two countries in 1672. The long war which ensued had very unfavourable consequences for Colbert's economic and financial policies; and in the end, at the Treaty of Nymegen, he was forced to reduce his tariffs.

Colbert looked enviously on the wealth which England and Holland derived from their great trading corporations, such as the English East India Company.[2] Like Richelieu before him, he attempted to follow their example by setting up similar companies in France. In 1664 he founded the *Compagnie des Indes Orientales,* which was given a monopoly of French trade with the East. Other companies were set up on similar lines to trade with America and Africa, with the Levant and with northern Europe. Yet, despite the example set by the king and the princes of the blood, who subscribed to their capital, the middle classes were by no means eager to risk their money in what seemed to them speculative ventures. In the end the monopoly of the *Compagnie des Indes Orientales*

[1] *Wealth of Nations,* Bk. IV, ch. IX.

[2] For these companies, see below, ch. XVII, pp. 398–402, 417–29.

was withdrawn, and trade with the Indies was left open to all merchants, on condition that they used the company's ships and trading stations. This company was the only one to survive Colbert.

Despite the unfavourable economic climate of the period, despite the failure of the privileged trading companies, and the enforced withdrawal of his high tariff system, Colbert did obtain some results, even though they proved to be much more modest than those of which he had dreamed. He did succeed in increasing the range of French industry and the quality of its products, and if there were considerable economic setbacks between his death in 1683 and the end of the reign, he had built for the future, since many of his dreams of a greater and more powerful French industry were to be realised in the course of the eighteenth century. He did something to improve internal communications; thus the famous *Canal des Deux Mers*, linking the Atlantic and the Mediterranean, was successfully completed two years before his death. The subsidies which he gave to shipowners resulted in a considerable increase in shipbuilding, and in course of time France developed a substantial merchant navy, with the result that overseas trade, especially with northern Europe, Spain, the Levant and the French colonies, greatly expanded, and France took her place alongside the great trading nations, England and Holland.

Seen in relation to the past history and traditions of France the work of Louis XIV and his ministers, from the time he took over power in 1661, takes on a revolutionary appearance. The break with tradition which absolutism at its height represented was in many respects a sharp one. No doubt the process which had raised the French Crown to this climax of its power had been very slow and gradual, extending over hundreds of years, and in the seventeenth century the contribution of Henry IV, Richelieu and Mazarin to the strengthening of its position had been extremely important. But with Louis XIV firmly in the saddle the monarchy raised itself, in its monopoly of power, above the princes of the blood, the great nobles and all the other notabilities, whom it pushed down into an equality of impotence with the masses of the nation. All the traditional checks on the royal power—the Estates General and provincial Estates, the independent powers of governors of provinces and the town councils, the political and administrative functions of the sovereign courts—all these were ignored or forced into the background to make way for the uncontrolled power of the king. At the centre there was no longer a prime minister of the stature of Richelieu or Mazarin; the king entrusted such powers as he thought fit to a small group of ministers and secretaries of state who, because of their modest origins and their utter dependence on his favour, were his faithful instruments; while in the provinces the writ of the central government was translated into action by the permanent establishment over the entire country of its agents, the *intendants*.

Yet, revolutionary as the new system was in several respects, supreme as Louis made himself at this period of his long reign, there were all manner of limits to his power and even to the changes which he sought to effect. He did not alter in any fundamental way the society which he found in existence when he took over power in 1661. He left untouched its deep divisions and its glaring inequalities, based on a subtle mixture of birth and wealth; if he encouraged rather than hindered the upward ascent into the nobility of the wealthiest section of the middle classes, if he stripped the aristocracy of all political power and made it entirely dependent upon himself, he left untouched its social and fiscal privileges, with all the abuses and injustices which these involved. At all sorts of levels the France over which he ruled was still very far from being really unified. There was the chaos of weights and measures and, more important, the confusion of Roman law and innumerable varieties of customary law. Economically, despite certain modest reforms of Colbert, the country was still divided by a complicated system of internal customs-barriers which were an obstacle to economic progress. There was no uniform system of taxation over the country as a whole; each province was taxed separately, with a different incidence of both direct and indirect taxation, levied by different methods and with varying degrees of favouritism or hardship. Some provinces had managed to hold on to their Estates, for what they were worth; others had lost theirs, while the majority had never had any such institution. The limits of the revolution effected by Louis XIV are clearly revealed if we stand back a moment and consider the picture of administrative chaos and fiscal injustice which ministers like Necker and Calonne were to paint a hundred years later. It was in fact left to the men of 1789 to complete the unification of France and to effect a real revolution in the economic and social spheres.

Louis XIV in these years of his glory is often depicted as the answer to the prayers of the mass of French people for a king who would be the incarnation of royal authority and the order which it brought with it. No doubt the masses were grateful for the contrast between the settled state of the kingdom and the disorders and devastations of the Fronde; pride in the military glory of these years of the reign no doubt strengthened these feelings of gratitude and admiration, even if we do not take literally the paeans of praise of the Sun-King poured forth by Racine and Molière, Boileau and La Fontaine, as well as a host of lesser writers. In the sphere of the arts there was revealed—for instance, in the writings of 'Moderns' like Perrault in the 1680's and 1690's—a new feeling of pride in the recent achievements of French civilisation, which was now felt to be superior to that of Greece and Rome or of such modern rivals as Italy and Spain. Yet if we do not question the sincerity of Louis's panegyrists at this period of the reign, we are left to wonder whether the mass of the French people were as thrilled to be alive in these years as some subsequent writers have suggested. There are hints, and often more than hints, of discontent among most classes of the community. The great nobles resented their exclusion from the royal councils and their dependence on the king; the judges of the *Parlements* and behind them the mass of lesser *officiers* were aggrieved by their loss of power and influence through the development of absolutism and the encroachments of the *intendants*. Wars meant a crushing burden of taxation and the bitterly resented billeting of troops on the civil population. The economic trends were unfavourable, and, rooted in the backward state of agricultural technique and transport, was the ever-present menace of grain-shortages, high bread prices, and even starvation. The expectation of life for the masses still continued to hinge on the uncertainties of the next harvest; it was not until the next century that this nightmare was to be lifted. A hundred years later, in the reign of the unfortunate Louis XVI, the masses might have to suffer privations in years of bad harvests; but they were at least spared the menace of famine and disease which in the France of Louis XIV could carry off thousands and produce a drastic fall in the birth-rate. A hundred years later there were riots in years of bad harvests or for other reasons; but the reign of Louis XVI saw none of the revolts, extending over whole provinces, which, in the age of Colbert and Louvois, were the result of grinding taxation and feudal oppression.

In these decades France was supreme in Europe. It is true that, as a result of the Fronde and of economic depression, her population would appear to have remained stationary or even to have slightly declined. Yet with her eighteen or nineteen million inhabitants she was numerically by far the strongest power in a Europe which was much less densely populated than it is today, and in which Germany and Italy were merely loose collections of States, each with a total population much inferior to that of France. Her chief rival was the House of Austria with its heterogeneous possessions, which had a population of some seven millions; France towered above the five (or at most six) millions of Spain and of England, and the fourteen millions of Russia. Judged by modern standards, towns were small; but in the conditions prevailing in seventeenth-century Europe a considerable number of French towns ranked as being of very respectable size, even though probably only two provincial centres, Lyon and Marseilles, had reached somewhere between 50,000 and 100,000 inhabitants. If Paris itself, with a population of almost 500,000, was smaller than London and came nowhere near containing some 10 per cent of the inhabitants of the country, it was far and away France's largest city. Along with London it held a unique position in the Europe of that day, being at once a great centre of communications and commerce, the seat of the administration, and the undisputed cultural capital of a highly centralised country.

When the landing of William III at Torbay in November 1688 once more plunged France and a great part of Europe into war, Louis XIV had held the reins of power for twenty-seven years. The inexperienced and unsure youth who had taken over power from Mazarin in 1661 was now a man of fifty, sobered by over a quarter of a century of almost unlimited power and responsibility, and yet bathed in an atmosphere of adulation because of his past triumphs. The twenty-seven more years which he had to reign were to bring him many setbacks and defeats abroad, while at home the economic consequences of almost incessant wars were to combine with agricultural depression alternating with rocketing bread prices and famine to bring criticism of the whole régime out into the open. The cost of his achieving such power both at home and abroad was to become plain for all Frenchmen to see.

CHAPTER XI

THE ACHIEVEMENTS OF FRANCE IN ART, THOUGHT AND LITERATURE

THE year 1660 was notable in the annals of French civilisation. Molière's *Les Précieuses Ridicules* was performed in the presence of the young Louis XIV, and Mademoiselle de Scudéry published the tenth and final volume of her *Clélie*, thus ending the four years of expectancy and suspense in which her many readers had been held. In the following year, France, disillusioned by civil wars and emancipated from the dominion of an unpopular minister, Mazarin, eagerly welcomed her young, energetic king, who gave promise of providing, in abundant measure, that military glory and national prestige which were the best antidotes to the national malady of *l'ennui*. In literature, a brilliant school of writers, endowed with intelligence and wit and supported by royal patronage, was to discredit the more prolix and sententious of their predecessors and to confer an enduring lustre on a court, the most magnificent in modern times.

Yet the glory was to prove short-lived. Thirty years later most of the great men had gone or had retired into obscurity. Molière died in 1673; Racine, who survived until 1699, was unproductive in the last decade of his life; Boileau, on retirement to his suburban house at Auteuil in 1685, could look back on his best achievements; La Fontaine, having lost his patroness in 1693, sought refuge in repentance and theological studies; even Madame de Sévigné wrote few letters after 1691, for in that year she joined her beloved daughter in Provence. At court, the buoyancy and vivacity of earlier years were replaced by a régime of sombre pietism, and France seemed to follow the mood of her king. There was still, it is true, much intellectual activity in France—who could prevent Frenchmen from thinking?—but the lead was no longer taken by Versailles.

Centralised control of every sphere of life was characteristic of the rule of Louis XIV. For the press there was the censorship, still exercised by the Sorbonne, and by the government, acting through the *Parlement de Paris*. Printing-houses in the cities were subject to licensing, and there were occasions, as in 1685, when heretical books were publicly burned. That the censorship of the stage was less strict than that of the press is an indication of the king's personal likings, but it should be added that, in general, interference with freedom of speech was fitful and capricious; moreover, the steady flow of books and pamphlets from abroad, particularly from Holland, helped to counteract the effects of the censorship.

In other spheres it was possible to ensure greater uniformity. Louvois created a disciplined army from what had been a rabble; Colbert regulated commerce and industry and legislated for every form of activity, including art; it was his object to bring even the highest imaginative effort within the control of a royal institution. The French Academy had been founded in 1634; then followed, in 1648, the Royal Academy of Painting and Sculpture, which was reorganised by Colbert and the painter Lebrun.[1] As Superintendent of Buildings, Colbert, with the help of the Academies, prescribed the rules to be observed by artist and sculptor, with the result that much of the imaginative life of the nation was as carefully cut to measure as its cloth. On the other hand, the institution of these Academies helped to raise the status of the artist. Hitherto, he had been a workman, a member of a gild; now, his association with a Royal Academy gave him a professional standing. As for the skilled craftsman, he might improve his prospects by a period of training in *Les Gobelins*, the royal factory where tapestry and furniture were made, and a high standard of excellence ensured by the personal supervision of the court painter and decorator Lebrun. Only the actor was left out of this purposeful co-ordination of talent. Louis risked the anathema of the clergy by his recognition of Molière; but, in spite of this royal support, difficulties were raised about conferring Christian burial on the great actor-dramatist.

The most concrete expression of this concentration of talent is to be seen in the palace of Versailles. In the course of the sixteenth century the influence of the Italian Renaissance had been clearly evidenced in French domestic architecture, especially in the châteaux of the Loire country; in the next century much was done, notably by Henry IV, Richelieu and Mazarin to embellish Paris, where the Palais Royal, the Pont Neuf and the Luxembourg were such notable additions that Paris rivalled Rome as a capital city. Outside the metropolis the greatest architectural achievement was the château of Vaux-le-Vicomte, designed by Le Vau, and completed for the Minister of Finance, Nicolas Fouquet, in 1661. Le Vau, assisted by a team of artists, sculptors and decorators, succeeded in making this edifice the most impressive of its kind in France, unmatched in its magnificent interiors and elaborately planned gardens; but unfortunately it provided the clearest evidence of that financial malversation which in 1661 caused the downfall of this phantastic minister. Vaux-le-Vicomte, designed in a style of Baroque more restrained than the Italian, was the model for Versailles; indeed, the artists, carvings, sculptures, and even many of the shrubs were taken from the one for the service of the other. The king, with his boyhood recollections of the Paris mob in the Fronde,[2] was resolved not to live in the Louvre; so he commissioned a number of artists to co-operate in the building of a palace which, if only

[1] For further details of the French Academies, see above, ch. VII, p. 161.

[2] For the Fronde movements, see vol. IV, ch. XVI.

by its size and cost, was an eloquent demonstration of what could be done with an unlimited amount of public money.[1]

The palace of Versailles, about twelve miles west of Paris, is notable, not for grace of design (this has been marred by additions and changes), but for its geometrically arranged gardens and its elaborate internal decorations. The gardens were planned by Le Nôtre, and much labour was spent in excavations to bring a water-supply to the fountains. The Grand Apartments, for the personal service of the king and queen, were decorated under the supervision of Lebrun in the years 1678–81. For Louis, it was a stage providing a setting for the glories of his reign, an emblem, not always of taste, but of over-rich, over-gilded display.

On the evolution of French pictorial art Versailles may have had an unfortunate influence. Lebrun, a good decorator but a mediocre painter, drew up a code of rules for the artist,[2] which, among other things, prescribed the 'postures' best adapted for delineating the various passions. The Academies helped to maintain this uniformity of precept and practice, and a table of precedence was established of the models to be followed—in sculpture, the Ancients; in painting, Raphael and the Roman school, and after them Poussin. Venetian artists, such as Bellini, were to be avoided because of their over-rich colouring; even more, Dutch and Flemish art were ruled out, as too *bourgeois* and literal. Insistence on such principles may well have diverted French pictorial art from its natural course. Already, Poussin and Claude Gelée de Lorraine had created a fine tradition in landscape painting, but as they spent the greater part of their working lives in Rome, they cannot be regarded as typically French. The same applies, though to a less extent, to Philippe de Champaigne, the portraitist, who came under the influence of Port-Royal;[3] his later portraits, well-known in engravings, show the austerity of the Jansenist ideal. To that extent Champaigne represents an aspect of seventeenth-century life not particularly suited to expression in pictorial art. Earlier in the century the three brothers Le Nain—Antoine, Louis and Matthieu—were producing work of a spontaneous and naturalistic kind, notably in their peasant scenes; and a similar integrity can be seen in the paintings of Abraham Bosse and of George de la Tour. All these artists gave proof of a power of individual characterisation; their work has the fidelity and conviction of true art. In contrasting these with the allegorical scenes used by Lebrun for the decoration of Versailles, one cannot but regret the departure from the old simplicity and directness; for, after all, in the scenes and people around him, however humble, the artist is more likely to find inspiration than in the Jupiters and Apollos

[1] In this and the immediately succeeding paragraphs the writer is indebted to Sir Anthony Blunt's excellent *Art and Architecture in France, 1500–1700*, Pelican Series (1953).

[2] *Méthode pour apprendre à dessiner les Passions.*

[3] For Port-Royal and the Jansenists, see above, ch. VI, pp. 132–4.

who usually provide little more than conventional patterns for tapestry or carpets.[1]

It may, therefore, be concluded that where, as in architecture and decoration, the inspiration or incentive came from Louis himself, the results were at best mediocre. But there were other spheres, notably drama, music and poetry, where the royal influence had more fortunate results. For the assessment of these it is necessary to indicate some of the elements in the rich intellectual heritage with which the civilisation of France was endowed. There was, first of all, the influence of Montaigne. Everyone read his *Essays*; everyone was familiar with his cultured scepticism, or pyrrhonism, as it was called; many disciples admired his robust common sense and moderation, so sharply contrasted with the excesses of the age in which he lived. Like many of his contemporaries, he had derived from Pomponazzi and the school of Padua a disbelief in miracles and revelation, an attitude which led, not so much to atheism or agnosticism, as to a contrast between faith and reason, the two extremes between which the mind may oscillate. Generally, he thought that Christianity had failed to create a civilisation worthy of comparison with that of ancient Greece and Rome, and accordingly he resorted to the Ancients for guidance and example. With his meridional egotism and keen appreciation of the sunshine of life, Montaigne, while admitting acquaintance with the vexed problems of civilization, refused to allow them to interfere with his digestion, an attitude which has commended itself to many generations of Frenchmen.

Equally important was the influence of René Descartes (1596–1650). To Descartes wisdom became the fruit, not of learning nor of experience, but of a chain of unbroken sequences; and religion, detached from revelation and mysticism, acquired the sterile validity of an algebraic equation. From the start, Descartes had taken the precaution of conciliating the Church, which did not quite know what to make of this uninvited bedfellow; and until about 1730 (when the Newtonian system came to be accepted and applied on the Continent) Cartesianism dominated European thinking—pointing obviously to Deism or Agnosticism, but involving no repudiation of accepted religious doctrines. This made it easier for the system to filter through into the mentality of western Europe, and helped to depreciate the imaginative or emotional element, without which there can be no true art. In consequence, poetry, as we know it, suffered; or rather, its place was taken by verse. Nor was this all. By its rejection of learning and tradition, and the substitution of the reasoning faculty, the whole field of philosophic inquiry was opened to all comers; we may have no Latin, but we are all sure that we have common sense. An academic passport was no longer necessary for travel in the world of thought. This, the equality of intelligence, was the first of human equalities.

[1] For further details of French painting, see above, ch. VII, pp. 160–2.

Cartesian rationalism was strengthened by its association with Jansenism.[1] Briefly, the Jansenists, notably Nicole and Quesnel, were Roman Catholics who adopted an attitude not unlike that of the Calvinists, in that they dated their theology from the Fall and repudiated those aids to salvation which, it was thought, the Jesuits were anxious to supply. The Jansenists, insisting on their orthodoxy, remained within the fold, and appear to have infected (for a time) even such staunch Catholics as Bossuet with their Puritanism—for want of a better word. Hence, drama and the stage (usually defended by the Jesuits) were bitterly attacked by the majority of the French clergy as well as by the Protestants. As the Cartesians dissected the mind, so the Jansenists dissected the heart; the two together account for that self-analysis, that probing into the recesses of human conduct which is so characteristic of the later seventeenth century. Moreover, Jansenism implied a certain fatalism, since man's fate has been predetermined by divine decree, a view according well with the Greek conception of necessity or destiny, two strands harmoniously combined in the poetry of Racine.

Another great writer can be connected with the influences derived from Montaigne, Descartes and Jansenism. Blaise Pascal (1623–62), whose achievements in mathematics and physics are recorded elsewhere,[2] associated himself with Port-Royal des Champs, the headquarters of Jansenism, because his sister was a nun in that convent, and because, like Descartes, he had experienced some kind of revelation which he interpreted in terms of 'conversion'. His *Pensées*, noted on scraps of paper, were collected and edited by his executors; these detached thoughts, in spite of the fact that they are not co-ordinated in any way, provide an interesting experiment in what is called Apologetics. Up to a point, Pascal was little more than a disciple of Montaigne and Descartes; right reasoning, he held, is the only true guide to the conduct of life. Reason shows the extreme artificiality of civilisation—truth on one side of the Pyrenees, error on the other; justice is merely what happens to be established; climate and chance determine a large part of human conduct. But while, in others, these facts caused acquiescence or even a certain degree of amusement, in Pascal they produced disquiet and depression. How few of our assumptions can be proved was the lesson he derived from Descartes; how few of our fellow-men are saved was the lesson he deduced from the Jansenists. Still more, Christianity, in contrast with other religions, as it insists on certain states of mind, is very difficult to practise; indeed, much of its spirit may conflict with the requirements of human physiology. These requirements may also be opposed to reason, and so there is a continual 'guerre intestine de l'homme entre la raison et les passions'.

More than any other apologist Pascal was morbidly conscious of the

[1] For Jansenism, see above, ch. VI, pp. 132–4.
[2] See vol. IV ch. IV.

difficulties confronting the acceptance of Christian doctrine and revelation by the man of education. In this respect he presented a striking contrast to his near-contemporary Bossuet, who enjoyed the felicity of attaining complete conviction by the simple device of excluding everything that was obviously incompatible with his beliefs. The *Pensées* were deeply concerned with these incompatibles; accordingly, in a spirit almost of desperation, Pascal ranged against his own beliefs everything that could be said on the other side, even if it had no more than a degree of probability; and so his evidence amounts to little more than a series of converging opinions, all pointing in the same direction. He never attained to that degree of certainty which his fellow mathematician Descartes claimed to have reached; indeed, at times he appears to imply that only by a surrender of reason and a mortifying of the flesh could the soul attain peace. His own peace of mind appears to have been affected by an overwhelming psychological experience, having consequences strong enough to resist the physiological pull. Racine may have undergone a similar experience; certainly many of the characters in his dramas are torn asunder by this 'guerre intestine'. Although he lived until 1662 Pascal has no kinship with the age of Louis XIV; nor can he be linked with any of the great traditions of Catholicism. He was indeed a 'solitary'.

Inspiration, as Pascal understood it, is the fruit of solitude; wit, on the other hand, is developed by contact with cultured men and women and finds its natural expression in conversation. In the later seventeenth century and throughout the eighteenth conditions favoured a high standard of conversation, because so many things which vex us today could then be left to other people—war to the soldiers and sailors, menial work to the servants. According to Boileau, it was not enough merely to write a book, one must live and talk in the right society; according to La Bruyère the spoken word might achieve a greater perfection than the written, because pronounced in circumstances (not capable of reproduction in a book) which gave it point and meaning. Hence a specialised application of the word *esprit*. A poem might have *esprit*, not in the sense that it was 'spirited', but because so many of its lines arrested the reader's attention by bringing together, in an unexpected and effective manner, things not usually associated. This is what Louis XIV meant when he said that Racine had lots of *esprit*, a conversational quality which became a definite goal of literary art.

In all this the women were playing an essential part. The seventeenth century did little to emancipate their sex; but, in France, the wives and daughters of the dukes and peers had already emancipated themselves in the middle years of the century, when the Fronde of the nobility[1] provided them with opportunities for publicity. Match-making and memoir-writing were the spheres in which the ladies of that period found adequate

[1] For this, see vol. IV, ch. XVI.

self-expression; but already in the earlier part of the century women had brought people together in salons, that of Madame de Rambouillet being a notable example. In these gatherings a man might try out his opinions before expressing them in print, or he might become acquainted with a new idea before it had passed into circulation; or he might write an intelligent history of civilisation because his patroness complained that history books are so stupid. The salons were an important and comparatively new factor in civilisation. In order to conduct a salon successfully, a woman did not have to be highly educated; all she needed was her femininity. She could easily stir up emulation among her masculine devotees; she would be likely to discourage coarseness or vehemence; by an exercise of mother wit, she could discredit extravagance and exaggeration. She might listen patiently while an over-credulous abbé kept repeating how many steps had been taken by a decapitated saint, holding his head in his hand; but she would break in with the devastating: 'Monseigneur, ce n'est que le premier pas qui coûte.' The Cartesian apotheosis of reason accorded well with this domination of good sense in France, and helps to justify Dryden's remark that the French were better critics, and the English better poets.

From the civilisation in which women were playing an important part there emerged the *philosophe*, or intellectual inquirer, as distinct from the professed metaphysician; hence also the vogue of more or less serious books among idlers and society women, who formerly had been content with gazettes and romances. La Bruyère may have had this in mind when he said that, in France, the great subjects were forbidden, and so men of letters had often to resort to satire or irony. These modes of expression have always been less popular in England where, after 1689, Church and State were *comparatively* tolerant; but it was otherwise in the France of the *ancien régime*, where government and hierarchy always provided a background of actual or potential repression. On the principle that *litera scripta manet*, the more daring spirits may have preferred the spoken word to the published book; and so, in many salons, revolutionary maxims may have been commonplaces long before the Revolution.

This socialisation of life in France, intensified by the domination of Versailles, was reflected in the French language. Throughout the seventeenth century, as the vernacular was displacing Latin, men were ceasing to be bilingual and had to adapt their mother tongue to requirements which hitherto had been met, however inadequately, by Latin. The significance of this was expressed by Descartes in his *Discours de la Méthode*: 'If I write in French, the language of my country, rather than in Latin, the language of my preceptors, it is because I hope that those who use only their natural reason will better judge my opinions than those who believe only in old books.' This triumph of 'natural reason' over 'old books' was one of the greatest achievements of the century and was most clearly evidenced in the progress of science.[1] But it was not accomplished without a considerable expansion of the vernacular which had now to take over the task previously performed by an international jargon. Inevitably, the process was a lengthy one, and many words, new to the vernacular, retained such close associations with their Latin progenitors that they never became fully naturalised in the language of everyday use. Hence two vocabularies came into use: one for concrete things and simple emotions, the other for abstractions and more recondite modes of thought—the first simple and direct, the second often nebulous and elusive, qualities not without their value in the academic world. Sometimes the one or the other of these vocabularies predominated in writers who were contemporary or nearly so: for example, Bunyan and Dryden in England, Molière and Bossuet in France. Here is one of the respects in which French exercised a strong influence on both English language and thought—an influence by no means limited to the period covered by this chapter—for it was through this medium that many Latin words connoting abstract ideas entered into English usage and so facilitated the discussion of philosophic or semi-philosophic themes.

In this period also the French language acquired greater flexibility. Already it had this advantage over English that it made freer use of the subjunctive, simply by change of a few letters in the verb, so that one might, even in the same sentence, pass easily from a categoric to a hypothetical statement; whereas in English, where the subjunctive can only be denoted in the inflexions of the verb *to be*, one is obliged to use words like 'should' or 'might' in order to indicate the change of mood. One consequence is that, in French, one can readily express oneself in contours rather than in a flat slab, an immense advantage for the lucid exposition of an abstract theme, since different degrees of emphasis or implication can be employed, with no danger that the statement of a contingency or of someone else's opinion will be mistaken for an assertion of categoric fact. Witness the example set in the *Lettres Provinciales* which Pascal produced in 1656. The Letters were a brilliant exposure of the abuses of casuistry. Their author was concerned to show the methods, such as the half-truth and the deliberate omission, by which you can prove whatever you want to prove, and his exposure was all the more effective because so restrained. In achieving this, Pascal showed how formidable a weapon is the French language, because of its suppleness; he delighted his readers with raillery and sarcasm, where earlier controversialists would have indulged in vituperation. He showed, for perhaps the first time in history, how easy it is to pervert truth and even common sense by a skilful manipulation of words. It is significant that he suddenly stopped the Letters, because, as a good Catholic, he feared that their success might do irreparable injury to the Jesuits and even to the Church. He was right.

[1] See above, ch. III, pp. 47–72.

It was in the *Lettres Provinciales* that Voltaire and the *philosophes* found a clear demonstration of the potentialities of their mother tongue; even more, the theological absurdities, which formerly had been decently veiled in Latin, were now exposed to the ridicule of the vulgar, in language as clear as sunlight. It is not unreasonable to suggest that the scepticism of the eighteenth century derived as much from the God-fearing Pascal as from the agnostic Bayle; for a clever book written in French might, in one period, endanger a vast theological edifice; as, in a later period, it might prove a declaration of war on the *ancien régime*.

These considerations may help to clarify the distinctive achievements of the French genius in the reign of Louis XIV. It is greatly to the credit of the king that he exercised a patronage, without which the imaginative achievements of Versailles might have been considerably less. This is particularly true of Molière. Louis perceived his genius, he conferred an official status on his company of actors, he stood godfather to the dramatist's son and shielded him from interference and possible persecution by the clergy. J.-B. Poquelin, commonly called Molière (1622–73), was the son of a merchant upholsterer, a fact of some interest, since this was one of the few instances of rise to fame from the ranks of commerce. Molière's early education was good; at the famous law school in Orléans he acquired that intimate knowledge of law which was afterwards to stand him in good stead; and, like Dickens after him, he knew the legal world and its underworld. He formed a company of players which toured the provinces and in 1659 settled in Paris. His career was made by the instant success of *Les Précieuses Ridicules* which the king witnessed in 1660; but his daring *Tartufe* (1664) brought on him the renewed enmity of the clergy, and its public representation was forbidden. Then followed in quick succession: *Don Juan* (1665), *Le Misanthrope* (1666), *Le Médecin Malgré Lui* (1666), *L'Avare* (1668), *Monsieur de Pourceaugnac* (1669), *Le Bourgeois Gentilhomme* (1670), *Les Femmes Savantes* (1672), and *Le Malade Imaginaire* (1673). It was while performing the leading part, that of the hypochondriac Argon, in the last-mentioned play that Molière had a seizure and died.

Molière's fame dates from *Les Précieuses Ridicules*, a one-act comedy which ridiculed 'preciosity', or affectation of speech. Every civilised nation at some time produces this literary excrescence. In France it was preciosity, and the school which Molière had in view was the salon of the Marquise de Rambouillet who, from 1610 onwards, had opened the *chambre bleue* of her house in Paris to those more refined spirits who resented the vulgarity of the court. In this coterie certain words and phrases acquired special favour, and a romantic world, having its own conventions and heightened vocabulary, took the place of the sordid world outside. In *Les Précieuses Ridicules* we have a fast, rollicking comedy, in which the two young ladies Magdelon and Cathos are at last brought down to earth by the exposure of two bogus noblemen, actually the lackeys of two honest suitors whom the young ladies had found dull and commonplace. In the background are Gorgibus, father and uncle of the heroines, who is unable to make anything of their extravagances, and Marotte, the servant girl, whose caustic realism helps to dispel the vapourings of her mistresses. But even Molière did not succeed in destroying preciosity, and in 1672 he again used the same theme in *Les Femmes Savantes*.

Les Précieuses Ridicules has been briefly analysed because it set the pattern to which most of Molière's dramas conform: the interplay of emotions and idiosyncrasies within the intimacy of family life. In France family life has always been secluded and sacrosanct; in penetrating its intimacies, the dramatist achieved an intensity and relevance which otherwise would have been unattainable. In these domestic dramas each member of the family acts as a foil to the others—it may be the incongruity of husband and wife, of parents and children, of brother and sister, or of suitor and mistress; and always the servant maid is the exponent of that common sense fundamental in the French character. Within the framework of the family Molière ridiculed certain types, such as the miser, the hypochondriac, the *bourgeois* aspirant to nobility, the neurotic pessimist and the religious hypocrite; in laughing at these aberrations as the dramatist depicted them, many Frenchmen were laughing at themselves; and healthy laughter is one of the most sanative things in human life. Nor did he spare the learned professions; indeed, *Le Malade Imaginaire* is the most scathing indictment of the medical practice of his time, a practice from which only those of strong constitution could hope to survive.

Of this interplay within the family *Tartufe* is probably the best example. It is scarcely necessary to say that the author was not attacking religion, nor even religiosity, but the homage which vice often pays to religion by assuming its outward trappings. In seventeenth-century France there had existed, until the 1660's, an organisation intended to enforce a higher standard of morality and conformity, the *Compagnie du Saint-Sacrement*,[1] which did not hesitate to use the spy and informer against erring husband or free-thinking citizen; but its excesses appear to have caused its disbandment, though something of its spirit survived. In the two leading characters—Tartufe and Orgon—Molière showed how the religious cheat can play on the minds of the simple; the first is the prototype of the Stigginses of literature, while the second is the credulous victim of the pietistic confidence-man. This process of 'spell binding' results in a deterioration of the victim's character, so that he fails to see that his wife has been seduced by the villain; even worse, he forces his daughter to marry Tartufe, who has broken up and corrupted the family. Molière

[1] See above, ch. VI, p. 132.

was taking a great risk when he suggested that the externals of religion might be no more than a cloak for gluttony and lust, and that such iniquities might be 'accommodated' by recourse to a particular brand of casuistry countenanced by the respectable.

Molière, however, was much more than a satirist. His early career had been one of poverty and struggle; he was saddened by domestic misfortune, and a constitutional melancholy caused him to ponder deeply over the mysteries of human existence. His laughter often concealed his tears. His portrait shows a face not commonly found in the seventeenth century, for the eyes are expressive of both humour and sorrow, and the face lacks that complacency so common in the portraits of the period. Racine called him *le contemplateur*. He found cruelty and injustice, not so much in the abstract relations of men to men, as in the bonds of personal relationship. These bonds often account for tragedy, as when an avaricious parent thwarts the natural instincts of a daughter, either because her marriage would necessitate a dowry, or because the choice of her heart is financially undesirable. In this way he advocated one of the most elementary of woman's rights. Generally, he was the sworn enemy of those conventions and prejudices, insistence on which accounts for so much unhappiness; he was the friend of all that is genuine, natural and spontaneous. This may in part be accounted for by the fact that as an actor he was, for the greater part of his life, a social pariah; and few things are more likely to encourage individuality than ostracism. In this respect, and in the fecundity of his imagination, he recalls another pariah, the English Nonconformist Daniel Defoe: both of them ardent social reformers, both of them acutely percipient of evils so difficult to dislodge, because condoned by the herd.

As man and dramatist Molière is in striking contrast with Jean Racine (1639–99). Like so many of his famous contemporaries, Racine originated from the professional middle class and might well have gone into Law or the Church. But, instead of studying at one of the well-known colleges or lycées, he went at the age of fifteen to *l'École des Granges*, a school close to Port-Royal des Champs, dominated by that Jansenism so characteristic both of the convent and of the group of laymen who had gathered in the vicinity. For a time, Racine was the solitary pupil, so that there was a certain concentration and even intensity in his education, a fact which accounts not only for his minute knowledge of Greek drama, but for his sensitivity and preoccupation with himself. His training included exercise in the vernacular—an unusual subject in the curricula of that time; even more, he imbibed from Port-Royal a sympathy with that austere Puritanism and fatalism which were to influence so much of his creative output. Racine's ancestry included a Scandinavian element, which is said by some writers to account for a certain callousness or even ferocity in his temperament; while from French forbears he may have derived his feminine delicacy and suavity. He had thoughts of entering the Church, provided he could obtain a good benefice; but, though he held for a time a priory in Anjou, he had to give up the idea of an ecclesiastical career. He showed himself a false friend in his temporary desertion of Port-Royal and in his treatment of Molière who had befriended him in earlier days. He had affairs with women, not always creditable to his reputation; indeed, in these liaisons he showed a callousness sometimes attributed to men who are supposed to have an intimate knowledge of the other sex. In his analysis of a woman's heart, particularly that of a woman in early middle age, he revealed the connoisseurship not of the lover, but of the anatomist. His was an unusual and not always likeable character.

Racine was also a mystery. The failure of *Phèdre* in 1677 was due to professional rivalry, organised and directed by that great mischief-maker, the duchess of Bouillon (a niece of Mazarin), whom he may have antagonised. The effect of this incident on the dramatist appears to have been devastating. For the next twelve years he was silent; then another woman appeared on the scene, Madame de Maintenon, wife of Louis XIV, who asked him to compose a sacred drama, to be performed by the young ladies of her seminary at Saint-Cyr. The result was *Esther* (1689), followed shortly after by *Athalie*; then another period of silence until his death in 1699. Meanwhile, he had married and had a family; he also made up his differences with Port-Royal. It is said that he lost favour at Versailles because of his veiled references to dictators in *Esther* and *Athalie* and because of his openly expressed sympathy with the peasants; or he may have undergone some psychological experience, similar to that which had been accorded to Pascal, which obliged him to forsake the stage. These things have occasioned many conjectures, some of them far-fetched. What seems certain is that his genius, less easily appreciated than that of Molière, was shown in his penetrating exposition of emotional crises and acute situations, executed with a remorseless logic and inevitable fatalism, and expounded in verse, usually devoid of imagery, but abounding in those antitheses which create a feeling of staccato precision and crystalline clarity. There is nothing like it in English literature; Racine has never been fully appreciated outside France.

That Racine had successfully explored the mysteries of a woman's heart is attested by the great appeal made by his dramas to the other sex. A good example is *Phèdre*, based on the *Hippolytus* of Euripides. The heroine, Phèdre, wife of Thesée and daughter of Pasiphaë, falls in love with her stepson Hippolyte, an illicit passion which she confesses to her nurse and confidant, Oenone. The rumour of Thesée's death raises false hopes, and the sense of impending tragedy is deepened by Phèdre's discovery that Hippolyte is in love with Aricie, and so jealousy is added to the passions which wrack the mind of the heroine. In her self-analysis Phèdre detests her passion and dreads its pre-ordained consequences; in vain her will struggles against fate. Hippolyte dies a violent death;

Phèdre takes her own life. Only a great artist could have redeemed such a theme from banality.

This searching analysis of a woman's mind is seen also in *Iphigénie en Aulide*, *Bérénice*, and in his later plays, *Esther* and *Athalie*. In February 1689 Madame de Sévigné attended a representation of *Esther* given by the young ladies of Madame de Maintenon's school at Saint-Cyr. To her daughter she wrote:

> I can hardly tell you how much I was moved by this play; it is something not easy to represent, something which will never be matched; for it consists in a harmony of music, verse, chants and actors so perfect that nothing is wanting; the girls who personify kings and great personages seem made for their parts; one's attention is held, and the only regret is that such a beautiful piece should come to an end. Everything in it is simple and innocent, sublime and moving. Its faithfulness to the Holy Scriptures commands one's respect; all the chants are suitable to the words, which are taken from the Psalms and the Book of Wisdom; and, in their context, they are of a beauty which one can hardly bear without tears.

Other spectators did not share this whole-hearted enthusiasm for the play; indeed, some interpreted it as an allegory, with Esther as Madame de Maintenon, Vashti, her rival, as Madame de Montespan, and the arrogant Aman (Haman) as Louvois. The following lines of Aman, spoken in Act III, were thought by some to portray the unfortunate relations of the king with his minister Louvois:

> He knows that he owes everything to me, and that, for his glory, I have crushed under foot remorse, fear and shame; and that, wielding his power with a heart of brass, I have silenced the laws and caused the innocent to groan.

It is possible that, by 1689, Racine, like so many of his intelligent contemporaries, was disillusioned.

There were two great writers who, though not mere devotees of the king, were brought into such close relationship with him that their views may be taken as semi-official pronouncements of the royal opinions about history, politics and poetry. These were Bossuet and Boileau. The character of Jacques-Bénigne Bossuet (1627–1704), who became bishop of Meaux, was many-sided. Though of unimpeachable orthodoxy, he sympathized with Cartesians and Jansenists in so far as these schools favoured a stricter and more reasoned morality; but, on the other hand, he had no sympathy with the Quietists, a fact which led to his estrangement from Fénelon. As a controversialist, he made effective use, in his *Histoire des Variations* (1688), of what was considered the weakest point in the Protestant cause, namely its division into innumerable and usually hostile factions, in contrast with the ostensible unity of the Catholic Church. Nor did he make any secret of his view that, whatever else they might be, Protestants could not be regarded as Christians, an opinion in which the bishop was by no means alone.

It was in his capacity as tutor to the Dauphin that Bossuet completed two notable books for the edification of his royal pupil. The *Politique tirée des propres paroles de l'Écriture sainte* provided the most ample demonstration of the doctrine of Divine Hereditary Right, derived from the Old Testament, wherein, it was held, God had provided a model to be followed by kings and subjects.[1] The other book, the *Discours sur l'histoire universelle*, is an interesting example of the attempt to write a general history of civilisation, with a complete explanation of why things happen. For the bishop the answer was easy. Neither economic nor cultural conditions, he held, have anything to do with the rise and fall of empires, these changes being merely manifestations of divine will and intention. God had revealed Himself only to Jews and Christians; even the Greeks had been accorded but a small portion of divine beneficence; all other civilisations were merely idolatrous. The history of humanity was thus the record of the progress of Christianity, and it is significant that the historical portion of Bossuet's survey ended with Charlemagne. For the author, as for most of his contemporaries, the medieval world provided little more than the twilight preceding the noonday sun of Louis XIV's reign. Bossuet's *histoire universelle* is the last important book of its kind; his successors have been obliged to suggest other and very different explanations, in language less magisterial and sonorous than that which distinguished the bishop of Meaux.

In another branch of literature Bossuet achieved uncontested preeminence, the *Oraison funèbre*, or funeral oration, commemorating the virtues of a deceased person, always a notability. Few forms of composition are more likely to be insincere than the obituary notice of a celebrity because it is an occasion when flattery can do no harm, and we are all agreed in our respect for virtue; but the old type of funeral oration had at least this to be said for it that it was intended, not merely as a contribution to an already loud chorus, but as an opportunity for inculcating moral lessons derived from the example set by the deceased. Bossuet's predecessors in this highly specialised branch of literature had often been characterised by their use of forced or even absurd similes, and their funeral sermons did not always have the dignity which the occasion demanded: a fault which cannot be imputed to the bishop of Meaux, whose obituary sermons have not only dignity, but even a certain majesty. His main theme was the contrast between the vanity of earthly life and the eternity of the soul; to him, Death was as much the Destroyer as the Deliverer; and it was in its presence that he most clearly expounded the essentials of his Catholicism, essentials to be practised in the details of everyday life. His was a theological system which allowed no room for doubt, but much for example, whether of the living or the dead; and in this way Bossuet was the semi-official exponent of much that was best in the religion of his time.

[1] For Bossuet and the theory of Divine Right, see above, ch. v, pp. 99–102.

Another semi-official expositor was Boileau-Despréaux (1636–1711), whose realm was poetry and taste. The son of a registrar, he attended the Collège de Beauvais in Paris, where he studied theology and law. After serving for a time in the *Parlement de Paris*, he devoted himself to literature, and speedily won recognition by his satires and his translation of Longinus, *On the Sublime*. In 1673, after years of careful revision, he published his *Art Poétique*, followed by *Le Lutrin*. In 1677 he was appointed together with Racine historiographer of the king, and in 1684 he was elected to the French Academy. In the contest of Ancients and Moderns, he sided with the Ancients, for his master was Horace, with whom he had much in common; indeed, it has been held that if you have anything worth saying, it has already been said much better by one of these two. In 1685 Boileau retired to his suburban house at Auteuil, where he never again experienced the inspiration of his earlier years, passed in the heart of the old Paris, under the shadows of the Sainte-Chapelle and the Palais de Justice, that *quartier* which later was to harbour Voltaire. Like Samuel Johnson, he was essentially a town dweller, to whom streams and fields were monotonous, and mountains abhorrent; like Johnson also, he lived almost solely for conversation and literature. The one was a staunch defender of English common sense and conservatism, the other of *l'esprit français* and of that impeccability of expression which comes only from devotion to literature as a serious, whole-time pursuit.

Boileau applied his exacting standards to all that was naïve or fatuous in the French literature of the two preceding generations; generations which, it is true, had included Corneille and Scarron, but also many mediocrities who had little more than membership of the French Academy to their credit. Among his immediate predecessors were many who had handled heroic or biblical subjects on the principle that length compensates for lack of inspiration; thus Moses, David, Clovis and St Louis had accounted for epics distinguished only for their edification, until in 1665 Chapelain came forward with *La Pucelle* in 24,000 verses. It was not difficult to burst these bubbles. This was effected in *Le Lutrin* (The Lectern), based on an actual series of incidents in the Sainte-Chapelle, involving two ecclesiastics, one of whom had objected that a lectern obscured his view of the choir. This was the origin of a titanic contest between two factions in the chapter. A specially large lectern was built and installed in order to obscure even more completely the view of the complainant; from words they came to blows, and there ensued a battle of the books, in which the folios of dreary epics and obscurantist commentaries provided the heavy guns brought up against the light artillery of octavos, including the ten volumes of Mademoiselle de Scudéry's *Clélie*. Like Voltaire, Boileau never neglected an opportunity for raillery, all the more welcome if his shafts hit two targets at the same time. *Le Lutrin* was a demonstration that seventeenth-century France was too old for an epic; indeed, by using grandiloquent language of ridiculous incidents, Boileau completely discredited those of his predecessors who, in less heroic times, had tried to perpetuate the muse of Homer and Virgil. He thereby insisted that poetry should be an expression of the age in which the poet lives. He also used the opportunity of satirising the clergy—their petty quarrels, their good appetites, their insistence on the deference due to themselves. Like so many educated French Catholics of his day, Boileau observed Easter, attended Mass, and ridiculed the hierarchy.

More important is *L'Art Poétique*. Though little more than a thousand lines in length, it had taken five years to complete. Drafts were submitted to friends for their opinion, and portions of the poem were read to the king who expressed his approval; accordingly, this poem may be regarded as a semi-official exposition of Classicism as it came to be understood in western Europe. The debt to Horace is obvious, but *L'Art Poétique* is much more than a mere reproduction, and it abounds in lines that are both easy to remember and worth remembering. Its chief injunction is that to write well you must think well—your thought must be of the logical Cartesian type, in which you proceed from one certitude to another. Nature, reason and truth, each an expression of the others, these provide the indivisible trinity of the poet's creed. The devotee of the art should be a cultivated as well as an educated man; he should have rounded off the corners of his temperament by contact with polite society, including female society. Conversation of the right kind is thus an essential amenity on the slopes of Parnassus, and well-balanced alexandrines take the place of those convulsive hexameters in which the oracle of Delphi had found ambiguous expression. The poet is not a visionary, but a social animal; and his compositions should have the aptness, the concision and the wit of the good talker. Inspiration there must be, but it should be rigidly controlled; the form must achieve that perfection which comes from long, skilful polishing; there must be no mediocre poems, as there are no mediocre diamonds. 'Qui ne sait se borner ne sait jamais écrire'; or, as Pope said, the last and greatest art is the art 'to blot', that is, to cut out. These principles retained their supremacy until late in the eighteenth century when they were displaced by the romantic school, which gave free expression to the individual and his strivings. Boileau's maxims imply a fairly static society, based on standard conceptions of character and conduct, unsympathetic to the exotic and the bizarre, and always acutely sensitive to the banal and the fatuous.

Hitherto those artists, dramatists and poets have been mentioned who can be closely associated with Versailles, because they were directly encouraged by the king. In one more sphere, that of music, it is possible to establish this harmonious and fruitful association.[1] The historians of

[1] For music, see vol. VI, ch. III, 2.

art and music make free use of the word 'Baroque' either as a general description of the artistic product of this period, or as a technical term implying divergence or even degeneration from some more restrained or 'classical' model. The word can be easily abused. Earlier in the century the ballet was popular and was so closely associated with the court that it was usually referred to as the *ballet de cour*. The Italian influence in France, so strong in the time of Mazarin, helped to transform the *ballet de cour* into opera, an evolution which was effected mainly by the Florentine Giambattista Lully (1632–87), who entered the service of the court in 1652; later he became Superintendent of the King's Music and acquired an almost complete monopoly in the provision of scores for theatrical performances. From the exercise of this absolutism he made a fortune. His autocracy was extended also to his orchestras, which were subjected to a discipline not unlike that which Louis exercised over his courtiers and subjects. Lully's services to the opera were mainly in the development of the overture and the march, both of them eminently fitted for conveying that sense of majesty which permeated Versailles.

Such were the high priests who ministered to Louis in the innermost recesses of the shrine. On the threshold were men and women of distinction who, though they did not join enthusiastically in the chorus of praise, were associated with the court, and so were part of the social order. In this category was François, duc de La Rochefoucauld (1613–80), a disillusioned survivor of the Fronde movement, whose *Maximes* were first published in 1665. These well-known aphorisms, which reduce virtue to a form of self-love, are characteristic of a society that had become acutely conscious of itself, intent on examining and exposing those principles which ensure success in a gregarious mode of life. They are of a hard, brittle brilliance: the product, not of meditation in the study but of sharp *riposte* in the salon. Their realism may owe something to Montaigne; their bitterness may have come from the mortification of the *grand seigneur* who had experienced the fiasco of the Fronde; their epigrammatic quality, so telling in conversation, loses some of its point as it appears on the printed page. The amount of this loss may be estimated by comparing them with the aphorisms of Oscar Wilde, which are so effective because they are interspersed with conversation. But we owe it to a woman that the *Maximes* are not even more bitter. Having parted company with his wife, La Rochefoucauld took up his residence with Madame de La Fayette, who also was unattached; in this new *ménage*, the duke somewhat moderated his cynicism, while the lady devoted herself to the writing of a historical novel, in which she showed that, even in the religious wars of sixteenth-century France, love and its complications were to be found (in high places). Of her gloomy partner she wrote: 'Mons. de La Rochefoucauld m'a donné de l'esprit; mais j'ai reformé son cœur.' It was a good exchange.

La Rochefoucauld may be conveniently classed with La Bruyère (1645–96) in so far as both were keen critics of the society around them; but, while the first was a duke, the second was a tutor in a noble family. His experiences in that capacity, in the service of the great but arrogant prince of Condé, induced him to ponder deeply the problems of life and conduct. Beginning as a translator of the Greek character-writer Theophrastus, he produced in his *Caractères ou les mœurs de ce siècle* (1688) a series of observations illustrative of the habit of self-examination so popular at the time, not without a realisation of the sacrifice entailed by this purely negative approach to life. When he wrote: 'the pleasure of criticism deprives us of the satisfaction of being strongly moved by very beautiful things', he was indicating one of the weaknesses of the French classical school, in so far as criticism may induce constraint as well as restraint. Still more, his words: 'a man born Christian and French finds himself forced into satire; the great subjects are forbidden him', show an awareness of the barriers which limited imaginative achievement in the reign of Louis XIV. La Bruyère had great powers of penetration. He summed up the requirements of good conversation as give and take: 'He who departs from a conversation with you pleased with himself and his wit is completely pleased with you.' Of women he naturally had a good deal to say. He thought that there were more extremes among them; they are either much better or worse than men. Their lives are regulated not by principles, but by the heart; and, when he wrote: 'it costs less to hate than to love', he was summing up that psychology of the passions which had such a fascination for his contemporaries.

Another, less conventional guide to the right conduct of life was Jean de La Fontaine (1621–95), the son of a superintendent of woods and forests. A keen student of the classics, he served for a time in his father's department; and, at his home in Château-Thierry (Champagne), he acquired an intimate knowledge of nature and wild life. It happened that the young and turbulent duchesse de Bouillon was in Château-Thierry, and there she met the poet, whom she took back with her to the capital. The result was that La Fontaine was introduced to polite society, particularly female society. Under the wing of the dowager duchess of Orléans he frequented a fashionable set at the Luxembourg, where he appears to have acted as a gentleman usher; and an introduction to Fouquet the great financier secured for him a pension, which ended with the disgrace of the minister in 1661. Meanwhile the poet had married and had a son; but he neglected his family as he did not wish to be encumbered by troubles. He also sold the office of keeper of woods and forests, as he wished to live in Paris. Completely amoral, but in an agreeable and even gentlemanly way, La Fontaine was relieved both from domestic worries and from the drab necessity of earning a living. Having become enamoured of Madame de Sablière, his 'Iris' and 'Turtle Dove', he took up residence with her in 1672 (she had parted company with her husband), an arrangement which was described thus by the lady: 'I keep a dog, a cat and La Fontaine.' Madame de Sablière, who specialised in science and philosophy, provided a home for the poet during the next twenty years, a home where he was able to share with the cat a solicitude for two things, comfort and survival, and where he could practise an agreeable naturalism, based on his instinct for the fundamentals of existence, taken from the world of wild life which he knew so well. It was a highly specialised equipment for a poet, particularly in this age of artificiality; and the French Academy showed unusual discernment when, in 1694, it elected him a member. In 1693 the death of Madame de Sablière obliged him to transfer to another and more pious household, where his last years were years of edification. The best comment on all this was made by a servant girl who ministered to him: 'God would not be so cruel as to damn him.'

The first edition of the *Fables* was published in 1668 in six books, and was completed with the publication of the twelfth in 1694; in the later books La Fontaine used his medium with somewhat greater freedom. In choosing this medium of expression he may have been influenced by the Socratic theory that morality can best be taught by the imagery of poetry and allegory; indeed, in the introduction to the first six books he stated that Socrates, in his last days, occupied himself in turning Aesop's *Fables* into verse. 'We are the abridgement of all that is good and bad in the animal kingdom'; in these simple stories of what is called the lower creation we can see ourselves as in a glass. It is probably vain to seek for any theory of their intention. Essentially a 'clubbable', social creature, La Fontaine consorted with Molière, Racine and Boileau, a quartet which, at convivial gatherings in the *Mouton Blanc*, discussed each other's work: and, for breach of the conventions, imposed the penalty of reading a verse or even a page of Chapelain's output.

In 1682 occurred a little-known incident which brought him to the fore, in the train, as usual, of a lady. That year is notable for the introduction into France of a new drug—quinine—which, under the name of Jesuits' Bark, was being used as a specific for fevers instead of the old purgings and bleedings, an innovation which caused a violent controversy between the Faculty and the amateur pharmacologists, who swore by the new remedy. Among those who plunged into the fray was that termagant, the duchesse de Bouillon, the first discoverer of La Fontaine, and now, apparently, the discoverer of quinine. She asked him to write a poem on the medical virtues of this substance. Always anxious to oblige, the old protégé of the duchess complied. In this way quinine is possibly the only drug to have the distinction of public advertisement by a poet; and, for its composition, the author appears to have dipped into the physiological learning of his day. 'My chief object is always to please', he had already declared with truth in the preface to his *Les Amours de Psyché* (1669), a collection of verse suitable for children; all that he wrote is suitable for the child in each of us. While other poets soared aloft in purposeful flight, he flitted about like 'a butterfly on Parnassus'; while his contemporaries were struggling with the subtle intricacies of human passion, he was concerning himself with those elemental realities—comprehensible even by a butterfly—which ultimately determine the conduct of the animal creation, whether we call it higher or lower. In this way he became expert in the simplest of all strategies: that which maintains a balance of population between the two main divisions of living things—the hungry and the well-fed, the astute and the over-confident, the quick and the dead.

But La Fontaine leaves his readers to draw their own conclusions. Verse came so naturally to him that he often lapsed into it in his letters; in this medium he achieved an aptness and pithiness unattainable in prose, an effect heightened by his resort to that rich vocabulary of sixteenth-century France which was now becoming outmoded. As well as language, and a sensitive ear for the sonority of line, La Fontaine had a sense of the dramatic, so that each fable is usually a self-contained tragedy or comedy, the story being told with inimitable concision and skill. As for the lessons to be learned from the *Fables*, they are of the simplest—we can learn most from the fox, the wolf and the rat; because, as everyman's hand is against them, they have had to develop a special technique directed against the vanity or simplicity of their more placid and more highly esteemed neighbours. 'Quiconque est loup agisse en loup';[1] it is not his fault that he is hungry and must eat. In the jungle there is a continual contest of wits, with death as the penalty; but the contest is often of a gentlemanly character, for there is much give and take, and we can all help each other. Death and suffering are inevitable, but we must submit with patience:

> Le trépas vient tout guérir,
> Mais ne bougeons d'où nous sommes;
> Plutôt souffrir que mourir
> C'est la devise des hommes.[2]

It is because so many of us derive our first lessons in worldly wisdom from them that the *Fables*, like *Gulliver's Travels* and *Robinson Crusoe*, have a special place in our affections; and it is evidence of the place assigned in French civilisation to La Fontaine that the name alone saved the poet's great-granddaughter from the guillotine in the days of the Terror.

The ethics of the seventeenth century were based on a sharp distinction between man and beast, the one having a soul, the other supposed to be devoid even of intelligence and entitled to no protection, save as an article

[1] 'Whoever is a wolf must act as a wolf.'

[2] 'Death comes to cure all; but let us not budge from where we are; better to suffer than to die—such is the motto of humanity.'

of human property. Descartes had propounded the stupid and cruel theory that animals are incapable of feeling; his contemporaries and many of his successors acted on this assumption. In consequence, the animal community seemed to Christians a most unlikely source for a theory of conduct, until La Fontaine showed how many and how close are the analogies between the behaviour of the best of us and that of the creatures which we profess to despise. If these analogies are valid, then we have need to revise our vocabularies, since words like *brutal*, *bestial* and *animal* are always used to denote human conduct so despicable that it can be correlated only with the conduct attributed to another order of creation. Even in the most highly polished society, the rule of tooth and claw, however skilfully disguised, may be the final arbiter; or, in the words of the fabulist: 'The less one puts oneself at the mercy of the fangs of others, the better.' By juxtaposing two worlds always kept apart, La Fontaine, who probably had no satirical intention, may unwittingly have been committing a heresy so great that it escaped unnoticed, even by himself. But, whatever meaning we may read into the *Fables*, everyone agrees that these are so exquisitely told as to be things of joy in themselves. The charm of the poetry is not in the rhymes, but in the cadence and simplicity of the lines, so effortless that La Fontaine—a poets' poet—must be considered the most spontaneous of all the writers in this age of artificiality and convention.

La Fontaine probably had as little appreciation of nature as have the wild creatures by which it is inhabited; moreover, it was not until a later age that men sought in nature a reflection of their more serious moods. But an exception may be made in favour of Madame de Sévigné, whose prose style resembles La Fontaine's in its richness of vocabulary, its abundance of expressive words and its supple adaptability to mood; it is not surprising therefore that, like the *Fables*, the *Lettres* have been acclaimed in every age and by every class. The high standard of letter-writing in the later seventeenth century is accounted for by several factors—by the comparative absence of journals and newspapers; by difficulty of communication which made the letter specially welcome, since its news was likely to be communicated to friends and neighbours; and by the gradual improvement of the postal services, notably in the later part of the century. The first edition of Madame de Sévigné's *Lettres* was published in 1697, the greater number of them having been addressed (in the years 1671–91) to her daughter, Madame de Grignan, who was then with her husband in distant Provence. The daughter, who appears to have been somewhat haughty and reserved, did not completely respond to her mother's affection. This affection inspired letters which have a unique place in historical literature. As in a panorama they enable us to follow at least the externals of Louis's reign—the trial of Fouquet in 1664; famous public executions, such as those of the two poisoners, the Marquise de

Brinvilliers and Madame Voisin (she shivered slightly at the execution of the latter); the social activities which graced a meeting of the Estates of Brittany in 1671; the trepidation produced in the following year by reports of French casualties in the passage of the Rhine (her son was in the fighting); the death in battle of the great Turenne (1675)—reading his exploits seemed to Madame de Sévigné like reading the history of Rome; her visit to the 'vallon affreux'—Port-Royal des Champs—where she listened to the edifying conversation of the nuns and thought of her own salvation. These are only a few of the more notable incidents which make an indelible impression on the mind of the reader.

Her letters show that Madame de Sévigné regarded the peasants whom she saw in the fields as barely human; but in this respect she was in agreement with the social class to which she belonged. Nevertheless, there was at least one interesting respect in which she was not of her age. She loved the seclusion of her château at Les Rochers in Brittany, where she took solitary walks in the moonlight, recalling sad thoughts which she was unwilling to reveal, even to her daughter. She loved the trees and was in the habit of inscribing sentimental messages on their trunks; she was a keen listener to the birds, and became thoughtful in the moonlight. All this shows an anticipation of the romanticism of the eighteenth century. But strongest of all was the love which she bestowed on an unresponsive daughter—'ma fille, aimez moi donc toujours; c'est mon âme'. Madame de Sévigné was the greatest mother in literature.

A certain vein of femininity can be detected in the writings of François de Salignac de La Mothe-Fénelon (1651–1715), archbishop of Cambrai, a vein which may have been developed by his experience as director of a school for girls of good family who had recently been 'converted' to Catholicism. The lessons which he derived from this occupation were embodied in his first book: *Traité de l'Éducation des Filles* (1687). Almost alone in his age he realised the importance of women in the State, and the need for providing them with a good education; but, like his English contemporary George Savile, Marquis of Halifax, he believed that the female sex is essentially subordinate, and that a woman can achieve happiness and usefulness only within the limits imposed by nature. It was this emphasis on nature that gave originality to his theories, for he claimed that the natural bent of the pupil should be followed as much as possible, and that education was not a process of filling the mind with information, but of drawing out and directing what was already there. In this way Fénelon's treatise anticipated *Émile*; the archbishop was also a precursor of Rousseau in what has been called 'poetic prose', a phrase relating to content rather than to form. Idealist and optimist, Fénelon believed in the natural goodness of man, most clearly evidenced in the supposed 'age of innocence', and most obviously contrasted with the corruption which underlies despotic government. In one more respect the archbishop was an apostle of nature. He anticipated the Physiocrats in his view that the soil is the source of all wealth; and he regarded as parasites all who batten on that wealth.

In 1689 Fénelon became the tutor to the duke of Burgundy, eldest grandson of Louis, as Bossuet had been tutor to the duke's father, the Dauphin. The parallel can be extended. Bossuet wrote the *histoire universelle*; Fénelon, in his turn, wrote *Télémaque*, which appeared in 1699. These two books, written by great ecclesiastics, for pupils who, it was hoped, would one day rule France, show diametrically opposite points of view; for, while the earlier volume claims to reveal the will of God in the evolution of absolute kingship, the later work shows how that will can be better interpreted by the exercise of humanity and intelligence in the ruler. Based on the *Odyssey*, *Télémaque* includes two Utopias: one, *La Bétique*, where happiness is secured by eliminating private property, and the other, *La Salente*, where the same result is achieved by confining power to an aristocracy by birth (as contrasted with one of money). Both types of State are based on agriculture; luxury and excessive wealth are prohibited; virtue is promoted by rulers who avoid display and seek their glories in activities other than war. The reference to Louis XIV is obvious. Fénelon's ideal State was not unlike a monastery dedicated to the cult of Socrates. Frugality verging on asceticism was the rule; as in Plato's Republic, music, drama and poetry were to be regulated in order to promote only the noblest impulses. The ruler must constantly interfere with the subject in order to promote virtue; man was forced to be good. A later age (arguing also from nature) wanted to force him to be free. It is not a far step from *Télémaque* to the *Contrat Social* and the French Revolution. The first effective blows at the *ancien régime* were directed not by atheists or radicals, but by the pious Pascal and the virtuous Fénelon.

Fénelon is thus representative of the transition in Louis's reign from the period of great imaginative achievement to that of criticism of the existing régime, when the attention of thoughtful Frenchmen was directed to the two evils following the royal despotism: misery at home and hatred abroad. It is possible that great literature cannot flourish in such an atmosphere, at least not in the France of that time, because so much of the creative life of the nation was centred in Paris and Versailles. This concentration may be contrasted with the more healthy diffusion of the eighteenth century, as exemplified by Voltaire who, though a Parisian, had his headquarters at Ferney, near the Swiss frontier; or Montesquieu who was so closely connected with Bordeaux; or Rousseau who lived an almost vagabond existence and detested society. In contrast, the Sun-King shed dazzling rays illuminating only a small circle; and when that light weakened, there remained only shadow and darkness. It may have been mere chance that brought together such a galaxy of talent as illuminated the first thirty years of the reign; or the phenomenon may be explained by the direct encouragement and direction given by king and court; or there may have been some incentive arising from the conviction that the nation was in the ascendant and on the threshold of a larger life. In English literature one can trace some such elements in the Elizabethan and in the Victorian ages. In France, they are not easily discernible after about 1700.

How can we characterise the wonderful achievements of the earlier years of the reign? These achievements were so richly diversified that we must be wary of accepting any single definition, if indeed definition is possible. But we can be sure of one thing, namely the influence of women. In France this influence was usually both stimulating and beneficent, in contrast with its counterpart in England, where so many of the women at the court of Charles II were merely mercenary and where, as a rule, women did not become associated with men of letters until a later date. France is one of those countries where the female is often more active and intelligent than the male; where sex and good food are matters, not of taboo, but of discriminating connoisseurship; where a partnership, not necessarily hallowed by the marriage vows, may nevertheless be based on some intellectual or spiritual exchange which commands respect rather than opprobrium. In England, where such partnerships exist they have to be kept discreetly veiled. It is significant of the part played by women in the history of France that, of her two great saints, one was a servant maid; and (if Molière be excepted) it may be hazarded that, but for the shrewdness, the insight and the charm of their feminine associates, the men of letters of the reign of Louis XIV would not have achieved so much.

In conclusion, it may be asked whether French influence can be detected in other European countries within the period covered by this chapter. Any attempt to answer this question must begin with acceptance of the fact that this period, and indeed the whole of the reign of Louis, was an era of French dominance which was based on threats and force. Against this dominance there was angry protest and reaction; and in every country menaced by Versailles innumerable pamphleteers and satirists engaged in scathing condemnation, not only of the Sun-King and his agents, but of the civilisation over which he presided. This antagonism was specially strong in Germany and Holland, which had special reason to detest the arrogance of their powerful neighbour; and so, in these countries, French character and culture were derided as corrupt and degenerate, in contrast with Teutonic 'honesty' and 'virility'. Throughout Europe, the exiled Huguenots added fuel to the flames by their contributions to a vast literature denouncing Louis and his subjects as modern Huns.

An exception, or an apparent exception, is provided by the England of the Restoration. This can be connected with the personal example and popularity of Charles II whose tastes were more French than English.

His preference for a *bon mot* to clinch an argument, his unfailing choice of the agreeable rather than the arduous, and his complete absence of shyness with the other sex—all these are Gallic rather than Saxon qualities. But the royal influence, so far as it was exercised in music and drama, was not always felicitous, nor was it even long-lived. He restored music to the churches from which the Puritans had driven it; but the music consisted of the somewhat shallow, voluptuous melodies which Lully had popularised and proved to be little more than a diversion from the main stream of a great tradition which was resumed, with such brilliant results, by Purcell and Blow. The same is true of Restoration drama, which collapsed, not from its obscenity, but from its inanity. In architecture, the palace of Versailles provided a model for England and many continental countries; in the decorative arts the achievements of *Les Gobelins* helped to ensure the high standards of furniture-making in the eighteenth century. The resources of horticulture were enriched by the cultivation of the pear and the nectarine; and it can be claimed that the amenities of life were enhanced by the introduction from France of what, at first, were regarded as insidious luxuries. It became fashionable to study French, even at a time when the two countries were enemies. Shortly after the Treaty of Ryswick (1697) advertisements appeared in London newspapers advertising establishments where French was taught 'as it is spoken at Versailles'.

It is not in these spheres of fashionable example or direct emulation, however, that one must seek for the abiding influence of French imaginative achievement. It was in the field of literary criticism, in the general conception of the functions of the poetic art, that France exercised a dominating influence in England. Two interesting personalities helped to facilitate this process. One was Charles de Saint-Évremond (1610–1703), a French exile in England who, in his capacity of informal literary ambassador, helped to make the dialogue more popular as a literary form and to give a personal illustration of the importance of conversation for the man of letters. He was credited with the aphorism that the ideal is the Frenchman who can think and the Englishman who can talk. Himself a voluminous rather than a distinguished writer, Saint-Évremond provided for Dryden and his contemporaries an example of that urbanity and fastidiousness so strikingly contrasted with the spontaneity and freshness of the native muse. Two ideals were brought into contrast, and some kind of compromise was effected.

'What, I beseech you, is more easy than to write a regular French play or more difficult than to write an irregular English one, like those of Fletcher or of Shakespeare?'[1] These are the words of Dryden who, nevertheless, proved to be the main channel through which French influ-

[1] *Essay of Dramatic Poesy* (1668), in *Essays of John Dryden*, ed. W. P. Ker (Oxford, 1900), I, 77.

ence passed into English literature. Well aware of the great literary achievements of his own country and of the banality of many foreign models, he selected and applied those excellencies of French theory and practice which he regarded as correctives of English insularity. A keen student of Corneille, he experimented with the use of rhyme in heroic drama, using it effectively in dialogue, and so preparing the way for the great vogue and high standard of the couplet in the Augustan Age. His progress can be shown by comparing his *Annus Mirabilis*, published in 1667, with *Absalom and Achitophel* (1681) and *The Hind and the Panther* (1687). The early poem reveals the genuine but less tutored inspiration of an older age, while the later compositions are distinguished by greater coherence, better structure and more incisiveness. It may well have been this French influence that prompted him to aim at 'an election of apt words and a right disposing of them';[1] to study form and expression as vehicles in which thought and inspiration must be confined.

It was Boileau, not Corneille, whom Dryden acclimatised in England. In 1680–1 he assisted Sir W. Soame in his translation of the *Art Poétique*, and this almost official acceptance of Boileau as the modern arbiter of taste, comparable with Aristotle and Longinus in antiquity, was signalised by the Earl of Mulgrave's *Essay upon Poetry* (1682) and the Earl of Roscommon's *Essay on Translated Verse* (1684). Under such skilled direction and such noble patronage the influence of French literary ideals was assured. 'Wit', declared Dryden, 'is best conveyed to us in the most easy language; and is most to be admired when a great thought comes dressed in words so commonly received that it is understood by the meanest apprehensions.'[2] This insistence on clarity and ease of comprehension is characteristic of French taste; and it was in this respect that the influence of France was most potent in England. It should be recalled also that the greatest intellectual impact on European intelligence was still that of Descartes; this was part of the scientific revolution which transformed the thought of the seventeenth century and penetrated to every nation where there were men sufficiently educated or intelligent to receive it. The Cartesian influence harmonised well with the principles advocated by Boileau and practised by Dryden, since all three illustrated the virtues of lucidity, order and precision, even if their achievement was at the expense of the original or the imaginative. These qualities were abundantly illustrated in the literature of eighteenth-century Europe.

Nevertheless, there remained something distinctive and inimitable in the intellectual product of France during the first three decades of the personal government of Louis XIV. Its mediocre products could be copied: its achievements of imaginative genius are unique. There were many fabulists, but only one La Fontaine; many letter writers, but only one Madame de Sévigné; many moralists and preachers, but only one

[1] *Ibid.* I, 95. [2] *Ibid.* I, 52.

Bossuet. Racine had neither predecessors nor successors; Molière must be classified, not with his contemporaries or imitators, but with Shakespeare. These writers, though showing unmistakable traces of the age in which they lived, are to be included in the heritage of western civilisation. Herein, it may be claimed, lies the enduring achievement of the reign, so sharply contrasted with the impermanence of the military and political dominance exercised by Louis XIV.

CHAPTER XII

THE DUTCH REPUBLIC

THE second half of the seventeenth century, which in many European countries witnessed rapid developments in the social, economic and political fields, was in the Dutch Republic a period of consolidation rather than change. The institutional, economic and social framework virtually remained what it had been in the early seventeenth century. The great statesmen who dominated the scene, John de Witt and William III, did not reorganise the political system, and even the issues which divided the Dutch political parties (the republican party and the party of the Orangists) differed only slightly from those which had separated Oldenbarnevelt and Maurice of Orange in 1618, Amsterdam and William II in 1650.[1] There were, no doubt, vehement political conflicts in the second half of the century, but on the whole these were conflicts between rival cliques and personalities within the governing class rather than between social groups and important political principles. It is not difficult to explain this situation. By 1650 the Dutch Republic had reached a point in its economic expansion beyond which it could not easily develop, but it had been unable to eliminate the uncertainties and tensions in its political system which had already caused dangerous clashes.

The complexity of Dutch life makes it very difficult to describe the social structure of the country. The differences between the various provinces were so fundamental that no broad generalisations can do justice to the facts. The interests, the power, even the language of the cattle-breeding gentlemen-farmers of Friesland, or of the nobility of Guelderland with its important feudal privileges, are hardly comparable with those of the urban patricians of Holland. The tenant-farmers of Guelderland and Overijssel, living in sparsely populated areas and working in the first place to supply their personal needs, had problems different from those of Holland—one of the most densely populated areas of Europe—who specialised in the cultivation of commercial crops for industry and in horticulture but did not grow corn. Holland, however, was by far the most influential of the seven provinces, and thus it may be justifiable to deal with the leading classes of Holland only. Its social hierarchy was, in fact, simple. The nobility was numerically weak and formed a strictly closed caste. It did not possess much political or economic power; most of the land was in the possession of urban capitalists. The nobility had no links with the great burgher families and did not challenge their leadership.

[1] For these conflicts, see vol. IV, ch. XII.

By the middle of the seventeenth century the Dutch *bourgeoisie* had acquired its typical form. The families which had grown wealthy through commerce and become influential in government during the early seventeenth century constituted the oligarchy which in fact ruled the province. They provided the men who served in the urban administrations, the States, the boards of the big trading-companies, and with these functions went the exclusive right of making appointments to numerous minor offices in the towns and the country. It is difficult to assess the total number of persons falling under the category of 'regents'; a rash estimate which cannot have the pretension of any precision, might suggest that in Holland one man in every 1000 belonged to a regent family. Little is known about their wealth, and it is obvious that the regents of a small town like Hoorn may have shared the prejudices and the social privileges of the Amsterdam millionaires but could, of course, not compare with them in power and influence on the level of provincial or national politics. By the middle of the century most of the regents had withdrawn from business and invested their money in life-annuities issued by the municipal, provincial and general governments, in country estates or in shares of the East India Company. They had consolidated themselves as a social group and as far as possible prevented other families from entering their ranks. Though they sometimes acquired titles of nobility and built beautiful country houses, they remained fundamentally urban patricians and had only slight interests in certain forms of intensive agriculture.

It is remarkable that the closing of the oligarchy led during these years in Zeeland and other provinces to a conception of public offices as private, more or less negotiable, property. Whereas in France it was the venality of the offices that brought into existence the nobility of the robe, in the Dutch Republic it was the growth of an oligarchic patriciate which led to practices which expressed exactly the same ideas. The ruling families began to divide public functions in the towns and the country according to certain rules previously agreed upon, in order to attenuate the bitter daily struggle for power and profit. This development had, however, not yet been concluded; it was rather slow in penetrating into the province of Holland and had not yet reached Amsterdam. During many years the chief burgomaster, Cornelis de Graeff van Zuidpolsbroek, a very subtle politician, defended John de Witt's régime against a group of rivals; but after his death in 1664 conflicts of the utmost vehemence broke out and the town wavered in its allegiance. Deep discords within the isolated, all-powerful minority of the regents paralysed the provincial government.

The political structure of the Dutch Republic was cumbersome and complicated: it did in fact not constitute one republic but a federation of seven sovereign provinces, each with its special characteristics. The federal government was weak. The most important of the federal institutions was the States General to which each of the provinces sent a delegation bound to vote as instructed by its principals. Unanimity was required for the States General to take a decision committing all their members. Yet the States General, meeting daily at The Hague for some hours, had important tasks to perform. They acted as the representative of the Union, conducted foreign affairs, controlled defence and federal taxation which was apportioned among the provinces according to a fixed key, Holland paying about 58 per cent. They nominated, finally, the captain-general and the admiral-general of the Union, offices usually held by the Prince of Orange. However, the States General were clearly not a sovereign body. Sovereignty resided in the States of the various provinces, the composition of which varied greatly. The States of Holland consisted of nineteen delegations each having one vote: the nobility and eighteen towns. In the States just as in the States General important decisions were normally taken unanimously: the principle of Dutch government was that none of its members could be coerced to comply with the majority. In practice a decision was reached only after long negotiations and thanks to the persuasiveness of the leading statesmen.

The centrifugal forces in the government were sometimes checked by two important officials: the Grand Pensionary and the stadholder. The Grand Pensionary was the legal adviser of the States of Holland who acted as the president of the States and of their committees, led the provincial deputation to the States General, often carried on the correspondence of the Republic with the Dutch ambassadors abroad and received their dispatches. An energetic and intelligent man who enjoyed the confidence of the urban administrations in Holland was able to wield decisive power not only in his own province but in the whole Republic. The function of stadholder was more ambiguous. The incumbent of the stadholdership of Holland was always the Prince of Orange. He was appointed by the sovereign States and was therefore in theory a provincial official just as the Grand Pensionary. But since he was always stadholder of more than one province at the same time (Holland, Zeeland, Utrecht, Overijssel and Guelderland normally nominated the Prince of Orange, Groningen and Drente, not represented in the States General, often did so, whereas Friesland always appointed a member of the Nassau branch of the family) and acted also as captain-general and admiral-general of the Union, he quite naturally participated in the making of federal policy. The enormous prestige, moreover, of his noble birth and the popularity of his great House gave him an influence and power not defined by any constitutional laws but none the less real and important.

Throughout the first half of the century there had been tensions between the States of Holland and the stadholder. During the 1640's the ruling oligarchy of Holland had opposed the militarist and dynastic policies of Frederick Henry, captain-general and admiral-general, stadholder of all the provinces but Friesland, because they were designed to continue the war with Spain and to enhance the position of the Orange family through the marriage of Frederick Henry's son, William II, to the daughter of Charles I, Mary. Fear and anger had been aroused by Frederick Henry's wish to support the royalist cause in the Civil War. But Frederick Henry died in 1647; in 1648 the regents had their way in making peace with Spain at Münster. His son William II, however, a young and adventurous man, appointed to all his father's dignities, felt frustrated by this victory of the States and soon considered himself strong enough to challenge Holland and Amsterdam. The conflict seemed grave and dangerous. But suddenly, on 6 November 1650, he died. The Dutch statesmen found themselves in a completely new situation. William II's only child, William III, was born on 14 November; the calm of his nursery was disturbed by the vehement conflicts between his mother, Mary Stuart, and his grandmother Amelia, the widow of Frederick Henry. In most provinces the idea of appointing Friesland's stadholder to the functions of William II did not even arise; only Groningen and the territory of Drente decided to fill the vacancy in this way. Thus for the first time in the history of the Republic five of the seven provinces represented in the States General were truly republican, although in some princely palaces at The Hague a group of Calvinist predikants and anglophile nobles and adventurers kept plotting on behalf of the greatness of the Orange dynasty.

The twenty-two years of almost completely republican rule, which followed, form a very distinctive period in Dutch history. In 1651 the States of Holland tried to lay the foundation of a new form of government by summoning to The Hague the so-called Grand Assembly and by proposing to attribute to this body, which was intended to be a joint session of all the provincial States and as such the sum total of sovereignty in the federated provinces, the right to decide arbitrarily on the cardinal problems awaiting solution. In the view of Holland the States General, still largely dominated by the protégés of William II, was not the proper place for so difficult a task. But the plan failed. The deputies sent by the provinces to the Grand Assembly had no larger powers than those sent to the States General, and what was intended to be a congress of sovereigns was in reality only a congress of ambassadors. Consequently the Grand Assembly (January–August 1651) was unable to produce any constructive plan and resigned itself to much classicist and confused oratory. The only decision of importance concerned the army. More than ever before military affairs were now to be dealt with as if they depended on the sovereign will of each of the seven provinces—with the result that the army was in great danger of being split into seven provincial armies. This was a victory for extreme particularism. Thus the real importance of the Grand Assembly was that it brought to a culmination and confirmed officially a tendency that undoubtedly was one of the main features of the confederation. The United Provinces—as John de Witt said[1]—were not a *respublica* in the singular but *respublicae* in the plural.

John de Witt, who soon became the leader of the republican party (owing to his office of Grand Pensionary to which he was appointed in 1653), exerted himself not only to defend the new stadholderless form of government but also to justify it intellectually. It was called by his adherents the System of True Liberty and de Witt availed himself of the services of excellent publicists like the brothers De la Court and of so systematic a philosopher as Spinoza. This literary activity gives the period the character of an intellectual adventure, of an attempt made by young men—de Witt himself was 27 years old in 1653—to break with a past marred by awkward compromises. Yet this rationalistic and doctrinaire aspect of the régime was but one of the elements in a very complex reality. John de Witt and his collaborators moulded into concrete form a variety of old and respectable tendencies. The dynastic policies of Frederick Henry and William II had aroused anger among the ruling classes, particularly those of Holland, because they led to adventures of incalculable consequences. The men upon whom, after the death of William II, power naturally devolved could devote themselves to the task of strengthening their own power. In principle they had always been in possession of sovereignty, but they had never fully exercised it. They immediately barred all the ways through which the authority of the stadholder had penetrated into the towns and the urban administrations. The various States decided that the annual elections of urban magistrates would in future be the affair of the towns only and in fact always be made by co-optation. All outside influence, especially that of the stadholder, who had in certain circumstances the right of selection from a number of recommended candidates, was eliminated and the power of a small group of ruling families was confirmed. This small group of ruling families formed the strongest support of de Witt's party. Not all of them were 'Wittians', but the most important among them, especially in Holland and Amsterdam, considered a régime which gave them practically a monopoly of power the best régime for the time being.

The régime was, however, not merely the dictatorship of a narrow class. It was deeply rooted in the life of the whole population, not because the ruling groups shared their power with the masses of the people, but because they turned away from them and left them alone. Thus the republican régime was silently supported by the numerous religious dissenters, who needed protection against the intolerance of the Calvinist minority. It was supported by Roman Catholics and Protestant sects, by intellectuals and wide strata of the *bourgeoisie*. It did not disturb the

[1] *Brieven van Johan de Witt*, ed. R. Fruin and G. W. Kernkamp (Amsterdam, 1906 ff.), I, 62.

turbulent, restless growth of numerous and very active small groups of religious innovators and considered it its sole task ingeniously to maintain the balance between extremes and to prevent excesses. The principle of toleration was utilitarian rather than founded on any philosophical principle. The regents never tired of repeating that foreign trade would inevitably be destroyed by the establishment of an exclusive Calvinist supremacy.

By the middle of the seventeenth century probably nearly half of the Dutch population (Brabant included) were still loyal to the Catholic faith. In the towns of the provinces of Holland and Utrecht numerous missionaries were allowed to carry on their partly secret activities. The majority of the rural population in these provinces was certainly Catholic: it is not surprising that Dutch civilisation continued to be permeated by Romish elements. This does not alter the fact that the situation of the Catholics continued to be precarious. The Dutch Republic was officially a Protestant State and the Catholics, though allowed to have their own religious services if they were willing to pay for the inattention of the authorities, found it increasingly difficult to keep their posts in the urban administrations. However, Calvinism was not the only alternative to Roman Catholicism. Of a total population of perhaps about two millions probably one-third belonged to orthodox Calvinism, a creed that consequently remained what it had been during the Revolt, though of course to a much lesser degree: the creed of a minority. Beside it innumerable small sects ventured to express extremely liberal interpretations of Christian dogma or even a de-Christianised religion to the point of transforming it into a general moral philosophy.

The dissenters no doubt supported the government of the tolerant regents, without being able to save it when it was fighting for its life. This would have required a solid organisation, but this they lacked. Yet the deep divisions of the Dutch people may help to explain a fact which must be regarded as one of the salient features of Dutch history in the seventeenth century: the fact that numerous changes of government took place without the violence accompanying the contemporary upheavals in France and England. It is indeed remarkable that the events of 1618–19, of 1650 and of 1672, all fundamental conflicts, did not develop into revolutions. The suppleness of the Dutch form of government and the general prosperity partly explain this; but the complex religious divisions, which made clear-cut conflicts almost impossible and in which party divisions disappeared like water in sand, certainly contributed a great deal to the fundamental weakness of all forms of government and to the ease with which one form was substituted for another.

It is difficult to understand the nature of the opposition to the domination of the regents, but some of its elements at least are clear. No imagination is needed to see that de Witt's way of eliminating the influence of the

Orange family in Holland, and as far as possible also in the other provinces, excluded a compromise with the clientele of the great House. It is also clear that the Orangists wanted to continue the policies by which Frederick Henry and William II had aroused so much antagonism. A small number of Calvinist pastors continued to nurse their ideal of an anti-Spanish crusade. These men were, of course, opposed to the religious tolerance of the regents, to their Erastian principles and to their complete lack of religious dynamism. Possibly the sharp social difference between the predikants of the lower middle class and the ruling families helps to explain the conflicts. Much more important, however, was the instinctive reaction of large groups of the population to the régime of the States in times of emergency. This reaction was often fostered by political speeches and pamphlets, but more often it arose spontaneously out of economic distress and political distrust. Sharp rises in the price of rye were caused by the Anglo-Dutch wars and, coupled with unemployment and deep suspicion, they led to vehement disturbances in the towns and a fairly general outcry against a régime suspected of treachery and inefficiency.

Yet these popular movements did not grow steadily during the years until—after the first disappointments of 1653—they became sufficiently strong in 1672 to overthrow the régime. On the contrary, their vehemence diminished. A more decisive factor contributing to the fatal weakness of the System of True Liberty in 1672 was the danger of being hollowed out from the inside. Orangist regents had retained much of their influence in some towns and provinces and their position became stronger as Prince William grew older. The sharp conflicts, moreover, within the town governments, conflicts often springing from the struggle for power, selfishness and personal hatred, naturally tended to expand and to merge with extra-mural conflicts. It was easy for a regent ousted by one of de Witt's friends to call himself an Orangist and so to infuse fresh vigour into the national party strife. Modern historians have carefully studied this phenomenon in Amsterdam and there is no reason to suppose that it did not occur in other towns also.

Thus an explanation of the political struggles in the terms of social contrasts is insufficient, although undoubtedly they formed one of the numerous elements from which the great conflict sprang. Neither is it possible to link the political development with the economic situation. It is perhaps surprising that the Orangist period before 1651 witnessed a considerable expansion of the Dutch economy, and that it came to a halt under the republican régime which was so eager to defend commercial interests. It was only about 1680 that the economy began to recover, a process which continued until the death of William III. This temporary slowing down of what had been such an amazingly dynamic development was not due to any fundamental change in the structure of Dutch commerce in general or of the Amsterdam staple market in particular.[1] It was caused by transient changes which after the middle of the century had a stagnating effect. Especially the Baltic corn trade, the 'mother commerce' of the Republic, suffered a serious decline in the years between 1652 and 1680, a decline not so much to be explained by increasing competition as by some bad harvests in the area of the Vistula, by the wars, by a fall in the demand for corn in western and southern Europe, and above all by the general depression afflicting the European economy during the 1660's and 1670's. It would be a gross exaggeration to speak of a crisis of the Dutch economy. The stagnation in the expansion of some important branches of commerce was accompanied by a sharp rise in that of others. Commercial relations with Spain became very close after 1648 and led to the development of Amsterdam as a leading bullion market. The Dutch economic hegemony in Muscovy was confirmed. Industry did not seem to suffer. It was precisely during these years that Leiden, the biggest European manufacturing town after Lyon, made its greatest advance in the cloth industry, and the industry of the area of the river Zaan in North Holland increased rapidly. Yet this does not alter the fact that the general expansion of the early seventeenth century was discontinued after 1650 and that de Witt's period witnessed economic difficulties and in some fields even a mild form of recession.

Thus in all spheres of Dutch life a similar phenomenon can be observed. The top seemed to have been reached; nothing remained but to attempt to retain the things acquired. De Witt's system, however fashionable it may have been intellectually, was in practice conservative. In a supremely intelligent way his conduct of domestic as well as foreign affairs tried to freeze the situation. In fact his whole policy was a reaction to disturbing tendencies and as such, the saturation of the Republic taken into account, a defence of fundamental Dutch interests.

The two disturbing elements which threatened the system and finally wrecked it were political. They were the closely related questions of England and Orange. Neither of them could de Witt eliminate and his ability to neutralise them was limited. England was a dangerous, but not necessarily a deadly enemy during the years in which the Dutch Republic, thanks to the uncertainties of the European political scene, was able to play the part of an arbiter. When it became clear that France was out to take over the Spanish heritage—European hegemony—English foreign policy became a very great danger because it contributed to a shift in the balance of power. The Orange question also assumed frightening proportions, and by the time Prince William came of age it dominated the situation. De Witt's greatness, the greatness of the Dutch Republic, lies

[1] For details of the character of the Dutch economy and the political institutions of the Republic, see vol. IV, ch. XII.

enclosed between Spanish and French hegemony, between the adult vigour of William II and that of William III. It fundamentally was a greatness *ad interim*.

The Dutch had not foreseen the forms English hostility would take. It was mainly economic hostility. The English, obsessed by the idea of a sum total of world trade, thought that the portion they desired must necessarily come out of the share of others, in practice that of the Dutch. Thus English hostility was aggressive, the Dutch reaction defensive. Much of this rivalry was strikingly mean: short-sighted irritations about daily competition, petulant touchiness, the desire to take Dutch ships and to sell them as prizes. But there were also contrasting principles: the idea of the domination of the British seas against the system, or the lack of system, which the Dutch called the principle of the free seas and which they upheld wherever their commercial power was or could be expected to be supreme. Only after many years and after the opening of new possibilities did it begin to be realised that world commerce itself could be expanded and that two capitalist and competing states could thrive without destroying each other.

The three Anglo-Dutch wars of the seventeenth century did not contribute to the solution of the economic problems. They sprang from a narrow interpretation of world affairs and did not bring much profit to either party. It was only possible for these economic hostilities to run riot and to force themselves to the front because in the short period of relative European calm between the Peace of Westphalia of 1648, which ended the Spanish hegemony, and the War of Devolution of 1667, which inaugurated the French hegemony, no wider political interests silenced these passionate jealousies or, at any rate, prevented them from developing into war. When in 1672 Charles II started the third war against Holland, it was felt that a policy which for twenty years seemed a reasonable programme of economic expansion was becoming a dangerous adventure.

Nobody had been able to foresee this either in England or in the Dutch Republic. The Dutch had followed the development of the Puritan Revolution with great anxiety and indignation. Few were those who did not regard regicide as a serious offence against religion, morals and public law. But the regents took grave risks to prevent William II from involving the Republic in the struggle. There is no doubt that the English revolutionaries felt greatly relieved when the stadholder suddenly died and the Dutch State seemed to become a pure republic. Cromwell made a vigorous attempt to raise Anglo-Dutch relations high above economic rivalry. In March 1651 he sent a mission to The Hague with far-reaching proposals: a close alliance between the two Protestant republics, a union even. It was a plan without a future. For the Dutch the realisation of the plan would have meant considerable economic loss because they had so much more to bring into the union, and it is easy to understand that the scheme was discarded. Yet the regents made a serious mistake in thinking that their haughty dismissal of Cromwell's attempt at finding a political solution to the problem of Anglo-Dutch relations, against the will of the London merchants, would be without grave consequences. The openly hostile attitude of the population of The Hague, stirred up by the court and its clique of predikants, intensified the feelings of frustration and bitter anger of the English envoys, who returned to London without any acceptable alternative to Cromwell's plan. Again the economic rivalry was given free scope. In October 1651 the Navigation Act was passed, in fact a declaration of economic war upon the Dutch. A Dutch embassy sent to England in December asked for its withdrawal, but failed to offer anything in exchange. The first Anglo-Dutch War followed (1652–4).

The war is of less interest for the history of Anglo-Dutch relations than for the internal development of the Republic. Neither party achieved a clear supremacy and after two years the struggle ended in a draw. Cromwell, moreover, in 1654 had more arguments at his disposal than in 1652 for bringing to an end this uninhibited outburst of economic jealousies. In 1652 there was some reason to suspect that the contemptuous rejection of his proposals sprang from stubborn pro-Stuart Orangism. In 1654 these anxieties no longer made sense. The republican régime in Holland had stood the test.

It had not been an easy victory. During the summer of 1652 it seemed likely that the popular movements would force the authorities to appoint William III to the dignities of his ancestors. There was, of course, no sound and considered Orangist solution to the problems of foreign and domestic policy. It was not political convictions which sought to express themselves in the innumerable, sometimes dangerous disturbances taking place in 1652 in the eastern provinces and in 1653 in almost all the towns of Holland and Zeeland, but suspicion of the government and despair, a result of the misery caused by the war. During 1651, but more still in 1652, the prices at the Amsterdam corn-exchange rose steeply, and the paralysis of trade and fishing brought serious unemployment. In the midst of this dangerous political crisis, which soon persuaded some Zeeland regents of the necessity of changing course and of making more room for the Prince of Orange, John de Witt was appointed to the office of Grand Pensionary of Holland. He knew how unpopular the republican régime was, supported in his estimate by less than one-tenth of one per cent of the 'common populace'.[1] But he also realized that the 'idle sound of the name of a child'[2] could only become dangerous if among the regents a party arose able to give political form to popular discontent. De Witt managed to overcome this danger by his adroit and courageous words.

[1] *Brieven van Johan de Witt*, ed. R. Fruin and G. W. Kernkamp (Amsterdam, 1906 ff.), I, 96.
[2] *Ibid.* p. 161.

To the relief of both de Witt and Cromwell the Orangist movement came to nothing. Moreover, de Witt proved willing, though with extreme reluctance, to have the States of Holland vote at Cromwell's request never to appoint a Prince of Orange stadholder or captain-general (Act of Seclusion, 1654). Although Cromwell was satisfied with this solemn assurance, it was nevertheless a very poor remnant of his ideal to bring both countries together in one united Protestant republic, a republic which obviously would exclude both Stuart and Orange. Thanks to this compromise the Peace of Westminster could be signed (1654), a peace which solved none of the economic problems.

The resistance of the other provincial States to the Act of Seclusion bore no proportion to the vehemence of the Orangist movements in 1653. The people were pacified now that the war, the cause of their misery, had come to an end. The States General were unable to take any action against Holland's decision, legally justifiable but—from the federal point of view—rather high-handed. In the province of Holland itself de Witt succeeded after 1654 in consolidating his party. The town garrisons were strengthened or, if necessary, replaced by more reliable ones, and in the urban administrations de Witt sought to establish friends—often his own relatives—through whom he could exercise influence. Through the Bicker family, to which his wife belonged, and his own family he dominated to a large extent the whole provincial government. Yet it was not without the utmost efforts that towns and States were persuaded to take decisions, and the legislative activity of the régime was remarkably slight. In two matters only was de Witt able to take determined action. He reduced the interest on Holland's debts from 5 to 4 per cent and set aside the amounts thus saved for amortisation, hoping that the whole debt could in this way be paid off within forty-one years. The States General adopted a similar measure. At the same time important parts of the army were disbanded. There is no doubt that these decisions were sound. The appalling decline of the Dutch army was not due to this reduction, but to the lack of a commander-in-chief, to the nepotism and particularism growing rampant in this State without a centre.

De Witt's influence outside Holland was of course smaller still, though it was fortunately more potent than his constitutional position and principles permitted. The Grand Assembly had opted for provincial independence, which benefited small cliques of regents, and de Witt was unable to do a great deal to counteract this development. He was, however, forced to intervene in the incessant conflicts which tore some provinces and led to years of anarchy. It is surprising that all the conflicts within urban or provincial governments, whether in Holland or in Overijssel and Groningen, seem to have been quite naturally absorbed by the antithesis of Orangism and the System of True Liberty. Yet the very fact that de Witt's régime in Holland was endangered by rival loyalties in other provinces made him an interested party in conflicts fought out in sovereign republics other than his own. It is indeed true that Holland's provincial republicanism could not be confined to its proper limits and, were it to live, would have to blot out the provincial frontiers which it was so eager to write in black on the map of the Northern Netherlands. If in this State broken by political barriers there was some kind of unity, it was not because a united government transcended them but because the political passions did.

Weak as this government was in domestic affairs, its foreign policy, when it acted as the representative of Dutch commercial interests and was able to make use of Holland's immense financial power, could be very vigorous indeed. After John de Witt had consolidated his party during and after the first Anglo-Dutch War, he could assert Dutch influence abroad in a more determined way. His intervention in the Baltic question, so vitally important to Holland because of the dependence of the Dutch economy on the Baltic trade, clearly demonstrates the character of his foreign policy. When the Swedes began to strive for hegemony in those areas it became necessary for the Dutch to take some action and to maintain the balance of power. Dutch policy now was based on friendship with Denmark, which demanded high duties in the Sound but did not aim at destroying Dutch trade. Already in 1649 an alliance was concluded between the Republic and Denmark, which inevitably had an anti-Swedish tendency, and the problem of the Sound dues was solved by Dutch willingness to pay an annual duty of 350,000 guilders. During the first Anglo-Dutch War these new relations asserted themselves. Sweden gave some support to England, Denmark to the Republic. Yet de Witt succeeded in staying neutral during the war started by Charles X of Sweden against Brandenburg and Poland (1655) and in obtaining a Swedish assurance that Dutch trade would not suffer any damage (Treaty of Elbing, 1656).

De Witt's reluctance to involve the Republic in the Baltic War sprang from his fear that England and France would almost certainly take Sweden's side. He abandoned his neutrality only after the danger had become less serious. In 1657 Denmark declared war on Sweden but Charles X kept the upper hand, laid siege to the Danish capital and by the Peace of Roeskilde (1658) acquired parts of Norway, the eastern shore of the Sound and the assurance that both kings would prevent foreign warships from entering the Baltic. This treaty did not end the war. In the summer of 1658 Charles X reopened his attack hoping to be able to dethrone the Danish king. The Baltic problem assumed the utmost gravity since it was intolerable from the Dutch point of view to leave both shores of the Sound under Swedish authority. At last de Witt sent the Dutch fleet to the Sound; it defeated the Swedes and relieved Copenhagen. Intensive diplomatic activity led in May 1659 to the Concert of The

Hague: England, France and the Republic made it clear that they considered the Peace of Roskilde, interpreted in a way unfavourable to Sweden, the basis of the situation in the Baltic and decided to force the two northern kings to preserve this agreement. Force was indeed needed, and the Dutch fleet provided it. The Swedish army capitulated and after Charles X's death in February 1660 the Peace of Copenhagen was signed which was to the great advantage of the Dutch.

De Witt, during this complicated episode, demonstrated high qualities of statesmanship. His position was difficult. Already during the first stages of the conflict Amsterdam was inclined towards drastic action, whereas the Grand Pensionary realised that sharp tension between the Republic, England and France would be the inevitable outcome of such high-handed proceedings. It was therefore only after England was weakened by Cromwell's death and France unable to give a demonstration of her power that de Witt took action. Thanks to this favourable international situation he was able to take the initiative for joint intervention by the three powers and to achieve the Dutch aims without risks. For the first time in its history the Dutch Republic acted as a great power. It did so cautiously and with moderation. It could act in this way because of the temporary weakness of its rivals.

The circumstances of 1658 and 1659 caused the end of the illusion nursed by the regents since 1648 that by careful neutrality the Republic could withdraw from the international struggle for power. Commercial interests forced the Republic into political activity. Dutch statesmen had learned to acknowledge, however reluctantly, the status of the Republic as a great power and to accept the responsibilities resulting from it. De Witt grew active. The Peace of the Pyrenees of 1659 and the Restoration in England cleared the sky of old troubles, and de Witt now saw the opportunity to realise a great plan. Since none of the great powers was any longer tied down by wars or alliances he attempted to bring about a defensive alliance between the Republic, England and France which, had it materialised, would have greatly strengthened the Dutch. De Witt was right in looking upon friendship with potentially greater powers as the only means for the Republic of maintaining its status. But the plan failed because England and the Republic were unable to achieve a compromise. De Witt apparently underestimated the vehemence of Anglo-Dutch economic rivalry and the difficulty of persuading the neighbours to accept a system of free trade which would enable the Dutch, with their better fleet and their incomparably greater financial power, to check the development of their competitors. The only possibility left was an alliance with France alone and de Witt did not hesitate. It was concluded in 1662 and linked with a commercial treaty in accordance with the wishes of the Dutch. It is difficult to see what else de Witt could have done. The vulnerability of the Republic compelled him to look for foreign support; English hostility, the weakness of Spain and of the Emperor limited his choice of allies. Moreover, the Franco-Dutch alliance meant a success for John de Witt in that the French statesmen, who had maintained intimate relations with William II and for long years had regarded the republican régime with great suspicion, now recognised its power and stability.

De Witt realised that his policy, however inevitable it might be, was fraught with danger. Franco-Dutch collaboration was extremely precarious, if not unnatural, in this period. From the Dutch point of view Colbertism was just as intolerable as was French territorial imperialism. The attempt to contain the latter by contriving a solution for the dangerous problem of the Southern Netherlands failed in 1664, notwithstanding de Witt's persistence and his great intelligence and resourcefulness: Louis XIV was unwilling to be tied by a compromise which would have strengthened and confirmed the Franco-Dutch alliance. Events proved that de Witt was right. Relations between England and the Republic did not improve after 1660. It soon became clear that Charles II wished to give a free rein to the economic struggle against the Republic, while the common religious interests of which Cromwell had never lost sight in his dealings with the States General no longer acted as a counterpoise. The tension between both maritime powers grew rapidly. In West Africa and North America the English African Company started an attack supported by the navy which brought such serious damage to the Dutch West India Company that the States General decided to order their fleet to reply. After the war in Africa had been going on for some time it broke out in Europe (January 1665), and after another couple of months official declarations of war were exchanged.

This was a purely commercial war.[1] In the first Anglo-Dutch War, too, economic interests had played a dominant part; but the situation then had been largely ruled by Cromwell's high idealism and by the dangers inherent in the Orange-Stuart connection. In 1665 no political element exercised any influence. The war found the Dutch ill-prepared, but much more confident than in 1652. Holland's finances were in perfect order. The province did not have the slightest difficulty, in 1664 and in 1665, in raising large amounts of money at low rates of interest and had sufficient quantities of cash at its disposal. The navy was not in very good condition, but it was easy enough to equip ships. With passionate determination de Witt set himself to improving the fleet, and after some initial disappointments he succeeded in making it so strong as to win supremacy. The army constituted a much more awkward problem. When in September 1665 the quarrelsome Bishop of Münster invaded the eastern provinces in the expectation of getting English support, no Dutch troops were available to stop him, and it was only due to French intervention that he ultimately was forced to withdraw. The usefulness of the French alliance

[1] See also below, ch. XIII, pp. 309–10.

was made clear. Although the French, notwithstanding their declaration of war (January 1666), did not participate in actual warfare against England their attitude helped to isolate Charles II. This isolation was complete when de Witt succeeded in winning Denmark by the payment of high subsidies, whereas lack of money prevented the Stuart king from drawing Sweden into the war.

The Dutch position was therefore favourable when in April 1667 peace negotiations were opened at Breda. Or did Charles II possess another card to play? It is possible that he promised to support Louis XIV, who just when the diplomats gathered at Breda invaded the Southern Netherlands and made his army advance rapidly northwards. But de Witt's prompt and effective action prevented Charles II from profiting by what seemed for him an advantageous development: the raid on the Medway (June 1667) ended the king's hopes. Thereafter it was easy to achieve a settlement. Thanks to de Witt's statesmanlike and realistic moderation the Peace of Breda (July 1667) was an earnest attempt to reach a compromise. Cape Coast Castle in Africa and the New Netherlands were ceded to England, Surinam and in the East Indies Pulo-Run to the States General. Some of the favourite Dutch principles were accepted. England recognised that the flag covered the ship, the search of ships for contraband was replaced by more civilised methods, and the definition of contraband itself was confined to implements of war. Yet in practice this arrangement did not open the way to any fruitful political co-operation of the two countries. The vehemence of the economic crusade against the Republic hardly subsided, but the vigour and the reasonableness of the Dutch helped to clear the atmosphere.

Louis XIV was impressed by this Dutch display of force and immediately invited de Witt to arrange with him a compromise concerning the Southern Netherlands. Negotiations proved difficult and slow. When they had virtually come to a halt Charles II decided to force de Witt into an anti-French policy which led to the notorious Triple Alliance of January 1668. De Witt had taken every possible care lest his relations with France should be disturbed by England, but he was unsuccessful. The Triple Alliance of Holland, England and Sweden, apparently a victory for Anglo-Dutch diplomacy because it held in check French expansion, was in fact only reluctantly signed by the Grand Pensionary. It was the end of his cautious policy with regard to France and enhanced the danger of isolation. But there was no alternative. Charles II as well as the States of Holland, greatly annoyed by Colbert's vehement anti-Dutch tariff policy, forced de Witt to acquiesce in an action of which he rightly feared the ultimate consequences.

Thus the Dutch Republic, while going from strength to strength, was beset by increasing dangers. De Witt's ingenious diplomacy could not prevent the great powers from gradually rising from their weakness and being irritated by Dutch wealth and Dutch influence which were in part due to their own shortcomings. In his domestic policy also de Witt's very successes helped to undermine his position. His handling of the Orange question was masterly. The Stuart Restoration could not be without consequences for the situation within the Republic. Charles II was William III's uncle and the Act of Seclusion was distasteful to the English king because it was Cromwellian, and to de Witt because it was brought about by foreign interference in Holland's policies. It was repealed in 1660; but the provinces of Zeeland, Friesland and Groningen, disturbed by Orangist hopes and Orangist intrigues, wanted to go much farther and proposed that William be assigned the offices of his ancestors. Yet as long as Holland refused their action was bound to remain fruitless, and Holland did refuse. De Witt understandably feared the restoration of the Prince not only because of the possible recrudescence of anti-republican tendencies, but also because it would reopen the channels through which Stuart influence could penetrate the Dutch State. Dynastic considerations were likely to become predominant again, and of that, precisely, he and his collaborators were most afraid. Something however had to be done. De Witt made a counter-proposal: Holland, he declared, though not prepared to tie itself to any firm promise, was willing to take over the burden of educating the young Prince for the functions held by his ancestors. This implied that the House of Orange was to be allowed a place in the State if it could be made to acquiesce in the strictly republican form of government and to sever its links with foreign princes.

The plan was not carried out. Charles II was naturally opposed to it. A Prince of Orange imbued with the *raison d'état* of republican regents would not be a means of weakening the hated State; it was far more advantageous to continue using him as pivot of paralysing conflicts. The English ambassador to The Hague, Downing, and members of the princely court started an elaborate pro-Orange propaganda campaign which was a contributory cause of several popular movements during the second Anglo-Dutch War. Though less vehement than in the early 1650's, they were strong enough to persuade some of the regents to ask for an Orange Restoration. Under these circumstances, with the English War going on, de Witt took up again his plan of having William III educated by the States of Holland and this was carried out in 1666. The princely palace was cleared of dangerous plotters; some months later the intrigues of some members of the Orangist clique were brought to light, and this led to the execution of one of them. De Witt himself took on the task of initiating the prince into the *arcana imperii*, the difficult political questions. It was certainly partly due to these measures that William III some years later proved to have largely detached himself from the dynastic, naïvely pro-English traditions of the Orange court. As a corollary the States of Holland decided in 1667 to declare the offices of provincial stadholder and tain-general and admiral-general to be incompatible and abolished ιdholdership of the province of Holland altogether (Eternal Edict). vas undoubtedly a success for de Witt, coinciding with his victory Charles II.

Eternal Edict, however, did not solve the constitutional problem. first place it was very difficult to extract similar decisions from the provinces; it was not until 1670 that de Witt succeeded in persuading to follow him, and even then only reluctantly and with reservations. s, moreover, doubtful whether this separation of military and cal power, however right in principle, made sense in a State like the blic. By what means was a Prince of Orange to be kept out of cs after having been appointed commander-in-chief of the provincial s? In 1668 William III was, in his quality of representative of the ity, recognised as a member of the States of Zeeland and in 1670 he entered the Council of State. Both functions were political functions.

De Witt's glory reached its zenith in 1667 and 1668. The States of Holland commissioned Wicquefort to write the history of the Dutch Republic from 1648 to 1668, a short period in the development of a small country, but so important as to be only paralleled by the most magnificent histories of past ages.[1] Yet serious dangers were threatening the Grand Pensionary even in Holland. His very power exposed him to the hatred of his former friends. Amsterdam seemed to move out of the reach of his party when in 1664, after the death of Zuidpolsbroek, who had done so much to support de Witt's policy, the shamelessly ambitious Valckenier acquired influence and ultimately turned away from the leader of the States. It was even suggested in Amsterdam to transform the office of the Grand Pensionary and to appoint a secretary of state for foreign affairs. The plan was not carried out.

It is not difficult to explain in general terms the decline of de Witt's power. Yet his fall in 1672, as a consequence of the French War, came as a surprise. On the whole the Dutch do not seem to have expected the French attack. De Witt's foreign policy was rather passive after 1668. But before criticising de Witt because of his carelessness, it has to be taken into account that the Dutch generally seem to have been unaware of the degree of jealousy and hatred they inspired abroad, which in 1672 was to lead to the joint attack of France and England upon the Republic. Throughout 1670 and 1671 the rate of interest was low. It is surprising how in their frequent negotiations with England the Dutch defended their own commercial interests—the freedom of the seas—without realising how much they irritated their adversaries. The Dutch hardly understood foreign countries although they were great travellers and The Hague was the centre of European journalism. They did not share in some of the most striking tendencies of the seventeenth century, in royal absolutism, in

[1] A. de Wicquefort, *Histoire des Provinces-Unies des Païs-Bas* (Amsterdam, 1861), I, 2.

mercantilism, in the Baroque. The form of their political society, the structure of their trade, the character of their culture, seem at times like a deviation from seventeenth-century patterns. Their conservatism, the late medieval ways of their life, with its glories of municipal and provincial independence, made them strangers in the world of their time. Their prosperity—exceptional in a period of vehement economic crises—their sober religious tolerance, their aristocratic liberty hardly fitted into the century. During de Witt's period of office this separateness from Europe seemed to grow stronger.

Therefore the attack of 1672 came as a painful contact with countries where baroque absolutism and baroque *raison d'état* ran wild. It is vain to ask what particularly had awakened the ire of the Stuart and Bourbon kings. The very existence of this Republic—announcing the Enlightenment notwithstanding its old-fashioned ways—with its defiant wealth was a paradox and a challenge. Colbertism, Louis XIV's hurt pride, Charles II's unscrupulous methods and his adventurous domestic policies, the traditional hatred of the Dutch among English businessmen, all this led to the Treaty of Dover (1670) whereby the French and English kings agreed to attack and divide between them this aristocratic republic—as Poland, that other aristocratic republic, was divided a century later. England was to acquire some towns and islands at the mouth of the Scheldt, but France did not yet define what she intended to take; William III was to receive in sovereignty whatever was left; and thus a peculiar anomaly would be abolished.

Attempts made by de Witt in 1671 to strengthen his diplomatic position did not meet with success. Neither the Emperor nor Spain were prepared to commit themselves and Sweden chose the French alliance. The Bishop of Münster and the Archbishop of Cologne, who also held the bishopric of Liège, were glad to open their territories to Louis XIV's triumphant march against the Republic. At the beginning of 1672 the diplomatic isolation of the United Provinces was almost complete. Towards the end of March England declared war, in early April France followed suit. While a Dutch medal of 1668 had depicted the *roi soleil* as the sun brought to a standstill by Joshua, in May 1672 Louis began to move against the United Provinces. Without any difficulty the French army of more than 100,000 men under the personal direction of Louis XIV crossed the Rhine near Elten on 12 June. The Dutch forces numbered about 30,000 men whose morale was bad and whose commanders were severely handicapped by the authority exercised by the States of the various provinces over the battalions paid from their contributions. Notwithstanding de Witt's resistance, the States General had in February 1672 appointed William III captain-general, but for one campaign only and under somewhat crippling conditions. Although it was decided in 1671 and again early in 1672 to increase the army, this had no immediate effect; and after the outlying defences on Dutch territory had been rushed the captain-general could only withdraw his troops behind the water defences which protected Holland (18 June).

As early as the end of June the fate of the Republic seemed to be decided. Louis XIV established his headquarters in the province of Utrecht. His armies were in control of Utrecht and Guelderland, whereas the bishops of Münster and Cologne held the provinces of Overijssel and Drente and part of Groningen. However, the town of Groningen offered stubborn resistance and thus saved Friesland. The fall of the eastern provinces looked like desertion. They seemed ready to leave the Union and to seek allegiance farther east. Early in June the nobility of Overijssel submitted to the Bishop of Münster, presuming that the dissolution of the Union had already come about. Everywhere in the areas occupied by Roman Catholic princes a religious revolution was carried out. The Roman Catholic clergy re-entered into the possession of their old churches and monasteries and showed themselves publicly at funerals and processions. The Jesuits founded schools in various towns. Yet Protestantism was not prohibited, and nowhere do tensions of any importance seem to have arisen. The Roman Catholic emancipation was carried out by order of the occupying authorities; but as Dutch Catholics were used to pinning their faith on Spain, now on the way to becoming an ally of the Dutch, and not on France, Louis XIV's troops were not hailed as an army of liberation, and his measures caused no repercussions among the Roman Catholics of the still independent provinces. Yet the zeal with which the Catholics in the conquered areas tried to return to their former position shows how definite in their opinion was the fall of the Protestant State.

In Holland also, traditionally not only the economic and cultural but also the military centre of the Republic, defeatism was rampant. Considering the catastrophic circumstances we may well wonder at its remaining within such narrow limits. For a few days the States of Holland were wavering to such an extent that it seemed possible they would give up the struggle before it had started. The cause of this hesitation was that de Witt, who had urged on the States the necessity of resistance to the utmost, withdrawing if need be to Amsterdam as a last redoubt, was suddenly removed from the scene of practical politics. On the evening of 21 June he was attacked by four youthful Orangist partisans and seriously wounded. Some days before, the States had agreed to open negotiations with the enemy, but it was only now that they were started. Soon, however, it became clear that France would not be satisfied with a reasonable compromise. When her excessive demands became known (1 July) it was no longer the States alone that stood before the task of deciding whether to accept the humiliating demands designed to bring to an end the greatness of the Republic.

During these fateful days, with the enemy near the very insufficiently protected frontier, the States of Holland were confronted with an additional problem of the highest importance. After the outbreak of the war the Orangists had started a formidable propaganda campaign. Popular movements were instigated in Dordrecht, Rotterdam, Gouda, Haarlem and other towns, which aimed at the restoration of the Prince of Orange to the traditional dignities of his ancestors. Most of the urban administrations resolved to abolish the Eternal Edict and to proclaim William III stadholder of Holland. On Sunday night, 3 July, the States of Holland took the difficult but inevitable decision. The States of Zeeland did the same one day earlier, and the States General hurried to appoint William III to be captain-general and admiral-general, abolishing the limiting conditions which had been imposed upon him (8 July).

One of the first political decisions made by the new stadholder was his advice to the States not to accept the peace conditions put forward by France and to continue the war. This advice was heeded and the negotiations were broken off. Meanwhile the tensions in Holland were increasing. The populace was by no means satisfied by the appointment of William III to the dignities of his ancestors. The Orangist successes of early July were considered insufficient, although the towns restored to the stadholder the right of nominating their magistrates. During July and August an uninterrupted series of popular disturbances, sometimes stirred up by the Orangists and never suppressed by them, undermined the authority of the urban administrations and the States. It was not so much hatred of the class of the regents as such which was expressed in these riots as suspicion of their policies. Early in August John de Witt, recovered from his wounds, handed in his resignation as Grand Pensionary, but he continued to be accused by Orangist pamphlets which were eagerly read. De Witt, it was thought, had stirred up the hatred of the Stuarts by his anti-Orangist policies and had wished to surrender to France rather than restore the Prince. On 20 August the great statesman and his brother Cornelis fell victims to the mob of The Hague, which neither the States nor the urban administration dared, and which William III did not desire, to disperse.

William III made use of the passions aroused. He rewarded some of the murderers; some predikants praised God's wisdom in punishing the hated man. Seven days after the abominable act the States of Holland decided to give the Prince a free hand in dealing with the urban governments. At last the wishes of the Orangist leaders were fulfilled. William III caused the regents who were most compromised by their adherence to de Witt's system to hand in their resignations. In September 159 members of the urban administrations—the total number of sitting regents in Holland was about 500—were replaced by Orangists. It was not a complete purge, nor was it a social revolution. The new members belonged to different families but to the same social group as the dismissed, who incidentally were not molested or annoyed. This was the end of the affair. On 27 September the States proclaimed an amnesty. The popular disturbances receded, and if necessary they were suppressed by the urban governments at last feeling safe. It emerges from this narrative that it would be wrong to call the events of 1672 a revolution. Not only had the constitutional forms been respected, the States having appointed William III in a perfectly legal way to perfectly legal offices; there had not even been a revolutionary programme, for the rare requests for democratic reforms made in the pamphlets can hardly be regarded as such. The outcome of these months of anger and suspicion was a murder, the replacement of some ruling families by other families, and the appointment of a Prince of Orange to the offices held by his ancestors.

The enemies had been looking at the events in Holland without making an attempt to profit by them. What was it that finally prevented Louis XIV from delivering the *coup de grâce*: premature self-confidence, impotence, or the water defences? Which of his expectations were disappointed? Towards the end of June he could probably have penetrated into Holland; but he did not move, haughtily waiting for a surrender which did not come in the form he desired. He did not resume the attack: towards the end of July he returned to France. His splendid army, reduced to 20,000 men, lay idle in a hostile country until, thanks to Holland's inexhaustible financial power, the military forces of the Republic had been strengthened and her diplomatic isolation broken by treaties with the Emperor, Spain, Lorraine and Denmark; thus in 1674 the French were compelled to withdraw. At the same time Charles II of England, forced by public opinion, made peace. He had achieved nothing. From the beginning of the war the Dutch fleet prevented English landings. In a series of important battles the Dutch admirals maintained their naval supremacy. The second Peace of Westminster (1674) was based on the *status quo ante*; it was accompanied by a commercial treaty recognising the validity of the liberal Dutch trading principles. It is, incidentally, noteworthy that now the English profited from them because, thanks to their neutrality, they were able to take the place left vacant in France by the Dutch. Some months later the bishops of Münster and Cologne also made peace.

These events completely changed the character of the war. Having started as an adventure of baroque power-politics, it continued after 1674 as the traditional conflict between the House of Habsburg and the House of Bourbon. It looked, however, as though the old French fear of being encircled by the House of Habsburg was gradually developing into a desire to win supremacy in Europe. This, in any case, was the opinion of William III who, while the Dutch regents soon lost interest in, and did not want to spend money on, a war which was no longer being fought on their territory and did not immediately endanger Dutch independence, came to be convinced of his mission to fight French attempts at hegemony. The means which the Dutch in their distress had been forced to use—the coalition of as many anti-French powers as possible—became an instrument of his policy.

The coalition was weak. The campaigns of 1675 and 1676 were indecisive; the attempts of the Dutch in 1676 to establish their maritime supremacy in the Mediterranean resulted in a minor Dutch victory in the battle of the Etna (in which Michiel de Ruyter fell) and the important French victory in the battle of Palermo. In 1677 the French captured some towns in the Southern Netherlands, but could not prevent William III from laying siege to Charleroi (which he did not succeed in taking). Yet the year 1677 was of great importance in the history of Europe because Anglo-Dutch relations suddenly improved. Charles II of England consented to the marriage of Mary, the daughter of his brother James, to William III: for him only motives of foreign policy counted, so that this second marriage treaty between the Houses of Stuart and of Orange was completely different in character from the first which had united, merely to the greater glory of the Orange dynasty, William III's father to the daughter of Charles I. William III acted in defence of the European balance of power and spent his whole life in serving the doctrine which had been advocated with such persuasiveness in the *Bouclier d'Estat et de Justice* by the famous Imperial diplomat de Lisola (who died in 1674). William understood that this system could never be established without active English support. In March 1678 an Anglo-Dutch defensive alliance was signed: a fact which was to dominate European history for many years.

In 1676 peace negotiations began at Nymegen, but they progressed very slowly. William III was firmly opposed to them because he saw how successful the French were in winning over the regents of the Dutch Republic and, above all, those of Amsterdam, to the idea of breaking away from the European alliance and of concluding a separate peace; for the war was highly prejudicial to the Republic, the financial burdens were heavy, and the merchants of neutral countries established themselves in the markets formerly dominated by the Dutch. In August 1678 the French and the Dutch indeed signed a separate peace. It was not unfavourable to the Dutch: Louis XIV abolished the prohibitive tariffs of 1667 and allowed the Dutch a measure of free trade, in flat contradiction to the protectionist system of Colbert. William III, however, who knew that peace was made, attacked the French army in a mood of desperate rage; but the battle of Saint-Denis (near Mons) ended with a near-defeat for him. The allies were reluctant to follow the Dutch example, but were unable to continue the war alone. Louis XIV abandoned most of his conquests, retaining only Franche Comté and Valenciennes, Cambrai and St Omer in the Southern Netherlands. Although he had not by a long way achieved his aims, the war ended with a diplomatic victory for him. The European alliance was broken, and it was not likely that it could easily be restored.

William III rightly considered the Peace of Nymegen a defeat. The following years were for him a period of frustration, during which the French took advantage of their excellent diplomatic position to annex the *dekapolis* in Alsace, Strassburg, Montbéliard, and Casale in northern Italy (1681). The Quadruple Alliance signed in the spring of 1682 by the Emperor, Spain, the Dutch Republic, and Sweden only purported to uphold the articles of the Peace of Nymegen, and the strong peace-party in the Republic, as well as the Emperor, engrossed in a new war against the Turks, were prepared to believe the assurances of Louis XIV that he did not want to break these terms. Nevertheless the danger of a general war constantly increased. In December 1683 Spain declared war on France and French armies began to operate in Luxemburg and, soon afterwards, in the Southern Netherlands. William III did his utmost to induce the Republic to help Spain. The differences of opinion between Amsterdam, supported not only by Holland but also by Friesland and Groningen, and the Prince of Orange seemed to come to a head. For a moment it looked as if he would use force to carry out his policy. But in the end, after months of bitter discussions, sharp measures and an enormous output of vehement pamphlets, he gave way to the wishes of his stubborn opponents. The direct result was that Spain and the Emperor signed the humiliating Armistice of Ratisbon (August 1684) whereby they ceded Luxemburg and Strassburg to the French for a period of twenty years.

It was only in 1685 that Louis XIV overstrained his forces and spoiled his splendid international position by reckless extremism. The Revocation of the Edict of Nantes and the emigration of numerous Huguenots, of whom many found refuge in the Dutch Republic, kindled among the Protestants the fire of the religious wars. Slowly a new anti-French coalition was formed. In 1685 Brandenburg and the Dutch Republic signed a defensive alliance. A year later the Emperor, Spain and most of the German States entered the League of Augsburg which obliged them to preserve the existing treaties. Louis XIV was fully aware of the reactions provoked by his policy; but instead of reasserting his prestige by caution and conciliation, as he had done in the late 1670's, he pursued his aims in the most uncompromising way. The spectacle of the persecutions in France, the many Huguenot refugees who settled in Holland and started a powerful propaganda, had a decisive influence. The reluctance to go to war which had dominated the Dutch Republic since 1678 began to recede. When William III saw the possibility of replacing his uncle and father-in-law, James II, he asked the States for support, and Louis XIV's over-confidence helped William to achieve his purpose. The king was convinced that his warnings would restrain the obstinate Prince of Orange, but Louis's German campaign in the autumn of 1688 provided William with an excellent opportunity. The States allowed the prince to sail, equipped him with a sufficient army and an excellent fleet, and on 12 November 1688 he left for England.

After 1674 William III's foreign policy belongs so clearly to European history in its widest sense that it is perhaps of less interest to the student of Dutch history than the analysis of the strength on which it rested. His domestic policy was, above all, remarkable for its negative character: he did not alter the organisation of the Republic. In a way this was unnecessary. The power he possessed was large; the war he had to fight demanded his entire attention. Yet it is surprising that this man of princely birth and almost reckless boldness maintained the narrow framework of the ruling oligarchy with its *bourgeois* outlook and its humanists' contempt for the populace; and it is paradoxical that he confirmed the oligarchic tendencies and abuses by exploiting them. The explanation lies perhaps not so much in his obvious indifference towards constitutional questions as in his insight into the nature of Holland's political system. It may be that his unhappy youth had inspired in him a certain aversion to the mentality of the regents; yet it was these early experiences which taught him how cautiously the regents had to be handled and how formidable their resistance could be. In 1674 he made an interesting attempt to acquire a kind of sovereign status. His popularity was then at its height. The States of Holland and Zeeland decided in February 1674 to make the stadholdership an hereditary function. In April 1675 the States General did the same for the offices of captain-general and admiral-general. Clearly these decisions only confirmed an old tradition broken by the events of 1650 and 1651 and did not contribute much to the solution of the constitutional problem. More important were the events in Utrecht, Guelderland and Overijssel.

When the foreign armies left these provinces Holland proposed not to allow them to reassume their seats in the States General, hoping to make its own vote in the assembly more preponderant. William III saw the danger and opposed the plan so strongly that it had to be abandoned. In April 1674 the provinces returned to the States General. But then Holland induced the assembly to grant William III the right of organising their internal government according to his own wishes. He not only radically changed the personnel of the governing bodies but introduced so-called 'administrative regulations' which, though maintaining the old forms, gave him almost absolute power in these provinces. Then, in January 1675, Guelderland offered to William III, who had certainly suggested this, the old ducal title which would have given him not only sovereign authority but also sovereign status. William III was right in not accepting this title without consulting the other provinces. In Holland and Zeeland reactions were generally very hostile. Public funds fell as though a *coup d'état* were imminent. Everybody realised that the prince if made duke of Guelderland could not be denied the sovereign titles of Holland and Zeeland. In Zeeland it was openly said that such a development would be detrimental to the economic position of the country, since arbitrary government was expected to undermine the confidence in institutions such as the discount banks and the East and West India Companies. The idea of one-headed government being by definition identical with arbitrary government—the stock argument of all Dutch republicans—proved to be current even among the Orangists. For in Holland and Zeeland it was precisely the towns which had most exerted themselves for the restoration of Orange rule that now most sharply turned against this plan. William III did not hesitate to draw his conclusions. On 20 February 1675 he informed Guelderland that he was unable to accept the sovereignty.

This was the Prince's only attempt radically to change the constitutional forms. Yet with his policy gradually concentrating on the one aim of putting an end to French imperialism his need of power and money grew; this could not be obtained by constitutional means only. It was inevitable that he would strain the constitution. Not only his ancestors Maurice and Frederick Henry had done this, even John de Witt had made his provincial function into something which formally did not fit into the constitution. But it is remarkable that William did not hesitate systematically to exploit the same oligarchic practices which de Witt had already used in order to strengthen his influence. However, what in de Witt's time was a government of relatives and friends was bound to degenerate under William III into a government of corrupt clients. He sought to fill the councils and governments of the towns, the States and the States General with people who promised to obey him blindly. In Zeeland his relative Nassau-Odijk used his position of princely deputy to exercise a completely unconstitutional power by the most unscrupulous means. In some of the other provinces scandals came to light which disclosed William III's tactics, but these exposures did not cause him to change his policy. At Rotterdam, for example, the 'griffier', William III's henchman, made a candidate for the town council promise to obey, if elected, all the directives of the stadholder on penalty of forfeiting a guarantee of 4000 guilders. William III, though not directly involved in such affairs, did not try to stop them, nor did he want to put an end to the rise of a closed oligarchy. On the contrary, by undermining the responsibility and the independence of the regents for the sake of his foreign policy, he accelerated this development.

Looking back upon the history of the Dutch Republic during these forty years one has the impression of seeing a climbing road. In de Witt's time the State, which had acquired full independence only in 1648, became a great power, and under William III it found an historical task of supreme importance. This impression, however, is incomplete; for the climax reached under William III was the beginning of the decline. The internal situation deteriorated; the oligarchic abuses increased; the finances were thrown into disorder. The personal union between England and the Republic—the term can of course be criticised from a strictly constitutional point of view—gave the competitor of Holland the opportunity of surpassing its rival in the economic as well as in the political field.

Before 1680 the creative geniuses of seventeenth-century Holland had already died: in 1669 Rembrandt, in 1672 de Witt, in 1675 Jan Vermeer, in 1676 Michiel de Ruyter, in 1677 Spinoza, in 1679 Joost van den Vondel. The inspiration of Dutch civilisation seemed to change. Huizinga has characterised Holland's seventeenth-century civilisation as a deviation from the European pattern, an exception rather than an example.[1] The realistic approach of the Dutch to nature, their distrust of baroque grandeur, the simplicity of their behaviour, and the disorder of their style of life and writing, unhampered by strict rules whether literary or political, their fundamental tolerance and mildness made them strangers in Europe. After 1680 this originality decreased. French classicism began to permeate Dutch culture precisely at the moment when William III succeeded in checking French imperialism. But it was not only that foreign influences deprived the Dutch Republic of its profound originality and made it conform to the dominating European fashion. At the same time foreign countries were beginning to adopt Dutch ideas and Dutch social patterns. The Enlightenment could lean on many Dutch achievements. And did not the social circumstances of other countries too gradually develop in the same direction? The strictly oligarchic régime, which was so queer and irritating a phenomenon in the eyes of absolute monarchs, was after all the prefiguration of a general European pattern. The political philosophy which developed in the Republic in the seventeenth century, and which led from Althusius's aristocratic constitutionalism towards Spinoza's democratic absolutism, sometimes gives the impression of having traversed the same course which was to be followed by the eighteenth century, from Locke and Montesquieu to Rousseau. The Dutch Republic ceased to be the economic, social, political and cultural anomaly which it had been, and this may in part be an explanation of its decline.

[1] J. Huizinga, *Verzamelde Werken* (Haarlem, 1949), II, 45.

CHAPTER XIII

BRITAIN AFTER THE RESTORATION

THE restoration of Charles Stuart to the thrones of England and Scotland in 1660 nearly coincided with the assumption of regal power by his cousin, Louis XIV of France. In each case, this meant the end of an interregnum and the beginning of an era of personal, monarchic rule. The two kings started with very different problems, for their countries were strikingly contrasted in temper and institutions; but, by 1685, the year of Charles's death, France and England showed an apparent approximation, since Stuart rule was no longer parliamentary in the true sense of the word; in both countries Protestants were subjected to active persecution, and there even seemed a possibility that England might become little more than a dependency of France. How that state of things was reached is the subject of this chapter; how it was averted by revolution is the subject of another.[1]

Cromwell's death in September 1658 had been followed by a period of about twenty months during which the army leaders, Fleetwood, Lambert and Monck, struggled for supremacy; until in January 1660 Monck, the most astute and secretive man of his age, marched into England at the head of the army of occupation of Scotland. Having left this army at nearby Finsbury, the general proceeded to 'countenance' (that is, extend unasked-for protection to) the remnants of the Rump at Westminster, now reduced to about forty members, who represented the elderly survivors of that Long Parliament which had initiated a great rebellion. Monck, who was perceptive enough to see that monarchy could be peaceably restored only by the civil power, brought back to the Commons (in February 1660) the survivors of the Presbyterians who had been expelled by Pride's Purge in December 1648, thereby completely swamping the small residue of republicans and visionaries to which the House had been reduced. On 16 March this reinforced Long Parliament effected its own dissolution with a declaration that the 'single actings' of the House were not to prejudice the rights of the House of Lords, thus anticipating the restoration of a two-chamber legislature. Thereupon the Council of State busied itself with drawing up a scheme of limitations which, it was thought, might be imposed on Charles, whose recall to the throne was now considered certain, since the Presbyterian majority in the Commons was monarchist. A general election returned a House of Commons in which the royalists were strongly represented; at the same time the Presbyterian peers took their seats in the Upper House, soon to be joined there by the

[1] See vol. VI, ch. VI.

returning exiles. The Convention Parliament, which began its proceedings on 25 April 1660, resolved that the government of the kingdom was in king, lords and commons; Charles was proclaimed king, the year of his restoration being reckoned not as the first but as the twelfth of his reign. The king's arrival at Dover on 25 May completed the Restoration.

The clue to much of the history of England under the last male Stuarts can be deduced even from this meagre summary of events. It will be noticed that the Restoration was not effected by armed intervention from abroad, such as Charles and his brother James had tried to arrange while in exile, nor even by a military *coup* at home, but by the prior reinstatement of the two Houses of Parliament (however attenuated in numbers); and it will be seen that, throughout, the lead was taken by Monck, with the help of the Presbyterians, who believed in monarchy, and with the concurrence of his army, which did not. In adopting a royalist policy Monck had betrayed his soldiers, who were republican and anti-Stuart. This largely accounts for long-continued resentment among the disbanded veterans, resulting in many plots, especially in the earlier years of the reign. It is for this reason that much of the legislation of this period can be considered panic legislation. The Presbyterians, unlike the Sectaries, were thinking in terms of an established church, a limited monarchy, and a powerful hereditary aristocracy. Throughout the Commonwealth and Protectorate they had remained distrustful of Cromwell; they had fought for the king in the second Civil War, and had taken a leading part in the restoration of his son; hence, they naturally assumed that toleration would be extended to them, even if denied to the Sectaries. In this, like Monck's soldiers, they were betrayed. Lastly, there was the general assumption that some at least of the lessons of the civil wars would be taken to heart, and that such limitations would be imposed on the Crown as to prevent the recurrence of events still fresh in public memory; might not the tragedy of Charles I be the starting-point of a new and more clearly defined prerogative? Unfortunately, however, there were many who deduced the exactly opposite conclusion from that tragic event, namely, that it must be avenged in blood. For long, opinion was sharply divided between these opposed schools of thought. Meanwhile Charles returned as a parliamentary sovereign, that is, as king in parliament, not king in person; but events, soon to be described, severed his and his successor's connection with the institution which had called Charles home from exile, and led to that irresponsible prerogative which was terminated in 1688.

Why did parliament fail to impose conditions on the restored king? The answer may be that Charles and his mentor Edward Hyde, afterwards Earl of Clarendon, were determined to submit to no conditions; on the other side were the Commons of the Convention Parliament who, after talking interminably of Magna Carta and the Petition of Right, came to no conclusion, possibly because no one among them had sufficient initiative or audacity to bring in a Bill, or even formulate a resolution. Already (April 1660) in the Declaration of Breda Charles had avoided any definite promise of toleration; and Hyde, in correspondence with friends in England, had urged that measures should be concerted in order to obviate, as far as possible, the imposition of limitations. Thus the restored king of 1660 was as unfettered as his father had been; and, until about 1675, Charles's sovereignty could be described as parliamentary only in the sense that, as the provision made by the Commons for the royal revenue was inadequate, there was always the hope (unfulfilled) that parliament would make good the deficiency. After 1675, on the other hand, the revenue originally granted in 1660 proved to be more than sufficient for peacetime purposes; and so, unless he went to war, Charles was independent of parliament. The same situation was created for James at the beginning of the session of his one and only parliament. Here is the cardinal fact which accounts for so much in the reigns of the two kings.

It came about in this way. The Convention Parliament wished to grant to Charles an adequate revenue for life in addition to that which he derived from Crown lands and royal perquisites. It was agreed that the sum necessary was £1,200,000 per annum, from which the king would have to pay not only for the upkeep of the royal estate, but also for the peacetime maintenance of the navy and the salaries of judges and ambassadors. It was not until 1697 that a Civil List in the modern sense of the term was established; until that date, the revenue granted by parliament was applied to both personal and national expenditure. In order to make up this agreed sum of £1,200,000 per annum, the Convention Parliament settled on Charles, *for his life*, the revenue from the customs, usually estimated at about £400,000 per annum, together with that from excise, about £300,000 per annum, of which an annual sum of £100,000 was settled on the Crown in perpetuity in compensation for the revenue surrendered by the abolition of the Court of Wards. Several miscellaneous items were added, such as revenue from the Post Office, from stamp duties and, after 1661, from the hearth-tax, all of them together supposed to yield about a million per annum. In actual fact the yield was less; and so, in the first twelve years of the reign, there was a steadily increasing debt which resulted in the Stop of the Exchequer of 1672, an admission of partial bankruptcy. Charles had not been treated fairly by the Commons. But the legislators of 1660 could not have foreseen that, with the great development of trade and commerce, the yield from customs and excise would so increase as to give the king a revenue of *more* than £1,200,000, which, moreover, could be lawfully collected without recourse to parliament. This became obvious after Charles's enforced withdrawal from the third Anglo-Dutch War in 1674, when the Dutch were left to carry on the war against Louis XIV and England enjoyed the unusual advantages of neutrality. By the time of James's accession this, usually called the hereditary revenue, amounted to about two millions. This is why Charles after 1675, and James, after the parliamentary grant of the life revenue in 1685, were financially independent of parliament; only thus can their policy be understood.

It has been noted that the arrangements made for Charles's revenue were bound up with the abolition of the Court of Wards. This court had been established by Henry VIII to exact from all who held their lands of the Crown by a free tenure a monetary equivalent for the services which they had formerly performed, and to impose on those tenants, more specially on their wards and widows, that personal supervision which had been the prerogative of the medieval suzerain. The tenants so affected were mainly those who held by knight service, and included practically all those who today would be described as members of the landowning class. By the statutory abolition of the court, this large class was emancipated from a system not unlike one of death-duties; and in this way many persons, including the most substantial in the land, were changed from nominal tenants into actual freeholders. The statute did not, as is commonly maintained, abolish all feudal tenures; for copyhold was untouched and remained an important tenure until its abolition in the twentieth century, so that English landlords, wherever they had retained manorial privileges, continued to exercise 'feudal' rights over their copyhold tenants. But meanwhile the landlords were emancipated at the expense of an additional excise falling on every consumer; and they were destined to experience another advantage, because, after 1660, although there were rebellions, there was no civil war, and so much less likelihood of forfeiture for treason. Except for the burden of the land-tax, which fell almost exclusively on them, the landlords after 1660 were in a particularly favoured and powerful position. Indeed, as landed freeholders they regarded themselves, not as one of several classes, but as the only fully authenticated and responsible element in the nation. This was a fact so implicit that it was seldom enunciated. It had several important consequences. Their freehold, which we are inclined to associate with privilege or monopoly, came to be identified with freedom, in a wide sense of the word, that is, freedom of action, whether as members of the Grand Jury or of the House of Commons, and this was regarded as the best safeguard, not against bribery, but against intimidation. This distinction was for long considered perfectly natural, and underlay both the revolution of 1688 and the politics of the eighteenth century.

The two main objects of the restoration settlement, as achieved by the Convention Parliament, were to end the period of constitutional experiment and to bridge the gap between the interregnum and the monarchy. With regard to the first object, it was tacitly assumed, and later enacted, that all Acts and Ordinances to which Charles I had not given his assent were invalid; but some of the most important of these measures were re-embodied in statute, with amendments or enlargements. An example is the Navigation Act of 1660. By the Act of Indemnity the surviving 'regicide judges' and about twenty other persons, who had failed to change their coats quickly enough, were exempted from mercy, of whom about a dozen, including Sir Henry Vane, suffered the death penalty. The land settlement caused much dissatisfaction, for there had been so much exchange and purchase of confiscated lands that no satisfactory solution could have been devised. Crown and Church lands were restored; the lands of several prominent royalists were recovered by special legislation, but the small fry were left to find what remedy they could in the law courts. In this way, many Cromwellians, who had acquired land cheaply during the Usurpation, obtained permanent places in the landowning class, and soon the Whig party derived strength from such new aristocratic owners of broad acres.

These facts help to explain why the events of 1660 are described not as a revolution, but as a restoration. In little more than eight months the Convention Parliament had bridged the gap and had dealt successfully with every urgent problem except the land settlement and the vague promise of toleration held out in the Declaration of Breda. Meanwhile, the royalist tide was steadily rising and reached its climax in the early sessions of the Cavalier Parliament, or Long Parliament of the Restoration, which lasted from May 1661 to January 1679. In the course of eighteen years this parliament completed the most notable evolution in English history. Its character was undoubtedly influenced by many by-elections, but its composition remained essentially the same, namely landowners and the nominees of landowners, with a sprinkling of merchants, lawyers, placemen, army and navy officers: a heterogeneous body, within which there was probably a hard core of young royalists who grew up into middle-aged and disgruntled Whigs.

The Cavalier Parliament began by passing measures intended to emancipate the king, as far as possible, from limitations or control. One statute conferred on him supreme control over all the armed forces by land and sea; another, by greatly extending the scope of the treason laws, made it easier for the Crown to dispose of critics and opponents; a Licensing Act created a new official, the Surveyor of Imprimery, with wide powers over authors and printers of unlicensed books; an Act against tumultuous petitioning limited the right of the subject to petition; lastly, the Corporation Act attempted to confine membership of corporations to Anglicans and loyalists. This last measure, usually, but not quite accurately regarded as part of the 'Clarendon Code', laid down the rules which, as later extended by the Test Acts of 1673 and 1678, came to be imposed as conditions of full citizenship, namely, swearing the oaths of allegiance and supremacy, with a non-resistance oath, together with the taking of the sacrament according to the rites of the Church of England at least once a year. By the Act of Uniformity (1662) all beneficed clergy who had not received episcopal ordination were obliged to give up their benefices, a measure which had the effect of increasing the strength of Protestant Nonconformity by adding to its numbers many clergy and laymen who today would be regarded as low church or evangelical. In this way was created an Anglican monopoly which extended to the Church, the universities, the schools and, later, to citizenship itself.

It remained only to penalise the Dissenters, including the Presbyterians. This was done in a series of measures, passed in the years after 1664 and known, with whatever justification, as the 'Clarendon Code'. The Conventicle Act of 1664 prohibited assemblies of five or more persons for a religious purpose; the Five Mile Act of 1665 forbade all teachers and preachers who had not taken the oaths to come within five miles of a corporate town. An intensive campaign against the Dissenters accompanied these measures, and the militia was employed to assist the civil power. For these severities, little, if any, blame can be attached to Charles himself, for at this time he inclined to tolerance; nor can the clergy of the Church of England be blamed, since they were not responsible for the legislation. The fact appears to be that the king was obliged to acquiesce at the price of special parliamentary grants. The responsibility lay with the majority of the House of Commons, who were thinking in terms of revenge—revenge for the death of Charles I. To them, all forms of Dissent—Presbyterian, Quaker and Baptist alike—appeared to be treasonable; only by adhesion to the Church of England could a man's loyalty be attested. As for the Roman Catholics, they were still subject to the harsh legislation of Elizabeth's reign; but in practice that legislation was neither uniformly nor harshly enforced on the Catholic laity who, though suffering from disability, were neither persecuted nor denied civil rights. Before the end of the reign, however, though their status remained the same, the attitude towards them completely changed, and there was instilled into English minds that distrust and hatred of popery which survived into recent times.

By April 1661 the Restoration in England can be considered as complete. In that month Lord Chancellor Hyde, who had served the king in exile and later acted as informal chief minister until his disgrace and exile in 1667, became Earl of Clarendon; General Monck was created Duke of Albemarle; Anthony Ashley Cooper, who had changed his allegiance in good time, became Baron Ashley and afterwards, as Earl of Shaftesbury, the founder of the Whig party and the most formidable opponent of the king. On St George's Day, 23 April 1661, Charles was crowned in Westminster Abbey and liberally anointed with holy oil; indeed, in no other instance did inunction prove so efficacious, for he was to win great popularity as a most successful 'toucher' for the King's Evil. Coronation was followed by marriage. This took place on 21 May 1662 at Portsmouth, where he married the Infanta Catherine of Braganza in two ceremonies, the one Anglican, the other Catholic. The young Portuguese bride brought, as part of her dowry, Tangier and Bombay, of which the first, after a precarious occupation, was surrendered in 1683, while the second became afterwards the basis of British power in India. The marriage was favoured by Louis XIV, anxious to secure English as well as Portuguese help against his father-in-law, Philip IV of Spain; indeed, so anxious was Louis to see this marriage effected that he provided a sum of about £50,000. Thus early in his reign was Charles pledged to furthering the designs of his French cousin.

Concurrently with these events the Restoration was completed in Ireland and Scotland. On the whole, Ireland was comparatively fortunate in the period 1660–88, mainly because the Stuarts sympathised with the Celtic Irish, and because they had at their disposal the services of James Butler, Duke of Ormonde, one of the best of Irish viceroys, who held office from 1661 to 1668, and from 1677 to 1684. The duke's political fortunes were at first bound up with those of his fellow statesman Clarendon, who was soon superseded in the royal favour by young, flashy men, such as Arlington and Buckingham; but fortunately Butler was restored to power in 1677 and succeeded in guiding the country through the difficult years of the Popish Plot and the Stuart reaction. Ormonde's task was to diminish, as far as possible, the traditional exploitation of Ireland by creatures of the English court. He also did much to encourage the development of native industries, notably the linen industry. For this purpose he introduced skilled workers from France and Flanders, but the industry was afterwards concentrated in Protestant Ulster. Generally, the restoration settlement in Ireland was similar to that in England. In 1662 by an Irish Act of Uniformity the recently revised Prayer Book was imposed on the (Protestant) Church of Ireland, and oaths of non-resistance and repudiation of the Solemn League and Covenant[1] were required of all teachers and clergy. The Roman Catholics were excluded from office, but they were not persecuted. The two Irish Houses of Parliament resumed their sessions, but their initiative in the introduction of Bills was seriously limited by the control exercised through the English privy council; accordingly, much of Irish legislation in this period was little more than a reproduction of English statutes, many of them in the interests only of the Anglo-Irish. In effect therefore the Irish Catholics continued to be pariahs, but at least their industries were encouraged, and they were not interfered with in the exercise of their religion.

As in England, the land settlement proved to be the most difficult problem, and for the same reason, because so much land, confiscated during the Usurpation, had changed hands several times. Further complications

[1] For this, see vol. IV, ch. XVIII.

resulted from the Irish Rebellion of 1641–3,[1] when so many Protestants had been dispossessed, and from the Cromwellian conquest, when many Catholics had been displaced by English soldiers and 'adventurers', that is, land speculators. This large class of (mostly small) landowners, supposedly of republican sympathies, was obviously objectionable in the eyes of Restoration statesmen; so too, at the English court were those who insisted on large grants of Irish acres, while in Ireland there were many 'innocent Papists' who had been unjustly deprived of their lands. The sympathies of Charles were with this last class, but he was obliged to sacrifice them to the courtiers. The general result was that, out of nearly 8000 dispossessed Roman Catholic landlords, only about 1300 were restored; while many of the soldiers and 'adventurers' had to quit possession. The land thus available was bestowed in large grants upon court favourites, many of them absentees; and the harshness shown by most of their bailiffs served, even in this comparatively beneficent period, to make the name of Englishmen detested in Ireland.

That name would have been equally detested in Scotland had not the northern kingdom been consigned to renegade Scots. Many of these had begun as opponents of episcopacy; but, now that the old altars were overturned, they were anxious to persecute the prophets whom they had formerly revered. These men would as willingly have become Turks had the Stuarts decided to establish Mohammedanism in the north. Notable among them was John Maitland, afterwards Earl of Lauderdale, secretary of the Scottish privy council who, in effect, ruled Scotland until 1680, a curious mixture of coarseness, pedantry and absolute loyalty to his royal master. The Stuarts had little love for the land of their origin; its Protestantism and poverty stirred their dislike; and, in the absence of institutions providing some protection for the liberty of the subject, the northern kingdom was helpless in the hands of agents of absentee kings. The harshness with which this system was enforced steadily increased. When in 1661 the 'Scottish Church' was restored this meant the restoration of the episcopacy which Charles I had so unwisely tried to enforce upon the Scots. At the same time a notable victim was found, when the Earl of Argyll, secular head of the Presbyterians in Scotland, was brought to 'trial' and executed; his offence having been that, in private letters sent to Monck (forwarded to the court by Monck) he had used terms implying approval of the Commonwealth. This was a foretaste of the treatment soon to be accorded to Presbyterians and Covenanters.

Historians emphasise that these royalists were bigots, but it should be added that they did not have a monopoly of that quality. In Scotland there was no vigorous local administration as in England; juries could be fined and imprisoned for their verdicts; with few exceptions, the judges deferred to the wishes of the executive in political trials. The ancient Estates of the

[1] For this, see vol. IV, ch. XVIII.

realm still met (in one chamber) in the Parliament House of Edinburgh; but, by law, the mixing of Estates was prohibited, and so the Third Estate consisted of merchants and tradesmen who, as they were limited to matters of trade and commerce, were debarred from expressing an opinion about the administration. That administration was directed by the Scottish privy council, taking its orders from Whitehall. Another body through which the Crown could enforce its will was the Committee of the Articles which, usually acting on instructions, decided on the measures to be put before the Estates. For these reasons there was practically no political life in seventeenth-century Scotland. Justice was administered by baronial, that is, semi-private courts; the supreme courts in Edinburgh were presided over by judges even more obsequious than those in Westminster Hall. Torture could be freely employed to extract 'confessions', and in this period the thumb-screw (imported from Muscovy) was substituted for the 'boot', which was unsuitable for people with thin legs. These things did not matter much, as Scotland was such a poor and undeveloped country; but they provide a significant comment on Stuart rule. It is not surprising that many Scots, fleeing from 'justice', took refuge in Holland, to return later with William of Orange.

At the time of the Restoration, however, these were still matters of the future. In England there was genuine relief that the rule of the army and the Saints was over, and that the country was at last restored to its rightful king. The king was determined to combine two barely compatible objects—to have his own way, and to avoid any more foreign travel; his comparative success in the first and his complete success in the second were the results of consummate skill and an instinctive political sense.

His contemporary popularity was slightly diminished by the conduct and events of the second Anglo-Dutch War.[1] Pepys was not the only observer of the desperate condition to which English and Scottish sailors were reduced by denial of pay and the provision of half-poisoned food; there was also the disgrace of the Medway in 1667, when some of the best ships in the navy were burned or towed away by Dutch small craft. For these things a convenient scapegoat was found in Clarendon, who was forced into exile. This second Anglo-Dutch War had created a diplomatic difficulty for Charles, because, at that time, Louis XIV happened to be committed by treaty with the United Provinces and went to their help as an ally. On the English side, the war had been entered into at the solicitation of the many trading interests which suffered from Dutch competition or open hostility—in this sense it was a national war, but Charles had entered into it unwillingly because it entailed hostilities with France. Nevertheless, Louis acted chivalrously with his cousin, giving as little help as possible to his Dutch partner, who was left to bear the brunt of the fighting, and assuring Charles that he fully appreciated the difficulties of

[1] See also above, ch. XII, pp. 288–9.

his position. The war was ended by the Treaty of Breda (July 1667): England obtained New York and New Jersey, but the Dutch retained Pulo-Run and Dutch Guiana, and the French Acadia and French Guiana; in other words, England failed to gain a footing in the spice trade, and the Hollanders were as formidable as ever at sea. A further strain on Stuart–Bourbon relations was imposed by the formation of the Triple Alliance of 1668, an alliance of England, the United Provinces and Sweden against the aggressions of Louis. Charles's private expressions of regret for this unfortunate alignment of forces were favourably received at Versailles, where it was well known that he was at the mercy of heretics and corrupt legislators. On the other hand, Louis had no doubt that the Dutch, who (it was alleged) owed their independence to France, had betrayed their benefactor. Accordingly, after 1668, the situation in western Europe was this: Louis's righteous indignation was directed against a former ally, to whom he had given only nominal support; and his friendship was extended to a former enemy, with whose king he was in secret sympathy. Why not join openly with Charles against the Dutch? And what advantages might not accrue to the cause of Catholicism in England if the Dutch were eliminated? The Stuart king, strengthened by a successful war against England's chief rival, would be in a position to promote the cause of the true faith among his turbulent subjects.

This view was not shared by Colbert, Louis's minister, who believed that Dutch prosperity could be destroyed, not by war, but by a commercial alliance of England and France directed against the United Provinces. Negotiations for such a treaty began, but they broke down mainly because of French insistence on English conformity with French standards of measurement. Accordingly, Louis stepped in where his minister had left off; emissaries from the two countries continued to cross the Channel, but for a very different purpose, namely to negotiate what came to be known as the Secret Treaty of Dover. By the end of 1669 it was agreed that Louis would supply money to Charles for two distinct enterprises—the restoration of Catholicism in England and a war of annihilation against the Dutch. The treaty was signed 22 May/1 June 1670. By its terms Charles agreed to join with Louis in hostilities against the Dutch, in consideration for which Louis promised to pay an annual sum of three million *livres* (about £250,000) and agreed that Charles's share of the spoils was to be Walcheren, Sluys and Cadsand. In the event of Louis's acquiring any fresh rights to Spanish territory, Charles was to assist in the enforcement of these rights. He further promised to declare himself a Roman Catholic, but in doing so was to choose his own time, and the reward for this was to be the equivalent of about £160,000, together with the services of 6000 troops for the suppression of disorders which might follow the declaration. Of the members of the Cabal (the name given to Charles's informal body of five advisers) only Clifford and Arlington were in the secret; the other three, Ashley, Buckingham and Lauderdale, knew nothing of the religious part of the bargain.

Between April 1671 and February 1673 parliament was prorogued. In this interval Charles tried a compromise which, it seemed, might have gone some way towards fulfilling the religious clause in the secret treaty. This was the issue, on 25 March 1672, of the Declaration of Indulgence, whereby the king suspended the execution of all penal laws against Dissenters and all who refused the oaths. Roman Catholics were to be allowed to worship in their own houses. By this measure, only the Crown would suffer, because it would have to sacrifice the revenue from the fines imposed on recusants. As regards the war on the Dutch, Charles was influenced by the steadily mounting debt which obliged him to acquiesce in the Stop of the Exchequer (January 1672); and so, two days after the Declaration of Indulgence he declared war on the United Provinces. Hence, unlike the two earlier Anglo-Dutch wars, the third was in no sense a national war, but was entered into by the king, on his own initiative, in order to qualify for the French subsidy.

When parliament reassembled in February 1673 a majority in the Commons, supported by an influential group in the Lords, demanded that the Declaration of Indulgence be withdrawn, on the ground that only the legislature could suspend penal laws in matters of religion. It is at this point that one can detect the beginnings of an opposition party in the Commons—the Country party—distinguished from the Court party in the sense that it was not honoured by the recognition of the Crown. At this time also, Lord Chancellor Shaftesbury was apprised of the secret clause in the treaty, and he now directed himself to the formation of an opposition in the Lords; and even Charles was unable to play off one House against the other. Rather than be sacrificed on behalf of the Catholics, the king withdrew the Declaration of Indulgence on 8 March 1673. He was just in time. Nor did he stop there. A few days later he gave his consent to the first Test Act which incapacitated from public office all who refused to take the oaths of allegiance and supremacy, together with the sacrament according to the rites of the Church of England, and a repudiation of the doctrine of transubstantiation. The immediate consequence of this was that James, Duke of York, a recent convert, was no longer able to hold the office of Lord High Admiral; a less direct consequence was that parliament obliged Charles to withdraw from the war by the Treaty of Westminster (February 1674). By this treaty the Dutch agreed to pay an indemnity, but otherwise its terms were inconclusive and left no opening for the English in the East Indies; on the other hand, England, now neutral, was able to seize some of the markets of her rival and enemy.[1]

Meanwhile in September 1673 an ominous event had occurred—the marriage of the convert James to the Catholic Mary of Modena. By his

[1] See also above, ch. XII, p. 295.

first marriage (with Anne Hyde) James had two daughters, Mary and Anne, who were being brought up in the Protestant faith; as for the king and his consort, it was now considered certain that they would never have an heir. It was also regarded as a certainty that James would have an heir by his new wife; indeed, this matter of presumptive fecundity had played an essential part in the duke's choice of a bride, a choice in which Louis had exercised considerable influence. Hence, it is of some significance that the emergence of an opposition party coincided with the beginnings of fears about the succession—fears that eventually England would be ruled by a Catholic dynasty, allied with kindred dynasties on the Continent and convinced that heresy was the greatest of all evils. This fear had already found expression in parliament's insistence upon the withdrawal of the Declaration of Indulgence and the speedy passing of the Test Act. It is important that the initiative for this step was taken, not by the Church but by the legislature, and for a secular purpose: to preserve, so far as that could be done by the imposition of a formulary, the two things which were then regarded as inseparable, the Protestantism and independence of England.

Inspection of the Test Act of 1673, as amplified by that of 1678, shows that of positive theology there was nothing, except the production of the sacramental certificate; of negative theology there was a good deal, namely rejection of certain doctrines fundamental in Roman Catholicism; the rest was made up of political safeguards intended to ensure the loyalty and obedience of the swearer. Lastly, by the Act of 1678, all these oaths and repudiations had to be taken 'in the plain and ordinary sense of the words'; which meant that this was a layman's profession of faith. The imposition of these Acts was not ended in its entirety until 1829; but long before that date the system was mitigated in favour of those Protestants who had held office without having taken the oaths; and, in a manner not easily explicable today, the Test Acts came to be regarded, by Anglicans, Roman Catholics and Dissenters alike, as a bulwark against the threats to English independence. Even more, the system came to be associated with enlightenment as well as a large measure of toleration,[1] and was praised by Voltaire,[2] because its effect was to create an Erastian Church where the clergy was kept in its place and debarred from that secret, irresponsible influence which it exercised in eighteenth-century France.

In this year 1673 the secret of the Treaty of Dover was still well kept; but the public events already enumerated caused many contemporaries to suspect that some hidden work of darkness was on foot. They were right. Nor would their fears have been allayed if the king had taken them into his confidence and explained that he intended to keep his promises as little as possible. The fears evidenced by Englishmen at this time were

[1] As exemplified by the Toleration Act of 1689. Roman Catholics were not included in this measure and continued to suffer from disabilities, but were not persecuted.

[2] In the *Lettres Anglaises*.

reasonable fears, justified by public events, and capable of substantiation by reference to secret facts. Accordingly, they cannot be dismissed as the result of 'propaganda'. In undertaking the commitments of the Secret Treaty of Dover, Charles II was concerned more about obtaining French money than about attempting to enforce Catholicism on England; but can we be equally sure about the character and intentions of the Duke of York? Charles, nationally popular almost because of his failings, was contrasted with his brother, who was formidable because of his virtues—the virtues of industry, religious fervour, consistency and determination to attain his ends at all costs. It is from this point that many Englishmen, Anglicans and loyalists, came to regard James as a menace, a menace soon to be elevated into a terror by the steadily accumulating suspicions of the years after 1673.

Why did the reasonable fears of 1673 become the wild panic and hysteria of 1678, the year of the Popish Plot? It may be doubted whether historians have ever given a satisfactory answer to this question. Part, at least, of the answer may be forthcoming from an unexpected source: one of the clauses of the Statute of Frauds, a measure passed in 1677, on the eve of the Plot. This clause included, as one of the conditions of the validity of contracts for the sale and purchase of goods above £10 in value, a note or memorandum signed by both parties. Here was an attempt by the legislature to deal, if only indirectly and in part, with what was known to be the chief social evil of the age—perjury. In a period of universal oath-taking, many shopkeepers were willing to come into court in order to swear falsely (usually with the help of their apprentices) that a prospective customer had verbally undertaken to make certain purchases; and so the Statute Book provides the best possible evidence of the prevalence of this evil. At that time perjury, for a first offence, was only a misdemeanour; hence, while a man who stole five shillings was likely to be hanged, if he obtained the same sum by perjured evidence resulting in the death of an innocent man he was punished only by a small fine and an appearance in the pillory. Unfortunately, the solitary voice raised against this iniquity had been that of the (reputedly) atheist Hobbes,[1] a fact which may have induced many good and pious men to tolerate an obvious evil. The same was true of forgery, which did not even begin to be a felony until the issue of Bank of England notes in the last years of the century obliged the legislature to change the law. Hence, in the reign of Charles II, to concoct a wild story of a plot, incriminating named and prominent persons, with the hope that they would suffer death on the strength of forged or perjured evidence, did not seem particularly mean or dishonourable, especially as one could obtain the services of professional perjurers so cheaply. Nor was it even a risky enterprise, since, if discovered, it might result only in an appearance in the pillory, possibly before sympathetic spectators.

[1] *Leviathan*, ch. XXVII.

In these circumstances, the discovery of 'plots' and their authentication by sworn evidence was almost a hobby in the seventeenth century. Titus Oates might never have been heard of but for a combination of circumstances very lucky for him and very unlucky for a number of perfectly innocent men, mostly Roman Catholics. His first asset was his wonderful memory—he could remember all his own lies; the second was his doctorate of Divinity, supposedly conferred upon him by the University of Salamanca; the third was his shrewd psychology which enabled him to perceive that the time was ripe for taking advantage of the fears and suspicions which had been mounting for nearly a decade. Then there was the 'gift' of the murdered body of the Protestant magistrate, Sir Edmund Berry Godfrey, discovered near Hampstead in October 1678. Godfrey had been unfortunate enough to be the recipient of the sworn depositions of Oates about a great 'plot', directed by the pope and the Jesuits, having for its main purpose the assassination of the king and his replacement by James. This was to be followed by a general massacre of Protestants. It seemed obvious to contemporaries that as Godfrey, the unwilling custodian of so much secret information, was too dangerous to live, he must have been removed by the Jesuits. So extraordinary was the wave of hysteria which passed over England in the following months that, with the exception of the king (who may have inherited the Highland gift of second sight), nearly all the prominent personages of the time believed in the plot—indeed, belief in the plot became a criterion of patriotism. In all this, a lead was given by Shaftesbury, who co-operated with Oates in the drilling of witnesses; and, in consequence, about a score of victims suffered death.

The influence of the plot can be seen in the creation of some kind of party distinction. There were many earlier examples of a dualism in public opinion, and as early as 1673 there was evidence of such a division in parliament, which for long refused to admit publicly the existence of any such distinction. But it was the Popish Plot which made popular and national a dualism that was ultimately to create our party politics. This was at first a simple contest between those who were for the court and those who were against. Supporters of the court included believers in Divine Hereditary Right, with its corollary of passive obedience or non-resistance, that is, obedience to the lawful commands of the anointed sovereign and submission to his unlawful commands. Advocates of these doctrines professed willingness to obey the sovereign even to the point of martyrdom, but in practice they were not so foolish; and the Anglican clergy, the main supporters of this view, contended that there was no need to provide a martyr from among themselves, as Charles I had already died on their behalf. As the Stuarts, at times, were credited with willingness to use Irish ruffians against Protestant Englishmen, the word Tory, or Irish cut-throat, was the nickname applied to these supporters of the prerogative. From their text-book, the Old Testament, they derived conclusive proof that the Lord's Anointed can do wrong; in fact, he is more likely to do wrong than right; but, as he is responsible to God alone, his subjects can do little about it, save recognise that in this indirect way God punishes the sins of humanity.

As Ireland supplied one term of abuse, Scotland supplied the other, there being nothing in English life sufficiently opprobrious for the purpose. It was in this period that events in the northern kingdom again acquired significance for English observers, events which have to be briefly recorded. In the south-west of Scotland were many Presbyterians who, as they refused to conform to the episcopal church, were proscribed and actively persecuted; and, early in 1678, an attempt was made to goad them into rebellion by quartering on their farms and homesteads a body of 6000 Highland robbers and bandits known as the Highland Host. This attempt failed; the clansmen retired with their booty, and many Scots migrated to northern Ireland. In May 1679 a crime was added which further embittered opinion and led to brutal reprisals; this was the murder of the hated James Sharp, archbishop of St Andrews, an event followed within a few weeks by the defeat of Graham of Claverhouse at the hands of a body of Covenanters (battle of Drumclog). This caused Charles's government to send Monmouth to the north in command of troops which were to be reinforced by Irish Catholics; but, before the latter arrived, the duke succeeded in defeating the ill-armed Covenanters at the battle of Bothwell Brig (June 1679). By this time the extreme Presbyterians, who had repudiated allegiance to the Stuarts and were either 'on the run' or in active rebellion, were known as Whigs—the nickname now applied to those English critics of Charles's government who had formerly been known as the Country party.

This party included a large proportion of wealthy merchants and Dissenters and was well represented in the House of Lords; indeed, it was an aristocratic party, deriving some strength from the fact that many of its devotees had the best racehorses. The Tory University of Oxford was a poor second to the Whig Newmarket. Protestants almost to a man, the Whigs dared to criticise the monarch on the ground that his policy was endangering the national faith and leading to the subordination of England to Louis XIV. Or rather they dared to criticise his ministers, such as Danby, whom they attempted to impeach late in 1678; but they failed because Charles gave him a full pardon in advance. The Whigs had deduced from the tragedy and futility of Charles I's execution the lesson that it was useless to press home an accusation of guilt on the king himself—the accusation must be directed against the royal agents; and so they revived the old common-law maxim: 'the king can do no wrong', applying it in the sense that, for all the public acts of the king, a minister must be responsible. As this responsibility could be enforced only by impeachment in parliament, the Whigs, from the start, maintained that parliament must be kept in regular session. They were therefore the party of Protestantism, parliamentary government and ministerial responsibility. In contrast, the Tories, who derived their strength mainly from the lower clergy and the squires, were insistent on unqualified submission to the personal prerogative. They were devoted to the Church of England; but here there was a complication, for the high-church party, in their detestation of Protestant Dissent, were reputed to be more sympathetic to Catholicism than to Protestantism, and many Anglican divines repudiated any connection with the churches of the Reformation. All that could be said with certainty was that Charles II based his power on the support of bishops and clergy, a support which was strengthened in proportion as the Dissenters were penalised.

It was natural that these two nicknames were rejected by many to whom they were applied; nor did there exist in either House of Parliament a definite party to which either label could be affixed, because politicians were not thinking in terms of party affiliation, and governments continued to be 'bottomed' not on party doctrine, but on groupings of families, interests and clans. Nor was there any distinction in regard to personal probity, for all parties, whatever their name, included some who were infamous and many who were corrupt. But this does not mean that the distinction between Whig and Tory was non-existent. By the nation outside Westminster, a simple, radical dualism was eagerly accepted, if only because so many people think in terms of two sides of a game; and in England two-sided games have always been more popular than anywhere else. Hence the first exponents of party distinction were the great unenfranchised and unwashed. The distinction could be pushed into so many recesses of life. Drinks, oaths, colours, patron saints, racecourses, watering places and coffee houses were all lined up on either side of the battle front, each of them, in the opinion of the other, led by a superhuman power: one side marshalled by the Devil who, as he was the first critic, was obviously the first Whig; the other having for its generalissimo the Whore of Rome, flaunting her scarlet finery in the face of 'true blue' Whigs, the whole providing a simple pattern, in bright colours, which even the meanest could understand. For a turbulent, adolescent people all this was a godsend, since everyone could take sides. Moreover, a safety valve was provided by the numerous racecourses, where superfluous enthusiasm could be dispersed over a wider range of contestants. English party politics first found expression, not in the polite platitudes of academic debate, nor in the calculations of parliamentary management, but in the scurrilities of the gutter and the scaffold; in this way Englishmen became politically-minded long before they acquired the vote.

Meanwhile the Popish Plot served to force on parliament a clear-cut question—should James, Duke of York, be excluded from the succession?

If he were excluded, who was to succeed? His eldest daughter, Mary (married to William of Orange)? Or Charles's illegitimate son, the Duke of Monmouth, who, if he succeeded, might rule by 'a limited command'? But these questions did not have to be answered in Charles's reign, because, mainly owing to the eloquence of Halifax, the elder statesman of the age, the Lords rejected the Exclusion Bill sent up by the Commons in November 1680. This saved the throne for James. The dissolution of the short-lived Oxford Parliament on 18 March 1681 marked the end of parliamentary government as far as Charles was concerned; at the same time, the renewal of the French subsidy provided some guarantee that English policy would be subordinated to the behests of Versailles. Now that parliament, exclusion and plot were out of the way, James came forward as the mentor and coadjutor of his brother, and in this sense James's reign began four years before his accession. The so-called Rye House Plot of 1683 provided a welcome opportunity or pretext for turning the tables on the Whigs; and, with the help of judge Jeffreys, it proved easy to obtain convictions for high treason against prominent opponents of the court. In this way Lord William Russell and Algernon Sidney were disposed of, and Jack Ketch the executioner was kept busy with the dispatch of humbler Whigs to another world. Shaftesbury, with many others, went into exile. Titus Oates went to prison, not for perjury, but from inability to pay the fine of £100,000 imposed on him for slandering the Duke of York.

For both Charles and James this was a period of revenge. A start was made with the parliamentary boroughs, many of which had returned to the Commons critics and even enemies of the court. Accordingly, their charters were subjected to *Quo Warranto*'s, and nearly all of them were remodelled in order to ensure the admission of only Anglicans and loyalists. In this way the walls of the corporations, including those of the city of London, fell before Jeffreys like the walls of Jericho. With these changes it was hoped that, if a parliament did have to be summoned, only the 'right' burgesses would be sent to Westminster; so, too, the sheriffs of the remodelled corporations could be trusted to summon the 'right' jurymen, who would give the verdict expected of them in cases where the Crown was concerned. Such at least was the theory behind this drive against the corporations. At the same time, the enforcement of the penal laws against Protestant Dissenters was intensified, and in one case[1] only the courageous conduct of the local authorities prevented the use of dragoons for the purpose of harrying the countryside. In Scotland, less fortunate, there was nothing to come between the populace and the executive; accordingly, in Presbyterian Scotland as in Huguenot France

[1] That of Shropshire. The evidence will be found in the Domestic State Papers of the reign, no. 29, bundle 438, letters of Charles Holt and other justices to Sunderland, 8 and 15 December 1684.

this was the 'killing time', and men condemned at two o'clock were hanged at five.

Charles II died on 16 February 1685 in his fifty-fifth year. His last years, which showed some decline in health and character, were, for him, a period of tranquillity and, for his country, a period of uneasy peace, to which his brother and the executioner contributed. 'Rien n'avance les choses comme les exécutions'; politically, England was reduced to the state of France and Scotland; only Ireland was unchanged. For however short a time, the British Isles were units in a system which aligned them with the respectable, 'well-conditioned' States of the Continent. Of that system, the most moderate and reasonable exponent was the great French bishop J.-B. Bossuet. In his funeral oration on the death of Henrietta Maria (1669), the mother of Charles and James, the bishop maintained that, for some years, England had been plagued by a disrespect for authority and a continual itch for change. This 'intemperance of mad curiosity' had arisen from the rejection of the Catholic faith, which alone 'has a certain weight capable of keeping people in their place'. God punishes nations which depart from the true faith. Henrietta Maria, according to Bossuet, had been convinced that only by the restoration of Catholicism would order in England be restored, and already her elder son had found his best servants among Catholics. Charles I's fault was neither his obstinacy nor his perfidy, as his opponents maintained, but his clemency.[1] Such were the principles, suggested with a delicacy and restraint, in accord with the solemn occasion on which they were pronounced, of that religious-political system in which the last male Stuarts implicitly believed. Charles had had to bide his time before acting on them; James was acting on them before his reign began. Nor was the system one that could be modified by experience, or even by defeat and disaster, for it had the cast-iron rigidity of theological dogma: a fact well illustrated by James himself when, in his exile, he regretted most of all that he had been too lenient. It is open to everyone to have his own views about the merits of such a system, by whatever name it may be called; but of its existence and its implications there can be no doubt.

Bossuet was right in thinking that the English were a turbulent people; but he knew nothing of the conditions which helped to control that turbulence, and even to give it some sense of direction, for his experience was only of France, a 'normal' country, in contrast with the abnormality of England. That abnormality was expressed in so many forms that most foreign observers were agreed that Englishmen were mad, the conclusive proof being that so many of them performed public services without payment. England was abnormal in her law and in her central and local government. The criminal law was nearly as harsh as that of continental States, for it was still held that the main purpose of law is to protect, not

[1] J.-B. Bossuet, *Oraison Funèbre de Henriette de France.*

the person, but his property. On the other hand, from Berwick-on-Tweed to Land's End the law was uniform, whereas in France there was a general distinction between the area of written law and that of customary law, the latter including about three hundred districts where different rules were enforced. Moreover, the jury system was characteristic of English procedure, and in 1670, by Bushell's case, there was vindicated for the first time the principle of the inviolability of the jury for its verdict. In addition to the petty jury which, as a result of this case, acquired some independence, there was also the grand jury, a body of substantial freeholders, which could not easily be intimidated. This body conducted a preliminary inquiry in order to determine whether or not a case should go for trial, and in this way provided some protection for the subject against the executive wherever it resorted to the law courts in order to penalise a critic or dissentient. A signal example was provided in November 1681 when the Crown tried to dispose of Shaftesbury by a trumped-up charge of high treason. The grand jury of Middlesex, composed of Whigs, threw out the Bill, on the ground that no reliable evidence of treason had been adduced, a signal defeat for Charles and his government. But the lesson was not lost on them; for, by the remodelling of the boroughs, they hoped to ensure that only Tory grand juries would be returned.

The Restoration had followed a period of Puritan experiments in law reform, experiments which were not brought to fruition until the time of Bentham; but meanwhile the reign of Charles II was notable for many additions to the statute-book. Among these was a Statute of Limitations passed in 1666. All wars create situations in which it may be impossible to determine whether a man is dead or alive, a doubt which may seriously prejudice wives and heirs; accordingly, this Act, passed in the second Anglo-Dutch War, imposed an arbitrary but not unreasonable time limit, seven years of absence abroad, without evidence of existence, after which death might be presumed. Shaftesbury's 'Act for the better securing the liberty of the subject and for prevention of imprisonments beyond the seas' is more widely known as the Habeas Corpus Amendment Act, and even as the Habeas Corpus Act. It was legalised by Charles in May 1679. The writ of habeas corpus was an ancient remedy for ensuring the production, before a court, of a detained person, in order that the causes of his detention might be publicly investigated; but, in practice, there were many ways in which the executive could interfere. Thus a procedure had developed whereby the writ was issued only by a judge of King's Bench, and only in term time. It might have to be applied for several times; and, even when granted, there might be long delays in serving it, as where the prisoner was confined overseas, for example, in Jersey. Shaftesbury's Act, which originated from earlier measures intended to prevent imprisonment overseas, remedied these defects and provided the basis for the modern application of this remedy: a remedy which, it may be claimed, is distinctive of the jurisprudence of English-speaking peoples, as contrasted with those systems where a political suspect can be imprisoned secretly and indefinitely. When James II announced that he wished to see the abrogation of the Test Act he added the Habeas Corpus Act.

These achievements would hardly have been possible but for the fact that the old common law of England—however much it may have been misinterpreted by Coke and other jurists—was held to provide rights and remedies for the subject against encroachment by the executive: rights and remedies, not of recent acquisition, but of (supposed) immemorial antiquity, unparalleled in the laws of other countries, including those of England's nearest neighbour, Scotland. Of these the High Court of Parliament was the ancient and revered custodian, a supreme tribunal and grand inquest of the nation, of which the king was an essential element, in contrast with the *Parlement de Paris* which was subject to the personal control of the Crown. The part played at this time by the Commons in parliament has not yet been fully elucidated by modern historians: can it be wondered at that it completely baffled contemporary foreign observers? It is true that most of the Commons were willing to accept bribes, whether from Danby, Louis XIV or anyone else; for private corruption is not always incompatible with public profession of high principle. But, in their corporate capacity, the Commons derived strength from their claim to speak on behalf of all the freeholders of England. Individually, only a minority were of distinctive personal interest; collectively, they had a prestige, at home and abroad, unparalleled by any other representative body in the world. These Englishmen could be bribed, but not bullied; Charles knew this, James did not. Moreover, they were representative, not in the modern sense that they had a mandate from tens of thousands of electors, but in the sense that, by their inclusion of squires, younger sons of peers, officials of the administration, army and navy officers, merchants and lawyers, they represented the classes which were predominant in the State.

Lastly, most remarkable of all was the English local administration. A great hierarchy of officials, exalted and humble, secular and ecclesiastical, co-operated in the task of keeping boisterous Englishmen in their place. They were headed by the lords lieutenant of the counties who, with the help of their deputies, supervised the militia; and, in what were like local parliaments, assessed property owners for their contribution to the support of this home defence force. At times these officials interfered with the course of elections; they also provided a channel by which the privy council was kept in touch with local feeling, and through which pressure could be exercised from the centre. In practice, the lords lieutenant were drawn from the nobility and the more important families of the gentry; and a king who was sure of these men was sure of the nation: hence the unwisdom of James II in depriving the majority of them of their offices.

Next in dignity came the sheriffs and the justices of the peace. The sheriff was responsible for the county gaol and officiated at executions; usually he held office for one year, and his office was considered both onerous and expensive. More numerous were the justices, who performed by far the greater part of the administrative and judicial work of the county. In exercising their various duties they acted singly, or in twos, or in quarter sessions, when all the justices of the county met together, to deal with the innumerable tasks imposed on them by statute, be it the licensing of ale houses, making affiliation orders, or sentencing recusants to fine or imprisonment. All of them freeholders and Anglicans, the justices usually had no more knowledge of the law than what could be picked up from such standard manuals as Dalton's *The Country Justice*. Many of them were oppressive and intolerant; but they were the unpaid enforcers of a system which was directed mainly to the maintenance of law and order in a high-spirited population.

Nor were these the only officials of the administrative system. The Church still exercised some disciplinary control over the laymen, usually in the diocesan courts of the bishop. For the villagers, there were the visitations of the archdeacon, when the scolds, the unmarried mothers, the sabbath breakers and, in general, the never-do-wells of the parish were disciplined by fine, penance or excommunication. Nobody was too humble for the attentions of this ecclesiastical mandarin. Moreover, it is not always realised that in many areas the old manorial jurisdiction, however attenuated, still survived, usually where there were copyholders, who were obliged to attend the customary courts held by the steward on behalf of the manorial lord: courts where the 'homage' or jury of copyholders might have to determine on a great variety of offences and infringements connected mainly with the cultivation of the soil. The countryside was subjected to supervision and control, not by appointees of the central government, nor by dragoons pursuing unarmed villagers, but by civilian residents, many of them poor and obscure, all of them habituated to that co-operation and public service which are among the essentials of self-government. Here was a closely knit, well-ordered world, as remote from the debauchery of Whitehall as from the subservience of Versailles. It was this dour, impenetrable world which James II, to his cost, attempted to overturn. Neither Bossuet nor Louis XIV could have imagined that Protestant England possessed in her local administration a system which effectively secured order by popular participation in a host of local offices, the great majority of them unpaid.

Such, in brief, were the royal policy and the central and local institutions of England in this period. From that policy the nation derived one great advantage—freedom from campaigns on the Continent, a freedom which enabled her to conserve resources and build up the wealth which served her afterwards in the long struggle with France. From her institutions she derived a spirit of enterprise which enabled her to take a prominent place among the nations. Of this increasingly prosperous and enlightened England London was the microcosm. But here a distinction is necessary. Today the two cities of London and Westminster are regarded as scarcely distinguishable, though they are still under separate administrations; historically, however, they are distinct and can even be contrasted. Westminster, with its abbey, its great royal hall and its two Houses of Parliament, was the embodiment, in Gothic architecture, of the alliance between Church, Crown, Legislature and Law, the four pillars of national history. London, on the other hand, with its docks, markets, shops and a population of about half a million, was a great trading metropolis, a closely knit civic community and the social centre of the realm. That these two centres were, for so many centuries, separate and distinct is of historical interest, for both parliament and the law courts developed in surroundings of sanctity and majesty, in contrast with the bustling, secular activity of the London streets. In consequence, English parliamentary procedure and judicial process have retained a dignity and high sense of tradition without parallel in other lands. Nor was there merely contrast between the two; there was also interaction. From the time of Elizabeth I it had become the practice for groups of members of the House of Commons, overawed perhaps by the solemn restraint of St Stephen's Chapel, to resort to London taverns, in order to discuss joint action, afterwards put into effect in the House, a practice of great importance in the history of parliament. Moreover, these opportunities for social concourse and discussion helped, as it were, to 'cushion' the impacts of political disagreement and to provide a broader basis for political life. London and Westminster, so far from being identical, were contrasted with and complementary to each other.

Of this fact the London coffee-houses provided a clear example. In Charles's reign they were becoming an important institution, and the government became apprehensive that they were a source of sedition; for newspapers, many of them suspect, could be read by their patrons, and there was no saying what plots might be hatched in such free and semi-secret intercourse of men who were presumably idle. Accordingly, several attempts were made to suppress them, but these were not persevered in, and indeed they provided useful places of resort for government spies. It was by the evidence of one of these that Titus Oates was convicted, not of perjury, but of slandering the Duke of York. On the other hand, several contemporaries praised the coffee-houses because they helped to make people sociable; the conversation often supplemented the information conveyed in books, and it was even suggested that, as educational institutions, they played the part of popular universities. Inevitably, there was some specialisation as men of similar opinions forgathered in the same place. Kid's Coffee House was favoured by Titus Oates and the Whigs,

Gray's Inn Coffee House by the Tories. Others had literary associations: for example, Wills' where Dryden presided. So too with clubs, of which the Green Ribbon was the most famous, frequented by supporters of Shaftesbury at the time of the Exclusion controversy.

The freemen of London had special privileges not shared by other cities. The chief magistrate, the lord mayor, had a place of unique dignity and power; the corporation over which he presided included the greatest commercial magnates of the realm; and there were occasions, as at the Restoration and the Revolution, when the city in its corporate capacity acted almost as an Estate of the realm. Moreover, its finances were so well managed that, before the changes of William's reign, the Chamber of London was considered to provide better security for investment than any government institution. In their wealth and mode of life the merchants rivalled the patricians of Venice and Amsterdam in their prime, and they mingled with professional men, such as lawyers and doctors, as well as with a host of brokers, insurance agents and middle-men, whose numbers were increasing so rapidly as to cause disquiet. Already London was becoming established as the world centre of marine and fire insurance; Lloyd's began in a coffee-house in Charles's reign; fire insurance commenced in 1680. There was no university; but the Inns of Court, where a collegiate mode of life was practised, provided what was claimed to be a third university, and so one more element was added to the numerous and contrasted components of the city's inhabitants. Another class—the nobility—was now taking up semi-permanent residence in the capital. Already, some of the bishops had town houses; with the development of the west end and the district of St James's, many members of the peerage spent a large part of their time in London, an innovation condemned by those holding older views about the function of the nobility. Generally, the governments of this period regarded the great expansion of London, not with pride, but with apprehension, since so many of the inhabitants were considered Whigs or Dissenters, and there were innumerable opportunities for plotting.

This increase in the population and importance of the city is partly explained by the fact that, after the rebuilding which followed the Great Fire of 1666, London was a much more pleasant place in which to live. The rebuilding was carried out on a definite plan enacted by statute; streets, lanes and houses were classified according to size and importance; the height of buildings and the materials to be used in their construction were prescribed. At the same time improvements were effected in street lighting and water supply. The result was that medieval London, with its narrow lanes and wooden houses, was swept away, and its place was taken by an array of streets, squares and buildings which, even today, can be described as comparatively spacious and substantial. St Paul's was still in process of rebuilding, and Wren was busy with those churches and halls which, before the second World War, stood out as jewels in a sea of masonry. With good reason, Englishmen must have felt pride as their renovated capital slowly took shape. England did not yet hold a commanding place in Europe, but the bases of power were there—the natural resources, the highly skilled labour, the well-built, well-manned ships, and a metropolis which might have rivalled Carthage in its commerce and Paris in its amenity.

The natural resources can be illustrated by a reference to the land. There was, first of all, the reclamation of marsh, as in the Fen district, an enterprise which had begun in the reign of Charles I and was resumed in 1663; the land thus reclaimed was particularly fertile and was at first devoted to the raising of vegetable oils. A similar improvement was that of enclosing which, at this time, was not necessarily for the conversion of arable to pasture, but often for the more profitable use of the soil: hence the frequency of enclosing round large towns or in mining districts. Chancery sanctioned several enclosures of this kind, insisting only on the consent of all the freeholders concerned, but there was no legislation which specifically encouraged landlords to enclose. Nevertheless, the 'improving' landlord was coming into existence and, in general, there was a more widespread interest in the potentialities of the soil. The cultivation of new crops, such as clover, lucerne and turnip, was suggested by at least one writer, and increased use was made of the potato. The best evidence of this more enterprising spirit in agriculture is seen in the investigations commenced by the Royal Society in 1664. In that year a 'Georgicall Committee' was appointed, a fact-finding committee which sent out questionnaires to prominent agriculturalists asking for information about types of soil, manures, farm implements, and the general level of cultivation in their districts. The replies showed that the level was fairly high, and that, especially in the sowing of the new grasses, much of the initiative of eighteenth-century farming was anticipated in the seventeenth.

The steadily increasing demand for corn benefited the landlord; indeed, it was in Charles's reign that the corn laws were inaugurated by an Act of 1673 which established a system of bounties, whereby an export trade in corn was started. A certain measure of stabilisation was thus created which made it worth while to grow corn, and so more land was brought under cultivation. Another development may be found in fruit growing. For long, the apple, basis of the extensive cider production, had been the most popular of English fruits. But, owing mainly to French influence, its monopoly was now threatened by the melon, pear, peach and nectarine; sheltered gardens in the south were decorated by these exotics, while the hardier fruits were grown in extensive orchards in Kent and in the Severn valley, thus adding to the variety so characteristic of the English countryside. This was enhanced by afforestation, encouraged by the demand for timber, and Evelyn's *Sylva* was found alongside Dalton's *Country Justice* in the thinly populated libraries of the squires. Their wealthier neighbours were becoming interested in landscape gardening, as evidenced in the layout of such new or rebuilt country houses as Euston (Lord Arlington), Althorp (Lord Sunderland) and Cliveden (Duke of Buckingham). But it is notable that these developments were to be found mainly in the midlands and the south, for the north was still poor, underpopulated and even unexplored, still devoid of those amenities which elsewhere were becoming such a distinctive feature of English life. On the Scottish border life and property were precarious; and the gaol at Carlisle was usually filled with northern cattle raiders, most of whom took the 'high road'[1] back to their native land.

Restoration England was still primarily an agricultural and pastoral country, its villages mostly given over to domestic industries. Throughout the country there were scattered areas which might be described as industrial, in the limited sense that their occupants were not dependent for a livelihood only on corn or wool, but might be engaged, in whole or in part, in some craft or industry. Thus there was considerable mining and metal-working, often located in districts other than the industrial areas of today—for example, the metal-working in the Forest of Dean and in the Wealden district of Kent and Sussex. Lead was still extracted in the mines of the Peak district in Derbyshire—later, lead became an important article of export. In contrast, tin-mining in Cornwall was a decaying enterprise, for the metal could be obtained more cheaply elsewhere. Copper, mined at Keswick and in Staffordshire, was coming into wider use and was the basis of a brass industry which had foundries in the Isleworth and Rotherhithe districts of London. Birmingham and Sheffield were already centres of metal industries, the one noted for its nails, guns and hardware, the other for its knives and cutlery.

Salt was relatively important. It was obtained from brine pits in Staffordshire and Worcestershire; after 1671 the rock salt of Cheshire was utilised, and on the north-eastern coast there were salt-pans where water was evaporated with the help of coal from the pits of Durham and Northumberland. Deposits of coal in the midlands helped to promote the metal-working of the Birmingham area; but the main sources of supply were the shallow pits of Durham and the western part of Cumberland, much of the product of the first source being conveyed by ship from Newcastle to London and up the Thames. Nevertheless, coal had by no means displaced wood or charcoal for smelting and heating, and so one cannot reasonably speak of an 'industrial revolution' in this period. Moreover, the steam-engine at this time was still a primitive device used mainly for pumping water out of pits, and industry continued to be dependent on water power. Transportation had developed little from its condition a century before because it was still dependent on river and

[1] That is, by the gallows.

coasting vessels, or on roads which were often little better than tracks. There was much improvement in rivers to make them more navigable; but not till nearly a century later were either industry or transport revolutionised.

The textiles were specially important. Manchester, an 'open' town like Birmingham, that is, free from the restrictions imposed in 'close' or corporate towns, was the centre of a cotton industry, dependent on an inferior variety of wool imported from the eastern Mediterranean. Cotton goods provided a valuable alternative to cloth, as they were more easily washable, and so more hygienic. But cloth-making was still the basic English industry. Its processes provided for the co-operation of all the members of the family; its products were the basis of the export trade; its regulation was the subject of statutes, passed in almost every year of the century. It was the belief of English statesmen that nature had conferred special advantages on England, most clearly evidenced in the great variety of wool to be found from one parish to another, a variety attributed to the great differences of rainfall and soil within the British Isles. Even in fuller's earth, obtained from pits in Surrey and used for removing oil from the finished cloth, it was thought that England had a monopoly, for it appears that this absorbent clay was not yet mined on the Continent. English cloth was usually made from the blending of wools from different areas; in this industry, it was variety as much as quality that was aimed at, each district specialising in the production of a fabric intended for a specific purpose or market. There was a similar variety in the degree to which capitalism had invaded the industry—it was making its appearance in the West Riding of Yorkshire, where small capitalists 'put out' the wool to cottage workers; it had progressed farther in the cloth towns of Wiltshire and the south-west, where there was large-scale production and more division of labour.

Much of the economic development of England was due to the dovetailing of industries at home with markets abroad. The link between the two was the ship and the seaman. The system was frankly based on exploitation of labour—of the 'poor' at home and of the negro in the West Indies—both pre-ordained by providence to their subordinate place in the scheme of things. Nor was there any conflict of interests, for the landlords were convinced that an expanding overseas trade was the best security for their own prosperity; and, unlike the French, they had no objection to putting their sons into trade, provided it was wholesale or overseas trade. For English products there must always be a sufficient 'vent'; only thus could bankruptcy be avoided. In addition to the private merchants, the great trading companies, such as the East India, the Levant and the Royal African Companies,[1] were providing such 'vents' in joint enterprises which, after the short period of relaxation in the later years of the Interregnum, were characterised by varying degrees of

[1] For the East India Company, see below, ch. XVII, pp. 417 ff.

monopoly. These three companies which, between them, covered a great proportion of the world's navigable waters, were alike in this that a major part of their exports consisted of cloth: cloth of innumerable varieties and textures, adapted to the different climates of foreign countries and to the needs of their markets. In order to ensure this variety each of these companies was accustomed to draw its supplies from groups of English counties, which were thus linked directly with an overseas market. But the system was precarious. The companies had to face fierce competition, notably from the French and Dutch. Changes of fashion influenced demand, and there were great fluctuations in the amount of English cloth which exporters could absorb, with the result that there might be prolonged unemployment in a district depending mainly on one or other of the companies. This precariousness may account for the fact that there is scarcely a year in the seventeenth century in which there was no complaint of the decay of the cloth trade—indeed, the workers were usually poised on the subsistence level—and this helps to explain England's adoption of an alternative, as evidenced by the Navigation Acts: encouragement of imports of raw materials from the southern plantations in America and from the West Indies, mainly for re-export.

The government was alive to this situation. Numerous committees of the privy council consulted with economic experts and merchants; legislation was drafted usually after consultation with the various interests involved. The Restoration period coincided with the beginning of some kind of imperial consciousness. While the Cromwellian Navigation Act had been intended mainly to limit Dutch penetration, the Act of 1660 was more constructive in character, since it imposed an oath on all the colonial governors and enumerated those raw materials, such as sugar, tobacco and cotton, which must be landed in England, mainly for re-export to other countries. English policy was thus a maritime policy, designed to ensure freights, to promote the building of large ships, to create opportunities for training in seamanship and, generally, to limit imports as much as possible to raw materials or 'unfinished' goods, in exchange for manufactured goods, notably cloth, leather goods, hardware, including clocks and watches, together with variable amounts of corn, fish, tin, lead and coal. Each part of the empire had its allotted place in this scheme of things. Virginia and Maryland received English manufactures in return for their tobacco.[1] The fishing fleets of Devon took cod-fish from Newfoundland to Spanish and Portuguese ports where they traded it for wine and oil. The slave ships carried negroes to the West Indies and returned with sugar which was exchanged in the London docks for manufactured goods intended for the West African market. The Levant and East India Companies, in return for cloth, imported silk, calicoes, muslins, fancy goods, porcelain and tea.[2] Scotland was debarred from trade with the

[1] See below, ch. XIV, pp. 348–9. [2] See below, ch. XVII, pp. 399–401, 409–10.

plantations, but Scotsmen were allowed to settle there, and a trade grew up in provisions between Scottish ports and the West Indies; moreover, the Scottish sugar refiners were allowed to import their raw material direct. Ireland was unfairly treated. By the Navigation Act of 1670–1 the 'enumerated' goods from the plantations could no longer be landed in Irish ports; and as the import of Irish cattle was supposed to prejudice English rents, this trade was prohibited by an Act of 1666–7. A similar restriction applied to wool and cloth, but large quantities of wool were smuggled to foreign countries, and the Irish economy was helped by a regular export trade in horses and provisions.

England's withdrawal from the third Anglo-Dutch War in February 1674 enabled English traders to seize several Dutch markets; and as Charles resisted the public demand that he should go to war with Louis, he indirectly benefited the cause of English overseas trade. The continuance of this policy of peace with France under his successor helps to account for the steady increase of English wealth and prosperity, derived mainly from overseas and re-export trade, in the years 1675–88. Although not yet a great European power, England was accumulating the resources which eventually enabled her to maintain her own in the long struggle with France and even to surpass the enemy, mainly because of her sea-power and a comparatively modern system of public finance. Yet by 1689, when the testing time began, English taxation tapped only a fraction of the available wealth of the country. Reference has already been made to the taxes which constituted the hereditary revenue of the Crown, granted to Charles and James in 1660 and 1685 respectively. Parliament also granted taxes from time to time, usually for specific purposes, such as the building of ships, or for war; of these, the most important was a levy, at first called an Assessment, falling nominally on property, but actually levied almost entirely on land. This was usually at a definite rate, such as two or four shillings on the pound rent, and it was estimated that a shilling rate produced about half a million pounds annually. This, as standardised in the reign of Anne, was called the land-tax, and became a permanent part of the fiscal system, because of the cost of the wars with France. With customs and excise, the land-tax was the most important tax of this period. There were many other taxes, such as the poll-tax, the hearth-tax, and special taxes on imports, such as wine; but the three main taxes continued to provide the bulk of the revenue in steadily increasing volume.

Most of the taxes were farmed—that is, their proceeds were mortgaged in advance to financiers and syndicates who made a bargain with the Treasury as to the initial advance of a lump sum and the payment of a rent for a term of years. In this way the government received large sums of ready money at once, but on expensive terms, since it was obviously in the interests of the farmers to make as much profit as possible in normal times, and to demand large 'defalcations' of the rent in abnormal times, as in periods of plague, or war, or alleged slackness of trade. The farmers recouped themselves by collecting the tax assigned to them, at a time when the State did not have the trained personnel for this purpose, and from the profits of old farms they were able to finance new ones. In these circumstances, the best that could be done by the Treasury was to make as good a bargain as possible with the farmers and to resist the demands for 'defalcations'. This was the policy pursued with much success by Thomas Osborne, Earl of Danby, who was lord high treasurer from 1673 to 1678. By prudent management he succeeded in diminishing the debts which threatened to overwhelm the administration, and this enabled him to conduct an organised system of bribing members of the House of Commons as a counter-campaign to the largesse bestowed by the French ambassador. Thus Danby rendered great service to Charles; later he was to prove one of the most effective opponents of James.

Charles's monetary difficulties derived from the fact that he was at the mercy both of female harpies and of an obsolescent system which had to meet the requirements of a comparatively modern State. The sources of national revenue were still kept in water-tight compartments, and each of these was saddled with an item of debt or payment. If the source failed, in whole or in part, then the payment failed in the same proportion; nor could a deficiency in one fund be made good from an excess in another. Not yet was there any consolidation of funds. This fact, more than dishonesty or negligence, accounts for much of the financial irregularity of the time. For example, a courtier or influential person whose pension failed because of deficiency in the fund supplying it would naturally beg the king to order the Treasury to transfer his pension to a better source. This 'switch' could be effected only by another 'switch'—transferring a debt or payment already based on a good fund to the insecurity of the bad one, a process by which the small men invariably were the sufferers. Such methods of accountancy, rather than actual dishonesty, help to explain why the humble and uninfluential—notably the sailors and their families—were unmercifully victimised; here indeed is the dark side of the Stuart medal.

It has been said that England advanced while the Stuarts stood still. The main interest of the reign of Charles II is the steadily increasing contrast between a system of personal rule based on unchangeable principles and a nation undergoing a remarkable development in every sphere of its life. We are too apt to assume that the career of the most popular of Stuart kings was identical with the best interests of the country; often these two things were in sharpest contrast. Experiment and experience in the organisation of industry, in the direction of overseas trade, in parliamentary government, in public finance, and in the highest spheres of intellectual achievement—all these helped to create an England well able to survive her last Stuart kings and to emerge eventually as the Great Britain of later times.

CHAPTER XIV

EUROPE AND NORTH AMERICA

THE domestic history of the restored Stuarts cannot be understood without an appreciation of the influence of the French and of the Dutch on English politics. This was equally true of the colonies in North America. There the French colony of Canada, if thinly peopled, was firmly established and vigorous. Indian alliances, the necessities of the fur trade, and the adventurous characters of the French missionaries and fur-traders, led the French towards expansion inland, while the character of the English settlers, their social and economic pattern, and the position of their colonies near open navigable water emphasised their tendency to settle in rigid communities. The English looked towards the Atlantic for trade and supplies, and when they spread inland it was a slow but possessive movement, taking Indian lands for settlement where the French were content to explore, to trade and to intermingle.

By comparison with the Canadian population of about 2000 in 1660, the English colonies were strong and populous. The New England group (Plymouth, Massachusetts, Connecticut, Rhode Island, New Haven, Maine and New Hampshire) had reached a population of about 20,800 by 1640, and the southern (Chesapeake) colonies of Virginia and Maryland about 17,300, while the British West Indies already had a total of about 38,000. But there were serious differences between the New England colonies, there was little in common between the New England colonies and the southern plantations, and even the English position on the coast was broken by the French colony of Acadia and by the Dutch colony of New Netherland, commanding the fine harbour of New Amsterdam. The alien shipping thus made available to the English colonists enabled them the more easily to trade as they wished, regardless of English laws, and in colonial affairs the main interest of the Restoration period lies in the efforts of the English government to reduce to conformity the North American colonies, with the French and the Dutch on their flanks.

The Restoration of the Stuart monarchy brought continuity rather than a breach in policy, for the Commonwealth and Protectorate governments had not only vindicated their statehood in Europe, but had asserted themselves on the high seas and overseas. The English colonists had tried to use the Civil War as an opportunity to assert a measure of independence, and the Commonwealth had tolerated many pretensions so long as loyalty to the Stuarts was not involved. But this did not imply indifference; as soon as the turmoil of the king's execution was over the colonies had been entrusted to the administrative care of the Council of State, and later of a series of special committees. There had been behind all this a feeling for the development of the coherence and balance of the empire and for integrating the economic, colonial and military aspects of such an empire as might be created.

It had been the Dutch rather than the English who broke the back of Iberian sea-power in the first half of the seventeenth century, and it was almost inevitable that it should be the Dutch who seized the colonial wealth which that Iberian sea-power controlled. The Dutch West India Company, however, failed to make Brazil into a Dutch colony; in 1654 the last outpost at Recife was subdued and the Dutch possessions in Brazil were surrendered.[1] This did not mean the end of the Dutch West India Company, for the West Indian islands had become more important than the mainland, and it was recognised that the English and French West Indian possessions were economically dependent on the Dutch. Amsterdam was the great sugar-refining centre as well as the great fur-mart of Europe; but despite its importance for the trade of the North American continent the Netherlands had not succeeded in establishing populous or viable colonies there. Yet the Dutch position, especially in bringing to market in Europe the products of other peoples' colonies, was such that the policy of France and England was framed in deliberate opposition to Dutch claims. If England was to profit by colonies, Dutch claims had to be rejected. Yet many Dutch practices had to be imitated—and this also was done. The period of accomplishment, however, was rather that of the restored Stuarts than that of the Cromwellian republicans; but they had enunciated an economic thesis of interdependence and a theory of sovereignty within which the whole might work. This was the epoch-making declaration of the Act of 1650 that colonies 'are and ought to be subordinate to and dependent upon England...and subject to such laws and orders as are or shall be made by the Parliament of England'.[2]

The period 1660–88 saw the adoption and adaptation of Cromwellian ideas and practices. There was, of course, a change of personalities and of emphasis, and the restoration period itself can be divided into two from the point of view of colonial policy; but throughout there was continuity of aim. Up to about the year 1675 a joint Anglo-French policy could be based on French approval of the Stuart monarchy and of their plans for re-establishing the Roman Catholic Church in England; the two countries were allied against the Dutch, and pursued a direct anti-Dutch policy in the Cromwellian pattern. From about 1675 onwards it became clear that a distinction must be drawn between the Stuart monarchy and the English people, that these would not stomach many of the French plans, however

[1] For details, see below, ch. XVI, pp. 385–6, 393.

[2] G. L. Beer, *The Origins of the British Colonial System* (New York, 1908), p. 362.

much the monarchy might accept them, and that English and French colonial ambitions must one day confront each other. During the second half of the period, therefore, Anglo-French rivalry replaced the alliance against the Dutch. In both phases the English colonies, and English policy with regard to them, occupied the centre of the scene. The English colonies were populous, purposeful and prosperous, in a way in which the French and Dutch colonies were not. Colonial issues were always intertwined with maritime power; it was the navy of Blake which challenged the Dutch and vindicated English claims in the Caribbean, and the navy of Samuel Pepys which assured the English position. The outstanding position of the English colonies was further emphasised by the mood of English governments.

This was a period of unremitting and purposeful experiment. Varying the method and the details, the constant aim was to cast the divergent and separatist colonial outposts in an imperial mould, to make of the many parts a single economic and military unit. There was continuity with Cromwellian policy, and indeed continuity of method. The Navigation Act was re-enacted, with emphasis on shipping, and with the 'enumerated' clause to drive colonial produce—sugar, tobacco, cotton-wool, fustic and other dyewoods—exclusively to England. And under the restored monarchy, as under the Commonwealth and the first Stuarts, colonial affairs were the proper concern of the Council and its various committees rather than of parliament—despite the declaration of parliamentary sovereignty in the statute of 1650. Officially the privy council was responsible for colonial matters, and a committee of that body was set up to deal with trade and plantations. A series of other committees followed; but Clarendon as Lord Chancellor was so preoccupied with domestic and European affairs that colonial matters were slighted; the outstanding feature of his régime, as far as the colonies were concerned, was the lack of effective governance which the multiplicity of councils and conciliar committees brought with it.

From 1667, when Clarendon fell from power, until 1676 when James, Duke of York, assumed effective control of colonial affairs, the reins were in the hands of Anthony Ashley Cooper, first Earl of Shaftesbury.[1] During this period the concepts of an imperial policy and economy were clearly formulated, and effective administration, not unsympathetic to colonial ambitions and interests, seemed likely to knit together the different elements in the empire. Shaftesbury's experience of colonial administration went back to the Cromwellian Council of State's Special Committee for Plantations; under his leadership the 1668 committee for trade, which included James, Duke of York, and Prince Rupert, above all tried to devise some means for enforcing the Navigation Acts. In 1669 they reported that neither the colonial governors nor the settlers were

[1] For him, see above, ch. XIII, pp. 306, 314–19.

observing the Acts and advised that agents should be sent to the colonies and naval vessels should capture ships contravening these laws. This recommendation, however, was not enforced effectively; although much of the Cromwellian emphasis on West Indian trade survived, Shaftesbury and his committees were not dogmatic on these issues except in their anti-Dutch connotation.

Even against the Dutch, Shaftesbury was not intransigent, and his approach to the vexed question of the Balance of Trade was marked by breadth of view and ability to consider the long-term problems of remittances and terms of trade. But if Shaftesbury and his committees for trade and plantations were somewhat illogical and far from dogmatic in framing and enforcing a policy to achieve a balance of trade by the full implementation of the Navigation Acts, he was firmly convinced that the interests of merchants must be consulted but that merchants must not dictate policy. The tone of his committees (amended to give small and effective membership in 1670 and 1672) was best summarised in the order that the trade of the plantations should be so regulated 'that they may be more serviceable one unto another, and as the whole unto these our kingdomes so these our kingdomes unto them'.[1]

Shaftesbury aimed at an imperial economy in which the relationships were mutually dependent, but the aim was pursued with tolerance and a readiness to acknowledge colonial interests and the claims of expediency. When in 1671 the colonists of Massachusetts seemed likely to break off their dependence, Charles II pressed for a strong tone to be taken (to quote the diarist Evelyn, who was a member of the Council of Plantations) 'which those who better understood the peevish and touchy humour of that Colony were utterly against', and so a 'conciliatory paper' or 'civil letter' was sent.[2] As Lord Chancellor Shaftesbury inveighed against the Dutch, aimed to seize their colonial trade, and told the Lords in February 1673 that 'the States of Holland are England's eternal Enemy, both by Interest and Inclination'.[3] By November Shaftesbury, an old Commonwealth man, was beginning to discover the secret implications of the Treaty of Dover[4] and to revolt at the necessities of the French alliance. He became the leader of opposition to the Roman Catholics, and even to the Dutch War which he had so vehemently supported. His fall was much more than a personal tragedy; it left the way open for the dogmatic assertiveness of James, Duke of York, and his associates in colonial matters. The Lords of Trade, an old committee of the privy council, again emerged as a powerful body, intent to be 'very strict inquisitors' in dealing with the colonies and to ensure the authority of the Crown. The question of sovereignty was

[1] P.R.O. 30/24/49/8–11.

[2] *Diary and Correspondence of John Evelyn Esq., F.R.S.*, ed. H. B. Wheatley (London, 1906), II, 260–2.

[3] *Journals of the House of Commons*, x, 246–7.

[4] See above, ch. XIII, p. 310.

argued round the regulation of vital trade relationships, not round abstract problems which might have left the colonists tolerant or indifferent. A detailed questionnaire was sent out to colonial governors, and the Customs Commissioners reported that all efforts to secure the co-operation of colonial governors and shipmasters in enforcing the Acts of Trade had proved entirely ineffective.

So far was the system from enforcing a trade in which England was the centre of exchanges that predominance seemed increasingly to lie with New England. The merchants and shipmasters of Boston, Salem and Providence prospered by taking the foodstuffs of New England and manufactured goods to the West Indies, where they could undersell English merchants and could buy indigo, tobacco, and sugar for shipment to New England or alien ports in Europe. An attempt to check the evasions was made in 1673 by an Act for the Encouragement of Trade. Shipmasters must give bond that they would carry the commodities which lay at the heart of colonial trade only to British ports or to another colony; in this case, they must pay a 'Plantation Duty' equivalent to the duty payable if they brought their cargo to a British port. Collectors and surveyors of the customs were appointed to act in the colonies; this introduced the problems of sovereignty in a particularly difficult form since these officers were not responsible to the local governments but to the Crown in England.

Towards the New England States even the Lords of Trade were a little cautious and circumspect; they did not know how much dependence Massachusetts and its satellites would accept. But for the West Indies, especially Jamaica and Barbados, they thought themselves in a stronger position. Overriding the claim that the laws of Jamaica were municipal, they denied the right of the island's Assembly to legislate, and reported that the king should retain power to alter or even to revoke laws which the Assembly passed. The Earl of Carlisle was sent out as governor in 1678, firmly believing in active and autocratic government and intending to set up a new and autocratic model for Jamaica without further consultation of the Assembly. He almost inevitably provoked protests and deadlock, and himself felt that the governor should not be tied too close to instructions issued at great distance. In Barbados also the activity of the Lords of Trade stirred up the Assembly against alien laws, and the governor against interference with his powers and patronage.

The Exclusion Bill controversy[1] brought Shaftesbury and the enemies of James, Duke of York, into power for a time in 1679; but the Lords of Trade remained substantially the same body pursuing substantially the same purposes, with scrutinies of laws and trade practices, and with constant interference in appointments. But they were at odds with the monarchy, irritated and ignored by the colonial governors. No solution could

[1] See above, ch. XIII, p. 317.

be found, but the Jamaican Speaker, Samuel Long, declared that 'as Englishmen' the colonists 'ought not to be bound by any laws to which they had not given their consent'.[1] At this juncture the Lords of Trade virtually abandoned their case: they accepted the reality of a revenue act in Jamaica in return for continuing the former constitution, and on the appointment of a new governor in Barbados they withdrew discreetly from the more dogmatically authoritative innovations. But colonial laws were to be sent home for confirmation; they were to agree 'as far as may be' with the laws of England; the king retained the right of disallowing them, and the governor the right of veto. The Lords had not changed their principles, and while the compromise with Jamaica was implemented they advised that a perpetual revenue Bill should be obtained, after which the governor and his nominated officers might pay but little attention to local opinion, and need seldom summon the Assembly.

The islands needed assurance that their revenues would be properly spent for their own purposes; but the Lords of Trade could only emancipate the governors from the assemblies if they could get for them some recurrent income. Revenue for Barbados and the Leeward Islands was put in the hands of commissioners in London, appointed by the Treasury; in Jamaica in 1683 the Assembly passed a revenue act, valid for twenty-one years, in return for tacit admission of the claim that the laws of England were in force there, while the demands for an annual session of the Assembly and a veto on forced military service were dropped. Thus in the West Indies control of revenue lay with royally nominated commissioners, and the Crown's right to confirm or reject laws passed by the assemblies was vindicated. The political balance was still uncertain; but at least the principles seemed to have been settled, and the Lords of Trade had asserted the claims to sovereignty, the appointment of officials, and the validity of the Acts of Trade upon which any idea of a co-ordinated imperial economy must rest. The Lords of Trade, however, as Charles turned against the Exclusionists who controlled that body, became merely an administrative committee carrying out the commands of the Secretary of State.

Vital as the West Indies appeared, North America was equally significant. Here Massachusetts was most important, and here also revenue and an appointed auditor played their part in precipitating disagreement; for trade, and taxation upon trade, mattered more in Massachusetts than in any other colony. By 1660 Massachusetts had a population of about 40,000 and was firmly established as a political, social, and economic entity. The spread of the English colonies had undoubtedly denoted internal dissensions, but also the strength and purpose of the settlers.

[1] A. P. Thornton, *West-India Policy under the Restoration* (Oxford, 1956), p. 199 *et passim*.

Although divergence from orthodox Puritanism was a primary cause for the establishment of the Providence Plantations on Rhode Island and of Connecticut, Massachusetts retained predominance; this made it inevitable that she should aim at pre-eminence in the imperial economy which was in process of creation. Not only were the Navigation Acts freely broken, with European goods taken direct into the colonies, but from the New England colonies such contraband goods went out to other colonies, especially to the West Indian islands. To meet the bills involved in such a system colonial produce was, despite the 'enumerated clauses' of the Navigation Acts, shipped direct to Europe instead of through an English port.

When the Commonwealth gave place to the restored monarchy Massachusetts was in a state of transition. As population increased the Puritan oligarchy more and more became a minority, and in 1662 the establishment was broadened by the 'Half-Way Covenant', by which children of Church members might be admitted to the Church and so might be freemen, even if they had not experienced conversion and were not qualified as full members of the Church community. The same year saw equally important changes in the other New England States. The communities of Providence, Portsmouth, Newport and Warwick had been established on the basis of separation of Church and State, and had to fear alike the hostility of Massachusetts and of the Indian population of Rhode Island (from which they had conscientiously purchased their lands). In 1644 they had secured a parliamentary incorporation as the Providence Plantations, giving them power to rule themselves, and in 1663 they vindicated their separate status and their democratic régime by a royal confirmation of the parliamentary grant.

Connecticut also showed important differences from the constitution of Massachusetts in that the franchise for voting at elections to the General Court was not based on religious conformity. A property qualification, imposed in 1657 at £30 personal estate and increased in 1662 to an additional £20 in real estate, disenfranchised more than half the adult male population. But the disqualification was not on religious grounds, and although the governor had to be a member of an approved congregation he was popularly elected according to the normal franchise. Government was markedly liberal: there was none of the theocratic aristocracy which ruled Massachusetts, and partly for this reason (but also on account of the rich soil and the fur trade) Connecticut prospered and by 1662 had fifteen towns and a population of about five thousand. While Massachusetts looked eastwards and to the development of maritime trade, Connecticut looked westwards and inward to the continent. When in 1663 Connecticut petitioned for a royal charter it secured not only a generous measure of self-government but a considerable extension: all the territory from Narragansett river to the South Sea, bounded on the north by Massachusetts and on the south by the sea, with the islands adjoining. This was interpreted as conveying Long Island, and later as extending Connecticut's boundaries to the Pacific; and although this was premature in 1663, the persuasiveness of Winthrop, the loyalty of Connecticut and its purposeful policy counted for much.

Connecticut triumphed, very largely at the expense of New Haven, which was predominantly mercantile and so in conflict economically with Massachusetts and with the Dutch and Swedes, and which had formed its federated government by admission of the towns of southern Connecticut and Long Island. But this government had no sanction from royal charter, and New Haven showed itself 'obstinate and pernicious in contempt of his Majestie' in harbouring two regicides who fled from England to America in 1660. In vain did the authorities proclaim the king and protest that they were faithful subjects; the colony was weakened by claims of the non-freemen to the franchise and by the dispute over boundaries with Connecticut. When the new charter gave Connecticut legal title to the territories of New Haven there was little strength to resist absorption: the cities which formed the federation of New Haven one by one submitted, joining Connecticut 'as from a necessity'.

At the Restoration it seemed that Rhode Island also might be absorbed by her more powerful or politic neighbours, Massachusetts, Plymouth and Connecticut, each of which claimed some of its territory. So, strongly stressing its loyalty and its breadth of religious toleration, Rhode Island petitioned for a charter in 1661, and although the Connecticut charter apparently gave it the Rhode Island territories, arbitration vindicated the claims of Rhode Island and set the boundaries between the two colonies. Rhode Island received a royal charter in 1663 which brought coherence and political stability.

Massachusetts, while undoubtedly superior to her neighbours in numbers and wealth, was not as easily able to effect a reconciliation with monarchist England. More noticeably than the other New England States she had ignored the Navigation Acts. Massachusetts, which had found it profitable to ignore the Cromwellian 'Act' of 1651, found that the 1660 Act required a bond and security from ships sailing to the colonies or bringing colonial produce to Europe, and that it offered to the governors a third of all goods confiscated for breaking its terms. Massachusetts, which had managed to evade commitment to either side during the Civil War and Commonwealth, found this impossible under the monarchy. In 1662 she was ordered to proclaim the king in the most solemn manner and to conform in all things; an order followed to grant full liberty of worship to Anglicans and to grant the franchise to all owning the necessary property, regardless of religion. This was indeed accompanied by a confirmation of the charter, but it struck hard at the power of Massachusetts' Puritan oligarchy and, in the circumstances of

1662, it held the threat that conformity in trade would be exacted. The favour shown to Connecticut and Rhode Island affronted Massachusetts, and the endless disputes which ensued caused concern to the royal government. In 1664, therefore, a commission was sent out charged with the task of inducing New England to submit to the king, settling boundary disputes, healing strife in the colonies, inquiring into their laws and governments, and also of subduing the Dutch colony of New Netherland.

The commission was not particularly hostile to Massachusetts, at least as far as its instructions went, and the commissioners made a good start there. But by 1665 the colony was denying their right to hear appeals or to exercise any jurisdiction, and they returned to England angry and thwarted, to advise Charles to take a strong line. Massachusetts was saved partly by the fear that it was on the eve of rebellion, partly by the fall of Clarendon, and partly by its protestations of loyalty and a present of twenty-six great masts for the navy. But it was due to the political situation rather than to any acceptance of the colony's protestations that a period of quiet prosperity and content followed the stormy departure of the commissioners; the trade of the eastern seaboard remained free from any serious effort to enforce the Navigation Acts.

From the point of view of the Lords of Trade the serious offence of the Dutch in New Netherland was that they controlled the fur trade of the Iroquois confederacy and allowed English settlers to sell tobacco and to buy European goods in defiance of the Navigation Acts. The Dutch occupied a strategic position on the coast; their boundary with New Haven had been fixed by treaty in 1650, but their claims extended down the coast from Cape Cod to Delaware Bay, and they controlled the mouth of the Hudson river, western Long Island, and the course of the Hudson inland to their outpost at Fort Orange. But they were divided among themselves; their chief city, New Amsterdam, had made itself independent of the government of the island of Manhattan, and the governor, Peter Stuyvesant, was unable to work with his fellow-Dutchmen and relied on the English and other aliens who had been admitted as residents after the failure to establish a Dutch-national colony. In 1663 the Council of Plantations appointed a special committee to report on the chances of ousting the Dutch, and early in 1664 James, Duke of York, received from Charles £4000 to achieve the conquest and a charter granting him the territory. Lords and Commons alike were aflame against the Dutch; the Commons inquired into the decay of trade and accepted the verdict of the merchant companies that the Dutch were the source of all difficulties, and it was claimed that it was quite impossible to enforce the Navigation Acts in the English colonies while the Dutch controlled New Netherland.

While England sent out a commissioner, John Scott, to assert royal authority, Connecticut laid claim to Westchester County and the Dutch towns on Long Island. Lacking support from Holland, Governor Stuyvesant was prepared to accept the claims; but Scott announced that Long Island was about to be granted to James, and while the Dutch, Connecticut and John Scott were engaged in negotiations which resulted in Connecticut throwing Scott into prison, the royal grant took shape in England. James appointed Richard Nicolls as lieutenant-governor of his territories; parliament agreed to support the king in a Dutch war (strongly urged by Shaftesbury); Charles appointed his commissioners to visit America and announced his intention of conquering New Netherland. Only four ships were sent, but the commissioners were empowered to demand help from the English colonists, and the fleet made Boston its first objective. Here they got little help, for Massachusetts well knew that her trade depended on the Dutch colony. A month spent at Boston dispelled all Dutch suspicions—to the extent that Stuyvesant allowed some ships to depart for Curaçao and himself went inland to settle an Indian rising. When the English fleet appeared off Fort Amsterdam at the end of August Stuyvesant, desperately though he wanted to fight, was forced to surrender; New Amsterdam passed without a shot fired into English hands, to become New York. The Dutch were promised that they might settle in Manhattan as freely as English subjects and that Dutch ships might freely ply to Holland; the Navigation Acts were waived to allow them to import from Holland the goods which the Indians had got to expect, and which the English manufacturers could not supply. But although New Amsterdam fell so easily, the English had to use force to subdue the posts at Fort Orange up the Hudson river and at Fort Amstel on Delaware Bay.

The war thus precipitated brought the English colonial frontier into direct contact with the French, secured control of the commercial and military centre of the Atlantic coast of North America, and brought the New England colonies into direct contact with Virginia and Maryland. The conquest made possible the vindication of imperial policy in a way which could not have been contemplated while New Amsterdam was in alien hands. It was, inevitably, a shrewd blow at the commercial independence of Massachusetts and the Boston seafarers.

The grant to James, and the use which he made of the grant, had further repercussions. Before the territory was captured he granted the lands between the Hudson and the Delaware to Sir John Berkeley and Sir George Carteret, both ardent royalists, active men, and deeply concerned in the efforts to expand the English colonies. The area, named New Jersey to commemorate the fact that Carteret had been governor of Jersey, was held to be the best land for agriculture in the whole of the York concession. It was sparsely settled; in the north the Dutch had achieved trade posts on the line of the Hudson rather than effective agricultural colonisation; in the south scattered communities of Swedes, Finns and Dutch were left in possession by the new régime. The proprietors, royalist and pledged to imperial unity though they were, were not illiberal. In February 1665 they issued a series of 'concessions' stating the terms upon which lands were to be allotted and guaranteeing liberty of religion, property and elections.

Secure government went far towards peopling New Jersey; but the governor of New York, Richard Nicolls, was equally liberal and anxious to attract settlers. He made liberal grants in the northern part of what was to become New Jersey, and thereby caused trouble between the New Englanders who took advantage of his offer and the governor whom the proprietors sent out, young Philip Carteret. Carteret brought with him French-speaking emigrants from Jersey, to settle in and around Elizabethtown and to rouse the suspicions of the Puritanical New England immigrants. The very liberalism with which the proprietors granted self-government, tolerance and trial by jury led to the development of town meetings, and efforts at reconciliation between the governor and the Puritan immigrants (who continued to people New Jersey) failed. They took their stand on the grants by Nicolls and on their purchases from the Indians and denied the proprietors' claims. There followed two years of confusion and riots, but the proprietors stood fast though they slightly modified the terms of the 'concessions', and Charles fully supported their title derived from James, Duke of York. The grants made by Nicolls were repudiated, and the settlers withdrew their claims.

The vindication of the proprietors was greatly helped by the fact that in 1673 twenty-three ships appeared off Staten Island and recaptured New York. The English garrison of Fort James was but eighty men, the governor was absent on Long Island, and the Dutch success was almost as easily achieved as the earlier capture by the English. An oath of allegiance to the United Provinces was exacted, an infantry soldier, Anthony Colve, was appointed governor of New Netherland, and the whole of Long Island was put under his jurisdiction. New Jersey was absorbed, and it seemed likely that the third Dutch War would effectively annul the one worth-while achievement of the second. Most settlers cheerfully accepted Dutch rule, which was not oppressive and exempted them from taking arms against any expedition from England. Since residents were in general secure in their lands and the attack by the New England colonies hung fire, it seemed that New Netherland might settle into a prosperous groove. It was now under the direct rule of the United Provinces, not of the West India Company; but Holland was hard pressed by the alliance of England and France, and in 1674 was ready to buy the neutrality and benevolence of England: the Treaty of Westminster restored New Netherland to English rule.

It was held that the Dutch re-conquest had extinguished the title of the

Duke of York and all grants which flowed from it, and that the resumption of English rule in 1674 was a new beginning. Thus in his instructions to Sir Edmund Andros, whom he appointed governor of New York in 1674, James gave him rule over all lands from the east side of Delaware Bay to the west side of the Connecticut river. This brought Andros into conflict with the two colonies of East and West New Jersey. Carteret had protested against the overriding of his grant; he secured from James a title to the eastern part of the former New Jersey, and young Philip Carteret was sent out as governor. He proved both efficient and popular, and Andros found it impossible to press the duke's claims against East New Jersey; indeed, he found that James himself would not support him. Despite the fact that he and Philip Carteret were personal friends, Andros carried Carteret off to trial in New York, only to find that the jurors accepted the claim that Carteret's jurisdiction in East New Jersey was legal and was derived from the king. The people of East New Jersey steadfastly rejected the domination of New York; when the affair was carried to England James disowned Andros, relinquished all claim to East New Jersey, and confirmed his grant to Carteret.

Berkeley, in the meantime, had sold the claim which he derived from James's grant to a group of Quakers, who had taken over the settlements on the Delaware as West New Jersey. The Quakers, however, were so much at odds among themselves that William Penn had to be called in to settle their disputes, and James's unsatisfactory attitude made tenures so uncertain that settlement in West New Jersey was slow. In 1676 the Quakers managed to settle their boundary with East New Jersey, and they got from Carteret a recognition of their title to their lands; but with Andros they could come to no agreement. He haled one of the purchasers of the Berkeley title, John Fenwick, off to New York for trial, like Carteret, to answer for his assumption of authority within the dominions of the Duke of York, and when the agreement of 1676 settled the boundary between the Carteret and the Berkeley claims he insisted that this did not override James's prior claim.

In 1677 a party of Quakers fresh from England were suffered to set up their town of Burlington up the Delaware river. They intended to found a self-governing community and had with them a draft constitution in the 'Concessions and Agreements' which Penn and his colleagues had drawn up for them before they left England. No man was to have power over another man's conscience. Subject to the laws of England and to the Concessions, all laws might be made or repealed by the colonial legislature. This was to consist of an executive nominated by Penn and his fellow-proprietors and an assembly freely elected by the inhabitants, with freedom of speech and full parliamentary privileges, and the executive was to have no power to levy taxes. Religious freedom, trial by jury, open courts of justice, and the right to petition were guaranteed; there was to be no imprisonment for debt and no capital punishment even for treason unless the assembly so decreed. The only limitations of local democratic control envisaged were the quit-rents paid to the proprietors, and their right to nominate the executive. Such autonomy was in conflict with the claims which Andros felt compelled to put forward on James's behalf; but despite this uncertainty the Quakers recruited so effectively that West New Jersey steadily increased. Yet the title was not settled until the period of the Popish Plot.[1] Then Penn put to James, with whom he was on terms of personal intimacy, the consideration that New Jersey offered an admirable opportunity of showing how just his rule would be if ever he came to reign. It was a shrewd and very worldly argument: thus James released all his powers of sovereignty over East and West New Jersey, and both were freed from the claims of New York.

James and his governors certainly showed a Stuart levity towards grants of proprietary rights and reluctance to cede the sovereign powers of government; but their approach to the settlers was not oppressive or resented. Colonel Nicolls, as first governor of New York, was conciliatory towards the Dutch settlers and moderate in his claims against Connecticut. Taken literally, the grant to James deprived Connecticut of all land west of Connecticut river; but Nicolls agreed on a frontier which ran north-north-west from a point on the coast twelve miles east of the Hudson river. He encouraged trade and shipping, organised judicial districts, made treaties with the Indians, and gained a reputation for gentle wisdom. But James forbade him to grant self-government to New York, and Nicolls was forced to formulate a code of laws himself. He could not provide for town-meetings, but he borrowed from the Dutch the idea of elective constables and overseers with limited local powers and made land-holding, not church-membership, the qualification for voting for these officers. Absolute religious toleration was granted, and within the limitations imposed on him Nicolls produced a liberal charter for the city. He followed this up by calling representatives from the towns of Long Island to an assembly, promising freedom and immunities equal to those of the New England colonies. According to the normal Stuart theory of sovereignty, the elected representatives were to sanction a code of laws already drawn up, and when they had done so they returned home to incur the wrath of their constituents. Nicolls could do nothing to meet their claims for revision of taxation, control of the militia, and election of magistrates; discontent bordering on sedition continued in the Long Island towns. During the period of renewed Dutch rule they managed to assert their independence, but as English rule was reasserted in 1674 they were forced back under New York, still without the self-government which they craved.

Andros, James's representative after the restoration of English authority,

[1] For this, see above, ch. XIII, pp. 313–14.

combined unquestioning acceptance of his orders with personal friendliness for the settlers. He failed to win their loyalty, but he improved the layout of the towns and the social and economic life of the colony, and he constantly tried to secure some concession to popular feeling. James, convinced that any concession would lead to further demands and would disturb good government, refused, and New York remained the only colony in which the settlers had no share in the legislative authority. The crisis, here as in the West Indies, came over matters of trade and revenue. By 1681 the merchants of New York were refusing to pay customs dues, as were the Quakers in West New Jersey and the proprietary settlers in East New Jersey. There was widespread disaffection; Andros was called home to answer the reports that, above all, the system was failing to produce revenue, and in 1682 James promised an assembly on condition that adequate revenue would be forthcoming.

The new governor, Thomas Dongan, an Irish Roman Catholic of the broadest sympathies and most tenacious purpose, was warmly welcomed in New York, for he brought with him a charter to convene a general assembly representative of the freeholders, with liberty of debate and power to consult the governor and council over taxation and legislation. Seventeen representatives duly met in New York in October 1683, passed some laws, and drew up a Charter of Franchises and Liberties on lines which closely followed the achievements of the English parliament. In the last months of his brother's reign James, as Penn had advised, was anxious that his conduct towards New York should persuade Englishmen how reasonable a king he would be. Despite his recent declarations, he accepted the charter, but, before the document could be sent out, Charles II died and New York became a royal province under the direct control of the Lords of Trade. James as king then rejected the charter which he had granted as heir to the throne and took up a plan to bring all the proprietary and charter colonies into closer dependence on each other and the Crown; it was partly economic but quite recognisably military in its purpose, and it overlooked the separate characters and interests of the individual colonies. It was a Dominion of New England into which James and the Lords of Trade wished to incorporate New York and the other northern colonies.

Interest was not entirely confined to the northern settlements nor (though this was important) was it entirely concentrated on meeting the French threat from Canada. To the south of Virginia stretched vast areas which ran down to the Spanish frontier and were as yet almost entirely vacant. A grant to Sir Robert Heath in 1629 had failed to people the land, and the area was neglected for a generation. When, however, sugar and over-settlement made Barbados look for some outlet for the emigrants who flocked there, and the Restoration government seemed to threaten the freedoms enjoyed under the Commonwealth, it was to the empty lands south of Virginia that the Barbadians turned, and in 1663 Charles II issued his charter for Carolina, a proprietary charter in unmistakable terms. The proprietors were those courtiers who gathered behind Shaftesbury, filled the Councils of Trade and Plantations and aimed to perfect a mutually dependent imperial economy on the basis of proprietary rights. Much the same group secured from the king in 1670 a grant of the Bahamas, and a further grant of Hudson Bay and its adjacent territories. They were well connected and purposeful; the grant of Carolina was probably their most significant achievement, to be put alongside the capture of New Netherland. It covered the territory from the thirty-first to the thirty-sixth parallel, and westwards to the south seas, and gave to the proprietors the lands in free socage; they were absolute lords, could set up a militia, exact customs dues, erect courts of law, make and execute laws, and grant freedom of conscience and of trade in so far as it was permitted by the laws of England. They might summon assemblies of the freemen or their representatives.

When earlier claims had been swept aside the way lay open to organise settlement from Barbados. But the Barbadians submitted a draft constitution with full powers of local government, to be met by a counter-proposal which embodied a governor and a council to be named by the proprietors, whose agents then set to work to draw up a compromise in the form of 'concessions'. With experience in Barbados behind them, the agents were more liberal than the proprietors would tolerate, and it was not until 1665 that a fresh set of concessions was put forward, liberal in matters of religion, free elections and the right to petition. Even then an expedition from Barbados in 1665 was a marked failure.

At this juncture Shaftesbury, with a new charter granted in 1665, came forward to dominate Carolina. A general assembly was called, and settler opinion soon demanded easier and more realistic methods of granting lands. The settlers wanted to be out, engaged in agriculture, not herded into towns by the proprietors; they wanted simpler forms of grant and generous estates on the model of Virginia (from which many of them had come). Under this treatment the settlement at Albemarle took firm root and Shaftesbury turned to foster the southern area at Port-Royal, while he and the proprietors' secretary, John Locke, drew up the famous Fundamental Constitutions for the colony: an academic blue-print for dividing the lands into counties, seignories, baronies and manors, with the people settled in precincts, four to a colony. A hereditary nobility of landgraves and caciques was to be created, the proprietors were to become hereditary officials, and the freeholders to hold minor offices and to elect their representatives to a parliament. Under the freemen were to be leetmen, bound to the soil in feudal style. This 'medley of feudal doctrine and seventeenth-century social theory' had little effect. A few baronies were laid out, but the chief value of the Constitutions was to show the ideas of enlightened men of the proprietary type. They wanted religious toleration, trial by jury and limited self-government, but also an aristocratic form of rule, and they thought that if a colony was to prosper it must have in England a parent-body of proprietors, or a company, to organise the supply of men and capital.

Meanwhile Shaftesbury got together a colonising expedition. The proprietors put up the money and, after reinforcement at Barbados, the expedition, defying the claims of the proprietors, founded Charles Town on Ashley river. Yet Shaftesbury, intent on building up an interchange of commodities between his three interests (at Charles Town, at Albemarle, and at Bermuda) could not afford to let the settlers depart. He recruited more settlers from England and Barbados, and the proprietors showed themselves willing to compromise as the colony's parliament began to sit in 1671. In 1672 there were about 400 settlers, by 1682 over a thousand, and by 1685 over 2500. The influx continued, from France where the Huguenots were forbidden to seek asylum in the French colonies, from Barbados and other colonies, and from England, organised by the proprietors; from 1682 onwards settlement began to spread inland while a new Charles Town, more commodious for trade and defence, was built at the junction of the Ashley and Cooper rivers.

Danger from a small Indian tribe, the Westoes, and from the Spaniards to the south delayed inland expansion, but economic life developed smoothly and steadily. Although the proprietors stood by the Fundamental Constitutions in theory they were realistic enough not to insist in detail, and government was 'simple and satisfactory'. But as the original proprietors either died or were disgraced as Stuart dynasticism triumphed over the Exclusionists, new ideas took hold. First came a complaint that a few privileged men were monopolising the trade in furs. Then the colonists rejected amendments to the Constitutions, not because they were harsh (for they were designed to limit the powers of the proprietors and to put more authority in the hands of the representatives of the people), but because they emanated from authority without discussion. The proprietors became more oppressive and heavy, and by 1684 they had driven their governor to resign by insisting that his duty was to govern, not to let the people govern him. With the accession of James II the new governor insisted that each member of the parliament must swear allegiance to James, fidelity to the proprietors, and acceptance of the Fundamental Constitutions: those who refused were excluded. Though the essence of the economy of Carolina was trade between separate colonies and between the colonies and the nearby Spanish settlements, the proprietors, through fear of losing their charter, adhered to the Navigation Acts and so increased the stress between them and the settlers. The colony was ready to revolt, the governor proclaimed martial law and refused to call another parliament. The Fundamental Constitutions were inoperative and a rival governor appeared, only to be disavowed by the proprietors. Clearly only military force would perpetuate the proprietors' English and authoritarian views where they conflicted with the settlers' needs.

Most of the care of the Carolina proprietors was, naturally, spent on the southern settlement at Charles Town. But in the north, on the fertile lands near Albemarle, was a competent settlement whose members had come mainly from Virginia, reinforced by some Quakers. Devoted largely to subsistence farming, they had little external trade save in tobacco and furs. This trade was almost entirely in the hands of New England merchants; the proprietors urged in vain that Albemarle should ship direct to England, or should trade with the southern settlement. Trouble came to a head in 1677–8, when the colonists resolved not to pay a tax of a penny a pound on tobacco exported to other colonies, imprisoned the governor, the president of the assembly and almost all the deputies, and took control for a year. The proprietors managed to evict a popularly appointed governor, but their own appointee was taken by Algerian pirates on his way out and did not arrive until 1683. By then Albemarle was in great confusion, and the settlers seized the governor and banished him. Carolina clearly revealed the power of the navigation policy to alienate overseas traders who needed intercolonial exchanges, and the inability of the proprietors to enforce their will.

Through all these changes the number of Quakers steadily increased, and by the time that their leader George Fox made a journey among them in 1672 there were communities in Virginia (with an offshoot at Albemarle), in East New Jersey, Rhode Island and Maryland. Normally they were without political influence and living under more or less hostile governments; but in Rhode Island the Quakers dominated the situation and supplied many of the governors and deputies. Early proposals to purchase territory in America, where the Quakers might lead their own lives without interference, all came to nothing until 1680, when William Penn petitioned the king for a grant of land north of Maryland, to extend north as far as was plantable. The Quaker's friendship with royalty ensured that the Lords of Trade would look well at his request, and in 1681 a royal charter gave to Penn the territory bounded on the east by the Delaware and to the 'three and fortieth degree of northern latitude'—a phrase which led to serious disputes later. To the south the boundary lay on a semi-circle running north and north-west from New Castle (which the Duke of York had insisted on keeping) until it cut the fortieth parallel; then westwards along the parallel for five degrees of longitude. Penn was anxious to have access to the ocean, and this brought him into dispute with Baltimore, which had a legal title to the Dutch and Swedish settlements on the west bank of the Delaware. Eventually, in 1682, James ceded to Penn New Castle settlement and all the territory on the right bank of the Delaware to its mouth; this brought forward Baltimore to deny his right to make such a grant, but at the end of 1685 the Lords of Trade decided that the land in dispute did not belong to Baltimore.

Penn had become lord of the province of Pennsylvania, could make laws with the advice and consent of his freemen, execute the laws, appoint judges and magistrates, grant pardons, and create towns and boroughs. His executive and judicial powers were almost unlimited, and generous though Penn was to his colony, he undertook the business of administration before embarking on law-making. He organised the dispatch of settlers and sent out orders which resulted in the planned layout of the city of Philadelphia, while his deputy-governor was instructed to call a council, to receive the allegiance of the people, to settle boundaries and to distribute lands, to keep the peace, to issue ordinances, but not to summon an assembly. Yet when he set out his Frame of Government for the colony, Penn revealed himself as a political philosopher of a high order; although outwardly using the same institutions as most colonial constitutions he gave great powers to his provincial council, an elected body, and gave his governor no powers independent of the council. Then Penn sailed to his colony in 1682, called an Assembly elected by the freeholders and, having settled the colony's boundaries and conferred citizenship on all residents, set out the principles of the colony in the Great Law. Capital punishment was to be inflicted only for murder and treason, and liberty of conscience was guaranteed. Democratic equality before the law was to be the mark of the new society.

Penn was intent to preserve friendly relations with the Indians, made treaties with them and paid them for the lands occupied. His touch was sure and confident, and he spent much time bringing his territory to fruit. When he returned to England in 1684 Philadelphia had over 2500 inhabitants and the colony over 8000, notable for their mixture of races and languages—Swedes, Dutch, Finns, Welsh, Germans, English, French, Danes, Scots and Irish. A prosperous trade developed, with its centre at Philadelphia and its markets in the West Indies and other colonies; town and country were fairly balanced, with manufactures of linen, glass and leather to supplement the agricultural surpluses. Yet after Penn's return to England religious and political quarrels developed, and the council showed a marked tendency to develop into an oligarchy. In 1685 Penn sent out a new governor, Captain Blackwell, who was not a Quaker and was determined to set up an efficient government; but the opposition secured his recall, and Penn promised to accept any governor whom the council might elect. Quarrels continued, helped by a split among the Quakers themselves; although the colony continued prosperous, as a 'Holy Experiment' it was a tragedy.

Virginia came but little into the discussions between the Lords of Trade and the colonies until a late date. Dependent largely on tobacco exports, Virginia continued surreptitious shipments to the Dutch who controlled the European tobacco-market. Reasonably prosperous and stable, the colony took advantage of the constitutional confusion of the restoration period to declare that supreme power was vested in its Assembly and to elect Sir William Berkeley as its governor. Under him it returned to the Stuart allegiance, and he was ordered to accept the Assembly as constitutional and to secure the passage of necessary laws, but also to ensure that the Navigation Acts were observed and to discourage over-much planting of tobacco. Berkeley soon became almost an absolute ruler, naming his own councillors and gathering round him a party of wealthy planters, while the House of Burgesses became a close and oligarchic body, divorced from the popular will which it was supposed to represent. The franchise was limited to freeholders, and ill-judged taxation, unwise spending and administrative abuses caused a situation which was made explosive by the unstable price of tobacco.

In 1675 a brutal scalping of two settlers by Indians caused a fierce punitive expedition, and the whole frontier was unsafe. Governor Berkeley was old and weak, and the Assembly proved as ineffective as the governor. The frightened settlers chose their own leader, young Nathaniel Bacon, and enlisted as volunteers under his command, but were declared rebels and ordered to disband. Bacon's rebellion lasted until 1676, when Bacon took and destroyed Jamestown, and then shortly died of fever. After his death the rebels surrendered, and although the king had promised an amnesty, the embittered Berkeley put several of them to death. A new governor, Captain Herbert Jeffreys, then arrived, while a commission was appointed to review the affairs of Virginia and a fleet with five companies of regular soldiers was sent to crush the rebellion (which had already died down). The new officers sent home a sympathetic report of the grievances of the colony, and the charter granted after the rebellion confirmed the right of the colonial Assembly to control taxation and left it to the king to make land grants in future. The economic unbalance could not easily be remedied; there seemed no solution to the tobacco problem save freedom of trade, but legislation limited the number of ports from which trade could be carried on, and angry planters began to impose their own quota system by destroying their neighbours' crops. The new governor was at loggerheads with the Assembly, and another revolt seemed inevitable when the news of the downfall of James II arrived. When William and Mary were officially proclaimed they were accepted with relief; for since Virginia needed England both for the sale of her tobacco and the purchase of her necessities she remained, if uneasily, at home within the empire.

Maryland was bound to be deeply involved in political disputes because the proprietor, Lord Baltimore, an avowed Roman Catholic, was deeply concerned to secure liberty of conscience and was, by virtue of his charter, the owner of rights and privileges which made him almost absolute. During the Commonwealth his authority was defied, and at one time it seemed likely that the Puritans would set up an independent government. But, as religious issues took second place after those of trade and defence, Baltimore managed to get his title recognised by the Committee of Trade, asserting his constitutional claims against the assembly of the settlers who were claiming the right to enact laws without his consent. Baltimore secured his position largely by appointing an effective and sympathetic governor, young Philip Carteret. In Maryland too tobacco was the sole industry. In the uplands the soil was fertile, and output was enough to keep planters and farmers content despite falling prices and unthrifty habits. Labour was got from servants and negro slaves, and tobacco was the currency for the payment of taxes, fees and dues. As Maryland possessed no shipping its tobacco was carried largely in the ships of the New Englanders engaged in purposeful evasion of the Navigation Acts. With this Baltimore was in the fullest sympathy, for he held that the trouble with tobacco was not over-production, but restriction of the markets by the Navigation Acts. Yet he officially complied, collected the payments due and enforced the giving of bonds by shipowners.

With the death of Lord Baltimore and the succession of his son Calvert in 1675 a far more authoritarian régime was instituted. He did indeed strive to increase trade and prosperity, but he ruled by manipulation of interests rather than by taking the people into partnership; his friends and relatives controlled the administration, and council and assembly were constantly at feud. Apart from this, Baltimore had to deal with Penn and the disputed claims to river frontage on the Chesapeake. The dispute took both proprietors to England in 1684, and there Baltimore was detained until the revolution of 1688. His declaration in favour of the 'Old Pretender' passed off quietly enough, for the people of Maryland were scattered and political action was difficult. But rumours spread of Jesuit activity to stir up the Indians and massacre the Protestant settlers, the Roman Catholicism of the proprietor and his attempts to govern in an absolutist manner roused suspicion, and suspicion increased when no orders for the acknowledgement of William and Mary were published. Discontent came to a head in 1689: an association was founded to defend the Protestant religion and to acknowledge William and Mary. Baltimore's efforts were weakened by his absence in England and lack of support from the Lords of Trade. He was not formally deprived of his charter, but neither did they support his claims; for they suspected him of opposing their plan of uniting the American colonies and of enforcing restraints of trade by the Navigation Acts and the customs system. Maryland in effect became a royal province and the proprietor's claims were ignored.

Although the political and economic balance lay with Massachusetts, New York and the problems of the Jersey settlements occupied English attention for some years. Only when Massachusetts became involved in a serious Indian war did the Lords of Trade take a more active interest. This was in 1675, when the Wampanoags under their King Philip attacked the Quaker-controlled colony at Rhode Island. Other tribes soon joined, Connecticut and Massachusetts were drawn into the war, and the whole frontier was terrorised by burnings, scalpings and murders. The great tribe of the Narragansetts, with whom relations had hitherto been friendly, was attacked by Massachusetts, Plymouth and Connecticut, in order to forestall Indian hostility. Rhode Island, Plymouth and Massachusetts suffered pillage until in the summer of 1676 King Philip began to find it impossible to keep his confederacy together and in August was himself killed. With this war ended the last serious attempt of the Indians to dispute European claims to the north Atlantic seaboard. But the Indians had penetrated to the heart of the settlements, destroying growing crops, towns and hamlets. Famine followed the war; the fur trade was ruined, as was the commerce of New England, both with England and the West Indian islands.

While King Philip's War was still in the balance, there arrived at Boston Edward Randolph as a special commissioner to inquire into and report upon the colony. He was a confirmed supporter of Stuart pretensions and of that unified system of imperial commerce for which the later Stuart councils stood. He was also a devoted member of the Church of England and could see nothing but evil in the Puritan government which had usurped power. To bring Massachusetts into closer dependence on the Crown he recommended a *Quo Warranto* writ. The old charges were revived. The suffrage had been restricted, the boundaries extended at the cost of Massachusetts' neighbours, taxes taken from non-freemen, appeals to England been denied; the Puritans had evaded the Navigation Acts, set up their own mint and coined their own currency, thereby diminishing the king's revenue and upsetting the imperial system of trade. The colony did nothing to mitigate the charges and seemed more set on its chartered rights than on allegiance to the Crown; and the agents sent to London were told to discuss nothing which called the charter in question. Massachusetts only passed a law enforcing the Navigation Acts when English merchants secured from the king (whose revenue they alleged was reduced by £60,000 a year) an embargo on the trade of New England.

To enforce the Navigation Acts Randolph acted as collector, surveyor and searcher of the customs, in which capacities he had infinite power to interfere with commerce but little to enforce compliance with the Acts. He was supported by the governors of Virginia and New Hampshire when he claimed that the merchants and shippers carried on illicit trade with alien territories and that the magistrates connived at these breaches of the

Navigation Acts. The Lords of Trade were determined, as they began to canvass the idea of uniting the New England colonies into one dominion, that Massachusetts' charter itself must be annulled, as the king successfully discounted the charters of many English boroughs.[1] The attorney-general was ordered to proceed against the colony; Randolph had the satisfaction of himself delivering the writ of *Quo Warranto*, and in October 1684 the charter was declared null and void.

This left the Lords of Trade with the task of framing a more suitable form of government. They were set on the unification of the colonies, and the annulment of Massachusetts' charter was part of a general move. Randolph's commission applied to all the New England colonies and, with him to urge them on, the Lords of Trade concluded that chartered and proprietary colonies in general could not be reconciled with their plans. Where some measure of sovereignty had been granted away, the right to legislate brought into question the Navigation Acts which conflicted with the interests of the commercial classes in the colonies. One after the other, the charters of Connecticut, Rhode Island, the Jerseys, Pennsylvania, Maryland, Carolina, the Bahamas and Bermuda were subject to *Quo Warranto* inquiries. The death of Charles II in 1685, the turmoil of Monmouth's rebellion, and the impossibility of creating so many alternative governments, staved off the blow from all except Connecticut, Rhode Island and the Jersey settlements. But already it had become clear that neither the money nor the men were available to give to each colony its own governor and administration, and that union would simplify the problems of defence and, above all, of the administration of the Navigation Acts. Anxious to form a union, the Lords of Trade agreed to annex to Massachusetts the colonies of Maine, New Hampshire, Plymouth, and the Narragansett country, and to add Rhode Island and Connecticut as soon as their charters should have been annulled.

Despite the annulment of its charter, Massachusetts was allowed to continue with its old forms of governor, magistrates and deputies, and when the Lords of Trade placed New Hampshire and Maine under Massachusetts in 1685, they accomplished under royal auspices an expansion which the colony had long sought in an independent fashion. Connecticut also was incorporated in this New England group, the council of that colony offering to submit to this solution although the General Court had asked for incorporation with New York. There remained New York itself. When Charles II died and James became king, he could evade granting the Charter of Liberties and Privileges to New York and consider his lands there a Crown colony, capable of being added to the envisaged union. Governor Dongan, fearing French moves, was convinced that New York could not provide adequate defence unless

[1] See above, ch. XIII, p. 317.

Connecticut and the Jerseys were added to her, and when he learned that Connecticut had been added to New England, it seemed to him that the only means of producing adequate military strength was to add New York to that group.

Dongan's suggestion carried great weight, and in 1688 a new commission was issued, joining all the English colonies from the Pemaquid river to Pennsylvania in the Dominion of New England. The constitution, as proposed by the Lords of Trade, was to consist of a governor and council chosen by the king, and of an assembly elected by the people. James, however, ruled out reference to the assembly, and governor and council were left with powers to legislate, levy taxes, set up courts of justice, and themselves sit as a court of first instance. There was to be a right of appeal to the courts in England, and colonial laws were to be submitted to England for approval. The abolition of the popular assembly savours of Stuart absolutism, but the distances involved, and the cross-interests within the colonies and between the colonies, made an assembly seem of doubtful value; and the popular assemblies, especially in Massachusetts, were not always democratic or representative of the majority. Their abolition was, as experience had shown, the only way of ending the dominance of the Puritans, and the constitutional stringency was alleviated by the grant of religious liberty and measures to regularise and stabilise the system of land-tenures.

The union of the colonies was advocated largely for military reasons. The Treaty of Westminster ended the Dutch War in 1674, but laid the country and the colonies open to French attacks and French intrigues. The Dominion of New England, with Connecticut, was held to control a force of 13,279 militiamen, and the inclusion of New York to add a further 2000. Thus a regular force of about two hundred soldiers was supported by a reserve of over fifteen thousand militiamen—a formidable force for defence, and a powerful machine for the capture of the French colony in Canada if that should at any time seem desirable. The governor was, significantly, given sole command of the troops. But the extension of the Dominion to include New York proved a weakness, not a source of strength; the area was too vast for adequate communication, and the advantage of consolidation, which the Dominion should have brought, was dissipated; it lost any chance of becoming an economic and social unit.

The choice of a governor for the Dominion fell on Sir Edmund Andros, honest and uncompromising, but with a background of unsympathetic authority during his governorship of New York and of disputes with the Quakers of West New Jersey and with the proprietors of East New Jersey. His task was difficult enough, for the Puritans refused to accept the new dispensation. Deprived of their assembly, they declared that they were 'abridged of their liberty as Englishmen'. With an empty treasury and no legal power to impose taxes, the provisional government was bound to be weak, and indirect taxes (import duties, excise and tonnage) were levied. Though this did not arouse serious opposition, as direct taxation might have done, the whole question of taxes upon trade was at issue. While the Lords of Trade wanted to bring New England into a comprehensive scheme for imperial trade, the merchants of Massachusetts were anxious to render the minimum of conformity and to secure modifications which would enable them to persist in their illegal trade. Something was done towards the enforcement of the Navigation Acts by making the four ports of Boston, Salem, Ipswich and Great Island the only places where goods might enter the Dominion and by creating a Vice-Admiral's Court for trying cases of smuggling. But Randolph got almost no support in his efforts to get the Acts properly enforced, and even the Vice-Admiral's Court could not be trusted to give uncorrupt verdicts.

Disappointed but determined, Randolph pressed for the dispatch of a regular governor, and the commission for Andros was hurried through so that he arrived in Boston in December 1686, as governor of all the New England colonies except Connecticut and Rhode Island, against which *Quo Warranto* writs were out, but whose charters meanwhile remained valid. Rhode Island submitted rather than have her charter annulled, and Connecticut was soon added. While the provisional government had been placatory and sympathetic and had done something to bring unity to the Dominion and to keep the colonists at peace, Andros had a much more intransigent outlook and started with the handicap that he was ordered to 'tear up a country's institutions by the roots'. Loyal to the Stuarts, he widely proclaimed the birth of the 'Old Pretender'; thus when the news of the Glorious Revolution reached America Andros was inevitably regarded as a royalist and rebellion broke out. Boston was the centre of the revolt; the fort, castle, and royal frigate were seized, Randolph was sent to the common jail and the governor himself imprisoned. The revolution was bloodless, but it overthrew the Dominion of New England. Connecticut and Rhode Island resumed their charters and reorganised their governments. Massachusetts was too deeply involved in conflict with royal authority for her opposition to count entirely in her favour or for the eloquence of her agent in England to achieve the restoration of her charter. Only in 1691 did William and Mary grant a charter, and then it was not such as it had been; voters qualified on a basis of property, not of religion, and appeals were allowed from the local courts to the King in Council. Yet the new charter pushed out the boundaries of Massachusetts to include Maine and New Plymouth, and thus perpetuated an important concept of the short-lived Dominion, that of defence against the French.

The power and stability of the French in Canada were negligible in comparison with the growing weight of the English colonies. The extent of the French threat depended on the determination of the rulers, the support obtained from Europe, and the determination to enlist the Indian tribes as auxiliaries. The vastness of the problem and of the possibilities of a French kingdom extending across the continent (whatever its width might prove to be) and for fifteen hundred leagues in longitude was realised. But the strength of France was fully committed to her struggles in Europe, and the achievement was as small as the possibilities were vast.

To achieve their supremacy in North America, and to maintain the fur trade on which their colony's livelihood depended, the French were convinced that they must break the power of the Iroquois confederacy—the 'Five Nations' of the Mohawks, Oneidas, Onondagas, Cayugas and Senecas; for the Iroquois were rivals of the Hurons and other tribes, through whose lands furs came to the French markets at Quebec, Trois Rivières and Montreal, and who were allies of the French. The Iroquois were tied to the fur trade of the Hudson river. They got their arms from, and took their furs to, the Dutch traders and were intent to harry and destroy the French colony. During the first Iroquois War, about 1640, the French accepted the conclusion that to free themselves from the Iroquois threat they must neutralise the Dutch colonies, either by conquest or by purchasing their lands. But France was racked by the Fronde. Weak government at home led to ineffective policy in the New World, where the French possessions in the Antilles were sold to private owners, the *Compagnie des Cent Associés* gave way to the *Compagnie des Habitants* in Canada, and in Acadia civil war was the prelude to the capture of the colony by the British in 1654. Montreal was almost abandoned, and succour arrived only just in time, with the Ursulines to supplement the inspired Christianity of the small settlement and a meagre reinforcement of soldiers.

There was in all this but little which portended any serious threat to British or Dutch colonial interests. Indeed, if the French were to reply effectively to the threat of Iroquois encirclement it must be by turning away from the areas of English and Dutch influence and recuperating their trade by routes to the north. The Ottawas, for example, welcomed French trade and the French alliance against the Iroquois. Even with allies among the Indians the French were hard put to it. By 1660 their total population in Canada amounted to less than 2000, and only the most tenuous and determined existence was possible there. The Iroquois prowled round the houses and fields of Montreal, women were seized as they went about their tasks, and the men carried arms at all times. In this year a band of Iroquois warriors descended the St Lawrence to extirpate the French and capture Quebec itself. But a devoted company of sixteen men, under the leadership of Adam Dollard, commander of the small garrison of Montreal, held them for eight days of bitter fighting at the St Lawrence above Montreal. They were all killed, but the Iroquois retired and the French colony was saved.

Later in the year a well-laden convoy of canoes manned by Ottawas brought to Quebec a supply of furs which enabled the colonists to maintain themselves. But the Iroquois remained an ever-present threat, and in 1661 Pierre Bouchier, commandant of Trois Rivières, was sent to France to solicit aid. Bouchier returned with about a hundred new colonists, but without military support. Although the governor pleaded for troops with which he could make Louis master of America, nothing was forthcoming until 1665, when, the Turks having been driven back in Hungary,[1] Louis sent the Carignan-Salières regiment of some 1200 men to Quebec: a magnificent addition to French strength, as previously the governor had only about thirty regular soldiers at his disposal. More important was the new sense of interest and urgency. Great concepts of a French-American empire were accepted, and the personalities of the governors and *intendants* in Canada gave weight and purpose to these concepts.

Under a new governor, an experienced soldier, the Marquis de Tracy, Canada experienced a reinvigoration which accorded well with the arrival of the troops. Montreal, which had enjoyed an independent status under the seminary of Saint-Sulpice, was brought under royal control in 1665. But a badly prepared winter campaign against the Iroquois did not defeat or annihilate them. Four of their five 'nations' accepted a treaty of peace, but the Mohawks held out. Tracy himself led another expedition which penetrated past Lake Champlain into the Iroquois territory, burned villages and destroyed provender, but could not come to grips with the Iroquois who withdrew and avoided decisive action. It was an impressive display by the most powerful army so far deployed in North America. Tracy had starved and humiliated the Mohawks. Whether they made a formal submission is not clear, but there was no further trouble between French and Iroquois until 1687.

Tracy's attacks on the Iroquois were defensive, for the existence of the colony was at stake; but they were also part of an ambitious plan for domination in the north. The display of French power followed hard on the English capture of the Dutch colony and was in a sense stimulated by the ambitions of the English. At New York James's governor, Nicolls, would gladly have attacked the French; but Massachusetts and Connecticut were not so eager, so that he held his hand. In Europe Louis, bound by treaty to help the Netherlands if they were attacked, offered mediation and, when Clarendon spurned his intervention, declared war on England in 1666. It was, however, only in October that the news was known in the English colonies, and by that time Tracy had safely extricated his army from the Iroquois territories.

The opportunity for an English attack on Canada was therefore lost, the more so since Louis, reluctant as he appeared to fight England, attacked with a will in the West Indies, where the English possessions in

[1] See below, ch. XXI, p. 511.

the Leeward Islands (especially St Christopher's) suffered heavily. Plague-ridden, fire-stricken, impoverished and divided, England was anxious for peace, and Louis was equally anxious so as to invade the Spanish Netherlands in vindication of his claim to the Spanish inheritance.[1] So the two powers agreed, early in 1667, on a restoration of the conquered Leeward Islands to England and of Acadia to France. England had not been defeated in the war as a whole, and the Treaty of Breda confirmed her in the possession of the Dutch colonies in America. Louis was more interested in the European aspects of the Spanish inheritance than in the vast possibilities of an empire in America. The loss of the Dutch colonies to the English, thus accepted by France, meant a change in the North American situation which cannot be overestimated; for Orange, Manhattan and the Hudson river were powerful rivals to Quebec and Montreal in the fur trade, and the *wampum*, which was the small currency of all Indian trade, largely derived from the beaches of Long Island. Moreover, the territory which passed to the Duke of York brought English and French into contact and rivalry and cut the French off from coastal advance to the south. From this time English fears were aroused whenever the French seemed likely to move south of the St Lawrence; and the French felt themselves threatened whenever the English colonists seemed ready to cross the Alleghenies and to emerge from the coastal lands into the hinterland through which the French must pass, by the Mississippi and the Ohio, if they would expand southwards.

The rivalry for position in America led to endless clashes; but France was absorbed in European projects, and although she was at the height of her power the English, almost in a client position in Europe, carried the day in America. But the French officials in Canada were not lacking in vigour or in vision. Jean Talon as *intendant* from 1665 to 1668 and from 1670 to 1672, and Frontenac as governor from 1672 to 1682 and from 1689 to 1701, brought to Canada a knowledge and a purpose which might well have changed the map of North America. For Talon the main problems were those of settlement. He brought the population of Canada, by organised recruitment of girls and boys, from about 3000 to almost 7000 souls, and when the Carignan-Salières regiment was called back to France about 400 of the men remained as *habitants*. The lands were granted in *seigneuries*, and the *seigneurs* had the duty of establishing fixed numbers of emigrants on their lands. But in 1666 Colbert told Talon that Louis thought it imprudent to deprive France of men in order to people Canada, and that he declined to accept his plans for making Canada a great and powerful State; and in 1672 he had to report that no revenue at all was available for Canada.

Yet there was real interest in France. In 1663 the Crown took over the colony as its property and adopted a plan for combining the French

[1] See above, ch. IX, p. 210.

interests in the West Indies and the north by establishing the great *Compagnie des Indes Occidentales*, so that the northern and the sub-tropical colonies should make good each other's wants on lines parallel to those which the English imperialists were accepting at this time. Talon's enthusiasms were always to some extent intermingled with his personal interests, and his lack of enthusiasm for the *Compagnie des Indes Occidentales* was imputed to his participation in trade. But serious efforts were made to encourage fishing and shipping, and industries began to take shape in weaving, leather-work, brewing and shipbuilding. For Talon such developments were but the preliminaries to expansion. He was inspired by the vastness of the American scene. Manhattan and Orange must be acquired, if necessary by war; the European wars offered great opportunities to conquer enormous and potentially wealthy lands in America, and he saw no reason why the French colony should not extend to Florida and the borders of the New England colonies, and even into Mexico. Fears of French intentions were fully justified.

The Treaty of Breda set a limit to the ambitions of both groups of colonists; all possessions were to be restored, and at least for the moment any French design on the key-area of New Netherland had to be abandoned. But the Mohawks had suffered a severe reverse and French prestige stood high; and there was a strong party within Canada which required little more than official connivance to carry French expansion through the Iroquois lands and into the south and west. The curbing of the Iroquois had been followed by a considerable movement to the west; the period in which Indians carrying furs for the French had been forced to run the gauntlet saw Frenchmen working outwards from the St Lawrence in pursuit of furs and French missionaries travelling in search of Indians. As the Hurons dispersed to the area near Lake Superior and Lake Michigan, and the Ottawas to the Mississippi, they made contact with new tribes and taught them the need of European goods and the potential market for their furs. The fur trade thus penetrated inland. The Sioux south-west of Lake Superior and the Crees to its north, expanding northwards towards Hudson Bay, were the two largest tribes brought into the French economic orbit.

Expansion to the north was not neglected, but priority lay with expansion to the south and west, if only because the Indians whom the French knew best reacted to the Iroquois check by a return to Lake Michigan and the surrounding area. The Sea of the South was much under discussion; whereas the normal fur-route, under Ottawa domination, veered northwards from the St Lawrence by way of the Ottawa river, Talon in 1668 sent a party to explore the southern route via Lake Ontario and Lake Simcoe and, in 1669, sent Louis Jolliet by the Ottawa river to the northern shore of Lake Huron, south through Lake Huron to Lake St Clair, to the narrows into Lake Erie, and overland to the western shore of Lake

Ontario. There Jolliet met a party of Frenchmen which was on its way through Lake Ontario to explore round Lake Erie and to seek the southern and western Indian tribes. Robert René de La Salle was its guiding spirit, but he was accompanied by two Sulpician missionaries whose presence indicated both the missionary zeal inspiring the French moves and the jealousy of the Jesuit pretensions. La Salle's overriding idea was to move south-west from the Iroquois country, with French control of the lakes at his back, and towards New Spain: an idea which occupied many French minds, including that of Talon. They hoped that the Mississippi (which figured in Indian reports as the 'Ohio') would lead to the south and west and into the Gulf of California and the Pacific Ocean. When the Sulpicians reached Lake Michigan they found the territory between Lake Superior, Lake Huron and the upper waters of the Mississippi full of fur-traders and a Jesuit mission established at Green Bay. While the fur-traders were fugitive and illiterate, so that the extent of their journeys can only be guessed, the Jesuits were determined and well co-ordinated, and by 1670 their mission was firmly established.

Talon spent the years from 1668 to 1670 in Europe, engaged in discussions with Colbert; he obtained moderate support for his expansionist plans and a Récollet mission to help him, and the Sulpicians, in curbing Jesuit influence. Stirred by the achievements of Jolliet, La Salle, the Sulpicians and the Jesuits, he sent an envoy in 1671 to Sault Ste Marie, where Lake Superior flows into Lake Huron, to claim for France the sovereignty of all lands bounded on the one side by the northern and western seas and on the other by the South Sea.

Thus French ambitions were given a definite and formal expression—and La Salle was moving south from Lake Ontario, while the Jesuits from Lake Michigan were ready for a journey south to the Mississippi. Even from France came the dictum that 'after the increase of the colony of Canada, nothing is of greater importance for that country and for the service of His Majesty than the discovery of a passage to the South Sea'.[1] The instruction was brought to America by Louis de Buade, comte de Frontenac, who arrived in Canada as governor in 1672 and became deeply imbued with a sense of its destiny, with the future of Quebec as the capital of a great American empire, with the ideas and plans of Talon. French expansion, nevertheless, could not be carried out according to plan. Frontenac himself was not hostile to the Jesuits; but Talon was, and Colbert and Louis were suspicious of their ultramontanism.

Jolliet spent the winter of 1672 with the Jesuits at their mission at Mackinac between Lake Michigan and Lake Huron and with the Jesuit Father Jacques Marquette crossed from Green Bay on Lake Michigan to the Wisconsin river and so, in June 1673, to the Mississippi. Disap-

[1] J. Bartlet Brebner, *The Explorers of North America* (London, 1933), p. 252.

pointed that the great river flowed straight to the south, when the Missouri joined them from the west they were doubtful whether they ought not to follow it upstream since Indians reported that it would lead to an open prairie and another river which ran into the Gulf of California. They went past the mouth of the Ohio, but then turned and began to work northwards. They were told by Indians, who were armed with guns which indicated that they had trading-contact with Europeans, that they were only ten days' journey from the sea and would run grave dangers, if they continued, from armed Indians and the Spaniards whom they would meet at their journey's end. They were convinced beyond doubt that the Mississippi ran into the Gulf of Mexico, not into the Gulf of California, and carried this news back to Canada.

The news set fire to the Canadian frontier, for it proved that there was substance in the rumours of a practicable waterway from Canada to the Gulf of Mexico, and that a French North America was not only possible, but would confine the English to the coastal areas bounded by the Alleghenies. Yet Louis, deeply committed to his wars in Europe, had little or nothing to spare for Canada. English neutrality was worth not only the support for the Stuarts which Louis promised in the Dover Treaties, but also a great deal of acquiescence in the New World, and Frontenac had to renounce all hope of succour from France. Even systematic emigration, especially of the young girls essential for developing a populous French colony, was not to be counted on. Forceful, ambitious, and convinced of the potential strength of Canada, Frontenac was compelled to adopt methods which were less direct and authoritative than he might well have chosen. During his first period as governor, up to 1682, he received no military reinforcements at all; it was marked by consolidation of the English position and by rivalry in the far north as the English Hudson's Bay Company began to develop a maritime route to the Crees and to the source of the finest furs which had hitherto come to Canada.

The initiative for the Hudson's Bay Company came from two enterprising Canadian *coureurs de bois*, Pierre Esprit Radisson and Médard Chouart, Sieur des Groseilliers. Both had come to Canada in their childhood and were familiar with the Indians in travelling and trading. In 1659 they pooled resources (they were brothers-in-law) for a voyage to the forests of Wisconsin, where they spent the winter with the Sioux and returned to Lake Superior in the spring to meet the Crees and to hear from them about the great Bay of the North and the wealth in furs which could be got there. They returned to Montreal convinced of the need to approach this Eldorado by sea, not by land from Canada, and anxious to rally French support. But the voyage from which they returned was contrary to a ban on trading with Indians in the woods; they were fined, forced to pay taxes on their furs, and derided. Determined to carry out their plan, they sought support in France and then in New England. While they were kicking their heels there they met the royal commissioners sent out from England to settle the boundaries of the English colonies and to bring them to loyal acceptance of the Stuarts. By George Cartwright the Canadians were persuaded that they could get support from England and were brought to London. They found Charles himself much taken with their stories and plans, and the group of nobles and statesmen engaged in formulating a balanced imperial policy ready to help them on a modest scale: in 1668 two ships set out from London, and one with Groseilliers aboard spent the winter at Hudson Bay and returned with a cargo of prime furs.

Spurred by the hopes of profit and urging the possibility of sailing through the Bay to seek a north-west passage, the group of courtiers and their city associates in 1670 secured an epoch-making charter for the Hudson's Bay Company, which set out an English claim as the counterpart of the French claim to the lands to the south; for Charles made the company absolute lords and proprietors of all lands on the shores of the Bay and drained by rivers running into it. Whereas the French were beginning to get some realistic notion of the lands which they claimed, the English had little idea of what was involved in this charter. Their posts in the Bay were insignificant, and their powers of penetrating into the hinterland negligible. They could indeed sail into the Bay with a disconcerting capacity for navigation in arctic waters, and their goods brought the Indians down to trade with them. But they did little or nothing to challenge the French or to assert title to their vast heritage, and even convinced themselves that their ambitions were reconcilable with French claims; for them the serious rivalry lay in the fur trade, not in any strategic claim to land—and so in fact the problem remained, for Hudson Bay never posed a military threat to Canada although it might seem (as at times it did seem to the French) to threaten encirclement from the north.

So little support was there in France for any expansion from Canada that the exploits of the Hudson's Bay Company were readily accepted. Colbert indeed fitted out an expedition to the Bay which might have anticipated the English had it ever reached its objective, and Talon sent an overland expedition from Montreal in 1671. A young soldier, Denis de St Simon, and an old Jesuit, Father Albanel, with Indians made their way to the shores of the Bay and formally claimed the land for the king of France. But when the English returned in 1672, to set up more permanent posts, they met no French opposition and slowly and unobtrusively established themselves on Rupert river, at Albany, and later at Nelson river. The French, however, followed up the expedition of 1671 and were soon trading furs on the headwaters of the rivers which ran into the Bay, and in 1674 Albanel reappeared, charged by Frontenac with the task of seducing to their French allegiance the two *coureurs* upon whom the English position depended.

Other explorers followed, and in 1679 Louis Jolliet himself visited the English posts. Though Frontenac was keeping a jealous eye on English development he was commanded from France to maintain 'good amity'; he was averse from supporting the Jesuits' plans, taken up with the internal struggles over the fur trade in Canada, and as much interested in southern expansion as in the development to the north. The *Compagnie des Indes Occidentales* had not succeeded in Canada; in 1674 its charter was revoked and Canada became once more completely dependent on the Crown—which confirmed the lack of reserves or support for expansion. As part of a policy of maintaining the colony without military support the *habitants* were to be concentrated in towns and villages and to be prevented from wandering off in search of Indians and furs. The fur trade was often carried on by giving spirits to the Indians, for whom brandy was an obsession and a grave danger. When drunk the Indian was murderously unpredictable, and from the start the Church opposed the trade in spirits; it was condemned as a mortal sin, and in 1669 Bishop Laval uttered an unequivocal condemnation with threat of excommunication. The secular authorities saw the dangers of drunken and riotous Indians but could not share in such complete condemnation, for too much of the life and trade of Canada was at stake. The long struggle for power came to a head in 1678, when Frontenac presided over a great debate in the Assembly of Quebec and a majority favoured freedom to trade spirits. In 1679 a compromise was arranged that spirits might indeed be traded to Indians in towns and markets, where allegedly little harm was done and supervision was effective; but none should be taken into the woods, for there trade could not be controlled and, if the Indians got out of hand, no remedy was available.

Even this compromise was modified by a system of *congés* which permitted some *coureurs* to trade in the woods. In theory their number was limited to twenty-five, and permission to trade spirits was not explicitly included. But in practice the number of *coureurs* always exceeded that of *congés*, and they always carried spirits. It was said that almost the whole of Canada was involved in illicit trade, and despite urgent commands from Colbert Frontenac did nothing effective to stop the evasions. He was strongly suspected of participating in the trade, argued that the only alternative was to let the furs go to the Dutch or English, and was a personal friend of some notorious *coureurs*. Thus the *coureurs* pushed French influence to the south and west against the policy of the French court. They met a real need, apart from grandiose schemes for creating a French empire; for the Iroquois were recovering and beginning to press into the Ohio country and the Ottawa territory, with a resultant diversion of furs to Orange and New York. To counteract Iroquois threats and to guard the Ottawas' route to Montreal, Frontenac himself in 1673 took a force of 400 soldiers to Lake Ontario and there built Fort Frontenac. It was well-sited for its purpose, impressed the Iroquois and prevented the Ottawas from joining the Iroquois–English alliance. In theory, Fort Frontenac should have been supplemented by another French post south of Lake Ontario, which would have dominated the routes of the Iroquois trading to New York. Lacking support from France, Frontenac built Fort Frontenac on his own responsibility, but not the southern fort, which would have been too clearly anti-English.

He did, however, support movements among the *coureurs* which opened the frontiers of Canada and presaged a threat to the English, particularly to any English notions of expansion into the interior. La Salle had ended his wanderings of 1669–72 without finding his way down the Mississippi, but his activity was by no means ended. He was a fur-trader rather than a pure explorer, anxious to develop the trade on a large scale on the Great Lakes, the Ohio and the Mississippi. A series of posts would give to France the right to the heart of the continent; having made such a claim and substantiated it with forts, she must then colonise and rule. La Salle was strongly supported by Talon and managed to work with the Iroquois, from whom he seems to have learned the art of covering long distances on foot, which freed him from the normal French dependence on canoes and rivers. The revival of Iroquois ambitions and the disturbances in the fur trade caused by war between the Iroquois and the Illinois set La Salle off down the Mississippi. He had spent the intervening years trying to organise transport to Lake Ontario and on to Lake Michigan by large boats, instead of by canoes, and had secured letters patent authorising him to discover the west, to erect forts and to enjoy a monopoly of trade on the Mississippi for five years as long as he did not trade to Montreal. He set out early in 1682, with a strong flotilla of canoes, which could take him past any opposition; in April he reached the Gulf of Mexico and took possession in the name of the king of France. This flaunted French pretensions against Spain rather than against England; but the English colonies would be enclosed and restricted if the French founded a defensible colony at the great river's mouth and made the river valley their own. Louisiana was to prove of no great value to France, but the river valley was now known, and the search for furs was to draw Frenchmen into the back-country behind the southern English settlements.

While this southern drive presented a real threat to any English ambitions for expansion, most of Frontenac's support was given to a thrust westwards by Daniel Greysolon, Sieur Dulhut, who intended to set up a fur trade régime in the area west of Lake Superior and to control the routes to the west, and perhaps to the Sea of the West, as La Salle hoped to control the way to the Sea of the South. He established himself among the Sioux of this area in 1679, but was diverted from westward exploration when he learned that a party of Récollet missionaries had been taken prisoner; he went south to rescue them, and then returned to Quebec to answer the charge that he was organising an unlicensed trade. His move to the west of Lake Superior took him to an area where his posts interrupted the flow of furs to New York and brought him into contact with the Crees and Assiniboines whose furs went by way of Lake Winnipeg or Lake Nipigon to Hudson Bay. For the moment his work was interrupted, for Duchesnau as *intendant*, while agreeing with Frontenac's aims, was in sharp disagreement over the dangers of dispersing population by connivance at the illicit fur trade (and the brandy trade that went with it) and responsible for accusations against Dulhut, and indeed against Frontenac himself. Both *intendant* and governor, equally convinced of the need to counter the Hudson's Bay Company, to watch the Jesuits, to get possession of New York and to hem in the English by control of the Mississippi valley, were recalled to France in 1682.

This recall was unfortunate, for the Iroquois were once more reaching for power. Although Antoine Lefebvre de La Barre, successor to Frontenac as governor, formerly lieutenant-general in the French West Indies, had shown strong hostility to English interests and belonged by nature and conviction to the expansionist party, the instructions which he received from France were dictated by fear that solid settlement might be sacrificed to expansion, and the settlements themselves be so thinly inhabited as to be insecure. Frontenac's remedy had been a policy of Christianising the Indians and intermarrying with them, so as to create a numerous and loyal population of *métis*. But although *métis* children were already a feature of life in Canada, they proved averse to agriculture and addicted to hunting and wandering. The French were rightly concerned with the consequences of dispersal, and La Barre was instructed that expansion would be disadvantageous and that he should refuse permits for voyages with the sole exception of La Salle's down the Mississippi. It was clear that the Iroquois would soon cause trouble again, that the English would support them, and that the potential danger of the English contacts with Hudson Bay was recognised in France.

La Barre's first problem was to rehabilitate Quebec after the disastrous fire of 1682. This threw him into the arms of the most energetic of the local inhabitants, and he came to rely on Charles Aubert de la Chesnaye. He was above all a fur merchant; he had dealings in most trades, and much of a hand in the finances of the colony; his chief object was to make Canada change from an overland approach to the American continent to fishing and a maritime approach to the fur trade of Hudson Bay. The Jesuit Albanel had been instrumental in drawing back Groseilliers and Radisson to their French allegiance, and the plan to send a French sea-borne expedition to Hudson Bay coincided with the debacle of the Exclusion Bill and with the fall from power of Shaftesbury and many of those interested in the Hudson's Bay Company and in the general organisation of English colonial interests. The Company survived the political changes, though with an almost complete change of directorate; but French opposition grew with changing circumstances and the powerful prompting of de la Chesnaye. In 1682 he secured in France the establishment of a *Compagnie de la Baie d'Hudson* and organised the expedition of two French ships from Quebec, taking Radisson and Groseilliers to Nelson river in Hudson Bay. With two such experienced men in the field the French had a great advantage although their ships and goods were not adequate for the task. The Hudson's Bay Company had not yet set up a post at Nelson river: their expedition of 1682 was anticipated by the French, captured and absorbed, as was an interloping expedition from Boston.

Thus the French *Compagnie de la Baie d'Hudson* held a minute post in the heart of the bay-side fur trade, and secured a substantial cargo of furs largely traded for goods taken from English and New English ships. The two countries were still at peace, and the incident at Nelson river resulted in endless diplomatic discussion. The French challenge was serious and might well have destroyed the English position by the Bay if it had been continuous, or if the French could have made profitable use of the furs thus obtained. But the prices at which furs might be bought or sold were rigidly controlled in the (supposed) interests of the financiers who farmed the revenues of the colony, giving a fixed revenue in return for the taxes on the fur trade and for the exclusive right to participate in that trade. The quantity of fur thrown into this system was limited only by the *habitants*' ability to get furs. Thus prices could not fall, the French fur market was glutted and inflexible and, attractive as the fine pelts from Hudson Bay were to the traders, they caused great difficulties within the colony.

The maritime approach to the Bay was, moreover, contrary to La Barre's policy; for soon after his arrival in Canada he declared that he would not challenge the English possession of the coastal trade, but if they advanced their 'noisome little forts' into the hinterland, he would oppose them. There was in fact no sign of such penetration by the English (and very little talk about it either), and La Barre's threat was part of the project outlined by Jolliet, Frontenac and Dulhut for cutting off the Assiniboines, the Sioux and the Crees, who would take their furs down to the Bay. The French could go far to stifle the English trade by occupying the headwaters of the rivers running into the Bay. This, rather than a frontal, sea-borne attack on the English posts, was their general policy; by 1684 Dulhut was set up in the Cree territory, in correspondence with the small French post at Nelson river and confident that he could drive the English from the Bay without laying a finger on them.

In 1684 La Barre began sending French emissaries overland towards the

Bay by way of Lake Nemiskau, where they were to build a post and to intercept the trade going down to the English, as Dulhut was intercepting it farther west. Simultaneously he allowed the organisation of a *Compagnie du Nord*, an active Canadian version of the official *Compagnie de la Baie d'Hudson*, which undertook a further maritime expedition to the Bay, to reprovision and reinforce the small post which the 1682 expedition had established. It was not a vigorous venture and met opposition of a type which it had not expected. Colbert's successors were anxious not to antagonise England and not only reprimanded La Barre for his part in the expeditions to Hudson Bay, but persuaded Radisson and Groseilliers to return into English service and to destroy the post which they had themselves set up. La Barre was in equal trouble for favouring a challenge in the west and south, where Dulhut was responsible for the establishment of French posts to the north of Lake Superior and on Lake Nipigon, and Michillimackinac and Detroit were developed into French posts. In addition, many undisciplined *coureurs* carried European goods in increasing quantities into the Great Lakes area and seriously disrupted the middleman trade of the Ottawas and other tribes, who turned to 'the Flemings and the English of New Yorck' for better and cheaper goods, and to the Iroquois for support against the French.

By 1683 La Barre was convinced that the Iroquois would always be hostile to the French and would incessantly try to starve the French fur trade and to overthrow their posts. A preventive war had universal support in Canada, and he got together a force of 800 men and embarked on a campaign, from which the French emerged with a peace virtually dictated by their enemies, though he had not been defeated in open battle. In his discomfiture he turned to Dongan as governor of New York, asking him to arbitrate between the French and the Iroquois. Their previous correspondence should have given La Barre ample warning that Dongan would be hostile to French pretensions, for he claimed that the French had no right to set up posts on Lake Erie, Lake Huron or Lake Michigan; for him the St Lawrence and the north shore of Lake Ontario were the boundary of Canada. He agreed to call the Iroquois to Orange, but in a way which emphasised that they stood under his government. In accepting this La Barre in effect renounced any French claims to suzerainty under the treaty concluded by Tracy with the Iroquois in 1667 and forfeited the good will of all ranks in the colony. He and his *intendant* de Meules, who had strongly supported his attack on the Iroquois, were recalled.

La Barre was replaced in 1685 by an experienced soldier, the Marquis de Denonville, who brought professional troops with him from France; it was expected that he would vindicate the French position against the Iroquois, the English of New York, and the English of Hudson Bay. Of these projects that against Hudson Bay took shape first and had the most spectacular success. The *Compagnie du Nord*, representing the most enterprising traders and merchants of Quebec as organised by de la Chesnaye, obtained a grant of the trade of Nelson river for thirty years in return for supporting a further venture to the Bay. This was to be a clear military attack on the English posts, to be conducted overland and not by sea. A hundred men set off from Montreal in canoes in March 1686, commanded by a young regular soldier, the Chevalier de Troyes; but the expedition derived its strength from the contingent of native-born Canadian *voyageurs* and the leadership of three brothers of the remarkable family of Le Moyne. When the French reached the Bay they found the English quite unprepared, and they captured the posts and ships, one after the other, in a series of exhilarating skirmishes. By mid-August, when de Troyes began his journey back to Canada, the small new post at Nelson river was the only post left in English hands and the French conducted an active trade with the goods taken from the English.

England and France were formally at peace, and de Troyes had not been instructed to capture the English posts, but only to secure the renegade Canadian Radisson. But his real object was well known (even the English knew the expedition was planned!) and his success was warmly applauded. Yet in ignorance of the actual state of affairs commissioners met in November 1686 to conclude a treaty 'for the quieting and determining all Controversies and Disputes that have arisen or may hereafter arise between the Subjects of both Crowns in America'. The French well knew of de Troyes's successes but concealed their knowledge until the treaty was signed, for it was based on an agreement to accept the *status quo* and therefore left in French hands the posts on the Bay which de Troyes had captured. The Edict of Nantes had just been revoked, English merchants were in grave difficulties in France, and though James II seemed reasonably secure on his throne, his pro-Catholic and Francophil policy was causing uneasiness; the talks preceding the treaty were kept secret for fear that parliamentary opposition would prevent a conclusion. When therefore it became apparent that the treaty sacrificed the English position in Hudson Bay, resentment against James considerably increased. The treaty also handed over the Indian position to the French, for each monarch agreed to refrain from assisting the 'wild Indians' with whom the other might be at war. No mention was made of the English claim to sovereignty over the Iroquois; the effect was to allow the French to use their troops for a full-scale punitive raid.

The French had secured the advantage, but the treaty was of little effect. Dongan was officially tied to the English policy of pacification of the French, but this was the period of the formation of the Dominion of New England and of the ill-concealed preparation of a military force to hold the French and, if desired, to overwhelm them. For Dongan an alliance with the Iroquois was essential, for the New England Dominion met with great opposition from the individual colonies; and early in 1686, while the French were making their way north to Hudson Bay, he convened an assembly of the Five Nations of the Iroquois and persuaded them that a French attack was inevitable and had best be anticipated. Dongan himself prepared to take the French posts at Niagara and Michillimackinac in the spring of 1687, so that at these vital points the French would be sealed off from expansion southwards.

Denonville for his part had early realised the need to acquire New York and was urging that James II, in his need, might sell it for French support. But though the posts in Hudson Bay might be sacrificed New York could not be bartered, and as it seemed probable that more and more of the furs on which Canada depended would be pillaged or diverted to New York, Denonville accepted the conclusion that a 'defensive' war was essential if Canada was to survive. While an ostensible peace reigned, hostilities could not long be deferred after the French had invited the Iroquois to a banquet at Fort Frontenac, seized between twenty and fifty and sent them as galley-slaves to France. It was a treacherous blow, but it seemed to promise success. As Dongan knew that the French had some 1500 regular soldiers at their disposal, whereas the English colonies were disunited and could depend only on the reluctant support of their militia, he was unwilling to provoke open hostilities by supporting the Iroquois. But when Denonville assembled his troops at Lake Ontario in July 1687, supported by Canadian militiamen and the Ottawas, he found it impossible to bring the Iroquois to battle. They retreated; he ravaged their lands and burned their crops; but their casualties were slight, and they returned as soon as he had gone.

Jesuit influence then induced the Iroquois to send ambassadors to Montreal to negotiate, but the Hurons of Michillimackinac massacred the ambassadors *en route*, and this was attributed to French bad faith. The Iroquois were bent on a war of revenge. At New York Governor Andros formally took them under English protection, some 2000 Iroquois armed with European weapons attacked Canada, and Denonville could do nothing but withdraw. The French outside Canada were recalled and all departures from the colony forbidden. The French posts at Detroit, Niagara and Frontenac were evacuated; the Iroquois demolished them and, arrogant with victory, spread out in bands which reached to the Atlantic and even to Florida. An appeal to France for more regular troops, with the prospect of overthrowing the English as well as the Iroquois, met with no response. Canada was on the defensive; governor and settlers were in real fear, not only of the failure of their ambitions, but of actual extermination. In August 1689 over a thousand Iroquois fell upon the French settlers at La Chine and massacred them. Over 300 victims, men, women and children were butchered, and terror seized the French. The massacre of La Chine completed the work which Denonville had begun.

At the end of a period marked by consistent plans for expansion, the colony was reduced to a few small posts in the St Lawrence valley. The Iroquois alliance, rather than the more grandiose Dominion of New England, had vindicated the English tenure of the strategically sited former Dutch posts; the danger of a 'defensive' policy of expansion from Canada was for the moment over; to save Canada it was thought necessary to recall Denonville and to send Frontenac out for a second term as governor.

CHAPTER XV

SPAIN AND HER EMPIRE

THE period between 1648 and 1688 was one of acute crisis for Spain: demographic, economic, social, political and spiritual. In 1648 the economic depression of the seventeenth century was in one of its most serious phases, while by 1688 recovery was already perceptible, especially in the eastern parts. This change, which reflected the general European development, operated also in demography, with a rise in population on the coasts, and stability or even decline in the interior. This was also a period during which the outlying areas, especially Catalonia, asserted themselves, and centralising tendencies suffered a set-back. When the Catalan rising was put down in 1652, Philip IV (1621–65), instead of imposing the full authority of the absolute monarchy, re-established the special position of Catalonia. This was in accordance with the new legalism which can be noticed in the Spanish State of Philip IV and Charles II (1665–1700) and parallel with the demographic and economic importance of the periphery.

In the international sphere, the Peace of Westphalia marked the collapse of the Spanish plan for a Habsburg hegemony. Spain abdicated her position as a great power and withdrew within herself. She was concerned only with defending her colonies, and especially her own territory, from the imperialism of Louis XIV, while Charles II's lack of an heir drew the covetous eyes of all western Europe towards Spain. This change had a powerful effect on intellectual life, stimulating meditation on the meaning of Spanish history, and rousing controversy between those who welcomed new ideas and those who remained faithful to the spirit of the sixteenth century.

There is insufficient evidence for a precise estimate of Spain's population in the period under review, and the experts disagree. Olagüe and Ruiz Almansa believe that the figure remained at about eight million throughout the century, while von Beloch and Earl J. Hamilton believe that it fell by 25 per cent to about six million. But in either case, the significant point is the contrast with the increase of the previous century, a contrast which is equally marked in the economic field. Recent studies indicate the recovery of Spain in the last quarter of the seventeenth century. The lowest point of the demographic curve seems to have coincided with the great plague of 1648–54 which, centred in the western Mediterranean, affected not only the eastern coasts of Spain—from Andalusia to Roussillon—but also invaded the interior from the south and from Aragon. Once the serious wounds inflicted by the plague were staunched, the population began to grow. There was a marked tendency for the population of the coastal regions to increase, while that of the interior declined: this was true of Catalonia as well as of Spain as a whole. Castile, despite the damage done to Aragon and Valencia by the expulsion of the *moriscos*, thus gradually lost its leading position. It is perhaps interesting that the first *pronunciamiento*, or *coup d'état*, of modern Spanish history, which raised Juan José de Austria, Philip IV's bastard, to power in 1669, began in Catalonia and was supported by the kingdom of Aragon. Not all regions of the periphery increased in population, however: Ruiz Almansa has shown that in Galicia there was a gentle decline in the first few decades of the century, and that this was accentuated during the protracted war with Portugal.

The economic depression intensified the polarisation of society into a privileged minority and a large number of poor people, while both law and custom made manual labour incompatible with honour. The middle class was ruined and began to recover only with the general economic recovery after 1680. Furthermore, the mania for nobility became even stronger in the seventeenth century, and the Crown was lavish in its conferment of patents of nobility and even of the title of Grandee of Spain, as in the case of Valenzuela, minister at the time of Charles II.[1] At the end of the century the duke of Osuna wrote to the king: 'previously up to 40,000 silver *pesos* were paid for a Castilian title, but today Your Majesty confers this honour on persons who pay 40,000 *vellón reales*'—that is, one-eighth of the original sum. The clergy grew equally in numbers, some entering the Church who had a genuine vocation, others in order to prosper, or merely to survive. Conservative estimates put the number of clergy about 1660 as high as 200,000. As to the poorer classes, all the authorities agree that the number of peasants and artisans diminished considerably, while that of rogues, vagabonds, beggars and bandits increased: a result of the economic depression. A characteristic of seventeenth-century Spain was the progressive concentration of property in a few hands, those of the great landowning nobility, which, together with the Church and the Crown, held 95 per cent of the land. Various schemes of agrarian reform were evolved, but they had no practical result.

Earl J. Hamilton's statistics show a serious decline in the import of precious metals from the Indies beginning in 1621–5: early in the reign of Philip IV, at the precise moment when the foreign policy of the count of Olivares required large financial resources and a healthy economy. This decline, accompanied by the exhaustion of other material resources, helped to impoverish the country and to deprive the Crown of the assets which had made possible so many enterprises in Europe. Thus the monetary policy of the last Habsburgs, with the Treasury thrown out of gear by the strain of Spanish intervention in Europe, and with no possi-

[1] See below, pp. 380–1.

bility of increased taxation, consisted in minting ever more copper coins. This was not an exclusively Spanish phenomenon. By about 1620, when the exhaustion of the American silver mines threatened, the days of the silver currency were numbered, and not long afterwards—at the time of the crisis of 1640—silver virtually disappeared from circulation. At the end of the century Brazilian gold restored the position of precious metals and contributed to the recovery already referred to; but up to 1680 some European States had to fall back on the issue of copper coins. Copper had become the means of credit of an impoverished economy. In Spain the inflation, interrupted by revaluations and deflations, disrupted the economy and injured trade. The great inflationary period of *vellón* (copper) covers the years 1634–56, which are those of Olivares's ambitious foreign policy, of the crisis of 1640, of the defeat for Spain brought by the Peace of Westphalia, and of the continuing wars on two fronts, with France and Portugal. The inflationary measures were particularly intense in 1642, taking the form of a restamping, at respectively twice and three times their nominal value, of the coins of four and two *maravedís*. This led to a sharp rise in prices and to a 190 per cent increase in the premium on silver. The result was a drastic deflation within a few months, coins of twelve and eight *maravedís* being reduced to two *maravedís*, and those of six and four to one. The needs of the war compelled the government in 1651 to resort once more to inflation, and this was followed by a new deflation in the following year.

The period between 1656 and 1680 has been described as a monetary disaster. The government took fresh inflationary measures until the Peace of the Pyrenees (1659) ended the war with France. Then there was an attempt to secure effective deflation by withdrawing the copper coinage, which had not circulated at par for forty years, and replacing it with 'strong copper' coins. Nevertheless, inflation went on, the minting of coins continued on a large scale, and the premium on silver rose by another 150 per cent. In order to avert complete disaster the government reduced to half the value of the coins issued three years before, and in 1664 the silver premium fell by 50 per cent; but between 1665 and 1680 inflation again reached dizzy heights. Unauthorised coinings and the introduction of counterfeit money drove the silver premium up to 275 per cent and made the drastic deflation of 1680 inevitable. This brought wholesale prices down by 45 per cent; its seriousness can be grasped if we remember that prices in the United States fell by only 38 per cent in the crisis of 1929. The severity of the deflation at last introduced order into the monetary chaos, and six years later the position could be regarded as stable.

Earl Hamilton has provided us with a reasonably complete statistical picture of price and wage movements during this period. It seems that the wars of Philip IV and Charles II had only a slight effect on them. For example, in 1650, at the height of the French war and after many years of incessant struggle in Europe, there was a substantial fall in prices, while their greatest rise of the century occurred in 1663–4, a time of comparative tranquillity despite the war with Portugal. The cycle of inflation and deflation, the monetary and economic chaos, and the disproportion between prices and wages—wages rising faster than prices—had a disastrous effect. All this applies to the kingdom of Castile. In Valencia, between 1651 and 1673, there was an appreciable fall in both wages and prices. Wages reached the highest point of the century in 1680, fell in 1681–7, and rose again in 1689–92; while prices fell in 1689 and remained more or less constant between 1690 and 1692. In Catalonia, we have information only on wages, which trebled between 1640 and 1659, under the influence of war, and became more stable in the last quarter of the century. From the figures of prices and wages we can conclude that wages nominally sufficed for the necessities of life in the reigns of Philip IV and Charles II; but the monetary chaos makes it almost impossible to estimate their real value. Further, the continual depreciation of copper, the only currency available to the poorer classes, whittled away their earning capacity, while the burden of taxation seriously reduced their actual income.

During this period the failure of the aristocracy as a ruling minority became obvious. It had monopolised power since the revolt of the *Comuneros* and *Germanías* was crushed at the beginning of Charles V's reign, and since the days of Philip III (1598–1621) the reins of government were in the hands of royal favourites (Lerma, Olivares, Haro) who belonged to the aristocracy; now it languished amidst the gilded magnificence of its coats-of-arms. The duke of Maura, who knew his subject well, described the Spanish nobility of the later seventeenth century as 'a limping, impoverished, importunate oligarchy'. There was indisputably an increase in the numbers of the nobility in this period, as much on its more dubious fringes (the great families augmented their property by advantageous marriage alliances) as among the simple *hidalgos*. These constituted a kind of proletariat among the nobility, and were—as in other western European countries—an element of political and social instability. The Spanish literature of the time provides ample evidence for the mania to be a knight and an *hidalgo* which obsessed the country. Some have blamed the *hidalgo* for his 'wretched pride', while others have seen him as the embodiment of a code of idleness. After the drastic deflation of 1680, there was a reaction against the idleness of the nobility: a royal decree stipulated that the possession of factories and manufactures was compatible with aristocratic status, provided that their owners had paid employees to run them. We must, moreover, remember that the tax-paying citizen, who received all the disadvantages and none of the advantages of society, had much to gain from buying a patent of nobility. The *hidalgos*, in exchange for their exemption from tax, had to render military services. When the urgent needs of the Crown compelled it to limit these exemptions, the *hidalgos* reconciled themselves to pay general but not personal taxes and clung to the legal fiction which exempted them from figuring in the tax lists.

The Spanish aristocracy seemed to have reached the limit of its creative possibilities when it assumed the direct responsibilities of power with the system which may be described as a 'collegiate aristocracy': a favourite presiding over government by the Councils. But it failed. The exaggerated cult of honour and the pejorative implications of work, hence the abhorrence of saving and of using capital in productive enterprises, exercised a fatal influence upon Spanish social life then as during earlier times. This example spread. On the eve of the financial catastrophe of 1680 the *tratadista* (social theorist) Alfonso Núñez de Castro wrote: 'Let London make the finest cloths; Holland, cambric; Florence, homespun; India, pelts; Milan, brocades; Italy and Flanders, linen...for our capital to enjoy; for this proves only that all nations produce craftsmen for Madrid, and that she is the Queen of Cities, since all serve her and she serves nobody.'

The number of clergy also increased, partly as a result of the crisis which impelled many to find in the Church a handy means of subsistence. There were, of course, outstanding figures whose virtues left a profound impression; but the vast increase in numbers did not mean a growth in quality. To remedy the ills arising from this development Charles II sent a circular to all his bishops in 1689: 'The number of those who have taken minor orders has recently been so great that in many villages it is hard to find a young unmarried man who is not in orders; many of riper years successfully seek ordination when their wives die; and almost all do this to enjoy exemption from the law, to live in greater freedom, to avoid taxes, and from other worldly motives.' Therefore he exhorted the bishops to suspend ordinations for the time being. It is needless to emphasise the Church's importance in political life, especially the influence of the royal confessors. Old religious and even political antagonisms set Dominicans against Franciscans and Augustinians, and Jesuits against the Inquisition and the Crown's power. Quietism was a movement typical of a period of religious ferment. As set out by the priest Miguel de Molinos in his *Spiritual Guide*, it regarded complete passivity and internal peace as the height of sanctity, so that the soul does not desire virtue or perfection and no external activity is undertaken. In this state man cannot sin, even if outwardly he appears to be sinning. Molinos carried on his activity in Italy, but his ideas exercised their greatest influence in France, in the circle of Madame de Guyon and Fénelon.[1]

We have very little information about the Castilian merchants and

[1] See above, ch. VI, p. 147.

burghers, though the depression must have aggravated their numerical weakness. Under the oligarchic régime, educated commoners wasted their energies in the bureaucratic posts of the Councils without being able to take a direct part in government, as Colbert, for example, did in France. Olivares's plan to replace the Grandees of Spain by commoners in positions of power had no positive result. We know more about the mercantile class of Catalonia. The war with France, begun in 1635, dealt a mortal blow to the great Catalan export trade to southern Italy; this threat to prosperity helps to explain the enthusiasm of the middle classes for Philip in 1640. The war of 1635 also affected the trade of Barcelona with the ports of Andalusia and the south-east, since French privateers were active in these waters. The later annexation of Catalonia to France ruined the Catalan merchants, who were incapable of resisting French competition and economic servitude. The feeling of the great *bourgeoisie* in Catalonia was strongly anti-French, and in 1652 the entry of Juan José de Austria into Barcelona was hailed as liberation. Only a small minority of 'new men', notably those interested in trade with Leghorn and Marseilles, were pro-French.

After the split caused by the events of 1640–59, the unity of the Catalan middle class was re-established and its collaboration with the monarchy firmly assured by the intelligent efforts of Juan José de Austria, the first Spanish politician to seek his main support in the eastern regions. Between 1653 and 1697 Barcelona paid the vast sum of 6,377,591 Catalan pounds to the Crown. As far as financial co-operation was concerned, Olivares's plans had been fulfilled. The merchants contributed decisively to the economic recovery of Catalonia in the second half of the seventeenth century. The principality's support for Charles II's monarchy went parallel with the abandonment of the economic conservatism which had tied the Catalans to Mediterranean trade. Henceforward they began to look towards northern Europe and America. A generation of Catalans, led by Feliu de la Penya, stressed the necessity of work and trade and urged the formation of a company to trade with the Indies. In 1674 the Aragonese writer Dormer held up the Catalans as a model of industry in Spain. Between 1680 and 1700 Seville's trade was almost halved, while Barcelona's almost doubled. Besides, the Catalan textile industry benefited from the free trade provisions of the Peace of the Pyrenees (1659) since, in order to meet French, English and Dutch competition, it was necessary to rival the products of these countries in price and quality. In these years the foundations of the future textile industry were laid.

Conservative estimates put the figure of foreign residents in Spain about 1650 at some 150,000. A policy of religious toleration was slowly beginning. The Anglo-Spanish treaty of 1630 stipulated that the religious beliefs of English subjects resident in Spain should be respected as long as they did not cause public offence. By the Spanish-Danish convention of

1641, Philip IV permitted the entry of Protestants into the country. A decree of 1679 aimed at increasing the immigration of foreign artisans without referring to religious issues. The strongest foreign group was the French—some 70,000 merchants, peasants (many helped to repopulate the valley of the Ebro and the Valencian fields after the expulsion of the *moriscos*), herdsmen and artisans. From the beginning of Philip IV's reign, the Portuguese gradually replaced the Genoese and in 1640 they had a prosperous colony of 2000 merchants in Seville. Thanks to their African possessions, the Portuguese had a ready supply of slaves for the Spanish Indies.[1]

The last foreigners to arrive in considerable numbers were the English and the Dutch. After the Peace of Westphalia, in which Spain recognised Dutch independence, the Spanish government favoured trade with Holland, largely as a weapon against France. Its flourishing trade with Lower Andalusia, the gateway to the Indies, contributed to the position of Amsterdam as Europe's chief money-market. The English were authorised by the treaties of 1665 and 1667 to establish businesses in Spain and to have a mercantile judge in the country. From 1648 onwards both Dutch and English merchants appeared in the Catalan ports to buy the spirits produced in Panadés and La Maresma. In the weak state of the Spanish economy, these foreign enterprises had a harmful effect since they almost monopolised the American trade. The *tratadistas* of the time noticed this and spoke of the wasting away of Spain. The economist Sancho de Moncada claimed with some justice that the foreigners were enjoying the best part of the country's assets, were dominating private and public finance and filling many benefices and offices.

The working class consisted of peasants and artisans, in the proportion of about four to one; their numbers fell during this period. The position of the peasants was very hard. The government took no effective action against the great landowning nobility, even though some *tratadistas*, like Bobadilla in his *Política de corregidores y señores de vasallos* (1649), urged the necessity of dealing with these 'powerful tyrants', by whom the peasants were completely crushed. The picture which contemporary authors paint is a sombre one: miserable dwellings, little food, and seigniorial oppression. The workers in the towns enjoyed a higher standard of living. The gilds lost their autonomy and were subordinated to the power of the State. The foundation of the *Junta de Comercio y Moneda* (Council of Trade and Currency) in 1679 involved the centralisation of artisan activities, since its functions included the supervision of gilds in their technical, economic and administrative aspects. The gild's exclusive and restrictive character was accentuated. But its privileges and its enmity towards freedom of work clashed with the beginning industrial system. In the *Cortes* of Calatayud (1678) an attempt was made to

[1] See below, ch. XVI, p. 386.

abolish the gilds altogether. Yet where money was plentiful the gilds flourished, as shown by the foundation of the Five Great Gilds of Madrid (which were to acquire considerable importance in the eighteenth century).

The prevailing economic crisis at times caused poverty to reach alarming proportions. The State reacted by fixing prices for essential foods, but this only made things worse, since the peasants found it harder to earn a living, abandoned the land, and swelled the numbers of the unemployed. The clergy also tried to alleviate suffering by providing food at monasteries; but the indiscriminate nature of this relief made begging no longer shameful and transformed it into a lucrative business. Nevertheless, some clerics reacted intelligently to the situation: thus at Palencia in 1664 an institution was founded which distributed food to sick workmen and to those unable to work because of the weather.

The severe blow sustained by Spanish agriculture through the expulsion of the *moriscos* (1609–14), and the subsequent slow and difficult repopulation, aggravated the results of the depression. Yields were low, and land which gave a net return of 5 per cent was considered very productive. Smallholders were progressively ruined. The close link between the Crown and the *Mesta* (the famous union of nomadic herdsmen) continued and enabled the latter to evade the attacks of the *Cortes*. A decree of 1680 recalled that half a century earlier there had been several flocks of 50,000 sheep, whereas 'now it is hard to find flocks above 10,000'.

Castilian industry was, in the period under review, in a critical condition, though there were hopeful symptoms after 1680 on account of government action. In 1655 the cities of Toledo, Seville, Valencia, Granada and Cordoba found it necessary to draw the king's attention to their plight. More than 7000 silk-looms closed down in the Toledo region between 1663 and 1680, and by 1685 only 500 remained. The production of woollen articles in Segovia declined similarly. In 1679 the duke of Medinaceli created the *Junta de Comercio y Moneda* and ordered Spanish envoys abroad to send technicians and craftsmen. The change which was affecting Castilian industry was symbolised by the decline of Burgos and the rise of Madrid, the latter being in contact with the Cadiz trade and the large estates of Andalusia and Estremadura.

The industrial depression explains the course followed by Spain's foreign trade. Between 1575 and 1675 trade between Spain and the Indies fell by 75 per cent. A French memorial of the late seventeenth century (1691) says that of 53 to 55 million pounds of merchandise which reached Cadiz, only 2,500,000 belonged to Spanish merchants; while 13 to 14 million were in French, 11 to 12 in Genoese, 10 in Dutch, 6 to 7 in English, 6 in Flemish, and 4 million in the hands of Hamburg merchants. Trading concessions to foreign nationals were a commonplace in the treaties signed by Spain after 1648 and were attacked by Spanish writers. For example, in the *Avisos* of Barrionuevo (October 1654) we read: 'A witty lampoon has lately appeared in Rome. It shows a fat cow with huge udders, and the inscription "Spain" on its forehead. The cow is suckling many calves, marked England, Flanders, Holland, France, Germany, Italy.'

The Crown's financial difficulties, leading to increasingly oppressive taxation, are revealed in reports to the king by the President of the Council of Castile. In 1654 Philip IV told the *Cortes* that of a revenue of 18 million ducats, which was collected by the Treasury, the Crown received only half, since the other half was already pledged, and that the debt had reached 120 million ducats. In the *Cortes* of 1662 it was stated that the tax payments of Castile had risen from 8½ to over 16 million ducats. The Crown's revenue came, above all, from the *impuestos* (taxes) of Castile and to a lesser extent from the *servicios* (voluntary payments) voted by the *Cortes* of the kingdom of Aragon. In 1610 Aragon, Catalonia and Valencia paid only 600,000 in *servicios*, and Navarre 100,000 ducats. To this must be added payments from Naples and Milan of 1,600,000 ducats. Revenue from Sicily, Majorca and Flanders was absorbed by the defence of those areas. Of the total revenue of 15,648,000 ducats in 1610, only 700,000 came from the non-Castilian kingdoms of the peninsula, while the Castilian excise alone brought in 5,100,000 ducats. In 1674 Castile provided over 23 million ducats out of the total revenue of 36 million. This alone does not prove inequality of taxation since there were also local taxes in the kingdoms. The very existence of separate systems of taxation, however, tended to produce inequality, and this was at the root of the struggle between Olivares and Catalonia which culminated in the war of 1640–52.

Since the middle of the century, Spanish America underwent an economic recession which had serious effects on western Europe. Financial reasons compelled the last Habsburgs to follow a 'cheap' policy in America. As Céspedes del Castillo wrote, the external result of this policy was a defensive attitude, which could not prevent certain losses, such as that of the trade monopoly in the New World and the establishment of foreign colonies in the Caribbean. The internal result was a decentralisation, which favoured the increasingly wealthy Creoles and which inaugurated the regional differences that became national characteristics after the Wars of Independence. About 1660, the population of Spanish America has been estimated at roughly 10,360,000: 3,800,000 of these in Mexico and 1,600,000 in Peru. The large majority (perhaps 80 per cent) belonged to the indigenous races; the rest were negroes, whites, mestizos and mulattos, in that order. By this time, the natives who lived under effective Spanish jurisdiction were converted to Christianity. Economic reasons explain the partial failure of the legislation designed to protect the Indians, and about this time the Indian population reached its lowest ebb. The consequent shortage of manpower had serious effects on production.

During the period under review money rather than birth largely conditioned the social structure of the Indies. The old aristocracy of the Conquest (*encomenderos*)[1] disappeared and was replaced by that of the great landowners, despite the *Leyes de Indias* of 1680, which forbade amortisations and the excessive concentration of landed property. The *haciendas* (plantations) flourished at the expense of the towns at a time of economic depression and restricted trade; they were complex and largely self-sufficient units. The leading group of Creole society consisted of their owners (*hacendados*), of administrators, and of *hidalgos*, the last being fairly numerous thanks to the extensive sale of titles by the Crown. On a lower level were merchants and artisans. Unskilled labour was supplied by Indians, negroes and mestizos, and slave labour was gradually giving place to free labour. Mineral production—for instance, the mercury concession at Huancavélica—took place in bad working conditions, and humanitarian considerations clashed with economic necessity. Heavy taxation explains the end of the old concessionary landowners of the Conquest; in 1687 a general lien of 50 per cent was imposed on them. Besides the Indians on the estates, there were settlements of converts, run by the religious orders, notably those of the Jesuits in Paraguay. During the seventeenth century the Spanish-American clergy concentrated great wealth and property in their hands. The Jesuits and the secular clergy became particularly numerous; many Creoles took Orders; and the Church produced such notable figures as Sor Juana Inés de la Cruz.

In the government of the colonies, all posts except the most important (that of Viceroy, for example) were sold. The rise in prices while salaries remained stationary resulted in an increasing corruption of the bureaucracy and increasing trade in offices. In 1688, for example, a Creole obtained an important post which he exchanged in Madrid for several mayoralties at a price of between 1500 and 4000 *pesos*. When he returned to Lima he sold them for between 15,000 and 56,000 *pesos*. The Spanish-American official was a businessman, who made capital out of his duties and diverted a good part of the State revenue into his own pockets.

The position of agriculture was difficult, since the mercantilist trade policies of the home country and the interests of the colonial producers often conflicted with each other. The mineral yield of Spanish America declined considerably after 1650. The Atlantic trade also suffered; after 1634 the Indies fleet no longer sailed every year. Everywhere the system of trade monopolies was breaking down, and towards the end of the century foreigners were the chief beneficiaries of trade between the Indies

[1] Spaniards to whom the government had entrusted the control and protection of native villages whose inhabitants had to render services to the *encomendero*: a system designed to prevent the enslavement of the natives.

and Lower Andalusia. Smuggling increased constantly; it has been calculated that, in 1686, legitimate trade could only have supplied one-third of the requirements of the Spanish-American market, and that the other two-thirds must have been smuggled. From 1623 to 1655, during the Thirty Years War and the subsequent Franco-Spanish War, English, French and Dutch colonies were established in the Lesser Antilles and provided excellent bases for smugglers trading with the Indian ports of the Caribbean. After 1680 the Portuguese colony of Sacramento was a focus of commercial penetration in the river Plate area. At the same time, any attempt to expand the economy of Buenos Aires was (until the liberal measures taken by Charles III in 1778) frustrated by the monopoly enjoyed by Lima.

The Spanish colonial system was characterised by an outlay insufficient to secure an even and reasonable return and succumbed to foreign competition. Once command of the sea was lost, the Crown relied exclusively, as a weapon against smuggling, on restrictive and totally ineffective legislation. Foreign interlopers could, of course, sell at much lower prices than legitimate traders: their goods could be produced more cheaply, since the rest of western Europe was more highly industrialised than Spain and the level of prices was higher in Spain. More important, the interlopers had no duty to pay and did not incur the overheads involved in the Indies fleet. There was a constant demand for their goods and the local population, and even the authorities, connived at their activities. The Crown reacted by trying to close the minor trade routes, thus splitting Spanish America into autonomous economic units (another factor which helps to explain the course of events after the achievement of Independence). The monopolies now breaking down were always in the hands of Castilians—a cause of discontent to the other peninsular kingdoms. Navarre, Aragon, the Basque Provinces and Catalonia frequently demanded a share in the administration of, and the trade with, America. The chief obstacle seems to have been not the Crown, but the powerful vested interests of the businessmen and officials of Lower Andalusia. The first move to admit these areas to a share in the benefits was not made until 1701, and really effective steps were not taken until 1778.

The political development of Spain under the Habsburgs reflected the same general tendencies as the economic development. There was a change from a centralising policy—which Olivares defined in a famous memorandum to Philip IV in 1626 and which caused the crisis of 1640—to one of decentralisation and return to legality under Charles II. The solution to the problem of the Spanish monarchy was delayed until the beginning of the eighteenth century (Philip V's *Decretos de Nueva Planta* of 1716) and was preceded by a civil war and the War of the Spanish Succession. Spain thus constitutes an exception to the general western

European tendency towards absolute monarchy, symbolised by Louis XIV: Habsburg Spain showed no change in her constitutional structure, except, of course, for the recognition of Portuguese independence in 1668. In Catalonia, Philip IV ratified the principality's charters and privileges in 1652 when the armies of Juan José de Austria occupied Barcelona. The failure of Olivares's centralising policy, and the pessimism which seized Castile after the military defeats in Europe, ruled out any immediate attempt to establish an absolute monarchy capable of imposing its will on the autonomous institutions of the non-Castilian kingdoms. In essence the constitutional structure which the Catholic kings gave to the monarchy in 1479 when—except for Portugal, Navarre and Granada—they unified the peninsula survived until the early eighteenth century.

The advocates of centralisation and of decentralisation were driven in the years 1640–52 to adopt more extreme positions. In Castile the legacy of Olivares's policy, and above all the reaction to the Catalan rising, aroused strong nationalist feelings which eventually proved to be the catalyst of Spanish unity. In Catalonia the reaction to Olivares's schemes strengthened local attachment to the old statutes and privileges which, although a guarantee of social and political security, impeded the recovery of the principality—a recovery which was leading the Catalans to play an increasing part in the political, and especially the economic, life of Spain.

The disasters abroad, and above all the Catalan and Portuguese risings, led to the fall of Olivares early in 1643. Philip IV was, however, incapable of governing himself and was strongly influenced by a nun full of virtues and good intentions, but with little political sense, Sor María de Agreda. The new favourite of the king was Olivares's nephew, Don Luis de Haro, who held effective power from 1643 to his death in 1661. In the last four years of his reign Philip IV made a supreme effort to reconquer Portugal, but failed because of the Portuguese victory at Vila Viçosa (or Montes Claros). Not long afterwards (17 September 1665) Philip died, naming as his successor his four-year-old son Charles; the regency was to be in the hands of the Queen Mother, Maria Anna of Austria, who was to be assisted by a regency council.

The regency lasted until 1675; in those ten years neither Maria Anna nor the members of the council could do more than struggle for survival against internal and external crises. Maria Anna handed over effective power to her confessor, the German Jesuit Eberhard Nithard, who was as politically incompetent as she herself. A rebellion against Nithard's régime was led by Juan José de Austria, the illegitimate son of Philip IV, and the actress María Calderón, the one hope of a society which had lost confidence in itself and longed for a Messiah. Juan José, unconditionally supported by the kingdom of Aragon, overthrew Nithard, but lacked the determination to take the reins into his own hands. A 'palace *pícaro*' (rogue), Fernando de Valenzuela, was given power by the regent. An excellent organiser of hunts and picnics, Valenzuela was able to supply the court with the amusements which were essential if it was to forget the state of Spain.

In 1675 Charles II attained his majority. His reign lasted for another twenty-five years, during which he was always ailing, several times critically ill, and subject to serious physical and psychological disturbances. Between 1675 and the Peace of Ryswick (1697) Louis XIV maintained a relentless pressure against Flanders and the Pyrenean frontier; while at home there was the choice between the Messianic approach of Juan José (who was saved from total failure by premature death) and the frivolity of Valenzuela. In the background were the queens, Maria Luisa of Orleans and later Maria Anna of Neuberg, neither of whom gave Charles II the hoped-for heir, the French and Austrian ambassadors, courtiers and confessors: all of them pestering the wretched king to achieve their own ends. In this corrupt atmosphere the efforts of a few statesmen, such as the duke of Medinaceli and the count of Oropesa, stand out all the more; reference has already been made to the establishment of the *Junta de Comercio y Moneda* and to the economic recovery which followed the deflation of 1680. The last years of Charles II's reign were dominated by the question of the succession; he reached real greatness in his defence of the Crown's dignity and his attempt to preserve Spain's territorial integrity.

Out of the Congresses of Münster and Osnabrück arose the Europe of Westphalia, replacing the conception of Austro-Spanish hegemony by that of the balance of power. The war with France continued for another eleven years, until the alliance between Cromwell and Mazarin compelled Philip IV to accede to the French demands. A new Spanish defeat, in the Battle of the Dunes (1658), led to the negotiations between Mazarin and Haro on the Isle of Pheasants, in the mouth of the Bidasoa. After long discussions the Peace of the Pyrenees was signed on 7 November 1659. This safeguarded the French frontiers and split Catalonia: France acquired Artois, Roussillon, part of Cerdagne, and a number of important fortresses on her eastern frontiers: Gravelines, Landrecies, Le Quesnoy, Avesnes, Philippeville, Marienburg, Thionville, and Montmédy. Bearing in mind the Emperor Leopold's rights to the Spanish throne, Louis XIV married the Spanish infanta Maria Theresa, who had previously been destined to marry an Austrian Habsburg. Although Philip IV stipulated that Maria Theresa should renounce her rights to the Spanish succession, this was conditional on a compensation of 500,000 gold *escudos*, which the impoverished Spanish Treasury could not raise. Half a century later this marriage was to give to the French Bourbons the throne of Spain. The Peace of the Pyrenees also gave France considerable trading advantages in the Spanish colonies.

Faced with the imperialism of Louis XIV, the Spain of Charles II had to wage constant war, while the European powers expected the dying out of the Spanish Habsburgs and even signed secret treaties partitioning Spain (in 1668 and 1688). In 1667 Louis XIV laid claim to the Spanish Netherlands on behalf of his wife, Maria Theresa, invoking a principle of Brabantine civil law as one of international law.[1] When Spain rejected the claim, Louis began the War of Devolution, in which he was opposed by a coalition of Spain, England, Holland and Sweden. In 1668 France restored to Spain Franche Comté, which her armies had occupied, but kept some strategic points in Flanders. The Spanish plenipotentiary, the count of Peñaranda, preferred to lose these and to retain Franche Comté, hoping to exchange this later for Roussillon and the lost part of Cerdagne. Also in 1668, Charles II was obliged to recognise Portuguese independence in the Treaty of Lisbon. After four years of precarious peace, Louis XIV began a new war against Spain, the United Provinces and the Empire. By the Peace of Nymegen (1678) Spain ceded Franche Comté and more places in Flanders to France. These weighty territorial losses clearly showed the catastrophic decline of Spain since the Peace of Westphalia.

There was, however, an entirely different picture in the fields of art, literature and learning. The Catalan philosopher José Ferrater Mora believes that what set Spain apart from the rest of western Christendom at this time was her stress on feeling, as against the prevailing rationalism of western Europe. The contrasting attitudes were personified by Cervantes (*Don Quixote*, 'a discourse on lack of method') and Descartes (*Discours de la méthode*). The Counter-Reformation certainly exercised a profound influence on the intellectual life, especially on Spanish literature; its pessimism and disillusionment may have been connected with the ideological isolation of the country since the reign of Philip II, the defeats of the Spanish armies in Europe, and Spain's loss of her position as a great power. The historian Claudio Sánchez Albornoz sees the Spain of Cervantes in opposition to the Spain of Calderón, saying that in the former reason conquers the spirit, while in the latter the roles are reversed. Américo Castro's thesis of a decisive Jewish and Moorish influence on the Spanish national character is now famous. In any case, the Spain of the code of honour and of the *autos sacramentales* (allegorical religious plays), the Spain of Calderón, made its cultural preferences quite clear. Constant wars against heretics caused the Spaniards to be preoccupied with religious issues. This helps to explain the predominance of theology and philosophy over experimental science, as well as the symbolism of mystical and ascetic poetry and of Calderón's plays. In a profoundly religious society, though one which was quick to find an outlet for its repressed passions, collective escapism produced mass entertainments like the theatre and the bull-

[1] See above, ch. IX, p. 210.

fight; while individual escapism retreated from the harshness of everyday life into private piety and the highly coloured world of the plastic arts. And when reality could no longer be kept out, biting satire and implacable denunciation were turned on the tinsel world of Philip IV's court, and on the frivolous Messianism of those who, in the reign of Charles II, looked to Juan José de Austria for a solution of all ills.

During the period under review literature flourished in Spain. Theology and philosophy did not reach their sixteenth-century heights. In the pure and experimental sciences, Spain had little to contribute. But an outstanding figure was the philosopher Baltasar Gracián, whose complex philosophical novel *El Criticón* won fame outside Spain. Saavedra Fajardo, Nieremburg, Ramos del Manzano and Solórzano Pereira were notable lawyers. In economics and sociology, Sancho de Moncada and Fernández de Navarrete were the most eminent. In the field of history, Solís, Melo, Nicolás Antonio, Lastanosa, Dormer, and Feliu de la Penya were important writers. The theatre was dominated by Pedro Calderón de la Barca, author of such diverse works as *autos sacramentales*, *La vida es sueño* (a philosophical drama conceived on the grand scale), and *El Alcalde de Zalamea* (an idealisation of religion, honour and the monarchy). In architecture, the Baroque triumphed completely with José Churriguera; and in sculpture, Spanish piety found interpreters of genius.[1] This was also a great period of Spanish painting: José Ribera, *El Españoleto*, of refined technique; Zurbarán, the painter of religious and mystical scenes; the pessimistic Valdés Leal; the Marian painter, Bartolomé Esteban Murillo; and, above all, Diego Velásquez, the portraitist of Philip IV's court and a master of historical painting, who produced works of outstanding importance in the history of the visual arts.[2] It was in these fields that Spain's greatness survived during the period of her decline.

In the sixteenth and at the beginning of the seventeenth century, Spain, under the strong leadership of Castile, played an essential part in the formation of the modern world—economically, socially and culturally. In the eighteenth century the outlying areas of the peninsula asserted themselves against the backwardness of Castile, so as to share in the new standard of living and in the enlightenment which was spreading in Europe. Between these two periods came the time of falling population, economic impoverishment and depression, a hardening of the social and political arteries, and spiritual isolation, particularly strong during the years from 1630 to 1690. Faced with the new world of capitalism and science, Spain remained aristocratic and introspective, disregarding the changes which were taking place in the world around her, and unable to respond to the check inflicted upon her by the Peace of Westphalia.

[1] For details of Spanish sculpture and painting, see above, ch. VII, pp. 173–4.
[2] For Velasquez, see vol. IV, ch. VII.

CHAPTER XVI

PORTUGAL AND HER EMPIRE

In Portugal in the second half of the seventeenth century a population of nearly two million occupied, as it had done since the mid-thirteenth century, an area of 34,000 square miles (55 to the square mile). Portugal's demographic position was thus stronger than that of Spain, whose density of population was only about 31–4 to the square mile (with a total of under six millions), and did not compare badly with that of the United Provinces, whose population was not much larger than that of Portugal. Yet, because of the injuries inflicted by war, there was no increase of population until the end of the century. Lisbon, the capital, had at least 165,000 inhabitants, a figure comparable to that of Amsterdam. Four towns had between 16,000 and 20,000 inhabitants: the university city of Coimbra, the great northern port of Oporto, and Évora, the grain centre of the south. A newcomer to this group was Elvas, the vital stronghold of the War of Independence. There were another thirty towns with more than a thousand houses each, most of them in the south.

The Portuguese Empire stretched from South America to China. In the vast territory of Brazil, which was being mapped by the *bandeiras*, the population, which had increased rapidly in the first third of the seventeenth century, later suffered seriously from the Dutch wars and the sugar slump and resumed a slow increase only towards the end of the century. The most densely populated areas were the north-east, Rio de Janeiro and São Paulo, the Amazon basin and the Maranhão. Europeans, Indians and Negroes together totalled half a million, about one-fifth of these being Europeans. The viceregal capital, Salvador (Bahia), had at least 8000 Europeans and a large coloured population. Rio de Janeiro was roughly the same size, while declining Olinda and growing Recife had about 2000 Europeans each; São Paulo was smaller still. Cape Verde, Guinea and São Tomé together had some 25,000 to 30,000 inhabitants. The population of Angola and Mozambique cannot be ascertained, but may have been between 80,000 and 100,000. In India, Goa, fallen into decline, had not more than 50,000 inhabitants, and in the whole of the Far East there do not seem to have been more than 10,000 Portuguese. Macao was undoubtedly the most thriving centre, notwithstanding the loss of the Japanese trade. Here some 6000 non-Christian Chinese rubbed shoulders with a few hundred Chinese converts and a thousand Portuguese families.

The axis of this empire, circling the world yet peopled by fewer than three million citizens, had been the Cape route; owing to Dutch expansion this was now reduced to a minor role and the Portuguese communities in the East lived largely by trading there. Some noblemen still set out for the East to make their fortunes: the Viceroy Luis de Mendonça, for instance, amassed 4 to 5 million *cruzados* in eight years, principally in the Mozambique trade. The trade in gold from Monomotapa grew from less than one ton per annum at the beginning of the century to 1½ tons by 1667. From 1675 onwards the Portuguese tried to direct this trade westwards and to make Mozambique the chief source of slaves for Brazil. The ships coming from the Indian Ocean generally put in at Bahia or another Brazilian port to load sugar and tobacco. This means that the empire became essentially an Atlantic one, based on Africa and Brazil.

In Brazil the sugar-mill owners and the merchants repeatedly emphasised that the sugar-plants were the sole foundation of trade. In 1645 there were some 300 mills in Portuguese Brazil, producing some 800,000 *arrobas* annually.[1] Dutch Brazil had about 150 large mills, with over half of the Portuguese output. After the final expulsion of the Dutch early in 1654 there were thus 400 to 500 sugar-mills (including a growing number of small ones) yielding over 1,200,000 *arrobas* a year. Three-quarters of them were concentrated in the area between Cape S. Roque and southern Bahia. While this region supplied the European market with sugar, the mills of Rio de Janeiro, though they too produced sugar, specialised in spirits for Africa. The sugar-cane was grown on plantations worked by slave-labour, which also supplied the manpower for the mills. This industry, manorial and capitalist in structure, contrasted with the cultivation and manufacture of tobacco, carried on in Bahia and Pernambuco by black and white, slave and freeman, rich and poor. With its tobacco Brazil bought the slaves it needed in Guinea and Angola. At the same time the consumption of tobacco in Europe and its export to the East Indies steadily increased. The tobacco monopoly in Portugal reached a value of 15,500 *cruzados* in 1638, doubled by 1642, doubled again by 1659, and continued to multiply in the following decades; 80,000 *arrobas* of tobacco reached Portugal in 1666, and 128,000 by 1672. The third most important export was Brazil wood, cut above all in the north-east; this was a royal monopoly. The *sertão* (hinterland) of Bahia, Pernambuco and Paraiba produced ox-hides—15,000 to 20,000 annually. From the extreme north came timber for joinery and cabinet-making and for ships. The total value of exports from Brazil to Portugal between 1654 and 1670 was 9 to 10 million *cruzados* a year.

The Restoration of 1640,[2] though it did not sever all links between Brazil and Spanish America, seriously injured trade. It is true that some small ships occasionally went to Buenos Aires; and the powerful governor of Rio de Janeiro, Salvador Correia de Sá, had family and financial links

[1] The Lisbon *arroba* contained about 32 English pounds.

[2] See vol. IV, ch. XV.

with Tucumán, on the Potosi road. But the Dutch seized São Jorge da Mina in 1637 and Luanda and São Tomé in 1641, holding them until 1648. Moreover, the Portuguese found it hard to provide Brazil with slaves, since for some decades they were unable to continue their previous practice of landing 2000 slaves a year at Buenos Aires; and they no longer had regular access to the Potosi road. Again, before 1640 the Portuguese had held the *asiento* (monopoly) of the supply of slaves to the Spanish Indies, and this trade was very slow in reviving.

Possession of Guinea and Angola had furnished the main link with Spanish America, thus gaining for Portugal much-needed silver *reales*. The Portuguese still held these African coasts, but from Cape Verde to Benin their position was very precarious and under constant Dutch pressure. The fact that they nevertheless held on was due to the supply of tobacco from north-east Brazil and of spirits from Rio de Janeiro. Angola, retaken in 1648, became the centre of the Brazilian slave-trade; but the hunt for slaves now had to penetrate deep into the *sertão* and became more expensive. The island of São Tomé stagnated: its sugar was no longer important and it lost its position in the Guinea trade with the loss of Mina. The Portuguese of the Cape Verde Islands, like those of Guinea, were closely connected with the negro world and the African trade of various countries in which they served as middlemen; beyond this, the islands played a part in the economy of the Atlantic because of their salt, exported to Germany, England and Denmark, and occasionally taken by the Dutch to the Antilles. Hides were the chief export to Portugal. Yet the islands sent little salt to Brazil, although they were on the trade route: metropolitan interests opposed this trade, but there was a small amount of contraband.

The Azores were a port of call on the voyage home from the Spanish Indies, Brazil and the East Indies and were thus favoured by smugglers and pirates. They supplied Portugal with grain, though wine was also important; but the Portuguese government restricted the supply to Brazil to three ships a year. Madeira was on the outward route to Brazil. Its production of sugar declined, but that of wine rose. Once more we find restrictions (2 to 3 ships) imposed on exports to Brazil. England and, to a lesser extent, Holland became increasingly important purchasers of Madeira wine.

The nerve-centre of the empire's economy was Portugal herself, and she adapted her economic structure to these conditions. More than three-quarters of her land lay fallow. Grain occupied some 2,250,500 acres, yielding about 15,000,000 bushels each year. It was thus necessary to import (from the Azores, France, Spain, and the Baltic) 2,250,000 to 2,750,000 bushels, or 15 to 18 per cent of the national consumption. It was the mills of Portugal which supplied the Brazilian and African colonists with high-quality flour. The cultivation of vines, olives, fruit and vegetables accounted for over 1,500,000 acres and grew with the demand from the colonial and foreign markets. About 1675 northern Portugal alone exported 30,000 pipes of wine. More important, this was the period when port was first produced; in 1678 408 pipes of port went to England. Further, in addition to the traditional exports to northern Europe of figs, raisins and almonds, from 1635 (when Dom Francisco Mascarenhas brought the Chinese variety to Lisbon) orange groves began to transform the coastal region of central Portugal; forty years later the export of oranges to England alone was worth 50,000 *cruzados*. France bought the same quantity, and Holland and the rest of northern Europe half the amount. Meeting the demand from colonial and northern European markets, olive plantations were spreading; this was all the more necessary since the battles of the War of Independence had devastated the olive groves of Alentejo.

The most significant export, however, was salt, especially from the Sado basin. In 1657 80,000 to 90,000 *muids* were exported;[1] in 1669 the treaty with Holland reckoned on a minimum of 107,000, worth 321,000 *cruzados*. Holland was by far the largest purchaser, accounting for four-fifths of the total. Apart from salt production, industry was on a very small scale. Portuguese fishermen had been ejected from the Newfoundland Banks, and the cod which was the staple diet of a large part of the people had to be bought from English fishermen. Shipbuilding, on the other hand, revived after the Restoration, with shipyards at Lisbon, Oporto, Pernambuco, Bahia, Rio and, for small ships, the Azores; but the oak and hemp used came from Danzig and Riga, and the Dutch were the chief suppliers of anchors, sails and cannon. Portuguese dependence on foreign sources was equally great in textiles.

Exports to Brazil, Africa and the islands comprised wine, spirits, oil, flour, salt and, to some extent, cloth and linen, produced at home, as well as fabrics, paper and metal goods received from other countries. At Lisbon, Oporto, Setubal and Faro, ships setting out for European ports loaded Portuguese wine, oil, fruit, salt, sumac, Spanish wool, diamonds and drugs from the East, sugar, tobacco and wood from Brazil, and hides from several colonies. Thanks to her sugar and tobacco, Portugal was able to acquire from Spain wool for re-export, corn, and above all the silver which enabled her to balance her trade and constituted the bulk of her coinage.

The movement of prices varied with different commodities, but the general tendency was one of stabilisation or a barely perceptible rise up to 1666–8; thereafter, corn, salt and olive oil held firm, while colonial products fell sharply during the recession from 1668 to about 1690. The basic difference between the two periods was clearly caused by a transition from war to peace. There is, however, another aspect to consider: if we express prices in terms of silver, there is first of all stability and then a

[1] The Lisbon *muid* (*moio*) contained about 23 bushels.

general fall, assuming dramatic proportions in colonial products. Monetary policy, then, acted as a brake on the fall in prices. In the late 1630's Portugal lost her two sources of gold, Mina and Arguin, to the Dutch, while Brazil and Mozambique were not yet effective sources of supply. Thus the currency depended on imports and during the period under review gold coins were scarce and silver plentiful; copper played only a minor part. The Portuguese financial system was closely linked to the Spanish. Fortunately for Portugal, the balance of trade was on the whole in her favour, sugar and tobacco balancing Spanish corn and wool; and the foreigners who sold their goods in southern Spain for Spanish coins paid with them for their Portuguese salt.

The international setting of the economy of the Portuguese Empire had changed profoundly since the end of the sixteenth century. The Dutch and English East India Companies had reduced the Portuguese carrying trade by the Cape route to less than a third of its previous size. Government and commercial circles realised that they were not equipped to face the competition of these great companies, and that State capitalism and the activities of individual traders had to be replaced by this new form of enterprise. Gomes Solis was its champion in oriental trade, but his company lasted only from 1628 to 1632. After the Restoration it was above all the Jesuit Vieira who urged the same policy for the Brazilian trade. The heavy losses of 1647 and 1648—an official, though perhaps exaggerated, report gives the losses as 108 ships in the first year and 141 in the second, out of a total of 300—led King John IV to create the Brazilian Trading Company, with a capital of 1,255,000 *cruzados*. The essential steps were taken in February 1649: immunity was conferred on the property of the New Christians sentenced by the Inquisition, and the administration of confiscated property transferred from the Holy Office to the *Conselho da Fazenda* (Financial Council). The company was granted the monopolies of exporting wine, olive oil, flour and cod to Brazil. Two squadrons, each of eighteen warships, were to be created and maintained, and a proper convoy system was to be organised between Portugal and Brazil. This was financed by duties on sugar, tobacco, hides and cotton, together with insurance and freight-charges on the warships. The company had some of the features of the limited company, grouping some of the strongest Portuguese trading houses—such as that of Duarte da Silva, the most powerful financier of the Restoration—with foreign, especially Italian, capitalists.

The company encountered strong and violent resistance. On the one hand, it threatened the prosperity of small ports by concentrating capital and trade in a few ports, thus impoverishing the provincial towns. On the other hand, the anti-capitalist, and to some extent anti-*bourgeois*, mentality of a society built round the aristocracy and moulded by the ideology of the Counter-Reformation and by hostility to the New

Christians, favoured the prerogatives of the Inquisition. Merchants were often, rightly or wrongly, accused of Judaism, and a hard-pressed and short-sighted State aimed at the confiscation of their goods. In May 1658 the export monopoly in the four commodities was ended, though compensation was paid to the company. In January 1659 the regent acceded to the demands of the Councils and the *Côrtes*: the Ministry of Finance was authorised to make use of the property of the sentenced New Christians, and in February the immunity which this property had enjoyed was lifted. The days of the company were numbered and in 1663 it was transformed into a royal council, with compensation for the shareholders. Despite the accusations levelled at it—insufficient convoys, inadequate supplies to Brazil—it had saved Luso-Brazilian trade at a time of great dangers. Once the danger was over, small ports and small firms saw their opportunities return.

December 1640 saw the restoration of the Portuguese throne, usurped in 1580 by Philip II and unlawfully retained by Philip III and Philip IV, to the only legitimate dynasty, whose rights were not diminished by the passage of time. It represented also a return to a legitimate system of State and government, ending the Spanish tyranny. An abundant politico-legal literature sprang up to prove the legitimacy of the Restoration, to secure recognition from foreign powers, and to establish the authority of the new régime at home. In the *Côrtes* of 1641 an official doctrine was formulated which was defined and developed in the *Consulta* of the Council of State of 1656: if power derives from God through the people as intermediary, the kingdom transfers full power and authority to the king. This is definitely a pact: it commits the subjects to obedience while the king rules justly and grants to the king the right to enforce obedience; on the other hand, it compels the king to respect natural law and the rules and customs of the country and permits revolt against tyranny or usurpation, the country being entitled in such cases to put a new king on the throne. Thus in 1640 a usurping tyrant was expelled and the rightful wielder of power restored. Significantly the Duke of Braganza was solemnly acclaimed king and took the oath before the *Côrtes* met, whereas in 1385 the *Côrtes* had elected a king, the throne being vacant; from 1580 to 1640 it was not vacant but usurped, and the Portuguese restored the government that had existed before 1580.

New taxes could not be levied without the approval of the *Côrtes*, specially convened; the heir to the throne had to take the oath during a session of the *Côrtes*; they had to decide doubtful cases of succession, and the king had to consult them in grave matters of State, vital to the national interest. The *Côrtes* had not met between 1620 and the Restoration, and only four times during the whole period of Spanish rule. Between 1641 and 1688, however, they met eight times, always in Lisbon, playing an important part in the reorganisation which followed the Restoration. Yet, even before the union of the Crowns, the role of the *Côrtes* had become far less important than in the Middle Ages (only seven sessions between 1500 and 1580). It was thus a State already absolute, with a hereditary monarchy and a bureaucratic machinery, which was restored in 1640, though better organised thanks to the administrative improvements under Spanish rule. The *Côrtes* consisted of representatives of the three Estates who met separately: the great lords and landed nobility; the archbishops, bishops and prelates; and two deputies each from 92 *cidades* and *vilas* (large and small towns). These deputies were elected by a meeting of the municipality consisting of *fidalgos* (noblemen), magistrates, citizens, representatives of the gilds (*Casa dos Vinte e Quatro*), the municipal judge,[1] etc.; nobles and ecclesiastical dignitaries were often chosen as urban deputies.

The role of the *Côrtes* being irregular and limited, Restoration Portugal oscillated between two forms of government: government by the Councils and High Courts, with the king restricted to appointing their members and to a very general guidance and supervision, and government by the king and his secretaries, with the Councils and High Courts as cogs in the administrative machine. There was, strictly speaking, no ministerial government, the functions of ministers being discharged by secretaries of state, *Vèdores da Fazenda* (Superintendents of Finance), and presidents of Councils and High Courts. During periods of personal rule by the monarch these functions were discharged by some favourite secretaries and councillors, and in either case an important part was played by the royal *Despacho*, those who took documents to the king for signature.

The Secretariat of State, dating from the sixteenth century, controlled the broad lines of domestic, colonial and foreign policy, and the armed forces. At the end of 1643 the king separated it from the Secretariat of *mercês e expediente* (which dealt with the appointment of officials, officers and magistrates up to a certain rank) and from the Secretariat *da assinatura* (dealing with the signature of documents coming from any Council). The secretary of state ensured continuity in government: Vieira da Silva, for instance, held the post from 1642 to 1662. But the head of the government was either a minister favoured by the king, or, as from 1662 to 1667, the *escrivão da puridade* (confidential secretary), a post revived by the count of Castelo Melhor and abolished on his banishment.

The Council of State, founded in 1569 and continuing the old King's Council, was clearly the supreme organ, deciding the issues of war and peace, and making the highest civil and military—and, in practice, ecclesiastical—appointments. The great lords had the title of councillor even when they did not perform the duties. Among the members we find dukes, marquises, counts, archbishops and bishops, but hardly ever magistrates or other commoners.

[1] The municipal judges (*juizes do povo*) were elected by the property-owners.

The Council of War was established in December 1640 and received its statutes three years later. All the councillors of state had the right to attend, but the regular members were the military governors of the provinces, important commanders, generals of artillery, the commander of the fleet, the viceroy of Brazil, and two judges of the Supreme Court, with a secretary. This Council appointed the officers of the army and navy, supervised fortifications, naval armaments, munition depots, foundries and hospitals, and was responsible for the general conduct of war.

The Council of Finance (*Conselho da Fazenda*) directed the financial, economic and mercantile administration. It was headed by the three *Vèdores* (Superintendents), all noblemen, representing specific interests. It consisted of three to five legally trained councillors, a Procurator Fiscal, and four secretaries. Subordinate to this council were the Court of Accounts, the *Casa da India*, the mint, civil shipyards and depots, consulates, the customs and other branches of the revenue, and the Brazilian Trading Company with its successor, the *Junta do Comércio do Brasil.*

Since the war against Spain required new financial efforts, and since the *Côrtes* of 1641 and 1642 wished to maintain control of supply, the *Junta dos Três Estados* was established, in January 1643, as a permanent organ representing nobility, clergy and towns. This had the task of fixing and repartitioning war taxation and of supervising the financial administration of the war. Its scope gradually broadened, taking in some sectors of commerce; but its original functions were slowly reduced to control of the less important taxes.

Also in 1643, the Colonial Council replaced the Council for India. Under a noble president it comprised six councillors (two noblemen and four lawyers), a secretary and two clerks. It was concerned with the government of all overseas possessions (excepting the administration of justice), the organisation of the merchant fleet, and colonial mercantile policy, except where Brazil was concerned.

Justice was the exclusive concern of the *Desembargo do Paço*, the Supreme Court originally presided over by the king, but since the late sixteenth century by a great noble, and composed of six *desembargadores* (judges), one of whom was an ecclesiastic, assisted by secretaries, clerks and a treasurer. The *desembargadores* enjoyed the status of *fidalgo*. This court nominated all higher magistrates and legal officials, could revoke certain decrees, resolved conflicts of civil and ecclesiastical jurisdiction, granted or refused appeals, decided on pardons, regulated livings, entails and privileges, and had to approve the briefs of papal nuncios. The Chancellery was subordinated to it. Below the *Desembargo* was the Lisbon *Casa de Suplicação e Relação*, the Court of Appeal for all civil and criminal cases in southern and central Portugal; cases in the north came before the Oporto *Casa do Civel e Relacão*, though some were reserved for Lisbon. The *Mesa da Consciência e Ordens* administered the Military

Orders and was consulted by the king on matters of conscience, such as the property of those condemned by the Inquisition.

Thus the machinery of State was firmly in the hands of the great nobility, the high clergy and the judges. Between the monarch and the people stood a bureaucracy well organised in the essential branches of war, justice and finance. But this structure embraced the remnants of feudalism and local rights: on the one hand, Commanders of Military Orders and those who had in their gift lands, revenues and appointments; on the other, the *câmaras* (municipalities) with their judges, and elective village judges. It was, however, the landed proprietors and merchants with a certain income who made up the *câmaras*, and in the large towns these were presided over by a nobleman. Elections were triennial. In the chief towns the representation of gilds was organised in the *Casa dos Vinte e Quatro* which, subordinated to the Senate of the *câmara*, was responsible for the economic administration and for the upkeep and policing of public places.

The annexation of Portugal by Philip II had been made possible by the benefits which noblemen and merchants expected to receive (silver from Mexico and Peru and the supply of slaves to the Spanish Indies); these classes were divorced from the ordinary people who favoured resistance. The economic and financial crisis of the empire which began in 1620–5, the new international situation, the centralised government which threatened privileges and careers—all this changed the attitude of nobles and merchants; but it was the pressure from below, the popular risings provoked by hunger and oppressive taxation, which drove them to revolt. The makers of the Restoration wanted to keep control of the situation and therefore sought popular approval only after the event. Some of them had taken part in suppressing the revolts of 1637: for example, Vieira da Silva, secretary of state from 1642 to 1662. Certain sections of the aristocracy, the higher clergy and the merchants remained attached to the dual monarchy and made several attempts to reunite the two countries. Reunion meant for them a strong combination against the new naval powers, American silver as a basis for the currency, a Spanish outlet for sugar and tobacco, the re-export of Spanish wool, the profits of the *asiento* and profitable trade between Rio de Janeiro and Buenos Aires. Further, there were many family ties with Spain. Leading Portuguese remained in Spanish service: Dom Francisco de Melo, the victor of Hannecourt (though defeated at Rocroi); Dom Felipe da Silva, the victor of La Motte; Gregório de Brito, the defender of Lérida. All this caused a political ambiguity among the ruling classes.

The Portuguese hoped that the Restoration would bring them peace with Holland and consequently the restitution of some lost territories. What in fact happened was a truce in Europe and continued fighting overseas. Thus Portugal had to wage two wars: one at sea against the Dutch

East and West India Companies, for the control of colonies and trade, from 1625 to 1661; and the other on land, against Spain, from 1640 to 1668. In order to carry on the Spanish war, Portugal needed good relations with the United Provinces, since that country was the main market for salt and Portugal's chief supplier of naval stores, masts, cannon and wheat. The Dutch, in their turn, could not do without salt for their fish, and Spanish wool came to them through Portugal. There was thus a mutually profitable truce in Europe, but this did not apply overseas. In the East, despite the accord of 1635 between the English East India Company and Portugal, the Dutch gained the advantage; the Cape route ceased to be the axis of the Portuguese Empire. In the Atlantic, however, the Portuguese won the upper hand. Angola and São Tomé, taken by the Dutch in 1641, were regained in 1648; and this decided the fate of Brazil, since the source of its slaves was now in Portuguese hands. The Dutch had to evacuate the Maranhão in 1644 after a revolt by Portuguese and natives which lasted eighteen months, and they never managed to control Bahia. In fact, their tranquil domination of the north-east (conquered 1630–5) lasted for only ten years. Pernambuco rebelled in 1645, and Haus was defeated at Tabocas by Fernandes Vieira. Guerrilla warfare began and help came from Portugal. In March 1648 Vieira and Negreiros won the first battle of Guararapes, and the reinforcements brought by Francisco Barreto secured the second victory in February 1649. Since the creation of the Brazilian Trading Company merchant ships enjoyed safe passage between Portugal and Brazil. In January 1654 the Dutch in Brazil capitulated. What caused their defeat? The Anglo-Dutch War of 1652–4 certainly hampered them; yet Portugal too was at war with England, from 1650 to 1654. Portuguese diplomacy secured some delay in the sending of Dutch reinforcements, but the fundamental reason for the inadequate help given to the Dutch in Brazil was the clash of interests in Holland between the West India Company and the salt and wool merchants. The central government was weak, and the decisive voice was that of Amsterdam, which preferred trade to colonisation. Moreover, demographic factors favoured Portugal, and the Dutch army in Brazil contained a high proportion of mercenaries. Finally, there was the spontaneous and fierce resistance of the Portuguese settlers and natives to Dutch domination.

Portugal was at the same time at war with Spain. Until the Peace of the Pyrenees (1659) Spain could not employ all her strength; but Portugal at the Restoration had neither a system of fortifications nor a modern army, she lacked generals (some of whom were serving in Catalonia or Flanders), and even the army's stud-farms had been closed by the Spaniards. This was a frontier war, with attacks on villages, seizure and recapture of livestock and crops, devastation of fields and olive groves. During this twenty years' struggle, however, Portugal became a network of fortifications and raised an army capable of winning pitched battles and led by able officers. Matias de Albuquerque, inspired by Rocroi, defeated Baron de Molinguen in the battle of Montijo (May 1644) and then defended Elvas against a strong army led by the Marquis of Torrecusa. Olivença was defended with equal success against the Marquis of Leganés in 1648. Heavy fighting, however, was resumed only at the time of the Franco-Spanish negotiations, for Portugal hoped to be included in the peace settlement. After a Portuguese defeat before Badajoz and the loss of Olivença and Moura, Dom Sancho Manuel and the count of Cantanhede won a striking victory at the Lines of Elvas (January 1659) over the Spanish favourite, Don Luis de Haro. In the War of Independence the field army numbered 4000 to 5000 cavalry, 10,000 to 15,000 infantry, and a score of cannon. Portugal was generally on the defensive: she aimed at recognition of her independence, not at conquest.

Her situation was indeed extremely difficult, abroad as well as at home. The Holy See stubbornly refused recognition. For twenty years no power helped Portugal, and she was not allowed to participate in international treaties. To France she was only a pawn in the struggle with Spain. Threatened by internal and external dangers, the king and the government vacillated and sometimes favoured desperate policies. They wished at one time, against the opposition of the Councils and High Courts, to cede north-eastern Brazil to the Dutch in exchange for silver, and at another considered abandoning the home country to the Spaniards and falling back on the colonies. The hard-pressed government created fresh difficulties for itself: its absolutist ideology led it to support the Royalists in the English Civil War, and this quixotic policy culminated in an open challenge to Cromwell in 1650. Blake intercepted the Brazil fleet, and in 1654 Portugal was forced to accept Cromwell's terms, opening her empire to English trade. The consequences of this policy continued after the English Restoration. The marriage of Catherine of Braganza to Charles II (May 1662), although it brought English support for Portugal, cost two million *cruzados* and confirmed England's privileged trading position (the present of Tangier and Bombay had only secondary importance). Expelled from Brazil and Angola, the Dutch, seeing the advantages won by England, attacked Portugal in the autumn of 1657, blockaded the Tagus with forty ships for three months, and in August 1661 secured a peace treaty which had a disastrous effect on the Portuguese economy. In return for their recognition of Portuguese ownership of Brazil, Angola and São Tomé (which was in any case firmly established), the Dutch received four million *cruzados* (to be paid out of the proceeds of the salt trade) and the same trading privileges as the English.

1661 was the nadir of Portuguese power, and the domestic situation helps to explain this. John IV at first ruled in collaboration with the *Côrtes* and the Councils; he then dispensed with the *Côrtes* and worked with the Councils through his ministers; and finally turned to personal rule through his secretaries, especially Pais Viegas, who had been his secretary since before the Restoration. John IV's death in November 1656 created a delicate dynastic position, since his eldest son, Dom Teodósio, had died in 1653, and the second son, Dom Afonso, was physically and mentally weak. There was thus a body of opinion which wished to summon the *Côrtes* so as to proclaim the incapacity of Afonso and the accession of his brother Pedro. The Queen Mother, Luisa, favoured this solution, but dared not take the decisive step. The majority of the aristocracy and the leading clergy were only too pleased with the prospect of a long regency under a woman, followed by the reign of a king incapable of ruling. They held the real power from 1656 to June 1662, exercising it legally through the Councils and High Courts which they dominated. Despite the victory of the Lines of Elvas, foreign affairs took a disastrous turn: Portugal was excluded from the Peace of the Pyrenees, the war with Spain continued, and the English marriage and the Dutch treaty put the economy of the empire under the control of foreigners.

The regency should have ended in 1657, Afonso being then 14 years old; but Dona Luisa prolonged her rule, hoping for Afonso's recovery or, preferably, for a chance to put Pedro on the throne. The failure of her attempts to strengthen the monarchy was due to her reliance on those very sections of the ruling classes which opposed changes in general policy and in methods of government. Thus the resounding defeats suffered by the existing policies and the unprecedented gravity of the situation led those who wanted a change to rely on Afonso, and in 1662 the count of Castelo Melhor was driven to transfer power from the queen mother to the king. Sousa de Macedo became secretary of state, and government by a ministry was imposed on the Councils and High Courts.

Profiting from the hostility of England (whose trade was suffering) to the Dutch treaty, Portugal postponed ratification until 1663, and actual payment until the new treaty of 1669. There was also an attempt to prevent the English from establishing themselves in the colonies. Castelo Melhor tried to use France in order to secure an advantageous peace with Spain, without being drawn too closely into French schemes. In 1661–2 the Spanish general offensive was halted; but in 1663 Spain, freed from other commitments, made a supreme effort, and in May Évora was taken. The reorganisation of Portugal's army and fortifications had, however, made great progress since Turenne had sent Schomberg with 600 French officers and men, followed later by some English regiments. In June 1663 Dom Sancho Manuel and Pedro de Magalhães won the battle of Ameixial and retook Évora: the reward of twenty years' preparation and of the firmness of the new government.

As Spain would not accept a treaty advantageous to Portugal, and as England, who was mediating, wanted a quick settlement at any price, Castelo Melhor signed in March 1667 a treaty of alliance with France.

The peace party and English diplomacy aimed at his fall, and—seemingly paradoxically—so did French diplomacy. The French realised that he wanted their alliance only as a means of bringing pressure to bear upon Spain, and that he would not co-operate with Louis XIV who wanted above all to oust the notoriously Anglophil secretary, Sousa de Macedo. At home, the ruling classes disliked the substitution of a ministry for government by Councils, since their power was diminished. The people, too, were dissatisfied because of the hardships of war. Castelo Melhor's power was not in fact as extensive as was believed: foreign envoys noticed that, through lack of decisive and informed support, his good intentions were not always carried out and that he was unable to resist the high nobility, especially the Marquis of Marialva who opposed him in the Councils. By his extreme legalism in 1662, which suited his rise to power, Castelo Melhor had delayed solving the problem of the succession. The majority of the nation would not resign itself to keeping an impotent madman as king, since this might cause a grave, perhaps fatal, crisis if Pedro were to die before his elder brother.

While apparently hostile, but in fact complementary forces united against Castelo Melhor, a romance developed between Dom Pedro and the young and beautiful queen, Marie Françoise of Savoy, daughter of the duc de Nemours, who had married the unfortunate Afonso in 1666 and doubtless wanted to rule as well as to reign. In September 1667 Dom Pedro and his partisans succeeded in achieving the dismissal of Castelo Melhor, who fled to a monastery and later escaped to England. Then the queen took refuge in a convent from where she began a suit for the annulment of her marriage. On the ground that he was incapable of having issue Afonso was prevailed upon by his brother and the Council of State to resign the Crown and was at once virtually imprisoned (which he remained until his death in 1683). The marriage was then annulled since it had never been consummated; four days later Pedro, who took the title of Prince Regent, and Marie of Savoy were married by proxy. In January 1668 the *Côrtes* declared Pedro prince and heir to the throne, while confirming the removal of Afonso because he was unable to govern and to produce issue. These events averted a war of succession in Portugal. On the debit side, the change led to a hurried peace with Spain in February 1668 and a treaty with Holland in 1669, confirming that of 1661. The triumph of the peace party was a rebuff for France, the fall of Sousa de Macedo and the marriage of Pedro a rebuff for England. The queen did not rule, nor did Pedro. As Saint Romain wrote in 1670, the government of Portugal was now in the hands of the *fidalgos*: they had achieved their purpose.

After the Restoration, Portugal itself was in fact much more aristocratic in government than were the colonies. It was certainly true that the people complained and sometimes intervened. In February 1641 some ten *fidalgos* fled to Spain: riots broke out against the nobility, but they were quietened by the suppression of the aristocratic conspiracy in July. In July 1657 the government's conduct of the war seemed equivocal, and the municipal judge and deputies of the gilds of Lisbon went to the French embassy to affirm Portuguese friendship for France and to accuse some of the ministers of being pro-Spanish. When Évora surrendered to the Spaniards in May 1663, the people of Lisbon took possession of the streets and demonstrated violently, thus helping the government of Castelo Melhor. In 1667 the Lisbon judge, the Senate of the *câmara* and the gilds played a far from negligible part in the fall of Macedo and Castelo Melhor: it seems that the people wanted to put Pedro at the head of the government and assure the succession, without deposing and exiling Afonso, but they were outmanœuvred by the nobility. In April 1672 the Lisbon gilds openly threatened the *fidalgos* with violence if they were drawn into Anglo-French intrigues, the judge again playing a political and diplomatic part.

Overseas, however, the *câmaras* had more influence than at home. It was the people of Tangier who in 1643 rebelled against the governor (who was still loyal to Spain), replaced him and recognised John IV. It was the people of the Maranhão who in 1642 began the revolt which ultimately forced the Dutch to withdraw. At São Paulo and Santos the Jesuits were expelled and the central authorities defied. In November 1660 the people of Rio rebelled against the powerful Correias de Sá and were subdued only in the following April, at which time São Luis and Belém rose against the Jesuits and expelled them. In Goa in 1652 a popular rising led to the expulsion of the viceroy, the count of Óbidos, and the people of Bombay delayed for some years the handing over of the town to England.

Thus in Restoration Portugal the government was in the hands of the *fidalgos* and of the higher clergy, who in any case formed one social class. The French consul noted in 1665 that the Church was extremely powerful, and in 1669 an Italian observed that the power of the Jesuits was abnormally great. Yet, in face of the political ambiguity of the ruling classes, it was the solidarity of the ordinary people, expressed by municipal judges, *câmaras* and gilds (even though the *Côrtes* did not allow them to intervene at the highest level) which sustained Portuguese independence by their threats and their actions.

CHAPTER XVII

EUROPE AND ASIA

I. THE EUROPEAN CONNECTION WITH ASIA

In the sixteenth century the Portuguese changed the course of the Asian trade with Europe, but did not significantly alter its content; they broke in upon the profitable port-to-port trade in the East, but did not fundamentally alter its pattern. From the end of that century their Dutch and English competitors more radically rearranged the Asian carrying trade, promoting the sale of Bengal silk in Japan and of Javanese sugar in Persia. They also put more Asian wares upon the European market, supplementing Malabar with Sumatran pepper, introducing indigo and sugar, opening a trade in that useful ballast commodity, saltpetre. The Portuguese had found coarse Indian cottons saleable in Africa and their Brazilian colonies; the newcomers found such cottons suitable for Europe—plain for sheets, towels and napkins, coloured for hangings, quilts and furnishing fabrics.

A still more dramatic expansion in the flow of Asian goods to Europe took place after 1650. Pepper and spices shared in that expansion, though they no longer dominated the sales in Amsterdam and London. Saltpetre continued to be important because in Bihar were found new sources of supply, capable of meeting the demand caused by the growing scale and intensity of war in Europe. A similar discovery, that of cheap raw silk in Bengal, also came to be exploited, as a succession of able Mughal governors progressively cleared the province of Arakanese and Portuguese pirates. The supply of Persian raw silk to north Italy and France had been partially diverted by the Dutch and English in the 1630's; the arrival of cheaper silk from Bengal further upset the old pattern. The cheaper and more plentiful supply, together with the influx of skilled refugees and the temporary protection caused by war in Italy, fostered the growth of a considerable English silk industry. As Sir Josiah Child boasted in 1681, the East India Company had 'of late years found out a way of bringing raw silk of all sorts into this kingdom, cheaper than it can be offered in Turkey, France, Spain, Italy, or any place where it is made'.

Sugar from Bengal and Java had seemed promising, but, like indigo, could not compete with West Indian production; but two new items in the trade between Asia and Europe, coffee and tea, did succeed. These two drugs, specifics respectively against sermon-time somnolence, and against corpulence and the vapours, became in time popular drinks as supplies increased and prices fell. In the 1660's the Dutch and English each bought twenty thousand pounds of coffee a year, one item in a wider Red Sea trade. By the turn of the century the English, French[1] and Dutch between them imported three million pounds of coffee, the trade was so important that their agents went up to the Yemen hills prepared to pay cash down, and special coffee ships sailed direct from Mocha for Europe. The fall in price and consequent rise in popularity of tea was a slower business; but by 1700 English imports from China reached a hundred tons a year, and the future importance of the East India Company's trade with China was already foreshadowed.

The popularity of the new drinks curbed drunkenness and led to new social institutions. Dozens of coffee-houses sprang up in Amsterdam; they became a London institution, informal clubs; and in Paris, complete with mirrors, candelabras and marble-topped tables, a recognised meeting-place for wits and writers. Coffee-houses, such as Lloyd's in Lombard Street, served as gathering points for merchant and shipper, where information could be collected and buyer introduced to seller. They also served as political centres where workmen and businessmen read their daily news.[2] The newspaper owed some of its power as a popular educator to the coffee-house in which it was read and discussed. Addison's hope was, through the *Spectator*, to bring philosophy 'to dwell in clubs, at tea-tables and in coffee-houses'.

The most startling development, however, followed from the realisation that Indian cottons, so long the dress of Asians from the Red Sea to the Moluccas, might also clothe Europeans. In the early seventeenth century cottons were used to cover African slaves, European walls and furniture, and, 'among those who could not go to the price of linen and yet were willing to imitate the rich', the English dead. In the latter half of the century Defoe noted a great change:

> the general fancy of the people runs upon East India goods to that degree that the chints and painted calicoes, which before were only made use of for carpets, quilts, etc., and to clothe children and ordinary people, became now the dress of our ladies, ...the chints were advanced from lying upon their floors to their backs, from the footcloth to the petticoat. Nor was this all, but it crept into our houses, our closets and our bedchambers, curtains, cushions, chairs, and at last beds themselves, were nothing but calicoes or Indian stuffs....[3]

Shirts, neckcloths, cuffs and handkerchiefs were of Indian cotton or silk, ruffles of muslin, stockings of cotton instead of silk or wool.

Nor was the fashion confined to England, though the English East India Company, with its narrower base in Asia and more limited choice of commodities than the Dutch, was the first to push sales at home. There was a European craze for things Indian: not only for Coromandel painted cottons or Gujerati brocades as high fashion fabrics, but for cottons whose washability and cheapness made them generally attractive. Here was

[1] The *Compagnie des Indes Orientales* had been formed in 1664.

[2] See above, ch. XIII, p. 322.

[3] *Weekly Review*, 31 January 1708.

another commodity, like sugar or tobacco, or tea at a slightly later date, which by its cheapness unlocked great new sources of demand. It was a situation which the companies proceeded to exploit. The English directors were soon ordering large quantities of cheap calicoes, and sail-cloth and long cloth shifts, 'to be strongly and substantially sewed for poor people's wear'. Calicoes became the common wear of country folk, of servants, and of the families of middling tradesmen.

The change was reflected in the import figures. Dutch imports rose from 55,000 pieces in 1650 to some 200,000 pieces in the mid-1680's; English imports, in the same period, from less than 100,000 to the boom figure of over 2,000,000. Further supplies were imported by the French, Danes and Portuguese, and from 1715 the Ostend East India Company actively purchased silks and cottons. Since the Dutch and English were large re-exporters of textiles—London Custom House records testify to an active trade to Spain, Germany, Italy, and the American colonies—the health and comfort of many people benefited considerably, for cheap cottons permitted a change of washable 'linen' on the person and on the bed.

Companies which imported textiles in such quantities—at the Rouen sales of 1686 textiles made 1,562,000 of the total of 1,713,000 *livres*—were obviously competing with the woollen, silk and linen industries of Europe, and were to suffer in varying degree from their hostility. In the United Provinces the imports of calicoes for local use were for a long time quite small; but an awareness of the profits made by the English gradually overcame all hostility. In France, where East India interests were weak and Louvois was busy fostering the textile industries, a ban was imposed in 1686 upon oriental silks and Indian printed cottons, as well as upon Indian calicoes printed in France. The barrier thus erected against the flood of Asian textiles required constant strengthening by new orders and edicts. The penalties imposed grew ever more severe; at Valence seventy-seven persons were sentenced to be hanged, fifty-eight to be broken on the wheel, six hundred and thirty-one to be sent to the galleys. Yet the use of printed calicoes continued to be widespread. The decisive effect of the ban was to cripple the French calico-printing industry, to the eventual advantage of the British cotton manufacturer. As for plain cottons—calicoes for tuckers, neckcloths or coverlets, muslins for the headdresses, kerchiefs and aprons of the *Midi*—these the *Compagnie des Indes Orientales* was allowed to import, though prohibitive duties were laid upon imports from England and the United Provinces. Because of smuggling even white cottons were banned in 1691, and the company was only permitted to import them again, under temporary permits, if they received a government stamp.

In England, where trade and industry were more evenly matched, it took twenty-five years from the Gloucestershire clothiers petition of 1675 to secure an Act against Asian textiles. During those years a varied opposition was mustered. The Turkey Company attacked the East India Company because Bengal silk competed with Persian. The silk weavers attacked the company, though it was the supplier of their raw silk, because it had encouraged a rapid expansion of silk weaving in Bengal, which brought down the price of Indian silks by 50 per cent within forty years. (The company had sent out English throwsters, dyers and pattern drawers to improve Indian silks.) The woollen manufacturers and the calico dyers and printers likewise resisted the invasion of their markets.

A first Bill to restrain the wearing of Indian silks and calico and calicoes printed in England passed the Commons in 1696. It was killed in the Lords by the counter-pressure of all those who handled or worked up the cottons and silks. A second measure also failed, and in 1697 a Spitalfields mob attacked the East India House and rioted outside the House of Commons. Rioting and a pamphlet war continued until, in April 1700, an Act was passed forbidding the use of 'all wrought silks, Bengalls, and stuffs mixed with silk or herba, of the manufacture of Persia, China or East India, and all calicoes painted, dyed, printed or stained there'. The Act differed in two ways from the French ban; it permitted imports of printed fabrics to be re-exported out of bond, and it permitted both the importation of plain calicoes and their printing in England. Since in the following session the duty on calico was also reduced, one result of the Act was to stimulate the English printing industry; nor in the event was the trade in silks and printed calicoes seriously affected. Some two-thirds of these had always been re-exported, and quite a number continued to find their way on to the English market. In 1719 David Clayton noted that calicoes were cheaper retail in coastal districts than they were wholesale in London. As the competition of Indian and English printed calicoes thus remained formidable, the next attack was directed against cotton as such. In 1720, after many petitions and riots an Act was accordingly passed '...prohibiting the use and wear of all printed, painted, stained or dyed calicoes except such as are the growth and manufacture of Great Britain and Ireland'.

One feature of the protracted struggle against the new commodity had been the long pamphlet war—a war in which the whole trade with the East had been under fire. The opposition to that trade was general, for it offended against almost every canon of bullionist, mercantilist or protectionist policy. A French memorial of 1686 stated the charge: Asian trade, instead of providing a market for French manufactures, and a return in money, swallowed infinite quantities of gold and silver, furnishing in return nothing but miserable piece-goods which, moreover, were ousting such good French manufactures as silks and woollens.

The denunciation of the drain of precious metals was not new; but changing trade patterns were making the problem more acute. Coffee had to be bought for cash. Fewer piece-goods were bought in Gujarat where there was a Mughal market for European goods, and more in eastern India where few European goods were taken in exchange. It became harder to extract gold for Coromandel, copper and silver for Bengal from the Asian port-to-port trade. Less gold and silver, drawn ultimately from the overland trade in silk and cottons, was coming from the Persian Gulf and Gujarat. Copper could normally be procured in Japan; but Japan stopped the important silver exports in 1668, and those of gold in 1685–6. By 1700 even the Dutch had to raise their modest exports of gold and silver to five million florins.

Against the 'bullionists', defenders of the East India trade used several arguments. The French directors declared that what they did not buy cheaply in Asia would have to be bought dear in Europe, and claimed that their re-exports recovered more than the original outlay of bullion; Seignelay told Louis XIV that all the company's bullion came from Cadiz in return for sales in Spain. But even if this were true of individual countries, it was not true of Europe as a whole. Not only was there no world-wide system of credit, so that money was needed to link several continental credit systems; but as Pieter de la Court stated in 1662, in his *Het Interest van Holland*, the trade with Persia, India and China could not be conducted by an exchange of goods and services, but only by exporting gold and silver. For until the Industrial Revolution there were no goods and few services which Asia would take in quantity from Europe.

But the trade with Asia not only exhausted Europe's treasure, it took away her people's work. That was what made the new trade in manufactures—textiles, chinaware or fans—so objectionable: it was contrary to the mercantilist stress upon production as opposed to consumption, upon exports as opposed to imports. In answering this attack the East India defence had to formulate arguments for 'free trade'. Child and Davenant stressed the value of buying in the cheapest market—as the linen-drapers put it, 'Free Trade makes all manner of commodities cheap; the cheapness of our commodities empowers our people to work cheaper; the cheapness of work encourages foreign trade, and foreign trade brings wealth and people'.[1] The *Considerations upon the East India Trade*, which appeared in 1701, anticipated that competition would foster the invention of labour-saving machinery, which, by cutting costs, would widen markets and increase production to the point where a further division of labour would again cut costs. But even arguments as advanced as these were of no avail when unemployment rose in the 1690's. When the woollen and landed interests seemed at stake there was little hope for calicoes, 'made the Lord knows where by a parcel of heathen and pagans that worship the devil and work for a half-penny a day'.[2] The old belief in the central

[1] *An Answer to Mr Carey's Reply* (1697).
[2] *The Female Manufacturers' Complaint* (1720).

importance of the woollen manufactures triumphed over the pleas of the East India interest.

Yet woollens, which in 1640 had formed between 80 and 90 per cent of London exports, in 1700 amounted to less than 50 per cent. By 1700 re-exports of Asian and American goods constituted some 30 per cent of the total export trade of England, and there were also the invisible exports of inter-port trading in the Indies. England was committed to the re-export and carrying trade almost as firmly as Holland. The interest of overseas and colonial trade had become a national interest, to be provided for in peace treaties, to be defended by force in Europe.

The marked change in the pattern of trade with Asia in the second half of the seventeenth century, which led to such notable argument, was mainly the work of the Dutch and the English. They had risen to a predominant position in trade and in military power; they had eclipsed the Portuguese and overshadowed the Spaniards. No similar change, however, took place in Christian missionary activity in Asia. Neither the Dutch nor the English showed an interest in spreading Protestant Christianity at all commensurate with their power in the East. The blows to Spanish and Portuguese commerce were blows to the mission work which that commerce sustained, but German, Italian and French missionaries did much to repair the damage. To its close the seventeenth century in Asia was predominantly Roman Catholic. For the Dutch and English advance was made not by governments, but by trading companies, for whom an attack on Asiatic religions spelt loss of trade. By contrast, the Roman Catholic missions were often vigorously supported by the French, Spanish and Portuguese Crowns, which in India and the Philippines placed considerable revenues at the disposal of the Church. In Europe Protestants, engaged in acrimonious controversy or subservient to indifferent princes, were not interested in providing an administration for foreign missions. The instruments of the Counter-Reformation, on the other hand, were also missionary agencies. Dominicans, Franciscans and Augustinians had worked in Asia since the opening of the sea-routes. The Capuchins, Theatines and Jesuits soon extended their activities overseas. Protestant missionary societies of comparable quality and vigour did not appear until the eighteenth century. Nor were there any Protestant parallels to the *Congregatio de Propaganda Fide* as a training and directive centre for missions, or even to the *Société des Missions étrangères* founded in Paris in 1658. Nor could Protestants have anything to compare with the ecclesiastical organisation—with its wealth of churches and seminaries, of universities, hospitals, libraries and printing presses—built up by Portugal and Spain during one hundred and fifty years. The Abbé Carré in 1672, from the house of the Portuguese Augustinians at Kung in the Persian Gulf, the Capuchin mission at Surat, the Recollects church at

Daman, the pretty Mahim church served by an Indian secular, the Dominican church at Bassein, the Jesuit college at Thana, the Carmelite house at Goa, right to the Theatines at Bicholim, everywhere found centres of Catholic communities. While crossing India he saw churches at Golconda, and on the east coast Jesuits at San Thomé and Capuchins at Madras; on the Dutch-held Malabar coast, from Quilon northwards, he found numerous Catholic communities under the care of Jesuit fathers or Indian priests. Other travellers furnish similar accounts of all the areas to which the power of Spain and Portugal had extended—or to which their nationals had penetrated as private traders, mercenaries or freebooters.

Under these circumstances the Dutch, while recognising their duty of preaching to the heathen, tended to be principally concerned with winning over Catholic native converts to the Reformed Faith; for the existence of strong Catholic communities linked by language and religion to the Portuguese constituted a political threat to Dutch supremacy no less than an affront to the true faith. Theirs was a large task. In western and northern Ceylon whole communities had accepted Catholicism, and almost every village had its church and school, supported by considerable land revenues. In Malabar, besides the churches established by the Portuguese, some forty-seven of the Syrian churches followed Catholic doctrine. The first step was to banish all Roman Catholic priests from Dutch possessions and to impose heavy penalties for harbouring them. But many continued their work from refuges in Kandy and Madura, while from Goa the Oratorian Joseph Vaz organised a mission to Ceylon. The second step was to prohibit the use of the Portuguese language and to order the people to learn Dutch. But as late as the 1730's a Dutch commander in Malabar complained, 'what can the zeal of a reformed preacher, whom nobody can understand, do to combat the bustle of a thousand Roman priests on this coast who are perfectly equipped with the necessary knowledge of the language?'[1] Until the nineteenth century English officials in Ceylon still learnt Portuguese; until the twentieth century Indian Christians in Calicut used Portuguese for their devotions.

The Dutch were successful only where they used the indigenous languages—Tamil or Sinhalese and, farther east, Malay—or adapted Portuguese works to their own purposes. They made a drive, using intensive catechising in the numerous schools, to instil Protestant beliefs in the children, though home influences undid much of this work. They also restricted government employment and licences to trade to adherents of the Reformed Faith, and put special pressure on such groups as the Muslims whose religion and economic competition made them particularly obnoxious. But, as in Holland, the commercial value of tolerance often prevailed over Calvinist zeal. The Dutch East India Company, indeed, showed itself determined not to allow its preachers to create a

[1] P. C. Alexander, *The Dutch in Malabar* (Annamalainagar, 1946), p. 181.

Calvinist Church with influence and interests of its own. No centralised mission administration, no church supervision of the schools, no direct communication with the Church in Holland was permitted. Preachers, it was made clear, were individuals employed by the company. And once the immediate military threat from the Portuguese had waned, not only were Italian Carmelites admitted to Dutch territory, but Portuguese Jesuits as well.

The English, with little territory and a Portuguese alliance,[1] had less need of a missionary effort than the Dutch. They appointed ministers to their factories, but did little to promote Christianity among the natives. The Society for Promoting Christian Knowledge (S.P.C.K.) was formed in 1699 and the Society for the Propagation of the Gospel in Foreign Parts (S.P.G.) in 1701; but it was not until the latter half of the eighteenth century that any very notable British missionary work was done in Asia.

The first true Protestant mission in Asia was the Danish Lutheran mission at Tranquebar on the Coromandel coast. This was started in 1706 by Plütschau and Ziegenbalg, who came out, not to minister to the Danish factory and garrison (though they did), but to convert the heathen. They took pains to master Portuguese, and Ziegenbalg became proficient in Tamil. Both were prepared to spend their lives in Asia. They had studied at the German Pietist centre, Halle, and it was through A. H. Francke at Halle that their work became well known. He had a wide correspondence, published their letters in the Halle *Reports*, and used the interest which they created to secure funds for the mission. Many now familiar methods were elaborated: mission boxes, house-to-house collections, the mission lecture. English interest was aroused through Böhme, the Lutheran chaplain of George of Denmark, Queen Anne's husband, and support was given to Tranquebar by the S.P.C.K. The first appeals for a more concerted Protestant missionary effort thus had some measure of success and important later mission work was foreshadowed.

The main new Christian effort in Asia, however, came not from the Protestant countries, but from France, Italy and Catholic Germany. In India Italian Carmelites established missions in the Deccan, and in China Italian Franciscans worked in Shansi, Shensi, Honan, Hupeh and Hunan. In 1660 three members of the *Société des Missions étrangères*, who had been appointed vicars-apostolic in China, Tonkin and Annam, were driven by war and weather to Ayudhya, the capital of Siam. They realised its advantages as a centre for their society and proceeded over the next twenty-five years to build a church, a substantial seminary and several mission schools with a hospital and dispensary attached. Their contacts with Phaulkon, the powerful Greek adventurer at the Siamese court, led Louis XIV, in the hope of the king's conversion and of profitable trade, to exchange embassies with Siam and to dispatch a military expedition. The

[1] See above, ch. XVI, p. 394, and below, p. 419.

death of the king and the fall of Phaulkon in 1688 ended the French and Jesuit connection with Siam, though the *Société des Missions étrangères* long continued to make Siam its main centre in the East. Some members of the *Société* went on to China, but the main French effort in that country came from the Jesuits who were sent out by Louis XIV. Five Jesuits chosen for their scientific attainments reached Peking in 1688 and were well received by the emperor, if rather coolly by their Portuguese colleagues. They were soon strongly reinforced and in succeeding years played a most important part as exponents of European science in China and as interpreters of China to Europe.

There was also a redeployment of forces by Spain and Portugal. When in 1614 the missionaries were expelled from Japan, the Portuguese Jesuits—and a number of their Japanese converts—moved to Tonkin and Cochin-China, where they established considerable missions and became court mathematicians. The Dominicans and Franciscans later joined the Jesuits or found new fields in the coastal provinces of China. Other missionaries displaced by the Dutch capture of Malacca passed first to Macassar, and then to Solor, Flores and Timor, where Dominicans and their converts successfully resisted a number of Dutch attacks. Barnabites worked in Burma, while the Theatines made Borneo their particular care.

All this was not achieved without conflict. French and Italian participation was made difficult by the existence of papal grants to the Crowns of Spain and Portugal. Both had shouldered responsibility for the maintenance of the Church and the extension of the faith in Asia. In return they had been granted extensive privileges which, in effect, extended into Asia the absolute control which the two rulers exercised over their national Churches. To the rights of *Padroado* and *Patronato real* Portugal and Spain jealously clung, whatever the strain imposed on their diminished resources, and however much the extent of their claims exceeded the political and commercial control which they could exercise over the countries of Asia. There had been disputes enough between the ecclesiastical authorities in Goa and Manila; but discord was multiplied and sharpened when non-Iberian missions appeared in the East. French missions were regarded as threats to political and commercial as well as to ecclesiastical monopolies. The establishment of the *Congregatio de Propaganda Fide* in 1622 and the dispatch of vicars-apostolic to Asia were considered to be attacks upon the royal control of the Churches of Spain and Portugal. Accordingly, the Spanish and Portuguese rulers exerted what pressure they could on Rome, did what they could to prevent ecclesiastical 'interlopers' from reaching Asia, and tried to curtail the effectiveness of those who arrived.

One Portuguese viceroy, João Nunes da Cunha, baldly announced in 1668 that he would hang any bishop who came to the East without Portuguese royal approval. On account of this attitude the three members of the *Société des Missions étrangères*, who in 1658 were appointed vicars-apostolic in China, Tonkin and Annam, thought it best to use the difficult overland route to the East which avoided areas under Portuguese control. In 1673 Pope Clement X signed a brief exempting vicars-apostolic from the jurisdiction of the archbishop and the Inquisition of Goa. An attempt was thereupon made to bargain with Rome: Portuguese recognition of the spiritual authority of the vicars-apostolic was offered, provided they were not French. The fear was plainly expressed that otherwise the French would become 'masters of the trade by reason of the ties which are necessarily formed between those who embrace the Catholic faith and those who announce it to them'. No compromise was reached, and the Papal Legate Charles Maillard de Tournon, who entered Portuguese Macao in 1717, was placed under house arrest on orders from Goa, from which only death released him.

These questions of jurisdiction were further complicated by rivalries between the Orders. For the Philippines the Spanish Crown early laid down the rule, one Order, one district, and even then did not escape disputes. Jesuits complained about friars from Manila who, ignoring royal orders, entered their province of Japan and later followed them to China. In Bengal the Augustinians protested when the Jesuits opened a mission there. The regulars were united, however, in opposing the building-up of an indigenous, secular clergy and the establishment of the ordinary process of episcopal supervision and visitation. The founders of the *Société des Missions étrangères* were convinced that only when the parish clergy were seculars and, like their bishops, of local stock, would the Church in Asia take real root and achieve a vigorous life of its own. They further believed that such a clergy must be created by seculars since regulars would always keep them in subordination to their Orders. This certainly was the case in the Philippines, where neither the demands of the archbishops nor the commands of the Crown could make the regulars transfer the settled parishes to the care of the secular clergy, though the two Philippine universities turned out many qualified men. The *Société*, at its central headquarters in Siam, trained a number of native priests for Siam and the adjacent States. A Chinese was created vicar-apostolic and later bishop of Nanking. In India an Oratorian of Brahmin stock was similarly appointed vicar-apostolic in Bijapur; but such appointments were rare and caused much friction. Considerable racial intolerance was, in fact, displayed by the European-manned and European-directed Orders. There were strict rules against the admission of half-castes. The Augustinian Fr Gaspar voiced the belief that Filipinos, and most other Asians, were an inferior lot, except the Japanese, 'who, as Gracian wisely remarked, are the Spaniards of Asia'.[1] But the fiercest attacks were

[1] J. J. Delgado, *Historia general sacro-profana, política y natural de las islas del Poniente llamadas Filipinas* (Madrid, 1892), pp. 273–93.

reserved for the Jesuits' methods. They were criticised for attempting to secure that influence in high places in Asia which they so often wielded in Europe. They were accused of using such influence against other Orders and of furthering their commercial interests. There were some reasonable grounds for criticism. The Jesuits maintained a mission at the Mughal court and hoped that the friendship of Father Busi with Dara Shikoh, in whom Sufi mysticism seemed to reach out towards similar trends in Hinduism and Christianity, would bring success to their North Indian mission. In China a similar policy appeared patently rewarding. Not only did the Jesuits force an entry into a country long closed to the missionary, but they rose to eminent positions in the service of the Chinese State. They even managed the awkward transition from the service of the Mings to that of the Manchus with the greatest tact. In 1692 the Emperor K'ang-hsi publicly proclaimed his appreciation of their official services and toleration for their religion. But the costs of such a policy were high. Christianity became tied to the fortunes of an individual ruler or a dynasty; in India the defeat of Dara Shikoh in 1658 at the hands of Aurangzeb, an uncompromisingly devout Muslim, ushered in a period of rapid decay for the North Indian mission. In Japan the Jesuit concentration upon the nobility had aroused political suspicion in the Shogun in a way that the humbler activities of the friars never did. In China, as in India, many of the ablest missionaries were condemned to live as courtiers, astronomers, gun-founders, map-makers, even as painters or musicians. In particular, the ambiguous status of those Jesuits who became civil servants of the Manchus was open to criticism. The Jesuits themselves were divided. In 1655 their Roman College condemned the acceptance of the office of reviser of the imperial calendar by Father Schaal; and although in 1664 Pope Alexander VII permitted Schaal's successors to work in the Board of Astronomy, the position of missionaries working on a calendar, the final function of which was astrological, was never a happy one.

Other aspects of the Jesuit approach caused even more bitter controversy. They had early felt the need to study the languages and civilisations of the East, and the schoolmasters of Europe proved apt pupils in Asia. Their learning made them good courtiers, their understanding of Asian societies made them aware of the strength of social forces. In South India de Nobili and his successors in the Madura mission realised the power of caste, and the association in Indian minds of Christianity with low caste. The meat-eating, hard-drinking, blustering habits of the Portuguese marked them as low caste, even if they had not usually married low-caste women. That association the Jesuits tried to break by cutting themselves off from the Portuguese on the coast, and by living the life of respected *sanyasis*, with due attention to such points as vegetarianism and ritual cleanliness. Their adoption of a manner of life so closely adapted to Hindu concepts of what was proper in a religious teacher, and so closely modelled in externals upon Hindu social customs, early brought charges of heresy against them. In 1704 de Tournon, *legatus a latere* to the Indies and China, condemned the Jesuit methods.

In China, too, the Jesuits sought outwardly to conform to the behaviour expected of a teacher or sage, though there they found that it was learning rather than asceticism which commanded respect. They stressed the concordance between the teachings of Christianity and those of the orthodox master Confucius whose works they indefatigably translated. They allowed their converts to continue to participate in the ceremonies connected with the honouring of Confucius and of the ancestors. Such an attitude was the very opposite of that of the Dominicans, whose uncompromising declaration that the rites were idolatrous led to their temporary expulsion from China. The *Société des Missions étrangères* took a similar stand, warning its members in its *Monita ad Missionarios* (1669) against sacrificing Christian doctrine to ease the way of the heathen.

The conflict was carried to Europe. Dominicans and Jesuits in turn laid their interpretations of the Chinese rites before the pope. The Jansenists entered the fray. Pontchâteau bitterly attacked the suiting of Christian doctrine to Chinese habits of mind. Of the Jesuits he said: 'they have in no wise announced to China Jesus Christ poor and crucified. They have taken it ill that the Dominicans place in their church, on the altar, the image of Christ crucified because, they say, the Chinese regard it with disgust.' The Jesuits countered by securing from the Emperor K'ang-hsi in 1699 a declaration that the cults of the ancestors and Confucius were as purely civil in their nature as the Jesuits claimed. But a pagan emperor's decision could hardly be allowed to be final. In 1703 de Tournon was sent out to investigate and in 1707, having decided that the rites were idolatrous, he condemned them. Though Chinese hostility had been aroused, and was later to result in the suppression and persecution of Christianity, the Legate's condemnation was reinforced in 1715 by the Bull *Ex illa die* and by the imposition upon all missionaries of an oath of obedience to the unequivocal provisions of the Bull.

The preaching of the Gospel in Asia provoked rivalries and conflicts over the Malabar and Chinese rites which, though at first waged within the Church, were eventually submitted, in a spate of publications, to the judgement of the general public. But the connection with the East also had less portentous by-products. There was a fruitful influx of new materials, new techniques, new designs, and new forms of art. If the tea trade with China was eventually to lead to an Opium War, its immediate effect was to encourage the use of porcelain cups and teapots, admired alike for their material and for their design. A single East Indiaman in 1700 brought home 146,748 pieces of chinaware—including those porcelain figurines and vases for which Queen Mary had developed a taste during her residence at The Hague. And when Meissen triumphed in 1710—producing a genuine European porcelain where Venice, and Delft with its blue and white ware, had failed—it continued to use the motifs made popular by China and Japan.

If 'china' became Europeanised, so did lacquer ware. French court inventories and cargo lists reveal the importation of lacquered chests and tables, dishes and fan sticks on a considerable scale. But by the end of the century there were do-it-yourself manuals on sale, and from Birmingham and Paris came excellent wares 'lacquered after the manner of Japan' with typical flower and bird designs.

The introduction of oriental textiles also led to the acceptance in Europe of new colour-schemes and designs. The grave full colours originally asked for gave way to brighter colours as the European eye adapted itself to them, and the dress chintzes and silks came to be admired for their novel oriental flavour. During the boom years of the 1680's the rule for English agents was to obtain 'whatever is new, gaudy or unusual'. The delight in the 'rambling fancies of the country' was largely reserved, however, for dress fabrics. For other textiles, the companies preferred to adapt traditional Indian designs to European taste. (The Dutch factor Daniel Havart considered that Coromandel craftsmen were too stupid to do anything but copy.) In 1677 'patterns in ruled paper for directing the weavers' accompanied English orders for branched velvets from Bengal, and there was a constant interchange of samples and patterns between India and western Europe.

The demands of the European markets thus produced changes of style which sometimes, as with Chinese porcelain, permanently affected the taste of the producer. The interchange could be very complicated. The embroidery designs of English crewel-work bed-hangings were long thought to have been taken from Indian fabrics. But it has been suggested that the English provided the patterns for the Indian fabrics, and that their oriental flavour was derived from an earlier period of Chinese influence in Europe.[1] Thus when in the eighteenth century patterns were sent from India for imitation in China, the Canton artisan was possibly offered his own twice-transmuted and unrecognisable designs.

The taste for things oriental was also seen in the pagoda towers, projecting eaves and pavilion-like plan of some European buildings. Internally houses might be furnished with imitations of Chinese wallpapers, externally with gardens bearing traces of Chinese and Japanese theories of garden design, as described by Le Comte or Kaempfer and admired by Addison. In those gardens might well be found such trees and shrubs, introduced from Asia, as the Aleppo pine and the white mulberry, the lilac and the hibiscus.

[1] See John Irwin, 'Origins of the "Oriental Style" in English Decorative Art', *Burlington Magazine*, XCVII (April 1955).

Other introductions of the period were perhaps more useful than aesthetically appealing: the castor-oil plant, the wild senna, tamarind, sarsaparilla, aloe and round-podded cassia. Whether useful or beautiful, they were part of that veritable flood of new plants which so stimulated botanical studies in Europe. Between 1678 and 1703 there appeared at Amsterdam the twelve-volume *Hortus Malabaricus* of Governor H. A. van Rheede tot Drakenstein—1794 plates of flowers, fruits and seeds, drawn full size by Indian artists. At the same time Paul Hermann, first physician to the Dutch East India Company, was having drawings made of the flora of Ceylon and was annually sending home the herbarium material, plants and seeds, which he was to grow and to examine for possible medical properties when he became director of the botanical gardens of Leiden University. G. E. Rumphius, who served the Dutch in the East from 1652 to 1701, prepared the materials for the monumental *Herbarium Amboinense* published after his death;[1] and the German doctor and botanist Kaempfer used his stay in the Dutch factory on Deshima island in Nagasaki harbour to explore the flora of Japan. The botanical works produced in Holland were the finest of their day, but there were keen botanists at work from all over Europe. Tournefort, in charge of the *Jardin du Roi* (now the *Jardin des Plantes*) in Paris made notable expeditions to the Middle East and discovered, while climbing Mount Ararat, that altitude had the same effect as latitude upon the distribution of plant species. James Petiver, using material collected at his direction, contributed several accounts of the flora of Madras to the *Philosophical Transactions of the Royal Society.*

Nor was the work done only by gifted amateurs. The Dutch East India Company regularly had material sent home from Batavia to the laboratories and physic gardens of Holland. Members of the French *Académie des Sciences* jointly produced a great history of plants. Such growing collections of botanical material intensified the search for a scientific basis of classification, which—after the discovery of the sexuality of flowers by R. J. Camerarius and the application of comparative anatomy to botany by Malpighi of Bologna—was first provided by Linnaeus. Similar effects can be observed in zoology. The opening of Asia to the collector and observer provided a tremendous stimulus. Private individuals and great companies brought home strange beasts or collected eggs, skeletons and skins. Evelyn, for example, in 1681 asked travellers to report their discoveries to the Royal Society; 'the particulars they collect are animals and insects of all sorts'. Lynx and deer from Mughal India were kept in St James's Park; pelicans, Indian geese and Malayan cassowaries were housed in Birdcage Walk. The menagerie at Versailles supplied the elephant and other exotic animals which Perrault dissected and classified according to the new science of comparative anatomy.

[1] *Het Amboinsche Kruid-Boek...Herbarium Amboinense*, 7 parts (Amsterdam, 1741–55).

Notable advances were also made in geography. The collection and collation of nautical data, as practised by the Spaniards and Portuguese, was taken up by the Dutch East India Company. Their cartographer at Amsterdam provided charts to pilots and corrected them in the light of their experiences. Pilots at Batavia sent home their observations 'lest what many by long industry have collected be lost'. The *Académie Royale des Sciences*, a creation of Colbert, from which he expected practical benefits as well as purely scientific results, sent out geographical expeditions whose findings were published in 1693.[1] In England the Royal Society got the Master of Trinity House to issue printed requests to ships' captains for geographical, meteorological and astronomical data. In such ways did the hopes of co-operative research of Bacon and Descartes find fulfilment.

Those parts of Asia which lay upon the main trade routes came to be well recorded; but little purely scientific exploration was undertaken. The Pacific, outside the narrow belt of trade winds used by the Manila galleon on its run to and from Acapulco, remained unexplored. The closing of Japan in 1638 to all but the closely guarded Dutch left unresolved the question of the lie of its northern islands, and of Kamchatka's relationship to Tartary and America. For a knowledge of the interior of Asia, beyond the ports and markets frequented by merchants, Europe depended mainly on the missionaries. The scientific training of the Jesuits proved invaluable in this field. In 1655 Martini produced an atlas of China, largely from Chinese sources. More information collected by Grüber and d'Orville on their journey from Peking through the Koko Nor to Lhasa, and thence by Katmandu to Agra, was published in Athanasius Kircher's *China Illustrata*. In 1688 the French Jesuit Gerbillon travelled to the Amur, and in 1696 and 1698 he accompanied Chinese officials to 'jirgas' of the Mongolian tribes. From these expeditions he brought back a number of fixes made by astronomical observations, as well as information about the Lake Baikal region gathered from Russian traders.

A major geographical undertaking was the mapping of China by a team of Jesuits using scientific methods and acting on the emperor's orders. The work was begun in 1707 by taking measurements and bearings along the fifteen hundred miles of the Great Wall. The work was then pushed to the borders of Korea, at last identified as an Asian peninsula, thence into the eastern provinces, and finally into Yunnan. Information about Tibet was obtained at second hand from specially trained lamas. The work, which ended in 1717, when combined with earlier information formed the basis of the maps which were first produced in Peking, and in 1735 published in Paris in the Atlas of d'Anville. In 1688, at Nerchinsk on the

[1] *Recueil d'observations faites en plusieurs voyages par ordre de sa Majesté pour perfectionner l'astronomie et la géographie...faites par messieurs de l'Académie Royale des Sciences* (Paris, 1693).

Amur, Russians, who had been advancing with giant strides across Siberia, met Jesuits who were in Chinese service. The European penetration of Asia by sea and by land was thus completed. Though the Russian material tended to be rough and ready, for much of it was provided by Cossacks who were trading in furs as far afield as the Pacific coast, it at last made it possible to complete the map of Asia.

The mapping of Asia was accompanied by an insatiable curiosity in Europe about the lands thus charted. Merchants were anxious to know more about markets and trade routes, about the vast miscellany of weights, measures and coins current in Asia. What Linschoten had been to one generation, men like Tavernier, whose *Voyages* provided a wealth of information about trade goods and trade routes, were to another. The curiosity of others was that of the armchair traveller. For the new middle-class reading-public created by cheaper printing there was an endless supply of *Travels* and of *Voyages round the World* (Dampier, Careri, Anson), in single volumes or in great collections, often lavishly illustrated.

Much of the travel literature gave only the stereotyped and superficial picture of Asia picked up in port and market-place by men who were not linguists. But there were also travellers with wider interests and a more scientific attitude reporting on Asia. Chardin, for many years jeweller at the court of the Shah, wrote about Persia with understanding and affection. Bernier made excellent use of his service with a leading Mughal noble, while Knox used his captivity in Kandy to produce an *Historical Relation of the Island Ceylon* (1681). There were also several semi-official Dutch works of great value, written by men whose long service in the East enabled them to utilise both company and native sources. Such were the works of Baldaeus on Malabar and Ceylon, of Havart on Coromandel, and of the botanist of Amboina, the scholarly Rumphius, on the history and ethnology of the islands.

The other interpreters of Asia to Europe were the missionaries. In some ways they were the best qualified for the task. They spent their lives in Asia; they were often excellent linguists, producing vocabularies and grammars, translating copiously and collecting widely for their rich libraries; they met all sorts and conditions of men. While French missionary scientists were busy at the court of Peking, Portuguese Jesuits laboured in the heart of the countryside—and yet found time to correspond with the Royal Society, the French Academy, and the Imperial Academy of Russia. If they had an inborn bias, it was far less marked than that of Anson, who made cunning and deceit an oriental monopoly.

All the Orders published mission reports to arouse interest in their work. The Jesuits did so most largely and methodically. Collections of the Annual Letters from their missions were published in many languages. There were special reports, such as that on the Mughal Empire produced by Botelho, Rector of the Agra College, and histories such as de Souza's

The Orient Conquered for Jesus Christ, published at Lisbon in 1710. Most popular and influential of all there were the *Lettres édifiantes et curieuses*, an up-to-the-minute encyclopaedia of information about Asia, laced with improving anecdotes, which appeared from 1702.

Through these Letters, through travel books, through a great web of learned correspondence between individuals, and after 1665 through the learned journals, Europe was made aware of the existence of Asiatic civilisations, with other histories, other social systems, other religions, as important as her own. Increasingly, as Hazard has put it, the notion of superiority had to give way to that of difference.

Because of the importance of Arabic for both biblical studies and the Levant trade—Edward Pococke, the first holder of Laud's chair of Arabic at Oxford, had served the Levant Company at Aleppo—this language was studied first and Islam was the first civilisation to be investigated in the new light. The Muslim world, revealed from its own sources, was viewed more sympathetically, so that Simon Ockley at Cambridge could even stress the debt which the West owed to it. Chardin's description of the splendour of Persian civilisation, Hyde's work on its religious antiquity, fortified the new impression.

There was less understanding of India, though the Mughal Empire was tolerably well known, for the key to her greatness was Sanskrit. But in North India merchant and missionary used Persian, in South India Tamil, Konkani, or some other vernacular. Not until the 1730's did the Madura mission secure Sanskrit manuscripts, and not until the end of the century were they read. Any understanding of Hindu religion and philosophy had therefore to be acquired second-hand from vernacular commentaries and digests. The wonder is how far the Dutch minister Abraham Rogers, or Bernier, or the missionaries Calmette and Pons, penetrated the confusing exterior of ceremonies and superstitions to an understanding of the *Vedas* and *Puranas* and of the main schools of Hindu philosophy.

The impact of China, however, was vast and disturbing. Information about her, learned and popular, poured into Europe. Descriptions such as those of Semedo (1667) and Avril (1692) (three French editions and English, Dutch and German versions were published within twelve years), histories, chronologies, accounts of China's sciences, and Jesuit translations of the works of Confucius arrived pell-mell. Travellers recounted the wealth and swarming population of China's cities; missionaries stressed the excellence and antiquity of her morals and administration. But whereas the civilisation of Persia or Egypt could be linked with the familiar worlds of the classics and the Bible, China's was completely distinct and strange. Remote, self-sufficient, her people and language affronted those concepts of monogeny to which Europeans were committed. The study of China made necessary a new attitude to the age of the earth and the origin of man, invited much questioning of established religious doctrine, and provided new models of society for the dissatisfied in Europe.

In a Europe where accepted history was being shaken by doubt only the exact chronology of the Vulgate had offered hope of certainty. Egypt and Assyria had with some difficulty been accommodated to it, but from China came news of a kingdom whose unbroken sequence of annals carried its origin far back beyond the Flood. Here was independent evidence to support the heretical view of Peyrère that Adam was the ancestor of the Jews only and the Flood a mere local episode. For the moment the use of the Septuagint might resolve the difficulty; but ideas of the scale of time and the duration of the earth were being radically altered.

If the world was older, it was also wider, no longer to be contained within the narrow confines of Bossuet's Universal History.[1] Because the idea of monogeny died hard attempts were still made to find a common origin for man and his civilisation, if not in the Jewish people, then perhaps in Egypt. But the spectacle of Asia's ethnic diversity suggested that perhaps civilisations were not given things, but the spontaneous products of local environment. Chardin suggested that the climate of each country was the principal cause of the inclinations and customs of men. Parrenin reported the Chinese belief in the influence of 'water and soil'. Here were the seeds of the eighteenth-century interest in the influences of geography and climate upon man. On the other hand, the search for a linguistic unity —Leibniz considered Chinese the possible mother language of the world—did produce some positive results. In the first half of the seventeenth century Arabic and Persian studies led men like Raphelengius and Elichmann to note the affinity of Persian to Greek and German. In the second half of the century Herbert de Jager identified Sanskrit and Tamil loan-words in Javanese, and Reland, at Utrecht, called attention to the fact that many of the languages of the islands of the Pacific, the Malay Archipelago and Madagascar sprang from the same Malay root. The study of comparative linguistics had thus got under way.

The religious problem posed by China went even deeper. The Jesuits, with an understandable enthusiasm for their charges, had painted a glowing picture—more particularly to the public—of the excellent morality and the virtuous lives of the Chinese. In the teachings of Confucius, which it would have been unwise to attack, they saw evident signs that the Chinese had worshipped the true God; 'who', asked d'Orléans in 1688, 'in reading his excellent morals could fail to believe that Confucius was a Christian?' The Chinese, without knowing Christ, had reached a Christian position. In India Ziegenbalg reached a similar conclusion with regard to the Hindus. He translated certain Tamil works especially to show 'how far a heathen, even without the Holy Scriptures,

[1] See above, ch. v, p. 99.

could come to the knowledge of the moral law by his natural intelligence'. The Jesuit Le Comte's claim, however, that the Chinese had practised the purest teachings of morality while the rest of the world was still in error and corruption, was formally condemned in 1700 by the Sorbonne, the Dominicans demonstrated that Confucian morality was an atheist one, and the papacy condemned the Chinese rites as idolatrous. The same conflict, which had ranged the Dominicans and the Jansenists against the Jesuits in Europe, thus occurred in China, the conflict between Thomism and Molinism, between belief in predestination and the need for God's Grace and the belief that salvation would not be denied to pagans who strove to live according to the moral law. The old complaint against the Jesuits' lax morality had again been pushed home.

The matter did not end there. The conclusion was drawn, as Le Comte had feared it would be, that a great empire could flourish and a people live virtuously without the aid of religion. Morals which were a practical summing-up of human experience and reason produced admirable political results. In China the Age of Reason had arrived. The *philosophes*, seeing how Confucius had 'put the sceptre in the hands of Philosophy and made Force quietly obedient to Reason',[1] rejoiced. Others, too, found instructive examples in Asia. Pierre Bayle did not fail to contrast the intolerance of Louis XIV with the tolerance of K'ang-hsi, and Montesquieu was to comment on how toleration flourished in the East. Vauban found in the Chinese national census the instrument for an improved management of the French economy. Bernier saw in the Morals of Confucius a text-book for princes, and in the Chinese government a model for that benevolent despotism which he hoped for in Europe. In India he noticed the fatal effects of the absence of powerful landowners. Europe, which was already busy comparing the political and economic institutions of its own States, thus drew upon the variety and experience of Asia as well.

The hold exercised over the European mind by China, and to a lesser extent by other States and civilisations of Asia, lay in this possibility of comparison. They provided examples to which to point and to appeal, statements of ideas otherwise not yet safe to express, external authority for new European beliefs. Their variety and strangeness stimulated inquiry and question. They provided answers in dangerous abundance. Not for nothing did satire choose the imaginary voyage as its favourite vehicle and put its most destructive criticism in the mouth of Turk, Persian or Chinese. Asia gave European man new clothes, new styles, new plants; she also gave him a new antiquity, a new perspective.

[1] F. de La Mothe le Vayer, *De la Vertu des Payens* (Paris, 1642), p. 283.

2. THE ENGLISH AND DUTCH EAST INDIA COMPANIES

By the middle of the seventeenth century the United Dutch East India Company (*Vereenigde Oost-Indische Compagnie*) was the most powerful European institution in Asia. The strength of the company was based on its seapower, but in the territorial sense its activities in Asia had their centre at Batavia, in West Java. From Batavia and the fortress of Malacca (captured from the Portuguese in 1641) the Dutch were able to dominate the Straits of Sunda and Malacca and the seas between Borneo and Sumatra, through which shipping moving from the Indian Ocean into the Eastern Seas, or coming from the Moluccas or the China Sea to the west, had to pass. From this centre they were able to prevent their Portuguese and English rivals from maintaining any significant trading connections with the Indonesian Archipelago, and were themselves well placed to develop a commercial system with factories stretching from Japan to Persia. In the eyes of the company's servants the most important part of this commercial system was the Moluccas, the fabulous 'spice islands'. The company's hold on the Banda Islands gave it a monopoly of the supply of nutmeg and its by-product mace, whilst Amboina, Ceram and its smaller neighbours in the southern Moluccas provided it with an ample supply of cloves. In the northern Moluccas the Dutch sought by agreements with the Sultan of Ternate, and by punitive military expeditions, to extirpate the cultivation of cloves on islands which they were not themselves exploiting, so as to obtain an effective monopoly of the product. By 1656, when the most ambitious of these expeditions had been concluded, and the Sultan of Ternate reduced to the company's vassal, its grip on the production of cloves may be regarded as effective; but its control over the northern Moluccas was not complete until 1663, when the Spanish outpost on the island of Tidore was withdrawn and its Sultan left without a protector. Another 'spice island' on which the Dutch were firmly established was Ceylon. Here, acting in name as the ally of Raja Sinha of Kandy, they had expelled the Portuguese from all their coastal fortresses by 1658, and in defiance of their agreement with the Kandyan ruler had occupied the most important themselves. Possession of Galle, Colombo and Negombo gave them *de facto* control over a large part of the rich cinnamon-producing areas of south-west Ceylon, and their agreement with Raja Sinha granted them a monopoly of the island's external trade.

There were a few other places where the Dutch company exercised in the middle of the seventeenth century a form of political control, based either on annexation or occupation by force or arms. The most important of these were the Cape of Good Hope (colonised after 1652 as a port of call on the route to Europe), a fortified factory on the north coast of Formosa (established in 1624) from which it was able to tap the China trade, and the previously Portuguese-held ports of Tuticorin and Negapatam, in South India, which the Dutch occupied in 1657 and 1658 to prevent the Portuguese from mounting a counter-attack against Ceylon. In the main, however, the Dutch establishments outside the areas of the spice monopoly were not of this kind, but were trading factories planted within the jurisdiction of independent Asian States. Such were the ten factories on the Coromandel coast of India, the so-called 'left arm of the Moluccas', which supplied cotton piece-goods to be used in place of bullion as a medium of exchange in the purchase of pepper from Sumatra and west Java. At Pulicat, their headquarters on this coast until the capture of Negapatam, the Dutch had built a fortress to shelter them from Portuguese attacks, and all the factories were to some extent fortified for defence. Yet, though in some places the Dutch factors administered the towns in which they lived in exchange for an annual rent, Dutch jurisdiction never extended inland. They did not control the areas of textile production, and in the last resort their position was dependent on the goodwill of the local rulers. This was even more the case with the factories up the Hugli river in Bengal, and in Gujarat in western India. Both these areas were within the boundaries of the Mughal Empire so that political independence from it was out of the question, and the trade though prosperous could be halted at any time if the financial demands of local governors were not met. In the same way the Arabian coffee factory at Mocha and the silk factories in Persia were purely trading settlements; so were the minor establishments in the countries of the mainland of south-east Asia. But the extreme case of a factory maintained at a political disadvantage for its commercial benefits was that in Japan, where the Dutch were the only foreigners allowed entry after Portuguese and Spanish missionary activities had frightened the Japanese government into forbidding all intercourse with the outside world. After 1639 the Dutch factors were confined to the small island of Deshima, off Nagasaki, and the number of ships allowed to call was severely restricted.

The position of the English East India Company in Asia at this time was far more modest than that of the Dutch. Without the resources or the inclination to pursue a policy of commercial monopoly based on naval and military power, it failed to make any headway within the Indonesian Archipelago against Dutch hostility, and after 1628 its only footing there was one factory at Bantam, in West Java, whose ruler was opposed to the Dutch. The company's factories on the east coast of India and in Bengal, though commercially important, were far fewer than those of their Dutch rivals. Like the Dutch factories in this area they had originally been established to provide piece-goods for the markets of the archipelago, and until 1652 they were administered from Bantam. From then onwards the seat of the Eastern Presidency was at Madras, where the company was allowed to build a fortress, Fort St George, and to exercise administrative control over the town in return for the payment of half the customs dues to the kingdom of Golconda. The company's main efforts in this period, however, were concentrated on the west coast of India, where it had been able to establish a position of relative commercial advantage in the earlier years of the seventeenth century while Dutch efforts were concentrated on the Indonesian Archipelago. The main English factory was at Surat, in Gujarat, but the English had also established trading centres inland at Ahmadabad, Broach and Agra. In return for co-operating with the Shah of Persia in the expulsion of the Portuguese from the island of Ormuz in 1622 they were able to obtain a privileged footing in the Persian port of Gombroon, free of tolls and with a share in the customs levied on others. This enabled them to develop a profitable exchange trade between Persia and western India. Their trade in this quarter was further stimulated by the political initiative of the president of the Surat factory, who in 1635 came to a local understanding with the Portuguese viceroy at Goa. The East Indies had not been covered by the English peace treaty with Philip IV of Spain in 1630; but the Accord of 1635 (extended by the Anglo-Portuguese Treaty of 1642 and confirmed by Cromwell's Treaty of 1654) not only brought peace between the English and Portuguese in the East, but opened all the Portuguese settlements, except Macao, to the trade of the East India Company. Relieved from the necessity of convoy, except in times of war with the United Provinces, the company could thus use small local vessels to develop the port-to-port trade of the 'western quarter' (as the Dutch called Indian and Persian waters); unlike the Dutch, who had their own supplies in the archipelago, it was able to tap the trade in pepper and other products of the Malabar coast.

The contrast between the achievements of the Dutch and English companies in Asia by the middle of the seventeenth century may be largely ascribed to the differences in their metropolitan organisation and the position which they held in Dutch and English society. The United Dutch East India Company was an amalgamation of the six previously existing companies of Amsterdam, Hoorn, Enkhuizen, Rotterdam, Delft and Middelburg. These remained in existence as separate chambers and sent delegates to the Court of Directors—the *Heeren Zeventien*—which provided the company with a permanent central administration. The company's resources were drawn from all the mercantile centres of the Netherlands. Its initial capital was about 6·5 million guilders, almost ten times as much as that with which the English East India Company commenced operations. The directors of the provincial chambers and the *Heeren Zeventien* were members of the ruling families of the towns. The central direction of the company was thus strong and able to exercise a preponderant influence over the individual shareholders; at the same time the company was intimately connected through these personal links with government circles and was in a very real sense the representative of the

State in Asia. Its charters, in addition to giving it a national monopoly of trade east of the Cape of Good Hope, empowered it to make treaties with Asian States, to take possession of territory in full sovereignty, to build fortresses, to raise military forces, and to wage war. So strong was the position of the directors that they were able to appropriate a large proportion of the capital and profits of the company to fixed investments of a political kind in Asia, without challenge from individual stockholders, who were denied access to the company's accounts.

The English East India Company was established at the beginning of the seventeenth century by royal charters which granted to 'the Governor and Company of Merchants of London trading into the East Indies' a national monopoly of trade east of the Cape of Good Hope and the power to purchase land, to sue and be sued, and to use a common seal. The company, however, did not have the wide military and diplomatic powers of its Dutch rival, and its charter did not extend to places in the possession of other Christian princes at peace with the English Crown, unless it was specifically invited to trade there; nor was it closely linked to the State. Stuart foreign policy often ran counter to the company's interests, and Charles I in 1635, when in need of money, granted a licence to trade within the area of the company's monopoly to a rival mercantile syndicate. The company's affairs were directed by a governor, a deputy governor and a treasurer, as well as by a court of twenty-four 'committees' or directors who were elected annually at the general court of all the stockholders; but for the first half-century of its existence the company had no permanent capital. Its members invested in a series of voyages and joint stocks; each of them was successively wound up, and the capital and profits were distributed. Continuity was provided by the fact that governors and 'committees' tended to be large stockholders, whose fortunes depended on the sale and re-export of eastern goods, and who were re-elected from year to year. In 1635 they held more stock than the four hundred small investors put together. Their authority was, however, restricted by the fact that all the stockholders, however small their investment, voted on an equal footing in the general court. The majority of the small stockholders, who were not directly interested in the company's activities except as an opportunity for profitable investment, viewed the governors and 'committees' as delegates rather than as managers. These had therefore continually to resist pressure for a distribution of profits, so that they would be able to finance fixed investment in the company's Asian factories and to keep trade going in bad years. Their difficulties were further increased by the disturbances and the uncertainty of the Civil War. The charter granted to the company by Oliver Cromwell in October 1657, however, marked a turning-point in its fortunes. It established for the first time a permanent joint stock and, by making votes in the general court proportionate to each member's stock-holding, secured the predominance of the company's officers and the large stockholders over the smaller ones. These elements of increased strength and stability were perpetuated by the charters of Charles II and James II, and the company's position was further reinforced by close personal links with the court and by the anti-Dutch foreign policy of the later Stuarts. After 1660 the English company was much more akin to the Dutch company in its ability to conduct a coherent trading policy.

So far as the Dutch East India Company was concerned the years between 1660 and 1684 were a time of vigorous consolidation, largely by the use of war as an instrument of policy. The company's directors were concerned with profits rather than with the acquisition of territory. They sought where possible to confine their authority to a minimum of important trading ports and to avoid involvement in the internal conflicts of Asian States. Yet, partly because of the unstable nature of local politics, especially in the Indonesian Archipelago, and partly because of their insistence on monopoly and the elimination of local rivals, the Dutch for most of this period had to extend their authority by arms. First, from their newly acquired bases in Ceylon, they reduced their Portuguese opponents in the Indian Ocean to a position of complete impotence. They had since 1636 conducted an intermittent blockade of the Portuguese headquarters at Goa. In 1661 they sent a fleet under Rijkloff van Goens against the Portuguese ports on the Malabar coast and captured the towns of Quilon and Kranganur, though they failed to take the main Portuguese position at Cochin. In the same year a peace treaty between Portugal and Holland was signed in Europe,[1] and had it been ratified promptly Cochin would have been saved. The negotiations were, however, prolonged by the intervention of Portugal's English ally, Charles II, who was unwilling to see the Dutch admitted to the trading privileges which the English enjoyed in the Portuguese settlements under the Accord of 1635. The treaty was not finally ratified until December 1662, and official news of this was not received in the east until several months later. This delay sealed the fate of Cochin. In September 1662 a large Dutch fleet sailed from Batavia for the Malabar coast, and after resisting several assaults the town fell in January 1663. The subsequent capture of Cannanore completed the conquest of the Portuguese ports, which were placed under the authority of the governor of Ceylon, thus giving the Dutch East India Company a virtual monopoly of the pepper production of the area.

In the Indonesian Archipelago the Dutch position outside the Moluccas rested on commercial treaties with local rulers which granted to the company complete or partial monopolies of various imports and exports. There were, however, a number of powerful Indonesian trading centres which refused to acquiesce in this state of affairs, and their influence the Dutch set out to reduce. One of these was the sultanate of Atjeh, at the

[1] See above, ch. XVI, p. 394.

northern tip of Sumatra. This State was the main centre of Islamic influence and trade in the area and exercised the overlordship of the tin-producing State of Perak, on the western side of the Malayan Peninsula, and of the pepper-producing areas of the west coast of Sumatra. A series of commercial treaties with Atjeh had been concluded between 1637 and 1659 granting the company a monopoly of the pepper exports and a share in the tin exports of Perak; but these were not kept, despite periodic Dutch blockades to prevent the sale of the commodities to other customers. In 1660 the Dutch therefore embarked on more direct action, establishing residents at several ports on the west coast of Sumatra and encouraging the Malay inhabitants to throw off Atjehnese control. In 1663 the Treaty of Painan brought the districts of Padang, Tiku and Indrapura under the company's protection in exchange for a monopoly of trade, and by 1670 the Atjehnese had been driven up the coast from Indrapura to the boundaries of the Atjehnese homeland. At the same time Dutch naval patrols and a Dutch fort on the island of Dindings, off the mouth of the Perak river, effectively shut them out of the tin trade. Meanwhile the Dutch company consolidated its position on the west coast of Sumatra. Opposition within the 'protected' districts around Padang was suppressed by the use of Ambonese and Bugis mercenaries. At the instigation of its agent on the spot, Jacob Pits, the company installed a chief of the Menangkabau people of the Padang Highlands as ruler of a Menangkabau State. They then acknowledged him as overlord of all the other petty States on the west coast, and received in return confirmation of their trading rights there and the grant of an area around Padang, which became the company's headquarters in west Sumatra.

A more dangerous threat to Dutch commercial supremacy than that of Atjeh arose from the Sultanate of Macassar, in south-west Celebes. The suppression of the independence of the Moluccan rulers had made it the most important Muslim centre in these seas, and it served as a base for Indonesian smugglers of cloves from the neighbouring spice islands. It was also a centre for other Europeans, English, Danes and Portuguese, whom the Dutch regarded as interlopers. There were clashes between Macassar and the Dutch in 1653 and 1660; but it was the attempt of its ruler to form an anti-Dutch coalition with other Muslim States and to conclude an alliance with the English company during the second Anglo-Dutch War that finally decided Johan Maetsuycker (governor-general, 1653–78) to embark on its conquest. This was undertaken by the young Cornelis Speelman between 1666 and 1668. The Treaty of Bongaya (November 1668) reduced the Sultan's jurisdiction to the town of Macassar and its environs. His former territories outside these limits and the dependent States of Boni, Buton and Sumbawa were brought under Dutch suzerainty. In Macassar itself the company imposed its monopoly over trade, expelled all non-Dutch Europeans, declared its own coins legal tender, and built in the centre of the town the fortress 'Rotterdam'. In view of the severity of these terms it is not surprising that a further campaign was necessary before the treaty could be executed.

The reduction of Atjeh and Macassar was followed by an extension of the company's authority in Java, largely caused by political instability in the States of Mataram and Bantam. Mataram had been founded at the end of the sixteenth century by a prince who brought under his suzerainty the highlands and rice plains of most of central and east Java, together with the formerly independent seaports of the north coast. The young Susuhunan (emperor) Amangkurat I (asc. 1645) continued the efforts of his predecessors to bring this large area under effective control and to reduce the power of the territorial chiefs and the influence of the Muslim teachers. His precipitate measures incurred the hostility especially of the semi-independent princes of the north coast, who rose in revolt in 1674 under the leadership of Trunajoyo, ruler of Madura. They were joined by elements driven out of Macassar by Speelman in 1669; emboldened by the difficulties of the Dutch during the third Anglo-Dutch War, they hoped to use this movement to strike at Dutch power in the archipelago. At the same time Sultan Abdulfatah Agung of Bantam, in west Java, sought to take advantage of his neighbours' troubles by occupying the western provinces of Mataram, to the south and east of Batavia. Abdulfatah (reigned 1651–83) was a formidable political and commercial rival of the company. His capital was a centre for European and Muslim traders, and his links with Mecca and Turkey made him a natural leader of Muslim opinion against the Dutch. The latter therefore felt themselves directly threatened by the prospect of their headquarters being surrounded by Bantamese territory. The final overthrow of Amangkurat I in 1677, despite the Dutch occupation of Surabaya and naval action, both designed to prevent supplies and reinforcements from reaching the rebels, precipitated a division of opinion amongst the company's officials. Rijkloff van Goens and Speelman both advocated intervention and the assertion of the company's supremacy in Java. Maetsuycker, older, and concerned to retain a reputation with the directors in Holland for caution and economic administration, disagreed. The debate was sharpened by the arrival as a refugee of Amangkurat's son, promising commercial and territorial concessions in return for Dutch support. It was settled decisively in January 1678 by the death of Maetsuycker. He was succeeded as governor-general by van Goens (1678–81) and Speelman (1681–4), who presided in turn over the implementation of the policy which they had advocated. Under van Goens, Trunajoyo's rebellion was subdued and Amangkurat II restored to his father's throne. In 1682 Speelman took advantage of a dynastic conflict in Bantam to depose Sultan Abdulfatah and replace him on the throne by his son Abdulkahar, known as Sultan Haji. Both of these new rulers were dependent upon Dutch support and heavily indebted to the company for the expenses of the campaigns which had placed them on their thrones. On its side the company secured a virtual monopoly of the external trade of Java, and the expulsion of all other Europeans, including the closing of the English East India Company's factory at Bantam. At the same time the Dutch company annexed the Preanger region, stretching southwards across Java from Batavia to the sea and separating Mataram and Bantam, and brought under its control the ports of Semarang and Cheribon. From 1684 therefore the Dutch were without any serious rivals in the archipelago. They had eliminated all the important centres of independent trade and were in a position to assert their control over the Javanese States. Although they had not yet become the direct rulers of any large stretches of territory, we may from this date speak justly of the area as 'Netherlands India'.

The year which saw the Dutch East India Company established in a position of absolute supremacy in the archipelago witnessed the beginning of a crisis in the affairs of the English company in India. There was for some years after 1660 a steady growth in the numbers and prosperity of the English factories and settlements in India. This prosperity was seen not only in the well-established centres at Surat and Madras, but also in the growth of the trade of the Bengal factories, and in the planting of several settlements on the Malabar coast to reopen the pepper trade which the fall of the Portuguese ports to the Dutch had cut off. The company's most important acquisition, however, was the island of Bombay. This had originally passed to Charles II as part of the Portuguese marriage settlement in 1661, but the king found it an unprofitable possession. The royal garrison sent out in 1662 did not actually obtain possession of the island until 1665, by which time its numbers had been reduced by disease from 500 to 102, and Charles was glad to make the place over to the East India Company in 1668 in exchange for an annual quit-rent of £10. The potential importance of Bombay lay not only in the fact that it had an excellent position as a trading and shipping centre on the west coast of India, but that it was not subject to the control of any Indian State or the whims of a local governor and was easily defensible against a land power. It was placed under the control of Surat, and chiefly owing to the exertions of Gerald Aungier (president at Surat, 1669–77) soon became a thriving settlement. The coins of the mint established there soon won general acceptance throughout western India; despite the prevalence of disease its population by 1671 had risen to 60,000, and the company's officials had developed the habit of speaking of it as a 'colony'. The royal connection which had given the company Bombay was not, however, without its embarrassments. There were divisions within the factories between the older Puritan elements and the Royalist officials sent out after 1660, and the latter were usually supported by the many king's officers in the settlements during these years. Conflicts developed between the two factions and between military and civil powers, resulting in a number of rebellions in India and at St Helena (permanently secured in 1673 as a port of call), in which the dissident parties endeavoured to take over the government in the name of the king. The last, and the most serious, was that led by Richard Keigwin, military commander at Bombay, in 1683 and 1684. In all these affairs Charles II loyally supported the authority of the company, and his influence was exerted to secure the submission of the malcontents.

The attempts of soldiers to claim a voice in the direction of affairs within the Indian factories were indicative of the increasing importance of the military element in the company's position there. Aungier, for instance, had to maintain the security of the west coast settlements against the formidable Malabar pirates, against the Marathas (who sacked Surat in 1664 and 1670), and against a Dutch attempt on Bombay in 1673. In the Madras area and in Bengal too, English interests were more and more placed in jeopardy by a decline in the authority of the Mughal central government during the reign of the Emperor Aurangzib (1658–1707). The war between Sivaji, the Maratha leader, and the Mughal armies kept the west coast in a state of upheaval. Sivaji was able at will to cut off the landward trade of Bombay and to plunder the English factories farther south, so that in 1674 the company's officials were compelled to come to terms with him. The Mughals, however, demanded the use of Bombay and its harbour for their mercenary naval auxiliaries, the Sidis of Janjira, and were capable of revenging themselves on the factory at Surat if refused. Bombay was thus caught between two fires. When the Mughal fleet sheltered in Bombay harbour and landed a force there the Marathas responded by taking reprisals against other English settlements. In 1679 both sides occupied different islands in Bombay harbour, and the neighbouring waters became the scene of fighting. On the Coromandel coast the Anglo-Dutch War of 1672–4 brought fighting between French and Dutch for the town of St Thomé, on the southern outskirts of Madras, and a Dutch naval squadron dislocated shipping. In 1677 Sivaji, with an army of 60,000 men, extended his activities into south-east India. The hinterland of Madras was kept in disorder by Maratha raids, and the town itself was threatened. So complete was the turmoil that in 1681 a local chief was able to blockade Madras and to bring it to the verge of starvation. It was only with the appearance of Aurangzib himself in southern India in 1683 and his conquest of Golconda that some semblance of order was restored, and the English factories on the Coromandel coast passed under the overlordship of the Mughal Empire (1687). In Bengal the weakness of the Imperial government expressed itself not in disorder, but in the freedom of the nawab or viceroy and his officials to levy their own dues on trade unchecked by higher authority. From 1656 onwards the East India Company had enjoyed freedom from all duties there in return for an annual payment of 3000 rupees. By 1672, however, the then nawab,

Shaista Khan, felt himself strong enough to disregard this compact and stopped the trade until his additional demands were met. The Bengal trade was particularly vulnerable to this kind of treatment, since it had to pass by boat from the inland factories down the river to the main factory at Hugli, some twenty miles above the highest point which the company's ships could reach. In 1677, when Shaista Khan temporarily resigned his office, the company repurchased exemption from dues for a payment of 21,000 rupees, and when he returned in 1679 it obtained from the emperor himself in the following year a *farman* confirming this arrangement. Shaista Khan, however, ignored this and again imposed his own duties, allowing his local officials to extort what additional sums they could for their own pockets. When in 1685 the company's officials at Hugli asked leave to move to a place lower down the river he refused and surrounded several of the factories with troops.

These developments in India, and the expulsion of the English from Bantam by the Dutch in 1682, led the company's governing committee to abandon the policy which they had followed faithfully for eighty years, of confining their activities to peaceful trade and relying upon local powers for the security of their goods and settlements. They resolved instead to fortify their settlements and to enforce the safety of their trade by arms. This change of policy is usually associated with the names of Sir Josiah Child, governor of the company five times between 1681 and 1687 and a preponderant influence in its committee, and his namesake Sir John Child, president of Surat and governor of Bombay from 1682 to 1690. In 1684 they replaced Bantam by the fortified factory of Benkulen, in south-west Sumatra. To implement their policy in India they dispatched an expedition of ten ships and some 700 troops. This force was instructed to withdraw the company's servants from Bengal, to capture and fortify Chittagong on the north-eastern shores of the Bay of Bengal, and to establish there a second Bombay, with its own mint, a secure centre for the trade of north-eastern India. This, and the cutting off of all local shipping on the west coast as well as in the bay, was expected to bring both the emperor and the nawab to such a state of mind that they would grant favourable terms for trade and henceforth show respect for English interests. Conceived in London, it was a plan which completely under-estimated both the still formidable power of the Mughal Empire and the geographical distances and difficulties involved. The expedition became separated on the voyage out, but in the autumn of 1686 part of it reached the Ganges delta, and 300 men were sent up to Hugli in boats. Their arrival provoked an attack by the local military commander, which they were able to beat off, but Job Charnock, the head of the factory, felt his position so insecure that he seized the opportunity to retreat down the river. There he maintained himself against attack and disease among the swampy islands of the delta, until he was taken off in September 1688 by a force designed for the capture of Chittagong. That place, however, was far too strongly defended to be taken by fifteen small ships and 300 men, and the English were left with no alternative but to retire to Madras, where they arrived in March 1689. Events elsewhere in India had been equally disastrous. Sir John Child's attempts to cut off Mughal shipping and to withdraw the establishment at Surat to Bombay, which had become the administrative centre for all the west coast settlements in 1687, provoked the seizure alike of the Surat factory and of those at Masulipatam and Vizagapatam, on the Coromandel coast. At the same time the Siddi fleet attacked Bombay, and when repulsed instituted a close siege. Child therefore sued for peace on behalf of the company, and Aurangzib—aware that, though he had the English factories within his grip, their ships were still capable of stopping the trade and pilgrim traffic between India and western Asia—granted it. His *farman* of 27 February 1690 readmitted the English to the trade of the Mughal Empire, provided that they paid a fine of 150,000 rupees (about £17,000) and that Child was dismissed from his post. The latter demand created no difficulty, because Child had already died at Bombay early in February. Charnock, however, refused to return to Bengal from Madras until in addition to the emperor's *farman* he had also secured from the nawab Ibrahim Khan (who had replaced Shaista Khan) a specific promise that the company would be allowed to trade free of duties and unhampered by local exactions in return for the old payment of 3000 rupees *per annum*. When he did return in August 1690 he established his headquarters not at Hugli, but farther down the river on the site which he had occupied between 1686 and 1688, within reach of the company's ships. This was fortified in 1696 under the name of Fort William, and eventually became the city of Calcutta.

The political and military activities of the English East India Company in these years were on a smaller scale, and less successful, than those of the Dutch company. It did, however, develop under the later Stuarts from a purely trading body into a nascent territorial power, with fortified settlements containing large local populations, with the right of coinage, the command of English and Indian troops, the authority to conclude treaties and to make war, and other attributes of delegated sovereignty. Moreover, its commercial activities between 1660 and 1688, in terms of its trade between England and Asia, the numbers of its ships sent out, and the size of its dividends at home, came to compare very favourably with those of the Dutch company. The Dutch in this period diverted a far larger proportion of their profits into political and military expenses and fixed investments as the price of their success in the archipelago. But even allowing for this, a comparison, until about 1688, with the accounts of the English company shows an increasing measure of commercial success on the part of the latter. After this date, however, the English trading and shipping figures fell, and between 1692 and 1700 the company paid no dividends whatsoever. In part this decline may be ascribed to the expenses of the unsuccessful Mughal war and to shipping losses during the French war of 1689–97. Mainly, however, it reflects changes in the political position of the East India Company at home as a result of the Revolution of 1688. Its close association with the Stuart court and the anti-Dutch and pro-French policies of Charles II and James II meant that it was increasingly alienated from the main body of English political opinion. After the Revolution it was faced with a hostile parliament which condoned the activities of interlopers, supported a bitter pamphlet war against the company's trading monopoly, and itself challenged that monopoly in 1694. The Scots Company (founded in 1695), which expended its resources in an attempt to establish a colony in the Isthmus of Darien, was no real threat to the English East India Company's position. In 1698, however, a rival 'New' East India Company was set up in London by Act of Parliament, and subsequently received a charter from William III. There followed a period of competition between the Old and New Companies in London and between their servants in India, where the New Company established factories alongside those of their rivals, which brought profit to neither. It was eventually ended in 1709 by their amalgamation into one 'United Company of Merchants of England trading to the East Indies'. This provided once more the element of strength in the conduct of English commercial affairs in Asia which had been lacking since the beginning of the 1690's.

By 1709 the main lines on which the activities and interests of the English and Dutch East India Companies were to develop in the eighteenth century may already be distinguished. The Dutch reinforced their political supremacy in Java by a further intervention in the internal affairs of Mataram between 1703 and 1705. They were able to use this supremacy to secure the delivery of large quantities of saleable products, such as pepper and rice. From the beginning of the eighteenth century they introduced new crops, most important among them coffee and sugar, which became the basis of a thriving export trade to Europe. Their establishment on Formosa had been lost as early as 1662, and the China trade had become of minor value to the company, although its officials in Batavia made handsome private profits from the trade by junk with Canton. The Dutch factories in India and the Japan factory were retained, but their trade became proportionately less important, and Dutch interests became more and more centred on the Indonesian Archipelago, and within the archipelago, on Java. The English East India Company continued to maintain factories on the west coast of Sumatra, but their establishment at Benkulen did not produce the large quantities of spices expected from it, and the trade became of minor importance. More significant was the development of the China trade; in the hope of profiting from it the company maintained struggling and unprofitable factories at

Tonkin, Amoy and on Formosa at various times between 1672 and 1697. The ship *Macclesfield*, sent out to Canton by the New Company in 1699, successfully established a trading-connection there, and from 1705 onwards this trade became increasingly important. It was in India, however, that the United Company's main effort was applied. Grants obtained from the Emperor Farrukhsiyar by the embassy sent to the Mughal court in 1714 won for the company a privileged position in trade, which it was able to extend to the administration of the areas around many of its factories. Thus the English East India Company was able to build up that position of strength which, when Mughal authority disintegrated, enabled it to contend with the French for supremacy in India.

CHAPTER XVIII

THE EMPIRE AFTER THE THIRTY YEARS WAR

When the Peace of Westphalia was signed on 24 October 1648 and the warring parties finally laid down their arms, a settlement was reached which, in its essential features, was to last until the dissolution of the Holy Roman Empire in 1806. For a century and longer civil war had been endemic in Germany, and there were to be many minor upheavals in the future; but until 1740, when Frederick II of Prussia chose to invade Silesia and to break the peace of the Empire, that peace was not disturbed by any major internal war. Yet, while the conditions of the Empire were settled by the peace of 1648, the same did not apply to the conditions of Europe. Wars continued in the west and in the east, against France and against the Turks; and Louis XIV found it easy to find allies among the German princes and to use them against the Empire which he was fighting. Internally, however, an equilibrium was reached between the Emperor and the princes, between Protestants and Catholics, between the centrifugal forces and those aiming at more centralisation. A compromise solution was found which, by its very durability, proved that it was not unsatisfactory.

In practice the Empire now consisted of Germany and the Habsburg hereditary lands: its frontiers had contracted; but Switzerland and the Netherlands had long ceased to be parts of the Empire, and the official recognition of this fact was an advantage, and not a loss. It was much more important that parts of Alsace were ceded to France, and western Pomerania with Stettin, Wismar and the duchies of Bremen and Verden to Sweden. This meant not only a loss of territory, but provided both powers with endless opportunities of making further claims and of fishing in troubled waters, of which France in particular was not slow to avail herself. Sweden not only gained those scattered territories and thus controlled the mouths of the Oder, Elbe and Weser, but she also received a war indemnity of 5,000,000 guilders which had to be raised by the impoverished principalities of the Empire. It was not until June 1650 that the Swedish army was disbanded and left the non-Swedish territories; it took another three years before it evacuated eastern Pomerania (which had fallen to Brandenburg), and only on condition that Sweden would receive half the revenue from the harbour tolls and customs. In 1652 the Swedish army opened hostilities against the Free City of Bremen which had not been ceded to Sweden—in contrast with the duchy of Bremen—and therefore declined to render homage to her. The burghers resisted with determination, and the Emperor as well as neighbouring princes tried to mediate. In 1654 a compromise was reached which left it open whether Bremen was a Free Imperial City, but obliged the burghers to render a conditional oath of allegiance to Sweden. After the death of King Charles X, however, they again refused to render homage to Charles XI as his subjects and instead sent deputies to attend the Imperial Diet. Thereupon the Swedish army in 1666 laid siege to Bremen; but the burghers' resistance and the intervention of Denmark, the United Provinces and several German princes forced the Swedish government to make peace and to recognise Bremen as a Free City. Until 1700, however, it was not permitted to send deputies to the Imperial Diet.

That the stipulations of the peace treaty facilitated the interference of foreign powers was shown even more clearly in the Rhineland. At the end of 1654 the archbishops of Cologne, Trier and Mainz, the bishop of Münster and the count palatine of Neuburg, who was also the duke of Jülich and Berg, concluded a Rhenish Alliance which was to protect its members against attacks and to become a mediating factor in European politics. Its importance was increased by the fact that the elder son and elected successor of the Emperor Ferdinand III had died in the same year, while his younger son, Leopold, was but fourteen years old. His youth provided Cardinal Mazarin with an argument for supporting the candidature of a non-Habsburg prince, either the Elector of Bavaria or the Count Palatine of Neuburg. When Ferdinand III died in April 1657 no successor had been elected, and the interregnum, which lasted for fifteen months, was filled with intrigues, threats and promises on the side of France. In July 1658, however, the young Leopold was unanimously elected Emperor by the Electors, having promised that he would render no support whatever to Spain in the war with France which was still continuing. Four weeks later many German princes—the archbishops of Cologne, Mainz and Trier, the bishop of Münster, the count palatine of Neuburg, the landgrave of Hesse-Cassel, the dukes of Brunswick and Lüneburg, and the king of Sweden as duke of Bremen and Verden—signed the Rhenish Alliance, which was joined on the following day by France. The army of the league was to number 10,000 men, 2400 of whom were to be French. The aims of the league were the maintenance of the peace treaty, of the liberties of the Estates of the Empire, and of a balance between France and the Habsburgs. But the German members were much too weak to pursue an independent policy or to form a third force, and in reality the league became an instrument of French foreign policy. It was renewed several times and joined by other German princes, among them the Elector of Brandenburg; but it was dissolved in 1668. By that time it had become clear that the German liberties were not threatened by the Emperor Leopold, but by Louis XIV. As the Crowns of France and Sweden were recognised as guarantors of the peace, and as Sweden acquired two seats in the Imperial Diet, both powers continued to play a very important part in the internal affairs of the Empire: until the reign of Louis XIV reached its end and the Swedish Empire collapsed in the Great War of the North.

During the Thirty Years War the Habsburgs had made strenuous efforts to increase the powers of the Emperor, to create a centralised monarchy, to subdue the Protestant princes, and to advance the cause of the Counter-Reformation—and they had come very close to success. The Peace of Westphalia buried these endeavours, but it also buried the opposite tendency: the attempts of the Calvinist princes to transform the Empire into an aristocratic republic, to carry the banner of Protestantism into the very heart of the Habsburg lands and to lay low the power of the Habsburgs. The Peace of Westphalia was a compromise. The unity of the Empire was preserved; the Imperial Crown remained in the Habsburg family as long as the House of Austria continued in the male line; its power was strengthened through the defeat of the Bohemians and the introduction of the Counter-Reformation in its hereditary lands; even in the Empire the power of the Emperor was by no means negligible. He continued to influence the decisions of the Imperial Diet, to defend the frontiers of the Empire against foreign attack, to act as arbiter in cases of internal conflict between the princes and within the principalities. His hereditary lands—soon to be expanded towards the south-east—made him a prince much more powerful than any of the Electors. Ferdinand III and Leopold I were far from showing political resignation and continued to focus their attention upon the Empire. The siege of Vienna by the Turks[1] led to a revival of Christian and Imperial solidarity, transcending the frontiers of the Empire. This feeling remained alive during the successful campaigns against the Turks, and the Emperor remained its living symbol. The people hoped that, after the end of the wars, he would restore the good old laws of the Empire and revive the authority of the Emperor. Nor was this entirely a pious hope: the century after 1648 saw a distinct revival of his authority, especially so under Leopold's successors, Joseph I and Charles VI. The rise of the Habsburgs in the power politics of Europe had clear repercussions within the Empire.

Yet the Empire after 1648 was incapable of acting as a unit and had no will of its own. The Estates of the Empire followed their own particular interests; they watched each other with jealous eyes and attempted to strengthen their own power, internally as well as externally, and to decrease that of the Emperor. It is true that the French policy of granting full sovereignty to the German princes had not prevailed at Westphalia: they had been accorded only a *jus territorii et superioritatis* by the terms of the peace. It seems doubtful, however, whether this made a great difference in practice. If the princes were granted the right of concluding

[1] See below, ch. XXI, pp. 515–17.

alliances amongst themselves and with foreign powers, this was a right which they had long exercised. If they were forbidden to conclude such alliances against the Emperor and the Empire, this prohibition could be interpreted in different ways. It is not surprising that the political writers of the time found it difficult to define what the Empire really was. Hippolythus a Lapide denied that the Emperor was a sovereign and held that the Empire was an aristocracy of the princes; while Samuel Pufendorf, in his *De Statu Imperii Germanici* (1667), aimed at a reconciliation of the different factors wielding influence in the Empire and declared that it was an '*irregulare aliquod corpus et monstro simile*'. It certainly was irregular, although perhaps not a monster but a marvel. So was the fact that, in spite of all tensions and rivalries, the internal frontiers fixed by the Peace of Westphalia remained substantially the same for more than half a century—only France continued to encroach upon Imperial territory in the west.

Even more stable proved the frontiers drawn between the warring creeds. Protestantism was eliminated from the Habsburg lands, Bohemia, and the Upper Palatinate, but the secularised abbeys and bishoprics were not restored. After 1648 very few German princes exercised their right of driving out those of their subjects who adhered to a religion different from that of the ruler. In their depopulated lands subjects were valuable, and the more enlightened princes tried to attract immigrants even if they belonged to different religious persuasions; the persecuted Protestant sects and the Jews found a home in Brandenburg and elsewhere. Many princes were not strong enough, or not fanatical enough, to enforce their religion upon their territories. Thus the Calvinist Electors of Brandenburg and the landgraves of Hesse-Cassel ruled over Lutheran principalities and did not attempt to make Calvinism the State religion.[1] When later in the century the Electors Palatine and the Electors of Saxony became Roman Catholics,[2] Protestantism remained the dominant religion of their principalities. The Counter-Reformation did not advance any further. Religious passions had cooled and self-interest dictated the adoption of a more tolerant course. Thus, to a very large extent, the religious map of modern Germany is that of 1648.

Many problems remained unsolved, or it took many years before a solution emerged. The restoration of law and order was a difficult task. The mercenary armies were paid off although there was extremely little money. But what should be done with the mercenaries, and how could they be fitted into civil life? There were as yet no standing armies into which they might be absorbed. During the disorders resulting from the war many people had taken to brigandage and crime, or had learned to live by their wits; bands of former soldiers roamed the country. Certain

[1] For further details, see above, ch. VI, pp. 126–7.

[2] See below, pp. 452, 454.

Estates of the Empire co-operated to suppress lawlessness and disorder. The continuing war between France and Spain and that between Sweden and Poland which broke out in 1655 absorbed some mercenaries who had not learnt any other trade; so did later the wars of Louis XIV. Even greater difficulties stood in the way of economic recovery. It was not only the fact, which has been emphasised so often, that the mouths of all the great rivers flowing through the Empire were controlled by foreign powers. It was not only that trade had dwindled or sought alternative routes to avoid the disturbed areas. It was, above all, the egotism and mutual jealousy of the princes and towns which, under the influence of the ideas of 'mercantilism', imposed more and more barriers upon trade and enterprise, erected innumerable customs stations at the frontiers of each principality and along the course of all the rivers, levied new impositions and taxes which drove away trade and delayed the recuperation by decades. If France recovered surprisingly quickly from long periods of war and civil war, this was partly due to the enlightened policy of a centralised government. The political disunity of Germany had grave consequences in the economic field.

A *Political Discourse on the real Causes of the Rise and Decline of Towns, Countries and States*, published in 1668 by Johann Joachim Becher, pointed to the wealth which the United Provinces derived from the sea: they would never have amassed their riches if they feared the sea as much as the German nation did. 'The result is that in Germany there is hardly any trade and enterprise, all commerce is ruined, no money is to be found either among the great or among the small people.' In the same year the officials employed to levy the wine-duty at Öttingen in Bavaria attributed the steep decline in the yield of the duty to the fact that 'in previous good years the sweet wines had been sent not only into the country, but frequently also into Austria, Bohemia and to Prague, even to Cracow in Poland, but at present times sales had nearly ceased on account of the manifold wars and widespread deaths which had caused the country's ruin and scarcity of money', and the same applied to the sale of Austrian wines.[1] At Munich, Augsburg, Speyer, Frankfurt and Leipzig the price of rye in the 1660's was between 13 and 34 per cent, and the price of oats between 15 and 29 per cent below the pre-war level. The depopulation of the towns, which lasted for a long time after the end of the war, led to a sharp decline of the consumption of corn, to a shrinking of the corn trade and to a severe fall in the price of land. In Berlin the price of rye and wheat remained depressed throughout the second half of the seventeenth century.

There can be no doubt that wide areas of Germany not only suffered severely from the war and its aftermath, but also lost a large part of their

[1] State Archives Munich, 'Altbayerische Landschaft', no. 1993: report to the deputies of the Estates supervising the levy of the wine-duty of 20 November 1668.

population. While the towns could protect themselves more easily against hostile forces, they suffered all the more severely from outbreaks of plague. Austria, the Tyrol, Salzburg and Switzerland were hardly touched by the war and their population grew. Large parts of north-west Germany—Slesvig, Holstein, Lower Saxony, Oldenburg, Westphalia and parts of the Rhineland—did not suffer much depopulation. Even in Silesia and Bohemia it probably amounted to only 20 per cent. But other parts fared much worse. In the various districts of Brandenburg between 15 and 60 per cent of the farms were deserted in 1652, on an average perhaps about 50 per cent. Berlin lost only 25 per cent of its population, but Potsdam and Spandau over 40, and the town of Brandenburg over 60 per cent. In six small towns of the Old Mark (to the west of the Elbe) 2444 hearths were counted in 1567: a century later there were 1021. In its most important town, Stendal, 2980 children were born during the first decade of the seventeenth century: during the seventh decade the number was 969; and Stendal was a town which had been neither conquered nor looted. But it has to be remembered that the decline of the Brandenburg towns had started in the sixteenth century. At the other end of Germany, in Württemberg, over 41,000 destroyed houses and barns were counted in 1652, and about one-third of the arable land was deserted, a total of 309,957 *Morgen* (about 241,000 acres). Fifty-one local districts reported that they had had 58,865 burghers before the war, but that only 19,071 remained; the other twenty-four districts merely reported that they had lost 18,546 burghers. The town of Nagold lost only 8 per cent of its population, but Urach 75 per cent. In Pforzheim in Baden so many houses were still deserted in 1667 that the margrave was forced to intervene. The population of Munich fell from 18,000 or more to 9000. Among the south-western territories the Palatinate and Württemberg suffered most; among those in the north-east, Mecklenburg and Pomerania. Many inhabitants migrated to the safer north-west where Hamburg and Bremen grew in importance, exporting corn overseas and receiving English and Dutch goods; the destruction of Magdeburg contributed to the rise of Hamburg, its rival. Ulm and Nuremberg, while declining in population, to some extent profited from the influx of Austrian Protestants and of the capital which they brought with them. In Augsburg, however, 143 people had paid between 50 and 100 guilders each in taxes in 1617, but in 1661 there were only 36; while the number of those paying more than 100 guilders fell from 100 to 20, although taxation was enforced more strictly. Thus no generalisation is possible, but the picture is grim enough.

The depopulation of the countryside had divergent effects in the different parts of Germany. In Bavaria the nobility, whose income consisted of peasant dues and rents, became impoverished and dependent upon money-lenders. Even the estates of the wealthier families were burdened with heavy debts. Those of the less well-to-do often came into the hands of the monasteries, of speculators, of officers or officials who invested their capital in real estate. At the diet of 1669 the nobility strongly complained about the buying-up of noble estates: if any came on the market the religious foundations offered the best price; their ready cash was pushing aside the nobility. Only a minority were still able to live according to their custom and to send their children abroad 'to learn the noble exercises'. On account of the prevailing low corn prices demesne farming held no attraction for the landlords; a tendency in that direction did not really develop and was later reversed. The Bavarian peasants, on the other hand, benefited from this situation. Because of the scarcity of tenants the landlords were forced to grant them better conditions. As the prelates put it in 1669, if they did not want their farms to become completely deserted, they had to accept whatever they were offered; if they wanted to put new tenants on their deserted lands, they had to improve their legal position, to allow them freedom from dues for many years, and to be content with what the peasants were willing to pay.

Exactly the opposite occurred in Brandenburg, Pomerania and Mecklenburg, where demesne farming had become prominent and the position of the peasants had deteriorated since the fifteenth century. The depopulation forced the nobles to take much more deserted peasant land under their own ploughs because they were unable to find new tenants. The peasants were burdened with much heavier labour services because their number had shrunk and the demesnes had grown. Their children were forced to serve as menials or labourers on the estate. The peasants with their entire families were not only tied to the soil—that had already happened in the sixteenth century—but many became personally unfree: even their bodies belonged to their masters (*Leibeigenschaft*). They equally controlled their peasants' private lives; their consent was required for marriages; many peasants were sold or exchanged like chattels. During the following decades many more peasants were evicted or bought out. In Brandenburg the size of the noble demesnes grew by about 30 per cent during the second half of the seventeenth century. In Lower Saxony, on the other hand, a strong and independent peasantry came into being at that time, because this area had lost only a small part of its population and benefited by immigration from the devastated districts. A purposeful government policy supported this tendency, while in north-eastern Germany the governments only too easily gave way to the demands of the nobility, which aimed at a complete subjugation of the peasantry and a further extension of its demesnes. It was only along the coast of the Baltic—in Mecklenburg, Pomerania, Brandenburg, the duchy of Prussia, Poland and Livonia—where there were easy facilities for export, that the *Gutsherrschaft* (large noble estates producing corn for the market with the help of the labour services of serfs) was established in the course of the seventeenth century. Even in Saxony and Magdeburg, which were equally 'colonial' in character and possessed easy facilities for sending corn down the Elbe, this was not the case. There peasant farming remained the preponderant form of agriculture, and serfdom never assumed the rigours which it acquired in the territories along the Baltic coast. There the local nobility did not become all-powerful, but its influence was balanced by that of the towns, especially of Leipzig whose fairs acquired European importance. Bohemia and Moravia, on the other hand, resembled the territories of the north-east, from which they were separated by Saxony and Silesia. The Bohemian nobility also possessed large estates, demesnes, sheep-farms, breweries and fish-ponds, which were farmed with labour services; the peasants were serfs and many had to serve as often as they were bidden by their masters, while in the Austrian lands their services were more limited, usually to twelve days in the year.[1]

Wherever demesne farming was less prominent and the noble estates small and scattered—as in western and southern Germany—serfdom had in practice disappeared and the labour services often been commuted into quit-rents. There the depopulation of the Thirty Years War could not lead to a revival of the manorial system, but the peasants' position continued to improve. These enormous differences in the social development can be illustrated by the figures of population density. About 1700 Brandenburg had only about 30 inhabitants per English square mile, the duchy of Prussia only 28, and Pomerania only 19; but Bavaria had about 73, Hanover 63, Magdeburg 78, Saxony 93, and Württemberg 105 inhabitants per English square mile, the latter figures approximating to those of the Netherlands and France and surpassing those of England and Wales. Clearly the condition of the peasantry was worst where the population was smallest. Not that the Thirty Years War had caused this uneven distribution of the population; it merely enhanced a tendency which had existed for centuries.

In north-eastern Germany there was no improvement in the condition of the peasantry in the century following upon the Thirty Years War. In the New Mark of Brandenburg, in the early eighteenth century, labour services of three days a week were considered a light burden: usually, they amounted to four, and often to six days a week, from sunrise to sunset, which left the peasants far too little time for their own farms. About two-thirds of the total arable land belonged to the nobility and another quarter to the royal domains. In the Brandenburg districts of Beeskow and Storkow 429 peasants were counted in 1746, while there had been 814

[1] Wolf Helmhard von Hohberg, *Georgica Curiosa. Das ist: Umständlicher Bericht und klarer Unterricht von dem Adelichen Land- und Feld-Leben*... (Nuremberg, 1682), I, 46, 53, 150. It is interesting that this Austrian nobleman considered the serfdom of the Bohemian peasants and their unlimited labour services as something that 'is not customary in the German lands', thus not taking into account the conditions in north-eastern Germany. For further details, see below, ch. XX, pp. 480–1.

before the Thirty Years War; but the number of cottagers had increased from 172 to 828. In eastern Pomerania there were 6514 peasants under the nobility at the end of the sixteenth century, but only 3419 about 1670 and 3584 in 1718. Many peasants escaped across the Polish frontier to seek better conditions. In 1684 a clergyman painted the following picture of the local peasantry:

The peasants are indeed human beings, but somewhat more churlish and uncouth than the others....In his movements, he would only seldom think of his hat and take it off,...but if he does so he turns it round like a potter's wheel, or spits into his hands and polishes it....When they eat they do not use a fork, but they dip their five fingers into the pot....If soldiers steal they do it out of extreme need; but most peasants who help themselves do it out of malice....It is also well known that those who keep on good terms with the vicar are maltreated by the other peasants, for they give them all kinds of bad names, call them traitors, lickspittles, toadies, talebearers....The peasants have that in common with the stockfish: these are best when beaten well and soft. The dear peasants too are only well-behaved when fully burdened with work; then they remain well under control and timid....[1]

And in 1710 a high Prussian official, von Luben, reported to his king:

Because in some places there is strict personal serfdom [*Leibeigenschaft*] and those of the nobility do not want to abolish it but want to retain the great power over their subjects, they plague them with heavy Egyptian services, with manifold corn and other carrying duties, harsh punishments and other dues to such an extent that they remain poverty-stricken; one cannot squeeze the contribution and other taxes out of them, or they run away; if they do so they are fetched back and things go worse with them; the people are punished and treated cruelly....They cannot obtain justice at the governments and regional and local courts because the nobles sit in them, and these have an interest on account of their own estates and peasants and do not want to prejudge their own cases....The rents, services, dues, billeting and contribution have been increased so often that the people can hardly maintain themselves; therefore the serfs have long been poor and get poorer still and remain so, and finally there is nothing left but to run away....[2]

Yet the pictures drawn of east-German noblemen were hardly more flattering. In a satirical story from Silesia there occurs this description of a young noble by his own mother:

The rogue knows already that he is a Junker; therefore he does not want to learn anything, but rather rides about with his stable-boy....But in the end I will have to buy a spelling-book for him....If only it did not cost anything and the learned chaps need not have so many books....I have always heard that in other countries there are not such proper noblemen as we have them....[3]

[1] *Des Neunhäutigen und Haimbüchenen schlimmen Baurenstands und Wandels Entdeckte Ubel-Sitten und Lasterprob*, von Veroandro aus Wahrburg (1684).

[2] *Friedrich Wilhelm I. in seiner Tätigkeit für die Landescultur Preussens*, Publicationen aus den K. Preussischen Staatsarchiven, II (Leipzig, 1878), pp. 213, 216–17: relation of 14 October 1710.

[3] Paul Winckler, *Der Edelmann*, in Verlegung Christoph Riegels (Nuremberg, 1697).

Another critic of the nobility wrote:

> If one visited another the beer mug immediately appeared on the table; it went round without distinction, whether the guest was thirsty or not....If they arrived in the afternoon the drinking started right away, with medium-sized mugs which held almost a jug; then the host drank to the guests, emptying either the whole mug, or half a mug, and the guest had to respond. Thus they got drunk before the evening, and in the early morning some drank ordinary spirits, others warm beer with eggs and ginger....[1]

Other observers too commented on the excessive drinking habits. From Hamburg it was reported about 1650 that 'nowadays people first send for spirits before they go to church' on a Sunday.[2] And from Ratisbon the English envoy, Sir George Etherege, wrote in 1686:

> the Gentlemen of this Country go upon a quite different Scheme of Pleasure... and they take more care to enlarge their Cellars than their patrimonial Estates. In short, Drinking is the Hereditary Sin of this Country, and that Heroe of a Deputy here, that can demolish (at one Sitting) the rest of his Brother Envoys, is mentioned with as much Applause as the Duke of Lorain for his noble Exploits against the Turks and may claim a Statue erected at the public Expence in any Town in Germany....They are such unmerciful Plyers of the Bottle, so wholy given up to what our Scots call Goodfellowship, that 'tis as great a Constraint upon my Nature to sit out a Night's Entertainment with them, as it would be to hear half a score long-winded Presbyterian Divines Cant successively one after another....[3]

A wide gulf separated the nobility from the commoners, and this distinction was equally upheld by the urban patrician families. At Augsburg, Nuremberg, Frankfurt and Ulm the noble families were strictly secluded from the burghers. At Nuremberg they considered it dishonourable to engage in commerce. At Frankfurt the Society of Old Limpurg demanded from new members proof of eight noble ancestors and abstention from all commerce. Apart from these old noble families there were many recently ennobled ones: officers, officials and merchants, whose families engaged in ostentatious display. They drove round in gilded carriages, their wives would wear lace only from Paris or Venice, their houses were luxuriously furnished. Those whose patents of nobility dated from an earlier time looked down upon the newcomers. An eighteenth-century writer, Johann Michael von Loen, critically compared the attitude of the German nobles with those of England, where 'even the sons of the greatest peers were not ashamed to become advocates, so that later they could become magistrates and be elected to parliament', and those of Spain, where 'young noblemen from the oldest families took doctorates...'. He also remarked upon the decline of the German nobility, which went hand in hand with more splendour and greater

[1] A. Tholuk, *Vorgeschichte des Rationalismus*, II, 2 (Berlin, 1862), 197–8.

[2] *Ibid.* II, I (1861), 121.

[3] *The Letterbook of Sir George Etherege*, ed. Sybil Rosenfeld (London, 1928), pp. 413–14.

expenditure, so that many noblemen had to enter military services. 'For this there is now the best opportunity because the *miles perpetuus et mercenarius* has been introduced in all European States....'[1] The economic difficulties which undoubtedly faced the nobility in the period after the Thirty Years War indeed explain the willingness with which that of Brandenburg and Pomerania entered the Hohenzollern army and became professional officers. The same was the case in some other German principalities. In Bavaria, however, the impoverished nobility showed a clear preference for civil employment and eagerly sought State and court offices and sinecures. As there were about 500 or 600 courts in Germany, not counting those of the Imperial Knights, there were indeed many openings for impecunious noblemen.

If, in many parts of Germany, the nobility was a declining class and had to seek offices and preferments, the towns were not in a much better position. With the exception of Hamburg and Frankfurt, which grew considerably in importance, the Free Imperial Cities were mere shadows of the past. After the loss of the Alsatian cities to France their number was fifty-one, the large majority situated in the south-west of Germany. Most of them were very small and unable to hold their own in the struggle with the principalities which surrounded them. But even the more important Imperial Cities—Augsburg, Nuremberg, Ulm, Ratisbon in the south and Cologne, Aachen, Bremen, Lübeck in the north—found it difficult to adapt themselves to changed conditions. The south-German towns were hard hit by the decline of the trade with Italy and the bankruptcies of the great banking houses of the Fuggers and the Welsers. The north-German towns suffered from overwhelming Dutch, and to a lesser extent English, competition. Foreign merchants exported German raw materials and produce and imported colonial and foreign goods. The Hanseatic towns had long declined under the double impact of foreign and noble competition. They no longer sent their own ships across the seas, but were satisfied if they could act as intermediaries between foreign visitors and the hinterland. Bremen and Cologne had to fight hard to preserve their status of Free Imperial Cities. The power of the princes and the rise of the principalities made any progressive development of the Free Imperial Cities impossible: hemmed in on all sides they survived, undiminished in number, until the *Reichsdeputationshauptschluss* of 1803, but the days of their power and splendour were past. Even the economic recovery of the eighteenth century did not lead to their revival.

The decline of the Free Imperial Cities did not result in a progressive development of the towns situated within the principalities and fostered by their princes. Their trade and industry had suffered severely. In Munich, for example, the number of cloth-makers fell from 148 in 1618 to 56 in 1649, that of cloth- and linen-weavers from 161 to 82, that of hat-

[1] Johann Michael von Loen, *Der Adel* (Ulm, 1752), pp. 271, 290.

makers from 23 to 9, that of tailors from 118 to 64. After the end of the Thirty Years War the Electors of Bavaria made strenuous efforts to revive the Bavarian cloth industry, but with little success, and the number of cloth-makers declined further. The heavy taxes and monopolies imposed by the princes only too often hampered the recovery of trade and enterprise. The import of many foreign goods was prohibited, as was the export of raw materials, such as wool or hides, before there were any domestic industries which could absorb these materials or supply the internal demand. Even if certain articles could be produced locally, the foreign goods were often cheaper and better. Thus many of the prohibitions and monopolies had to be rescinded, only to be reimposed later, with the same disastrous results. In Brandenburg the export of raw wool was prohibited no less than ten times during the reign of the Great Elector, but—as the nobility was exempt from this prohibition—it proved ineffective. The repeated prohibitions of the import of iron and metal goods were equally disregarded, even by the State officials. The trade down the Elbe was so burdened with tolls that even corn, 'the soul of commerce', was shipped along different routes and transport over land became cheaper. The Elbe tolls at Lenzen were farmed out for some years, with very bad results for trade; but matters did not improve when they were again managed by State officials. The Great Elector considered these heavy tolls entirely justified; three conferences summoned to discuss the Elbe tolls produced no result because, against the advice of his privy councillors, he refused to make any concessions. The commandants of Frankfurt-on-Oder and Spandau levied their own duties on passing carriages and ships, and others did the same with travellers, in spite of official prohibitions. The number of ships putting into Königsberg declined steeply on account of new duties and tolls imposed by the government.

Equally bad was the effect of the new excises, the favourite instruments of seventeenth-century governments. In Saxony an excise was introduced in 1640 and not rescinded after the end of the war. Therefore many goods by-passed Saxony and were transported along alternative routes. Silk and other costly goods from Italy went north through Thuringia, linen from Bohemia and Silesia went through Brandenburg (before the excise was introduced there). It was in vain that the Estates of Saxony complained that the excise caused the ruin of the country, especially of the cloth and linen industries, and favoured Saxony's neighbours. It was equally in vain that the Hanseatic and the south- and west-German towns repeatedly declared that under these conditions their trade with Leipzig could not revive. There was much passive resistance, but the excise remained; only on home-produced goods was it rescinded temporarily, but reintroduced in 1681. By that time the excise had also been introduced in Brandenburg, with even more negative effects. For there it was not introduced for the country as a whole, but only for the towns, so that each small town was surrounded by artificial customs barriers and the excise had to be levied at the town gates. Thus urban trade and enterprise were burdened with the new tax, while those carried on outside the town walls remained free and the tax-exemption of the nobility was preserved. It also meant that the towns had to carry a disproportionate share of the taxes: it is not surprising that their recovery was so slow. And this was the system which was gradually extended from Brandenburg to the other Hohenzollern territories. Other principalities were more fortunate. Following the Brandenburg example, in 1700 an excise was also introduced in the duchies of Jülich and Berg on the lower Rhine; but there the Estates and the towns got it rescinded after a few years, for urban enterprise was declining and trade was migrating into neighbouring territories.

The towns within the principalities also suffered from the efforts of their rulers to extend their sway over the towns. Since 1648 Archbishop John Philip of Mainz tried to enforce his prerogative over the town of Erfurt in Thuringia which vigorously resisted all his threats and even the ban of the Empire. In 1664 he decided to use force and, supported by France and the Rhenish Alliance, laid siege to Erfurt. A month later the town surrendered, rendered homage to John Philip and accepted a princely garrison. Two years later the Great Elector forced Magdeburg to do the same. In a similar fashion the city of Münster was subjugated by Bishop Christopher Bernard von Galen and the town of Brunswick by the dukes of Brunswick-Lüneburg. The opposition of Königsberg, the capital of the duchy of Prussia, and of the towns of the duchy of Cleves, which resisted the imposition of arbitrary taxes and the depredations of the military, was broken by military force. The introduction of the urban excise in the early eighteenth century spelled the ruin of their old prosperity. Within twelve years the most important town of Cleves, Wesel, lost over a quarter of its inhabitants and all the towns of Cleves over 11 per cent of theirs.

It is true that the rise of Hamburg continued during this period, that the fairs of Leipzig became a focal point of exchange between east and west and south; that the Silesian linen industry continued to prosper; but these exceptional cases merely emphasise the general stagnation. The continuing decline of many German towns, often caused by government action, provided great opportunities for foreign merchants and financiers. Already before the Thirty Years War Dutch merchants had penetrated up the Rhine and from the Baltic ports into the hinterland. After the war their influence increased and at certain places became predominant. The Dutch with their capital resources and trading connections, with their many ships and cheaper freight rates, were at an enormous advantage compared with the small merchants of petty German towns. The Thirty Years War and the collapse of the great banking houses had ruined all credit and consumed most of the capital. Timidity and narrow-mindedness were the characteristics of the day. For his naval and colonial enterprises the Great Elector had to use Dutch experts and sailors, Dutch companies and financiers, because no such resources were available in Brandenburg and Prussia. For the same reason he welcomed Jewish merchants, especially if they also represented Dutch interests. Thus Moses Jacobson de Jonge in 1664 received an important privilege which entitled him to take up residence at Memel—at a time when the Jews were still excluded from the duchy of Prussia. He soon established a flourishing trade with Poland, Lithuania and Livonia, almost monopolised the highly important trade in salt and successfully competed with the local merchants; in 1694–6 he paid 80 per cent more in customs duties than all the merchants of Memel together. No wonder that they as well as the Estates of Prussia violently complained about the newcomer. In Cleves the Gomperz family played an important part in financial matters, advancing sums to the government and to the Estates, anticipating the yield of taxes, and meeting the arrears of French contributions. In 1700 Ruben Elias Gomperz was appointed chief tax-collector for the principalities of Cleves and Mark, and under Frederick William I members of the same family were again employed on official business. Because there were so many courts and so many impecunious princes, because their splendour and their ambitions were continuously growing, because they had to have standing armies which had to be supplied with food and equipment, hundreds of court Jews had to try to meet the ever-increasing demands of the princes.

Thus the Thirty Years War exercised a profound influence on the course of German history, especially in the social and economic field. In popular opinion it became the cause of all evils; even the deserted villages of the later Middle Ages were attributed to destruction by the Swedes or to some other calamity of the great war. Naturally, the popular literature of the time, as well as of modern times, tended to over-emphasise the horrors and the hopelessness of the situation. If this picture is too one-sided and biased, so are the attempts of some modern historians to 'debunk' the Thirty Years War and to attribute much of the bleakness to later propaganda. It has also been alleged that contemporaries did not think of the war as one war, but divided it into a number of separate wars. But it can be proved that one name—'the great German war', or 'the Thirty Years War'—was used soon after the fighting had come to an end. It is true, of course, that the political disunity of Germany was not caused, but merely exacerbated, by the Thirty Years War, and that some of the negative features described above were due to political disunity. But it also remains true that the social and economic decline was at best local before the outbreak of the war and was made much more general by the war. It is equally true that the rise of the western European countries began long before the outbreak of the war; but it seems at least possible that

Germany might have been able to participate in that rise if the war had not intervened. In the sixteenth century Germany was still a flourishing country; it took her a century or longer to reach once more the level of development she had attained before the outbreak of the Thirty Years War.

If the economic and social development of Germany during the second half of the seventeenth century presented a picture of almost unmitigated gloom, the same is not entirely true of the constitutional field. The institutions of the Empire—in spite of all its decline and disintegration—continued to work better than might have been expected. A certain stability was reached which was to persist into the eighteenth century; and no serious efforts were made to upset the balance of forces which had come into being. Perhaps it was the continuous threat from France which brought about some cohesion between divergent forces, or the pressure from the Turks; but the latter were far less dangerous than they had been in the fifteenth and sixteenth centuries, and the siege of Vienna was only a passing episode. Louis XIV always had his partisans and clients in Germany: in that respect French power was an element of disruption, and not of cohesion. Only certain parts of the Empire were threatened by foreign foes. Yet it was not only the States of the Rhineland which combined against France—on the contrary, there Louis XIV found many more or less willing 'allies'—and not only those of the south-east which fought against the Turks. If one remembers that the Empire had about 360 different Estates—not counting the 1500 Free Imperial Knights—it seems a miracle that some unity was preserved in spite of so much disunity.

Not all the 360 Estates were represented in the Imperial Diet, which met at Ratisbon and debated upon matters such as the coinage, sumptuary laws, measures against vagabonds and beggars and, above all, military affairs and taxes to be levied for defence or other purposes. For, with the sole exception of a levy for the maintenance of the Imperial High Court, there were no permanent Imperial taxes, but only the 'Roman months' voted by the Diet.[1] Another weakness of the Imperial Diet was that it possessed no executive authority if some of the Estates declined to carry out decisions taken by the Diet. In that case, there was only the possibility of a trial before the Imperial High Court which was notorious for its delays and for creating complications. The Diet consisted of three houses or 'colleges'. The first was that of the Electors: in 1648 their number was increased to eight, but the Elector of Bohemia (the Habsburg Emperor) did not exercise his electoral dignity. There were thus four Catholic Electors—Bavaria and the archbishops of Cologne, Mainz and Trier—

[1] Originally levied to finance Imperial expeditions to Rome, the 'Roman months' since the sixteenth century were grants made by the Diet for the Imperial army, which were repartitioned among the Estates of the Empire according to a fixed quota.

and three Protestant ones—Lutheran Saxony and two Calvinists, Brandenburg and the Palatinate. In the Palatinate, however, a Catholic line of Electors succeeded in 1685, and twelve years later the Elector of Saxony also became a Roman Catholic. This was balanced only to some extent by the creation of a ninth Electorate for Hanover—granted in 1692 by the Emperor acting on his own authority, without any consultation with the Electors or other princes, who had no alternative but to acquiesce. Thus at the end of the century there were only two Protestant Electors, against six Catholics (excluding Bohemia). The Elector of Mainz was the leader of the *corpus catholicorum*, and the Elector of Saxony of the *corpus evangelicorum*; but in religious controversies neither side could outvote the other.

The second house was that of the princes, separated into ecclesiastical and temporal 'benches'. There were thirty-seven ecclesiastical and sixty-three temporal votes, six of which were composite: the Swabian and the Rhenish prelates and four groups of Imperial Counts each exercising one vote. In this house also the Catholics had a majority, but not a large one. The third house was formed by the fifty-one Free Imperial Cities, thirteen of which counted as Catholic, thirty-four as Protestant, and four as 'mixed'. Their influence, however, was very restricted because the Diet of 1653 granted them a *votum decisivum* only *after* an agreement had been reached between the two upper houses, so that they could no longer influence the outcome in case of a disagreement between the houses. As the English envoy, Sir George Etherege, wrote in 1685, 'the deputies of the towns serve only for form's sake, and have never any business transmitted to them till the other two Colleges have agreed... '.[1] In that case the deputies of the cities had practically no alternative but to consent, for it was an accepted principle that none of the houses could be outvoted by the others. As far as Imperial taxation was concerned, it became equally accepted since 1653 that a vote of credit required unanimity, for—as a decision of the Lower Saxon Circle put it in 1652—it would be 'entirely contrary to natural freedom...if someone by his vote could decree what someone else should give'.[2] The Emperor Ferdinand III had to give up his plan of making majority decisions in questions of taxation binding on the minority: the Estates' liberties triumphed once more and the opposition of the princes, led by Brandenburg, prevailed.

In 1654 the princes gained another point: paragraph 180 of the *Recess* drawn up at the conclusion of the Diet stipulated that the subjects of each Imperial Estate were obliged to make grants in aid to their prince or lord with respect to the manning and maintenance of the essential fortresses, places and garrisons. If this was a blow aimed at the local Estates, which in most principalities still exercised the power of the purse, a further step

[1] *The Letterbook of Sir George Etherege*, p. 61.

[2] Karl Lamprecht, *Deutsche Geschichte* (Freiburg, 1904), VI, 377.

in that direction was made after the death of Ferdinand III in 1657. Before the young Leopold was elected Emperor he had to make far-reaching concessions. The Electors of Brandenburg and Cologne, involved in complicated struggles with their own Estates, demanded that these should maintain the fortresses with their own resources and have no right to dispose of local taxes without the consent of the prince in question. Brandenburg in addition requested that the Estates should be forbidden to meet without a summons by the ruler or to make a complaint about him to the courts of the Empire; while the Palatinate, Saxony and Trier were satisfied with the preservation of the *status quo*. Saxony in particular opposed the prohibition of appeals to the Imperial courts, from which it would not have benefited: at that time only the possessions of the houses of Saxony and Bavaria, of the Electors Palatine and of Mainz had received a *privilegium de non appellando* which exempted them from the jurisdiction of the Imperial courts; but of the Hohenzollern territories such an exemption had been granted only to the Brandenburg Mark, not to their other possessions. Yet, if Leopold wanted to be elected Emperor, he had to accept the Electors' conditions. Hence it was stipulated that the local Estates were not entitled to refuse contributions to the 'necessary' fortresses and garrisons, to meet without a summons, or to dispose independently of local taxes. If in such cases they sent complaints to the Imperial courts, these should not be heard, nor should complaints against paragraph 180 of the *Recess* of 1654. If the Estates possessed privileges contrary to these stipulations they should be revoked, and equally alliances or unions between the Estates of several principalities. Only thereafter was Leopold elected Emperor by a unanimous vote. Henceforth the princes possessed a legal title which they could always employ against their Estates. Contrary to this prohibition, however, the Imperial courts, especially the Aulic Council, continued to entertain complaints of local Estates against their rulers: a factor which was to be of great importance.[1]

The dangers threatening from the Turks and domestic circumstances induced the Emperor to summon another Diet. It was opened early in 1663 and, after deliberations stretching over more than twelve months, consented to support the Emperor against the Infidel with an army of about 30,000 men. But only one-third of that number finally appeared in the field, and they participated only in the last stages of the campaign. The discussion of other subjects was even more prolonged—so much so that no *Recess* was ever concluded: the Diet became permanent, consisting of envoys of the princes, whose instructions they had to seek on each issue. It thus became a congress of diplomats wrangling over questions of rank and procedure, as described in letters of Sir George Etherege from Ratisbon in 1687–8: 'The business of the Diet for the most part is only fit

[1] See below, pp. 455–6.

to entertain those insects in politics which crawl under the trees in St James's Park....' And four months later: 'The cabals and intrigues for and against the Count de Windisgratz's pretensions have been the only business of the Diet this long while....' After another five months nothing had changed: 'Those who are unacquainted with the proceedings of this assembly would wonder that, where so many ministers are met and maintained at so great a charge by their masters, so little business is done, and the little that is so slowly....' The lot of the English envoy, who disliked the drinking bouts of the Germans and found their ladies 'so intolerably reserv'd and virtuous...that 'tis next to an impossibility to carry on an Intrigue with them...', was not an enviable lot.[1] What heights of folly the system could reach may be illustrated by the behaviour of the representative of the Elector of Mainz in 1701. When leaving his coach at the quarters of the Imperial representative he demanded to be led to him through a secret staircase because he had found in the files that this had been the previous practice. When he was informed that this was impossible for the simple reason that the secret staircase no longer existed, but had disappeared during building operations, he insisted nevertheless and declared that under these circumstances he did not dare to seek an audience, but would write to his master for instructions.

When the War of Devolution broke out in 1667[2] the Imperial Diet was confronted with the question whether the Spanish Netherlands, which formed the 'Burgundian Circle' of the Empire, should be protected. The French ambassador used all the means at his disposal to prevent such a decision, while the Imperial representative, the archbishop of Salzburg, tried to counteract his influence. Meanwhile Louis XIV conquered town after town, but the Imperial Diet remained silent. In September the Electors pronounced in favour of mediation, ignoring the question whether the Spanish Netherlands formed a part of the Empire. Among the princes the Salzburg resolution which affirmed the latter point obtained only thirty votes, while forty-one were in favour of mediation and thirteen without any instructions. During the following weeks both sides continued their efforts: as the influence of the French ambassador was gaining ground, the archbishop of Salzburg did not persist and the matter was quietly dropped. It was only in 1674, after new acts of aggression, that the Imperial Diet finally declared war on France. But even then only part of the Estates furnished the contingents to the Imperial army which this decision obliged them to provide, and the Franconian and Swabian Circles as well as Bavaria protested against the billeting of the Emperor's forces within their frontiers. After the Peace of Nymegen (1679) no fewer than six of the Electorates—Bavaria, Brandenburg, Cologne,

[1] The quotations are from *The Letterbook of Sir George Etherege*, pp. 210, 270, 328, 416.

[2] See above, ch. IX, pp. 210–12.

Mainz, Trier and Saxony—belonged to the French party, seeking to achieve their aims through an alliance with Louis XIV or compelled by their geographical position to remain on good terms with him. After 1680, however, the new Electors of Bavaria and Saxony adopted a more friendly policy towards Vienna and left the leadership of the French party to the Great Elector of Brandenburg.

It was during these years, when the power of Louis XIV stood at its height, that real progress was made by the Imperial Diet with the creation of an army to defend the Empire. An Imperial law of May 1681 fixed the figure of the *simplum* of the army at 40,000—12,000 horse and 28,000 foot-soldiers. The total was then distributed among the ten Circles of the Empire, the Austrian Circle having to contribute about 20 per cent, and the Burgundian, Lower and Upper Saxon, Swabian and Westphalian Circles about 10 per cent each. Within each Circle, the various Estates had to furnish their military contingents, the details of distribution being left to the Estates of the Circle in question. This meant that in the Swabian Circle, which had by far the largest number of Estates, contingents had to be provided by ninety-one different Estates, including thirty-one Free Imperial Cities. At the same time an Imperial War Chest was set up. The Emperor in person could command the Imperial army or nominate an Imperial Field-Marshal, while the Imperial Diet appointed a number of generals. The fortresses which Louis XIV had built on the right bank of the Rhine—Philippsburg and, after 1697, Kehl—were maintained and garrisoned as Imperial fortresses after their restoration by France. The *simplum* of 1681 could be increased in case of need, and was indeed augmented immediately by 50 per cent to 60,000. By a law of November 1702 it was increased to 120,000, 80,000 of which were to be kept in permanent readiness (*duplum*). Difficulties were, however, raised by those Imperial Estates which already possessed a standing army of their own, for example Brandenburg, because they did not want to furnish their contingents to the armies of different Circles. In practice, therefore, the whole organisation only functioned in the western Circles of the Empire which were directly threatened by Louis XIV. In 1697 the Bavarian, Franconian, Swabian, Westphalian and two Rhenish Circles concluded an Association which undertook—on the basis of the law of 1681—to raise an army of 60,000 men, reduced to 40,000 in peace-time, and regulated its organisation in detail. It was this army which for many years defended the Rhine frontier against France and garrisoned the Imperial fortresses on the Rhine. It thus proved that there was no need for each principality to acquire a standing army of its own, that the Empire was capable of defending its own frontiers, and that the institution of the Circles could be of great practical importance. Some of the Circles successfully dealt with matters of trade, customs, coinage, building of roads, law and police, health and welfare. In the south-west they took steps to bring about greater uniformity in legal and economic affairs—steps which were essential for the progress of the most divided region of the Empire.

The other institution of the Empire which showed signs of real life in the later seventeenth and eighteenth centuries was the Aulic Council at Vienna. For the subjects and Estates of the princes the Imperial courts were the remaining link with the Empire because to them they could complain or appeal, even against their prince, unless he had been granted a *privilegium de non appellando*, and that applied only to four or five princes, such as those of Bavaria and Saxony. The Aulic Council (*Reichshofrat*) was steadily gaining in importance because it dealt with cases more quickly and efficiently than the Imperial High Court, was freer in its rules of procedure and had better means of enforcing its decisions. Thus its jurisdiction was preferred by many parties. It was competent to deal with questions of fiefs and privileges and was the last court of appeal within the Empire. It depended entirely on the Emperor, who nominated its president, its vice-president, and its eighteen councillors, six of whom had to be Protestants. In 1654 he issued on his own authority regulations for the procedure of the Aulic Council which excluded the Imperial Estates from all participation and influence. The jurisdiction of the Aulic Council was instrumental in protecting the subjects of several German princes against the worst excesses of princely despotism and prevented the dukes of Mecklenburg, Württemberg, and Jülich and Berg from making themselves absolute. Its field of competence, however, was progressively curtailed in the eighteenth century by the grant of *privilegia de non appellando* to several princely houses, even outside the Electoral group.

The other Imperial court, the *Reichskammergericht* (Imperial High Court), was steadily declining in importance. Until 1688 it was situated at Speyer, and after the second devastation of the Palatinate it was transferred to Wetzlar. It was the last court of appeal for the subjects of the princes, but a court of first instance for those who were not the subjects of any prince, for example Free Imperial Knights, and in cases of denial of justice. It stood much less under the influence of the Emperor, who nominated its president, and much more under that of the Imperial Estates. Twenty-four of the judges were to be nominated by the Electors, twenty-four by the Circles, and only two by the Emperor. Because of lack of funds, however, the number of judges never exceeded eighteen and was often much smaller. The Imperial High Court was notorious for its dilatory procedure: cases dragged on for decades, and sometimes for centuries, without ever reaching a conclusion. The devastation of the Palatinate and internal strife further contributed to its decline and to the rise of the Aulic Council, which was favoured by the Emperor. An Imperial Deputation was appointed to speed up the appeals pending, but did not start its work until 1767. Apart from the two Imperial courts, there was an Imperial Chancery, under a Vice-Chancellor, which served the Emperor as a secretariate for purposes of the government of the Empire—as distinct from that of his hereditary territories, which were administered by organs such as the Imperial Privy Council, the Privy Conference, and the Court Chancery.[1]

If the Empire had almost lost the character of a State, the weight of political life had shifted into the principalities. The major princes, adopting the principles of absolute government, tried to gain more power at the cost of weaker neighbours and of their own subjects. Their policy of consolidation and of becoming 'more considerable' was bound to lead to conflicts with those institutions which acted as a brake on such endeavours, especially their own Estates. In most principalities these possessed far-reaching privileges, above all the power of the purse which made the ruler dependent on their voting of taxes, whether it was for his growing court expenditure, for his military forces, or for the waging of war. Furthermore, in many principalities the local Estates had acquired a strong influence in the field of administration: by taking over more and more debts of the prince they had gradually built up their own organs of administration, with their own officials and permanent committees, side by side with, or superseding the machinery of the State. In some principalities they had acquired the privilege of periodical meetings, or could meet without a summons by the ruler. Such privileges were extremely irksome to princes who wanted to be independent of any fetters and aimed at the building up of their own administration. This tendency clearly emerged before the election of Leopold I to the Imperial throne, but many princes were not satisfied with the concessions gained. They wanted to extend the rights obtained through the *Recess* of 1654 to all their military enterprises and to see the Estates' power of the purse abolished. In 1670 the Imperial Diet passed a proposal to this effect, but the Emperor refused to give his assent. Therefore the princes with particularly strong inclinations towards absolute government—Bavaria, Brandenburg, Cologne, Palatinate-Neuburg, etc.—in June 1671 concluded an alliance to help each other if their Estates resisted them by force of arms, or if they refused to pay what was necessary for defence purposes or the conservation of fortresses, or what the Empire and the Circles had agreed upon. Against their own Estates the German princes found it easy to co-operate: thus the Great Elector of Brandenburg and the Count Palatine Philip William, the duke of Jülich and Berg, jointly tried to achieve the repeal of the hereditary unions which bound the Estates of Jülich, Cleves, Berg and Mark together.

It was the example of Louis XIV and of his unlimited power which inspired many German princes. If they could not hope to rival the splendour of the French king, if their armies remained woefully inferior to his, they at least had to build a little Versailles on the banks of the Neckar or

[1] For these Habsburg organs of government see below, ch. xx, pp. 477, 485.

the Spree. John George II of Saxony built an opera-house and maintained an orchestra with one conductor-in-chief, two assistant conductors, four Italian composers, and forty-six singers. In Württemberg in 1684 a French opera with a ballet was enacted by the court under the title *Le rendez-vous des plaisirs*. A visit to Versailles became almost obligatory for the sons of the German princes, and their example was soon followed by the higher nobility. In 1671 the president of the Württemberg privy council, full of pride, described to the deputies of the Estates the grand tour of the Württemberg princes in France. After their arrival in Paris the two princes

> were immediately visited in their lodgings by the highest grandees and frequently entertained magnificently in their palaces; until finally Marshal de Turenne conducted them in his carriage to an audience in the royal Louvre where they were received in the most friendly fashion by His Majesty; before they were admitted to his presence they were informed that the King would not wear his hat during the audience, but would talk with them bareheaded; and thus it was done in his private closet where he entertained them for a full half hour discoursing with them most graciously, which otherwise was quite unusual....[1]

The sun of Versailles lent lustre even to very minor stars. French fashions and French modes of government penetrated across the Rhine, and French money was an extremely powerful influence at many a princely court. In Berlin, after 1679, the French ambassador, Count Rébenac, wielded enormous influence and distributed his largesse among the servants of the Great Elector, exactly as the French ambassador to the court of St James's did among the supporters and opponents of Charles II.

Among the German principalities the four lay Electorates continued to be the most important ones. Yet during this period the Palatinate lost the leading position which it had occupied for so long. When the Elector Charles Louis in 1649 returned to his devastated lands he used the methods of absolute government; he tried to revive trade, to direct the economy, to improve education, and to settle the religious strife. He also founded a standing army—which in wartime grew to over 8000 men—and a military administration with a war council. For their maintenance permanent taxes on wine, fruit and meat were introduced. The Elector was strongly opposed to all privileges and to any curtailment of the power of the State. Under his strict rule the country began to recover from the ravages of the Thirty Years War, but in 1673 the taxable capital and property were estimated at only about one-quarter of the figure of 1618; in the different local districts it varied from one-sixth to three-fifths of the pre-war figures. Yet the worst was still to come. In 1685 the Simmern branch of the Electors Palatine died out and was succeeded by the Neuburg branch which also ruled in the duchies of Jülich and Berg. Already

[1] State Archives Stuttgart, *Tomus Actorum*, vol. LXXI, fo. 270: report of 13 February 1671.

in 1674 the Palatinate had been terribly devastated by the French; now Louis XIV claimed it in the name of his brother who was married to Elisabeth Charlotte, the sister of the last Elector of the Simmern line. The result of the ensuing war was a second devastation, even more thorough and deliberate than the first. Among the many towns and villages destroyed was the capital, Heidelberg, with its ancient university and beautiful palace. From these repeated blows the Palatinate was unable to recover. In addition, the new Elector, John William, was a Catholic and soon began to oppress the Calvinists, many of whom sought refuge abroad. Thus the Palatinate lost its leading position among the German principalities and became one among many minor States; even in the eighteenth century it was unable to resume its former place.

The other Wittelsbach Electorate, Bavaria, emerged from the Thirty Years War considerably strengthened, in spite of the ill-effects of the war. Maximilian I was the acknowledged leader of the Catholic League, gained the Electoral dignity and conquered the Upper Palatinate, where he suppressed the Estates and introduced the Counter-Reformation. In Bavaria also he followed the principles of absolute government. As he wrote shortly before his death in the 'Information' which he left to his wife: in almost every country there was a clash of interests between the prince and the Estates, for they always tried to increase their privileges and liberties and to escape the burdens and taxes to which the prince was entitled by right, or at least to whittle them down by all kinds of means; therefore, it was not advisable to hold diets without a highly important cause, because the Estates only used them to raise their grievances and new pretensions.[1] In spite of the Estates' demands, no diet was summoned after the end of the war, but they were successful in achieving the disbanding of the army, with the exception of only a few garrisons. Maximilian's successor, Ferdinand Maria (1651–79), continued his father's methods of government. Its heart and soul was the privy council; the other central authorities, for financial, military and religious affairs, were made subordinate to it and became its executive organs. For the supervision of the local authorities and matters of 'police', agriculture, trade and industry, the Church and the schools, the *Rentmeister* were used as the long arm of the government, their manifold functions corresponding to those of the *intendants* in France. The Elector administered the country as though it were his private estate and ruled his subjects as if he were their guardian. Through the introduction of new taxes and the judicious use of monopolies the electoral revenues grew considerably and were partly used to encourage music and the arts. A standing army of a few thousand men came into being, but only during the wars against Louis XIV did it reach a

[1] Christian Ruepprecht, 'Die Information des Kurfürsten Maximilian I. von Bayern für seine Gemahlin vom 13. März 1651', *Oberbayerisches Archiv für vaterländische Geschichte*, LIX (1895–6), p. 317.

more substantial size. After many years and repeated petitions of the Estates' committee Ferdinand Maria consented to summon a diet. It met in 1669, after an interval of fifty-seven years: the last in the history of the *ancien régime*. The Estates granted 372,000 guilders a year for nine years and took over most of the Electoral debts. They further empowered their twenty deputies to grant another 200,000 guilders in case of need and, if this was insufficient, to summon the Estates; but some days later the Elector changed this clause by a decree which empowered the deputies to decide with him what was necessary and to co-opt new members in case of any vacancy. Thus the Estates' deputies continued to meet several times each year, to grant the taxes required by the government, to raise grievances, and to supervise the financial administration of the Estates and the work of their officials. Ferdinand Maria's successor, Max Emanuel (1679–1726), paid even less regard to the privileges of the Estates: he considered them a useless institution and an obstacle to his ambitious foreign policy. During the War of the Spanish Succession he sided with Louis XIV, was put under the ban of the Empire and, after Blenheim, driven out of the country.[1] After his restoration in 1714 he continued his absolutist policy; but he did not dispense with the remaining rights of the deputies of the Estates.

Even more than Catholic Bavaria, it was the two Protestant Electorates in the east of Germany, Brandenburg and Saxony, which came to the fore in the period after the Thirty Years War. More will be said about Brandenburg in another chapter,[2] but at this time Saxony was still the much more developed, wealthy and populous of the two. As a result of the war it had acquired Lusatia and the secularised bishoprics of Meissen, Merseburg and Naumburg. Soon a much greater prize, Poland, was to loom large in the policy of the Electors. But it was a gain of very doubtful value, for vast sums of money had to be spent in Poland, partly on bribes to the electors; and the kingdom absorbed the energies of the House of Wettin which thus could not concentrate on the development of their own State—the policy to which the Hohenzollerns adhered so faithfully. Poland and the wars in which the Electors found themselves involved because of Poland—especially that against Sweden in the early eighteenth century, during which Saxony was occupied by the Swedish army[3]—contributed to the decline of Saxony. From the point of view of Brandenburg it was extremely lucky that the ambition of the Great Elector and his eldest son to become king of Poland was not fulfilled. In contrast with Brandenburg and with Bavaria, the Estates of Saxony did not lose their powers: on the contrary, the enormous debts of the Electors forced them to make new concessions to the Estates. In 1661 their deputies were granted the right of free assembly on their own initiative to discuss

[1] For these events, see vol. VI, ch. XIII.
[2] See below, ch. XXIII, pp. 543 ff.
[3] See vol. VI, ch. XX.

important affairs; if the Elector attempted to change the established religion, Lutheranism, the Estates' votes of credit were to be null and void. The religious issue stiffened their resistance to absolute monarchy; for in 1697 Frederick Augustus I, to secure the Polish Crown, became a Roman Catholic and thus lost his rights of supreme headship over the Saxon Church which were transferred to the privy council. He had to sell or pawn many lands and prerogatives; but he made his capital, Dresden, a centre of the arts and founded the Meissen porcelain manufactory, the first in Germany, soon to become famous. A standing army of about 10,000 men came into being in the later seventeenth century. During the wars against the Turks, in which it took a prominent part, it was increased to nearly 20,000: less only than that of Brandenburg. Yet the growth of the *miles perpetuus* did not destroy the power of the Estates, and diets continued to be summoned at fairly regular intervals. Their influence only declined when, early in the eighteenth century, the general excise was introduced on the pattern of Brandenburg. The need of money and more money, the religious opposition, and the Electors' preoccupation with Poland prevented them from following the Hohenzollerns' example more closely; the standing army remained comparatively small, and Saxony remained a constitutional monarchy—in contrast with the kingdom of Prussia.

The development of Hanover, which in 1692 became the youngest Electorate, was considerably delayed by conflicts among ducal brothers, so common in German princely families, and the resulting divisions of their territory. New partitions were effected in 1641 and in 1665; but in 1683 Ernest Augustus of Hanover introduced primogeniture for his possessions, and in 1705 his son, the Elector George Louis, succeeded in reuniting the ducal territories, nine years before he mounted the British throne. In the later seventeenth century dukes John Frederick and Ernest Augustus of Hanover built up a strong army which enabled them to participate actively in the wars against Louis XIV and the Turks and the rebellious Hungarians. The elevation of Ernest Augustus to the Electoral dignity by the Emperor Leopold was a reward for services rendered. The former also supported the expedition of William of Orange to England. The administration of the Electorate was carried on, under the Elector's control, by the privy council, with four colleges responsible for finance, law, war, and the Church respectively. The court was under the influence of the philosopher Leibniz.[1] The ruling group, however, consisted of the nobility, and this prevented the establishment of a completely absolute government. This tendency was strongly reinforced in the eighteenth century, because the Electors were so often absent abroad and the government was in the hands of regents drawn from the native nobility. All important posts were reserved to a few families, social dis-

[1] For Leibniz, see above, ch. IV, pp. 82–5; ch. V, pp. 114–17; ch. VI, pp. 145–6.

tinctions were rigidly upheld, and the Estates dominated by the nobility in practice ruled the country. Even the historical divisions remained a reality; the Estates were divided into seven different corporations for the several duchies and counties which made up the Electorate. Exactly as the preoccupation of the Electors of Saxony with Poland prevented them from playing a leading part in Germany, so the preoccupation of the Electors of Hanover with Britain prevented them from concentrating on the development and unification of their German possessions.

In the duchy of Holstein, to the north of Hanover, on the other hand, the Estates lost all their influence in the later seventeenth century. There the joint rulers—the dukes of Holstein and the kings of Denmark—used to the full the rights granted by the Imperial *Recess* of 1654,[1] which were backed by a decision of the Lower Saxon Circle. The rulers maintained that they alone were entitled to decide upon the maintenance of fortresses and garrisons, while the Estates declined to grant them the necessary means. After the accession of Duke Christian Albrecht in 1659, however, a tax for military purposes was demanded regularly every spring: if the Estates did not consent to it, it was nevertheless levied by the government. When the Estates referred to their privileges the government declared that these constituted only a private law, while the decisions of the Empire and the Circle were fundamental and public laws. When the Estates insisted that their grievances be redressed first, the rulers refused and proceeded with the compulsory levies. In 1675 the last diet was summoned: after renewed disputes it was adjourned, never to meet again, and the Estates lost all their influence. Very similar was the development in the margraviate of Baden-Durlach, in the south-west of Germany, which had suffered severely from the Thirty Years War and was to suffer even more during the wars of Louis XIV. There also the diet met for the last time in 1668: without any opposition it transferred the power of the purse and the administration of the debts to Margrave Frederick VI. The constitution was not abrogated, but the diet was no longer summoned because its usefulness had disappeared. The country was ruled by the methods of patriarchal absolutism which eliminated all conflicts and promoted economic recovery. A memorandum drawn up in 1771 pointed out correctly that the very name of the Estates had long been forgotten.

In some other principalities, however, exactly as in Saxony, the Estates during and after the Thirty Years War succeeded in retaining and even extending their powers. In the duchy of Mecklenburg, to the east of Holstein, the dukes also claimed the right of levying taxes for military purposes without a grant by the Estates. In 1659–63 these complained to the Emperor Leopold and the Aulic Council where their privileges were confirmed. Encouraged by this support from the highest authorities of the Empire they refused in 1671 to pay the aid granted by the Imperial

[1] See above, p. 445.

Diet to the United Provinces, whereupon the dukes levied it by force. When the Estates renewed their complaint to the Aulic Council it was rejected; yet the conflict went on. In 1698 the Aulic Council decided that, if the issue was a tax for the Empire, the Estates were obliged to pay. Three years later it was agreed that for such purposes 120,000 thalers were to be levied annually, one-third of which was to be given by the nobility, the towns, and the ducal domains respectively; and this was confirmed by the Emperor, but rejected by a part of the nobility. New conflicts broke out during the War of the North in which Duke Charles Leopold participated on the side of Peter the Great and Russian troops occupied the duchy.[1] The Estates refused to grant the large sums demanded and Rostock, the only important town of the duchy, again appealed to the Aulic Council; but in 1715 the town had to surrender and to accept the ducal conditions. In the same year the Emperor Charles VI, after petitions of the Mecklenburg Estates and the Elector George Louis of Hanover, decreed an 'Imperial Execution' against Charles Leopold and entrusted its execution to the princes of Hanover and Brunswick. Their troops occupied the duchy after the departure of the Russian troops and virtually deposed Charles Leopold. By a decision of the Aulic Council the government was in 1728 entrusted to his brother, and the constitution was restored with the help of the Estates. In the middle of the eighteenth century the conflict was renewed; but the Estates, backed by the Aulic Council, were again victorious over the duke and their privileges remained in force.

If the Mecklenburg Estates were dominated by the nobility, the opposite was true of the duchy of Württemberg in the south-west: there the Estates consisted only of the deputies of about sixty towns and fourteen secularised monasteries and were unicameral—a very exceptional development, due to the fact that the noblemen had become Free Imperial Knights. In Württemberg also the main issue between the dukes and the Estates was the question of the standing army. The Estates strenuously refused to grant the means for its maintenance in peace-time and achieved its reduction to a few hundred men as soon as the wars came to an end. When Duke Frederick Charles in the 1690's transformed the militia into a regular army the Estates declared that this was unconstitutional and complained to the Aulic Council, but without much success. The conflicts continued in the eighteenth century during which the Estates at first steadily lost ground, but finally succeeded in re-establishing their influence, thanks to support from the Aulic Council and the kings of Prussia and Britain. In Württemberg also, the fact that, from 1733 onwards, the Estates were fighting against Roman Catholic dukes strengthened their resistance to despotic government.

Thus constitutional developments varied enormously in the different

[1] For these events, see vol. VI, ch. XX.

parts of Germany, with repercussions which have lasted into the twentieth century. But the events in the Palatinate and Baden, in the south-west, and in Mecklenburg, in the north-east, show that it was by no means the south-west which remained more constitutional and 'liberal' and the north-east which became more autocratic. The divergent developments cannot be explained by factors of geography, nor by differences of social structure; for the Estates of Mecklenburg—like those of Poland and of Hungary—were dominated by the nobility, and those of Württemberg by the burghers of small towns. Only in Saxony did there exist a balance between the nobility and the towns, among which Leipzig was by far the most important. In Brandenburg and Prussia, on the other hand, where the nobility was as predominant as in Mecklenburg, absolute government triumphed, and a standing army was established which was far larger than in any other German principality. This was due, above all, to the determined policy of the Hohenzollerns: their single-mindedness helped them to overtake the Wittelsbachs and the Wettiners during the century following upon the Thirty Years War. The personal factor was of vital importance in this respect. Outside Prussia, the standing armies remained small, and the Estates with their ancient liberties and constitutional rights disappeared only in a few of the other principalities. Wherever their influence was preserved, and wherever that of the army did not permeate the whole State, a tradition remained alive which was to facilitate the establishment of modern self-government and representative institutions.

CHAPTER XIX

ITALY AFTER THE THIRTY YEARS WAR

BEFORE the Peace of Westphalia Italy was an organic part of a vast network of European interests. It was the centre of the Catholic Counter-Reformation and one of the main bases of Spanish imperialism. Spanish-Catholic political interests were connected with widespread economic interests in which the shipping, banks, industry and merchants of Genoa, Milan, Tuscany, Naples and Sicily played an important part. The Peace of Westphalia maimed Spanish imperialism and halted the Counter-Reformation. As an indirect result, Italy was relegated to the margins of European history and confined to a very minor place among the countries of Europe. Thus the Peace of Westphalia was also a date of fundamental importance in the history of Italy, although its effects came to be seen only with the passage of time. It did not at once terminate the conflicts in which the peninsula and its States were involved, the war between France and Spain and the War of Candia between Venice and the Turks; nor did it change the political map of Italy, the essential features of which were settled by the Peace of Cateau-Cambrésis (1559) and modified in some details by subsequent events, in particular by the Treaty of Cherasco (1631).

Spain remained mistress of her traditional domains, Milan, Naples, Sicily and Sardinia. By means of a series of strategic points she retained control of the Tyrrhenian Sea, which was vital to imperial communications, and of the States along its coast. The Genoese republic, with its own territories of Liguria and Corsica, continued to be a pawn of Spanish policy; it was watched over by the strategic strongholds of the Marquisate of Finale (on the Ligurian coast and under direct Spanish rule) and of the Lunigiana valley (between the Po valley and the Tyrrhenian, an area dotted with fiefs of the Malaspina family, who were theoretically vassals of the Empire, but in practice dependants of the Spanish governor at Milan). From the Lunigiana the Spaniards also controlled the very small neighbouring States, the Cybo principalities of Massa and Carrara and the republic of Lucca, and overlooked the grand duchy of Tuscany. Moreover, by the direct control of the *Presidios* dependent upon the viceroys of Naples, and indirect control of the principality of Piombino (a fief of the Ludovisi since 1634), Spain also contained Tuscany from the south. Finally, these strongpoints safeguarded the route from Naples to Genoa and indirectly dominated the Papal State itself.

To the massive Spanish power in Italy was opposed a French power which was unimpressive territorially, yet most effective in political and military respects. By the Treaty of Cherasco France had acquired the fortress of Pinerolo and the adjacent Alpine valleys in Piedmont. She was thus able to send troops into Italy at any time and control the duchy of Savoy, with its territories of Savoy, Piedmont, Nice and an enclave in Liguria which included Oneglia. The Duchess Christina, regent for her son Charles Emanuel II of Savoy (1637–75), who was a minor, had hoped that the terms of Cherasco would be revoked at Westphalia, but in vain. On this point the Emperor Ferdinand III had yielded to the claims of France, and Piedmont remained a battlefield for the French, who occupied the citadel of Turin, and the Spanish forces of Caracena, the governor of Milan, which garrisoned Vercelli. All the minor States of Italy turned upon the axis of this great struggle, some supporting France and others Spain, according to their interests and ambitions.

During the decades which preceded the Peace of Westphalia the policy of the Italian States had been one of internal consolidation which often took the form of the absorption of smaller principalities, anachronistic survivals of the Middle Ages, by their larger neighbours. This process naturally caused a number of local conflicts which in their turn became linked with the major struggle between France and Spain. There was a sort of permanent 'cold war' between pro-Spanish Genoa and the House of Savoy, vassals of the French, who at the same time were in open conflict with the Gonzaga-Nevers, the ducal family of Mantua and Monferrato, over the latter territory which lay in a strategic position between Lombardy, Piedmont and Liguria. France, by the Treaty of Cherasco, had become the arbiter of this quarrel and reduced Savoy to vassalage, meanwhile guaranteeing Monferrato to the Gonzaga-Nevers on condition of their ceding Alba and Trino to their opponents. Spain, however, opposed this solution by force of arms, and the Gonzaga-Nevers, in spite of their French origin, were unwilling to give up Alba and Trino. Accordingly, in 1648 the French were garrisoning Casale, the largest fortress of Monferrato, and Caracena was trying to win over Charles II of Gonzaga-Nevers (1647–75). At the same time he was playing a similar game with Francis I d'Este (1629–57), duke of Modena, utilising his aspirations to the principality of Correggio. France, for her part, was supporting Ranuccio II Farnese (1646–94), duke of Parma and Piacenza, in his conflict with the Holy See which sought to deprive him of his fief of Castro in Latium.

Furthermore, Mazarin had sent an expedition to Tuscany to occupy Piombino and the *Presidios*. But Ferdinand II de' Medici (1621–70), grand duke of Tuscany, continued to incline towards Spain while preserving a cautious neutrality. He thus hoped to continue the traditional policy of his ancestors, who had sought to strengthen their frontiers in the two strategic zones of the Lunigiana and Maremma. In the latter the Medici had acquired the counties of Pitigliano (1604) and Santa

Fiora (1634), while in the former they coveted Pontremoli, formerly a fief of the Malaspina, the key to the Cisa Pass and hence to the entire valley.

The Holy See also had followed a policy of annexation, acquiring the duchies of Ferrara (1598) and Urbino (1631), and now aspired to Castro. But Innocent X Pamphili (1644–55) was above all interested in securing peace among the Catholic powers in order both to re-establish papal prestige, which had suffered seriously at Westphalia, and to oppose the Turks who were attacking the Venetians on the island of Candia (Crete).[1] Thus the Holy See and the republic of Venice were moving towards an agreement upon political objectives—in spite of the many conflicts of the past—inasmuch as both desired peace and a common Christian front against the Porte. For the present Venice conducted a neutral policy between France and Spain and aimed at profiting from its traditional friendship with the former as well as from the latter's traditional hatred of the Turks.

It was Richelieu's intention that the Treaty of Cherasco should enable France to follow an ambitious policy of conquest in Italy similar to that of her sixteenth-century kings. But in 1648 the country lacked the material means needed for such a policy. Both France and Spain were so exhausted by the Thirty Years War that their struggle in Italy was reduced to an inconclusive exchange of blows. During the first phase, the crisis of the Fronde[2] enabled the Spaniards to drive the French from the key positions of Casale and Piombino and to attach several Italian rulers to their party by satisfying their ambitions. Thus Innocent X was able to gain Castro from the pro-French Farnese (1649), while Ferdinand II de' Medici was freed from the threatening presence of the French at Piombino and in 1650 obtained Pontremoli. Caracena allowed Francis I d'Este, who became an ally of Spain, to annex Correggio, and Charles II of Gonzaga-Nevers also joined the Spanish side and in 1652 regained Casale. Immediately after this, however, Mazarin returned to power (1653) and succeeded in neutralising these Spanish successes; but he in his turn failed to persuade the Italian States to form a league sufficiently strong to withstand the Spaniards. This was largely due to the refusal of the Venetians to participate; they were too fully occupied in Candia to be willing to enter into adventures elsewhere. Thus the Cardinal had to seek decisive diplomatic success elsewhere, and he turned towards an alliance with Cromwellian England.

At this point there occurred an episode in Italy which was small in itself, but important for Anglo-French relations owing to the great impression it made on English opinion. In 1655, with the connivance of Mazarin, the House of Savoy dispatched a military expedition against its own Pro-

[1] See below, pp. 461–3.

[2] See vol. IV, ch. XVI.

testant subjects in the Waldensian valleys of the Piedmontese Alps. This force ravaged the valleys, committing every sort of atrocity, but was unable to extinguish all resistance. The 'Waldensian Easter' enraged opinion in the Protestant countries, and Milton celebrated the victims in one of his best known sonnets. Cromwell threatened to send a fleet to carry out reprisals on the Italian coast, and Mazarin, in order to gain his friendship, offered to act as mediator between him and the court of Turin. The Waldensians were permitted to live in peace, and for the first time Italy became aware of the growth of British naval power. Meanwhile Mazarin had also succeeded in winning over the duke of Modena, who married one of the cardinal's nieces and broke off relations with Caracena. Under the duke's command a French army advanced into Lombardy and won several victories, but in mid-campaign (1658) Francis died, and Mazarin, successful in Flanders thanks to his alliance with England, did not press home his Italian offensive.

The Peace of the Pyrenees (1659) restored the *status quo* in Italy. Spain retained her traditional territories, and France kept Pinerolo and with it control over the duchy of Savoy. The Spaniards evacuated Vercelli and the French had already left the citadel of Turin. Yet it was clear that the political and military weakness of Spain was increasing, and no less evident was the decline in the prestige of the Holy See: Pope Alexander VII Chigi (1655–67) was not admitted to the negotiations preceding the peace. The pillars of the old Spanish-Catholic régime in Italy were silently crumbling, and no new order was forming to take its place. Although during the following decades Spain's decline continued, France made no serious attempt to drive Spain from Italy and take her place in governing its people. There was not even any attempt to link Italian interests organically with her own. She was content to remain encamped at Pinerolo and occasionally to frighten the States of the peninsula by a display of military strength. It was enough that Italy should remain inert, creating no problems, while French armies pursued more important objectives in other theatres of war. Thus from 1659 to 1690 Italy lived through a time of political immobility during which, at least to all outward appearances, virtually nothing happened.

This political immobility was emphasised by the fact that Venice, the strongest of the autonomous Italian States, was so involved in the War of Candia that for a quarter of a century it could play no part in Italian affairs. In contrast with Spain's bellicose policy of crusading against the Turks, Venice had always followed a pacific policy towards them, based on rational considerations of commercial utility. Moreover, as a traditional opponent of Spanish-Catholic policy, Venice had obviously benefited from the weakening of Spain and the papacy brought about by the Thirty Years War. Before she could reap any reward from this, however, she was suddenly forced into an all-out war against the Porte which caused a decisive change in Venetian history.

Despite Venice's care to avoid any quarrel with the Turks, she had not been able to prevent the Porte sending a strong expedition in 1645 to capture the Venetian island of Candia. The time was a favourable one for the Turks, since the Christian powers were too deeply occupied with fighting against each other in the Thirty Years War to send aid to Candia; in particular Spain, the most formidable opponent of the Ottomans in the Mediterranean, had been bled white. Venice itself was quite unprepared from the military point of view. As if this were not enough, the bad Venetian colonial administration had so enraged the population of Candia that they took no part in the defence of the island. Within a few weeks (June–August 1645) the Turks captured the town of Canea and then advanced across the island to besiege its principal strongpoint, Candia itself. In similar circumstances Spain and the papacy had in the past succeeded in raising a really large force; this time they could only send a fleet of Neapolitan, Tuscan, papal and Maltese ships under Niccolò Ludovisi, prince of Piombino, and this fleet arrived too late to save Canea. Neither then nor later was any really effective help given to the Venetians. Even after the Peace of Westphalia Venetian diplomacy could not achieve anything; Spain and France continued to fight each other, and the formation of a united Christian front remained a hopeless dream.

Candia was the richest of Venice's possessions, however, and the republic was unwilling to yield it. The Venetians were prepared to adopt all sorts of financial expedients, such as opening the patriciate to anyone offering large money payments, in order to equip a considerable fleet. With this fleet they won back control of the sea, cut off the Turkish forces besieging Candia and, from 1647 onwards, carried the war into the enemy camp. In 1648 they captured Clissa in Dalmatia, and they defeated the Turkish fleet on a number of occasions. In the great battle of the Hellespont (1656) they lost their captain-general, Lorenzo Marcello, but destroyed a large part of the enemy fleet and blockaded the Turks in the Dardanelles. A Turkish attempt to break this blockade met with a bloody defeat in 1657, and Lazzaro Mocenigo, the new captain-general, even succeeded in forcing his way into the Straits. His advance on Constantinople was finally checked by the fire of coastal batteries which destroyed the Venetian flagship and caused the death of her courageous commander.

After twelve years of war, however, the republic was exhausted. It had failed to break the unrelaxing determination of the Turks, who had been reinvigorated by the iron government of Mehmed Köprülü.[1] The Venetian fleet lost command of the sea, and what had been a war of movement became a war of attrition around besieged Candia, in which the Ottoman

[1] See below, ch. XXI, pp. 507–9.

Empire enjoyed the advantage of possessing superior resources. The Venetians fought on for another twelve years with extraordinary tenacity, but the War of Candia became for them what the War of the Netherlands had been for Spain, a bottomless pit into which they poured men, money and supplies endlessly and without effect.

The efforts of Venetian diplomacy were of no avail. The Peace of the Pyrenees (1659) left Spain exhausted, and Mazarin's France sent only a single contingent which Francesco Morosini, the new captain-general, contrived to add to the garrison of Candia, but to small effect (1660). The outbreak of a new war between the Porte and the Habsburgs at last brought a certain relief to Candia since it drew off the bulk of the Ottoman forces. In 1664, however, the Venetians were again fighting alone, succoured only by the meagre aid offered by some Italian princes, such as Charles Emanuel II of Savoy, who hoped in this way to induce the Venetians to accord him equality of treatment with crowned heads. Later Pope Clement IX Rospigliosi (1667–9) recruited assistance zealously among the Italian and Imperial States and by the Treaty of Aix-la-Chapelle (1668)[1] put an end to the War of Devolution in the hope that Louis might at last place France's formidable military strength at the service of the Christian cause. But her commercial interests in the Levant were too important for her to be willing to become the bulwark against the Turks which Spain had been. French intervention was limited to the dispatch of a single force, which fought under the papal flag to avoid an open rupture with the Porte; its principal purpose was to gain prestige, or rather perhaps to exert pressure on the Porte to improve the terms on which the French were permitted to trade. The French abandoned Candia after a few months, leaving Morosini alone with a mere three thousand survivors, exhausted by fighting and the deprivations which they had suffered. In September 1669 Morosini had at last to evacuate Candia, after a siege of twenty-three years in which about 100,000 men died.

The Venetians certainly put up a very strong defence, and the terms granted to them on their surrender were fairly favourable; they retained the fortresses of Suda, Spinalonga and Carabusa, as well as Clissa and the Ionian island of Zante. Serious accusations, however, were made against the men regarded as responsible for the defeat; among those brought to trial was Morosini, but he was acquitted. The war had consequences far deeper than these superficial manifestations of discontent. Venice had entered it as a great trading power and as a firm adversary of the Habsburgs and of the papacy. In the course of the war she lost almost all her Levant trade to the French, English and Dutch and was transformed into a pillar of Catholicism and an ally of the Habsburgs. It was symptomatic of this change that the Jesuits, who had been driven from Venice half a century before, were readmitted in 1657 to ingratiate the city with

[1] See above, ch. IX, p. 213.

Alexander VII. Equally significant was the transfer of Venetian capital from shipping and trade into land. The patriciate was ceasing to be an oligarchy of adventurous capitalists and becoming instead an aristocracy of conservative landowners.

During this period the decline in the papacy's moral and political prestige was becoming more marked. This decline was already evident by 1648, and the Peace of Westphalia was in practice a defeat for the Holy See. Innocent X had been the butt of much bitter criticism and many pasquinades for his weakness, in particular on account of his avaricious relatives. It was notorious in Rome that one could obtain anything from the papal administration so long as one satisfied the thirst for money of his arrogant sister-in-law, Olimpia Maidalchini. Venality and maladministration were rampant in the Papal State. While Bernini, the pope's favourite architect, continued to embellish St Peter's with the products of his dazzling genius, there was miserable poverty in the Roman Campagna, the prey of malaria and brigandage. None of these matters improved under the following popes.

Relations between the Holy See and France were unfriendly, partly on account of the affair of Cardinal de Retz, archbishop of Paris, who was persecuted by Mazarin because of his participation in the Fronde. In order to placate the pope, Mazarin gave his agreement to the papal condemnation of Jansenism (1653).[1] Jansenist agitation did not come to an end, however, and the problem of Franco-papal relations was threatening to become a permanent danger to the popes. On the death of Innocent X the successor elected as Alexander VII was the Sienese Fabio Chigi (1655), who had been the papal nuncio at the congress of Westphalia; his support of the Society of Jesus and his ideological views exacerbated French Gallicanism. He issued frequent condemnations of Jansenism, received Christina of Sweden with great pomp after her conversion from Protestantism and, as we have seen, secured the return of the Jesuits to Venice. But he fell foul of Mazarin, who was personally hostile to him, resented the reception given in Rome to Cardinal de Retz when he fled from France, and objected to Alexander's appeals to the French clergy to support his attempts to make peace between the Christian monarchies. The Holy See thus suffered another moral defeat at the Peace of the Pyrenees (1659) and failed to provide help for the Venetians. Worse was to follow after Mazarin's death and Louis XIV's assumption of personal power. In 1682 a futile little brawl between some papal soldiers and servants of Créqui, the French ambassador to the Holy See, was made the pretext for a violent onslaught: Louis occupied Avignon and even threatened to send an army into Italy. So weak was the pope's position that in 1684 he had to accept an utterly humiliating settlement of this

[1] See above, ch. VI, p. 133.

quarrel, and his brother, Mario Chigi, was sent to France to make Louis a formal apology.

Louis XIV's overbearing pressure was felt in the conclave after Alexander VII's death in which another Tuscan was elected: Giulio Rospigliosi, who took the name of Clement IX (1667). Clement was the last of those Tuscan administrators who had played so great a part in papal history. Thanks to his diplomatic ability and gentle character Clement was able to diminish tension with France, thus to help in the negotiations leading to the Treaty of Aix-la-Chapelle with Spain in 1668 and to secure a temporary settlement of the Jansenist question ('the peace of the Church' of 1669). But his attempts to induce Europe to assist Venice against the Turks were completely unsuccessful, and this failure so depressed him that he died soon after. French pressure, even more shameless in the next conclave, was responsible for the election of the fragile and elderly Roman Altieri, who took the name of Clement X (1670–6). Clement did his best to please the *roi soleil* and avoid further disputes; but even his willing submissiveness could not shield him from painful humiliations, in particular at the hands of the haughty French ambassador d'Estrées who on more than one occasion publicly insulted the aged pope. In the conclave after Clement X's death the French emphasised that the late pontiff had fallen into disgrace with Louis by insisting that no cardinal who had been friendly with Clement should be elected. In the end the choice of the Lombard Cardinal Odescalchi as Innocent XI (1676–89) was permitted only because he was represented as an opponent of his predecessor.

But Innocent XI differed from Clement X in his greater courage and decisiveness in the defence of papal prerogatives. An austere pope of rigid principles, Innocent undertook important work in the sphere of doctrine, condemning moral casuistry and the obscure mysticism of the Quietists, the disciples of the Spaniard Miguel de Molinos, who had acquired a certain following in Italy. Even more notable was his struggle against Gallicanism, despite its protection by Louis XIV, particularly in the Four Articles controversy of 1682.[1] Innocent also took up the old papal scheme for a coalition against the Turks, and when Turkey attacked the Empire he persuaded John Sobieski, king of Poland, to intervene as an ally of the Habsburgs.[2] He celebrated Sobieski's victory at Vienna by instituting the new feast of the Name of Mary (1683). In 1684 he brought into being the Holy League between Austria, Poland and Venice which is discussed below. Meanwhile he also fought against nepotism, corruption and crime in the Papal State and set about the restoration of its finances which had suffered under the shocking administration of his predecessors. In his zeal for reform he was even willing to face yet another dispute with a French ambassador (Lavardin) over the latter's intolerable abuse of diplomatic

[1] See above, ch. VI, p. 137. [2] See below, ch. XXI, p. 514.

immunity (1687), and he was not intimidated when Louis XIV again threatened to send an army into Italy.

Thus ended a period of forty years during which French policy towards the Holy See consisted exclusively of intimidation and the use of force. This policy gravely damaged papal prestige in the eyes of the Italians and did nothing whatever to link French power with the Catholic cause in the way that the Habsburgs had linked Spain with the cause of the Counter-Reformation. Despite his pose as the champion of Catholicism against the Protestants, Louis XIV found himself without allies and threatened with imminent war against the League of Augsburg.[1] French policy had been merely negative; it had helped to discredit the old order of things without contributing to the birth of a new one.

The merits of Innocent XI could not conceal the slow decay of Italian Catholicism which had become mummified, as it were, in the attitudes adopted during the Counter-Reformation and gave no indication of realising a need for reform. Superficially, the Church had achieved complete victory. No opposition to it survived in Italy except for some small quietist conventicles, which were dogged by the Inquisition, and some offshoots of French Jansenism. In reality, beneath the lazy, somnolent conformism and superficial, festive religiosity of the Italians there was a complete void, a void filled less by new ideas than by slothful scepticism and often by an ignorant brand of anticlericalism. Characteristic of the latter was Gregorio Leti (1630–1701), an adventurer who travelled between Geneva, Paris, London and Amsterdam and for several decades flooded Italy with innumerable scandalous pamphlets which, though worthless, met with enormous success.

Italy's political stagnation was in part the consequence of the appalling condition to which she had been reduced by the Thirty Years War. In 1648 the peninsula was in a state of economic and intellectual decadence and her population was declining. During the next forty years this decadence was aggravated by Italy's isolation from the main currents of European history. It was a long time before the lowest point of decline was reached and a certain stability achieved at a level much lower than that which had prevailed earlier.

The population of Italy had suffered gravely from the terrible epidemics of the war, from the devastations and from the resultant poverty. The gaps were only slowly filled during the next forty years, for epidemics, although less serious, continued until at least 1660, while other negative factors, such as the disproportionate growth of a celibate clergy and the general poverty and wretched living conditions of the lower classes, had effects over a longer time. The long period of peace after 1659 did eventually bring some improvement, but the cities did not attain their former

[1] See above, ch. IX, pp. 220–1.

levels of population. In the late sixteenth century Milan and Venice had had about 250,000 and 200,000 inhabitants respectively. Both were decimated by the epidemics of the early decades of the seventeenth century, and although later both cities made a certain recovery, their populations did not rise above approximately 125,000 and 135,000. The loss was all the more striking compared with the increase in the populations of Paris and London during the same period.

The decline of the urban centres was part of a more general phenomenon. In the early years of the seventeenth century Italy was still an active country in commerce, industry and banking, which were centred mainly in the towns. By the end of the century it was an almost exclusively agrarian country, whose small and lethargic towns were for the most part administrative centres or places of residence for the landowners. Italian finance —except for that of Genoa—had vanished as an international economic factor. Italian trade was mainly a memory of the past: Italians played no part in the colonial trade which was the chief commercial activity of the time, and their ports were in full decline. The loss of the Levant trade of Venice has already been discussed, and Messina's disappearance from the list of great Mediterranean ports will be considered below. Even Genoa was severely affected by the decline of the Spanish Empire of which it had been one of the traditional economic centres. Leghorn remained active, but mainly as an entrepôt for foreign trade, particularly for the Dutch and English. Industry also declined: the number of cloth factories in Milan fell from seventy in the early years of the century to fifteen, while the Florentine silk industry virtually disappeared. Factors in this appalling decline were the collapse of the Spanish Empire, dragging three-quarters of Italy after it, the competition of foreign powers, in particular of England and Holland, and the aggressive mercantilism of France. Louis XIV's acts of violence against the Italian States were accompanied by silent economic warfare, for example in the competition of Marseilles with Genoa and the manufacture in France of the mirrors for which Venice was famous. Here was another instance of Louis's failure to create organic links between France and Italy.

Agriculture was left as Italy's main economic activity, but for the most part it was of an unambitious, conservative nature, with only here and there an occasional attempt at improvement; in Sicily, for instance, some of the magnates built entire new villages to house the workers on their estates. The growing rigidity of landed property also tended to discourage technical improvements. More and more land passed into the hands of the Church, while the noble estates were increasingly burdened by trusts and entails. Finally, the increasing tendency on the part of the merchant families to abandon their traditional activities and their gradual transformation into a landed nobility led to the disappearance of the habits of economic enterprise, industriousness and parsimony and their replacement by aristocratic habits of economic parasitism, idleness and extravagant show. In the seventeenth century the Italian nobility regarded the income from their lands as a means of enabling them to live without working and to maintain a costly way of life; they were less likely to invest in agricultural improvements than they were to spend their money in building a luxurious villa. Social habits too reveal the importance of landed property and the decline of the towns. People went to the country for *villeggiatura*, to display their fashionable elegance: the ability or inability to afford a *villeggiatura* was often regarded as the dividing line between the upper and the lower ranks of society. The importance of land had little to do with its economic exploitation.

Society itself was becoming more rigid in structure. Italy was turning into a country of neglectful, affable gentlemen and resigned, fatalistic peasants. Apart from the nobles and the clergy the only class of any importance was a small professional group of teachers, lawyers and officials. On the other hand, the long peace and the general tendency towards deflation brought to an end the disorders caused by monetary inflation and the worst forms of pauperism, crime and vagrancy which had appeared in the late sixteenth and early seventeenth centuries. Food prices fell. Life was more stable; the people suffered from poverty and exhaustion, but they managed to live, and in comparative tranquillity.

Towards the end of the century the peace began slowly to bear fruit. Capital accumulated quietly in some parts, particularly in Lombardy owing to the natural fertility of its soil and the decay of the Spanish government, now too feeble to do much harm. In Tuscany a certain administrative and intellectual tradition survived, and the descendants of the Florentine merchants, transformed into a landed patriciate, were not all negligible men. Naples had a class of lawyers who enjoyed social prestige and occasionally showed considerable intellectual ability. Slowly the ground was being prepared in which would germinate the enlightenment of the following century. Yet although intellectuals, professional men and officials might possess ability, they had no economic or political power themselves and could only hope to exert influence in so far as the machinery of the State allowed them. It is not surprising that they should soon have begun to identify themselves with the cause of enlightened despotism and to give it enthusiastic support.

Reforms and vigorous political action were still far in the future. Italy was no longer capable of continuing in her high intellectual traditions after the disappearance of the great generation of Galileo, Campanella, Sarpi and Boccalini. Venice was still an important publishing centre, and Italian universities could boast a few teachers of European fame, such as Marcello Malpighi (1628–94) of Bologna, one of the founders of modern biology. Galileo's heritage lived on in Tuscany with the foundation of the *Accademia del Cimento* (1657) and the excellent studies of its members—

among them the Aretine doctor Francesco Redi (1626–97)—especially in the field of biology. But the major currents of European thought and learning were outside Italy. The lively scientific and philosophical interests of the Neapolitan class of wealthy lawyers and liberal-minded noblemen showed themselves mainly in a concern with English, French and Dutch culture. In contemporary opinion Italy was still the great country for art and for refined pleasures. It was the country of the Baroque masters, Bernini and Borromini,[1] and its painters and architects swarmed across Europe, influencing profoundly the taste of their time. It was the country of virtuoso singers and of delightful musicians, of Lully and Scarlatti, of Baroque Rome, with its gorgeous ceremonies, its churches and cardinals' villas, of Venice, with its enchanted palaces along the Grand Canal and its famous gaieties. It was no longer a country that might be expected to provide literary, philosophical or political guidance. A journey to Italy was still thought indispensable for the education of young noblemen and artists, but the peninsula was becoming a country for tourists, a museum.

The ruling houses and their courts putrefied in the futile routine of a pointless existence, a decadence which was physiological as well as political and moral. We have already observed the disappearance of the class of Tuscan officials of the papacy which had once been so active, and the fatal weakness of many of the popes of the second half of the seventeenth century. By the end of the century the families of Este, Gonzaga and Farnese, too, present a depressing spectacle of half-wits and scoundrels. Ferdinand II de' Medici, though weak and timid, had achieved a certain reputation as a statesman owing to the skill with which he piloted his own small State through the stormy waters of the Thirty Years War. But his son Cosimo III (1670–1723) was a pathetic case of mental disorder, whose subjects suffered through his morbid religious mania. Few of the Italian States can be said to have had an internal policy. They confined themselves to drawing some money from their subjects through fiscal arrangements, which bore heavily on the poor by indirect taxes on articles of general consumption, and hindered all forms of trade by multitudes of duties and tolls. These revenues were then squandered on yet another new palace or sumptuous Baroque church and on the maintenance of a handful of courtiers and parasites, and that was all.

The sole exception was Piedmont, after the weak regency of Christina had come to an end. The period of activity under Charles Emanuel II was clearly the result of an intention to imitate Louis XIV: hence certain reforms in legislation, finance and military affairs, combined with a rigid absolutism aiming at the humiliation of the nobility, and an ambitious mercantilist policy. But in practice these ambitions proved to be beyond the country's means—or beyond the duke's real political capabilities.

[1] See above, ch. VII, pp. 156–9.

Charles Emanuel was filled with the desire to rank with crowned heads, hence the dispatch of troops to distant Candia and his fantastic plans for conquering Geneva and Genoa. The acquisition of Genoa was intended as the culmination of Savoyard mercantilism, and the duke's plan was to take advantage of Louis XIV's preparations for the Dutch War of 1672.[1] Counting on Spain being immobilised by this other commitment, Charles Emanuel invaded Liguria in 1672; he also tried to organise a revolt in Genoa itself through a Genoese adventurer, Raffaele della Torre. But the plot was strangled at birth and the troops of Savoy suffered a humiliating defeat at the hands of the Genoese. Charles Emanuel II had to withdraw as rapidly as possible from his ill-fated adventure, helped by the mediation of Louis XIV. Mercantilist dreams failed to transform Piedmont's economic structure which was agricultural and archaic. Despite their temporary check, the noblemen remained the dominant class. The unhappy duke died in 1675, and there followed a new regency, even more feeble and inglorious than the last.

The disintegrating Spanish administration of Naples, Milan, Sardinia and Sicily became, if possible, still more inefficient and corrupt. Spanish rule survived less through its own strength than through French lack of interest in Italy. Spanish officials still felt some interest in the peninsula because it could provide a career and a salary for them, but this was not true of France, intent upon other objectives. French interest was renewed at the time of the Dutch War, but even then it took the form of sudden, capricious interventions, not of a rational and organic policy.

Messina was the only place in Spanish Sicily to retain a considerable degree of economic prosperity. Its port was still active, there was a lucrative silk trade, and its ancient privileges made it a sort of independent merchant republic. The Spanish government, however, was jealous of this autonomy and encouraged the popular faction, the Merli, against the dominant patrician party, the Malvizzi. In 1674 the Malvizzi replied by organising a Messinese revolt. The Spanish troops were driven out, and the Malvizzi offered the city to Louis XIV, who not only accepted it but sent troops to assist in its defence. The French fleet won a victory over the Spaniards off the Lipari Islands (1675) and another over de Ruyter's Dutchmen off Augusta (1676). It looked as though the French would soon conquer the whole of Sicily. But England saw this situation as a threat to her interests in the Mediterranean, and Louis did not hesitate to sacrifice the Messinese rather than arouse English hostility: in 1678 he withdrew his troops. Thousands of Messina's citizens took to flight, in grim conditions which Louis did nothing to relieve. Depopulated, punished by bloody Spanish reprisals, and deprived of its privileges, Messina lost all its former prosperity.

[1] See above, ch. IX, p. 215.

Instead of supporting those who had trusted him, the *roi soleil* now renewed the French claim to Casale, taking advantage of the financial difficulties to which Ferdinand Charles, duke of Mantua (1669–1707), had been reduced by his dissipations. In 1678 the duke promised to cede Casale for a money payment by an agreement which was kept secret to avoid possible action by other powers. The secret was betrayed by one of the duke's ministers, Count Mattioli—again for money. Louis XIV then succeeded in capturing Mattioli by a trick and in imprisoning him: he was probably the famous 'man in the iron mask'. Louis renewed his negotiations with the duke and finally secured Casale in 1681.

Encouraged by this success, Louis attempted next to gain Genoa, where he built up a pro-French 'fifth column' and tried to provoke incidents to justify armed intervention. When war again broke out between France and Spain in 1683 Louis ordered the Genoese to discontinue their traditional assistance to Spain and made other far-reaching demands. The republic did not yield, however, even when a French fleet appeared before Genoa—without any declaration of war—and subjected the city to a fierce bombardment lasting five days (17–22 May 1684). Louis's aggression and Genoa's costly resistance had a considerable effect on Italian opinion, arousing indignation against his bullying attitude. Yet the Spanish weakness enabled him to disguise the substantial failure of his scheme of conquest under the dramatic appearance of success. By the truce of Ratisbon (1684) Louis promised to respect Genoa's independence, but was left free to exact a sop to his pride. In May 1685 the doge of Genoa had to travel to Versailles to perform a solemn act of humiliation and beg the king's forgiveness for having incurred his anger.

By that time the international situation was again altering. Innocent XI's crusading policy had achieved its first successes with Sobieski's victory at Vienna (1683) and the constitution of the Holy League—the Empire, Poland and Venice—against the Turks (1684). To strengthen the Empire against the Turks meant also, implicitly, to strengthen the Habsburgs against the Bourbons. Soon the league was gaining brilliant successes. Fifteen years after his evacuation of Candia Francesco Morosini was again appointed captain-general; his fleet, reinforced by Tuscan, Maltese and papal ships, attacked Santa Maura (an island in the Ionian Sea) and the fortress of Prevesa. The inhabitants of Albania and the Epirus, and the Morlacchi of Dalmatia rose in rebellion against the Turks, and in 1685 Morosini's fleet began the attack on Greece by taking Koroni. The conquest of the Morea was completed in 1687, and Morosini was acclaimed as *Peloponnesiacus*. Before the end of that year the Gulf of Corinth had been crossed and Athens itself was in the hands of the Venetians. Thus 1688 began under the best of auspices for the arms of Venice and her allies of the Holy League.

Events now maturing in northern Italy threatened Louis XIV more directly. Louis had long been able to dominate Savoy, particularly after the death of Charles Emanuel II (1675), when the French princess Jeanne-Baptiste of Savoy-Nemours acted as regent for her young son Victor Amadeus II (1675–1730). She attempted to retain control after her son had reached his majority, keeping him away from power and relying on the support of the French king. Victor Amadeus, precociously expert at dissimulation, kept secret his feelings against his mother and the French: he had real political talent as a 'Machiavellian' prince, a talent which was maturing during this silent, lonely phase of his life. His State, however, was still declining rapidly, both in external and internal affairs. In 1680–2 Mondovi and the surrounding countryside was the scene of the bloody 'salt war', a revolt against court taxation which was suppressed only after much fighting and harsh military repression. In 1687 Jeanne-Baptiste renewed on behalf of herself and her son the terms of subjection to France stipulated in the Treaty of Cherasco: Victor Amadeus was to marry a French wife, chosen for him by Louis XIV, in 1684. The young duke used this marriage as the occasion for a *coup d'état*, depriving his mother of power and himself taking over the government of his State, but Louis repaid this energetic action by many humiliating vexations.

After the Revocation of the Edict of Nantes (1685)[1] Louis forced Victor Amadeus to persecute his Protestant subjects, the Waldensians. Faced with the choice of immediate conversion to Catholicism or expulsion from Piedmont, the Waldensians organised resistance, led by one of their pastors, Enrico Arnaud. Louis thereupon sent an army under Catinat to Piedmont under the pretext of assisting the duke against the rebels. Waldensian resistance was overcome by methods of hideous cruelty, and the entire population of the valleys, including women and children, was rounded up and imprisoned in various Piedmontese fortresses; two-thirds of the twelve thousand people involved died as a result of hardship and disease (1686). But a handful of guerrillas continued to hold out in the Alps, until at last the duke decided to release the surviving prisoners and to send them to Geneva where they were generously succoured by fellow-Protestants.

By this time the League of Augsburg and the great European alliance, which was to wage a general war against Louis XIV after the landing of William of Orange in England, was already in process of formation. With extreme caution, lest his action should become known and provoke Louis to revenge, Victor Amadeus began to contact secretly the enemies of France. At once the perennial Waldensian question was raised, this time by Arnaud, who began to organise the 'Glorious Return' of his people with the aid of William III under whose flag they now fought. In August 1689 their force started from Lake Geneva under Arnaud's command; an extraordinarily daring march took them over the Alps and into their own

[1] See above, ch. VI, p. 141.

valleys, where they resumed their guerrilla campaigns. These were marked by episodes which seem to come straight from adventure stories, such as the defence of Monte Balziglia by the Waldensians against a besieging army of 11,000 Frenchmen. In June 1690, when Arnaud's men were decimated by the fighting and their cause apparently lost, they were visited by a ducal emissary who offered them peace on condition that they joined the forces of Savoy against the king of France.

On his usual pretext of fighting the Waldensians Louis XIV had again dispatched Catinat with an army into Piedmont. In reality he now suspected that the duke had come to an agreement with his enemies. Catinat made ever more onerous demands, culminating in an order that Savoy should give up its principal fortresses and send its army to France as a guarantee of good faith. Victor Amadeus won time by pretending to negotiate with Catinat while covertly negotiating with Spain and the Empire. A secret agreement was signed whereby Savoy joined the League of Augsburg in return for a promise of immediate military assistance against France and the restoration of Pinerolo at the end of the war (3 June 1690). A few days later Catinat demanded the handing-over of the citadel of Turin without further delay and Victor Amadeus replied by openly starting hostilities. Thus began a new phase in European and in Italian history.

CHAPTER XX

THE HABSBURG LANDS

DURING the two years that followed his election as Emperor in 1519 Charles V handed over to his brother Ferdinand all the hereditary Habsburg lands in central Europe. By securing his own election to the thrones of Bohemia and Hungary in 1526 Ferdinand I completed the Habsburg Empire. His was the cadet branch of his House and his dominions were remote from the Atlantic seaboard, economically backward, riven by social and domestic strife, devastated and crippled by the Turks. During the Thirty Years War, except for Wallenstein's brief heyday, Austria played only a secondary part and emerged from that war maimed, depopulated and impoverished. But by the end of the century the Habsburg monarchy became one of the great powers, hailed as the saviour of Christendom in the last and only permanently successful crusade, wooed as an ally by the maritime powers, feared as a rival by France. It is true that the Habsburgs climbed to this position of power by destroying the Bohemian nation and abrogating the liberties of Hungary, but the means and the persons engaged in this achievement make the history of the Habsburg lands in the second half of the seventeenth century an important and illuminating chapter in the history of European society.

Few dynasties have bred more truly to type than the Habsburgs. The three rulers whose reigns, uninterrupted by dynastic disputes or debilitating minorities, extended from 1619 to 1705 all exhibited the virtues and weaknesses typical of their line; they were conscientious, convinced of the dignity, rights and responsibilities of the office to which they devoutly believed themselves to be divinely appointed; they were sincere Christians and devoted Catholics; their private morals were impeccable. Leopold I, whose long reign occupied most of this half-century, was, like his ancestors and successors down to Joseph II, a collector of books and pictures, an amateur of music and a devotee of the chase. Though his chosen policy compelled him to tax his subjects into poverty and to recruit them in hundreds of thousands for his wars, he was not devoid of Christian and human sympathy for their sufferings on the rare occasions they were brought to his notice. When in 1680 the peasants of Bohemia were able to present their petitions direct to him he wrote to Count Humprecht Černín: 'In these evil times it is indeed necessary to do something for the peasants and to deal with them kindly, since after all they are men like us.'[1] Their fervent belief in the divine origin of their royal office made

[1] Quoted in *Československá Vlastivěda*, vol. IV, 'Dějiny', ed. V. Novotný (Prague, 1930), p. 531.

both Ferdinand III and Leopold I look enviously at the unlimited autocracy of some of their contemporary sovereigns. On the death of his tutor and chief minister, Prince Giovanni Porzia, in 1665, Leopold declared his resolve 'to be himself his own prime minister'.[1] But Leopold was not of the stuff of the Great Elector or Peter the Great. He suffered from an agonising inability to make up his mind, so much so that the papal nuncio Albizzi was driven to say: 'If I were permitted to say so, I would personally wish that the Emperor's trust in God were a bit less, so that he might deal with somewhat more foresight with the dangers which threaten, and when he has decided, act.'[2]

In dealing with the history of the Habsburg lands it is essential never to forget that the Austrian Habsburgs were the wearers of the crown of the Holy Roman Empire continuously from 1556 to 1740. They themselves never forgot it. It enhanced their sense of vocation and convinced them that as the secular heads of the whole Christian society they were especially responsible for restoring both the confessional and the territorial integrity of Christendom. Leopold especially was very conscious of the rights and duties that his Imperial position entailed. He jealously regarded every acre of the Empire and, after the dismissal of his Gallophile minister Lobkowitz in 1674, he did not hesitate to engage the lives and wealth of his Austrian, Bohemian and Hungarian subjects in three long wars with France for the defence of Germany. On the other hand, he firmly believed that as Emperor and German king he had the right to call on the Imperial Diet to vote him men and money for his wars as well against the sultan as against the king of France; the Diet, as far as its now diminished competence and resources permitted, usually complied. It is true that the Emperor could no longer summon the German princes to do him military service; but nevertheless the sense of common danger, the skill of François Paul de Lisola's ubiquitous diplomacy and the still surviving sense of their duty to the Christian Empire combined to bring most of the great princes of Germany into active alliance with the Emperor in his French and Turkish wars. Four princes of the Empire, Charles duke of Lorraine, Max Emanuel elector of Bavaria, Louis margrave of Baden and Frederick Augustus elector of Saxony, commanded the armies which expelled the Turks from Hungary, the first three with distinction and success.

When the Peace of Westphalia was concluded in October 1648 Ferdinand III was forty years of age. The worry of war, the cares of government and the gout made him already think of himself as an old man with not long to live. Much of his concern during his remaining nine years was to secure the Imperial succession for one or the other of his sons in his own

[1] 'Sein eigener Primado selbst zu sein': *Privatbriefe*, I, 105, of 18 February 1665, quoted by O. Redlich, *Geschichte Österreichs* (Gotha, 1921), VI, 112.

[2] Quoted by Redlich, *ibid.*

lifetime.[1] The Thirty Years War left Ferdinand with diminished territories, for his father had sacrificed Lusatia to purchase the defection of Saxony from the Protestant coalition in 1635. Even so Ferdinand's dominions were numerous and extensive. As direct descendant of Rudolph I he was duke of Upper and Lower Austria, margrave of Styria, duke of Carinthia and Carniola and hereditary lord of scattered lands in Swabia. His cousin, the archduke Ferdinand Charles, was *Landesfürst* of the county of Tyrol, the last of the Habsburg apanages, which was to escheat to the Crown with the death of the last of the Tyrolean branch, the archduke Sigismund Francis, in 1665. This completed the reunion of all the Habsburg territories in the hands of the head of the family and so the conditions for the completion of the experiment in centralisation were fulfilled.

Ferdinand III and Leopold I were also kings of Bohemia and therefore rulers of all the lands of the Crown of St Wenceslas: the kingdom of Bohemia, the margraviate of Moravia and the many and tiny dukedoms which constituted the political patchwork of Upper and Lower Silesia. By the Renewed Land Ordinance of 1627, which had given legal definition to the subjection of the kingdom after the defeat of the Bohemian rebellion at the White Mountain in 1620, the Crown of St Wenceslas was made hereditary in the House of Habsburg. The complete defeat of the Bohemian rebellion provided the Habsburg kings of the seventeenth century with an ideal field for a preliminary exercise in centralised autocracy. It was carried out by implicit agreement between the Habsburg king and the Bohemian nobility, many of whom were the mercenary officers who had fought for Austria in the Thirty Years War; they had been belatedly but lavishly paid by the grant to them of the estates of Czech landlords who had suffered death or exile as traitors or heretics. The Bohemian Estates continued to meet, but only at and for the king's convenience. To the traditional Chambers of magnates, gentry and towns was now added a First Chamber of prelates. But the Estates had been deprived of most of their initiative; they appointed only powerless dignitaries and minor officials; they might question the budgetary proposals presented to them by the *Hofkammer* in Vienna, though rarely did any of the Chambers do so except the prelates, and never effectively. The Bohemian Estates in this period were chiefly concerned with making lawful the exploitation of the serfs and legalising the economic privileges of the landlords at the expense of the towns. Since 1627 the last remnants of the autonomy of the towns had disappeared; their magistrates were appointed by the Crown or the lord, their landed property, which had been extensive, was forfeited, and the privileged competition of the lords' breweries, inns, shops and manufactories almost ruined the economy of the towns. From 1632 the margraviate of Moravia had been governed, with no pretence of maintaining the rights of its Estates, by a nominated

[1] See below, p. 486.

tribunal which sat in Brno. As Silesia had taken no part in the rebellion of 1618 it was allowed to retain its two diets and no formal constitutional change was imposed. The administration of Bohemia itself was carried on from Vienna by the Bohemian Chancery, composed of a High Chancellor and Councillors, some of them Bohemian aristocrats, some Austrians or Germans, but all nominated by the Crown.

The uneasy head of Ferdinand III was also dignified and encumbered by the royal and apostolic Crown of St Stephen, the battered crown which the Habsburgs had fished out of the swamps of Mohács in 1526. In virtue of it Ferdinand was nominally king of Hungary and Transylvania, Croatia, Slavonia and Dalmatia. In fact, of the great Hungarian kingdom which Suleiman I had shattered, only little more than a quarter, merely the western and northern counties, was under Ferdinand's rule. About five-twelfths were ruled by the prince of Transylvania, often under the suzerainty of the sultan, but always, until 1687, outside Habsburg control. The remaining third of Hungary, a wedge of territory with its broad base on the Sava and Danube and its blunt apex in southern Slovakia, was directly ruled by the Turks, constituting the vilayets of Kanizsa, Buda and Temesvár, each under a resident military governor or pasha. Though both the Hungarian capital cities, Buda and Székesfehérvár, and the seat of the primate, the archbishop of Esztergom (Gran), were in Turkish hands, the Turks had acquired only the poorest and most sparsely populated part of the country. The mineral wealth of Slovakia was in royal Hungary and that of the *Siebenbürgen* in Transylvania. In 1648 royal Hungary still enjoyed the national autonomy it had exacted from the quarrelling Habsburgs in 1606 and 1608. It had a parliament of two *tabulae*, one composed of the great officers of State, the magnates and the prelates, the other of representatives chosen by the gentry of the counties, and the Hungarian Estates had much more real power than their enfeebled counterparts in Bohemia and Austria. It elected the Palatine (*Nádor*), who commanded the national armed forces, and legislated profusely on social, economic, legal and religious matters. It is true that the Hungarian Chancery sat in Vienna, but the Hungarian Chamber (the treasury) was in Pressburg and the independence of both was jealously guarded by the Hungarians. The only Imperial organs of State which exerted any authority in Hungary were the Court War Council (*Hofkriegsrat*) and the Court Chamber (*Hofkammer*) which had certain powers, such as the administration of the mines of Slovakia.

Ferdinand's kingdom of Croatia was treated as what it was, an outpost against the Turks and the last foothold of a Christian prince in the Balkans. The eastern part of the kingdom was in Turkish hands and formed part of the vilayet of Sirmium. The western half of Croatia and the northern part of Dalmatia constituted a precariously exiguous strip of Christian territory running down to the Adriatic. The Estates of Croatia still met in Zagreb, but the government of the country was a military one, conducted by the royally appointed *Ban*, in 1648 the great Hungarian soldier-poet Miklós Zrínyi.

Transylvania had been independent of Austria since Ferdinand I had divided the kingdom of Hungary with King John Zápolyai in 1538. Amid the storms of the first half of the seventeenth century the Transylvanian princes, Gábor Bethlen and György Rákóczi I, had preserved and strengthened the principality. György Rákóczi died in 1648. His son of the same name had already been elected prince by the Transylvanian Estates in 1642. György Rákóczi II was twenty-seven years old when he began to reign in 1648. He inherited vast estates in Transylvania and in north-east Hungary both from his father and his mother, Zsófia Báthory, as well as the domains that went with the princely office. He was a spoilt, vain and rash young man, ambitious to become king of either Hungary or Poland. Beside Transylvania he ruled the large adjoining counties of Szatmár and Szabolcs. The principality was still formally a federation of three 'nations': the Magyars, the Magyar-speaking Szeklers of its eastern part, and the 'Saxons', the townsfolk of German origin and speech.

The material state of the Habsburg lands after the Thirty Years War was bad. Vast sacrifices of men, money and requisitioned goods had been made by every part of the monarchy where the Emperor's writ still ran, though not all parts had been within the field of military operations. It was Austria north of the Danube and particularly Bohemia and Moravia which had suffered from the presence and the conflict of the rival armies. The war had begun with the defenestration of Prague in 1618 and it had ended with the battle of the Charles Bridge in Prague in 1648. In the intervening years half a dozen bloody and destructive campaigns had been fought on Czech soil, for the most part between the Imperialists and the Swedes. Wallenstein's armies had battened on the country; the Swedish occupiers were even more exacting and destructive. The Swedes were still in Bohemia in 1648, and it was another two years before the Treaty of Nuremberg and the payment of five million guilders induced them to go home. Even then they took with them as booty the great art collection which Rudolph II had made in Prague as well as many manuscripts of Wyclif and Hus.

The effect of the war which was of the greatest consequence was depopulation. The destruction of life directly due to the war, the mortality of soldiers in battle and in camp, the starvation and death from cold due to the requisitions and depredations of the armies which had been for twenty years quartered in the country, the plague which persisted into the years of peace, the drop in the natural state of reproduction due to the absence of so many men on military service for so long, all had conspired to reduce the population by hundreds of thousands. To these losses directly due to the war must be added those due to enforced or voluntary emigration. After the victory of Crown and Catholic Church in Austria as well as in the Czech lands Protestants were compelled to conform or to depart. Concrete evidence of the extent of destruction and depopulation in Bohemia is afforded by the great tax roll (*berní rŭla*) which itinerant committees of the Estates compiled for most of the country in 1654 and 1655. In form, content and purpose it is much like Domesday Book, listing the tenants of holdings and their land and stock. Though only about half of the *berní rŭla* has been published it suffices to confirm what other evidence suggests, that the destruction of life and property since 1618 had been enormous, though perhaps not as great as has sometimes been said. Czech historians today estimate that the population of Bohemia declined from some 1,700,000 in 1618 to something more than 900,000 after 1648. The decline in Moravia was in similar proportion. The Austrian lands also lost many exiles for religion's sake after the repression of the rising of 1626 and 1627. A patent of Ferdinand II of the latter year ordered the knights and nobles of Upper Austria to conform or to depart, and in 1628 much the same treatment was meted out to Lower Austria. In 1645 the Swedish army had gone plundering and burning through the Austrian arable lands north of the Danube. Hungary's population probably declined less than that of the western part of the monarchy. Nevertheless its losses had been and continued to be considerable. In Turkish Hungary the Christian population was decimated by the sheer poverty and starvation due to a sandy or marshy soil, backward husbandry and the demands of the landlord, the tax-collector and the sultan's recruiting officers, as well as by the flight of many of the better off to northern and western Hungary.[1] Hungary as a whole had not been invaded and devastated by the armies of the Thirty Years War. Officially there had been peace between the Emperor and the sultan since the Treaty of Zsitvatorok of 1606. But neither the Christian nor the Muslim emperor was able to control the commanders on his distant frontiers. Throughout the fifty years of nominal peace there were constant raids by ambitious and avaricious pashas into Christian territory in which peasants and townspeople were murdered, robbed or carried away into slavery. Preventive or retaliatory incursions across the undefined border by the commanders of the Hungarian frontier fortresses often were less harmful to the Turks than to their Christian subjects. Hungary also suffered from the plague which was pandemic in the second half of the seventeenth century.

In all those parts of the Habsburg lands where tillage or forestry was the predominant economy the shortage of labour which resulted from this

[1] The researches of Professor H. Inalčik have recently shown that the Turkish fiscal system was not as harsh to the Christians of the Balkans as has hitherto been assumed. Whether this is also true of Turkish Hungary awaits investigation.

depopulation was crucial because it coincided with an increasing demand for rural labour. Throughout central Europe landlords were discovering that if they used their land not merely to feed and clothe their own households but also as a source of production of commodities which could be sold, they would gain a money income which would satisfy growing appetites and wider ambitions. Markets for agricultural and forest products were growing: the western European States, increasingly engaged in commerce and manufacture, were demanding corn and timber; Vienna, Prague and the south-German towns needed to be fed and clothed; the huge standing armies maintained by the Emperor and the sultan and the many permanent garrisons on the Turkish frontier afforded a considerable market, as did the courts of princes, magnates and prelates. All these markets the landlords were monopolising. This exploitation of the land for sale and profit went further in Poland,[1] but it was important in Bohemia, Hungary and Austria also. The landowners produced and sold corn, timber, pigs, poultry, wine, beer and spirits. By using their predominance in the various Estates they were able to grant themselves monopolies and trading privileges. They built frontier granaries and corn barges. They rafted timber down the Hron and the Vah to the Danube. The Bohemian lords built many large and highly profitable fish-ponds. This transition from an economy of manorial self-sufficiency to one of production for the market involved a fundamental agrarian revolution. The landlord was no longer content to allow his peasant tenants to occupy nearly all his estate with their holdings. He needed not their customary and often paltry rents but their labour. He therefore took every opportunity to increase his demesne, the land which he did not let out but which he kept in his own hands to produce marketable crops. The demesne was increased by strictly interpreting the law and custom which regulated the escheat of peasant holdings for defect of direct male heirs. Peasants' holdings left vacant through war or pestilence were also brought into the demesne.

Demesne farming, if it was to be profitable, needed abundant cheap labour. The fall in the value of money made it uneconomical for the landlord to hire labour for wages. His only recourse was to force the peasants to labour on the demesne land without pay, and because there were now fewer labourers the predial service demanded from each peasant holding had to be increased; hence arose the enormous growth in the labour services demanded from the peasants of central and eastern Europe which characterised this period. For Bohemia we have the evidence not only of the legislation of the Estates, but also of contemporaries such as J. E. Wegener and the Dutch Jesuit Jacob des Haies, that serf labour (*robota*) on the lords' demesnes, rent, taxes and tithes consumed three-fifths of the serfs' labour; more than a quarter of them worked every day except

[1] See below, ch. XXIV, p. 565.

Sundays and saints' days for their lords. Whereas before 1620 the peasant tenant had usually done only some four to twelve days' boon work a year for his lord, after 1627 week work, at first exceptional but later usual, was enforced and the norm came to be three days a week of predial work from each peasant holding. Those who had larger holdings were bound to do 'draught *robota*', that is, to provide beside their labour two horses and a cart or heavy plough. The landlords usually had no draft animals of their own and owned beasts for fattening only; all the carting of the goods to market or river port was done by unpaid peasant labour. The peasants were compelled to buy their corn, wine, beer and spirits, often also their cheese, fish, cattle, poultry and salt, solely from their own lords. Payments for the use of the lord's mill and for licences to leave his estate were heavy. In royal Hungary there was a parallel worsening of the conditions of the serfs, Magyar, Slovak and Croat alike.

The economic and political predominance of the landowners was also a potent factor in the calamitous decline of the towns in the Habsburg lands. The implication of the towns in the Bohemian and Austrian rebellions of 1618 to 1626 had provided the opportunity for the restriction of their civic liberties and the undermining of their manufactures and trade. They were forbidden to sell to the peasants goods of the kind produced on the lords' estates. Plans for the development of industry and commerce propounded by publicists such as Wegener, the enlightened and patriotic Czech Jesuit Bohuslav Balbín, P. H. Morgenthaler and F. S. Malirský were ignored. The royal towns were oppressed by debts and taxes, neglected by the Chamber, and therefore made little if any progress. The 'subject' towns, that is, those which were part of the property of some lord or prelate and which together had more than twice the population of the royal towns, recovered somewhat more rapidly, for it was to the lords' interests that they should do so. Nevertheless when industry began to recover after 1650 in the Czech and Slovak lands, it did so rather in the countryside than in the towns.

The lingering consequences of the Thirty Years War, the continual hostilities on the Turkish frontier, unofficial at first, but from 1661 to 1699 open, general and almost uninterrupted, the drain of men and money for the standing army, the garrisons and Leopold's long wars with France, and the degradation of town life, all combined to arrest the cultural development of the Habsburg lands. Writing in German or Czech contributed little to poetry and nothing to drama. Only the Latin plays produced in some of the Jesuit colleges and schools, the Latin writings of Balbín, some treatises in German and Italian on politics or the art of war, and, exceptionally, the Magyar poetry of Miklós Zrínyi, afford any presage of the flowering of the following century. In painting, sculpture. architecture and music Leopold and the aristocrats of his dominions were just beginning to import the Italian, German, Polish and French artists who laid the foundations of the Baroque of Prague, Vienna and the Slovak towns. It was the fault and the loss of the Habsburg kings of Bohemia that the two best Czech painters of the seventeenth century, Karel Skréta and Wenceslas Hollar, did most of their best work in exile in Germany, Holland or England. That was also the fate of an even more eminent man, Jan Amos Komenský, known to the world as Comenius, the last bishop of the Bohemian Brethren, whose pioneer works on education were written during his restless wanderings from Leszno in Poland, to London, Stockholm, Elbing in Prussia, Sárospatak in Hungary, to Amsterdam where he died in 1670. After the expulsion or conversion of the Austrian and Czech Protestants higher education remained in the hands of the Jesuits, whose achievements were not entirely destructive. Whereas one Jesuit, Antonín Koniáš, boasted of having burned 60,000 Czech books, his younger colleague, Balbín, was the only man within the kingdom who showed any interest in the history or language of the Czechs. His *Dissertatio apologetica pro lingua slavonica praecipue bohemica* was brave and eloquent, but no one dared publish it until 1775, more than a century after it was written. In northern Hungary Jesuit teachers wrote on biblical, historical and contemporary themes, occasionally in the Slovak language.

By 1648 the first stage of the Counter-Reformation had been almost completed in the Austrian and Czech lands; that is to say the open practice and preaching of Protestantism had been stopped by the expulsion of ministers and school-teachers, by the execution or proscription of all gentry and burgesses who had been treasonably or heretically active, by the resumption or demolition of the property of the Protestant communities, and by compelling the mass of the Protestants to conform to the Catholic Church on pain of forfeiture and exile. The task was the easier because Czech and Austrian Protestantism had been primarily a landlord's interest; as patron of the parish church the landlord had determined the confessional allegiance of the incumbents he appointed and therefore also the type of service and the spiritual allegiance of the parishioners. Once the Protestant landlord had been replaced by a Catholic or had himself become a Catholic and had installed a Catholic priest who conducted a Catholic service, it was the easiest and usual thing for the parishioners to accept the new state of affairs. Recatholicisation was easier in Austria, for there Protestantism was more recent and less widespread than in Bohemia. Only in Lower Austria were landowners allowed to hold Protestant services in their own houses, but they could not admit their neighbours or even their tenants. By the middle of the century only forty-two lords and thirty-two knights exercised this privilege.

In Bohemia and Moravia the task of recatholicisation was bigger and more difficult. It was not only that the majority of Czechs had been heretics and schismatics since the early fifteenth century, but also that the Catholic Church had been so diminished and impoverished in property and in talent that it had to be rebuilt almost from the foundations. Bohemia was the only predominantly Protestant State which was ever brought back wholly into the Catholic fold. Ferdinand III was devoutly convinced of his duty towards his erring subjects. He was the patron of the Marian cult, the promotion of which in all his dominions was one of the most effective instruments of the Counter-Reformation. A 'Marian pillar' still dominates the central square in many a Czech, Slovak and Austrian town or village. Professors in the University of Prague, no longer *Carolina* but *Ferdinandea*, had annually to swear their belief in the Immaculate Conception of the Virgin. The final campaign in the crusade against the Hussites was inaugurated by two decrees of the regents of Bohemia published in September 1639 and February 1650, pronouncing that all must conform within three weeks. There was some rioting and so many flights from the country that the landlords, troubled as ever by the shortage of labour, got some relaxation of the peremptoriness of the decree. The archbishop of Prague, Cardinal Adalbert Harrach, and some of the more prudent Jesuits restrained the haste of the zealots and stopped some of the beating and imprisonment of recalcitrants. Harrach saw the need for a more positive policy and therefore set on foot the reorganisation and expansion of the ecclesiastical structure. A third and a fourth Bohemian bishopric were created, at Litoměříce in 1655 and at Hradec Králové in 1664.

It was more difficult to persuade the lords, Catholic though they now were, to disgorge the property which their Protestant predecessors had confiscated from the Church and to provide enough good Catholic priests, for many landlords were still reluctant to let the sons of their serfs go into the Church. In Bohemia, as in Hungary, the parishes had often to be manned by regulars. In 1651 Ferdinand set up in Austria and Bohemia 'Reformation commissions', composed in each district of a lay royal nominee and a cleric, usually a local abbot or prior, who chose local clergy to carry out 'instruction'. Registers were compiled of non-Catholics, who were summoned to undergo six weeks of instruction and then given the choice of conformity or exile. It usually depended on the local lord whether this sanction was enforced. Many recalcitrants were ingenious in evading obedience to such a summons and often the lords helped them to do so. Nevertheless the steady labours of the Jesuits were undoubtedly successful with the mass of the people, deprived as they were of spiritual and temporal leadership. By 1664 the Czech lands, with the exception of a few mining villages in the Ore Mountains, had at least outwardly conformed. Secret Protestant services, hymn-singing, prayer meetings and Bible readings continued, particularly in the northern and north-eastern parts of the country where clandestine visits from exiled pastors and the smuggling in of forbidden books from Saxony and Silesia were possible. This underground Protestantism, not very widespread, survived to re-emerge when Joseph II issued his patent of toleration in 1781. In Silesia alone of the lands of the Bohemian Crown was Protestantism officially tolerated, for the Elector of Saxony had insisted that by the terms of the Peace of Westphalia Lutheranism should be allowed in the Silesian principalities of Öls, Brieg, Liegnitz and Wohlau and in the towns of Breslau, Schweidnitz, Jauer and Glogau. The bishop of Breslau, Ferdinand's brother Leopold William, had little time to foster the Counter-Reformation in Silesia, for he was also bishop of Olomouc and governor of the Spanish Netherlands.

The great effort to recatholicise Hungary and Slovakia had been made before 1648 by Cardinal Péter Pázmány, archbishop of Esztergom. With the zealous help of the Jesuits and the Franciscans he had won over many of the nobles of western and north-western Hungary to the Catholic Church, and they had normally brought their tenants and serfs with them. But the military and political successes of the Calvinist princes of Transylvania, Gábor Bethlen and György Rákóczi I had arrested the process. By the Treaty of Linz of 1645 between Ferdinand and Rákóczi royal Hungary was confirmed in the enjoyment of the measure of toleration which had been conceded by Matthias II at his coronation in 1608: freedom of confession to all of noble birth and to the royal towns. This toleration was extended at Linz to the inhabitants of all towns and, in theory, even to the subject tenants of lords whose faith was different from theirs. In Turkish Hungary the Christian sects languished under the toleration of Muslim indifference. Here the Catholics were in the worst state, for the prelates whose sees were in Turkish territory had long before departed, the archbishop of Esztergom to Trnava, the bishops of Eger, Pécs, Nagyvárad (Grosswardein), Gyulafehérvár (Karlsburg) and Veszprém to some western asylum, but itinerant Franciscan and other missionaries kept the Catholic Church alive during the hundred and fifty years of Turkish occupation. The Calvinists managed to maintain some local organisation under the Turks and were helped by the continuance of relations with their fellow-believers in Transylvania. Transylvania itself throughout the seventeenth century preserved its peculiarity of virtually complete religious toleration. Its princes were Calvinists, and Calvinism was the faith of most of the Magyar lords and gentry, and therefore in practice, though not in law, of their serfs. The strength of Lutheranism lay in the 'Saxons', the German inhabitants of the Transylvanian towns. A diminished minority remained faithful to the Socinian anti-Trinitarianism which had flourished in Transylvania in the last decades of the sixteenth century and managed with some difficulty to avoid complete absorption in either the Reformed or the Catholic Church. The position of the surviving Roman Catholics was almost as precarious, but despite the flight or expulsion of the Roman prelates and the opposition of the Estates and princes to Jesuit intrusion, the Catholic community in

Transylvania survived until it was reinvigorated by the return of the principality to its allegiance to Leopold I at the end of the century. The growing number of Rumanian-speaking Transylvanians was permitted its Greek Orthodox churches, hierarchy and liturgy. All this variety of religious practice in Transylvania was rather the result and symbol of the weakness of the State than an expression of any precocious attachment to the theory of toleration which John Locke was only then beginning to formulate.

With the territories, peoples and problems described in the foregoing pages, Ferdinand III and Leopold I tried to deal in informal alliance with the greater landowners and the prelates, who, with their officials and the county and manorial courts, played the part of a civil service in local administration and jurisdiction. The central government of the monarchy the Emperor carried out with the help of the existing advisory and administrative bodies. Policy was made by him in consultation with his privy council (*Geheimer Rat*), composed of the president (*Hofhochmeister*, who came nearer to being prime minister than anyone else), the High Marshal of the Court, the Court Vice-Chancellor and two or three other councillors (*Vertrauensmänner*). The privy councillors were usually Austrian, German, Bohemian, Italian, and occasionally Hungarian aristocrats or prelates. The administrative organ of the central government was the Court Chancery, since 1620 separated from the Imperial Chancery. It dealt with the domestic affairs of the monarchy as a whole and of Austria in particular. From 1667 to 1683 an able and assiduous Rhinelander, Dr Johann Paul Hocher, the son of a professor of Freiburg, was chancellor. The functions of a central treasury were performed by the Court Chamber (*Hofkammer*), which had been set up in 1527 as a financial organ superior to the Chambers of the various lands of the monarchy. The *Hofkammer* fixed and apportioned the budget and had general control of commerce, manufacture, mints, and the gold and silver mines. Military affairs were administered by the Court War Council (*Hofkriegsrat*) which had been competent for all the Habsburg lands since 1556. In addition to its military functions it conducted diplomatic relations with the Porte. The *Hofkriegsrat* had a series of able presidents, Lobkowitz, Hannibal Gonzaga, Marquis of Mantua, Raimondo Montecuccoli and Hermann, margrave of Baden; it was characteristic of Habsburg government that none of these was an Austrian or an Hungarian.

Once peace had been made in 1648 the immediate concern of Ferdinand III was international. The welfare of neither his House nor his monarchy had been advanced by either the war or the peace. The hereditary enemy, France, was more powerful and dangerous than at any time since Cateau-Cambrésis (1559) and was still engaged in fighting successfully against Ferdinand's Spanish kinsman. Fortunately there was no immediate danger from the sultan, except to the wretched Magyars, Slovaks and Croats of the marches. The Turkish Empire sank to its nadir when in 1648 Ibrahim I was deposed and his seven-year-old son Mehmed IV set up in his place.[1] Transylvania too for a brief period ceased to be a trouble, for György Rákóczi I died in the same year and it was seven years before his son and successor, György Rákóczi II, found the opportunity to make his bid for a royal crown. Ever zealous for his House, Ferdinand's chief concern in his premature old age was to secure the succession of his eldest son Ferdinand to all his titles and crowns. He had without difficulty already got him crowned king of Bohemia in 1646 and of Hungary in 1647. But the succession to the Imperial Crown was not so easily to be had, partly because of the selfishness and greed of the Electors, flushed with their recent successes at the peace conferences, partly because of Mazarin's lavish energy in seeking the election of anyone except a Habsburg. The Electors after six months haggling elected the younger Ferdinand in May 1653 at Augsburg and crowned him at Ratisbon in June. But the death of Ferdinand IV in July 1654 made vain all the patient diplomacy and the money taxed out of the peasants of Bohemia and Spain. His younger brother Leopold was brought from his theological studies in Spain and the wearisome, costly business was begun again. Leopold was crowned in Pressburg in 1655 and in Prague in 1657, but a renewal of war prevented Ferdinand III from getting him elected Emperor before his own death.

The war, which began in June 1655 with the invasion of Poland by Charles X of Sweden,[2] concerned Austria not only because it threatened to extend the hegemony of Protestant Sweden to central Europe, but because it was a direct threat to the monarchy. Charles X was ambitious to become king of Bohemia as well as Poland, a plan by no means chimerical less than forty years after the Bohemian rebellion, especially for a Protestant soldier-king of the genuine Gustavian stamp. Even more immediately dangerous was it for Ferdinand when the reckless and ambitious prince of Transylvania, György Rákóczi II, saw in Charles of Sweden the ally who might help his plans. As soon as Charles had captured Warsaw, Rákóczi in August 1655 sent envoys to him, and in December 1656 an alliance was concluded which promised to Rákóczi southern and south-eastern Poland. Alarmed at this prospect of the Protestant partition of the country Ferdinand began negotiations with the fugitive and childless Polish king, John Casimir, but Ferdinand was dying and could do no more. Rákóczi took a Transylvanian army by way of Przemysl to Cracow and Sandomierz where he joined forces with the triumphant Charles on 11 April 1657. Nine days earlier Ferdinand died and his sixteen-year-old son succeeded to a situation as critical as that

[1] See below, ch. XXI, pp. 504–5.

[2] See below, ch. XXII, p. 521, and ch. XXIV, p. 566.

which had faced his grandfather on his accession in 1619. Within a month he was at war with Sweden as Poland's ally. Fortune favoured the new ruler. First the Danish attack on Swedish territory in May 1657 caused Charles X to desert Rákóczi in order to deal with this threat to his communications; secondly the Turks turned on Rákóczi. This was the first warning Christendom had that there had been a revolution in Turkey. There Mehmed Köprülü had become Grand Vizier in 1656. He ruthlessly purged court and army of their sloth and corruption and was already looking round for the opportunity to restore and extend the sultan's empire.[1] Köprülü had no desire to see the prince of Transylvania create an independent kingdom for himself, and therefore, when Rákóczi deposed the voivode of Moldavia and summoned his successor and the voivode of Wallachia to send him auxiliaries as if he were their lord, the sultan ordered his vassal, the Khan of the Crimean Tatars, to drive the Transylvanian invaders out of Poland. Rákóczi, deserted by his Swedish ally and his Cossack auxiliaries and anxious about his homeland, in July 1657 hastily bought peace from the Poles at the cost of an indemnity of 1,200,000 florins and hurried back to Transylvania. He left part of his forces in Poland under the gallant János Kemény, but they were too few to withstand the Tatar onslaught. At the battle of Trembowla, south of Tarnopol, on 31 July Kemény's troops were either slain or taken, together with Kemény, to imprisonment in the Crimea.

It was at this point that Austrian troops first began to participate in the war. They assisted the Poles to recover Cracow and to restore John Casimir. Another Austrian army, in co-operation with the Poles and Brandenburgers, began a successful campaign against the Swedes on the Baltic coast. Here the commander of the Austrian force, Montecuccoli, first distinguished himself by his successful actions at Neumünster, Thorn and on Alsen Island.

It was not an inauspicious beginning to Leopold's reign, but the demands he had to make on his subjects for men and money from the day of his accession were ominous. The taxation was made still heavier by the enormous cost of bribing the Electors not to yield to the seductions of Mazarin to elect, if not Louis XIV as Emperor, then some princeling who would be a French puppet. Leopold and his fellow Habsburg, Philip IV of Spain, were fearful not only of the loss of the Imperial dignity, but also of the implied imperialism of France. Ultimately the stream of Habsburg gold and the half-conscious fear of the German princes of French aggression secured the election of Leopold in July and his coronation at Frankfurt in August 1658.[2]

The most dangerous development during Leopold's early years was the revival of Turkish aggressive power by the Grand Vizier Mehmed Köprülü. As long as it threatened merely Transylvania the government in

[1] See below, ch. XXI, pp. 507–8. [2] See above, ch. XVIII, p. 446.

Vienna was not disturbed, even by the desperate appeals which began to come from royal Hungary. There, ever since 1648, the sporadic Turkish incursions had continued, threatening the frontier strongholds of Léva and Győr in 1652, which were saved only by Ádám Forgách's victory over a force of 5000 Turkish marauders at Nagyverekés. A bitter struggle continued on the middle Danube frontier in south-west Hungary, waged by the local magnates with no support from Vienna. Miklós Zrínyi, the Ban of Croatia, boasted in Tassonian verse of Magyar bravery and bewailed in prose the indifference and inaction of Leopold's advisers, of whom he said: 'The blowing of the winds can no more still the raging of the sea than princes can go against the advice of their councillors.'[1]

It was the subjection of Transylvania to the Turks which at last aroused Vienna to the danger. After Rákóczi's calamitous Polish adventure the Transylvanian Estates, hoping to appease the Turks, elected Ferenc Rédei prince in November 1657. But Rákóczi was determined to save his country and his title and in his turn bullied the Estates into recognising him again in January 1658. The feeble Rédei abdicated. Rákóczi fought and defeated the Turkish invaders at Lippa in May. But in September a double assault, by the Tatar Khan from Wallachia and the Grand Vizier himself from the south, led to the sack of Karlsburg and to the capture of three of the most powerful strongholds of western Transylvania: Jenő, Lugos and Karánsebes. In the same month the Grand Vizier proclaimed Ákos Barcsay vassal prince of Transylvania, and in November the cowed Estates recognised him. Rákóczi meanwhile was feverishly recruiting forces on his Hungarian estates, whence in 1659 he advanced into Transylvania and drove his rival Barcsay to flight, and was again recognised by the Estates. But in the same year Ahmed Sidi, the pasha of Buda, led a Turkish army through the south-eastern counties from Temesvár to Torda and Szeben (Hermannstadt), systematically sacking the frontier fortresses in his path. It was clear that the Grand Vizier was going to persist in his designs and that Rákóczi was too weak to save Transylvania by himself. He turned to the king of Hungary in Vienna, and at last Leopold was ready to help. His Imperial election had been accomplished; Montecuccoli was bringing the Baltic war to a successful end; the new president of his privy council, Johann Adolf von Schwarzenberg, was ready for action against the Turks. In return for restoring to the Crown the two counties of Szatmár and Szabolcs, Rákóczi secured the promise of military help. Leopold's troops occupied Szatmár and Kálló, but they made no attempt to fight the Turks until after the Austrian army of the Baltic was released by the death of Charles X and the Peace of Oliva early in 1660.[2] It was already too late. In the spring the pasha's army had made a great tour of destruction in north-eastern Hungary, beyond

[1] Quoted by Szekfű in 'Hóman Bálint és Szekfű Gyula', *Magyar Történet* (Budapest, 1935), IV, 163.
[2] See below, ch. XXIV, p. 568.

Debrecen and then down into the heart of Transylvania to Kolozsvár (Klausenburg). Rákóczi tried to stop the destructive tornado at Fenes, some ten miles west of Kolozsvár, in May 1660, but was defeated and fled mortally wounded to Nagyvárad where he died a fortnight later at the age of thirty-nine. Ahmed Sidi came to Nagyvárad and besieged this greatest of the cities of Transylvania. The Austrian general, Louis de Souches, cautiously brought his force to neighbouring Rakamaz, from the ramparts of which he idly watched the final assault on Nagyvárad when the pasha took it on 27 August.

Even the fall of Nagyvárad did not end the death agony of Transylvania. Kemény having returned from his Crimean imprisonment, on new year's day 1661 the Transylvanian Estates elected him successor to György Rákóczi II. He prudently asked Austria for help and Montecuccoli was appointed to lead the army of assistance. He would have preferred to attack the Turks in Esztergom and Buda to distract them from Transylvania, but the War Council ordered him to join forces with Kemény, whose position was desperate. The Estates had arrested and executed his rival, Barcsay, in September 1661, but the Turks were no longer willing to tolerate a prince who was not their creature. The Grand Vizier Mehmed died in October, but his son and successor, Fazil Ahmed Köprülü, was no less able than he and no less zealous to complete the subjection of Transylvania. Montecuccoli with 10,000 men had joined Kemény on the upper Tisza, but had done nothing to interrupt the great raid which the sirdar, Ali Pasha, together with the Tatar Khans and the voivodes of Wallachia and Moldavia had made into eastern Transylvania, in the course of which the sirdar proclaimed as prince yet another Transylvanian magnate, Mihály Apafi. All Montecuccoli had done was to advance cautiously to Kolozsvár where he found the city in the hands of the Turks; he had no provisions or pay for his troops; the Magyars and Saxons were both unfriendly. The Austrians therefore retired, leaving garrisons in the northern Transylvanian fortresses. In 1662 the tragedy ended. A Turkish army set out from Jenő under Mehmed Kučuk, caught Kemény on 22 January at Nagyszöllös near Segesvár (Schässburg) and there defeated and killed him. The century of Transylvania's meteoric and singular greatness was over. Its fall shocked and frightened not only the Emperor Leopold but the whole of Christendom. They realised that Transylvania had been a dam, the destruction of which laid open royal Hungary to the concentrated assault of the triumphant and eager Turks. The Grand Vizier Fazil Ahmed gave Leopold no time to find allies or augment his army. In April 1663 he set his forces in motion. His plan was to drive up the Danube directly to Pressburg and Vienna. Nothing stood in his way but the strong fortress of Neuhäusel (Nové Zámky), which had imposed a limit to the Turkish advance for more than a century. Within was a garrison of Austrians and Hungarians under Ádám Forgách. Behind him on the Vah stood Montecuccoli with a small force. In November the straitly besieged garrison in Neuhäusel forced Forgách to surrender; but the stout defence had forced the Turks to postpone their assault on Vienna till the next year.

Desperately the Emperor's emissaries appealed to the rulers of Christendom to come to save Austria, and so obviously urgent was the need that even the Imperial Diet and the king of France responded. Pope Alexander VII, Philip IV of Spain, Frederick William the Great Elector, and other German princes sent men and money. Bohemia paid 2,000,000 guilders in taxes in this year 1664. Louis XIV allowed 6000 valuable 'volunteers' to go to the war. Before the Turks renewed their attack in January 1664 Zrínyi tried to cut Fazil Ahmed's lines of communication by launching an attack into Turkish Hungary. But when in the summer Fazil Ahmed at last moved, Zrínyi's small Hungarian and Austrian force had to retreat and the Grand Vizier was able to take the fortress of Zerinvár, the last great stronghold in western Hungary. It was already June and this southern campaign had given time for Montecuccoli to assemble the motley army of Christendom to defend the line of the Raab, some fifty miles east of Vienna. There on 1 August 1664 Montecuccoli destroyed the great army of Fazil Ahmed as it tried to force a crossing of the Raab near the monastery of St Gotthard.[1]

The battle of St Gotthard was a great victory for Christian arms. It did not indeed end for ever the threat to Vienna; it merely postponed it for nineteen years. Leopold and his advisers made no attempt to follow up the victory by pursuing the demoralised Turks to Buda and Transylvania, but within ten days they concluded the Peace of Vasvár.[2] The terms provided for a twenty years' truce; Transylvania was to be free of both Turkish and Imperial occupation but to remain under the suzerainty of the sultan; Leopold was to give a compensation of 200,000 florins to the enemy he had just signally defeated and, what was even more dangerous, was to allow the Turks to continue to occupy Nagyvárad and Zerinvár and the three fortresses in western Slovakia which had hitherto provided an insuperable barrier for the upper Danube: Neuhäusel, Nitra and Léva. The Peace of Vasvár at once began a heated argument which is not settled today. On the one side, Austrians and Germans argued that it would have been folly to attempt to expel the Turks from Hungary with the relatively meagre forces available in 1664; to run the risk of another Mohács might have been fatal to Christendom. On the other side, Hungarians have always regarded Vasvár as typical of Habsburg treachery. They argued that once the Turks were demoralised by defeat and on the run they could have made no effective stand anywhere north of the Sava and lower Danube. They accuse the government in Vienna of having no desire to see Hungary free and reunited; they also maintain that the peace was made

[1] See below, ch. XXI, p. 511. [2] See *ibid.*

hastily and disadvantageously because Leopold had suddenly been distracted by the prospect of something far more attractive than the liberation of Hungary or the expulsion of the Infidel. At the same Imperial Diet of January and February 1664 which had been persuaded to send help to Leopold in his great peril, John Philip von Schönborn, the Elector and Archbishop of Mainz, had drawn the Emperor's attention to the probability of the imminent demise of the Spanish king and of his only and sickly infant son. Human motives are rarely unmixed and it may be suggested that military caution and dynastic ambition combined to induce Leopold and his advisers not to seize the opportunity presented by St Gotthard.

Leopold's interest in the future of Spain was fostered by his chief ministers. The death of his mentor and first minister, Prince Porzia, in 1665 brought to the head of the privy council first Count Johann Auersperg and on his fall in 1669 Prince Wenzel Lobkowitz. These two statesmen, the dour, cautious German and the intelligent, volatile Czech aristocrat, were alike only in their devotion to the dynasty and their belief that it would be foolishly hazardous to quarrel with Louis XIV when so much might be obtained by agreement with him. When it was a question of a successor to the childless John Casimir of Poland, who abdicated his throne in September 1667, Habsburg diplomacy, in accordance with old habit, supported the claims of a prince of the Empire, Charles, the son of Duke Charles IV of Lorraine, against the younger Condé, the French candidate. But when, after the death of Philip IV, Louis XIV sought to anticipate the dissolution of the Spanish Empire by embarking on the War of Devolution in May 1667,[1] Leopold did not join the Triple Alliance, but sought to agree with his adversary. Leopold's ablest diplomat, Count Lisola, warned him that the French attack on the Spanish Netherlands was 'the beginning of the march of the enemy towards the gates of Vienna',[2] but he was unheeded. In January 1668 Leopold made a secret treaty of partition with Louis XIV which would have given to him Spain, Spanish America, Milan, Sardinia, the Balearic and Canary Islands, and to France the Spanish Netherlands, Franche Comté, Naples and Sicily, Navarre, the Philippines and the Spanish posts in Africa.

Leopold's preoccupation with the Spanish succession nearly cost him his Hungarian Crown. The indifference to the fate of Hungary indicated by the Peace of Vasvár convinced the Magyar magnates that they had better make terms with the sultan if even the torso of the kingdom was to be saved from Turkish conquest. Even those like the Palatine Ferenc Wesselényi who had hitherto been loyal to Leopold now turned to conspiracy and treason. Louis XIV was quick to perceive what profit might

[1] See above, ch. IX, p. 210.

[2] Quoted by A. F. Pribram, *Franz Paul, Freiherr von Lisola, 1613–1674, und die Politik seiner Zeit* (Leipzig, 1894), p. 311.

here be gained for France. He was already making his plans for the destruction of the United Provinces and he was therefore pleased that the Emperor should be distracted. His ambassador in Vienna, Jacques Gremonville, by the expenditure of many words and a little money fanned the flames of Hungarian discontent. He approached Miklós Zrínyi, but he refused to betray his allegiance. Fortunately for him perhaps he was torn to pieces by a hunted boar in September 1664. With the others Gremonville was successful. The most reckless of the conspirators was Péter Zrínyi, the successor to his brother Miklós's estates and title, who was ambitious to become prince of Transylvania. The Chief Justice of Hungary, Ferenc Nádasdy, who hoped to succeed Wesselényi as Palatine, joined the plot. Some of the leading Protestant clergy of Slovakia and north-eastern Hungary, fearful for their religious liberties, were also persuaded to give their support.

As it became clear that Gremonville had no authority to commit Louis XIV to any promise of effective support, the conspirators looked more and more to the sultan for help. In August 1666 Wesselényi presided over a meeting of the disaffected lords where it was proposed to collaborate with Apafi and get the Porte to promise to defend the liberties of Hungary, which should be free to elect its own king and be independent in foreign affairs in return for a fixed annual tribute to the sultan. Rarely has a conspiracy been so long gestating and so soon betrayed by so many of its participants. When Apafi sent an emissary to seek out the Grand Vizier, Fazil Ahmed Köprülü, in the spring of 1667, one of the interpreters of the Imperial embassy in Constantinople heard of the plot and reported it to Vienna. The death of Wesselényi in April 1667 left the conspiracy without any authoritative leadership. But for three years more the wretched and confused business of intrigues, betrayals and quarrels went on. Any patriotic character the movement had once had was destroyed by the ambitious rashness and the abject cowardice of the plotters. The Turks were too busy with the long siege of Candia and their war with Poland[1] to give any help. In turn Nádasdy, Wesselényi's widow and Péter Zrínyi betrayed every ramification of the plot to the Austrians. Zrínyi confessed, was pardoned and then intrigued again with the Turks. Lionne and Gremonville revealed all they knew to Leopold. When at last the young Ferenc Frangepán took to arms and tried to capture Zagreb, this, the only military gesture of the whole conspiracy, was easily repressed by an Austrian force in April 1670. Too late the northern counties set military preparations afoot, but when they heard that Péter Zrínyi had been arrested they desisted. The entire movement collapsed before midsummer. Procrastination, fatuity, inability to collaborate or organise, conflicting personal ambitions, treachery and treason had put Hungary helpless into the hands of its enemies.

[1] For these see below, ch. XXI, pp. 510, 512.

Lobkowitz eagerly accepted the opportunity to 'put the Hungarians into Czech trousers'. He entrusted the inquiry to an old enemy of the Hungarians, the Austrian Chancellor Johann Hocher. Ignoring their constitutional privilege of being tried by their Hungarian peers the government arraigned Péter Zrínyi, Nádasdy and Frangepán before a purely German court which, after playing cat and mouse with them for some months, condemned them to death. They were beheaded in April 1671. An Hungarian court presided over by the new primate, György Szelepcsényi, archbishop of Esztergom, tried the lesser conspirators, three of whom were executed. The treasury was greatly enriched by the confiscation of the traitors' estates. Some two thousand persons fled, mostly to Transylvania, there to plot vengeance. All this made possible the use of Montecuccoli's old prescription for Hungary, military occupation. In May 1670 Austrian troops crossed the Vah and reduced the kingdom to the status of a conquered country. The principle of Austrian policy was expressed by the Imperial Vice-Chancellor Leopold Wilhelm Königsegg in the words: 'The Magyars rebelled and thereby have lost all their privileges; henceforward they must be treated as *armis subjecti*.'[1] In March 1671 the counties and towns were ordered by royal decree to maintain the occupying troops stationed in them. Archbishop Szelepcsényi was nominated the king's lieutenant in Hungary and a notorious enemy of the Magyars, Leopold Kollonitsch, bishop of Wiener-Neustadt, was made president of the Hungarian Chamber. In March 1673 Leopold nominated a *Gubernium* to sit at Pressburg composed of four Germans and four Hungarians. Its president and the real ruler of the kingdom was Johann Gaspar Ampringen, titular Grand Master of the Teutonic Knights. The Council governed by means of the army of occupation, whose rapacity and cruelty were such that the papal nuncio in Vienna, Francesco Buonvisi, expressed his alarm as to what the consequences might be.

The abrogation of the political liberties of Hungary seemed to the Catholic prelates a heaven-sent opportunity to put an end to the galling existence within the apostolic kingdom of the Protestant Churches. Kollonitsch brought 12,000 soldiers from Vienna to assist Archbishop Szelepcsényi and his suffragans to suppress the Protestant churches and schools in Pressburg, Sopron, Szentgyörgy and the mining towns of Slovakia. The soldiers were followed by Jesuits, Franciscans and Augustinians who set up their religious houses and schools. Efforts to stop Protestant worship in the frontier fortresses, however, met with such resistance from their Hungarian garrisons that in 1674 the government in Vienna called a halt to forceful recatholicisation. The prelates had recourse to judicial process. From September 1673 until April 1674 Szelepscényi conducted in Pressburg a *judicium delegatum* to try those Protestant

[1] O. Redlich (ed.), 'Das Tagebuch Esaias Pufendorfs', *Mittheilungen des Instituts für österreichische Geschichte* (1916), p. 589.

clergy who were suspected of having been party to the Wesselényi conspiracy. More than two hundred of them were induced to sign an undertaking to leave Hungary and never to return to preach or teach. Forty pastors obstinately refused to sign and were condemned to the Neapolitan galleys. Their sufferings there evoked loud protests from Protestant States whom Leopold at this juncture least wished to alienate, such as the United Provinces, Brandenburg, Saxony and Sweden. After more than two years in the galleys the wretched convicts were rescued by Admiral de Ruyter and were afforded asylum in Holland.

From 1671 to 1681 Leopold was unusually free from eastern problems. Hungary had been crushed; the Turks were too much preoccupied with their wars against Poland and Russia[1] in the struggle for the Ukraine to be an immediate threat to Austria. The Emperor was therefore able to devote his attention to the problem created by Louis XIV's imperialism. Leopold was not easily weaned from Lobkowitz's policy of friendship with France as the most promising means of getting the Spanish Crown. But Louis's obvious determination to destroy the United Provinces, his occupation of the Imperial duchy of Lorraine in 1670, his alliance with Sweden and his invasion of the United Provinces in the spring of 1672[2] at last convinced Leopold that the Empire was threatened. He let Lisola off the leash and in 1672, 1673 and 1674 alliances were made with the Dutch, Spain, Brandenburg, Brunswick and Saxony.[3] In August 1672 Montecuccoli set out from Eger with 15,000 men, and for the next seven years the wealth and the manpower of the Habsburg lands were deployed in the costly and inconclusive struggle to reconquer Alsace and to prevent Turenne and his successors from breaking through to the Danubian high road to Vienna.

The maintenance of 50,000 men on the upper Rhine for so long a period drained all Leopold's realms of men and money, especially his kingdom of Bohemia. Unhappy is the land which has no history. Bohemia under the autocratic Habsburg rule was living through its age of darkness, the *Temno* as the Czechs call it. But the gloomy decades were in the year 1680 briefly lit up by the lurid flames of peasant rebellion. There had been small, local stirrings of rural discontent in 1652, 1668 and 1673 as the lords' demands for labour increased. The more general agitation was provoked by the dearth of 1679 and the plague which invaded the Habsburg lands from the Balkan peninsula. It ravaged Hungary in 1678 and Austria in 1679; despite some belated, primitive and ineffective precautions the plague reached Bohemia in 1680. Fifteen thousand, a third of the population, died in Prague, 3500 of them in the Jewish ghetto. Leopold's presence in Bohemia, whither he had fled to escape the plague in Vienna, seemed to some of the Bohemian peasants an opportunity for a

[1] See below, ch. XXIV, p. 569.
[2] See above, ch. IX, pp. 215–17.
[3] See above, ch. IX, pp. 217–18.

direct appeal to his benevolence. Early in 1680 a group of serfs living in northern Bohemia presented a petition to the king which he accepted. But when other serfs from all parts of the country were thereby encouraged to follow suit the lords, fearing lest the kindly Leopold might be moved to do something, began to arrest and imprison the deputations elected by the peasants and induced Leopold to issue a patent which forbade direct appeals to the king and directed them to the presidents of the district courts. A proclamation followed which declared that all servile privileges and liberties dating from before the 'foul rebellion' of 1618 were abolished.

Thereupon some of the more radical of the peasants' leaders began to preach open revolt. In many districts of northern and western Bohemia the serfs refused their predial services and made armed demonstrations against the landlords and their stewards. At once a force of soldiers under Colonel Christopher Harant was sent to repress the rebellion. He went from eastern through northern to western Bohemia; most of the peasant bodies dispersed at the mere news of his approach. There were a few skirmishes, but as it was illegal for a serf to own arms, the peasants, armed for the most part only with scythes, flails and sickles, could not withstand Harant's well-trained troops. The only fighting on anything but the smallest scale was at Čeliv in the Plzeň district, where two companies of cuirassiers supported by artillery dispersed the peasants, and near Čestina in the Časlav district. More than a hundred peasants were killed in these two skirmishes. All those who were captured with any sort of arms in their hands were hanged forthwith. By the end of April the rising had been suppressed. A criminal commission supported by troops was sent round the disaffected districts to discover and try the leaders. Some hundred persons were convicted and executed by hanging, beheading, quartering or impaling. Ten times that number were sent to forced labour or to prison in the lords' or Hungarian gaols. In June 1680 the king issued a *robotní patent* which, while it acknowledged the inhumanity of some of the lords, yet recognised as legal most of the innovations made since 1620. The patent fixed the normal maximum of *robota* at three days a week from each peasant holding, except for the corn and hay harvest and for harvesting the fish-ponds, 'but the lords should see to it that the serfs should get some reward for these extraordinary services'.[1] On those estates where less than three days' work a week was customary it was not to be increased. This patent of 1680 afforded only temporary and imperfect relief; in many places it was disregarded.

The autocratic Austrian rule of Hungary by Ampringen and the *Gubernium* proved unable to conciliate the nation or to give it peace and order. The exiles of 1671, organised into an army of patriots (the famous

[1] See *Československá Vlastivěda*, vol. IV, 'Dějiny', ed. V. Novotný, p. 531.

kurucok) by Count Mihály Teleki, supplied with money by the Transylvanian prince, Apafi, who like Teleki was a zealous Calvinist, made their base in the no-man's-land of north-eastern Hungary where they held out, homeless, landless, quarrelling, robbing, constantly hunted by General Spankau's mercenaries. Teleki tried to take advantage of Louis XIV's anti-Habsburg diplomacy which was endeavouring to get John Sobieski, king of Poland, Apafi and the 'exiles' to harry Leopold from the rear. The attack was launched by Teleki's fellow exile, Imre Thököly, a clever, restless young aristocrat of twenty-two. His birth, education and wealth attracted many to the ranks of the *kurucok*: proscribed landlords and peasants, Slovaks as well as Magyars. In the summer of 1678 Thököly with the help of French officers and Polish mercenaries began his attempt to drive the Austrians out of northern Hungary. It was a merciless war on both sides, disgraced by the exacerbation of religious zeal. Archbishop Szelepcsényi had eighteen Protestant pastors put to death for supporting Thököly; he on his part wherever he came suppressed the religious orders and handed over Catholic churches to the Protestants. The Catholics closed the Protestant schools at Prešov and Sárospatak; Thököly closed the Jesuit colleges at Užhorod and Košice. Neither of the two Austrian generals, the veteran Walther Leslie or his successor Aeneas Sylvius Caprara, was able to prevent Thököly and the *kurucok* from occupying the mining towns of central Slovakia or from raiding as far to the north and west as Silesia and Moravia. By 1680 he had occupied nearly all the counties of northern and western Hungary.

It was clear to the more far-sighted statesmen of Christendom that the situation was very dangerous. The Turks, frustrated in the Ukraine, were much interested in the potentialities of Thököly's campaign. There was a feeling that Ampringen would never succeed in taming Hungary. It was the new pope, Innocent XI, who took the lead in the reconciliation of Leopold, Louis XIV and Hungary. Innocent was the most zealous crusading pope since Pius II. In 1677 he sent Buonvisi to Vienna to win over the Emperor and within a year the nuncio got the Hungarian magnates to confer in Vienna with Leopold's ministers. After peace had been made in the west at Nymegen[1] Leopold summoned the Hungarian Estates to meet at Sopron in May 1681. There he purchased the support of the Hungarian lords by restoring the liberties of the kingdom. The Estates recovered their right to elect a Palatine; the Lieutenancy and *Gubernium* were abolished; the Hungarian Chamber was made independent once more; the principle that offices of State should be filled by Hungarians was recognised; the Estates were to meet every third year; finally, the Protestants were given back the liberties of 1608 and the exiled pastors were allowed to return.

This dramatic *volte face* was made only just in time. Thököly realised

[1] See above, ch. IX, p. 219.

that the conciliation of Leopold and the Estates meant that he could not remain master of Hungary without Turkish help, and Kara Mustafa, Fazil Ahmed Köprülü's successor as Grand Vizier, was now ready to interfere, for he believed that the time was ripe for the overthrow of the Habsburg Empire. Thököly was received with great pomp by the pasha of Buda in the summer of 1682 and at once a joint army of *kurucok* and Turks embarked on the conquest of Hungary. They speedily captured the north-eastern strongholds of Košice, Prešov, Levoča and, at the cost of 4000 Turkish dead, Fid'iakovo. Thereupon the pasha Ibrahim delivered to Thököly the *athnam* of Mehmed IV which declared Thököly to be king of all Hungary and Croatia, as tributary vassal of the sultan. The new conquerors of upper Hungary proved to be a plague worse than the Austrian army of occupation had been. Tatar and Szekler horsemen burnt villages and carried off the people to slavery; the Turks' camels devoured gardens and vineyards; the frontier fortresses were demolished. At the end of 1682 Leopold was glad to purchase time to find allies and an army by making a truce with Thököly which left all Hungary east of the Hron in his hands. All was ready for the sultan and his Grand Vizier to embark on the campaign which they believed would accomplish what Suleiman the Magnificent had failed to achieve in 1529.

Leopold was still anxiously watching the activities of Louis XIV's *Chambres de Réunions*[1] as he was the preparations of the Turks, and it was the pope who through his nuncios played the greatest part in creating the Christian coalition of Austria, the princes and Diet of the Empire, and the Poles. The crucial alliance with John Sobieski was not concluded until 31 March 1683, the very day that Mehmed IV and Kara Mustafa set out with their great host from Adrianople. They were joined in Hungary by Apafi and the Transylvanian army. Thököly renewed the war in western Slovakia but failed to take the key point of Pressburg. When Duke Charles of Lorraine, the commander-in-chief of the Christian army, heard of the approach of the enemy towards Győr he withdrew westwards, leaving Hungary to its fate and Vienna to withstand a siege. From July the garrison of Vienna under the leadership of Count Rüdiger von Starhemberg bravely defended itself, until on 12 September Sobieski's relieving army swept down from the heights of the Kahlenberg to rout the Turks and to deliver Christendom for ever from the spectre of Muslim conquest which had haunted it for three centuries.[2]

The great victory of Vienna stilled as many fears and evoked as much rejoicing as Lepanto, with greater justification, for its consequences were much more substantial and enduring. Like Lepanto it was a joint victory of pope and Emperor. Moreover it marked the advent of Austria to the position of a great power. It was Leopold, and not Louis XIV, who now

[1] For these, see above, ch. IX, pp. 219–20.

[2] For details of the siege and relief of Vienna see below, ch. XXI, pp. 515–17.

stood at the pinnacle of glory, and in the years that followed, while Louis's great armies were struggling obscurely and unsuccessfully in the labyrinth of the War of the League of Augsburg, Leopold's army under the aegis of the refurbished Crown of St Stephen was hammering the Infidel back beyond the Danube and the Carpathians. The war of Hungarian liberation was veritably a crusade, the final achievement of the victorious Counter-Reformation. It was Innocent XI who organised the Holy League of the Emperor, the king of Poland and Venice at Linz in March 1684; it was his plan that the allies should attack simultaneously in Hungary, in Moldavia and in Greece. The pope brought the Curia almost to penury so that he might spend every florin on the war; the monasteries of the monarchy were taxed a third of their incomes. Cardinal Buonvisi not only administered all this money; he prepared military plans and kept the irresolute Leopold up to the mark.

The expulsion of the Turks from Hungary was not a short or an easy task.[1] It occupied sixteen years, and at one point, when in 1688 Mustafa Köprülü, brother of the great Fazil Ahmed, became Grand Vizier, it looked as if all the gains of six victorious years might be lost. But despite this dying spasm of energy, the Turks had been fatally crippled by the political disasters which followed on their defeat before Vienna.[2] What ensured their expulsion from Hungary was the size of the Christian army and the skill with which it was deployed. In the terrible battle which led to the recovery of Buda on 2 September 1686 an army of 40,000 men took part: Austrians, Czechs, Hungarians, Brandenburgers, Swabians, Franconians, Bavarians, Swedes, Italians, Spaniards, and even a few Englishmen and Scots. The superiority of the Imperial generals was shown in such battles as Charles of Lorraine's great victory in 1687 at Nagyharsány, almost on the field of Mohács, which restored southern Hungary to the Habsburgs after nearly a hundred and fifty years of Turkish rule.

The expulsion of the Turks was a mixed blessing for Hungary, for by 1687 Leopold was sufficiently master of the whole country to think the time ripe for putting an end to the liberties which he had been compelled to grant in 1681. He summoned the Estates to Pressburg in October 1687 and coerced them into declaring the Hungarian Crown to be no longer elective, but hereditary in the male line of the House of Habsburg. The treasured paragraph 31 of the Golden Bull of 1222, which gave the Hungarian lords the right of *insurrectio* against any king who offended against the charter, was abrogated. The Estates ceased to meet and Hungary was at last reduced to the provincial status in which Bohemia had already existed for sixty years.

The principality of Transylvania was more fortunate in the conse-

[1] For a fuller account of the expulsion of the Turks from Hungary see vol. VI of this History, ch. XIX.

[2] See below, ch. XXI, pp. 517–18.

quences of its liberation from the Turks than was the rest of Hungary. When Mustafa Köprülü became Grand Vizier and embarked on the great counter-offensive of 1690 he saw that he must secure Transylvania as a bridgehead north of the lower Danube. Therefore, when Prince Apafi died in April, the sultan nominated Thököly as prince of Transylvania and sent him with a force which defeated the Imperial and Transylvanian army at Zernyest in August. Louis of Baden was therefore compelled to turn to Transylvania with his main army, even though it meant allowing the Grand Vizier to reconquer Vidin and Belgrade and all the recently recovered territory south of the Sava. The battle which decided the fate of Transylvania was fought on 19 August 1691 at Zalánkémen near the confluence of the Tisza. Louis was completely victorious. Twenty thousand Turks and Mustafa Köprülü were killed, though Thököly escaped. The constitutional position of Transylvania within the Habsburg monarchy was defined in the two *diplomata Leopoldiana* published in Vienna in October 1690 and December 1691. The principality was not reincorporated in Hungary, but was subordinated directly to Vienna, though it was allowed to enjoy some vestiges of autonomy. It owed allegiance to the Habsburg king. The co-existence of Catholic, Calvinist, Lutheran and anti-Trinitarian faith and practice was allowed to continue. Though the Transylvanian Estates continued to meet and to legislate, the principality was in fact administered by a governor and council appointed by the king. This was to remain its constitutional position until 1848.

The Turks did not easily concede victory to Leopold. For six years after Zalánkémen they fought desperately and sometimes successfully against the incompetent successors of Louis of Baden and the Imperial army now further diminished by the demands of the western war against France. The election of Frederick Augustus, Elector of Saxony, as king of Poland in 1697 sealed the fate of the Turks, for it brought as his successor to the command of the Imperial forces Eugene of Savoy. On 4 September 1697 he destroyed the last effective Turkish army at Zenta on the lower Tisza. Through Lord Paget, the English ambassador to the Porte, Sultan Mustafa II began negotiations for peace. The maritime powers urged Leopold to terminate the eastern war in view of the imminence of the death of Charles II of Spain. Near the ruined village of Carlowitz on the lower Drava the plenipotentiaries of the Emperor, the sultan, Poland, Russia and Venice concluded the peace by which the Turks renounced the whole of Hungary and Transylvania to Leopold, with the exception of the so-called Banat of Transylvania, that is the area in south-east Hungary between the Maros, the lower Tisza, the Danube and the Wallachian frontier. Belgrade remained in Turkish hands. With the exception of the Banat and of Lusatia Leopold I now ruled all the lands of the Empire which Ferdinand I had created, and he ruled them with an absolute authority which Ferdinand would have envied.

CHAPTER XXI

THE OTTOMAN EMPIRE UNDER MEHMED IV

SULTAN MEHMED IV who ascended the throne in 1648 inherited a vast empire which had been conquered by the sword of his ancestors and stretched over three continents. In Europe the frontier of the Ottoman Empire was a mere eighty miles from Vienna; in North Africa only Morocco did not belong to it; it included Upper Egypt and extended to Aden; the Black Sea and the Red Sea were Turkish lakes; in the east it stretched to the shores of the Caspian and of the Persian Gulf. It is impossible to give the exact figure of its population, but in the seventeenth century it amounted to approximately 25 or 30 millions. The Turks, although the dominant race, were only a minority. Probably the Muslims —Turks, Arabs, Kurds, Bosnians, Albanians, Circassians, Crimean Tatars and Turkic peoples of the Caucasus—were stronger than the Christians—Greeks, Serbs, Hungarians, Bulgars, Wallachians and Moldavians. Outstanding among the Turks of this period were the famous historian, geographer and bibliographer Kâtib Tchelebi (1609–57) and the renowned traveller Evliya Tchelebi (1611–78), who described the cities, customs and peoples of the Ottoman Empire in his huge ten volumes. Its heart was the city of Constantinople (Istanbul), the seat of the military and administrative institutions of the empire, the centre of commerce and culture as well as amusement and pleasures. It was inhabited by more than half a million people, Muslims, Christians and Jews, all living side by side for centuries, observing their own customs. The city contained the palace of the sultans, the Serail, the splendid mosques of Sultan Ahmed, Suleymaniye, Bayezid, Selimiye and Sultan Mehmed the Conqueror, many *Medresse*'s (colleges), libraries, public baths, hospitals, inns and food distribution centres, maintained by pious endowments. The 'second capital' of the empire was the city of Adrianople, where the sultans spent many of their leisure hours, and which served the army as a base at the beginning of a campaign against the Christian powers. The holy cities of Mecca and Medina stood under the sultan's special care, for as the caliph it was his duty to protect these places, which were visited every year by hundreds of thousands of pilgrims from every corner of the Muslim world, and to give large donations to them.

Basically the empire was an agricultural country with many fertile areas, and taxes on land and farming were the principal source of revenue. The methods of agriculture, however, were very primitive and the tools used were rudimentary. The status of the peasants was that of serfs; the Muslim peasants gave the tithes from corn and were subject to many other obligations, while the Christian peasants in addition had to pay the *Djizye* or poll-tax which exempted them from military service, its amount varying according to the peasants' status and incomes. As the empire dominated the main trade routes from the Mediterranean to the East, trade, although hampered by many obstacles, played an important part. Constantinople and Smyrna were the main centres of trade with foreign countries, while Adrianople, Brussa and Thessalonica were famous internal trading centres. The customs duties were another source of large revenues. There were many Jewish, Greek and Armenian merchants, for the Turks as a rule considered trade derogatory to their honour and preferred military and administrative appointments. Foreign merchants too were extremely active and enjoyed a privileged position, for example with regard to the payment of customs for imported goods. The leading position was held by the English Levant Company which had succeeded in ousting the Venetians and the French. Venetian cloth, however, was imported side by side with English cloth for the use of the upper classes, as were precious furs from Russia. Coffee came from the Yemen, and tobacco was imported by English and Dutch merchants: although severe penalties were imposed for smoking it spread rapidly, and tobacco cultivation began at this time.

The stability and security of the empire rested on its army, an ancient institution going back to the fourteenth century. It consisted of the standing army known as the Janissaries and provincial feudal levies raised by the tenants of fiefs held on a military tenure. Each tenant according to the amount of his revenue was obliged to equip and mount a certain number of horsemen and to participate with them in the campaigns. This system provided the army with something like 100,000 horsemen, but it had become corrupt and inefficient. Fiefs were often distributed illegally, and the obligations to render military services were ignored although legally such a refusal should have ended the period of tenure. The corps of the Janissaries (*Yenitcheri* or new troops) had been founded in the fourteenth century and was based on the system of *Devshirme*, the conscription of Christian children from the Balkans. They were converted to Islam, educated and trained under special regulations and a severe discipline: this highly superior force had enabled the Turks to make their great conquests. The corps was divided into more than 150 *orta*'s of varying size, known by their numbers and with their special standards and ensigns. The soldiers wore uniforms, lived in barracks, and received wages according to the length of their service as well as a special *bakhshish* on the occasion of the accession of a new sultan. The total strength of the corps amounted to about 50,000 men, but its discipline and power as a fighting force had declined. The problem of controlling the mutinous

Janissaries was of vital importance, for their outrages shook the foundations of the empire. Furthermore, during the reign of Mehmed IV the system of *Devshirme* was abolished, and only Muslims, especially the sons of Janissaries, were conscripted for the corps, another factor contributing to its decline. Apart from the Janissaries, the standing army had smaller numbers of gunners, bombardiers, sappers, drivers and armourers.

The navy too was of great importance, the admiralty occupying a large area at the Golden Horn where new ships were built and damaged ones repaired. The sailors were mainly recruited from the Greek population and known as *Levend*'s (a corruption of the Italian word *Levantino*). But the Ottoman navy had equally decayed, so that the Venetians could establish their mastery not only in the Mediterranean but even in the Aegean Sea, with fatal consequences for the Ottomans. In other fields too their innate conservatism prevented them from making the necessary changes and adjustments. No attention was paid to the rapidly changing economic conditions and the technical advances made in Europe. Many important posts were given to unqualified people and administrative appointments often went to the highest bidders.

The Ottoman Empire had reached its zenith during the reign of Suleiman the Magnificent (1520–66); it then possessed well-developed and efficient institutions which matched its political greatness. But Suleiman's successors, with only two exceptions, lacked the gifts and the enthusiasm of their predecessors and no longer played a conspicuous part in public life, preferring to stay behind the walls of the Serail. As early as the later sixteenth century, the reign of Murad III, there were signs of decline. The government was subject to intrigues by the sultan's favourite wives or to the influence of the queen mother. The chief of the harem, a black eunuch, often played a part in the most important affairs of State, while the sultan ceased to be an active ruler. According to the established tradition the government rested in the hands of the Grand Vizier, who exercised far-reaching powers. Yet, until the accession of the Köprülüs in 1656, the intrigues of the Serail and the interference of the sultan's favourites caused a decline of the Grand Vizier's authority and of the whole system of government. The *Divan* (Council) which was presided over by the Grand Vizier and was attended by certain other Viziers and high dignitaries, such as the Kadis of Rumelia and Anatolia, was only a consultative organ.

As the empire was a Muslim State the Mufti (Sheikh-ul-Islam) played an important part in the government. He was the head of all Muslim legal and spiritual institutions and enjoyed a privileged status. His approval was required for many important decisions, such as the declaration of war, the conclusion of peace, or the deposition of a sultan. In contrast with the Grand Vizier, the Mufti was never executed if found guilty, but only exiled. Less important than the Mufti were the Kadis (judges) who also had many other duties. In their districts they had to carry out the instructions of the central government and to supervise the municipalities and the supply of food. The highest among the Kadis was the Kadi of Rumelia, and after him the Kadi of Anatolia; they were the judges of the army and judicial matters concerning the army came under their jurisdiction. The legal system was based on Islamic law, the *Sheriat*, a knowledge of which was essential in the judicial and administrative spheres.

The empire was divided into thirty-two provinces, the most important of which were Rumelia, Anatolia, and the territories along the coasts of the Aegean and the Mediterranean. The latter stood under the jurisdiction of Kapudan Pasha, the Grand Admiral, while the other important provinces were administered by *Beylerbeyi*'s, appointed by the central government, who received high salaries and large lands as fiefs. They exercised legislative and executive powers, had to supervise the fulfilment of certain military duties connected with the levy of troops and to participate in campaigns as the commanders of the troops of their provinces. Among the military obligations which they supervised was the institution of *Timar* which obliged their holders to render feudal services. The smaller provinces were governed by *Vali*'s, also appointed from Constantinople. The provinces were subdivided into *Sandjak*'s (standard of an army unit) which corresponded to the districts from which a certain number of troops was recruited. The *Sandjak* was in the charge of a *Sandjakbeyi*, the political and military representative of the central government, who also held a large fief, was responsible for recruiting in his district and commanded its troops during a campaign. The system thus combined military and administrative functions to an extraordinary degree; it appeared to be highly centralised, but in reality it proved impossible to maintain order in the remote provinces and to control the powerful governors. Incompetent men were frequently appointed governors of provinces and districts, who then extorted illegal impositions from the population.

Certain provinces, such as Damascus, Yemen, Abyssinia and Egypt, enjoyed a special status and separate privileges. The system of taxes and obligations which were imposed on the Turkish provinces, for example the institution of *Timar*, was not applied in Egypt and the Arab provinces. Egypt was not only one of the principal sources of revenue, but also an important centre of commerce and the granary of the empire. Almost the entire burden of maintaining the government and the armed forces fell on the Turkish provinces proper; but only Muslims had to render military services, while non-Muslims paid instead the *Djizye* or poll-tax. The Christian principalities of Moldavia and Wallachia possessed autonomous status. Their princes were appointed by the Porte, but their subjects were not obliged to military services, nor were the principalities garrisoned by Turkish forces. They had to provide corn and sheep for the Ottoman army and owed tribute to the Porte, otherwise they were administered according to local customs. The same applied to the Khanate of the Crimea, which was an autonomous Muslim state whose Khans were installed and deposed by the Porte. They were watched by the Ottoman governors of Kaffa and Özü, who intervened when necessary. The Tatar Khans paid no tribute, but were obliged to participate in Turkish campaigns with some 20,000 to 30,000 horsemen, who served as the advance guard of the army, and had to defend the Ottoman territories against the raids of the Dnieper and Don Cossacks. In their turn, the Tatars nearly every year raided Poland and Russia and took many prisoners whom they shipped from Kaffa or Azak to sell them as slaves in Constantinople or Egypt. Looser still were the links of the Barbary States—Tripolis, Tunis and Algiers—with the Ottoman Empire. They were more or less independent, had their own military and administrative organisation, and their obligations towards the Porte did not exceed certain presents which they sent to the sultan.

While in Europe new ideas were developing in many fields, the institutions and society of the Ottoman Empire lost their dynamic character and began to stagnate and to decline. The gap between Orient and Occident became wider, especially in the field of technology, but the Ottomans were not aware of this fact. They continued to regard their empire as the strongest in the world, and their Islamic way of life as the best. Nor did the European powers notice the weakness of the Ottoman Empire—until the catastrophe before Vienna opened the eyes of the contemporaries and the real situation began to be appreciated.

As the empire was governed in the form of a medieval despotism with the corresponding institutions, the ability and the competence of the sultan and of the Grand Vizier were vitally important. When, in the person of Murad IV (1623–40), an energetic and competent sultan ascended the throne the Ottomans' financial and military power revived. The anarchy and corruption of the preceding reigns were brought to an end, and the lands which had been lost to Persia were reconquered at the cost of much bloodshed. During the reign of Murad's brother Ibrahim (1640–8), however, the signs of decline became more marked. The sultan spent his days and nights in the pursuit of his passions and his mental health deteriorated quickly. The misgovernment and abuses spread to the provinces where local rebellions broke out. In addition to these mutinies the Venetians and the Cossacks invaded the Ottoman Empire. The Venetians soon succeeded in occupying the islands of Lemnos and Tenedos, and thus in blockading the Dardanelles and threatening Constantinople itself. In these circumstances, which threatened the spread of anarchy and the outbreak of revolution, some influential persons persuaded the Grand Mufti and Kösem sultan (the sultan's mother) that Ibrahim must be deposed.

This was accomplished in August 1648, and Ibrahim's son Mehmed, then seven years old, ascended the throne. Eleven days later Ibrahim, to prevent him from regaining power and challenging the succession of Mehmed, was murdered. As Murad IV had killed three of his brothers, Ibrahim being the only exception, Mehmed and his younger brother were indeed the only surviving male members of the Ottoman dynasty, so that the news of Mehmed's birth had been greatly welcomed throughout the empire, in spite of certain bad omens.

Mehmed was much too young to assume the government himself, and it remained in the hands of successive Grand Viziers as well as Mehmed's grandmother and his mother Turhan who was of Russian descent. Therefore the instability of government continued and intrigues were rife at the palace; this was soon reflected in the spread of robberies and rebellions in the provinces. In the war with the Venetians the fortress of Canea on the island of Crete had been conquered by the Turks during the reign of Ibrahim; but it was now necessary to send reinforcements to Crete and to lift the blockade of the Dardanelles which the Venetians had imposed in return. Thus in 1649 the Turkish fleet set sail from Chanak, only to suffer another defeat at the hands of the Venetians. Thereupon the Grand Vizier Sofu Mehmed Pasha was dismissed and executed. But the struggle for power between Kösem, Mehmed's grandmother, and Turhan, his mother, continued. In this struggle Kösem relied on the support of the Janissaries and planned the elimination of the other party through the accession of Mehmed's younger brother, Suleiman. When her plans were nearing completion and an agreement had been reached with the leaders of the Janissaries, she was murdered in September 1651 by the partisans of Turhan. This was followed by the execution of her accomplices, so that the Janissaries lost their influence for the time being and that of Turhan, supported by the palace eunuchs, became supreme. The Grand Viziers and government officials were appointed according to their wishes, while the education and training of the young sultan were completely neglected. He spent most of his time with toys and games and soon developed an interest in the hunt which became the great passion of his life. This tendency was encouraged by his mother who thus achieved complete mastery in the State. Therefore Mehmed IV was called 'the Hunter' by the Ottoman chroniclers: a passion he was unable to give up even when his army was marching on Vienna and when it had been annihilated before its walls—a passion which became the cause of his deposition and imprisonment. He never showed much interest in literature or the art of government.

In the person of Tarhondju Ahmed Pasha a Grand Vizier of great honesty was appointed by Turhan in June 1652. At this time the revenue for the following two years had been anticipated and the coinage debased. The new Grand Vizier attempted to restore the shattered economy of the

Empire and put forward a budget, according to which the revenue was estimated at 14,503 purses of silver and the expenditure at 16,400, leaving a small deficit of 1900 purses;[1] but the real difficulty arose from the fact that the taxes of the two following years had already been levied so that very little revenue could be expected for the time being. The bulk of the expenditure—about 10,000 purses—was allocated to the army and the navy; of this sum, 3866 purses went to the corps of Janissaries which then numbered 51,647 registered soldiers, and only 988 purses to the navy which comprised fifty galleons and thirteen galleys. 966 purses were allocated to the Imperial kitchen and 255 to the Imperial stables. In view of the financial situation a veritable hunt for money set in, for the soldiers had to be paid regularly. New arbitrary duties were introduced and even the estates of rich people were confiscated. Drastic measures were employed to curtail favouritism and the illegal levies made by followers of the Grand Mufti. But these proceedings antagonised many influential people: their intrigues were eventually successful in bringing about the downfall of Tarhondju Ahmed Pasha, and with him fell his policy of reform. He was dismissed from office after only nine months and immediately executed.

His successors were equally unable to solve the administrative and financial difficulties of the empire. The Grand Vizier Ibshir Pasha was executed in August 1655. Revolts broke out in Asia Minor; taxation continued at a very high level; the provincial governors showed an entirely irresponsible attitude. The threat from the Venetians did not diminish and their admiral, Lazzaro Mocenigo, gained a great victory over the Turkish navy, while the struggle for the possession of Crete continued unabated. On account of the Venetian blockade of the Dardanelles the transport of food and supplies to Constantinople nearly came to a standstill and prices rose steeply. Among the citizens there was grave anxiety and dissatisfaction because the government failed to take any security measures to protect the capital against an attack through the Straits. Many complaints were made to the palace and the officials concerned; but the Grand Vizier Mehmed Pasha was unable to decide what measures should be taken, and the sultan was busy hunting at Scutari, on the opposite side of the Bosporus. The *Divan* met, but with no result. It became clear that the government was incapable of dealing with the internal and external dangers, that an able man must be appointed Grand Vizier, and that drastic measures had to be taken to cope with the situation. Those who realised its gravity approached the sultan's mother, Turhan, because no important decisions could be taken without her assent. The chief architect of the palace suggested to her that the appointment of Köprülü Mehmed Pasha, an Albanian like himself, to the post of Grand Vizier would solve the difficulties. This was accepted by Turhan,

[1] The 'purse' (*kese*) of silver was worth 500 piastres.

and the seal of the office was offered to Köprülü who was then seventy-one years old. Previously he had served in various official posts, in the palace and in the Treasury, on the staff of a former Grand Vizier and as the governor of several provinces, but he had been out of office since 1655. He lacked the education required for the post of Grand Vizier, but he was shrewd, very experienced and had a sound knowledge of the government machine and its defects. Accordingly he put forward several conditions on which he would be prepared to accept the office: no criticisms of the Grand Vizier should be permitted or taken into account; no vizier should be entitled to oppose the proceedings of the Grand Vizier; there should be no interference with the appointment of officials, regardless of rank; and all the reports presented to the court should go through the hands of the Grand Vizier. Turhan, on behalf of her son, agreed to these terms and Köprülü was installed in office in September 1656: the eleventh Grand Vizier of the reign which until then had lasted only eight years. He remained in office until his death in 1661, and during that time he was in an extremely strong position.

On his appointment Köprülü carried through a purge of the government offices. Those notorious for their irregularities were dismissed, among them great dignitaries such as the Chief Treasurer and the Grand Mufti, as was also the commander-in-chief of the navy. The Chief Eunuch, the principal engineer of intrigues in the Serail, was exiled to Egypt. Many new Kadis and magistrates were appointed. Köprülü, however, not satisfied with the removal of those whom he distrusted, had many of his opponents and potential rivals exterminated. The admiral, who was considered responsible for the fall of Lemnos, and the commander of the Janissaries, who was found guilty of lack of discipline, were executed. So were a tax-collector accused of cruelty towards the people and the governor of Silistria indicted for his ill-treatment of the Tatars. The Orthodox Patriarch, Parthenios III, was hanged, being accused of having provoked the Hospodars of Moldavia and Wallachia to revolt against the Turks. Many pashas, viziers, agas and senior provincial officials who had incurred the Grand Vizier's enmity suffered the same fate. Altogether the number of the victims is said to have reached 50,000 to 60,000. All unnecessary expenditure was curtailed, and a campaign against corruption was launched. According to the budget of 1660 the revenue was estimated at 14,531½ purses (hardly more than in 1652), and the expenditure at 14,840 purses, leaving an insignificant deficit. In contrast with 1652, however, the revenue had not been anticipated so that the financial situation had greatly improved. In general, Köprülü was no innovator but was satisfied with making the existing machinery of government work well and with the strict enforcement of the existing laws.

Rebellions against the government were put down with great severity. Among these the revolt of Abaza Hasan Pasha in Asia Minor constituted a real danger to the government in the years 1657–8. Its centre was at Broussa from where it spread into the neighbouring provinces. Many viziers, pashas, agas and other government officials participated in the movement which found support among the people and was not just another rebellion of outlaws. Abaza Hasan aimed at establishing his power in Asia Minor, and a rebel government was formed there. Köprülü had to be recalled from Transylvania where he was engaged in the suppression of another, equally dangerous uprising. A large force was dispatched against Abaza Hasan and succeeded in crushing the revolt after heavy fighting. Many rebels were killed or executed. Thirty-one heads were sent to Constantinople—among them those of Abaza Hasan, four pashas and two viziers—to be publicly displayed.

Köprülü was equally successful in the field of foreign policy. He dispatched the navy against the Venetians, who were still threatening the Dardanelles, and after some initial failures they were forced to lift the blockade which they had imposed. Then Köprülü without delay undertook to recapture the islands which had fallen into Venetian hands. He himself directed the embarkation of the force sent to reconquer the island of Tenedos which fell in August 1657; Lemnos followed in November. Thus a great victory was gained: not only were the Dardanelles freed from the Venetian threat, but the Ottoman navy regained its superiority in the Aegean Sea so that it became possible to send reinforcements to Crete. At the entrance to the Dardanelles two great castles, Seddülbahr and Kumkale, were built to protect the Straits against future attacks.

Even more important from Köprülü's point of view was the struggle over Hungary and Transylvania—the key to central Europe and a bone of contention between Ottoman and Habsburg since the days of Suleiman the Magnificent. More than half of Hungary was under Turkish rule, and the princes of Transylvania often sought the sultan's consent and sanction for the exercise of their government. For the maintenance of Ottoman rule in Hungary and the securing of Turkish influence in Poland Transylvania was of supreme importance. The result of the decline of the Ottoman Empire in the early seventeenth century was that its hold on Transylvania became very loose. During the years of crisis at the beginning of the reign of Mehmed IV Prince György Rákóczi II attempted to liberate his country from Turkish rule.[1] During the War of the North (1655–60), when large parts of Poland were occupied by Sweden, Rákóczi aimed at seizing the Polish throne,[2] and equally at intervening in Moldavia and Wallachia. As these projects were prejudicial to the interests of Turkey, Köprülü decided on intervention. He demanded the deposition of Rákóczi and the election of another prince. In November 1657 Ferenc Rédei was duly elected, but two months later he was expelled from Transylvania by Rákóczi; Köprülü then decided to lead an expedition

[1] See above, ch. xx, pp. 487–8.

[2] See above, ch. xx, p. 486.

into the principality. Before he left Constantinople he succeeded in imposing firm discipline upon the Janissaries and many whom he distrusted were executed. The Crimean Tatars and the Cossacks, who had recently accepted Ottoman protection, joined the expedition, and a great force was assembled. In spite of Rákóczi's resistance the Turks were soon in complete control of Transylvania. An agreement was concluded with the new prince, Ákos Barcsay, according to which the annual tribute was to be increased from 15,000 to 40,000 florins and several fortresses were to be occupied by Turkish garrisons. Rákóczi had to seek refuge in Habsburg territory and appealed to Leopold I as king of Hungary for support; but he had to continue his struggle alone, was wounded in an engagement in May 1660 and died a fortnight later. Yet his supporters in Transylvania did not give up the fight. Early in 1661 they elected János Kemény as Rákóczi's successor and succeeded in kidnapping and killing Barcsay, his pro-Turkish rival. As Köprülü in 1658 had had to return to Constantinople to deal with the revolt in Asia Minor, Transylvania could not be brought under control for many years. The Porte in its turn proclaimed Mihály Apafi prince of Transylvania, who disputed control of the country with Kemény. In 1662 the latter was killed in an encounter with Apafi who then succeeded in bringing Transylvania under his control, and thus Turkish suzerainty was restored.[1]

Köprülü did not live to see the consummation of his policy in Transylvania; in October 1661 he died, more than seventy-five years old. His achievements indicate that the Ottoman Empire was capable of surmounting great difficulties if competent men were employed in the offices of State; but a régime of terror had to be established to obtain that end. In the eyes of the contemporaries he was an 'atrocious and ruthless man' and not a great statesman, as later historians have argued. He was particularly criticised for the killing of many innocent people and the confiscation of the estates of the executed, not for the sake of reform of the empire, but for that of enriching the Treasury. Yet it cannot be denied that he halted the decline and that the power of the empire revived rapidly. The sultan and his mother, Turhan, were especially pleased with Köprülü's conduct of affairs which relieved them from the burdens of government. Thus Mehmed IV could devote himself entirely to hunting at Scutari or at Adrianople; or hunting parties were arranged for him in the Balkans where more than 10,000 of his Christian subjects had to leave their occupations and serve the royal pleasure as beaters or in some other capacity. Vast numbers of pedigree hounds and falcons, often brought from Russia, were provided for him. In accordance with Köprülü's advice, his son, Köprülü Fazil Ahmed Pasha, was appointed his successor at the age of twenty-six; he remained in office from 1661 to 1676.

Fazil Ahmed was entirely different from his father. As a provincial

[1] For further details, see above, ch. xx, pp. 488–9.

governor he had acquired administrative experience. He was intelligent and wise as well as a distinguished commander and clearly was one of the great statesmen of the time. As Grand Vizier he did not adopt a policy of terror and soon became popular on account of his fair methods of administration and his humane conduct; his modesty and politeness earned him general respect. He refused to take bribes and through his good example succeeded in curtailing corruption. He was opposed to religious fanaticism; Christians and Jews were well treated and protected from injustice. In spite of many military expeditions the treasury was not short of money. Owing to his administrative skill and his patronage of the arts the Ottoman Empire experienced one of its golden eras: he was perhaps the most successful Grand Vizier after Sokollu Mehmed Pasha who was in office under three different sultans between 1565 and 1579.

In the field of foreign policy Fazil Ahmed's greatest achievement was the conquest of Candia which had been besieged by the Turks since 1647. After a struggle lasting for more than twenty years the Venetians found it impossible to withstand the large forces brought to Crete and surrendered the fortress in 1669.[1] The conquest of Crete transformed the eastern Mediterranean into a Turkish lake and considerably strengthened the Ottoman Empire.

On land the Turkish forces were almost equally successful. The Habsburg intervention in Transylvania caused considerable tension between the two empires. In order to maintain Turkish influence there Fazil Ahmed with an army moved from Constantinople to Belgrade in the spring of 1661. Thereupon the Austrians sent an envoy to Belgrade to open negotiations. Fazil Ahmed demanded that the Austrians should evacuate Transylvania, demolish their castles facing the fortress of Kanisza, release all their Muslim prisoners and terminate all military operations. When the Turkish forces reached the river Drava he in addition demanded the payment of the annual tribute of 30,000 florins which the Habsburgs had paid in the time of Suleiman the Magnificent. When they refused to comply the advance was resumed. In the summer of 1663 at the head of an army of 100,000 men the Grand Vizier marched through Buda and laid siege to the fortress of Nové Zámky (Neuhäusel) in north-western Hungary, which was under Habsburg rule. There was little resistance. The Austrians were satisfied with a show of force—Montecuccoli assembled 6000 men near Pressburg—and no succour was sent to Neuhäusel. The garrison defended the fortress with determination, but when further resistance became impossible an agreement was reached in September 1663 by which it was permitted to evacuate the fortress. After this victory Fazil Ahmed returned to Belgrade to spend the winter there.

The revival of Turkish military strength and the threat this entailed for Europe had important repercussions. The Imperial Diet at Ratisbon voted

[1] For further details, see above, ch. XIX, pp. 462–3.

unanimously in favour of granting the Habsburgs financial and military aid.[1] Not only Spain, but even Louis XIV, contrary to his pro-Turkish reputation, promised to send help, in spite of his recent quarrels with the Habsburgs; and a French contingent of 6000 men was dispatched to Hungary, as were those of many German princes. Under the auspices of Pope Alexander VII a Holy League was formed against the Infidel. Thanks to this aid the Austrians were able to take the offensive in the spring of 1664. Montecuccoli reinforced the fortress of Raab (Győr), an important frontier post, to protect the Habsburg lands against a Turkish advance. Fazil Ahmed crossed the Mur, occupied Zerinvár, and arrived before the fortress of Komárom on the Danube, intending to occupy all the castles which barred his advance on Vienna. This enterprise was known to the Turks as *Kyzyl Elma*, the 'Red Apple', and became a symbol of their political aspirations. In view of this threat the Austrians decided to reach a peaceful settlement. Negotiations began at Vasvár at the end of July: according to the terms agreed upon the Austrians were to acquiesce in the Turkish occupation of Neuhäusel and Nagyvárad (Grosswardein), to recognise Apafi as prince of Transylvania, which was to be evacuated by both sides, to terminate all military activities, and to present the sultan with a gift of 200,000 florins, while the latter would also make a suitable gift to the Emperor. This treaty was to be valid for twenty years (beginning in 1662), but until its ratification by both sides the Turks retained their freedom of action, in order to force Leopold to agree without delay. While the text was on its way to him for ratification Fazil Ahmed crossed the Raab and advanced westwards up its left bank where he encountered Montecuccoli's army; if this force had been destroyed the advance on Vienna could have been resumed and the capital might have fallen. On 1 August 1664 the Turks attacked Montecuccoli's army at St Gotthard with superior forces, but made the mistake of not bringing all their troops across the Raab. They were at first successful against the Imperialists' centre, but were finally repulsed and forced back to the river. They lost about 5000 men and fifteen guns, but their enemies also suffered heavy losses and Montecuccoli did not dare to follow the Turks across the Raab, who then retreated to the Danube. The battle of St Gotthard indicated the Austrian superiority in arms and tactics; it became obvious that Turkish military strength was not as formidable as had been feared. With the battle of St Gotthard hostilities came to an end, for in spite of the victory Leopold ten days later confirmed the terms of the Treaty of Vasvár which gave Neuhäusel and Nagyvárad to Turkey and guaranteed Turkish influence in Transylvania.[2] Only western and northern Hungary was retained by the Habsburgs: there was as yet no indication of the eastward spread of Habsburg power, and Fazil Ahmed was received in Constantinople as a victorious general.

[1] See above, ch. XVIII, p. 446.

[2] See above, ch. XX, p. 490.

At this time Turkish influence also extended into the Ukraine. The Cossack hetman Petr Dorošenko sought the protection of Mehmed IV who undertook to defend it against both Poles and Russians and to protect it against the raids of the Crimean Tatars. After the armistice of Andrusovo, by which Poland and Russia temporarily settled their differences,[1] Dorošenko entered into even closer relations with Turkey, hoping to conquer the Russian Ukraine with Turkish help, but the aid promised proved insufficient. In 1672, however, a large Turkish army, supported by the Khan of the Crimea and 15,000 Cossacks, marched into Poland, conquered the fortress of Kamenec and advanced as far as Lwów. Yet a treaty, by the terms of which Poland would have had to pay an annual tribute to the Porte, was not ratified by the Polish diet; neither was the independence of Dorošenko recognised by Poland, nor did Podolia—between the rivers Dnieper and Dniester—become a Turkish province. In 1673 Sobieski's victory of Chotin[2]—like that of St Gotthard nine years before—revealed the military weakness of Turkey. Yet the Turks succeeded in reoccupying Chotin and in capturing other castles in Podolia. By the terms of the peace of 1676 they retained the fortresses of Chotin and Kamenec as well as Podolia, so that they were able to put pressure on Poland and to oppose the seizure of the Ukraine by Russia. Ottoman power was established to the north-west of the Black Sea, but a few months later Fazil Ahmed died: Turkish domination between the Dnieper and the Dniester only lasted for a few years.

Fazil Ahmed's successor was Kara Mustafa Pasha, then forty-three years old, who had been educated with his predecessor and had married his sister, thus entering the Köprülü family. He had held various posts under both Köprülüs and during Fazil Ahmed's campaigns he was appointed deputy Grand Vizier. He was very ambitious and spiteful and at times mean, making many enemies for himself, among whom were the Chief Eunuch and the Marshal of the Imperial Stable. Continuing the methods of his predecessor Kara Mustafa succeeded in maintaining internal order and peace as well as the economy through his great authority. But his real desire was the achievement of fame through victory and conquest. The Turkish claims to the Ukraine were not maintained, although in 1678 he led an expedition thither which captured the fortress of Chihirin, the capital of the Dorošenko Cossacks: the Turks left it in ruins and withdrew. In 1681 a treaty was signed with Russia; the Turks renounced their claim to the Ukraine, which they considered of little value, and the campaigns for which had brought them little satisfaction. Kiev and the left bank of the Dnieper remained Russian, and Podolia and the right bank (with the exception of Kiev) soon became Polish, while the Turks withdrew from this contested area. The problem which began to

[1] See below, ch. XXIV, pp. 568–9; ch. XXV, pp. 575–6.

[2] See below, ch. XXIV, p. 569.

attract all the attention of Kara Mustafa was the advance westwards, the 'Red Apple', the conquest of Vienna.

The Treaty of Vasvár of 1664 was valid until 1682, but the struggle for influence in Hungary and Transylvania was continuing. The Magyars of Hungary were reluctant to submit to Austrian rule, and the Protestants of the area feared the Catholicism of the Habsburgs—factors which played into Turkish hands. As the Hungarians under Turkish rule were allowed religious toleration, the Protestant Hungarians were hoping for Turkish support in their fight against the Catholic Habsburgs. The Hungarian leader, Imre Thököly, sent an envoy to Constantinople who was to seek Ottoman protection, but this request was at first refused by Kara Mustafa. Yet in 1682 he recognised Thököly as king of western Hungary and promised him help in case of need, and a small Turkish force actually went to his aid. With its support Thököly attacked and captured two Austrian fortresses. To avert this new threat to their territory the Austrians sent an envoy, Count Albert de Caprara, to Constantinople to renew the Treaty of Vasvár which was due to expire in August 1682. His proposals, however, were rejected by Kara Mustafa who was bent on war: he was only willing to abide by its stipulations if the Austrians surrendered the fortress of Győr and refunded the expenses the Porte had made in preparation for war. In order to reinforce his threats he persuaded Mehmed IV to spend the winter with the Janissaries at Adrianople, whither the Austrian representatives repaired to continue the negotiations. But the Turkish attitude remained uncompromising. The commander of the Janissaries once more demanded the surrender of Győr, whereupon the Austrian envoy replied: 'a castle may be taken by force of arms, but not by force of words'. Thus war became inevitable. The sultan himself led his army as far as Belgrade whence Kara Mustafa led it into Hungary. The most important campaign in Turkish history had begun.

The number of Kara Mustafa's army is not exactly known. Together with a maintenance force of 150,000 it has been estimated at about 500,000, but some chroniclers give the figure of 200,000. According to Silâhdar Mehmed Aga, the Ottoman historian, the engineer and artillery units alone had 60,000 men. The Crimean Tatars mustered 40,000 to 50,000 horsemen. But all these figures have to be treated with caution and the real numbers were probably much smaller. The fighting units were accompanied by many artisans and tradesmen and a great number of pack-animals, so that the army appeared larger than it actually was. According to the Turkish sources the plan was to conquer the fortresses of Győr and Komárom and not to march on Vienna, and some Ottoman historians have asserted that Mehmed IV was not aware of the intention to extend the campaign as far as Vienna. It has also been asserted that it was the Foreign Secretary, Mustafa Effendi, who was aware of Kara Mustafa's thirst for glory and fame and urged him to undertake the expedition. Yet it seems very unlikely that the capture of the two fortresses would have satisfied the Grand Vizier while such a large army was available, and it seems much more likely that he intended from the outset to march on Vienna. Probably the intervention of the Foreign Secretary was adduced later as proof that Kara Mustafa was not alone responsible for the failure. What he did was simply to make use of the might of Turkey which had re-emerged as a great military power under the two Köprülüs. But in order to keep his strategic plan secret the name of Vienna was not mentioned and the targets announced were the fortresses of Győr and Komárom. It was indeed of the greatest importance to reduce all enemy garrisons barring the way to Vienna before attempting an assault on the capital. Muradgerey, the Khan of the Crimea, criticised Kara Mustafa for advancing on Vienna before Győr and Komárom were taken, but thus made himself the Grand Vizier's enemy. Ibrahim Pasha, the aged commander of Buda, suggested that the two fortresses should be reduced now and that in the following spring the moment would have come to attack Vienna. Kara Mustafa, however, was irritated by these suggestions and—arguing that after the fall of Vienna 'all the Christians would obey the Ottomans'—gave the orders for an attack on the capital.

Before the declaration of war by the Porte the Austrians did not consider a siege of their capital likely, but believed that Kara Mustafa would engage in military activities in Hungary. Only when war was imminent did the Habsburgs call on the other European powers for help. Yet the situation in Europe was not propitious for this purpose. Louis XIV, in particular, did not conceal his hostility to the Habsburgs; if the Austrian armies were defeated by the Turks this would enable him to become the champion of Christendom and after an overwhelming success to win the Imperial Crown. The attitude of Frederick William, the Elector of Brandenburg, who was the close ally of Louis XIV, was equally doubtful. But Max Emanuel, the Elector of Bavaria, and John George III, the Elector of Saxony, promised to send help. Pope Innocent XI, as the head of the Catholic Church, made strenuous efforts to provide aid for the Habsburgs. He appealed to the sovereigns of many Christian countries and sent large sums of money to Leopold I. Following his appeal many Italian cities contributed, as did Portugal. The most effective aid, however, came from John Sobieski of Poland, who had fought the Turks successfully in the past.[1] On 31 March 1683 Austria and Poland signed a defensive and offensive alliance; if Austria were attacked Sobieski promised to come to her aid with 40,000 men. Austria's own military strength was insufficient to withstand the Turkish invasion, for after the Peace of Nymegen (1679) she kept only 30,000 men under arms; General Montecuccoli, the victor of St Gotthard, died in 1681, and his successor, Duke Charles of Lorraine, the brother-in-law of Leopold I, was not of the same calibre.

[1] See below, ch. XXIV, p. 569.

The Ottoman army advanced up the right bank of the Danube, reached Stuhlweissenburg (Székesfehérvár) and crossed the Raab on ten bridges, which were constructed on the spot, without encountering any resistance. Only a small force was left behind as a pretence of laying siege to Győr. When the Turks crossed the Raab Leopold I left Vienna with his family and court and fled to Passau, while Charles of Lorraine retreated with his forces from the vicinity of Nové Zámky, which he had intended to besiege, to Linz higher up the Danube. After a week's march the Turkish army approached Vienna and began to surround it. Its walls enclosed the *Burg*, and, by the standards of the seventeenth century, the fortress was easy to defend and difficult to conquer. But when the Turks appeared the defence measures were far from complete and there were only 12,000 to 13,000 soldiers within the walls of Vienna. Its defence was entrusted to Count Rüdiger von Starhemberg, the governor, who, together with the mayor, Andreas Limberg, played a prominent part in the operations. It may be that the Turks, if they had advanced quickly from Győr, could have taken Vienna by storm; but the army moved very slowly and only arrived before Vienna on 14 July; three days later the town was completely surrounded. The Turkish camp was pitched to the west of Vienna, between Grinzing and Schönbrunn: with its 25,000 tents it looked like a large town. The tents, the 50,000 carts and the pack-animals—mules, camels and buffaloes—made it appear extremely crowded.

The Turkish batteries were placed in position on the evening of 14 July in preparation for an attack on the following day. Before it began, according to custom, a message in Turkish and Latin was shot by arrow into the town demanding its surrender and the conversion of the citizens to Islam. If they refused but consented to abandon Vienna, a safe-conduct was guaranteed to every inhabitant. Count Starhemberg, however, sent no reply to this proposal. Therefore the Turkish artillery opened fire—154 years after the first siege of Vienna by Suleiman the Magnificent. Then the Turks had possessed no heavy guns, and this mistake was repeated in 1683. According to Silâhdar Mehmed Aga, who took part in the campaign, the Turks had only nineteen small guns, some howitzers and 120 guns of medium calibre. But the heaviest Turkish gun, the *Balyemez*, was not used. This lack of heavy guns may be attributed to the fact that the avowed target of the campaign was only the capture of the fortresses of Győr and Komárom. The Viennese, on the other hand, were superior in artillery, both in quality and quantity, and this fact was to play a decisive part in the defence. The Turks intended to make up for this deficiency by mining the walls and bastions and thus opening breaches for an assault. This they had done successfully at Chihirin five years before; but the walls of Vienna were much more solid and its defenders much more courageous, determined, and better disciplined than those of the Cossack capital. The garrison did not adopt merely static defensive tactics but made sorties which caused heavy losses among the Turks. The long duration of the siege caused dissatisfaction among them; since many had already collected enough booty they wished to return home as soon as possible. During the siege the Crimean Tatars penetrated westwards to the vicinity of Krems and Stein and as far as the frontiers of Bavaria, their raids causing panic among the people. If Kara Mustafa had attacked with all his strength Vienna might have been taken; but he feared that, if the city fell as the result of attack, there would be no booty left on account of the soldiers' plundering. His greatest mistake, however, was his disregard of the forces sent to relieve Vienna.

Since the beginning of the siege the allies of the Habsburgs doubled their efforts to send help, and Charles of Lorraine awaited reinforcements from Poland and Bavaria. He was in continuous contact with the beleaguered city and was successful in opposing the Tatar raids towards the west and in preventing the capture of Pressburg by Thököly. Thus John Sobieski succeeded in joining the Austrian forces without encountering any resistance. The two commanders met at Hollabrunn to the north of Vienna, where the Bavarian and Saxon contingents also joined them. Although Sobieski led only 20,000 men into the allied camp, the command of the army which numbered some 70,000 in all was left to him because of his royal rank. But the strategical planning was in the hands of Charles of Lorraine and his soldiers had to bear the brunt of the fighting. News of the advance of the allied army reached the Turkish camp on 4 September. It would have been possible to try to prevent it from crossing the Danube, and allegedly Kara Mustafa ordered the Khan of the Crimea to do so, but the latter, out of animosity towards the Grand Vizier, permitted the enemy to cross safely to the right bank. In fact, however, the Khan could not achieve much against an army which possessed artillery, and Kara Mustafa committed a grave mistake in not himself commanding this operation and in not using more troops and artillery for it. After the catastrophe the Turkish chroniclers used the Khan as a scapegoat. Before the arrival of the allied army Vienna was living through its most critical days, for early in September the Turks succeeded in the mining of some bastions, in opening several breaches in the walls and in forcing their way to the inner precincts of the *Burg*, so that the fall of the city seemed imminent. Count Starhemberg urgently demanded aid, but would hardly have been able to withstand a major assault. Yet before any materialised the desperate Viennese were informed of the arrival of the allied army by bonfires lit on the slopes of the Kahlenberg. From there the allies launched their attack on 12 September. Kara Mustafa thought that cavalry would be sufficient to repulse it—in contrast with the Khan of the Crimea who advised him to use the Janissaries for a counter-attack on the allies. These proved far superior in every respect: they chose an eminently suitable terrain for their attack, their artillery and manœuvres were perfect, and their fighting morale was very high, since the deliverance of Vienna was deemed a holy duty. By the evening the Turkish forces were defeated and the Polish cavalry entered the Ottoman camp. Then the Turks began to flee towards Győr, but the allies did not pursue them because they believed that this speedy retreat was a ruse. The Turks suffered more than 10,000 casualties—against about 5000 or fewer of the Christians—and lost their whole camp with its treasure and provisions.

The result of this Turkish catastrophe was the occupation of Hungary by the Habsburgs. As early as mid-October the Austrians captured Gran (Esztergom), the first of many Turkish fortresses that were to fall into their hands. Kara Mustafa eventually reorganised his panic-stricken forces, but was unable to stop the Austrian advance into Hungary. He therefore returned to Belgrade, intending to spend the winter there and to start a new offensive in the following spring; but his harsh measures had created many enemies. The Chief Eunuch and the Marshal of the Sultan's Stables persuaded Mehmed IV to sanction the execution of the Grand Vizier, who was strangled in Belgrade on 25 December 1683. Yet his execution was a loss to Turkey, for he alone would have been capable of taking revenge on the enemy, as was admitted by many of the pashas in spite of their intense dislike of Kara Mustafa. Mehmed IV, however, had no longer the peace of mind to go hunting. He asserted that Kara Mustafa had failed to ask his permission for laying siege to Vienna and made him personally responsible for the defeat; but none of the later Grand Viziers possessed his ability.

The situation of the Ottoman Empire was indeed alarming. The Austrians drove the Turks out of Hungary, and the Venetians occupied the coast of Dalmatia and even the Morea.[1] But Mehmed IV did not change his mode of life. The people were saying that the country was lost but that he never sacrificed his hunting: if he took no account of the people, did he not fear God? Meanwhile Mehmed, while hunting at Davud Pasha near Constantinople, invited a certain Sheikh to deliver a sermon at the local mosque, but the latter declined, for in his opinion he could only preach on the necessity of the sultan's giving up hunting and occupying himself with the affairs of the State. The clergy then took up the case, the Grand Mufti, Ali Effendi, putting himself at the head of the movement. Thereupon Mehmed IV dismissed him and appointed Mehmed Effendi as his successor; but the new Grand Mufti warned the sultan that there would be an uprising if he did not give up hunting. This Mehmed did for one month, but felt so desperate and had so many sleepless nights that he announced his intention of hunting again within the neighbourhood of Davud Pasha. Then the army, blaming him for all the setbacks which the empire had suffered, joined the opposition. When the sultan was faced with this critical situation he promised that he would

[1] For these events see volume VI, chapter XIX.

never hunt again, dissolved all the hunting establishments, distributed his hounds, sold his horses, and undertook to observe the maximum economy in all his expenditure in future. Several hundred women were released from the harem. But it was too late. The mutinous army marched on Constantinople and deposed the sultan on 9 November 1687. He spent the rest of his life as a prisoner in the 'cage', to die five years later. He was succeeded by his younger brother, Suleiman II, who had been imprisoned since September 1651 when his grandmother had wanted to put him on the throne in place of Mehmed.

With the close of Mehmed's reign Turkey ceased to be a threat to Europe, and the Christian powers assumed the offensive.[1] The military reforms in the European armies and the battle of St Gotthard indicated the changes which had taken place. It was indeed fortunate for Turkey that the European powers did not realise their superiority until the catastrophe before Vienna, a superiority caused by the scientific and technological advances of western Europe. The two Köprülüs, for all their successful administration, only put the out-of-date institutions of the Ottoman Empire into working order. They deserve credit for transforming a declining empire into a great power reminiscent of the days of Suleiman the Magnificent. But with the mistakes of Kara Mustafa the tide of decline returned: the main objective of his campaigns was the gaining of booty and prestige, and not the annihilation of the forces that threatened the security of the Ottoman Empire, but in doing this he merely revived its classical policy. The exit from the Ukraine and the failure of the ambitious siege of Vienna made the decline of Turkey obvious; but much more so did the great victories of Prince Eugene at the beginning of the eighteenth century.

[1] See vol. VI, ch. XIX.

CHAPTER XXII

SCANDINAVIA AND THE BALTIC

THE Peace of Westphalia considerably strengthened Sweden's position in Scandinavia and the Baltic. To the earlier conquests in the east—Ingria, Estonia and Livonia—were added western Pomerania, Bremen, Verden and Wismar in the Empire; the total population amounted to about 2,500,000 people, half of whom were Swedish. The peace did not, however, solve Sweden's problems at home and abroad, but created fresh problems. The new German provinces made Sweden a member of the Empire and she became more deeply involved in the intrigues and negotiations between the princes and the Emperor. Moreover, the new provinces were coveted by others. Brandenburg remained discontented because she failed to gain western Pomerania. Denmark and the Lüneburg princes wanted Bremen and Verden. In the east the fear persisted that Russia—after the 'Time of Troubles'—would renew her attempts to break through to the Baltic.

Furthermore, Swedish successes in the Thirty Years War had not terminated the struggle for hegemony in the north between Sweden and Denmark, which dated from the fourteenth century. By the Peace of Brömsebro (1645) Denmark ceded to Sweden freedom from customs dues in the Sound as well as the Baltic islands of Gotland and Ösel, Jämtland, Härjedalen and Halland (the latter for thirty years). The gains of 1648 also meant that Sweden could attack Denmark from the south; but even so Denmark still constituted the greatest threat to Sweden's position. Denmark was eager to reconquer the provinces lost in 1645 and—since the struggle was fundamentally one over hegemony in the north—she necessarily considered it a fight for existence. Thus the Scandinavian countries, during the whole period to the outbreak of the Great Northern War in 1700, attempted to isolate each other by concluding alliances with each other's enemies among the European powers.

The struggle for hegemony in the north was closely linked with the Swedish aim of gaining the *dominium maris Baltici*, the command of the Baltic, considered necessary for Sweden's continuation as a great power. The prerequisites of Swedish naval supremacy in the Baltic were the command of the Baltic ports and the conversion of the Baltic into a *mare clausum*, by denying the western fleets access to it. This could be effected either by a complete defeat of Denmark, which would give Sweden command of the Sound and the Belts, or by collaboration with Denmark. In either case the interests of other powers had to be taken into account. English and Dutch trading interests were engaged to such an extent that neither power could tolerate its fleet being shut out of the Baltic, nor the domination of that sea by either Sweden or Denmark. This was a salient factor in Baltic diplomacy during the second half of the seventeenth century.

Sweden's struggle to achieve command of the Baltic had important economic aspects. In harmony with the mercantilist ideas of the time it was stressed that without commerce this command was 'dead and wasted'. Axel Oxenstierna's instructions for the newly established Board of Commerce of 1651 give the clearest indications of these hopes. The Chancellor visualised the Swedish ports along the Baltic as import and export centres for large parts of Europe. By controlling the export of corn and naval stores from the Baltic to western Europe the revenue of the Swedish Crown would, it was hoped, increase manifold through customs and excises.

The issue of the command of the Baltic was inextricably linked with the problem of defence and the domestic problems confronting Sweden after the long wars. The defence of the scattered conquests, threatened by neighbours bent on revenge, demanded a fleet with command of the Baltic, as well as an army ready at all times and fortresses furnished with garrisons strong enough to contain an initial attack by the armed forces of any of the neighbours. The income of the Swedish Crown did not suffice to maintain so strong a defence. The solution advocated by Oxenstierna and the majority of the Swedish nobility was that the new trans-Baltic provinces should pay for their own defence through the customs whose yield would increase with the growth of trade. There was much wishful thinking in this plan whose realisation would in any case require time; and a *dominium maris Baltici*, as far as trade was concerned, was an illusion. It is true that some 40 per cent of the ships which passed through the Sound from the Baltic had loaded their cargoes in Swedish ports, while some 35 per cent came from Polish ports—Sweden's closest competitors; but 65 per cent of all ships passing through the Sound in the middle of the seventeenth century sailed under the Dutch and only 10 per cent under the Swedish flag.

Therefore the increased demands for Sweden's defence must, as before, be met from taxation. During the long war, however, the revenue from taxation had declined catastrophically. The Crown lands as well as the taxes due from the landowning peasants had passed into the hands of the nobility, especially the high nobility, for the recruiting of regiments or in lieu of unpaid salaries. This applied especially to the newly conquered provinces; but even in Sweden and Finland the loss of Crown land reached such proportions that in the year 1655 two-thirds of all farms were reckoned to be in the hands of the nobility. Since the nobility, because of its privileges, enjoyed tax-exemption, taxes were paid from every third farm only, and the resulting deficit had to be covered by extraordinary contributions formally voted by the Estates during a session of the diet.

Dissatisfaction with the constantly recurring contributions and the demand for fresh recruits for the army increased amongst the clergy, burghers and peasants, and also among the lower nobility who looked with resentment at the large estates of the high aristocracy. When, after the peace of 1648, the pressure of taxation increased further discontent became vocal. Against the Crown's request for supply the lower Estates demanded a resumption of Crown lands, a *reduktion* of the great donations and fiefs. It was argued that the fruits of Sweden's great victories must not be confined to a few noble families while the nation as a whole grew poorer. The struggle over this issue, which had begun earlier, grew ever more intense in the years 1648–55.

The differences between the Estates were exploited by Queen Christina (1632–54) who had decided to abdicate because of her conversion to Catholicism, for it was unthinkable that a Catholic should sit on the throne of Gustavus Adolphus. When the queen wanted to secure the succession in the person of her cousin Charles Gustavus, she was opposed by the Council, led by Axel Oxenstierna, since the high nobility wanted to use this opportunity to increase its own power. Through a skilful use of the dissensions among the Estates the queen succeeded in having Charles Gustavus declared her heir after her death; then, at the remarkable diet of 1650, where the struggle between the Estates reached its climax, she forced the Council and the nobility—threatening to approve the demand for a resumption of Crown lands—to recognise Charles Gustavus unconditionally as heir to the throne. In 1654 she solemnly relinquished the Crown and left Sweden.

Charles X (1654–60) came from the House of Palatinate-Zweibrücken. His brief reign was dominated by an expansionist foreign policy, partly due to his military profession: he had been the commander-in-chief of the Swedish forces in the last decade of the Thirty Years War. Other circumstances also forced Sweden into a new war. Russian successes against Poland were so sweeping that Poland's disintegration seemed imminent.[1] It was a matter of life and death for Sweden that the west-Prussian harbours, particularly Danzig, should not become Russian, but Swedish. Finally, one way of solving the problem of supporting the forces necessary for defence was by waging war abroad, where they could live off enemy resources. The war in Poland (1655–7), which began with Swedish attacks from Livonia and Pomerania, initially brought great successes to Charles X. In alliance with Frederick William of Brandenburg he defeated the Polish army in the famous 'three-day battle' at Warsaw; but neither this battle nor the long marches across Polish territory proved decisive. As the war progressed, Charles learnt how concerned other European States were with a proper balance of power in this area. Brandenburg demanded increased compensation for her collaboration in the Polish campaign and

[1] See below, ch. XXIV, p. 566, and ch. XXV, p. 574.

finally went over to Poland. The Dutch, who were determined to deny Sweden the west-Prussian harbours, moved closer to Sweden's enemies. The Emperor Leopold intervened on the side of Poland, and Russia proceeded from defence to attack. In the summer of 1657 Denmark declared war on Sweden, hoping to use the situation to reconquer the territories lost in 1645.

The ensuing war proved that the military situation had changed decisively in Sweden's favour through her possessions in the Empire. Her position had been further strengthened by Charles's marriage to Hedvig Eleonora of Holstein-Gottorp, which became the foundation of an alliance, destined to last into the eighteenth century, and the corner-stone of Swedish policy towards Denmark. Conversely, this alliance made it a matter of life and death for Denmark to free herself from an encirclement by Sweden and Holstein-Gottorp. At the news of the Danish declaration of war, Charles hurried by forced marches from Poland to Holstein and then conquered the whole Jutland peninsula. With the onset of winter, however, the situation became critical because the fleet could not transport the Swedish army to the Danish islands, while Charles's enemies prepared to attack him from Germany. One of the boldest exploits in Scandinavian military history—the marching of the whole Swedish army across the frozen Great and Little Belts—decided the issue. The Danes were taken completely by surprise. Faced with the threat of an attack on defenceless Copenhagen, they speedily agreed to peace negotiations and made peace at Roskilde in February 1658.

This peace, only slightly modified by the Peace of Copenhagen of 1660, became decisive for the domestic and external developments of Scandinavia. The whole eastern part of the Danish State, Scania, Halland and Blekinge, and the Norwegian province of Bohuslän were permanently ceded to Sweden. Thus the main entry to the Baltic, the Sound, became the border between Sweden and Denmark and the Danes were no longer entitled to demand tolls in the Sound. Sweden realised her old dream of gaining a coastline which gave her direct access to the North Sea, a victory of great importance, especially for Swedish trade; but fear of Danish revenge remained, as did fear of popular risings in the former Danish provinces in case of a Danish attack on Sweden.

For Denmark, the loss of her eastern provinces had consequences beyond the economic ones, since the war with Sweden led to radical constitutional changes. The position of the Danish nobility, and their influence on government and administration, was even stronger than in Sweden. Their power was based partly on the great noble estates (about half of Denmark's soil belonged to some 150 noble families) and partly on their customary control of local administration. On their estates the Danish nobility enjoyed even greater privileges than their Swedish counterparts, for example, a wider freedom from taxation for their tenants. This, together with the unlimited labour services of the peasants (the institution of *hoveri*), facilitated the growth of demesne farming. The Danish nobility, receiving preference in official appointments, also dominated the entire administration. The Council, which consisted of representatives of the highest noble families, exercised the decisive influence at the expense of the Estates (nobility, clergy, burghers). The provincial governors, all members of the nobility, controlled the collection of taxes. In Norway, where there were few noblemen, the peasants had maintained their traditionally independent position; but the country was at times governed rather insensitively by the central government in Copenhagen.

After the death of Christian IV in 1648 a struggle lasting several months broke out between the heir, Frederick III (1648–70), and the Council. As the price of his election by the diet the new king had to sign a comprehensive privilege which guaranteed to the Council and the nobility that economic and political influence which they had gradually acquired without legal foundation. The king's declaration was meant to inaugurate a long period of uncontested noble government; but soon after its signature friction arose not only between the king and the nobility, but also among the leaders of the nobility. The Grand Marshal, Korfitz Ulfeldt, was accused of peculation, joined Charles X and accompanied him as an adviser during his Danish campaigns. Throughout the period the financial difficulties of the Danish Crown increased. Extensive alienations of Crown land gave temporary relief, but in the long run made the situation worse. The heavy taxation caused discontent among the lower Estates, which in the first place was directed against the privileged nobility and its control of the government.

Charles's triumphant campaign against Denmark in 1657–8 and the hard peace terms exposed the inability of the nobility to provide peace and security. Frederick III and the burghers, on the other hand, showed courage and heroism at the siege of Copenhagen, thus preparing the ground for change. When the Estates met in Copenhagen in the autumn of 1660 the revenue had been reduced to a fraction of the peacetime level, while the national debt amounted to nearly 5 million Danish *daler*. The hostility between the Estates came into the open when the Council suggested an excise on certain goods; for while the clergy and burghers championed the principle of equality and demanded that everybody should pay the new tax, the nobility claimed exemption not only for themselves but also for some of their tenants. The determination of the two lower Estates forced the nobility to retreat step by step and further demands for reform were raised, for example, for a change in the system of administration which left the provincial governors too free from royal control.

While these reforms were discussed, a proposal to declare Frederick III hereditary king of Denmark was put forward. Although the details are not known, it is certain that the initiative came from an inner court circle. Its leader, Christoffer Gabel, penned the anonymous proposition for the introduction of hereditary kingship, apparently after consultation with the leader of the clergy, Bishop Hans Svane, and the mayor of Copenhagen, Hans Nansen, the spokesman of the burghers; the king was a passive observer. Clergy and burghers were persuaded to petition the Council for a change in the constitution. When the Council refused to debate this and the nobility remained silent, Frederick III declared that he would allow himself to be proclaimed hereditary king against the will of the Council and the nobility. The gates of Copenhagen were closed and the wartime burgher militia was called out. These moves weakened the opposition and all three Estates granted Frederick the hereditary government. This change did not immediately lead to the establishment of absolutism. A committee was formed to submit proposals for a new constitution and the diet, at the suggestion of this committee, agreed to return to Frederick the privilege which he had granted at his accession and to ask him to draft a new constitution; thus power was put into his hands. The king took a further step when he let himself be proclaimed 'sovereign king'. By 1665 the new constitution was complete and promulgated as the 'King's Law'. Its ideological foundation lay in the principles of natural law: power had been transferred to the king through a treaty of the Estates with the ruler.

The introduction of absolutism was accompanied by drastic changes in the central and local administration. The driving force behind the reforms was the Grand Treasurer Hannibal Sehested, who was impressed by the collegiate form of administration introduced in Sweden in 1634. He organised the different branches of the central administration into colleges with presidents and a fixed number of assessors. With the introduction of absolutism and collegiate administration the Council of the high nobility ceased to function. It was resurrected in a new form during the early years of the reign of Christian V (1670–99), when Peder Griffenfeldt introduced a privy council (*Gehejmeraad*) on the French model. In the realm of local administration the old *len* (fief) divisions were in 1662 transformed into *amt* (local district) divisions, administered by *amtmenn* instead of *lensmenn*, whose powers were severely curtailed; for while the old provincial governors had combined civil and military authority, the *amtmenn* were purely civil administrators. Even there their powers were circumscribed, since the collection of taxes was transferred to separate officials, the *amt*-secretaries. Effective central control of the local administration, hitherto lacking, was now established.

This reorganisation was closely connected with financial reforms which were initiated by Sehested after 1660. The problem was to reduce the national debt while retaining sufficient forces for defence. The debt consisted, above all, of loans contracted during the war, of unpaid salaries, and of payments due to army contractors from the war. Sehested employed methods used earlier, though never on such a scale: he ceded Crown lands to mortgagees and other creditors, corresponding to a sum roughly equalling the national debt. So much land was alienated that the Crown was forced to look for other sources of revenue. It was also realised that the customary taxes burdened the peasants too heavily, while the nobility were exempt. The noble privileges in respect of existing taxes could not be altered, since the king at the introduction of absolutism in 1660 had promised to maintain them. To provide a basis for new taxation a land survey of all Denmark, the so-called *matrikulering*, was undertaken in the early 1660's, which was superseded by a new, vastly improved survey in 1688. In accordance with this a general land-tax for towns and country alike was introduced, which brought to the Crown a much higher revenue than that formerly derived from Crown lands. Thus Denmark's financial dilemma was in the main solved by increased taxation of land or, alternatively expressed, through a change from a revenue based on a natural economy to one based on money.

The men who introduced absolutism in Denmark carried out reforms with enthusiasm in many fields. The work on the new constitution awakened interest in civil law. There had never been one common law for the whole State, the medieval laws of the different parts forming the basis of the legal system. In 1661 a commission began to draft a new civil law; several others followed, and in 1683 the 'Danish Law' was completed. In the economic sphere these men represented the ideas of mercantilism. They tried to loosen the ties which restricted trade and crafts. They subsidised the establishment of factories and workshops. Their initiative produced some results, particularly in Copenhagen, which grew to a town of over 60,000 by the end of the seventeenth century. The growth of trade and industry, however, should not be exaggerated; for the export of corn and oxen, which was very important, declined and could not be compensated for by the rise of Copenhagen. A favourable balance of trade resulted from increased exports of timber and fish from Norway.

Interest has concentrated on the changes affecting the agrarian classes, nobility and peasants alike, and their relationship. The old nobility remained important though it lost its political power. Even when the *len* was changed to an *amt*, the new officials came at first mainly from the old families. These posts were, however, not as lucrative as they had been. Some members of the high nobility remained in the central administration, though most noblemen preferred to leave the capital and live on their estates. The nobility retained its economic and social privileges, but the former were made illusory by the new taxes based on the *matrikulering*. The trend was clearly towards a decline of the old nobility, both in influence and income.

Alongside the old nobility, and partially replacing it, a new nobility developed, partly a service nobility, partly a landowning nobility. It consisted mainly of immigrant Germans. The introduction of absolutism did not, as was the case in Sweden, mean a transfer of land from the nobility to the Crown and the peasants. On the contrary, the new Danish nobility became partly a landowning nobility at the expense of the Crown through the alienation of Crown lands mentioned above. By 1688 there were in Denmark 58,000 farms. Of these only just over 1000 were farmed by peasant proprietors. The Crown possessed 25 per cent of the land, but two-thirds belonged to noble or burgher landlords, and the remainder to the university, the Church and schools.

Parallel with this development went a change in agricultural methods; for the production of oxen for export became less profitable than the cultivation of corn and, to some extent, than the more recent dairy farming. As a result old farms and villages were abandoned; large estates appeared, corresponding to forty average farms, and cultivated as a single unit. The condition of the peasants deteriorated and the landowning peasantry virtually disappeared. The Crown's need of more money meant increased pressure of taxation, which fell most heavily on the peasants. Tenants received worse conditions from their new lords. The change to big-estate farming demanded more labour on the demesnes. The Germans among the new nobility introduced into Denmark the harsher treatment of the peasants customary in northern Germany. The burghers who owned estates were usually absentee landlords, and supervision was exercised by bailiffs who in their own interest squeezed the peasants. Similar conditions obtained on many noble estates. Some attempts were made to improve matters, but the reformers, in accordance with their mercantilist principles, had no interest in improving the peasants' lot.

In Sweden, at this time, there occurred a movement in the opposite direction—though less sweeping. Charles X died at the beginning of 1660. On his death-bed he dictated his will, arranging the government of the country during the regency, which was inevitable since his heir, Charles XI (1660–97), was only four years old. The government was entrusted to the Queen Mother, Hedvig Eleonora, and five high State officials. As some of the five offices had been left vacant, Charles X appointed persons who could be expected to safeguard the interests of the dynasty as against those of the high nobility; among them was Charles X's brother, Duke Adolphus John, and Herman Fleming, the leading spirit behind the partial resumption of Crown lands decreed in 1655, which had been largely ineffective because of the war. As early as the autumn of 1660, however, the nobility prevailed upon the other Estates to have Charles X's will declared invalid. The five high officials were forced to resign and make place for others more amenable to the aristocracy. The Council, composed exclusively of members of the high nobility, increased its influence. In foreign policy leadership devolved on the Chancellor, Magnus Gabriel de la Gardie. In domestic affairs the Treasurer, Gustav Bonde, urged a programme of strict economy; but the central aim of the new government was to preserve the landed wealth of the nobility.

The most urgent task was to put an end to the war inherited from Charles X. The peace with Denmark-Norway has already been mentioned. With Poland peace was concluded at Oliva in 1660, on the *status quo* principle as far as territory was concerned. The Polish royal House finally relinquished its claims to the Swedish Crown which it had maintained since the time of Sigismund Vasa. A Swedish–Russian peace was concluded at Kardis in 1661, again without territorial changes. These three peace treaties marked the zenith of Swedish power in the Baltic. The complete domination of the Baltic and of Scandinavia, which had been the aim of Charles X and others, was not achieved; the various parts of the Swedish empire had not been linked up territorially, nor had the empire been stabilised. The danger remained that Russia might break through to the Baltic, either across the Swedish barrier on the Baltic littoral or across Poland. There were several German States, especially the dynamic Brandenburg, eager to wrest from Sweden her German provinces. But Danish plans for revenge constituted the most serious threat; yet the regency government considered a Danish attack on Sweden unlikely, because of the changes in Danish foreign policy after the introduction of absolutism.

Denmark's traditional foreign policy up to 1660 had rested on alliances with the Emperor, Poland and the United Provinces. This was natural, because her main rival, Sweden, since the Thirty Years War had tied herself to France, the chief opponent of the Habsburgs. During Sehested's period of power a reorientation took place which meant that Sweden, in the short run, had nothing to fear from Denmark. In his efforts at financial economy Sehested reduced the standing army, a move which provoked strong opposition from the officer corps. Denmark had been disappointed at the lack of help from her allies during the war and, no less than Sweden, suffered from Dutch trade dominance in the Baltic. Therefore, Sehested began to turn towards France and England. Both countries were able to pay subsidies which would make possible increases in the Danish armed forces in case of war. In principle Sehested believed that it would be to the advantage of both northern Crowns to co-operate in foreign affairs; but he was not unaware of the danger implied in Swedish hopes for hegemony in the north and thus, by his alignment with France and England, wanted to move closer to Sweden's ally and potential ally. Through such a grouping Sweden might be contained, since she would either become isolated or would have to suffer Denmark as an equal partner in an alliance. As early as 1661 Sehested made a commercial treaty with England which for long proved an obstacle to an Anglo-Swedish agreement. With France he concluded a treaty of mutual defence and trade in 1663, but this worked mainly to the advantage of Louis XIV and the subsidies which Sehested counted on were not paid. The final setback for this policy came in 1665 when a mere accident prevented Denmark from entering into the hoped-for alliance with England and drove her on the side of the Dutch into the naval war between the maritime powers. Even if the political system of Sehested had disciples after his day of power, the traditional Danish orientation towards Sweden's enemies became increasingly dominant, especially after the accession of Christian V. His long reign was governed, as far as foreign relations were concerned, by a threefold aim: to destroy the independent position of the ducal house of Holstein-Gottorp, to end its close alliance with Sweden, and to reconquer the lost eastern provinces; in other words, to end the Swedish dominance in the north by war.

While Danish foreign policy aimed at isolating Sweden, Sweden strove to make anti-Danish alliances. These efforts led to a temporary co-operation with the enemies of Louis XIV. Owing to her German possessions Sweden was to some extent dependent on the Emperor, who at this time was willing to buy Swedish support against France. Swedish resentment at Dutch trade dominance in the Baltic, and even more at the Dutch policy of curbing Swedish commercial expansion, predisposed Sweden towards friendly relations with the foremost rival of the United Provinces, England. Swedish overtures were welcomed there because relations with the Dutch were particularly strained, and in 1665 a treaty was concluded whereby England guaranteed the independent position of Duke Christian Albrecht of Holstein-Gottorp. Since Denmark, partly in consequence of this Anglo-Swedish treaty, in 1666 allied herself with the United Provinces, and since France shortly before had declared war on England, the northern Crowns had once again moved into opposing camps. Sweden, however, did not intend to join a power 'bloc' in such a way that she would be involved in war. The army sent to Germany was to make a military demonstration rather than participate in a war. Sweden was helped by the fact that French diplomacy aimed at preserving the peace in the north. France prevented Denmark from attacking Sweden and, at the same time, through concessions dissuaded Sweden from joining the Habsburgs. In 1666 Sweden declared her neutrality in the Anglo-Dutch War and acted as a mediator during the peace negotiations at Breda in 1667.

Between 1667 and 1672 Sweden's position in the constantly shifting alliances changed as frequently as that of England. Her moves and counter-moves, among other factors, depended on opposing views within the Swedish Council. In principle the Council was agreed on the need to maintain peace and a balance of power in Europe; there was also agreement on the need to keep Denmark isolated while avoiding Swedish isolation. There was, however, no agreement as to how far Sweden dare go without risk of being involved in war, or on the advantages and disadvantages of one power group compared with another. The factors which finally made her decide for France included the successes of Louis XIV in Germany, England's change from the Triple Alliance to co-operation with France, and the fear that Louis XIV might move closer to Denmark if Sweden maintained a negative attitude towards French overtures. A Franco-Swedish treaty was signed in 1672: against a promise of large subsidies and a French guarantee of the position of the duke of Holstein-Gottorp, Sweden agreed to send an army to Germany. By threatening not to pay subsidies Louis XIV forced Sweden to attack Brandenburg, the ally of the United Provinces, and in June 1675 the Swedish army suffered a defeat at Fehrbellin. Against her will Sweden had been dragged into the struggle of the great powers.

Meanwhile Danish diplomacy remained non-committal, though negotiations were started with various powers to prevent the isolation of Denmark. After Sweden had definitely joined France, and while Louis XIV's fortunes visibly declined in 1673–4, Denmark entered into an alliance with the Emperor whereby she undertook to declare war on France if yet another power, that is, Sweden, attacked the Dutch. Efforts made by Sweden and France to keep the Danes neutral were unsuccessful. At the news of the Swedish defeat at Fehrbellin Christian V arrested the duke of Holstein-Gottorp, forced him to renounce the sovereignty over his lands and to cede his fortresses to Denmark. By this *coup* Christian V deprived Sweden of her valuable base in Denmark's rear.

The war of 1675–9 opened badly for Sweden, who suffered reverses unequalled in the opening stages of any war during her period of greatness. The battle of Fehrbellin, an insignificant clash of arms, robbed the Swedish army of that nimbus of strength which had surrounded it since the Thirty Years War. As the Swedish fleet could not prevail against the Danish fleet reinforced by a Dutch squadron, Sweden's German provinces were doomed. Pomerania was occupied by Brandenburg. The Lüneburg dukes, helped by Brandenburgers and Danes, conquered the duchies of Bremen and Verden. Wismar had to capitulate after a siege and blockade by the Danish army and navy. In 1676 the war was carried on to Swedish soil, when Christian V moved an army across the Sound in order to regain the provinces lost in 1658. All but one of the Scanian fortresses fell into his hands. The population of Scania, still loyal to Denmark, made common cause with her. What saved the situation for Sweden was above all the energetic work of Charles XI—declared of age in 1672—ably supported by Johan Gyllenstierna, who soon achieved a dominant influence. In the late autumn of 1676 a Swedish army marched into Scania and beat the Danes in the bloody battle of Lund. Christian V had to surrender one after another of the Scanian castles, while the bitter guerrilla warfare between the population and the Swedish troops continued for years.

In spite of Swedish setbacks in Germany the peace of 1679 brought only slight territorial losses. This was due in part to Louis XIV's clever diplomacy, and in part also to the circumstance that neither the Dutch nor the Emperor desired Swedish losses. Thus Louis XIV, without any real consultation, made peace on Sweden's behalf with her enemies: the Lüneburg princes received some small gains from Bremen and Verden, Brandenburg was given a small strip of eastern Pomerania, and Denmark gained nothing at all.

Louis XIV's failure to consult Charles XI was resented. France had also gone back on the promise, given in the alliance of 1672, not to make peace with the United Provinces till Sweden had received certain concessions in respect of tolls, and had included in the peace treaty with the Dutch a trade agreement so disadvantageous that Charles XI refused to ratify it. Sweden in 1679 was therefore equally dissatisfied with France and the United Provinces. Christian V was similarly disillusioned. The United Provinces had betrayed him in 1678 and made a separate peace, while France had forced him to end the war without any gain. Sweden and Denmark thus found themselves united in anti-French and anti-Dutch sentiments. In Sweden Johan Gyllenstierna now controlled foreign policy. In the Council before the war he had consistently warned against the French alliance and he shared the king's resentment at Louis XIV's treatment of Sweden. Nor did he favour a policy of co-operation with the United Provinces. It is against this background that the peace negotiations with Denmark took place which, on Gyllenstierna's initiative, were started at Lund and led to a treaty between Charles XI and Christian V in the autumn of 1679. The clauses of this treaty corresponded exactly to the terms laid down by Louis XIV; the real significance of the treaty is to be found in its secret articles which envisaged a far-reaching co-operation between the northern Crowns. Neither partner was to make any agreement or enter into any alliance with another power without informing and consulting the other. If either ally found it necessary to begin a war of aggression, the other must be informed and, if a joint war were undertaken, the gains must be shared. Admittedly each State had its own particular spheres of interest, where co-operation was neither essential nor possible, for example, Sweden's relations with Russia; but in respect of the German Empire collaboration became obligatory. The alliance was sealed by the renewal of the engagement between Charles XI and Christian's sister Ulrika Eleonora.

The remarkable change from traditional opposition, intensified by a ruthless war, to a close alliance has been much discussed among historians since the secret articles became known in the 1870's. There was a common Scandinavian interest, for example, against the United Provinces; but that community of interest was not new. In reality the alliance was neither so new nor so startling as appears at first sight, but there were several precedents. Even Johan Gyllenstierna had in the debates preceding the war of 1675 stressed the advantages of a united northern front; but the policy of co-operation was then—as later—indissolubly linked with the rivalry for domination of the north. In 1679 this rivalry showed itself most clearly in respect of the duke of Holstein-Gottorp, who at the peace had been reinvested with his possessions. While Denmark vainly tried to get binding assurances that Sweden would not in future interfere in the duke's relations with Denmark, Gyllenstierna carefully avoided any such promise. Indeed, at the very time of the treaty negotiations, Sweden was attempting to remove those ducal advisers who were considered too pro-Danish and to replace them by partisans of Sweden. Holstein-Gottorp was still regarded as essential to Sweden. What Gyllenstierna intended was a close Scandinavian alliance, but an alliance in which Sweden should be the dominating partner. Thus his policy was not so very different from that of Charles X who attempted to unite the north by force of arms. As soon as this became clear, Christian V disengaged himself from the Treaty of Lund, and the efforts of the northern Crowns to isolate each other were resumed.

More revolutionary and, above all, more lasting effects of the war appeared in Swedish domestic developments. Exactly as the war of 1657–60 gave the impetus to the introduction of absolutism in Denmark-Norway, the war of 1675–9 led to absolutism in Sweden. Account must also be taken of the financial predicament of the regency government during Charles XI's minority. In 1660 troops had to be paid off, officers had to be rewarded, and the expenses of a strong defence had to be met. The high nobility dominated the government, and therefore the solution advocated by the non-noble Estates and by some of the lower nobility, namely a resumption of alienated Crown lands, was not adopted. Indeed, in spite of attempts at economy, the alienation of Crown lands continued, especially in the provinces gained from Denmark. In general the government tried to uphold the existing social order and privileges against the demands of the non-noble classes. It hoped furthermore to prolong its power beyond the time when the king would be declared of age, and tried to limit the royal power by demanding from Charles XI an assurance which would in fact curtail the power of the Crown. This attempt failed because of the opposition it met, especially from the lower nobility; but until the outbreak of war the young monarch remained dependent on the Council of high nobles and especially on the group led by Magnus Gabriel de la Gardie.

The war brought about a remarkable development of the king's personality. In the autumn of 1675 he left Stockholm to put himself, according to custom, at the head of his army. Thus he became isolated from the Council, which remained in the capital, and surrounded by men of the lower nobility and commoners. Under the influence of Gyllenstierna, the king's dominating adviser, he increasingly took decisions before submitting matters to the Council, so that by the end of the war the Council had in reality lost power. Charles XI publicly maintained that he was not bound to heed its advice. As Sweden had been dragged into the war badly prepared and armed, it was natural to blame the regency government. Already at the diet of 1675 the Estates demanded an inquiry into the regency administration and a commission was constituted for this purpose. Its findings were complete by 1680 and hung like a cloud over the high officials and the Council, threatening also the economic position of regents and councillors by the prospect of fines for maladministration and bad advice.

During the war Charles XI and his advisers had determined to make impossible a recurrence of that state of unpreparedness in which Sweden found herself in 1675–6. The regency government had shown great concern for the building of new ships and for the navy in general; but the war demonstrated that the main naval station, Stockholm, though suitable for action in the eastern Baltic, was unsuitable for action in the rest of the Baltic. The need for a naval station in the former Danish province of Blekinge was obvious; work was begun in 1680 and the station was called Karlskrona after the king. Lack of trained troops seemed to Charles XI and Gyllenstierna the main reason for the setbacks of 1676 in Scania, and therefore plans for the creation of a standing army were prepared. After the war Charles XI and his advisers were ready with an important programme of military reorganisation. Its realisation demanded much money, and Sweden's financial situation—precarious already before the war—had meanwhile further deteriorated. Repeated contributions and conscription hit not only the non-noble Estates, but also the nobility, so that the Estates demanded a relief from the burden of taxation. Paradoxically, Charles XI and Gyllenstierna saw in the steadily mounting dissatisfaction with heavy taxation a means that could be used to solve the Crown's financial difficulties. Among the non-noble Estates and the lower nobility demands for a reduction of the larger fiefs were once more voiced. Such a resumption of Crown lands, as the king and his advisers realised, could provide the financial basis for a standing army, so that the levying of extraordinary contributions would become less frequent. The domestic reforms had already begun, though they had not yet received their final sanction by the diet, when Johan Gyllenstierna died in the summer of 1680.

At the diet which met some months later, the Estates asked to have communicated to them the findings of the commission of inquiry into the regency government. This was done and a committee of the Estates was appointed with full powers to sentence the members of the regency government. During the following years they were ordered to refund large sums on charges of maladministration and self-interest. Hardest hit was the great Chancellor, Magnus Gabriel de la Gardie, one of the biggest landowners, who lost practically all his fortune. When the Estates answered Charles XI's question, whether he was obliged to consult the Council in affairs of the State, in the negative, its political decline was confirmed. During the diet the resumption of Crown lands was brought up for discussion, first in the Peasant Estate. In the House of the Nobility the reformers succeeded in winning over the lower nobility to the principles of the reduction programme. All the large ducal and baronial fiefs would be resumed, and the conquered provinces would be declared 'inalienable places', which meant that all fiefs which had been granted there would be resumed and the bestowal of new ones would be prohibited. Elsewhere all fiefs which produced an annual income of more than 600 Swedish *daler* would be resumed. These proposals caused consternation among the high nobility; but faced with the defection of the lower nobility and the threat of being outvoted by the three other Estates they gave way. The reduction was thus agreed upon in 1680, and a commission was appointed to work out the practical details.

The power of the Estates remained formally intact, in respect of legislation, the voting of supply, and in questions of foreign policy. At the next diet, in 1682, the king was given unlimited legislative authority and power over the resumption of Crown lands. The method was the same as that used against the Council in 1680: the king posed the question whether he was not, according to the constitution, empowered in times of need to resume alienated lands, and whether he was not 'permitted to make laws and regulations, rules and decrees' without consulting the Estates. In either case he received an affirmative answer. There was still room for the extension of royal power in respect of foreign policy and the voting of supply. During the last diets of his reign Charles XI secured sole control of these two fields. The diets of 1686 and 1689 were made necessary by the Crown's need of money. Their relatively short duration, compared with those held earlier, reflects the decline of the Estates. The diets of 1680 and 1682 sat for two and a half and three months respectively, and that of 1686 for about two months; but that of 1689 lasted only six, and that of 1693 only three weeks. There was no longer anything to negotiate. When in 1686 foreign affairs were, according to custom, to be debated, the Estates were told that the king did not desire any answer to his address; he would in future only inform the Estates of the foreign situation if he needed supply. Consequently the Estates after 1686 limited themselves to thanking the king for 'his great care, industry and concern', without adding any opinions or advice of their own.

Through the resumption of Crown lands and other permanent financial arrangements voted by the Estates, the royal finances improved so much that Charles XI, at the diet of 1693, could give the hitherto rare message that 'no supply was necessary'; but he demanded a general permission to levy contributions and to float loans under the guarantee of the Estates in case of need. The fines imposed upon the members of the regency government, the resumption of Crown lands and the reorganisation of the administration made the king independent of the Estates in times of peace. The first are reckoned to have amounted to 4 million Swedish *daler*. According to figures which were put forward at the accession of Charles XII in 1697 the resumption increased the yearly revenue by 2 million Swedish *daler*; to this sum Sweden-Finland contributed 700,000 *daler* and the trans-Baltic provinces the rest. The public debt, estimated in 1681 at 44 million *daler*, had by 1697 been reduced to 11½ million. About 80 per cent of all the farms alienated to the nobility returned to the Crown or to peasants who paid taxes to the Crown. On this basis the military and civil administration was rebuilt by the so-called *indelningsverk*: the income from certain farms was earmarked for certain officials, officers were assigned farms to live on, etc. The permission granted in 1693 to levy contributions and float loans made the king independent of the Estates even in times of war; since the Estates at the same time agreed to leave all matters pertaining to foreign policy completely in the king's hands, they need no longer be summoned. The consummation of this development appeared in the Declaration of Sovereignty of 1693, which called the king 'an absolute, all-commanding and governing sovereign king', who was not responsible to anyone on earth for his actions.

The economic system which was established by the resumption of Crown lands certainly gave a greater stability to Sweden's finances. It could not be foretold, however, how the system would function under the stress of a great war. The resumption and the fines imposed upon regents and councillors also brought about changes in the structure of society. Complete misery, even for individual noblemen, rarely resulted, since it was usually possible to retain the manor farm, the *säteri*, by ceding to the Crown tenant-farms. The difficulty of paying in cash large fines and other sums demanded by the Crown forced many noblemen to sell their land at too low a price. This created an opportunity for the new service nobility, which was developing under State protection, to acquire estates cheaply. While the nobility in 1655 possessed two-thirds of the total number of farms inside Sweden-Finland, the proportion at the end of the seventeenth century inside the new borders (that is, including the provinces conquered from Denmark-Norway) was: 33 per cent of the farms was owned by the nobility, 36 per cent by the Crown, and the final 31 per cent by the tax-paying peasants. Thus a large number of peasants, who had been dependent upon the nobility, became either Crown tenants or, if they owned their land, tax-payers to the Crown. When the Crown tenants in the eighteenth century were permitted to buy the land which they farmed, the free peasant population increased. Since the tax-paying peasants were freed from dependence on the nobility, this meant the saving of the Swedish peasant class as a landowning and politically active Estate. Through the *indelningsverk* the peasants became dependent upon the holders of royal offices or commissions instead of upon the nobility; thus there was no immediate improvement, and peasant complaints were as numerous as before. In fact, however, the free peasant Estate was safeguarded, and the *indelningsverk* of Charles XI remained the basis of the military organisation of Sweden down to the early twentieth century.

If the factors which brought about the change of régime in the two Scandinavian States are considered, the similarities are striking. In either case the king could play off the lower Estates against the nobility. A destructive war, in both cases between Denmark and Sweden, had exposed the weak points of the régime and had destroyed the financial foundations of the State so that sweeping changes in the administration proved essential. Frederick III during the siege of Copenhagen of 1658–9 and Charles XI in the Scanian war of 1676–9 made personal contributions to the war which were enhanced by royalist propaganda. The traditional tendency of the lower Estates to seek the support of the Crown against the nobility was intensified. The course of events at the decisive meetings, the diet of Copenhagen of 1660 and that of Stockholm of 1680, therefore developed along similar lines: co-operation between a court circle and the lower Estates forced the aristocracy to retreat. But there the similarities end. Danish absolutism was introduced all of a piece and was then codified in the King's Law of 1665. Caroline absolutism advanced step by step, sometimes as if by accident, during the diets of the 1680's, to be consummated in the Declaration of Sovereignty of 1693. The reason for this can be found in the different constitutional ideas which motivated the change. Danish absolutism was founded on natural law; power was transferred to the king through a treaty between people and ruler. This was done under certain conditions, and the king was in his exercise of power bound by the existing laws. Swedish absolutism, on the other hand, grew out of a reinterpretation of the existing fundamental law, the medieval law of the land. When finally it was given a theoretical foundation in the Declaration of Sovereignty this was done through an antithesis of natural law, the theocratical conception of the State: the words of the declaration of 1680 that the king must govern 'according to the law' were replaced by the words 'according to his pleasure and as a Christian king'. He was not tied by temporal laws and was responsible only to God.

The measures which the two absolute governments took to solve their difficulties were also diametrically opposed. In Denmark-Norway Hannibal Sehested tried to balance the budget by cutting down the army; while Charles XI, as soon as the war was over, increased the army to a total of about 63,000 (25,000 serving in garrisons outside Sweden-Finland and about 38,000 recruited in Sweden on the basis of the *indelningsverk*).

Sehested made big alienations of Crown lands to the creditors of the Crown and organised a new tax system founded on money, a change in the spirit of mercantilism; whereas in Sweden the resumption of Crown lands and the 'registration' of the resources at the disposal of the Crown seemed to point in the opposite direction. In Sweden the introduction of absolutism implied that the fiefs of the nobility and many noble estates were transferred to the Crown or to landowning peasants. In Denmark the area of land owned by the nobility and other owners of large estates increased at the expense of the Crown and the peasants. While Caroline absolutism in the long run led to the liberation of the peasants, Danish absolutism worsened the condition of the peasants. In both countries absolutism led to the creation of a new service nobility; but in Sweden this nobility did not remain as separate from the old nobility as it did in Denmark. Members of the old Swedish families continued to serve the State in various capacities and the new families were quickly assimilated. Although there was a German element within the Swedish service nobility, that element never became as important as it did in Denmark.

There remains to be considered the relation between the Swedish Crown and the provinces on the Baltic. Ever since their conquest the degree of their incorporation with Sweden had been debated. The issue was whether they should receive Swedish laws and privileges and be represented in the Swedish diet, or whether they should continue to live under their own laws and privileges and keep their own local Estates. The Swedish nobility was opposed to the former alternative, since its members had acquired estates in these provinces where the nobility had a more dominating position, particularly in relation to their peasants, than was the case in Sweden. The situation was different in the provinces conquered from Denmark-Norway, where the social structure far more closely resembled that of Sweden than in the Baltic and German provinces. Charles X had clearly intended to incorporate these provinces with Sweden, yet little was done in this direction during Charles XI's minority, and thus the population was still pro-Danish when war broke out in 1675. The revolts in northern Scania and Blekinge made it clear to Charles XI and his advisers that a more radical policy was essential. Already during the war it was decided that Swedish law and religious services in Swedish were to be introduced as soon as peace was restored. Conscious and patient efforts were made after the war to make the Estates of these provinces desire greater uniformity with Sweden, and the foundation was thus laid for a change in nationality which seems more striking than almost any other case in Europe. Most influential was the change in the religious services at a time when the Church constituted the sole effective instrument of State propaganda. But the efforts of the bishop of Lund, Knut Hahn, and of the governor-general of the southern provinces, Rutger von Ascheberg, to gain the confidence of the local population were equally important.

The attempts at Swedification were not limited to the provinces conquered from Denmark-Norway, but were extended to Livonia and Estonia which—with their corn and timber exports—were of great economic importance for Sweden, producing about one-third of the revenues of Sweden-Finland. The Livonian diets persistently refused to recognise the validity of the Swedish resumption decrees for their province since they were not represented in the Swedish diet which agreed to the resumption of Crown lands. This attitude angered Charles XI; it seemed presumptuous to him that he should be hindered in the exercise of his power by a provincial diet while 'His Majesty's Estates' in Sweden had fully accepted his absolute power. Since it was the German nobility, prominent in the province ever since the days of the Teutonic Order, which led the opposition it was tempting for the Swedish Crown to break the opposition by collaboration with the Livonian people. This could be achieved, it was hoped, by the introduction of Swedish institutions. In 1690 the Swedish church law of 1686 was introduced both in Livonia and Estonia. In the same year the Academy of Dorpat was founded, with Swedish professors who taught in Swedish, and it was decreed that only those who had studied for no less than two years at the Academy could hold administrative offices in Livonia. The authorities tried to exclude German students from the Academy, and Swedish and Finnish students were in a majority. It was further decreed that these should have preferential rights compared with the Germans in the filling of ecclesiastical appointments in Livonia. In 1694 Charles XI proceeded farther on the path of Swedification by issuing a regulation for the government of Livonia. He had contemplated complete incorporation of Livonia with Sweden, but had given in to warnings against so radical a step and the Livonian diet was therefore maintained. Its only remaining function, however, was to meet when the king desired extraordinary contributions, so that it lost its importance and became 'a registration office for the royal tax decrees'. In this way absolutism was introduced also in Livonia. At the same time it was decided that Swedish civil law should be applied as much as possible; the official correspondence should in future be conducted in Swedish so that the Livonian nobility should 'increasingly become used to the language'. These measures caused an open breach with the German nobility. Soon a group of noblemen, led by Johann Reinhold Patkul, began to conspire with the enemies of Sweden.

The policy of Caroline absolutism at home and abroad during the period up to the outbreak of the Great Northern War can be characterised with the words 'consolidation' and 'defence'. The resources of the State were used for the upkeep of a standing army, a completely new phenomenon in Swedish history. The army was constantly exercised under the command of officers whose names became famous in the Great Northern War; but it was not meant to be used aggressively. The government seems never seriously to have entertained the idea of continued expansion as a means of maintaining the great power of Sweden, nor to have harboured plans for a complete domination of the Baltic. The government aimed at maintaining the *status quo* and at welding together the different provinces with their various nationalities. After the death of Gyllenstierna Swedish foreign policy was directed by the head of the Chancery, Bengt Oxenstierna, who must be regarded as the most skilled Swedish diplomatist of his time; but the absolute king not infrequently made his will felt in foreign affairs. In some questions he had strong convictions, in others he was on occasion influenced by advisers. Bengt Oxenstierna was very familiar with the politics of Europe, and especially of the Empire, and was concerned with the safeguarding of Swedish interests in Germany and the exploitation of the possibilities offered by changes in the political groupings of the great powers. The king's horizon was, of necessity, more limited. His own bitter experience had taught him that Sweden's main enemy was Denmark. Louis XIV's annexation of Charles's hereditary principality, Palatinate-Zweibrücken, as well as his memories of the peace of 1679 made him look upon France with suspicion.

Denmark's finances had been ruined by the war; but the great change to royal absolutism had taken place twenty years earlier and the reforms which were instituted after 1679 to remedy the financial situation were less drastic. It is noteworthy that, while Charles XI in Sweden created a standing army of native soldiers, Denmark decided to get rid of the militia and to rely on mercenaries only. Much work was done in improving the Danish fleet, which was facilitated by the rapid growth of her merchant navy. Christian V was determined to put an end to the independent position of the duke of Holstein-Gottorp and to reconquer the provinces lost to Sweden. Danish foreign policy was conducted by the great Chancellor Frederik Ahlefeldt until his death in 1686, though his caution was bitterly opposed by those who desired a more active policy. After 1680 it became clear to both countries that a close alliance between them could not be realised, and each returned to the policy of seeking allies for protection against each other: a policy which became increasingly evident in the years before 1700. The choice before each was between France and the United Provinces.

As long as Sweden hoped to achieve collaboration with Denmark against Dutch demands for trade privileges in the Baltic, Charles XI refused to ratify the peace treaty of 1679 with the United Provinces; but eventually Bengt Oxenstierna, hard pressed by the Dutch, had to accept their terms. Arguments against a *rapprochement* with France, apart from Charles XI's suspicions of Louis XIV, were the improbability of obtaining support for the Gottorp policy and Sweden's need of naval support in the Baltic, while her fleet was being rebuilt. Experience from the last war had shown that the French fleet had not dared to enter the Baltic, while the

Dutch had given the Danes effective and, for Sweden, fatal support. Therefore in 1681 the peace treaty with the United Provinces was ratified and was followed by the far-reaching commercial treaty which the Dutch desired. In the autumn of 1681 the Treaty of The Hague was signed, by which the contracting parties bound themselves to work for the maintenance of the treaties of Westphalia and Nymegen, to offer their mediation if any power acted against the terms of the treaties and—if mediation failed—to defend them by force of arms; if either party were involved in war because of the alliance, the other was obliged to render assistance. Sweden's association with the United Provinces had important consequences. The commercial treaty implied a complete retreat for Sweden: Sweden had to dissolve her privileged companies, the Dutch were to be treated as the 'most favoured nation', and the favourable conditions which they had enjoyed in Swedish ports during the years 1659–67 were reimposed. The attempts of Sweden to introduce restrictions in the form of tolls on foreign trade in Swedish ports had to be abandoned.

The ratification of the peace treaty with the United Provinces meant a clear break with the Dano-Swedish treaty, since according to its stipulations the two allies should carry on negotiations jointly. The Swedes had not only negotiated secretly with the Dutch, but had renewed the Swedish-Dutch alliances of 1640 and 1645 which guaranteed the position of the duke of Holstein-Gottorp and therefore implied Sweden taking up a position in favour of Denmark's enemies. The Treaty of The Hague further implied that Sweden had gone over to the enemies of France. Louis XIV tried, with all the means at his disposal, to prevent the conclusion of these treaties and had most skilfully used the domestic opposition, both in the United Provinces and in Sweden, but failed to achieve his aim. Louis XIV, therefore, to counteract the consequences of the Treaty of The Hague, began negotiations with Sweden's potential enemies, Brandenburg and Denmark. Both had in 1679 lost conquests in Germany, made at Sweden's expense, which they had expected to keep. Against a promise of subsidies, Frederick William of Brandenburg at the beginning of 1682 renewed his alliance with France. Shortly afterwards Louis concluded an alliance with Denmark, promising her large subsidies and agreeing neither to guarantee the northern peace-treaties nor to prevent Denmark from attacking Holstein-Gottorp.

During the years 1682–4 Brandenburg and Denmark were both keen to take the offensive, but Louis XIV restrained them. His purpose was not to start another war in the north, but to create a counterbalance to the Dutch-Swedish alliance. Nevertheless Christian V—now completely under the sway of a belligerent group—in the autumn of 1682 invaded Holstein-Gottorp. In 1684 Denmark officially deprived the duke of his part of Slesvig and declared it for ever incorporated with Denmark.

Sweden watched this action against Holstein-Gottorp with apprehension. Charles XI was, however, not ready to give military aid and the duke's appeal for help according to the treaty of alliance was answered with vague promises. Sweden dared not risk a direct attack on her German possessions, for in 1683 an offensive alliance between Brandenburg, Denmark and France had been signed. Although it was never ratified by Louis XIV, the presence of a French squadron in the Baltic, while a Dutch fleet cruised in the North Sea, shows the critical situation in the summer of 1683.

During the armistice negotiations at Ratisbon in 1684[1] Sweden failed to gain support for her claim that the restitution of Palatinate-Zweibrücken and of Holstein-Gottorp should be included in the settlement; she was equally unsuccessful in her demand that a specific guarantee of her possessions should be included in the armistice. Hence Sweden continued negotiations with other powers trying to find support for her demands. Negotiations with the Emperor led to Sweden's accession to the League of Augsburg of 1686. More important were the diplomatic consequences which resulted from Brandenburg's change of policy: a treaty of alliance was signed between her and Sweden in 1686 which echoed the terms of the treaties which the Elector had concluded with the Dutch and Leopold I: the Westphalian peace and the Ratisbon armistice were to be maintained; Frederick William promised help to solve the Holstein-Gottorp question, preferably by peaceful means; both parties guaranteed each other's possessions in Livonia and Prussia respectively.

Through Brandenburg's change into the anti-French camp and her alliance with Sweden, Denmark became isolated, and after the death of Ahlefeldt her policy became more aggressive. A conflict between the Lüneburg duke George William of Celle and the Free City of Hamburg seemed to offer Denmark an opportunity to consolidate her position in north Germany. She proceeded to attack Hamburg, where Denmark could put forward legal claims similar to those which Sweden claimed in respect of the Free City of Bremen.[2] The Lüneburgers, however, joined forces with Hamburg, and even Brandenburg hurried to the support of the city. Since Denmark seemed bent on aggression—she continued to occupy the lands of the duke of Holstein-Gottorp—the north-German princes determined to stop Danish expansion. Only Charles XI's cautious attitude and Brandenburg's opposition prevented open war. In the spring of 1687 a defensive alliance was signed between Charles XI and Dukes George William and Ernest Augustus of Lüneburg.

The conflicts of the north were taking place while Louis XIV prepared his attack on the Rhine Palatinate. Because of the impending conflict both France and the Emperor strove to avoid complications in the north. Thus all interested parties were brought by pressure from the great powers

[1] See above, ch. IX, p. 220.

[2] See above, ch. XVIII, pp. 430–1.

to accept a proposal for mediation in the Holstein-Gottorp conflict which was put forward by Leopold I, Brandenburg and the United Provinces, and in the autumn of 1687 the congress of Altona met. As neither Christian V nor Duke Christian Albrecht of Holstein-Gottorp would give in, the congress achieved no result for a considerable time; but in 1689 a threat of armed intervention by Sweden and Lüneburg decided the issue. They concluded a new alliance to attack Denmark unless the duke of Holstein-Gottorp were restored by a given date. The Swedish diet was called and military preparations began. With no hope of receiving armed support from France, and with both Brandenburg and the United Provinces working for a peaceful solution, Christian V had to give in: Christian Albrecht was restored to all his possessions. This, however, left the essential questions unsolved, especially the duke's rights to build fortifications and to maintain garrisons in Slesvig. Swedish foreign policy in the 1690's continued to be dominated by suspicion of Denmark, and in particular of her relations with Holstein-Gottorp.

The Anglo-Dutch dynastic union of 1689 and the consequent strengthening of the anti-French forces had important results for Scandinavia. The union lessened the commercial rivalry between England and the United Provinces, which the northern Crowns had been able to exploit; it was no longer possible to play one off against the other. When the maritime powers in the autumn of 1689 declared a blockade of the French ports, without this blockade being made effective and without application of the principle 'free ship makes free goods', this action caused intense dissatisfaction both in Sweden and Denmark. Although Swedish direct trade with France was at this time practically non-existent, Swedish statesmen and merchants were alive to the possibilities created by the war: the importance of the Baltic ports for the trade in Russian goods increased, and it was correctly assumed that the war would bring particularly favourable conditions for the goods needed by the belligerents. In 1691 Swedish-Danish negotiations led to a treaty of armed neutrality; the two countries agreed to demand compensation for merchantmen seized, to apply reprisals if compensation was not forthcoming, and to fit out convoys for mutual protection. This treaty was renewed in 1693.

The successes of the allies in the Nine Years War as well as pressure from pro-French circles in Sweden led Charles XI at some points to moderate his anti-French attitude. Debates took place as to whether Sweden ought not to take the initiative for the formation of a 'third party' to force the belligerents to make peace, and a *rapprochement* with France followed, especially during periods of allied superiority in the field. During the years 1693–4 the allies in principle accepted Swedish mediation on condition that the coming peace would be based on the treaties of Westphalia and Nymegen. France for her part tried to gain advantages from Sweden by concessions with regard to Palatinate-Zweibrücken.

Shortly before the death of Charles XI the official request for Sweden to act as a mediator reached Stockholm. The peace negotiations at Ryswick thus permitted Sweden to enjoy the position of a great power, though in reality the mediation meant little. It might be argued, moreover, that Swedish preoccupation with Denmark and the Danish relations with Holstein-Gottorp, as well as with western European issues, to a certain extent prevented her from paying attention to the developments in the eastern Baltic and from seeing the dangers which were arising there.

CHAPTER XXIII

THE RISE OF BRANDENBURG

UNTIL the beginning of the seventeenth century the Electorate of Brandenburg—stretching from the Old Mark (west of the Elbe) to the New Mark (east of the Oder)—was one of the largest German principalities and, as one of the seven Electorates, possessed a certain influence in German and Imperial affairs. But it was situated in the most backward corner of the Empire, the 'colonial' north-east, thinly populated and cut off from the sea and all important trade routes. Its towns were small and declining, had lost all contacts with the Hanseatic League, and had been reduced to obedience by the Hohenzollern Electors in the fifteenth century. The country had no natural resources; its soil was proverbially poor, much of it being either sandy or water-logged. The peasants had been reduced to serfdom; and on the ruins of their freedom and of the towns' wealth the nobility had established its rule, not only over the peasants, but also over the Electors and the towns. This rule was exercised, as elsewhere in Germany, through the Estates which dominated the financial administration, the domestic, and even the foreign policy of the Electorate. The east-German—and the Polish—noblemen were interested in demesne farming and in the sale of their produce, especially corn and beer, hence opposed to any ventures in the field of foreign policy and to any military duties. Because of their trading interests, they were in favour of the maintenance of peace and good relations with their neighbours. They constituted a kind of squirearchy which treated the Elector as *primus inter pares*—as the Polish nobility treated their king. Within the Estates, the towns were much too weak to render any effective opposition to the ruling nobility, the prelates having disappeared as an Estate with the introduction of the Reformation. The Reformation, as elsewhere in Germany, had not resulted in the strengthening of the powers of the prince. Many of the dissolved monasteries and nunneries had passed into the hands of the nobility, and the disappearance of the Estate of the prelates had deprived the Elector of the possibility of playing off one Estate against the other and of using clerics in high offices of State. As the largest landowner of the Electorate he had the same interests as the other landlords; for his domains, exactly like the noble estates, were farmed with the labour services of serfs, and the beer brewed by his stewards was sold, as that from noble estates, to the detriment of the urban brewing industry. Indeed, until the later years of the Thirty Years War the powers of the Elector continued to decline. He had no army, through which he might have gained influence during the war, and his country was occupied by foreign troops which showed scant respect for his rights.

It is one of the marvels of German history that suddenly, in the later seventeenth century, a strong centralised State arose on such an unpropitious basis, for Brandenburg seemed to be predestined to go the way of Poland or of Mecklenburg. It is true that during the first half of the seventeenth century the Hohenzollerns had made important acquisitions. It was their policy, as it was that of the Habsburgs, to conclude dynastic marriages which opened the possibility of inheriting the dominions of other princes if their male line failed. Through his wife, the Princess Anne of Prussia, the Elector John Sigismund (1608–19) could lay claim to the highly important duchies of Jülich, Cleves, Berg and Mark on the lower Rhine after the death of the last native duke in 1609, and equally to the duchy of Prussia itself (the later East Prussia) after the death of her father in 1618. While the Hohenzollern claim to the duchy of Prussia, which was still a Polish fief, was indisputable, the duchies on the lower Rhine had to be shared with another claimant, the count palatine of Neuburg: Brandenburg only received the duchy of Cleves and the counties of Mark and Ravensberg when the inheritance was divided provisionally in 1614—terms which were confirmed by the final partition of 1666. Thus the Hohenzollerns acquired principalities of great political and strategical importance: those in the west closely connected with the United Provinces and, after the outbreak of the Thirty Years War, occupied by Dutch garrisons; those in the east situated on the Baltic coast and coveted by Poland and Sweden alike. Further important gains were made at the Peace of Westphalia. Thanks to French support, the Hohenzollerns received the secularised bishoprics of Cammin, Halberstadt and Minden, the expectancy of the rich archbishopric of Magdeburg on the Elbe, and most important, the eastern half of Pomerania—but without Stettin, the important harbour at the mouth of the Oder, which with western Pomerania went to Sweden. Thus the Hohenzollerns emerged from the Thirty Years War as the most important German ruling house after the Habsburgs, and this with hardly any military effort of their own.

Yet these large possessions, scattered over the whole of north Germany, from the Meuse to the Niemen, did not form one State. The gaps between them were much larger than the territories themselves. In the centre the Brandenburg Mark, with eastern Pomerania, Magdeburg and Halberstadt, formed a fairly contiguous block of territory. The remainder were outposts which could hardly be defended in case of war and were threatened by many European powers. Furthermore, they had little in common with Brandenburg. It is true that the social structure of the duchy of Prussia and of eastern Pomerania was the same as that of Brandenburg and that Lutheranism was the predominant religion. But, since the Hohenzollerns were Calvinists, this was a factor which strengthened the opposition to Brandenburg rule, especially in the duchy of Prussia. Moreover, all these small principalities had their own governments and Estates, their own traditions and ties. They had no more in common than, within the Habsburg territories, the Breisgau or Tyrol with Bohemia or Silesia, or England with Scotland. The mere possession of more lands could be a source of weakness, as the example of the Habsburgs was to show. The question was whether the Hohenzollerns would succeed in welding these heterogeneous lands into one State. This task was undertaken by the young Elector Frederick William who came to the throne in 1640, in the midst of the Thirty Years War, at the age of twenty, and who was called 'the Great Elector' by posterity. The task was completed by his successors in the eighteenth century.[1] When he came to the throne most of Brandenburg was occupied by the Swedes who were the real masters of the country; his army consisted of mutinous mercenaries who had to go without pay; the country had suffered terribly from foreign occupation and the depredations of the soldiery; it looked as though it might disintegrate completely. When he died in 1688 he left a well-trained standing army of about 30,000 men, had been victorious in long-drawn-out conflicts with the Estates and had created the first centralised institutions for all his territories. The importance of his reign does not lie in foreign conquest, but in his internal policy of consolidation and centralisation. From that point of view he was the most important of the Hohenzollern rulers.

Frederick William looked upon his many widely scattered territories as *membra unius capitis*, as he put it in 1650.[2] Through his possessions on the Rhine and on the Baltic he would be drawn into the great power conflicts of Europe—be it those between France and the Dutch, or those between Poland and Sweden. Naturally, he would desire to use the resources of all his lands in the defence of one or the other against foreign aggression. But such a policy was bound to clash with the local Estates: why should those of Cleves be interested in the fate of Pomerania, or those of Prussia in the aggression of Louis XIV? In 1650 even the Estates of Brandenburg declined to vote any money for the dispute with Sweden over the Pomeranian frontier, stating quite correctly that those of Pomerania or Cleves would not help them either if they were threatened: why should they get mixed up in the quarrels of foreign provinces?[3] If the Elector wanted to defend his possessions he needed an army, and an army he could raise only if his Estates granted him the necessary means. Early in 1652 he therefore decided to summon a general Brandenburg diet, attended by the entire nobility and all the towns of the Brandenburg Mark: usually only small deputation diets were called, or the committees

[1] For Prussia in the eighteenth century, see vol. VII, ch. XIII.

[2] *Urkunden und Actenstücke zur Geschichte des Kurfürsten Friedrich Wilhelm von Brandenburg* (Berlin, 1880), X, 194.

[3] *Ibid.* X, 196.

of the Estates met to transact current business. To this large assembly the Elector proposed the introduction of a general indirect tax, the *modi generales*, to which rich as well as poor would contribute and which would thus do away with the tax-exemption of the nobility. It was a tax similar to the Dutch excise, which the Elector knew from the years he had spent in the United Provinces during his youth, and it was appropriate to the conditions of a flourishing commercial community; it was likely to become a permanent tax and thus to deprive the Estates of their power of the purse. Some Brandenburg towns, indeed, were in favour of the excise because they hoped it would bring them an alleviation from the crushing burden of taxation (the towns having to contribute 59 per cent to each tax). The opposition of the nobility, however, was so strong that the proposal had to be dropped. The Estates then offered the comparatively large sum of 500,000 thalers payable over six years if their grievances were redressed, and on this basis a compromise was finally reached in May 1653, after eight adjournments of the diet. Frederick William got his money grant and could thus recruit a small army; but he had to make far-reaching concessions to the nobility, especially with regard to their rights over their peasants. He also had to promise that he would neither introduce the excise nor conclude an alliance without the consent of the Estates and would hear their advice in all important affairs: their *condominium* was once more confirmed. The outcome of the diet was not a victory of the Elector, nor did it bring about any real change.

This change was brought about, in Brandenburg as in the other electoral territories, by the War of the North which broke out in 1655.[1] It was in this war that Frederick William, by cleverly changing sides and first allying with Sweden and later with Poland, made the only gain of his reign in the field of foreign policy. At the Peace of Oliva in 1660 Sweden as well as Poland confirmed him in the sovereign possession of the duchy of Prussia, which thus ceased to be a Polish fief and later provided the name for the new kingdom. But the War of the North also brought about fundamental changes in the relationship between the Elector and his Estates. Everywhere troops were recruited and taxes were levied, if need be by military force, without waiting for grants by the Estates. During the first two years of the war 717,766 thalers were raised in Brandenburg, not counting supplies in kind; and the burden increased until, for some time in 1659, 110,000 thalers a month were levied. In Cleves and Mark 1,500,000 thalers were collected during the war years: an even heavier burden considering the small size of the two principalities. The duchy of Prussia suffered terribly from the fighting, looting, burning, and an outbreak of plague. In spite of this, new tolls and taxes were introduced against strong local opposition, and the trade of Königsberg, the capital, declined sharply.

[1] For this war, see below, ch. XXIV, pp. 566–8, and ch. XXV, pp. 574–5.

After the end of the war Frederick William was in a much stronger position. The army was not disbanded and the Estates did not regain their former influence. In Brandenburg 22,000 thalers a month were still levied, about three times as much as before the war, although the Estates had never agreed to such a sum. When they complained that the Elector did not consult them in important matters, as he had promised to do, he curtly replied that it was impossible to discuss confidential affairs with a general diet: after the experiences of 1652–3 he was determined not to repeat the experiment. In the duchy of Prussia there was strong opposition to the continuation of heavy taxes and to the recognition of the electoral sovereignty over Prussia. While the nobility was conciliatory, and the small towns even more so, Königsberg—the only large town of the duchy—refused to give way. Inside Königsberg the urban commons, led by Hieronymus Roth, an urban official, strongly insisted that their consent should be obtained in a general *sejm* of Poland and that a deputation should go to Warsaw to seek support there. They eventually appealed to King John Casimir and made military preparations to defend their freedom, claiming that they could no longer bear the 'yoke of tyranny'. In their opinion, the transfer of sovereignty was legally void because their agreement had not been obtained. The aldermen of Königsberg, however, dissented and struggled to maintain their authority against the rebellious lower orders. This disunity proved fatal. The urban commons alone were unable to withstand the Brandenburg army, and the abduction and imprisonment of their leader, Roth, sufficed to bring popular resistance to an end. The diet recognised Frederick William's sovereignty and granted him substantial taxes, but only against weighty concessions. In 1663 he had to confirm all the Estates' privileges and to promise that he would hear their advice in all important matters, hold triennial diets, levy no tax without their consent, and leave the administration of taxes in the hands of the Estates. In spite of these promises, however, they had suffered a decisive defeat: disunited and deprived of support from Poland, they were unable to hold their own against the electoral army.

Even more striking was Frederick William's success in Cleves and Mark. There the position of the Estates was particularly strong, thanks to the weak government of the last native dukes, the struggles over the succession during which the Estates had emerged as one of the decisive factors, and the Elector's policy of aggression against his co-heir, the duke of Jülich and Berg, which had been strongly opposed by the Estates of all four principalities. The result was that, in 1649 and in 1653, Frederick William had to make far-reaching concessions to the Estates. They were granted the rights of free assembly on their own initiative and of negotiating with foreign powers; no troops were to be brought into the duchies without their consent; all officials were to be natives of either principality, and no taxes were to be levied without their consent. During the

War of the North, however, these privileges were violated continuously, and a régime of military force was erected which aroused such opposition that the government feared a general uprising. As the Dutch garrisons no longer supported the burghers, they were unable to render any resistance. The Estates were no longer united because many noblemen had entered the electoral service or had received other favours from their master. This disunity and his own armed strength enabled Frederick William to abandon the policy of bargaining with the Estates. A new *Recess* was drawn up in Berlin and sent to Cleves signed and sealed. An ultimatum was then put to the Estates either to accept this *Recess* as it stood, or their prince would arrive with his army and treat them as they deserved. These tactics were entirely successful. The majority gave way and accepted; a minority left the diet, but were soon brought to heel. In the new *Recess* many of the previous concessions were revoked, especially those relating to foreign powers and the introduction of troops. But the Estates' power of the purse and their rights of free assembly (after due notification of the government) and of limiting official appointments to natives of the duchies were recognised specifically. Like the Brandenburg *Recess* of 1653 and the Prussian *Recess* of 1663 it was a compromise solution. There was no longer a *condominium* of the Estates, but they retained certain definite rights. In contrast with Brandenburg and Prussia, however, these remained in force during the subsequent period. As the Estates made substantial money grants and no longer tried to follow an independent policy, the Hohenzollerns left these far-away provinces largely alone. The reforming zeal of Berlin found little echo in the Rhineland with its entirely different problems and traditions. Cleves and Mark continued to be outposts of the Hohenzollern monarchy, not only in the geographical sense.

In Brandenburg, on the other hand, decisive reforms were carried through during the second half of the Elector's reign, reforms which completely destroyed the influence of the Estates. At the diets of 1661 and 1667 he reverted to the plan of introducing an excise instead of the antiquated contribution, a direct tax on property, but again met with strong noble opposition; the nobility declined to give up their exemption from taxation and thus to become the equals of the lowest *plebeji*. The Elector was contemplating another retreat, but a popular movement inside the towns forced his hand. The result was another compromise. In 1667 the excise was introduced by decree, but only for the towns directly under the ruler, not for those under the nobility. Even these 'immediate' towns were given the option whether they would accept the excise or not. Only in 1680 was it made compulsory for the towns, and two years later it was extended to the towns under the nobility, which had escaped it hitherto. In this way the privileges of the nobility were not violated, but preserved into the nineteenth century. The Estates, however, lost their political influence. As the nobility had feared, the excise became a permanent tax and made the summoning of diets unnecessary: their *raison d'être*, from the ruler's point of view, had been the voting of supply. As the excise was a permanent tax which could be increased and extended to more goods at the pleasure of the Elector, the towns need no longer be summoned. The land-tax paid by the country districts could be assessed and repartitioned by local assemblies of the nobility, the so-called *Kreistage*.

The collection and administration of the excise was at first left in the hands of the urban authorities, but soon passed into those of electoral officials appointed to supervise matters relating to the excise: the military and tax commissars of the Hohenzollern monarchy. An entirely new bureaucracy came into being, divorced from the Estates and their interests and subservient only to the prince. In the eighteenth century these new officials became the all-powerful masters of the towns; whatever was left of urban self-government and autonomy was destroyed by the bureaucracy. The towns remained weak, politically as well as economically. No strong middle class could develop under these conditions, but only obedient burghers who expected everything from above and looked to the State for protection and inspiration. This was the system which was slowly extended from Brandenburg to the other Hohenzollern provinces.

In Brandenburg the resistance of the Estates to the reforming policy of the Elector was weak, and he was able to play off one Estate against the other. As the privileges of the nobility were confirmed and the State did not interfere with the management of the noble estates and the position of the serfs, the nobility acquiesced. The rapid growth of the army enabled them to solve the problem of providing for their younger sons who could no longer enter the Church. The Brandenburg nobility was poor and their estates could not be further and further subdivided. State service presented a solution of their economic difficulties, especially at a time of depressed corn prices. The nobility of the duchy of Prussia had to solve the same problems, but they were less poor and by tradition more independent. Their ancestors had risen against the Teutonic Knights when their rule became oppressive, and the connection with Poland had made them accustomed to enjoy the position of their Polish counterparts. Opposition to a foreign Calvinist prince was strengthened by the native Lutheranism. Even after 1663 there existed a pro-Polish faction among the Prussian nobility which aimed at the restoration of the links with Poland. Against them the Great Elector used all the severity he could muster. In 1670 their leader, Lieutenant-Colonel Christian Ludwig von Kalckstein, was abducted from Warsaw by the Brandenburg envoy, tortured and executed: a violation not only of international law, but also of noble privilege.

Opposition in Königsberg was also crushed. When the town refused to accept the electoral tax demands a 'military execution' was ordered against it in 1674. Soldiers marched in and were billeted on the burghers; if necessary, force was to be used to obtain the payment of arrears. Soon the town consented not only to pay all arrears, but even the costs of the 'military execution'. Its resistance was broken and its trade declined. The leaders of the nobility, however, realised that unity among the Estates had to be restored if they wanted to regain their influence and avoid the continuation of heavy taxes; for in Prussia the noblemen were not exempted from taxation as they were in most German principalities. To bring to an end the separation of the Estates, which raised their taxes by different modi, the nobility proposed that a general excise be adopted, thus taking a leaf out of the Elector's book. In that way the diet would retain the power of the purse and Königsberg would be brought back to amity with the other Estates. By this time, however, the Great Elector had come to realise the advantages of the Brandenburg system which guaranteed a permanent separation of the Estates. He thus gave up his policy of reform and preferred one of 'divide and rule'. During the 1680's the nobility repeatedly voted a general excise, but was forced by the new military authorities to adhere to the customary land-tax. The powers of the new military Commissariat, headed by Brandenburg officials, began to supersede those of the older authorities of the duchy and to make the diets a farce. The Estates lost the power of the purse and were in practice split into four parts: the nobility, the free peasants, the small towns and Königsberg. Only among the nobility opposition continued for some time, but without gaining any success. Gradually, they also entered the service of the Hohenzollern monarchy.

It was not in the duchy of Prussia, however, but in the Brandenburg Mark that the urban excise was first introduced, the new military authorities came into being, and the Estates were pushed back most energetically. There the privy council had been founded at the beginning of the seventeenth century to advise the Elector in matters relating to the new acquisitions in western and in eastern Germany. In practice the privy council, during the first half-century of its existence, dealt mainly with the affairs of Brandenburg and only to a very limited extent with those of the other Hohenzollern territories. Slowly, however, it extended its sphere of activities. While it remained the government of the Brandenburg Mark, it became an organ superior to the governments of the other territories; their affairs and matters of foreign policy were discussed in the privy council, side by side with purely local issues. It had no departments, and there was no proper division of functions between the privy councillors, the large majority of whom were noblemen. Originally, all matters of State came within the purview of the privy council. But during the War of the North, which brought about such decisive changes in the internal history of the country, a new military authority came into being, the *Generalkriegskommissariat*; it became responsible for all matters of finance and taxation connected with the army, which it had to pay, equip and provision, and it soon acquired numerous subordinate officials in the different territories, the military and tax commissars mentioned above. During the wars against Louis XIV a central military chest, the *Generalkriegskasse*, was added into which the foreign subsidies and the taxes of the electoral principalities had to be paid. It thus became a central treasury for the whole State, superior to the provincial chests which had to render their accounts to it. As the existence of the standing army depended on the payment of taxes, the supervision and control of their levy remained the most important task of the officials of the *Generalkriegskommissariat*. This applied especially to the excise, from the administration of which the urban authorities were excluded. As the Estates everywhere were reluctant to grant the heavy taxes demanded, the new officials soon got involved in conflicts with the Estates and their representatives. These officials, in contrast with those of the various local governments, had no ties with the Estates. They were the organs of the new State, active and ruthless, eager to assert their power and executing the orders of the prince without any inhibitions. They became the 'soul of the State', the ancient privileges disappeared, and 'no shadow of liberty seemed to be left', as the Brandenburg nobility put it in 1683.[1]

From the field of taxation the *Generalkriegskommissariat* in the last years of the reign of the Great Elector extended its activities into that of economic life in general. The supervision of trade and manufactures, the financing of new enterprises, the control of the gilds, the undertaking and financing of naval and colonial ventures, belonged to its tasks. As so much of the economic activity was financed or controlled by the State, in the absence of private initiative, and as the army became the centre of all State activity, the *Generalkriegskommissariat* became the most important authority of the Hohenzollern State. As the population had shrunk owing to the Thirty Years War and the heavy burdens imposed upon it, the new authorities were made responsible for the promotion of immigration and the settlement of foreigners, and this became an important function of the State. More settlers meant more taxpayers, more production, new industries and new skills, hence more money. During the last two decades of the seventeenth century more than 20,000 Calvinists from France and the Palatinate were settled in Brandenburg and Magdeburg. Especially the textile industries—the manufacture of cloth, linen, cotton, silk, velvet, lace, braid, stockings, ribbons, etc.—benefited enormously. The manufacture of candles, soap, paper, mirrors, watches, optical articles, buttons, gloves, shoes, hats, vegetable oils, tobacco, iron, copper and brass was encouraged. Thus the officials of the *Generalkriegskommissariat* fulfilled many of the tasks of the French *intendants*, but the accent of the new authority was a military one. While in France too *intendants* were attached

[1] *Urkunden und Actenstücke*, x, 595, 600.

to the armies and responsible for the levying of contributions in occupied countries, their Brandenburg counterparts had above all to provide the army with what it required and to foster enterprises which were useful from the point of view of the army. Even the promotion of economic recovery and the settlement of immigrants came under this heading. Yet the growth of the standing army, too large for the country's resources, considerably delayed the economic recovery.

When Frederick William came to the throne in 1640 the Brandenburg forces numbered only 4650 men and soon had to be reduced further because of lack of money. After the conclusion of peace in 1648 hardly any soldiers were retained. In 1653, after the end of the Brandenburg diet which granted the Elector money for six years, the army numbered only 1800 men. During the War of the North, however, it quickly grew to about 22,000 and enabled him to play an important part in that war. At Warsaw in 1656 it gained its first important victory, together with Sweden, over Poland. After the Peace of Oliva the army was not disbanded, but only reduced to 12,000 men—a considerable force. Although it had to be further depleted during the following years, it soon regained its former strength. The wars against Louis XIV after 1672 caused a new substantial increase to about 45,000. After the Peace of Nymegen the army was again reduced, but only to 25,000—a force much larger than that maintained by any other German principality. In 1688, the year of the death of the Great Elector, it numbered over 30,000 men. It twice conquered western Pomerania from Sweden and in June 1675 at Fehrbellin gained a renowned victory over the Swedes who had invaded Brandenburg. It equally distinguished itself in the wars against the Turks. It was a force to be reckoned with by the powers of Europe and partly built up with the help of Dutch and French subsidies. But over 90 per cent of the military expenditure came from internal sources. In 1688, a year of peace, the roughly one million subjects of the Great Elector had to raise 3,382,000 thalers, or almost 680,000 pounds sterling: an enormous burden for the population of a very poor country and, above all, for the serfs who constituted its major part. The officers of this army were mainly native noblemen who began to identify their interests with those of the State. Although many of them were unruly and ill-disciplined, a spirit of loyalty towards the Elector and a strong monarchical feeling began to permeate their ranks. He was their commander-in-chief, and they his loyal vassals: because so many of the officers came from the native nobility a feudal bond tied them to their master. A working alliance was established between him and the nobility which thus forgot the loss of its political privileges, exercised through the Estates. But it retained its social privileges and remained the ruling class, albeit in a new form. It was the nobility of Brandenburg, Pomerania and Prussia which occupied the leading positions in State and army, especially in the eighteenth century.

If the army and its administration owed much to the Swedish example—Frederick William was a nephew of Gustavus Adolphus—his economic policy was strongly influenced by western European ideas, those of Colbert as well as of the Dutch. Yet the principles of 'mercantilism' when applied to small, open and scattered territories could not have any beneficial effect; nor could the money be kept in the country, as Frederick William desired, for Brandenburg depended on imports of essential commodities. Yet some of his measures had the desired effect. This applies in particular to the construction of a canal to link the rivers Oder and Spree in order to divert traffic from the Oder, the mouth of which was in Swedish hands, to Berlin, his capital. In spite of counter-measures taken by the towns on the Oder—Frankfurt, Stettin, Leipzig, etc.—the work was completed during the 1660's, to the detriment of Saxony and the Oder towns. Many goods from Silesia and Poland, which used to be transported via Leipzig overland, now took the cheaper route through the canal and down the Elbe. Frankfurt-on-Oder declined, but Berlin—hitherto very unimportant—developed, partly because all goods had to be trans-shipped there. Brandenburg might have benefited more if it had not been for the heavy and obnoxious tolls levied at Lenzen and Werben on the Elbe which made the carriers of less bulky goods prefer the land routes. The many electoral prohibitions, regulations and monopolies equally had a nefarious effect on trade; but in this respect the policy adopted by Brandenburg did not differ from that of its neighbours.

Alone among the German princes, however, Frederick William, owing to his close connections with the United Provinces, seems to have realised the great importance of a naval and colonial policy. Projects for the foundation of an East India Company were made in the early years of the reign. During the wars against Louis XIV he employed privateers, equipped by the Dutch merchant Benjamin Raulé, to attack Swedish and Spanish ships. After the Peace of Nymegen (1679) the first expedition was sent to the Gold Coast, financed by a Dutch company whose chairman was Raulé. In 1682 an Africa Company was founded with the modest capital of 50,000 thalers (about £10,000) to which Raulé contributed 24,000 and the Elector only 8000. In the following year its seat was transferred from Pillau near Königsberg to Emden, much more favourably situated on the North Sea and close to the United Provinces. The Estates of East Frisia contributed a further 24,000 thalers, as did the Elector of Cologne; but lack of capital remained a great handicap. In the same year the first Brandenburg factory was founded at the Gold Coast, 'Great Frederick's Burg', soon to be followed by others. From Denmark a trading post on the island of St Thomas in the West Indies was bought, for the slave trade was the most lucrative branch of these activities. Friendly relations were established with native chiefs, but the Dutch West India Company was bitterly hostile. In 1684 Frederick William bought from Raulé nine men-of-war for 110,000 thalers and thus founded his own navy to protect the colonial enterprises. An East India and an America Company were launched during the last years of his reign. Yet Brandenburg was much too poor to maintain so many enterprises and to raise the required capital. No profits were made by the shareholders and the Africa Company soon went bankrupt. In 1717 Frederick William I, much more realistic than his grandfather, sold the possessions on the Gold Coast to the Dutch West India Company for the paltry sum of 6000 ducats. The State, preoccupied with manifold other tasks, could not be a substitute for a strong middle class.

In his foreign policy Frederick William was not much more successful. The one great gain of his reign—the sovereignty over the duchy of Prussia—was made in the War of the North; but after 1660 there were no further gains. From 1672 onwards he was engaged in the wars against Louis XIV on the side of the United Provinces, from which he received substantial subsidies. Because he had no good harbour on the Baltic, the Elector tried to win Stettin from Sweden by all the means at his disposal. The town was conquered in 1677, but at the Peace of St Germain two years later it had to be restored to Sweden. If Frederick William until that time had tried to advance his interests by fighting against Louis XIV in alliance with the United Provinces, he then dramatically changed his policy and became the ally of Louis XIV. Against the payment of an annual subsidy of 100,000 *livres*, or 33,333 thalers, the Elector promised to allow French troops to march through his territories and to vote for Louis XIV at the next Imperial election. Yet his hopes of gaining Stettin through French support were disappointed; nor did the French alliance bring him any tangible profit. During the following years the relations between France and Brandenburg became closer still; Frederick William supported Louis XIV's policy of the *Réunions* and opposed the taking of military measures against France.

Only after the Revocation of the Edict of Nantes did his policy change once more. The Edict of Potsdam of November 1685 invited the Huguenots (his co-religionists) to settle in Brandenburg—a step bound to arouse the displeasure of Louis XIV. Thousands came and brought their native skills to Brandenburg; Berlin in particular greatly benefited from the influx. In March 1686 a secret alliance was concluded with the Emperor Leopold against France. By its terms the Elector undertook to defend the Spanish Netherlands, to put 8000 men at the Emperor's disposal, to support the Austrian claims to the Spanish inheritance and to vote for Leopold's son when the Imperial throne became vacant, and received an annual subsidy of 66,666 thalers in peacetime. It was a tortuous foreign policy, dictated by the weakness of Brandenburg and by its need of foreign subsidies. It showed no German patriotic motives, either consciously or unconsciously; but German patriotism was an impossibility at a time when there was no Germany. It was nevertheless a realistic policy, aiming at the strengthening of his own State and his own army, and changing from one side to the other as the interests of his State seemed to demand. If territorial gains eluded him this was due to the weakness of Brandenburg, and not to any faulty policy.

During the reign of the Great Elector Brandenburg gradually became one State, held together by one army and one bureaucracy. Frederick William was successful in making himself an absolute ruler, although he had no preconceived plan of doing so. He was rather driven by circumstances in that direction, above all by the resistance of the Estates to his policy of unification and of becoming 'more considerable'. For this policy he required a standing army; this army required taxes and more taxes, and it could be used to levy them if the Estates proved reluctant to make large money grants. Thus the army and the new military bureaucracy became the favourite instruments of the Elector's policy. It was the army which made Brandenburg-Prussia a great power and which imprinted its stamp on the whole State. It was the Great Elector who founded both the army and the State. But how little he himself thought of Brandenburg as one State can be seen from the fact that in his will he set aside separate principalities for the sons of his second wife, Dorothea of Holstein, under whose influence he stood. Bitter conflicts between her and the sons of his first marriage dominated the last years of his life. After his death, however, the will was declared invalid by his successor, Frederick III. On his death-bed in May 1688 Frederick William had the words 'Amsterdam' and 'London' on his lips: he was one of the German princes who supported William of Orange's expedition to England.

Frederick III continued his father's policy, although with less energy. He supported William of Orange's expedition and participated in the wars against Louis XIV on the side of the Emperor. In 1689 he commanded the forces which took the fortress of Bonn on the Rhine. The Brandenburg army continued to grow and numbered about 39,000 men when the reign came to an end in 1713 after many years of war against France. Exactly as during the previous reign, however, the military efforts on the side of the Grand Alliance brought very little reward. At the Peace of Ryswick (1697) Brandenburg neither received any territorial compensation nor even the arrears of the subsidies due to her. This ill-success and the intrigues of the Electress Sophia Charlotte, the sister of the Elector George Louis of Hanover (the later George I), brought about the downfall of Frederick's powerful minister, Eberhard von Danckelman, who for the past nine years had directed the affairs of State in the spirit of the Great Elector. He was soon replaced by a new favourite, Count Colbe von Wartenberg, who remained in power until 1710. Danckelman was dismissed in the most gracious manner, but arrested a few days later and put on trial. Although the evidence against him was entirely insufficient, although the courts of all instances refused to condemn him and even the privy council voted that he should be released, an electoral decree sentenced him to imprisonment and the forfeiture of his property. He regained his liberty in 1707, but his property remained confiscated.

Count Wartenberg, however, was equally unsuccessful in obtaining any large territorial gains. From the rich inheritance of William III of Orange the Hohenzollerns secured only the small counties of Lingen and Mörs in western Germany, Neuchâtel, and later part of Guelders. But he was successful in promoting one overriding ambition of his master. Because Frederick Augustus of Saxony had become king of Poland, and because it seemed likely that George Louis of Hanover would become king of Britain, Frederick desired not to be out-distanced by his rivals and to become himself a king. As he was the sovereign ruler of the duchy of Prussia which was situated outside the Empire, he could make himself a king there without the consent of the Emperor. But he did not want to do so without the latter's approval, and to obtain this lengthy negotiations were started in Vienna. When the outbreak of the War of the Spanish Succession seemed imminent Leopold finally agreed.[1] In November 1700 a treaty was signed which renewed the alliance of 1686 between Vienna and Berlin against France. Frederick undertook to support the Emperor for the duration of the war with a contingent of 8000 men, while Leopold promised him a subsidy of 100,000 thalers and the immediate recognition of his royal dignity. Two months later, on 18 January 1701, the coronation was celebrated at Königsberg with magnificent splendour, Frederick crowning himself and his wife, to mark the independence of the Prussian Crown of the Emperor and any spiritual power. Thus the duchy of Prussia, the ancient domain of the Teutonic Knights, gave its name to the new kingdom: Frederick was now king *in*, not of Prussia. The change of name, however, did not mean that the duchy became of any greater importance for the monarchy as a whole, or that the centre of gravity shifted from Berlin to Königsberg. Berlin remained the capital of the Prussian monarchy, and the Brandenburg Mark its core and most important province. In 1697 Brandenburg contributed 32 per cent of the total revenue from taxation and the duchy of Prussia only 16·4—to be followed by the much smaller Magdeburg with 15·7 and Cleves and Mark with 10·2 per cent; these figures also indicate the relative importance of the different territories for the State as a whole. Nor did the new kingdom inherit the traditions of the Teutonic Knights who had once ruled in Prussia. Their State had been secularised in 1525, and the Estates which became the real rulers of the duchy during the following century were in no way influenced by the ideas and practices of the religious order which they had superseded. Their orthodox Lutheranism was far removed from the Order's crusading

[1] For the war and Prussia's participation in it, see vol. VI, ch. XIII.

zeal; their Polish sympathies were alien to any Teutonic spirit. The black eagle of Prussia replaced the red eagle of Brandenburg as the insignia of the new monarchy, but that was the only link which connected it with the 'Prussian spirit'.

The elevation to the position of a king brought out Frederick's love of pomp and splendour. Of the Hohenzollern rulers he was the most strongly influenced by the 'grandeur' of Louis XIV. The court ceremonial became far more elaborate. A magnificent palace was built in Berlin by Andreas Schlüter[1] to replace the older and simpler one. When the building was completed the king immediately desired the number of the state rooms to be doubled. Other palaces and new wide streets began to adorn the capital. Outside, at Lietzenburg (to be renamed Charlottenburg after her), Sophia Charlotte had another palace built with a park and an opera house. There comedies were enacted by the ladies and gentlemen of the court and the philosopher Leibniz became a regular visitor. There the Crown Prince, the later Frederick William I, played the part of Cupid and sometimes performed a solo dance. To foster the development of painting, sculpture and architecture an Academy of Arts was founded in 1696 after the example of Rome and Paris, where Dutch and other painters taught and Schlüter found employment. A few years later there followed, after Leibniz's plan, the Academy of Sciences which also had its more practical functions: to supervise the whole system of education and to promote agriculture and enterprise, for example the cultivation of silk. A new university was founded at Halle where well-known scholars received appointments. The new Crown thus became a protector of the arts and of scientific progress. The Muses seemed to find a home in Berlin, especially at the court of the queen, soon to be chased away again by more martial tunes. Frederick William I was not cast for the role of Cupid.

If the arts flourished owing to royal support, expenditure increased by leaps and bounds. Between 1688 and 1700 that on food and wine nearly doubled, that on liveries more than trebled. The king informed the French ambassador that the jewels on his clothes were estimated at more than one million thalers. He developed a veritable passion for jewellery and other precious objects. He loved to make presents of gold and silver plate, of swords, sticks, rings and miniature portraits adorned with diamonds, to embellish his new palaces with costly decorations and furniture, to arrange splendid entertainments and displays. An enormous deficit soon resulted, for Brandenburg-Prussia was still a very poor country, and the subsidies of the great powers were quite insufficient to close the gap. The royal favourites and the faction struggles at the court were contributory factors, and the finances and administration suffered badly. Matters began to be remedied during the last years of the reign, and the impending conclusion of the War of the Spanish Succession

[1] See above, ch. VII, p. 172.

provided an opportunity for a considerable reduction of the army; for in the long run the kingdom was quite unable to maintain a large standing army and to spend vast sums on the court and the promotion of the arts. The king who ascended the throne in 1713, however, had already made his choice: the army was not reduced, but augmented to 45,000 men in peace-time, while the expenditure on non-military objects was severely curtailed. Mars became the god of the new kingdom. Yet its first king, in spite of all his obvious faults, perhaps deserves a better name than he has been given by the Prussian historiography. His inclinations were, on the whole, pacific and cultural; his capital was beginning to become a metropolis; industry was at last beginning to develop, thanks to the efforts of the Huguenots, nearly 14,000 of whom found a home in the Hohenzollern lands. It might have been better for Prussia and for Germany if Frederick's successors had shown similar inclinations, if the army had not become the heart and centre of the whole State. It was this feature which came to distinguish eighteenth-century Prussia from all the other German principalities.

CHAPTER XXIV

POLAND TO THE DEATH OF JOHN SOBIESKI

IN the middle of the seventeenth century Poland-Lithuania (that is, the kingdom of Poland and the grand duchy of Lithuania) covered some 350,000 square miles and was, after Muscovite Russia, the largest State in Europe. It extended from the basin of the Warta to the most westerly tributaries of the Volga and probably had about 10 million inhabitants, of whom less than half were Poles. To the east of the Polish Bug and the San there lived Lithuanians, White Russians and Ukrainians, each settled in separate regions. The Poles in this eastern territory were chiefly resident in the towns, but elsewhere they were scattered throughout the country. Poles were strongly represented among the nobility of the eastern regions, owing partly to the Polonisation of the native Lithuanian, White Russian and Ukrainian nobility in the seventeenth century. Of the remaining non-Polish nationalities only the Jews and the Germans were of numerical significance. The Jews, estimated at 5 per cent of the total population of Poland-Lithuania at that time, were predominantly to be found in the eastern regions of the country; the Germans, on the other hand, resided chiefly in the western districts, particularly in Greater Poland and Polish Prussia. The German element in the population increased during the seventeenth century as a result of further immigration from Germany. The ratio of the nationalities corresponded by and large to that of the creeds. Apart from an insignificant percentage, the Poles and Lithuanians were members of the Roman Catholic Church, whilst the White Russians and Ukrainians belonged partly to the Uniate[1] and partly to the Orthodox Church. Amongst the Germans Lutheranism had a strong following.

As far as its social structure was concerned, Poland-Lithuania was predominantly a land of peasants. Many urban dwellers also engaged in agriculture. The percentage of the population living in towns was higher in the west than in the east; in the western districts, according to some estimates, it reached some 20 per cent. However, the most striking characteristic of the social structure of Poland-Lithuania was the high percentage of nobility among the population. It has been reckoned that in Poland proper in the seventeenth century almost one in ten of the total population was a nobleman. Among the nobility the small number of magnates was of special importance. They possessed vast estates, occupied the most important public offices, and to a large extent controlled the

[1] See below, p. 572, n. 1.

policy of the State. The remainder of the nobility (the *szlachta*) for the most part owned only modest landed property and were frequently dependent upon the great magnate families. The nobility as a whole held a privileged position *vis-à-vis* the other classes.

The leading role of the nobility found its clearest expression in the fact that the diet (*sejm*), which existed since the late fifteenth century, was not an assembly of Estates but exclusively a parliament of nobles. Membership of one of the two chambers of the diet, the senate (*izba senatorska*), was reserved to holders of high ecclesiastical or secular offices, that is, to magnates. In the other chamber, that of rural deputies (*izba poselska*), sat representatives of the *szlachta*. Those few deputies from the towns who were admitted to the chamber of rural deputies played no part in its proceedings and had only limited voting rights. The diet exercised virtually legislative functions, and it also possessed the power of granting taxes and dues. In this way, ever since the close of the Middle Ages, the power of the king had been greatly restricted to the advantage of the nobility.

Poland's internal evolution in the latter half of the seventeenth century was characterised by a further weakening of the monarchy and by a decay of the legislative power. The weakening of the monarchy was connected with the practice of choosing the sovereign by a free election, which had become customary since the Jagellon dynasty died out in 1572. At the beginning the nobility, all of whom were entitled to vote, upheld the principle that only members of ruling dynasties were candidates eligible for the Polish throne. On several successive occasions kings had been elected from the same dynasty (that of the Vasas) and in the first half of the century, despite adherence to the principle of elective monarchy, the State had not been severely shaken by the question of the succession. But already on the first occasions when the throne fell vacant after the abdication of John Casimir, the last Polish Vasa (1648–68), the dangers inherent in an elective monarchy became clearly evident. Party strife and the intervention of foreign powers in electoral contests amongst the Polish and Lithuanian nobles threatened to make the king a tool of individual groups of magnates or of foreign powers. In 1669 Austria, France, Sweden, Brandenburg, and also Muscovy attempted to exercise influence upon the Polish election. The first four of these powers had agreed to support the candidature of the Count Palatine Philip William of Neuburg. But France secretly encouraged Condé's aspirations to the Polish throne, whilst the Habsburgs supported the candidature of Duke Charles of Lorraine. Amongst the *szlachta*, surprisingly enough, those opposed to the election of a foreigner prevailed. The principle hitherto observed of only considering members of ruling dynasties was abandoned, and a Polish-born magnate, Michael Wiśnowiecki (1669–73), was elected king. This understandable and politically ingenious reaction to foreign intervention, however, yielded no benefit at all to the Polish State, since the nobility from the outset impeded any consolidation of the royal power by electing as sovereign a man who, although a member of a distinguished family, was undistinguished as a person. Nor was foreign influence upon the king eliminated by the decision in favour of a 'Piast', for the vote had first and foremost been directed against the French candidate, and the result was that Michael Wiśnowiecki fell ever more under the influence of the pro-Habsburg party amongst the Polish nobility and eventually married a Habsburg, the Archduchess Eleonora. The election of 1669 subsequently turned out to be a victory for Vienna.

In 1674 the struggle to fill the vacant Polish throne was again chiefly determined by the antagonism of France and the Habsburgs. In addition, the candidature of the electoral prince of Brandenburg, Charles Emilius, at first played a far from insignificant part. But on this occasion too, none of the candidates who enjoyed the open support of foreign powers (Charles of Lorraine, Condé, John William of Neuburg) was victorious. Instead the throne went to a Polish-born magnate, John Sobieski (1674–96). He belonged to the pro-French faction within the Polish nobility, but during the course of his reign gradually broke away from his allegiance to this party. In contrast to Michael Wiśnowiecki, he was a man of strong character, though not a great statesman, and must be regarded as an exception amongst the Polish kings of the later seventeenth and the eighteenth centuries. His election was a consequence of the emergency in which the State at that time found itself. The threat which the Turks, Tatars and Cossacks presented to the south-eastern districts of the country necessitated the appointment of a general to the position of supreme authority in the State, and in these circumstances there was no one to rival Sobieski, the victor of Chotin.[1] But as a result of the principle of elective monarchy, the choice of an energetic ruler, conditioned as it was by the particular circumstances of the moment, did not lead to the creation of a strong national monarchy, which would have been the essential prerequisite for the strengthening of the Polish State at home and abroad.

The decline of the legislative authority found its clearest expression in the fact that the principle of unanimity came to be accepted for decisions taken by the diet. In theory this had already been the case in the sixteenth century, but the rule had not been strictly observed. If the number of opposing deputies was small, it was usually disregarded by the majority. However, from the mid-seventeenth century onwards, an entire diet could be broken up by the opposition of a single deputy (*liberum veto*). The first case of this kind occurred in 1652. At the session of 9 March one of the deputies, Siciński, lodged a protest against a motion to prolong the debates by one day over the customary period of six weeks. At first the other deputies paid no heed to this protest; obviously some of them realised how much the working of the diet would inevitably be impeded if

[1] See below, p. 569, for Sobieski's victory over the Turks.

the objection of a single member were taken into consideration. But the upshot was that the deputies made the extension of the session dependent upon Siciński withdrawing his objection. Since he did not do so, the diet adjourned without taking any decisions. Undoubtedly Siciński's veto would have had no success had not the matter been turned into a precedent by those nobles who were opposed to the court. The incident of 1652 did not result in a 'split' of the diet, that is, an adjournment prior to the expiry of the six-week time-limit legally established for debates. It was not until 1669 that a *liberum veto* was exercised before the termination of the customary period. In 1688 the diet 'split' for the first time right at the beginning of the proceedings, even before a Marshal had been elected. Thus the principle of the *liberum veto* had now been developed to its logical end. Whatever form it took, it did much to cripple the activity of the diet. Already in the reign of John Sobieski half the diets summoned were not brought to a successful conclusion. The bad example set by the diet was rapidly followed by many provincial diets (*sejmiki*).

The baleful effect which the *liberum veto* exercised upon the activity of the diet was most evident in matters of finance and the army, both of which were dependent upon resolutions passed regularly by the legislature. For there were at this time no permanent taxes in Poland. Instead, taxes were voted by the diet for certain definite purposes and for a limited period of time. Although the provincial diets had certain rights in this sphere, the granting of taxes and loans was primarily a matter for the central diet. Principally, these regular monetary grants kept in being the small standing army which during the course of the seventeenth century took the place of the old general levy of nobles. The reckless use of the *liberum veto* sometimes jeopardised the success of important military operations.

With the triumph of the principle of the *liberum veto*, foreign powers had an excellent opportunity to exercise influence upon the activities of the diet, all the more so since several of them commanded a political following amongst the magnates. This was especially true of the two powers whose rivalry determined the pattern of European politics at this time: Austria and France. The tensions brought about by the formation of such factions could lead the country close to civil war. Thus in 1672 the confederation of Gołąb, formed by the partisans of the Habsburgs, stood in threatening opposition to the confederation of Szczebrzeszyn formed by the army and the French party. During the reign of the Great Elector, Brandenburg also had a strong following not only among the nobles of Greater Poland, but also among leading magnate families in the grand duchy of Lithuania. Moreover, in the eastern districts of the country Muscovite Russia succeeded on certain occasions in obtaining far from insignificant support, as was shown during the Polish-Russian negotiations of 1656–8, and again after John Casimir's abdication in 1668. Nothing characterises better the internal political conditions in Poland-Lithuania during the latter half of the seventeenth century than the growing endeavours of neighbouring states to maintain 'order'—that is, internal weakness—in Poland. In 1667 Sweden and Brandenburg signed a treaty to maintain the existing relationship between king, Senate and nobility in Poland. In 1675 representatives of the Emperor and the Tsar signed a treaty—albeit one that did not come into force—which *inter alia* was directed against Sobieski's efforts at reform, in other words against any limitation of the liberties enjoyed by the nobility. Similar intentions formed the basis of a Swedish-Brandenburg and an Austrian-Brandenburg convention of 1686.

During the second half of the seventeenth century there was no lack of attempts to strengthen the State by internal reform. This objective was pursued, although not consistently, by John Casimir throughout his reign. His consort, Louise Maria of Gonzaga-Nevers, devoted herself to the same cause with even greater vigour. She was influenced by the ideas of French absolutism, but simultaneously by dynastic considerations which had a detrimental effect upon the efforts to promote reform. The court succeeded in gaining the support of some of the magnates for its plans, which were primarily concerned with the election of the sovereign, the voting procedure in the diet, and the establishment of a permanent council of senators and delegates of the *szlachta* to act as an advisory body between sessions of the diet. With regard to the election of the sovereign, the reformers went no farther than to suggest that the successor to the throne should be chosen during the lifetime of the reigning king (*rege vivente*), which would have spared the State the dangers resulting from an interregnum. With regard to the voting procedure in the diet, it was suggested that a drastic change should be effected by abolishing the principle of unanimity and introducing a system of majority voting. But the attempts at reform, and in particular the proposal for elections *rege vivente*, were eventually opposed by most magnates and above all by the *szlachta*. The attitude adopted by the nobility can be attributed in no small degree to the fact that the court sought to appoint a Frenchman as successor to John Casimir. A Frenchman, they feared, might display absolutist tendencies and represent a threat to their liberties. Because of their opposition to France, Austria and Brandenburg backed the opposition of the Polish nobility to the electoral project put forward by the court. Thus in 1661–2 the schemes of reform put forward by John Casimir and his adherents suffered an initial defeat. Despite this setback, the king refused to abandon his endeavours, with the result that in the following years a new conflict broke out between him and the anti-reformist faction amongst the nobility led by the Grand Marshal of Poland (*marszałek wielki koronny*), George (Jerzy) Lubomirski. Although hostilities with Muscovy were not yet concluded, the two parties did not shrink from civil war, and consequently the king was again compelled to renounce his plans for reform. His abdication in 1668 denoted that the cause of reform had suffered a decisive defeat.

John Sobieski resumed the efforts to consolidate the position of the monarchy in Poland, but like John Casimir he was thwarted by the resistance of the magnates and the *szlachta*. The reformist aspirations of both kings were in essence very moderate. But the nobility of Poland-Lithuania would not consent to a modernisation of the State, even on a modest scale. This demonstrates the lack of a proper sense of responsibility amongst the majority of representatives, at least, of the class which dominated the political, social and economic life of Poland. During the sixteenth century the Polish nobility had been more responsive to political innovations, but in the course of the seventeenth century their attitude stiffened. It is certainly no accident that in the Poland-Lithuania of the latter half of the seventeenth century there occurred several gross examples of political treason by leading magnates, such as the case of the Vice-Chancellor of Poland, Hieronymus Radziejowski. He came into conflict with the law and the sovereign, was forced to flee the country, eventually went to Sweden, and reappeared in Poland in 1655 together with the invading Swedish troops.

Polish literature and science could boast of no renowned representatives during the second half of the seventeenth century. But, on the other hand, Polish culture spread extensively to the east and south-east, beyond the territory which was ethnographically Polish. The religious situation was characterised by a further decline in the number of Protestant churches and communities and by intensified conflict between the Orthodox Church, on the one hand, and the Roman Catholic and Uniate Churches on the other.

Despite considerable losses the Protestant churches were able to maintain their position amongst the German population and to preserve a firm nucleus of parishes. But amongst the Polish population the Protestant churches and communities had only insignificant support which dwindled further under pressure from the State and the Church of Rome. From 1666 onwards, no Protestant had a seat in the Senate. The measures taken by the State were directed chiefly against the radical group of Arians (Socinians). The war with Sweden created a climate of opinion favourable to such repressive measures. Like most Polish nobles, the Arians amongst the *szlachcici* had rallied to Charles X after his great initial successes. Many Arians felt especially drawn to the Swedish king because they expected to receive tolerant treatment at his hands. In general, those who forsook John Casimir at the outset of the war were subsequently amnestied; but in 1658 the diet resolved that the Arians must leave the country within a period of three years, and only converts to Catholicism were allowed to remain. The majority of Arians seem to have availed themselves of this opportunity, while their spiritual leaders went abroad. Whereas the Protestant churches and communities were entirely forced on to the defensive, the Church of Rome succeeded in consolidating its dominant and privileged position. In 1668 a law was promulgated which made apostasy punishable by expulsion from the country.

Under Władysław IV the Orthodox Church in the eastern districts of Poland-Lithuania recovered appreciably from the blow which it had suffered by the Union of Brest in 1596. In the middle of the seventeenth century it had five dioceses: Kiev, Lwów, Lutsk, Przemyśl and Mogilev. It enjoyed strong support from the Cossacks; after the commencement of Chmel'nyćkyj's rising[1] the position of the Catholic and the Uniate Churches in the south-eastern provinces was weakened to the advantage of their Orthodox rival. But the Treaty of Andrusovo (1667),[2] whereby Poland-Lithuania renounced part of her territories, including Kiev, which were inhabited by adherents of the Orthodox Church, automatically deprived it of much of its strength. Consequently the Uniate Church again improved its position. In 1691 the Orthodox bishop of Przemyśl was converted to it, and several years after Sobieski's death the bishops of Lwów and Lutsk followed his example. From the mid-seventeenth century onwards the tsar displayed a keen interest in the position of the Orthodox Church in Poland-Lithuania. By the 'eternal peace' concluded with Muscovy in 1686, the Orthodox population was guaranteed religious liberty; no pressure was to be exercised to convert them to the Uniate or the Catholic Churches. Thus the ecclesiastical situation in the east of Poland-Lithuania began to assume an important role in Polish-Russian relations—a role which it was to resume during the events leading to the partitions of Poland.

After the middle of the seventeenth century the economic development of the country was badly affected by the incessant wars, particularly the struggles of the 1650's and 1660's which took place predominantly on Polish soil. In these two decades the population declined sharply; according to some estimates the loss was as much as one-third. The economic decline was evident in the countryside as well as in the towns. Between the 1640's and 1660's the area under tillage shrank considerably in some parts of the country. The reduced harvest yields caused an appreciable fall in corn exports. This unfavourable development in agriculture was accompanied by changes in the social structure. The number of land-hungry peasants increased considerably, for at the same time the demesnes (*folwarki*) of the landlords became more important. Their labour was provided as before by peasants' labour services, but in addition the landlords could now obtain labour from the impoverished rural population. In the western districts of Poland attempts were made to counteract the decline in agriculture by attracting new peasants, chiefly from Germany. Amongst the Polish peasantry there were a number of

[1] For these events see below, pp. 566–7.

[2] See below, pp. 568–9.

local uprisings; but only the revolt of Kostka Napierski in Podhale (on the northern slopes of the Tatra) in 1651 gained a short-lived success.

The decline of the towns brought with it a decline of trade and handicrafts. The metal industries of Little Poland were likewise affected by this general tendency. The slow recovery of the various sectors of the economy from the damage wrought by the wars was doubtless largely due to the prevailing political and social conditions, for example, the discrimination against the towns by the *szlachta*. Thus Poland-Lithuania fell behind her neighbours, not only in her constitutional, but also in her economic development.

Until the mid-seventeenth century Poland-Lithuania could maintain her international position with regard to most countries, and *vis-à-vis* Muscovy even improve it in the first decades of the century. But a fundamental change took place after the middle of the century: as a result of interminable wars Poland-Lithuania lost her position of hegemony in eastern Europe. Poland entered upon a period of decline which was above all due to the internal developments described above.

The armed conflicts began in 1648 with the revolt of the Dnieper Cossacks, under hetman Bogdan Chmel'nyćkyj, who were joined by the peasants of Poland's Ukrainian districts. Since neither side was able to gain a decisive victory, the Cossack question became an international one in which neighbouring States intervened. The alliance which ultimately came into being between the Cossacks and Russia had momentous consequences for Poland-Lithuania. In 1654 Chmel'nyćkyj and his army accepted the suzerainty of the tsar of Muscovy. This inevitably caused a war between Russia and Poland-Lithuania to whom the territory of the Dnieper Cossacks still—nominally at least—belonged.

The Muscovite armies which invaded the grand duchy of Lithuania and the south-eastern regions of Poland achieved notable successes. Within a few months they occupied the territory up to the Dnieper and the Dvina. In the following year they advanced farther. In the north they captured Minsk, Wilno, Kaunas and Grodno, and in the south, supported by Chmel'nyćkyj's forces, they advanced to the gates of Lwów. In the central sector Muscovite and Cossack units took Lublin and even reached the Vistula. Never before had Poland suffered defeats of such magnitude in her struggles with Moscow. It now became apparent how fundamentally the balance of military power had shifted to Poland's disadvantage since the abortive Muscovite attack on Smolensk in the 1630's.

These momentous events in eastern Europe brought about the intervention of King Charles X of Sweden. In the summer of 1655 Swedish troops marched from Pomerania into Poland and from Livonia into the grand duchy of Lithuania. Within a few months Charles X was master of most of Poland. On 25 July Greater Poland capitulated since the local nobility did not even attempt to offer any serious resistance. On 8 October

Warsaw fell into the hands of the Swedes, and on the 19th they marched into Cracow. King John Casimir left his country and sought refuge in Silesia. Most of the Polish provinces submitted to Charles. In the grand duchy of Lithuania a group of magnates led by Janusz and Bogusław Radziwiłł went over to the Swedes and concluded with them the Treaty of Kedainiai, whereby the grand duchy became united to Sweden. Thus in the autumn of 1655 the Polish-Lithuanian kingdom was in a state of complete disintegration.

The fact that the country was almost wholly occupied by foreign troops did not lead to a partition of Poland-Lithuania, as was the case over a century later. The threat to Poland's existence passed, for the acute antagonism between her neighbours very rapidly turned the scales in her favour. This reversal of fortune had begun by the end of 1655. The Crimean Tatars, who since 1648 had been allied with Chmel'nyćkyj's Cossacks, went over to the Poles, and in November 1655 the Muscovite-Cossack army operating in south-eastern Poland was compelled to raise the siege of Lwów and to retreat eastwards. There thus emerged in the south of Poland a large zone free from foreign troops. There John Casimir returned in December 1655, and there he rallied a Polish army to resume the war against the Swedes. This development was aided by the fact that a national spirit of resistance began to manifest itself amongst the Polish people. The best known, if not the first, example of this was the successful defence of the Jasna Góra monastery near Częstochowa against the Swedes at the end of 1655.

At the same time the Habsburg-Swedish enmity began to have a favourable effect upon the situation in Poland. The Emperor Ferdinand III, anxious to prevent Sweden from dominating Poland, mediated successfully between the tsar and the king of Poland. The Russo-Polish negotiations thus brought about through the aid of Imperial envoys in November 1656 led to the conclusion of a treaty of friendship. John Casimir, however, had to purchase this friendship by a risky concession: a promise to promote, at the next diet, the election of Tsar Alexis as king of Poland, that is, as his own successor. But the Poles deliberately dragged out the subsequent negotiations on this point, so that they had no result. Yet with regard to Poland's military situation the treaty was of considerable significance, since it brought about a truce in the east until the summer of 1658 and thus gave perceptible relief to the Poles in their struggle with the Swedes. For all the efforts of the Habsburgs the suspension of hostilities between Poland and Moscow would hardly have come about had not the tsar himself since April 1656 been at war with the Swedes in Finland and Livonia and thus had reasons of his own to seek an interruption of the war with Poland.

As a result of the new political and military situation in eastern Europe Poland was virtually obliged to fight only Sweden and her ally Brandenburg and was thus able to register several victories over Charles X, whose hands were tied by his war with Russia. With the assistance of new allies (Chmel'nyćkyj, the Cossack hetman, and György Rákóczi, prince of Transylvania) the king of Sweden did succeed in again overrunning the whole of Poland early in 1657; but the victories of the anti-Polish coalition now induced two of Sweden's adversaries to intervene in the war: Austria and Denmark. The entry of these two powers into the war delivered Poland from her distressing position almost by a single stroke. Charles X now turned against Denmark, merely leaving garrisons in several Polish towns. Rákóczi retreated to the south and was compelled by Polish troops to capitulate. In the light of the new situation the Elector Frederick William of Brandenburg, through the mediation of Austria, entered into negotiations with Poland which led to a Polish-Brandenburg alliance against Sweden. As a reward the king of Poland renounced the suzerainty over his fief, the duchy of Prussia, and surrendered Bütow and Lauenburg to the Elector as Polish fiefs (treaties of Wehlau and Bromberg).

In the final phase of the Polish-Swedish war there were no further major engagements on Polish soil. At the peace negotiations which began early in 1660, with French mediation, at Oliva near Danzig between Poland, Austria, Brandenburg and Sweden, the Poles were able to maintain the *status quo ante bellum* with regard to Sweden, as a result of the diplomatic and military shift in their favour which had taken place in 1657. According to the peace treaty (3 May 1660) Poland retained Polish Prussia (Pomerelia), whilst Sweden kept possession of Livonia, apart from so-called 'Polish Livonia' (the south-eastern part of the country, including Dünaburg). As far as relations between Brandenburg and Poland were concerned, the treaties of Wehlau and Bromberg were confirmed; thus Poland's renunciation of suzerainty over the duchy of Prussia was endorsed by an international treaty.

After the Peace of Oliva Poland-Lithuania could devote herself with increased energy to the war against Russia. Fighting between Polish and Muscovite troops was renewed in the autumn of 1658. In the Ukraine Poland was able to improve her position, since an anti-Muscovite tendency temporarily prevailed amongst the Cossacks. This resulted in the tsar retaining sovereignty over the part of the Ukraine to the left of the Dnieper and recognising Polish sovereignty over the part to the right of the Dnieper. In the north too, thanks to the Peace of Oliva, which made it possible for John Casimir to concentrate upon the war against Moscow, the territorial position could be altered in Poland's favour. In 1661 Polish-Lithuanian troops reconquered Grodno, Wilno, Gomel' and Mogilev. With the armistice of Andrusovo (near Smolensk) in 1667 the war came to an end. By this treaty Poland-Lithuania renounced the territories of Smolensk, Starodub, Chernigov and Novgorod-Seversk, as well as part of the Ukraine, that is, she ceded to Russia most of her territory east of the Dnieper and, on the western bank, Kiev with its adjacent territory for two years; but it was never returned to Poland.

The consequences which the wars of 1648–67 had upon Poland-Lithuania's international position cannot be fully appreciated merely on the basis of the territorial changes agreed on at Oliva and Andrusovo. The Polish-Lithuanian kingdom lost approximately one-fifth of its territory, but the ceded lands were primarily border areas, where Polish or Lithuanian rule had not lasted long without interruption, or where it had only existed in the form of suzerainty. Far more serious for Poland was the loss of her position as the most powerful State in eastern Europe. With the conflicts of the 1650's and 1660's the balance of power shifted against Poland in favour of Muscovite Russia. But both in the war with Sweden and in that with Russia Poland had on several occasions shown that she was far from incapable of asserting her strength.

Owing to the Turkish wars of the following decades the Polish State had no opportunity of regaining its strength. In the 1670's the Ottoman Empire, which since the mid-seventeenth century was experiencing a political revival and was resuming its expansionist policy for the last time,[1] directed its attacks against Poland. This war, like the war against Russia, originated in a conflict between the Polish State and the Cossacks, in this instance those Cossacks who had remained under Polish rule in the Ukraine to the right of the Dnieper. Urged by hetman Dorošenko, the Porte intervened in this conflict and took this part of the Ukraine under its protection. In the summer of 1672 a large Turkish army marched into Podolia, conquered Kamenec-Podol'sk, which was garrisoned by only a small Polish force, and threatened Lwów. King Michael Wiśnowiecki refrained from offering any resistance, and in October 1672 concluded with the Turks the Treaty of Bučač. By this treaty Poland pledged herself to pay tribute to the Porte and to cede Podolia to Turkey, and most of the Ukraine to the right of the Dnieper to hetman Dorošenko, a vassal of the sultan.

The events of the following years, however, proved that Poland was not so weak as she appeared because of her failure to defend herself against the Turkish attack. In November 1673 Sobieski won a glorious victory over the Turks at Chotin and in 1676 parried a new Turkish thrust near Żuravno (Galicia). But in the treaty concluded there the Porte retained almost all the gains which it had made by the Peace of Bučač. The readiness of the king of Poland to compromise was partly connected with his diplomatic plans. These were directed against Brandenburg. In accordance with this policy John Sobieski concluded secret treaties of alliance with France (1675) and Sweden (1677); the former *eo ipso* required him to take account of France's reluctance to see any weakening of Turkey.

[1] See above, ch. XXI, pp. 508–10.

Sobieski finally abandoned these diplomatic plans and from 1679 onwards adopted a systematic anti-Turkish policy. The alliance with Austria of 1683 for several years provided a workable basis for his foreign policy. Through the participation of a Polish army and of the king himself in the victorious battle against the Turks outside Vienna, in September 1683,[1] Poland achieved her last great triumph in the diplomatic and military fields. But soon it again became clear that she was no longer in a position to compete with the other European powers. The remainder of the war against the Turks was waged by the Holy League, formed in 1684 by the Emperor, Poland, Venice and the pope. But in the subsequent struggle against the Ottoman Empire Poland played a subordinate part, and Sobieski did not succeed in achieving any further striking victories. He sought to reconquer the Polish territories which were still in the hands of the Turks, and thereafter to subjugate at least the principalities of Moldavia and Wallachia which were under Turkish suzerainty. But his two advances into Moldavia (1686 and 1691) failed, as did the attempts to wrest from the Turks the fortress of Kamenec-Podol'sk. It was only at the Peace of Carlowitz (1699), after Sobieski's death, that Poland regained Podolia and the Ukraine to the west of the Dnieper.

In view of Poland's military and diplomatic position in the last quarter of the seventeenth century, it stands to reason that Sobieski had no opportunity to effect a revision of the treaties of Oliva and Andrusovo. Indeed, by the 'eternal peace' of 1686 he was compelled to renounce permanently the territories ceded to Muscovy in 1667. The shift in the balance of power to Poland's disadvantage, which had come to pass in eastern Europe during the 1650's and 1660's, remained an irrevocable fact.

[1] See above, ch. XXI, pp. 516–17.

CHAPTER XXV

RUSSIA: THE BEGINNING OF WESTERNISATION

THE accession to the throne of the second tsar of the Romanov dynasty, the sixteen-year-old Alexis Michailovich, took place without any incident. At home the dynasty was firmly established. In her foreign relations Russia maintained, during the first years of Alexis's reign (1645–76), the peace so dearly bought by Michael Feodorovich: in 1617 Moscow had resigned the Baltic littoral to Sweden, and in 1634 had ceded to Poland the districts of Smolensk and Novgorod-Seversk, the key to the Dnieper basin.[1] Peace with the Ottoman Empire, overlord of the Tatars, had been assured by the abandonment of Azov (1642). Though Moscow endeavoured to utilise the Don Cossacks as a shield against Tatars and Turks, she was ever ready to disavow their actions in Constantinople, to avoid a serious attack upon her southern borderlands. With the exception of the region of the Don Cossacks, the European frontiers of Russia remained essentially the same as at the death of Ivan IV (1584).

In Siberia, on the other hand, the area under Russian sway had been greatly extended: in 1645 Poyarkov reached the Amur; in 1648 Okhotsk was founded on the Pacific shore and Dezhnev sailed around the north-eastern tip of Asia. A few fortified strongpoints sufficed to maintain Russian rule over the sparse nomad population. In the remoter areas Moscow's actual authority was of course weak, but such political organisation as existed was from the start highly centralised; from 1637 onwards Siberia was governed from a special office in Moscow. The Russian settlers enjoyed neither political nor judicial autonomy, nor did they have any special colonial status. Siberia was treated as an Imperial province whose political structure evolved only gradually.

For Russia expansion into Siberia did not have the effect of broadening horizons, as colonial expansion overseas did for western Europe: Russian settlers were not completely isolated from their homeland, nor were they faced with an entirely different terrain. Moreover, they did not encounter highly developed cultures, whose strength and alien character might have stimulated reflections on their own culture. From the beginning the extent and uniformity of the country exercised a fatal influence upon Russian history, by slowing down the process of concentration and intensification. The role of space was enhanced by the annexation of Siberia, for the open frontier prevented economic, political and religious

[1] For these events, see vol. IV, ch. XIX.

tensions from becoming too acute: it was closed only by modern technology under Soviet rule. Economically, Siberia was of marginal importance, apart from fur-trapping and some transit trade with Asiatic countries (including, after 1653, China). Politically, until the mid-nineteenth century, Siberia remained, so to speak, Russia's backyard: a place for exiles and fugitives, divorced from the European field of Russian foreign policy.

Alexis's first diplomatic task was to settle the dispute with Denmark over the projected marriage between the Danish prince Waldemar and Irene, sister of the tsar, which had broken down over the refusal of the prince, a Protestant, to accept conversion to Orthodoxy. This ended Denmark's hopes for an alliance with Russia against Sweden. Similar hopes were entertained by Poland, whose hegemony in eastern Europe had been undermined by Sweden. But again Russia, anxious to avoid a war with her formidable neighbour, refrained from committing herself; whilst the Poles in 1646 rejected a Russian proposal for an alliance against the Tatars because of a Turkish attack on southern Poland. The threat from Sweden and Turkey did, however, bring about a *rapprochement* between Moscow and Poland, so that the Polish envoy in 1646 could speak of the common factors in both States, whose peoples shared 'the same Slav blood and the same Slav tongue'—one of the first appeals to Panslav sentiment in Russo-Polish relations. Moscow's internal weakness necessitated a defensive policy; it had to be abandoned as a result of political developments in the Ukraine.

The Ukrainian Cossacks were fighting to extend their political and social rights within the framework of the Polish State. From 1620 onwards, when (among others) an Orthodox bishopric was re-established in Kiev by the Patriarch of Constantinople, this struggle became increasingly a religious one of the Orthodox against the Catholics and Uniates.[1] Until the late 1640's the Polish State succeeded in suppressing Cossack revolts and in curtailing the liberties which they enjoyed; but in 1648 the Cossacks united in a great uprising, led by Bogdan Chmel'nyćkyj, a nobleman from Chigirin and the 'chief secretary' (*voyskovoy pisar'*) of the Cossack host. At first the Cossack army triumphed, helped by bloody uprisings of Ukrainian peasants against Polish landowners and officials. The Peace of Zborów (near Lwów) in 1649 resulted in a maximum of Polish concessions: an increase in the number of 'registered' Cossacks from 6000 to 40,000; withdrawal of all Polish troops from 'Little Russia'; election of officials from the Orthodox *szlachta* in the provinces of Bratslav (Bracław), Kiev and Chernigov; abolition of the ecclesiastical Union; expulsion of Jesuits and Jews; and admission of the metropolitan of Kiev to membership of the senate. But owing to the resistance of the Church on the

[1] Acknowledging the supremacy of the pope, but retaining the Greek liturgy and rites (Union of 1439).

Polish side and of the non-registered Cossacks, the treaty was not implemented, and from 1650 onwards the tide of war turned against the Cossacks: in 1653 the encircling of the Polish army near Zwaniec (near Chotin (Chocim)), was vitiated by the unreliability of their Tatar allies, who clearly did not wish the Cossacks to become too strong.

In this steadily deteriorating situation Chmel'nyćkyj strengthened his links with Moscow. From 1649 onwards the Cossacks engaged in negotiations, hoping to secure effective support from the tsar; but, as with the Don Cossacks in the Azov crisis, Moscow reacted with extreme caution, limiting herself to the occasional dispatch of supplies. A. L. Ordyn-Nashchokin, who was in charge of foreign policy, regarded it as Russia's prime objective to gain access to the Baltic and was therefore anxious to avoid a breach with Poland. However, the defeats inflicted upon the Cossacks raised the possibility of their becoming subject either to Poland or to Turkey, thereby exposing Moscow's southern border. Thus in 1653 a national assembly (*zemsky sobor*) decided that, to safeguard the Orthodox faith, the tsar should take the Cossacks 'under his mighty sovereign hand'. In January 1654 a solemn Cossack council (*rada*) approved Chmel'nyćkyj's proposal for union with Moscow, 'that we may all be one until eternity'; on 8 January they swore the oath of allegiance. The details of the settlement were agreed upon in Moscow in March: the Cossacks were to elect their hetman and other leaders; the number of registered Cossacks was increased to 60,000; existing property and judicial rights were confirmed, as were the towns' rights to such municipal self-government as they possessed; the estates of the Polish Crown and magnates and of the Catholic Church were confiscated and distributed amongst the Cossack nobility or granted to the Orthodox Church; the position of the peasants was improved.

The agreement of 1654 was no alliance: the Cossacks sought the protection of the tsar, he took them into his service; the tsar promised the Cossacks his 'favour and defence against enemies and protection'. They demanded from the Muscovite envoys that 'the Tsar should not deliver them, the hetman Bogdan Chmel'nyćkyj and the whole Zaporog host to the king of Poland, but should stand up for them and not destroy their liberty. And whoever has hitherto been a nobleman (*szlachcic*), or a Cossack or a townsman (*meshchanin*), or whoever possessed rank or estate, all that shall be as before. And that the sovereign may deign to command that title deeds should be drawn up for them with regard to their estates.' The Cossacks listed their rights as individuals and as a group; they made no demand for new law, and had no thought of a Cossack State. The tsar's envoys were requested to take an oath that these rights would be maintained. When they refused, and the Cossacks reminded them that 'the kings of Poland always swore an oath to their subjects', the Moscow boyars explained: 'never has it been demanded that sovereigns (*gosudari*) should take an oath to their subjects. And as concerns [the fact] that the kings of Poland used to swear an oath to their subjects, it is improper to quote this as an example, since these kings are heretics and are not autocrats (*samoderzhtsy*).' Thus Moscow expressly repudiated any treaty relationship, any partnership between equals. It guaranteed the specific rights that had existed under Polish rule, but did so as an act of grace by the tsar in favour of certain individuals and social groups.

The Cossacks were not simply incorporated into Russia as subjects, since the hetman was allowed to exchange embassies with other countries—although not with the most important States, Turkey and Poland, and all such exchanges had to be reported to Moscow. Thus even in the sphere of foreign policy the Cossacks enjoyed no genuine sovereignty; one could best regard them as having been incorporated into Russia with confirmation of their rights of military self-government. They actually continued to enjoy a far-reaching *de facto* autonomy because the central government was only able to assert itself gradually in the Ukraine.

Moscow had first to defend Kiev and the regained territories against Poland. The war began in May 1654. Russian armies captured Gomel', Mogilev and Polotsk; in September Smolensk capitulated, and in November Vitebsk was taken by storm. In 1655 the succession of victories continued. Minsk and Wilno (Vilna), the Lithuanian capital, were conquered in July, by which time the Cossacks, having taken Ostróg, Równo, Turów and Pinsk, had reached the gates of Lwów. Poland was also attacked by the Swedes who were concerned at Russian expansion in Lithuania. Swedish troops occupied Dvinsk, before which the Russians were already encamped. Sweden and Russia, after first pursuing a parallel policy, inevitably came into conflict. Invading the kingdom of Poland, the Swedes compelled Poznań, Kalisz and Warsaw to recognise their sovereignty. The king left the country; the power of Poland seemed destroyed. In the summer of 1656 Russia's policy changed: after concluding an offensive alliance against Sweden with Denmark and a security treaty with Brandenburg, she entered into peace talks with Poland. Though these negotiations broke down over Russia's demands (for cession of Lithuania and acceptance of the tsar as king of Poland on the death of John Casimir), they did lead, in October, to an armistice: all unsettled questions were temporarily shelved and agreement was reached on military collaboration. The main Russian army seized Dvinsk from the Swedes and then captured Dorpat; but the siege of Riga (August to October) failed, since the town was supplied by sea. In the meantime Poland had time to recover: the people rose *en masse*, and the king was able to return. In the winter of 1657–8 Poland and Russia resumed peace negotiations, but without result.

In the Ukraine the death of Chmel'nyćkyj (July 1657) was followed by disturbances which were extremely disadvantageous for Russia: under their new hetman, Ivan Vygovsky, the Cossacks went over to Poland. By the Treaty of Hadziacz (September 1658) Poland promised an extension of the Polish-Lithuanian Union of Lublin (1569) to the Ukraine: the palatinates of Bratslav, Kiev and Chernigov were to be included in the Polish State as a 'Grand Duchy of Russia'; the figure of registered Cossacks was to remain at 60,000; the hetman was to be chosen from candidates nominated by the Cossacks; their representatives were to sit in the senate; they were to have their own administration and currency; and the Orthodox were to enjoy the same rights as other Christians. In November 1658, under the influence of this dangerous turn of events, Moscow concluded a three-year armistice with Sweden. Despite the favourable terms of the Treaty of Hadziacz, the Cossack rank and file remained loyal to Russia; in October 1659 they elected as hetman Chmel'nyćkyj's son Yury, a partisan of Moscow. In contrast to Poland, Moscow imposed conditions harsher than those of 1654: the election and deposition of a hetman required the tsar's consent; his diplomatic rights were rescinded; he could only pass sentence upon a Cossack leader with Moscow's approval, and the Cossacks were granted the right of direct appeal to the tsar; the rank and file had to be consulted when filling senior appointments in the Cossack administration; tsarist voivodes were introduced into the chief townships in Cossack territory; and the Cossack army could henceforward be employed on military service by the tsar without any limitations.

Even the hetmanate of Yury Chmel'nyćkyj, however, did not give Moscow a firm hold over the Ukraine. His vacillating attitude was all the more dangerous once Poland, after the Peace of Oliva (1660),[1] was in a position to concentrate all her forces against Russia. This prompted Moscow to conclude with Sweden the Peace of Kardis (June 1661), in which she recognised the former Russo-Swedish frontier, while Sweden undertook not to intervene in the Russo-Polish war. Though now safe from the risk of attack in the north, Russia was unable to maintain her position in Poland, and Polish troops pressed back across the Dnieper into Novgorod-Seversk. In the Ukraine fighting broke out between rival hetmans. The most capable of them, Petr Dorošenko, decided in October 1666 to place himself and his Cossacks under the Khan of the Crimea. Against this background the Russo-Polish peace talks, resumed in the summer of 1666, led to the conclusion of an armistice at Andrusovo in January 1667. It was to last for 13½ years, during which a 'perpetual peace' was to be prepared; Russia retained Smolensk; Poland recognised Moscow's sovereignty over the Ukraine to the east of the Dnieper, while the western Ukraine and White Russia remained Polish; Kiev, together with some territory on the right bank of the Dnieper, was ceded to Russia

[1] See above, ch. XXIV, p. 568.

for two years; the Zaporog *sech'* was to be administered jointly by Poland and Russia.

The war, which the Cossacks had begun to consolidate their military and political organisation under the protection of one of the neighbouring powers, ended in their being divided between them. The Cossacks failed in their attempt to unite the area on the borders of Muscovite Russia, Poland and the Tatar Crimea into a single State. Apart from this local significance, the war had an effect upon the general situation in eastern Europe. While Sweden maintained her position as a great power, Poland lost hers. The Polish State was hollowed out from within by its obsolete structure, and this created a vacuum which attracted Poland's neighbours. Complete catastrophe had been averted only by the conflict between Russia and Sweden. Russia had shown herself incapable of waging a two-front war: she was neither able to consolidate her position in Poland nor to break through to the Baltic, but her offensive did bring her the strategically important frontier on the Dnieper and the old Russian capital of Kiev, a significant gain. The Russians did not evacuate Kiev, and Poland was unable to assert her rights because even under the brilliant military leadership of John Sobieski (1674–96) she could not prevail over the Turks, whose advance also threatened Russia, in particular during the reign of Alexis's successor, Feodor Alexeievich (1676–82). After 1676 Dorošenko, under pressure from the rank-and-file Cossacks, ceased his resistance to Moscow, with the result that the western Ukraine also came under Russian sway; but the Turks asserted their claim to the Ukraine in two successful campaigns (1677–8), in which their forces reached Chigirin. In 1681 Russia had to recognise Turkish rights to the Ukraine west of the Dnieper, with the exception of Kiev. The armistice of Andrusovo thus did not bring Poland any aid from Moscow, nor did the victory at Vienna in 1683[1] bring her relief. Sobieski's plan of regaining for Poland her old greatness as a bulwark of Christendom by forming an anti-Turkish coalition with the Empire, Venice and the papal curia required, if it were to be successful, the inclusion of Russia. Sobieski reluctantly decided to obtain Russia's adherence to the alliance by converting the armistice of Andrusovo into a 'perpetual peace'. In April 1686 Poland finally renounced Kiev and the Ukraine east of the Dnieper and undertook to grant her Orthodox subjects religious freedom. Russia paid a compensation of 1,460,000 gold roubles and promised to provide military assistance against the Turks. It was only with this treaty, concluded during the regency of the tsarina Sophia (1682–9), that the achievements of Alexis's policy were made secure.

The acquisition of strength and territory brought in its train a broadening of Moscow's political horizons. In 1645 Alexis notified his accession only to neighbouring Poland and Sweden and to Russia's old commercial

[1] See above, ch. XXI, pp. 516–17.

partners, England, Holland and Denmark. In 1673 Moscow for the first time put forward the idea of a European coalition, in view of the danger threatening from Turkey. The move failed, owing to Russia's ignorance of the situation at western courts; it nevertheless showed how she was extending her diplomatic contacts: the Emperor, Brandenburg, Saxony, Venice, the papal curia, France, and Spain were now added to the States mentioned earlier. Yet Russia was still a passive rather than an active participant in European affairs. Whereas Sweden, Denmark, Poland and Holland maintained permanent representatives in Russia (from 1631, 1672, 1673 and 1677 respectively), she was represented only in Poland (from 1673). However great the importance of trade with Russia for her commercial partners in northern Europe, by and large Russia still lay outside the European political system and its shifting alliances, partly on account of distance, and partly because in the West her faith was regarded as heretical and her form of government as despotic. Accounts of the country by western travellers, ever more frequent during the seventeenth century, did little to modify this view until, to a more rationalist age, the differences of religion and historical background became less potent. Russia knew far less about the political situation in the West. The first man to gather information systematically about foreign countries and to expand contact with them was Ordyn-Nashchokin, head of the Office of Ambassadors (*posol'skiy prikaz*) from 1667 to 1671. He considered it expedient to make borrowings from abroad, attempted to escape from traditional prejudices, and sought to conduct relations with Poland on the basis of *Realpolitik*—a policy with Slav unity as the ultimate goal.

The nature of Moscow's foreign policy was dictated by her internal weakness. The country had not yet recovered from the Time of Troubles (1605–13) and the government's approach was thus necessarily defensive. At home the autocracy continued on the course followed since the sixteenth century: a policy of centralising the administration, building up a strong military machine, and creating various social classes which could be controlled by the State and had to perform State services. Foreign invasions had shown the necessity of an effective army to protect Russia's extended frontiers. The Troubles had also demonstrated the military superiority of her neighbours and brought home the need of modernising the army on a European pattern, by engaging foreign instructors and mercenaries and by importing and manufacturing equipment and supplies. Between 1632 and 1680 Russia's active fighting force grew from 34,600 to 129,300 (the total strength in that year amounting to some 170,000 to 190,000 men).

The most aristocratic element in the army—though one whose relative importance declined from 34 to 8 per cent of the total strength during these years—was the traditional levies supplied by the court, the capital ('Moscow'), the provincial and the Tatar nobility. The nobility held estates on full or conditional tenure and were obliged to perform services upon succeeding to their property. Service was also obligatory for the garrison troops, the archers (*strel'tsy*), artillerymen and Cossack fortress guards, who lived in special quarters of the towns and maintained themselves by agriculture or crafts, with the benefit of tax privileges. In addition to these groups came the so-called *datochnye lyudi*, soldiers 'given' by ecclesiastical lands and the court and State domains. From these lands, as from those of the service nobility, the number of men to be provided was determined at first by the acreage, but later (ultimately from 1679), owing to the varying density of population, by the number of homesteads. For service of a specialised nature there were foreign mercenaries, Russian troops under foreign officers, which at the same time acted as model troops, and the Cossacks for frontier protection. Russia was moving towards the creation of a standing army: the introduction of a permanent officer corps, military settlements and drill were steps calculated to enhance the army's striking power. The offices concerned with the control of service obligations and the allotment of estates (*razryadnyy* and *pomestnyy prikaz*) were amongst the most ancient central administrative organs. To these, other offices were added in the course of the seventeenth century to deal with the various specialised units and with military equipment.

The autocracy owed its rapid rise at the end of the fifteenth century to the absence of Estates of the realm such as existed in western Europe. Already in the sixteenth century it had attempted, with the support of the serving nobility and the bureaucracy, to impose State service upon society. This basic trend of development led, in the seventeenth century, to the creation of centrally controlled service classes, each of which had its specific duties towards the State, without any corresponding rights to exercise political influence. This creation of distinct social groups at the behest of the State differed radically from the western European pattern of autonomous Estates based upon birth, privileges and legal traditions, conscious of their ancient political rights and special local status. The Russian State insisted on clearly differentiating between the classes which served it, not from respect for their legal status, but from concern that each should perform its allotted tasks: the nobility had to serve in the army and administration, the peasants had to enable them to do so by rendering labour services and paying taxes, and the townspeople above all had to provide revenue. The danger existed that some individual might escape the burdens of State service by becoming unfree and dependent upon someone else. In order to prevent this shrinking of its servitors, the State sought to enforce individual freedom by legislative action.

The influx of new families into the service nobility during the Troubles had given a new lease of life to the practice of *mestnichestvo*, whereby a noble, on being assigned a State post, would compare the proposed appointment with those held in the past by his superiors and his and their ancestors, and would refuse to serve if he considered it inferior to what he was entitled to by his rank. Already in the sixteenth century this custom had demonstrated its perniciousness, especially in the filling of commanding posts in the army during campaigns, but the constant disputes within the nobility had helped the autocracy to consolidate its power. In the seventeenth century the autocracy, wielding uncontested authority, could devote itself to combating the harmful aspects of *mestnichestvo*: with increasing frequency it was suspended during campaigns, until it was eventually abolished by a decree of January 1682. The distinction between estates held on full tenure (*votchiny*) and those held conditionally (*pomest'ya*) disappeared, since owners of either were required to serve, and *pomest'ya* could be inherited. Apart from the Church and monasteries only the service nobility were permitted to possess lands with peasants, and in 1649 the Church was forbidden to extend its holdings. Already in 1642 impoverished noblemen were prohibited from becoming the servitors of more prosperous noblemen; in 1649 the government also banned the practice of 'pledging' oneself (*zakladnichestvo*, that is, agreeing to work for a creditor until one had repaid a loan), which often led to permanent serfdom for the pledger as well as his descendants.

To make it economically possible for the nobility to serve, their peasants were tied to the land. Without labour, land was worthless. The free peasant, impoverished by heavy taxation, sought to escape by fleeing to the border areas, by settling on the estate of a more prosperous landowner who could pay his debts and afford him better conditions, or by binding himself and his family by contract to serve a master until the latter's death (*kabal'noye kholopstvo*). The latter practice often led to his service becoming hereditary, so that the distinction between free and unfree peasants became blurred. Another way in which this could come about was through landowners, faced as they were with a constant shortage of labour, settling their unfree menials on the land as peasants (*zadvornye lyudi*). As early as 1592 the government had attempted to prevent peasants from escaping, or being bought out by landowners, by establishing a legal term within which peasants had to be returned to their former owners. This time-limit, re-established after the Troubles, was annulled in 1649. Henceforward any owner could secure the return of a runaway peasant at any time. Thus the peasants were bound to their masters. The revision of the survey registers (*pistsovye knigi*) in the 1620's, which determined the tax assessments in rural districts and in the towns, had the same effect: it was naturally in the interests of a community to prevent any of its taxpaying members from leaving. All these circumstances combined in making the Russian peasant a serf by the mid-seventeenth century. The government had sought only to tie the peasants to the soil, not to reduce them to serfdom. Thus, from this time until the nineteenth century, the State refrained from interfering with the personal relations between a master and his dependants, although its own measures, designed to create a service nobility, had been to a large extent responsible for the development of serfdom.

The townspeople, likewise, were turned into a service class. Russian towns were small and poor, did not possess the immunity or the privileges enjoyed by the towns of western Europe, and were not clearly differentiated from the villages. Within the town, not all plots of land were 'black', that is, subject to taxation; they were 'white' if, for instance, they belonged to some boyar or monastery outside the town. There were houses which became 'white' through their owners becoming unfree dependants of a lord outside the town, but the owners continued to engage in crafts or trade, contributed nothing to the town's revenue, and even undermined the urban economy by competition. Equally, artisans living in the immediate vicinity of a town took part in its economic life without assuming any share of its fiscal obligations. Already during the preceding reign the government had attempted to remedy this state of affairs. In 1649 it was decreed that only taxpayers could live in the towns and carry on their trade; they were prohibited from leaving the town, and all property from which no taxes were paid was incorporated into the towns. In Russia it was not a strong class of burghers, but the State which separated the towns from the countryside and formed them—but without granting the municipal liberties characteristic of medieval western Europe. The uppermost group in the urban population, the wealthy merchants (*gosti*), who in the mid-seventeenth century numbered about thirty, were State functionaries rather than private entrepreneurs. They came under the direct jurisdiction of the tsar and administered on his behalf the customs, the iron trade and liquor monopolies, and the revenue from Siberian sables. They enjoyed fiscal privileges, but answered with their property for any losses incurred. Below the *gosti*, as their partners and agents, came the members of the organisations of less wealthy merchants, the *gostinnaya* and *sukhonnaya sotnya*. They, too, had to perform tasks on behalf of the Treasury. Thus it was only the State and the handful of *gosti* who disposed of any considerable amount of capital.

Owing to the lack of demand and the prevailing natural economy, the domestic market was generally limited in area and not particularly profitable. Foreign trade held out the prospect of better returns, but it was mainly in the hands of foreigners (Englishmen, Dutchmen, Germans, Frenchmen and Danes) or agents of the tsar. Russia imported manufactures of every kind, especially metal goods, arms, cloth and luxuries, and exported raw materials, such as wood, pitch, hemp, flax, potash, furs and hides. The first ironworks and cannon foundries, as well as the first mines, owed their establishment to foreign entrepreneurs. The government promoted their activity because of the revenue it yielded and the example it set, and constantly sought to recruit technicians from abroad. From the 1620's onwards Russian merchants were continually complaining about the competition of foreigners, who were better organised and had more capital. The government responded with mercantilist measures. In 1649 the English were once more deprived of their privileges, some of which dated back to the sixteenth century, and again lost the right of engaging in the transit trade with Asia. The commercial statute of 1654 abolished almost all internal tolls and protected merchants from interference by local officials. In 1667 a 'New Commercial Statute' restricted trade by foreigners to certain frontier points and fixed higher dues, payable in foreign currency, for permission to engage in internal or transit trade. The standing ban on foreigners conducting retail trade, which was continually circumvented, was now reaffirmed under penalty of confiscation of goods, and duty-free trade between foreign merchants was prohibited.

The only genuine Estate in society was the clergy, who formed a separate, legally defined entity and had their own representation in the patriarchate. But they also had to pay tax upon, and provide troops from, their secular property and were subject to regimentation by the State.

The Russian administration can be called centralised in so far as the ultimate responsibility for decisions lay with the tsar and the highest authorities (*prikazy*) situated in Moscow; but one can hardly speak of centralisation according to function. During the seventeenth century the *prikazy* multiplied and became more differentiated, but they were not systematised according to any theoretical plan, and there was no clearly defined hierarchy of authority or allocation of competence between the various offices. It may be assumed that business in a *prikaz* was to a large extent managed by the boyar in charge; but the tsar would often entrust a boyar with several *prikazy* at once, and the differentiation became obscured. Some *prikazy* dealt with a particular topic, others with a particular region. A *prikaz* would often concern itself with matters which were hardly related at all, or which had only been related in the past; on the other hand, the same matter might be dealt with by several institutions. In the 1680's military affairs, for example, were the concern of no less than eighteen *prikazy*. Almost all the more important *prikazy* had their separate financial administration and exercised judicial authority over their own personnel. In addition to the permanent offices for foreign affairs, military and financial matters, the administration of the court, etc., there were others which were subordinate or temporary, for example, for collecting money and grain in time of war. In Alexis's reign there were some forty *prikazy*, but the figure varied, since offices would be set up, combined, or dissolved according to need.

The Siberian Office, carved out of that for Kazan' in 1637, was temporarily incorporated into the Main Revenue Office between 1661 and 1663. Similarly, matters concerning Little Russia were after 1649 first dealt with in the Office of Ambassadors, a separate office being established only in 1663. In 1649 the department for ecclesiastical affairs in the Main Court Office became an independent body, the Monasteries Office. Thus all the judicial privileges which the Church had gradually accumulated were abolished, except for the patriarch's jurisdiction over his own immediate domain. The Monasteries Office, at first directed jointly by churchmen and laymen, soon came to be manned by laymen alone; it supervised the Church's finances and its jurisdiction in secular matters. The Church resented this control and in 1677 obtained its suspension. To the military departments (for the *strel'tsy*, Cossacks, artillerymen and serving foreigners) there was added, in 1651, a Cavalry Office. The judicial offices for cases involving serving men in the districts of Moscow, Ryazan', Vladimir, and Dmitrov were integrated in 1685 into the Moscow Judicial Office. Amongst the new departments was the *prikaz schetnykh del* for financial supervision, founded in 1667, and the supreme organ of control, the Office of Secret Affairs. This was not only the tsar's private chancery, dealing with his personal affairs (correspondence, falconry, etc.) and solely responsible to him; it was also responsible for control and espionage within the administration, indispensable in any autocracy; its competence was not circumscribed.

The isolation and threat to which individual districts had been exposed during the Troubles led to the concentration of all authority in the hands of the local military commander, the voivode. Administration by voivodes became universal during the seventeenth century. The voivode, generally a member of the service nobility, exercised power over a district (*uyezd*) from its principal centre, to which he was assigned by the central government with specific instructions and was in charge of all local administrative matters. His short tenure of office (from one to three years), and the fact that he received a salary from the central authority, distinguished the voivode from his predecessor, the 'lieutenant' (*namestnik*) of the sixteenth century, who had to be provided for locally—although even now there were continual complaints about extorted 'gifts' to the voivode. Occasionally the government took notice of such grievances, but there was no permanent control over the voivodes. By the mid-seventeenth century there existed more than 250 districts. Most voivodes administered their districts from an office in conjunction with a secretary (*d'yak*) responsible for current business. In larger districts there were from two to four voivodes, one of whom was senior to the others, and several *d'yaki*: thus the government hoped to establish mutual supervision, which was naturally not conducive to amicable co-operation.

The voivode administration was superimposed upon the institutions of local self-government which existed since the latter half of the sixteenth century. The voivode was given authority over the representatives elected by the peasants and townsmen: the *gubnye starosty* and *tseloval'niki*, who exercised police and penal functions, and those with general administrative competence (*zemskiye starosty*, *lutchiye lyudi*). As a rule the voivodes, as agents of the central power, turned the local self-governing institutions into subordinate executive organs. Thus self-government continued to exist, but in effect as a part of the State administration—the more so because since the sixteenth century self-government had become not a right but an obligation towards the State. Therefore the government could even afford to dispense temporarily with the voivodes, as it did in the 1660's, returning to this system in the following decade.

The establishment of large administrative regions (*razryady*) illustrates the prevailing tendency towards the creation of a system of local government as standardised and as closely linked to the centre as possible. This process originated in frontier areas where the co-ordination of military and general civil functions was particularly important. The Tula *razryad*, which had existed from the sixteenth century, was reformed in 1663 into the *razryad* of Belgorod, in accordance with the extension of the frontier southwards. *Razryady* were established at an early date in Siberia, and the war with Poland and Sweden brought about their institution in Smolensk, Novgorod, and Sevsk (1654, 1655, 1665). Later in the seventeenth century they were also introduced into the central districts of the country (Moscow, Vladimir, Tambov, Ryazan' and Kazan'). This created the outline of an administrative hierarchy, since the local voivodes were made subordinate to those of the *razryady* (or to the chief voivodes); but the system remained anything but uniform: the voivodes were responsible to various *prikazy*; the *razryady* did not cover the whole country; and many voivodes still communicated directly with the centre. The problem of strengthening local government whilst maintaining central control remained a crucial one for Russia, with its vast territory, until recently.

The building up of a centralised, salaried administration and a modernised standing army, and finally the long wars, imposed financial burdens which the country's agrarian economy could not carry. Taxation was assessed according to the *sokha*, re-established in the 1620's, a unit which took account of the area of land possessed or (in the towns) the size of the homesteads; it varied both according to the quality of the land or the state of one's trade, and according to the class of service. In 1646 and 1678 the entire male population was registered—a sign of the importance attached to manpower, as distinct from ownership of land. From 1679 onwards taxes were levied not upon arable land, but upon each homestead. The government raised dues, introduced indirect taxes, issued regulations and used military force, all of which served to augment popular discontent. In 1646 the salt-tax was quadrupled, but the fall in receipts showed that the tax-bearing capacity of the population was overstrained.

Discontent at the heavy fiscal burdens and the arbitrary methods of the evergrowing bureaucracy arose, as was to be expected, in the towns. In June 1648 Moscow was the scene of violent disturbances lasting several days, in which the townspeople were joined by the *strel'tsy*. Several high officials lost their lives, and the boyar V. I. Morozov, the tsar's brother-in-law and tutor, who exercised paramount political influence, had to give up his post temporarily. Similar revolts against excessive taxation and the extortion practised by dishonest officials occurred in many other towns. The immediate causes were varied, and the disturbances remained local, but the revolt in Pskov in February 1650 represented a political threat to the government. Linking up with Novgorod, and mobilising the surrounding countryside in their support, the inhabitants of Pskov for three months withstood a siege by government troops; their demands aimed at greater local autonomy.

At the beginning of the Polish war the government provoked a further crisis by debasing the silver coinage and minting copper coins at a forced rate of exchange. To make matters worse, the officials did not hinder the private minting of copper coins. The value of the copper rouble fell, especially since the government and foreign merchants demanded to be paid in silver. In 1660 one silver rouble was worth two, but in 1663 fifteen, copper roubles. In July 1662, after handbills had circulated in Moscow, a revolt broke out. Popular anger was directed against the highest officials around the throne and threatened even the tsar himself. The brutality with which the disturbances were suppressed revealed the government's helplessness and undermined its reputation.

The people sought in their usual fashion to escape from the pressure of the central power by fleeing to the border areas, particularly to the region of the Don. As the Don Cossacks, formerly free and untrammelled, were hemmed in by the Turks who, after the Azov affair, had sealed off the mouth of the Don, the Cossacks raided the area of the lower Volga, in Muscovite territory. In 1668 the Cossack leader Stepan Razin embarked upon a spectacular campaign of plunder, which extended into Persian territory on the Caspian Sea. In 1670 he turned against Moscow. In April, with 7000 men, he took Tsaritsyn, in June the well-fortified city of Astrakhan, in July Saratov and Samara. Some troops went over to Razin. In September Razin's advance came to a halt before Simbirsk, although some of his detachments reached the district of Nizhny Novgorod; but with the relief of Simbirsk in October by government forces his aura of invincibility disappeared. In April 1671 Razin was seized by Cossacks in the Don area, handed over to Moscow and executed in June. The great threat which the rebellion presented to the government lay in the fact that Razin's appearance provoked similar risings throughout the east of European Russia, from the Donets in the south to Galich (near Vologda) in the north. Cossacks, fugitive peasants, unpaid mercenaries, impoverished noblemen, even village priests and non-

Russian nomads flocked to Razin, whilst local uprisings broke out against hated landowners and officials. The constant unparalleled pressure exerted by the State had unleashed a struggle against State authority of any kind. In his appeals Razin called upon the people to fight for the 'good tsar' against the 'traitorous' boyars, voivodes and officials. His political programme was confined to the introduction of the primitive Cossack administration; it contained no principle which went beyond that of the existing State. Understandable though this desperate revolt was against the background of hopeless misery, it was nevertheless anarchic and, compared with the autocracy, retrogressive.

The government attempted to check administrative arbitrariness by codifying the laws and, especially, judicial procedure. After the Moscow rising of June 1648 a government commission began to compile a code of law, which was laid before an assembly (*zemsky sobor*) in September and completed by January 1649.[1] The commission's draft and the proposals of the various groups were thoroughly discussed. This code (*ulozheniye*), the first to be printed (in an edition of 2000 copies), came into force at once. Its twenty-five chapters contained 967 articles. It was not drafted according to systematic legal principles, but was a codification of selected legal traditions to which were added some innovations due to political expediency. Since the last legal code of 1550 successive tsars had issued a large number of decrees (*ukazy*) having the force of law, known only to the relevant *prikazy* where they were kept. These decrees, the code of 1550, the main maxims received from Byzantine law, and the Lithuanian Statute, a compilation of ancient Russian law with some western elements, formed the basis of the new code concerning the political and social order and legal procedure. Mention has already been made of its most important provisions: the segregation of the service classes, the abolition of the peasants' right to leave and to give themselves in pledge, and the establishment of the Monasteries Office. Apart from these, the *ulozheniye* was important on account of the detailed provisions designed to secure impartial administration of justice, to which 287 articles were devoted, and because it brought uniformity into existing law and made it more widely known. It did not contain a definition of legal concepts, nor was it comprehensive. The absence of a tradition of Roman law and of a class of lawyers trained in this tradition decisively hindered legal development in the legislative and administrative spheres.

In particular, there was no definition of the autocracy itself. After the Time of Troubles the traditional concept of the ruler was revived: he was the source of all judicial, administrative and political decisions, the owner of the country and the protector of the Church; his authority was neither limited by law nor by the existence of Estates with their own privileges. As in the sixteenth century, the autocrat remained the embodiment of the

[1] For the *zemsky sobor*, see below, p. 586.

State; nevertheless, the autocracy did now possess more pronounced institutional features, which made it more independent of the personality of the individual ruler. Russia's disintegration during the Troubles deepened the traditional view of the autocratic power of the tsar into a hope for a strong State above the contending factions. The consolidation of the autocracy gave Russia a firm central authority, but one where all the political initiative came from the State. The tsar continued to be assisted in the work of government by a consultative and executive body, the council (*duma*) of boyars. In 1668 the council had a membership of sixty-eight, who were nominated by the tsar for life. Only twenty-six, however, came from the ancient and important boyar families; most of them were 'new men', some of whom did not even belong to the service nobility. Here, as elsewhere, State service was coming to replace tradition and birth as the criterion for advancement.

Characteristic of the 'restorationist' autocratic tendency in Russia's internal development was the decline of the national assembly (*zemsky sobor*). During Michael's reign it had been convoked relatively frequently, and it might have developed into a political institution representing Russian society. But in Alexis's reign it met only seldom: in 1648–9 to discuss the *ulozheniye*, in 1650 to decide the measures to be adopted against Pskov, and in 1651 and 1653 to discuss policy with regard to Poland and the Ukraine. The *sobor*, convoked as required by the tsar, consisted of the tsar, the council of boyars, the ecclesiastical synod, and deputies elected by the lower nobility and the towns. No fixed rules existed to determine the *sobor's* composition or activity. The number of participants varied, reaching a peak in 1648 with 290 elected deputies; the peasants were not represented, and neither, in 1650, were the provincial towns. Deliberations were either in common or, as in 1648–9, separate for elected and *ex officio* members. The deputies apparently brought no instructions from their electors; their function was consultative, but could on occasion assume a legislative character, as in the framing of the *ulozheniye* or the decision to annex the Ukraine. The decision always rested with the tsar and the *duma*. Without periodicity or definition of election and procedure, the *sobor* was unable to represent consistently the interests of individual social groups, let alone those of the people, against the government—especially because it was itself part of the *sobor*. Participation in the assembly's deliberations was a duty, not a right. After 1653 the government only summoned committees of experts with advisory functions, and the *sobory* faded out.

During Alexis's reign one attempt was in effect made to limit the autocracy—by Patriarch Nikon. The son of a peasant, he gained Alexis's favour and rose with astonishing rapidity, becoming metropolitan of Novgorod in 1648 and four years later, at the age of 47, patriarch. The young impressionable Alexis at first venerated the strong-willed, zealous and eloquent Nikon like a father and accorded him a position similar to that held by Filaret under his son Michael: he received the title of 'Great Sovereign' (*Velikiy Gosudar'*), generally reserved for the tsars alone; his name appeared after that of the tsar in State documents; and it was he who was given charge of the government in 1654 whilst the tsar was absent during the Polish campaign. He earned the hatred of churchmen and laymen alike on account of his limitless ambition, and particularly his aim of elevating the patriarch above the tsar. When, in July 1658, the tsar formally deprived him of his title of Sovereign, he withdrew to the Monastery of the Resurrection near Moscow. Alexis, who approved of Nikon's reforming activity, wished to retain him as patriarch, whilst restricting his authority to purely ecclesiastical matters; but Nikon would neither recognise any secular limitation upon his ecclesiastical office nor resign as patriarch. This uncertain situation lasted from 1658 to 1667, during which time Nikon formulated more clearly his earlier views on the supremacy of the ecclesiastical over the secular power, the derivation of the latter from the former, and the separation of Church and State. This undermined the traditional Russian idea, inherited from the Byzantine Nomokanon and Epanagoge, of the ruler as protector of the Church and of 'symphony' between Church and State. In Russia, as in Byzantium, there had always been a sharp dividing-line between the spheres of piety and politics, unlike the West, where faith and action in the world of realities were inseparably interconnected; but in law the Eastern Church had no precisely defined dominion within which it was master, as it had evolved in western Europe during the Middle Ages.

It was not surprising, therefore, that Nikon should be accused of papism, especially since he recognised the achievements of the papacy in maintaining its position *vis-à-vis* secular rulers and, echoing Innocent III, compared the Church to the sun and the State to the moon, which obtained its light from the former. In particular he attacked the establishment, by the *ulozheniye*, of the Monasteries Office, which involved the subjection of the Church to secular jurisdiction in non-ecclesiastical matters, and the ban on further land grants to the Church.[1] As early as February 1660 an ecclesiastical council, attended by Russian prelates only, declared Nikon to have forfeited his office, but this resolution was not put into effect. A further Russian council was held in 1666; it paved the way for an oecumenical council (November–December 1666), attended by the patriarchs of Alexandria and Antioch, representatives of the patriarchs of Constantinople and Jerusalem, and the metropolitan of Serbia. Nikon was solemnly deprived of his patriarchal dignities, on the grounds that he had disrespectfully made baseless charges against the tsar and his council of boyars, failed to carry out the obligations of his office, and acted in an un-Christian fashion towards his clergy. The council agreed that the tsar

[1] See above, pp. 579, 582, 585.

could not alter the traditional rights and customs of the Church, but that the Church was subordinate to him in all secular matters. Thus the Russian Church was again confined within its traditional spiritual sphere, and the autocrat assured of his right to participate in deciding secular matters of the Church.

This council, in a second session (February–June 1667), confirmed Nikon's 'reforms'; these originated in the desire of responsible churchmen, stimulated by the experience of the Troubles, to eliminate the formalism in religious observance, the ignorance of the clergy, and the moral degeneration amongst laity, priests and monks. The situation was particularly acute because the Russian Church was faced, as never before, by the challenge of other Christian creeds: Protestantism chiefly in the central districts, as a result of the contact with foreigners from northern Europe, and Catholicism in the south-western border areas. This gave rise to doubts amongst the Orthodox themselves: there were Uniates and sectarians, and the subordination of Kiev to the patriarch of Constantinople had led to a strengthening of Greek influences. With the establishment of the Moscow patriarchate by the patriarch of Constantinople in 1589, the Muscovite hierarchy could no longer accuse the Greek Church of betraying Orthodoxy. The uniqueness of Moscow's position as the depository of the true faith, the Third Rome, was narrowed down to the claim that it was the only Sovereign Orthodox State. There now developed a burning question: how did the idiosyncrasies of theology and custom that had developed in the Russian Church, since it had become autocephalous in 1448, stand in relation to the Greek Church? For the first time the Russian Church, for which tradition had always been decisive, had to formulate and defend the true faith against Churches with a stronger theological foundation. All the reformers agreed upon the need for a more profound attitude to religion and morals; what was in dispute was whether this should be realised within the framework of the Muscovite ecclesiastical tradition or through adaptation to the Greek Church. The traditionalists put their trust in a renewal from within of the old Muscovite faith. The Graecophil group thought it essential to go back to the—as they thought—more ancient, and thus correct, Greek tradition. But the traditionalists regarded any changes on the Greek model as innovations, whilst to the Graecophils the preservation of Muscovite liturgical usages seemed an act of defiance against the oecumenical Church. Both groups were rooted in tradition. The State supported assimilation to the traditions of the Greek Church, a prerequisite of Moscow's leading position within the Orthodox world, and essential for the spread of education in Russia which the State sought to promote.

Around Alexis there gathered a group of Graecophil reformers, who dispatched to the provinces priests distinguished for their piety and strict morals. Their sharp criticism of the laxity and indiscipline common amongst clergy and laity frequently led to persecution. As far as their theological education was concerned, these priests were simple people who clung to the Muscovite tradition and thus soon drifted into opposition to the better-educated Graecophil reformers in Moscow. Already Patriarch Iosif (1642–51) consciously desired an approximation to Constantinople, and during his tenure of office scholars were brought to Moscow from Kiev, then the centre of Orthodox learning. It was the great contribution of the Ukraine to seventeenth-century Russian history that, having acquired the elements of religious and secular education through controversy with the rich literature of Catholics and Uniates, it transmitted this knowledge to Muscovy and stimulated the establishment of colleges and the compilation of textbooks, sermons and apologetics. In 1651 Iosif was obliged to resign because he opposed the reformers' demand for the abolition of polyphony (*mnogoglasie*) in the Muscovite liturgy, that is, the practice of curtailing the inordinately lengthy liturgy by reciting the various parts simultaneously. Although Iosif authorised the abolition of this senseless formality in monasteries, he refused to do so in ordinary churches, since the length of the liturgy, if recited in full, would have deterred the church-goers. It was significant that the reformers sought the sanction of the eastern patriarchs; Iosif's place was taken by Nikon.

Nikon, once a traditionalist, later a member of the group of reformers at court, now took over the leadership of the Graecophil reform party. The despotic manner in which he carried out by decree the assimilation of the Russian Church to the Greek helped to intensify opposition amongst the traditionalists; but the stubbornness of their resistance can only be explained by the ritualist character of Muscovite piety and its magic conception of rites—for the absence of any theology had endowed tradition with sanctity. On the other hand, Nikon was concerned, not with deepening religious feeling, but with replacing the ritualism of Moscow with Greek rites which he interpreted in the same formalistic manner (making the sign of the cross with three fingers instead of two, as prescribed by the Moscow Council of 1551, singing three hallelujahs instead of two, reducing the sixteen genuflexions in the Great Lenten prayer to four, removing the four-pointed Latin cross from communion wafers, and destroying icons painted in the Latin manner). The faithful were horrified not only by these and other trivial changes in the rites, but also by the fact that ancient religious works, chiefly service-books, were repudiated if they differed from the Greek originals; in 1655 a new liturgy was introduced. Nikon's reforms were endorsed by the crucial councils of 1666 and 1667, the second of which annulled the decisions of the council of 1551 and excommunicated those who adhered to the old Muscovite rites.

The hierarchy had brought about a schism (*raskol*). The Old Believers (*starovertsy*), as they came to be called, were expelled on account of differences of ritual, not of dogma. Even after Nikon's deposition they were persecuted cruelly by Church and State. Some stoically accepted the penalties inflicted upon them; others fled into the wilderness or to the border, or even set fire to their prayer-houses, perishing in the flames. The most moving literary monument of the Old Believers is the life of the priest Avvakum, the first autobiography in Russian literature, which depicts vividly the passion of the sufferer wrestling with his soul. The most notable physical resistance was offered by the monks of the Solovetsky monastery, who held out against government troops from 1668 to 1676. In many places the protest of the Old Believers intensified and gave a religious meaning to social discontent. In their eyes patriarch and tsar appeared as agents of Antichrist, whose rule had visibly begun. Eschatological tracts were widely distributed, announcing the end of the world. Indeed, for Russia the end had come of a world rooted in sanctified tradition.

The *raskol* was more than a mere conflict within the Church. Until the seventeenth century the Church had been the sole intellectual force in Russia; it had taken over from the Byzantine Church its pure transcendental orientation and its monasticism, though without the complement of a secular culture based on the heritage of antiquity. The Russian Church had not attempted to state its faith or explain the outer world in theoretical terms and had developed neither a theology nor standards by which to judge the existing historical and political reality. As a result tradition had become the guiding principle in religious and secular life. With Russia's emergence from isolation it became necessary to define the ancient Russian tradition and to formulate its relationship to other creeds. Tradition ceased to be accepted blindly and unthinkingly, and the problem arose of determining what the correct tradition was, and how it compared with the tradition of the Greeks. The doubts as to the soundness of the liturgical formula, the heart of the old Russian Church, dissolved the rigidity of tradition, the conservative principle of life in old Russia. The *raskol* thus marked the end of old Russia.

It occurred at a time when Russia was drawn ever more closely into contact with western Europe, with its superiority in the military, technical and economic fields, which rested on a theoretical recognition of historical reality and a relative readiness to accept it. The Russian Church was in no position either intellectually to digest the fact of western superiority, or to develop corresponding forces itself. For this reason the government was forced to accept western instructors and technicians and soon began to appreciate the need of a secular elementary education. A small group of educated men in leading political positions believed that the fruits of western culture could be taken over without damage to the Orthodox religious outlook. Yet the incompatibility of the traditional old Russian piety with independent western thought was demonstrated ever more frequently from the middle of the seventeenth century onwards by such phenomena as individual lapses from Orthodoxy, and even flight abroad. The mass of the people, however, rejected the European influences fostered by the government and refused to abandon the sanctuary of religious tradition; in this respect many shared the attitude of the Old Believers.

The Church was incapable of blending the values and methods offered by the West with the native heritage. At a juncture when the historical evolution compelled Russia to draw comparisons between herself and western Europe in the sphere of secular culture, instead of merely in the religious sphere, the spiritual purity of the Russian Church inevitably revealed itself as a fatal weakness. If the attempt were to be made, in practice and in theory, to let Russia compete with the West, in the prevailing circumstances this would have to be done by leaning upon the West; if, on the other hand, the attempt were to be made to maintain Russia's traditions by sealing her off from the heretical western world, this would involve the risk of Russia, owing to her material backwardness, falling victim to western expansion. This fundamental option produced a breach in Russian society, between a slowly expanding ruling class which looked towards the West, and the mass of the people who remained loyal to their traditions. At the very heart of the period of Russian history described here lies a feeling of religious insecurity, arising out of the challenge to tradition and the first contacts with the historically orientated Christianity of the West. The life of old Russia, self-contained, backward-looking, and stamped by the Church, broke down under pressure from the West: the decisive factor in modern Russian history was a continual interchange and tension between Russia and the West.

INDEX